Grace and Life

Grace and Life

Studies in the Pastoral Letters

PAUL E. DETERDING

WIPF & STOCK · Eugene, Oregon

GRACE AND LIFE
Studies in the Pastoral Letters

Copyright © 2025 Paul E. Deterding. All rights reserved. Except for brief quotations in critical publications or reviews, no part of this book may be reproduced in any manner without prior written permission from the publisher. Write: Permissions, Wipf and Stock Publishers, 199 W. 8th Ave., Suite 3, Eugene, OR 97401.

Wipf & Stock
An Imprint of Wipf and Stock Publishers
199 W. 8th Ave., Suite 3
Eugene, OR 97401

www.wipfandstock.com

PAPERBACK ISBN: 979-8-3852-4569-7
HARDCOVER ISBN: 979-8-3852-4570-3
EBOOK ISBN: 979-8-3852-4571-0

09/24/25

Scripture quotations marked "ESV" are from The ESV® Bible (The Holy Bible, English Standard Version®), © 2001 by Crossway, a publishing ministry of Good News Publishers. Used by permission. All rights reserved.

Scripture quotations marked "RSV" are from the Revised Standard Version of the Bible, copyright © 1946, 1952, and 1971 National Council of the Churches of Christ in the United States of America. Used by permission. All rights reserved worldwide.

Scripture quotations marked "CSB" have been taken from the Christian Standard Bible®, Copyright © 2017 by Holman Bible Publishers. Used by permission. Christian Standard Bible® and CSB® are federally registered trademarks of Holman Bible Publishers.

The Scriptures marked "NET" are from the NET Bible® https://netbible.com copyright ©1996, 2019 used with permission from Biblical Studies Press, L.L.C. All rights reserved"

To the faculty of Saint Paul Lutheran High School,
Concordia, Missouri:
The excellence with which you carried out your vocations has been
an inspiration to me in carrying out mine.

Contents

Permissions	ix
Author's Preface	xi
Principal Abbreviations	xv
A Note to the Reader	1
Introduction to the Pastoral Letters	3
Introduction to 1 Timothy	39
Commentary on 1 Timothy	46
Introduction to Titus	209
Commentary on Titus	214
Introduction to 2 Timothy	291
Commentary on 2 Timothy	295
Essays	401
Extended Notes	471
Bibliography	513
Subject Index	519
Scripture Index	529

Permissions

Unless otherwise indicated, translations of Scripture are those of the author.

Scripture quotations marked ESV are from the ESV Bible (The Holy Bible, English Standard Version), copyright © 2001 by Crossway, a publishing ministry of Good News Publishers. Used by permission. All rights reserved.

Scripture quotations marked CSB have been taken from the Christian Standard Bible, copyright © 2017 by Holman Bible Publishers. Used by permission. Christian Standard Bible and CSB are federally registered trademarks of Holman Bible Publishers.

Scripture quotations marked NET are from the NET Bible, copyright © 1996, 2019 by Biblical Studies Press, L. L. C. http://netbible.com. Used by permission. All rights reserved.

Scripture quotations marked RSV are from the Revised Standard Version of the Bible, copyright 1952 [2nd edition 1971] by the Division of Christian Education of the National Council of Churches of Christ in the United States of America. Used by permission. All rights reserved.

Earlier versions of the following sections appeared in Paul E. Deterding, *Colossians*. Concordia Commentary. St. Louis: Concordia, 2003, and are used by permission of Concordia Publishing House.

"The Nature of the Heresy" (14–21) first appeared in *Colossians*, 7–12.

"For the Sake of the Elect Ones" (330–33) first appeared in *Colossians*, 75–79.

"With Eternal Glory" (333) first appeared in *Colossians*, 139–40.

The Extended Note "In Christ" (485–88) first appeared in *Colossians*, 23–25.

The Extended Note "Mystery" (492–94) first appeared in *Colossians*, 73–75.

The Extended Note "Slavery in the New Testament World" (502–8) first appeared in *Colossians*, 171–76.

Author's Preface

You might have a different opinion, but it seems to me that the Pastoral Letters have often been regarded as the "red-headed stepchild" of the New Testament.¹ Some dislike certain things that are said therein and so subtly or even overtly reject them.² Skeptics deny their authenticity as letters of Paul and in so doing relegate them to a second-class status in the New Testament.³ Some see them as belonging to a supposed era of rigid and formal institutionalization of the church, when the living voice of the gospel was allegedly being replaced.⁴ Some bristle at their straightforward insistence that the pastoral office is to be reserved for men. Their catalogues of requirements for certain positions in the church and of ethical standards for various classes of people cause some to think of these epistles as being mainly collections of rules and regulations, perhaps even with the implication that these letters are legalistic rather than evangelical. Even for those who regard them as belonging to the

---

1. C. K. Barrett (*Pastoral Epistles*, 32) is somewhat more guarded in expressing this: "The Pastorals cannot be said to be one of the more exciting parts of the New Testament."

2. Luke Timothy Johnson (*First and Second Letters to Timothy*) puts it this way: "There is much in them that present-day readers find distasteful and even offensive" (xi). "The Pastorals have managed to offend scholars committed to reformation theology as well as feminists committed to liberation theology" (14).

3. "The issue of Pauline authorship shades imperceptibly toward the question of canonical status and theological authority" (Johnson, *First and Second Letters to Timothy*, 14). "The decision against authenticity means that the Pastorals are automatically secondary (perhaps even tertiary) witnesses to Christian life, since they do not come from the first Christian generation. They are not technically outside the canon, but they may as well be for all the attention they receive.... In a milder form, those who reject authenticity often spend so much energy demonstrating the ways in which these letters are *not* by Paul that they can find little positive to say about them" (Johnson, *First and Second Letters to Timothy*, 57 [emphasis original]).

4. Johnson (*First and Second Letters to Timothy*) alludes to (and dismisses) such an approach (256, 342, 353-54).

AUTHOR'S PREFACE

Scriptures that they love and revere, the Pastorals may not be among the portions of the Bible to which they most readily turn.

It is my hope that the reader will come away from the present work with a more positive view of these letters. As especially the essays toward the conclusion of this volume demonstrate, the Pastorals offer a rich tapestry of teaching regarding some of the most central articles of the Christian faith: Christology, soteriology, eschatology, the doctrine of God, the relationship of doctrine and ethics, worship, and of course the pastoral ministry. It is my belief that a thorough study of these letters will pay rich dividends in terms of growth in both faith and Christian living.

A word of appreciation is in order to Matthew Wimer and the entire staff at Wipf and Stock Publishers for putting this volume in print. A debt of gratitude is also owed to Faith Viera Lutheran Church in Rockledge, Florida, for providing financial support for the publication of this work.

To an extent that only the Lord of the church could fully comprehend, a man's years of serving as a pastor will have affected his view of the pastoral ministry and will have influenced his carrying out the duties of that office. The same is true of my own years of serving as a pastor. As important as such experience is, it would be presumptive of me (or any pastor) to think that in my life I have covered the gamut of what it means to be a pastor. While my own experience will flavor the way in which I write about it in this volume, I have endeavored to let the texts speak about the pastoral ministry and to have my experience be illustrative rather than normative for what I offer on these pages.

The last eleven years of my full-time ministry experience were spent as a faculty member at Saint Paul Lutheran High School in Concordia, Missouri. It was at that time when I first put fingertips to keyboard for the writing of this commentary. During my years at Saint Paul about 40 percent of the student body consisted of students from outside the United States. This meant that during those years I was involved in ministry with a wide variety of students. There were usually a tiny minority of missional atheists, students who not only believed (that is the correct verb) that there is no God, but who saw as their mission in life proclaiming this to anyone within earshot. Then there were students whose first encounter with Christianity was at our school. There were others whose worldview included animistic/spiritualistic influences of one sort or another. Of course, there were Christian students who ranged from those whose faith was feeble and poorly informed to stronger believers and even to future professional church workers. Ministering to such an across-the-board sampling of faiths shaped my own proclamation of God's word. Laboring alongside the outstanding members of that school's faculty also had a wholesome influence on my ministry then and thereafter.

Although I began writing the present volume in Missouri, I completed it after I had relocated to Brevard County, Florida, the same county where I had begun my years in ministry. Brevard County is also known as the Space Coast, even being located within area code 321, as within it are located Patrick Space Force Base, Cape Canaveral Space Force Station, and the Kennedy Space Center. When there is a space launch in Brevard County, one can go outside and see the rocket on its way toward orbit. So it was that on the cold morning of January 28, 1986, I was watching the launch of the Space Shuttle Challenger and saw it explode, killing everyone on board, including Christa McAuliffe, the first teacher in space. However, what I remember most about Christa McAuliffe was not that tragedy but how she described her profession: "I touch the future; I teach."

I intend no disrespect to the memory of Christa McAuliffe. Nevertheless, I can say that those who labor in the gospel of Jesus Christ can go her one better, for we can say, "I touch the future, and I reach eternity, for I speak of Christ."

Perhaps the most exciting thing about writing a work of Christian theology has to do with reaching eternity—for the author, for those who read these words, and for those to whom those who read these words will minister. As these words help to proclaim the word of him whose word endures forever and does not return to him empty, they may enable readers whom I will never meet in this life to reach eternity and in turn assist them in bringing the eternal benefits of that word to still others.

May our great God and savior Jesus Christ bless you as you go about the task of touching the future and reaching eternity.

Principal Abbreviations

BOOKS OF THE BIBLE

Gen	2 Kgs	Isa	Nah	Rom	Titus
Exod	1 Chr	Jer	Hab	1 Cor	Phlm
Lev	2 Chr	Lam	Zeph	2 Cor	Heb
Num	Ezra	Ezek	Hag	Gal	Jas
Deut	Neh	Dan	Zech	Eph	1 Pet
Josh	Esth	Hos	Mal	Phil	2 Pet
Judg	Job	Joel	Matt	Col	1 John
Ruth	Ps (pl Pss)	Amos	Mark	1 Thess	2 John
1 Sam	Prov	Obad	Luke	2 Thess	3 John
2 Sam	Eccl	Jonah	John	1 Tim	Jude
1 Kgs	Song	Mic	Acts	2 Tim	Rev

BOOKS OF THE APOCRYPHA

Tob	Wis	1–3 Esd	Sg Three	Bel	3–4 Macc
Jdt	Sir	Ep Jer	Sus	1–2 Macc	Pr Man
Add Esth	Bar				

PRINCIPAL ABBREVIATIONS

REFERENCE WORKS

ABD	*Anchor Bible Dictionary*. Edited by David Noel Freedman. 6 vols. New York: Doubleday, 1992.
ACCS	Ancient Christian Commentary on Scripture
AE	*Luther's Works*. St. Louis: Concordia, and Philadelphia: Fortress, 1955–present.
ANF	*The Ante-Nicene Fathers*. Edited by A. Roberts and J. Donaldson. 10 vols. Reprint. Peabody, MA: Hendrickson, 1994.
BDAG	Bauer, W., et al. *A Greek-English Lexicon of the New Testament and Other Early Christian Literature*. 3rd ed. Chicago: University of Chicago Press, 2000.
BDF	Blass, F., et al. *A Greek Grammar of the New Testament and Other Early Christian Literature*. Chicago: University of Chicago Press, 1961.
CD	Damascus Document
CSB	Christian Standard Bible
DNTB	Evans, Craig A., and Stanley E. Porter. *Dictionary of New Testament Background*. Downers Grove, IL: InterVarsity, 2000.
DPL	*Dictionary of Paul and His Letters*. Edited by Gerald F. Hawthorne and Ralph P. Martin. Downers Grove, IL: InterVarsity Press, 1993.
Epi	Epitome of the Formula of Concord
ESV	English Standard Version of the Bible
FC	Fathers of the Church. The Catholic University of America Press, 1947–present.
LCC	Library of Christian Classics
LSB	*Lutheran Service Book*. St. Louis: Concordia, 2006.
LXX	Septuagint
MM	Moulton, James H., and George Milligan. *The Vocabulary of the Greek Testament*. London, 1930. Repr., Peabody, MA: Hendrickson, 1997.
MT	Masoretic Text of the Hebrew Bible

PRINCIPAL ABBREVIATIONS

NET	New English Translation of the Bible
NPNF[2]	*The Nicene and Post-Nicene Fathers*. Series 2. Edited by P. Schaff and H. Wace. 14 vols. Reprint. Peabody, MA: Hendrickson, 1994.
PG	Patrologia Graeca [= Patrologiae Cursus Completus: Series Graeca]. Edited by Jacques-Paul Migne. 162 vols. Paris, 1857–86.
RSV	Revised Standard Version of the Bible
SD	Solid Declaration of the Formula of Concord
TDNT	*Theological Dictionary of the New Testament*. Edited by G. Kittel and G. Friedrich. Translated by G. W. Bromiley. 10 vols. Grand Rapids: Eerdmans, 1964–76.

A Note to the Reader

As one who served as a parish pastor for more than twenty-five years and who has been a guest pastor a number of times since then, I realize that rather than being read from page 1 to the end commentaries are more often read in bits and pieces to prepare for preaching or to answer some question. Even so, it may be that you might be inclined at some point to read the present volume cover to cover.

In the event that this should be the case, let me make the following suggestions: Begin by reading the Introduction to the Pastoral Letters. After that, read the Extended Notes at the end of this volume; this way you can read the rest of the book without having to consult the Extended Notes each time that they are mentioned. Then, beginning with the Introduction to 1 Timothy, read the commentary proper. After that, conclude with the Essays.

As I will suggest elsewhere in this work, it seems likely that the order in which the apostle wrote these letters is 1 Timothy, Titus, 2 Timothy.[1] Therefore, I have ordered this commentary so that you will read the letters in what I would argue is their chronological order.

It is my prayer that through this volume the Lord of the church would bless you and your service in his name.

---

1. An opinion with which Towner agrees (*Letters to Timothy and Titus*, 30–31).

Introduction to the Pastoral Letters

SIGNIFICANCE

The Letters to Timothy and to Titus have much to say about the place and work of pastors in and for the church and for the world. For this reason, since the eighteenth century these three collectively have been known as the Pastoral Epistles or Pastoral Letters.[1] In and of itself their instruction regarding the church and its pastors is reason enough for them to have been cherished by many Christians.

Nevertheless, these relatively brief New Testament documents are much more than a sort of set of instructions for pastors. As the essays elsewhere in this commentary demonstrate, these letters make a substantial contribution to the scriptural witness regarding significant doctrines and topics of the Christian faith and life. That being the case, a devoted investigation of these letters will provide great spiritual and practical benefits for those who give their attention to them.[2]

---

1. Easton, *Pastoral Epistles*, 1; Guthrie, *Pastoral Epistles*, 17. Guthrie traces the origin of the term to D. N. Berdot (1703) and to Paul Anton (1726).

2. C. K. Barrett, who himself takes a somewhat critical view of these letters, says it this way (*Pastoral Epistles*, 33): "The Pastorals instruct us in what is our own task. . . . It is our duty to 'join the struggle in defense of the faith, the faith which God entrusted to his people once and for all' (Jude 3). If therefore the Pastorals insist upon the primary importance of maintaining in its purity the Gospel message of God's gracious activity—past, present, and future—in Jesus Christ; if they insist upon the necessity of Church discipline, and high standards of Christian obedience; if they require that Christian ministers shall be men of irreproachable character and competent attainment: from these affirmations the Church of every generation may learn its own task."

TEXT

"The textual evidence of the letters shows no obvious insertions or dislocations that would compromise their textual integrity."[3] Only a handful of textual variants call for comment; these will be considered at the appropriate place in the textual notes.

AUTHENTICITY AND INTEGRITY

The acceptance of the Pastoral Letters as a part of the New Testament canon presupposed their Pauline authorship. In his *Ecclesiastical History* Eusebius quotes Serapion, bishop of Antioch (191–211),[4] to this effect: "We receive both Peter and the other apostles as Christ, but pseudepigrapha in their name we reject" (6.12.3). This judgment regarding 1 Timothy, 2 Timothy, and Titus was all but universally accepted throughout Christendom, with only a few heretical teachers, among them Marcion, rejecting the assertion that Paul was the author.[5]

Beginning in the nineteenth century and continuing to the present day, many have raised objections to the Pauline authorship of the Pastorals. Their arguments fall into four main categories.

The Historical Setting

One criticism against the authenticity of these letters is that they refer to events that do not correspond to the history of the life of Paul as given in the book of Acts. The conclusion is drawn that these are things that never took place; rather, the unknown author of the Pastorals simply fabricated them.[6]

It is illogical to think that the book of Acts would have recorded every event in the life of Paul. The list of his sufferings that he gives in 2 Corinthians (11:23–27), a letter whose Pauline authorship is all but universally recognized, demonstrates that.

---

3. Achtemeier et al., *Introducing the New Testament*, 464.
4. See Orthodox Wiki, "Serapion of Antioch."
5. *DPL* 659.
6. For example, Debelius and Conzelmann, *Pastoral Epistles*, 3.

Moreover, the way in which the book of Acts ends points to the apostle being released at the end of his two-year house arrest.[7] There are multiple indications in the narrative that the charges against him were completely fabricated.[8] Acts ends where it does because the conclusion completes the narrative that the author of Acts had set out to tell. Luke had indicated the outline for his narrative by quoting the words of Jesus about where his followers would be his witnesses (1:8). His people would bear witness to Christ not only in Jerusalem to their fellow Jews (1:1—6:7), and not even only in Judea and Samaria to those half-Jewish, half-gentile Samaritans (6:8—9:31), but to the end of the earth, that is, also to the gentiles (9:32—28:31). Paul's bold and unhindered proclamation of Christ in Rome fulfills the promise of the proclamation of Christ to the end of the earth. Luke's account is complete; there was no need for him to report anything further about the life of Paul.

The narrative of Acts was complete, but that did not mean that the apostle's ministry came to an end at the conclusion of his first Roman imprisonment. After the end of his incarceration in Rome, he may indeed have taken up his proposed mission to Spain (Rom 15:24, 28)[9] before carrying out the various travels that are indicated in the Pastoral Letters. At some point after his release from prison he may have made his planned visit to Philemon (Phlm 22). Thus, the historical setting implicit in the Pastoral Letters does not disprove their Pauline authorship.

The Ecclesiastical Circumstances

Another objection to the authenticity of the Pastorals is that they presuppose a formal ecclesiastical structure that postdates the time of Paul.[10]

---

7. Bruce, *Book of the Acts*, 534–36 (also nn48 and 49); Reicke, *New Testament Era*, 220; Ramsey, *Historical Commentary*, 20–25.

8. The charges were not true (21:27–29); not even the members of the Jewish Sanhedrin could agree on his guilt (22:30—23:9); the tribune Claudius Lysias attested that Paul had done "nothing worthy of death or imprisonment" (23:26–29); his two-year imprisonment in Caesarea was due to his unwillingness or inability to pay a bribe to the Roman governor Felix (24:26–27); the governor Festus and king Herod Agrippa, after hearing him, agreed that he could have been freed, had he not appealed his case to Caesar (26:30–32).

9. Clement of Rome (*1 Clem* 5:5–7) is among the post-New Testament authors who attest to Paul's release from his first Roman imprisonment and/or his journey to Spain ("the limits of the West"); Mounce, *Pastoral Epistles*, lv–lvi.

10. *DPL* 660; Guthrie, *New Testament Introduction*, 591–93; and Johnson, *Letters*, 74–75, all provide an overview (591–93).

The claim is made that whereas the spiritual leadership of the Pauline churches was informal, even charismatic (1 Cor 14:20–33), the Pastoral Letters assume a formal ecclesiastical structure with a monarchical episcopate (1 Tim 3:1–2) headed by a bishop (ἐπίσκοπος), under whom deacons (διάκονοι) served (1 Tim 3:8–13).

This objection reads into the Pastorals what is not there. In these letters an ἐπίσκοπος is simply another name for a pastor, as demonstrated by the Letter to Titus, where ἐπίσκοπος is used synonymously with πρεσβύτερος, "elder" (Titus 1:5, 7). The ecclesiastical structure of the Pastorals is no different than that of the book of Acts, where the terms ἐπίσκοπος and πρεσβύτερος are also used synonymously (Acts 20:17, 28), or that of the Letter to the Philippians (1:1), which is addressed to the "saints" (Christians) there "along with the overseers [note the plural] and deacons" (σύν ἐπισκόποις καί διάκονοις), or that of the First Letter to the Thessalonians (5:12–13), which directs the addressees to esteem "those who labor among you and are over you in the Lord and instruct you." Therefore, the organization of the churches presupposed by the Pastorals is no obstacle to their having been written by Paul.[11]

The Linguistic Problem

The claim is made that the language of the Pastorals is significantly different from that of the undisputed Pauline Letters. This assertion is based on the significant number of words that occur in the Pastoral Letters but which are not found in the other letters of Paul, and on the amount of words that do occur in the other letters of the apostle but which do not occur in 1 and 2 Timothy or Titus. As many of the words from the first group are attested in second-century authors, it is asserted that the Pastorals must have been composed after the time of Paul. P. N. Harrison, basing his calculation on a words-per-page methodology, was the trailblazing advocate of this argument rejecting the Pauline authorship of the Pastorals.[12]

---

11. "To judge from what we know of Paul's apostolic and mission *modus operandi* and of the functions performed by his mission colleagues (Rom 16:1–3; 1 Cor 4:17; 2 Cor 8:23; Phil 2:19; Eph 6:21; Col 4:7–8; 1 Thess 3:2), the instructions communicated to Timothy and Titus and the roles they were to play within the communities to which they had been dispatched conform perfectly to a Pauline pattern"; Towner, *Letters*, 86. Mounce, *Pastoral Epistles*, 186–92, provides multiple examples of differences between the ecclesiastical organization of the Pastorals and those of succeeding generations.

12. Harrison, *Problem of the Pastoral Epistles*; see also Debelius and Conzelmann,

INTRODUCTION TO THE PASTORAL LETTERS

However, Harrison's methodology and conclusions have been rightly critiqued. It is questionable at best to think that one author would be so limited in his vocabulary that he could not have gone beyond his past universe of words, particularly if he were writing on new and different subjects.[13] Furthermore, Harrison does not take into account a sizable number of words that are found in both the Pastorals and in the other ten letters.[14]

There are differences in vocabulary between any given Pauline Letter and the rest of them; these are easily accounted for by differences in subject matter. Romans and Galatians have much in common, but there are also noticeable differences between the two of them and the other Pauline Letters.[15] The two letters to the church at Corinth, especially 1 Corinthians, contain unique terminology due to the unique company of problems and issues which faced that congregation. The Letters to the Thessalonians addressed the unique issues in that church. Philippians is somewhat different from Romans and Galatians, and Colossians and Ephesians tackle a new set of issues.[16]

Variety in language can be seen among all the letters of Paul. Different subject matter, not a different author, accounts for the variation in vocabulary between the Pastoral Letters and the apostle's other letters.[17]

The Theology of the Letters

Similar to the previous objection is the assertion that the theology of these letters differs from that of the "authentic" Pauline Letters. Certain

---

Pastoral Epistles, 3–4; Easton, *Pastoral Epistles*, 9–15.

13. Paul "was certainly able to adopt various styles and forms of expression" (Reicke, *Re-Examining Paul's Letters*, 31; similarly, Ramsey, *Historical Commentary*, 15). Donald Guthrie has given an in-depth critique of all the challenges to the Pauline authorship of the Pastorals, especially those raised by Harrison. On the linguistic arguments in particular, see his *Pastoral Epistles and the Mind of Paul*, 12–14 and Appendix E (41–44), and his *Pastoral Epistles*, 224–40.

14. See Appendix: Parallels Between the Pastoral Letters and the Other Letters of Paul at the end of this Introduction.

15. For that matter, in spite of the obvious similarity between these two letters, there is also considerable difference in the vocabulary utilized in each one. See Guthrie, *Pastoral Epistles and the Mind*, 14.

16. On the relationship of Colossians and Ephesians see Deterding, *Colossians*, 193–94.

17. Johnson, *Letters*, 69–71, offers a number of specific examples of differences in vocabulary and style between the "undisputed" letters of Paul.

characteristic Pauline doctrines such as the believer's existence "in Christ" and the work of the Holy Spirit are in short supply if not entirely lacking, while there exists a new emphasis on "the faith" and "sound teaching."[18]

The answer to this objection is similar to the rejoinder to the linguistic problem (see above). The variety of topics and terminology displayed throughout the Pauline corpus demonstrates that the apostle could and did speak to many theological topics and did so with a variety of expressions. These letters are written for new situations with new issues that the apostle had to oversee. It is to be expected that Paul would need to speak to new matters and to do so with new vocabulary.

Moreover, this objection (like the previous one) ignores language and concepts that are common to both the Pastorals and to the apostle's other letters. These include major theological concepts, some of which are characteristic of Paul, as well as various turns of phrase. The appendix at the end of this Introduction to the Pastoral Letters lists these, by my count 103 of them; a few of them call for further comment.

The expression ὁ Χριστός occurs in the New Testament as the Greek equivalent of the Hebrew הַמָּשִׁיחַ and Aramaic מְשִׁיחָא, "the Messiah," the name the Jewish people of the first century were using to refer to the Savior promised from the line of David (2 Sam 7:1–17; 1 Chron 17:1–15); in this way the New Testament proclaimed Jesus to be that promised Messiah. In time the title ὁ Χριστός morphed into a name for Jesus, so that the authors of the New Testament might name him as "Christ" or "Jesus Christ." The apostle also uses these names for our Lord. However, in addition to these Paul also identifies him as "Christ Jesus," and he is the only biblical author to do so.[19] The Pastoral Letters contain many instances of this distinctly Pauline way of referring to Jesus of Nazareth. As there is no obvious difference in meaning between "Jesus Christ" and "Christ Jesus," the use of both terms would be a characteristically Pauline way of speaking and serves as a strong pointer to the authenticity of the Pastorals.

---

18. Moffatt and Easton are among those who advocated this position; Guthrie, *New Testament Introduction*, 593–94.

19. The only "exception" to this is found in Acts 24:24, but since this reports Paul's own testimony, it is not really an exception. The use of "Christ Jesus" is found in Rom 1:1; 2:16; 3:24; 6:3, 11, 13; 8:1, 2, 34, 39; 15:5, 16, 17; 16:3; 1 Cor 1:1, 2, 4, 30; 4:15; 15:31; 16:24; 2 Cor 1:1; Gal 2:4, 16 (2x); 3:14, 26, 28; 4:14; 5:6, 24; Eph 1:1 (2x); 2:6, 7, 10, 13, 20; 3:1, 6, 11, 21; Phil 1:1 (2x), 8, 26; 2:5; 3:3, 8, 12, 14; 4:7, 19, 21; Col 1:1, 4; 2:6; 4:12; 1 Thess 2:14; 5:18; 1 Tim 1:1 (2x), 2, 12, 14, 15; 2:5; 3:13; 4:6; 5:21; 6:13; 2 Tim 1:1 (2x), 2, 9, 10, 13; 2:1, 3, 10; 3:12, 15; 4:1; Titus 1:4; Phlm 1, 9, 23.

INTRODUCTION TO THE PASTORAL LETTERS

The use of the phrase "in Christ" (ἐν Χριστῷ) and its equivalents to describe a saving relationship with Jesus Christ is virtually unknown outside the apostle's letters;[20] this expression and concept seems to have originated with Paul himself.[21] The Pastorals also contain instances of this phrase.[22]

Another uniquely Pauline way of proclaiming salvation is with the phrase "with Christ" (σὺν Χριστῷ).[23] With this formulation and certain verbs compounded with the preposition σύν, which the apostle creates as his thought requires it,[24] Paul indicates that Christians were with Christ as he carried out his saving actions, so that they thereby received the benefits of these.[25] This uniquely Pauline expression is attested in the Pastoral Letters: "If we died with him, we will also live with him; if we endure, we will also reign with him" (2 Tim 2:11-12).

In the New Testament "justification" and "righteousness" as a way of speaking of salvation is for the most part characteristic of the apostle Paul.[26] All three of the Pastoral Letters contain examples of this Pauline way of speaking.[27]

Paul's special calling and obligation to bring the gospel of Jesus Christ to the gentiles is well attested in his letters.[28] In the Pastorals the apostle also takes note of this distinctive vocation of his (1 Tim 2:7; 2 Tim 4:17).

In Summary

The common element to all of these arguments is that they allegedly demonstrate that the Pastoral Letters date from a time well after the life of Paul and therefore could not have been written by him. However, the

---

20. The only possible exceptions are 1 Pet 3:16; 5:10, 14; 1 John 5:20.

21. Bouttier, *En Christ*, 25.

22. 1 Tim 1:1, 4; 3:1, 3; 2 Tim 1:1, 9, 13; 2:1, 10; 3:12, 15.

23. The only possible exception is Mark 15:32; however, the equivalence seems to be merely of vocabulary rather than significance.

24. Bouttier, *En Christ*, 39.

25. Rom 6:4, 5, 6, 8; 8:17, 32; 2 Cor 4:14; 13:4; Gal 2:20; Eph 2:5, 6; Phil 1:23; 3:10, 21; Col 2:12, 13, 20; 3:1, 3, 4; 1 Thess 4:14, 17; 5:10.

26. This can be seen by looking at the entries δικαιοσύνη, δικαιοῦν/δικαιόω, and δικαίωμα in a Greek concordance of the NT and noting that the vast number of occurrences are to be found in the letters of Paul.

27. 1 Tim 6:11; 2 Tim 2:22; 3:16; 4:8; Titus 3:5-7.

28. Rom 11:13; 15:16, 18; Gal 2:7-9; Eph 3:1, 8; 1 Thess 2:16.

arguments fail to prove their assertions. Dating the Pastoral Letters after the apostle's lifetime "fits neither with the concrete names and dates that they contain nor with the problems that occupied the postapostolic generation."[29]

Some who deny the Pauline authorship of these letters regard them as entirely fabricated. A strong argument against the inclusion of such pseudonymous works in the New Testament is Christianity's universal rejection of works—such as 3 Corinthians, the Letters of Paul and Seneca, and the Letter to the Laodiceans—that claimed to be the work of Paul.[30]

Others who reject the genuineness of the Pastorals postulate that certain genuine Pauline fragments have been incorporated by a later author into these works.[31] The notable lack of agreement among scholars as to what portions of these letters are the genuine fragments tells fatally against the theory.[32] Furthermore, the apocryphal Letter to the Laodiceans,[33] whose spuriousness is evident upon a first reading to anyone familiar with the genuine Pauline Letters, demonstrates what such a "cut-and-paste" approach would have been like. In contrast, such slavish copying of the other letters of Paul is completely missing from the Pastorals.[34]

It is also worth noting that certain "offhand" comments in these letters bear the mark of authenticity. In these letters the author drops names of people otherwise unknown to readers of the New Testament.[35]

29. Reicke, *Re-Examining Paul's Letters*, 34.

30. As noted by Johnson, *Letters*, 84.

31. Both *DPL* (659–60) and Guthrie, *New Testament Introduction* (590–91) provide an overview.

32. Reicke, *Re-Examining Paul's Letters*, 34; Guthrie, *New Testament Introduction*, 590–91.

33. Found in Hennecke et al., *New Testament Apocrypha*, 2:128–132.

34. Kelly, *Pastoral Epistles*, 225; even Debelius and Conzelmann (*Pastoral Epistles*, 4–5) express the strongest skepticism toward any hypothesis of the incorporation of Pauline fragments into the Pastorals.
Note also the remark of Johnson, *Letters*, 89: "Our author, in short, is not a hack who writes the same thing over and over in three segments, but an author of considerable literary skill, beyond any we find evidenced in the extant writings of Ignatius, Clement, Polycarp, or any other author of the early to mid-second century. His skill is immediately evident by comparison with the 'Pauline letters' that were universally rejected as spurious. It is an artistry sufficient to convince critical readers from Origen through Erasmus to Grotius that the same author who wrote Romans also wrote the Pastorals."

35. Hymenaeus (1 Tim 1:20; 2 Tim 2:17); Phygelus (2 Tim 1:15); Hermogenes (2 Tim 1:15); Onesiphonus (2 Tim 1:16; 4:19); Philetus (2 Tim 2:17); Crescens (2 Tim 4:12); Carpus (2 Tim 4:13); Eubulus, Pudens, Linus, and Claudia (2 Tim 4:21); possibly also Alexander (1 Tim 1:20; 2 Tim 4:14).

INTRODUCTION TO THE PASTORAL LETTERS

There is no reason for this, unless these letters are, in fact, compositions by none other than the apostle. Paul's instruction to Timothy to "bring the cloak that I left in Troas with Carpus" (2 Tim 4:13) serves no purpose if this letter is a fabrication designed to give apostolic sanction to a later work. The very nondescript character of this portion of the letter points to it having been composed by Paul himself.

The absence of the Pastorals from the earliest papyrus document containing the Pauline Letters (P^{46}) is sometimes offered as an argument against their authenticity. However, this is offset by several factors: (1) P^{46} also lacks 2 Thessalonians and Philemon; (2) an equally early papyrus document (P^{32}) contains portions of the Letter to Titus (1:11–15; 2:3–8); (3) 2 Corinthians, whose authenticity is widely accepted, is found in only one papyrus document (P^{46}); and (4) patristic citations of the Pastoral Letters as Scripture give evidence for their acceptance that predates any manuscript evidence.[36]

For those who accept the Scriptures as God's word, the testimony of these letters themselves as the work of Paul is the strongest evidence of their authenticity. Even beyond that, we have demonstrated that the arguments against the Pauline authorship of the Pastorals are not nearly as convincing as their proponents would suggest; objections to the authorship of these letters by the apostle often tell us more about the presuppositions of those who reject the genuineness of the letters than about the letters themselves.[37] Furthermore, we have seen that on a purely academic basis a strong case can be made for the authenticity of these letters.

THE MAN PAUL

The book of Acts informs us that Paul was also known as Saul (Acts 13:9). As a "Hebrew of Hebrews" (Phil 3:5) he was born into a deeply religious family, who gave their son the Hebrew name שָׁאוּל/Σαούλ (Acts 26:14), the Greek version of which was Σαῦλος. But he was also born a Roman citizen (Acts 16:37–38; 22:25–28), and as such would have had

---

36. Johnson, *Letters*, 17–18.

37. Towner, *Letters*, 9–10: "Until about the nineteenth century, the letters to Timothy and Titus went relatively unchallenged as letters from Paul the apostle to his co-workers. Their status as canonical Scripture was never seriously in doubt. What comes to light through the succession of commentaries is the way in which their authors' own cultural and philosophical frameworks conditioned their exposition of the letters for the church."

a three-part Greco-Roman name, one part of which would have been Παῦλος, Paul, the name by which he is most well known.[38]

Even though he was a citizen of Tarsus in Cilicia (Acts 9:11; 21:39; 22:3), he was educated in Jerusalem by the renowned Jewish rabbi Gamaliel[39] (Acts 22:3) and was thereby instructed according to the traditions of the Pharisees (Acts 23:6; 26:5; Phil 3:5). As a "Hebrew of Hebrews" and one who had been educated by a rabbi, he would have been well acquainted with the Hebrew Scriptures. On the other hand, the language of his letters and his ability to quote Greek sources (Acts 17:28; 1 Cor 15:33; Titus 1:12) demonstrate that he was quite at home in that language as well. As much of Galilee and Judea was trilingual, "with Aramaic the language used for many day-to-day activities, Mishnaic Hebrew used for religious worship and learned discussion and Greek the normal language for commerce, trade and administration,"[40] it is reasonable to conclude that the apostle was at home in all three languages.

Thus, in terms of both language and culture Paul was a man of two realms: the religious community of Judaism and the culture of the Greco-Roman world. As such he was ideally suited, once his religious orientation had been completely transformed by his encounter with the risen Lord on the road to Damascus, to bring the gospel, which had begun among Christ's fellow Jews, to the world at large.

THE CHRONOLOGY OF PAUL'S LIFE

During his ministry in Corinth on his first missionary journey the apostle appeared before Gallio, who was then proconsul of Achaia. From fragments of letters discovered at Delphi in Greece it is possible to date Gallio's tenure in Corinth to AD 51–52.[41] This provides an anchor date

---

38. Cranfield, *Romans*, 48–50. It is perhaps worth noting that the book of Acts says nothing about his name being *changed* to Paul. Up until Acts 13:9 Luke has always designated him by his Hebrew name. At this point in Acts the narrative of Paul's life and ministry is about to take up his seminal outreach to the gentiles. In keeping with this, from this point forward the author of Acts always refers to him by his Greco-Roman name, Paul.

39. The high status in which Gamaliel was held by his fellow Jews is seen in Acts 5:33–42 as well as in the *Mishneh* (Sotah 9:15): "Since Rabban Gamaliel the Elder died, there has been no more reverence for the law, and purity and piety died out at the same time."

40. *DNTB* 472.

41. The reconstructed text reads as follows: "Tiber[ius Claudius Cae]sar Augustus

for the life and ministry of Paul, so that we can have a reasonably accurate chronology of the events of his life, as follows.

AD 1?—birth

AD 30—involvement in the death of Stephen (Acts 7:58—8:3)

AD 32—Paul's calling on the road to Damascus (Acts 9:1-31)

AD 35—first visit to Jerusalem (Acts 9:26-30; Gal 1:18-24)

AD 45—work in Antioch with Barnabas (Acts 11:25-26)

AD 46—famine visit to Jerusalem (Acts 11:27-30; 12:25; Gal 2:1-10)

AD 47-48—first missionary journey (Acts 13—14)

AD 49—the apostolic council in Jerusalem (Acts 15:1-35)

AD 49-51—second missionary journey (Acts 15:36—18:22)

AD 52-56—third missionary journey (Acts 18:23—21:17)

AD 56-58—imprisonment in Caesarea (Acts 23:33—26:32)

AD 59—voyage to Rome (Acts 27-28)

AD 60-61—imprisonment in Rome (Acts 28:30-31)

AD 62-67—further missionary work in Spain, Crete, Ephesus, and elsewhere (Rom 15:24,28; 1 Tim 1:3; Titus 1:5; 3:12)

AD 67—imprisonment and martyrdom at Rome

The writing and sending of the Letters to Timothy and Titus would have taken place between his release from his first Roman imprisonment and his martyrdom. For a discussion of the dates of the individual letters see the introductions to each of them.

Ge[rmanicus, invested with tribunician po]wer [for the 12th time, acclaimed Imperator for t]he 26th time, F[ather of the Fa]ther[land . . .]. For a l[ong time have I been not onl]y [well-disposed towards t]he ci[ty] of Delph[i, but also solicitous for its pro]sperity, and I have always guard[ed th]e cul[t of t]he [Pythian] Apol[lo. But] now [since] it is said to be desti[tu]te of [citi]zens, as [L. Jun]ius Gallio, my fri[end] an[d procon]sul, [recently reported to me, and being desirous that Delphi should retain [inta]ct its for[mer rank, I] ord[er you (pl.) to in]vite well-born people also from [ot]her cities [to Delphi as new inhabitants]." Murphy-O'Connor, *St. Paul's Corinth*, 161.

THE NATURE OF THE HERESY[42]

It is evident from a reading of the Pastoral Epistles that there were false teachers present who were troubling the churches served by Timothy and Titus (1 Tim 1:6–7; Titus 3:10–11). The critique common to all these letters that Paul makes of these heretics and their false teaching demonstrates that his two coworkers were each dealing with the same type of heresy. From the various places in the Pastorals where the apostle speaks against this false teaching, we can gather something of its claims and its doctrines.

Paul refers to a teaching that "is falsely called knowledge" (1 Tim 6:20). He characterizes its proponents as those who are "never able to come to a knowledge of the truth" (2 Tim 3:7) and its adherents as those who claim to "know God" (Titus 1:16). This indicates that the heretics claimed for themselves a religious "knowledge" that others supposedly did not have. Yet for all their claims to knowledge the apostle asserts that they deny God by their works (Titus 1:16), that they hold "to deceptive spirits and teachings of demons" (1 Tim 4:1), and that they are "never able to come to a knowledge of the truth" (2 Tim 3:7).

In order to promote their so-called "knowledge" the heretics resorted to impressive-sounding rhetoric and fine-sounding arguments. Paul speaks of their "futile talk" (1 Tim 1:6), their "morbid craving for controversies and disputes about words" (1 Tim 6:4), their "corrupt, meaningless talk and the contradictions of what is falsely named knowledge" (1 Tim 6:20), their "foolish and uninformed speculations" that "give birth to disputes" (2 Tim 2:23), and to their "useless speculations" (1 Tim 1:4). He asserts that they "know neither what things they say nor the things about which they insist" (1 Tim 1:7). While their talk and disputes about words may have made them seem astute and learned, the apostle evaluates their doctrines as "foolish controversies . . . and disputes and arguments about the law" that "are unprofitable and futile" (Titus 3:9).

In these letters Paul often identifies his teaching as "the truth."[43] In contrast he speaks of "myths" that are troubling these churches.[44] He also speaks of these as involving "genealogies" (1 Tim 1:4; Titus 3:9), and he characterizes these false teachings as "speculations" (1 Tim 1:4;

---

42. An earlier version of this section appeared in Deterding, *Colossians*, 7–12.
43. 1 Tim 2:4, 7; 3:15; 4:3; 6:5; 2 Tim 2:15, 18, 25; 3:7, 8; 4:4; Titus 1:1, 14.
44. 1 Tim 1:4; 4:7; 2 Tim 4:4; Titus 1:14.

2 Tim 2:23). He notes that these false teachings stir up controversies, which cause dissension and quarreling.[45]

The apostle also critiqued the heretics for their way of life. Some of the false teachers practiced a false piety that involved living according to human commandments and regulations, forbidding such things as marriage and the eating of certain foods (1 Tim 4:1–3; Titus 1:14). Others were guilty of all manner of vices (2 Tim 3:2–7; Titus 1:16).

A peculiar doctrine of the heretics had to do with the resurrection of the dead. At least some of the false teachers (Paul names two of them) held to the notion that the resurrection had already taken place (2 Tim 2:17–18).

This false teaching was more than an academic or hypothetical problem for the churches served by Timothy and Titus (and Paul). The heretics had already enticed some people away from sound teaching (2 Tim 4:3–4; see also 3:2–7). There were those who had swerved from the faith (1 Tim 6:21); certain ones (the apostle names some) had lost salvation altogether by going contrary to conscience (1 Tim 1:19–20).

We should also note that this heresy had some distinctively Jewish elements about it. Among the deceivers were "those of the circumcision [party]" (Titus 1:10). Paul notes that among the dangers to the faith of these Christians are "Jewish myths" (Titus 1:14), and when he warns Titus to avoid "disputes and arguments about the law" (Titus 3:9), this may also point to a Jewish element to the heresy troubling his churches.

From this we see that the heresy besetting the churches served by Timothy and Titus bore a number of similarities to the Gnosticism of the second and third centuries AD. This suggests that like several other New Testament documents[46] these letters were written against a point of view that later developed to become (at least an element of) the religious movement known as Gnosticism.[47]

---

45. 1 Tim 6:4; 2 Tim 2:24, 23; Titus 3:9.

46. Although it is by no means universally accepted, the case can be made for the Gospel and Letters of John, 1 Corinthians, Colossians, 2 Peter, and/or the Letter of Jude as having been written against some early precursor of Gnosticism. There is considerable similarity between the heresy combated by Paul's Letter to the Colossians and that which he opposes in the Pastoral Letters (Knight, *Pastoral Epistles*, 72). The origin of the Johannine writings from the same area as that to which 1 and 2 Timothy, as well as Colossians, were written suggests that an early form of Gnosticism was prominent in that part of the world and supports the identification of the heresy dealt with in these letters as having significant elements in common with the Gnosticism of the second and third centuries.

47. Along these lines see Easton, *Pastoral Epistles*, 2–8; Arnold, *Syncretism*, 1–3.

Grace and Life

For centuries our knowledge of Gnosticism was limited to the antignostic polemics of second- and third-century church fathers, particularly Irenaeus in his work *Against Heresies*. However, with the discovery of various gnostic documents, especially those contained in the library of gnostic writings found near the modern Egyptian town of Nag Hammadi (the findings are sometimes referred to by the name of the ancient, neighboring locale Chenoboskion), scholars obtained access to gnostic teachings as the gnostics themselves presented them. This led to a substantial confirmation of the picture presented by the fathers.

It would be anachronistic to think that the heresy opposed by the Pastoral Letters conformed in every respect to the elaborately developed gnostic systems of later centuries. Nevertheless, a knowledge of basic gnostic teachings, as drawn from the Nag Hammadi sources as well as the fathers, will most likely cast light on the false teaching being combated by the Pastorals.

We must, however, speak of Gnosticism in rather broad, general terms. There was great variety among the gnostic teachers and much fluidity in what they taught. Irenaeus, for example, complains of "the inconsistent views of these men, since there are two or three of them anyway, how they do not even agree on the same topics, but vary from each other about things and about names"[48] and that "because it [gnostic soteriology] is fluctuating, it cannot be described simply or in one account, as each one of them hands it down as he chooses. Each of these mystagogues has his own ceremony of redemption."[49]

Despite this variety we can identify certain tenets typical of many gnostics.[50] The foundational teaching of all forms of "Gnosticism" is that

---

Arnold briefly sketches various points of view on the identification of the Colossian heresy, from those who have confidently identified it with Gnosticism to those who deny any substantive connection between it and later Gnosticism.

48. Irenaeus, *Against Heresies* 1.11.1, in Richardson, *Early Christian Fathers*, 1:362.

49. Irenaeus, *Against Heresies* 1.21.1, in Richardson, *Early Christian Fathers*, 1:354.

50. A concise introduction to gnostic writings and teachings may be garnered from the articles on "Gnosticism" and "Nag Hammadi Codices" in the *Anchor Bible Dictionary*. Representative gnostic sources can be found in the following volumes:

Hennecke and Schneemelcher, *New Testament Apocrypha*. Especially the first volume of this standard reference tool contains translations of a number of important gnostic documents.

Nag Hammadi Library in English, 3rd ed.

Rudolph, *Gnosis*. This in-depth study of Gnosticism, past and present, contains numerous quotations from primary gnostic sources, especially the Nag Hammadi literature, whose discovery is also recounted.

since God is pure spirit (πνεῦμα), matter (the flesh) is inherently evil.[51] The origin of matter is explained as resulting from a series of "emanations" who came from God; each of these was slightly less than its predecessor.[52] Sometimes these lesser beings are given names such as αἰῶνες, θρόνοι, κυριότητες, ἀρχαί, or ἐξουσίαι[53] and at times may be identified with angels.[54] The name πλήρωμα is sometimes applied to God alone or to the total pantheon of deities emanated from him;[55] the totality of these emanations might be referred to as genealogies.[56] The last of these emanations, the demiurge, was so far removed from and inferior to the pure πνεῦμα that he performed the horrible act of creating the material (and hence evil) world:[57] "The world came into being through a transgression. For he who created it wanted to create it imperishable and immortal. He failed and did not attain to his hope. For the incorruption of the world did not exist and the incorruption of him who made the world did not exist."[58] In some forms of Gnosticism (Marcionism) this creating emanation was identified with the God of the Old Testament,[59] who is sometimes known by the name Ialdabaoth [Yaldabaoth],[60] a compound name of Semitic origin meaning "he who begets" [יָלַד] "the heavenly hosts" [צְבָאוֹת].[61]

In this scheme redemption involves the escape of the spiritual (πνεῦμα) from the material (σάρξ) in order that there may be unification with God, who is pure spirit (πνεῦμα); one who accomplishes this is said to become perfect. This escape can only occur when one has knowledge [γνῶσις, from which the name "Gnosticism" is derived]; this escape becomes realized at the time of death, the abandonment of the material body of flesh.[62] This knowledge is hidden from humanity and so must

---

51. On the Origin of the World 99:2–22.

52. On the Origin of the World 99:23—103:32.

53. On the Origin of the World 100:1–9, 29; Apocryphon of John 7:30—11:10; Irenaeus, *Prescriptions Against Heretics* 14.7, 33 (ANF 3:246, 259).

54. Apocalypse of Adam 85:1–18.

55. Gospel of Truth 16:31—17:4.

56. Irenaeus, *Against Heresies* 1, Preface.

57. On the Origin of the World 100:29—103:32; Gospel of Truth 17:4—18:11; Irenaeus, *Against Heresies* 1.1, in Richardson, *Early Christian Fathers*, 1:358.

58. Gospel of Philip 75:2–9; translation in Rudolph, *Gnosis*, 83.

59. Rudolph, *Gnosis*, 314.

60. On the Origin of the World 100:19–24.

61. Rudolph, *Gnosis*, 73.

62. Gospel of Truth 21:11—22:19; *Book of Thomas the Contender* 139:28–30; *Authoritative Teaching* 32:16—33:2.

be revealed; the task of revealing this saving knowledge is the work of the redeemer. The redeemer may be identified with one of the emanations, perhaps even the highest of these, and may be said to have first himself been redeemed; sometimes the redeemer/revealer is identified as Christ:[63] "Jesus appeared.... He who was redeemed in turn redeemed (others)."[64] "Even the Son himself, who has the position of redeemer of the Totality, [needed] redemption as well—he who had become man—since he gave himself for each thing which we need, we in the flesh, who are his Church. Now, when he first received redemption from the word which had descended upon him, all the rest received redemption from him, namely those who had taken him to themselves."[65]

Gnostics put great stress on the hidden and secret nature of the saving knowledge, which they maintained could only be revealed through their philosophy:[66] "These mysteries which I shall give you, preserve, and give them to no man except he be worthy of them. Give them not to father nor to mother, to brother or to sister or to kinsman, neither for food nor for drink, nor for woman-kind, neither for gold nor for silver, nor for anything at all of this world. Preserve them, and give them to no one whatsoever for the sake of the good of this whole world."[67] Possession of this knowledge meant that as one's spirit made its way to the πνεῦμα, he would know what to say (like a password) to each of the emanations by which he would have to pass on his way to union with God.[68] Of those without the saving knowledge it is sometimes said that they will be annihilated[69] or eternally punished;[70] other sources claim that these will be subject to reincarnation until they obtain knowledge.[71]

The attitude of the gnostics toward the material led them to hold one or the other of two different (and contradictory) views toward life in

63. Apocryphon of John 1:5—2:25; Gospel of Truth 23:18—24:9.

64. Gospel of Philip 70:34—71:4; translation in *Nag Hammadi Library*, 152.

65. Tripartite Tractate 124:32—125:9; translation in *Nag Hammadi Library*, 97.

66. Apocryphon of John 31:32—32:5; Gospel of Thomas 13.

67. *Two Books of Jeu*, 43; translation in Hennecke et al., *New Testament Apocrypha*, 1:263.

68. First Apocalypse of James 32:29—35:25; Gospel of Thomas 50; Apocalypse of Paul 23:1-28.

69. Gospel of Truth 21:34-37.

70. *Book of Thomas the Contender* 142:6—143:7.

71. Epiphanius, *Panarion* 26:13, 3. The reference in the *Panarion* of Epiphanius is to an otherwise unattested citation attributed to a Gospel under the name of Philip; a translation may be found in Hennecke et al., *New Testament Apocrypha*, 1:273.

this world. Some gnostics insisted on the strictest asceticism (such as no sex or certain foods being forbidden) to tame the flesh, lest contamination with worldly things pollute one's spirit.[72] Others claimed that since matter and the flesh had no place in redemption, one with knowledge could live as licentiously as he pleased.[73] In general, gnostics regarded themselves as superior to those who did not have knowledge and frequently would have nothing to do with them.[74]

These tenets of Gnosticism required its adherents to neglect or even to deny the incarnation[75] and to interpret the death and resurrection of Christ in some other fashion than as events in history.[76] The resurrection of the redeemed also had to be "spiritualized" or otherwise explained as having already taken place (cf. 2 Tim 2:17–18).[77]

In expounding upon its esoteric doctrines gnostic philosophy made much use of favorite technical terms. Two especially common ones were "light" and "truth."[78]

While it would be rash to assume that all of these tenets of second- and third-century Gnosticism were also a part of the heresy against which the Letters to Timothy and to Titus were written, there does seem to be enough common ground to suggest that the heresy afflicting these churches was an early form of Gnosticism. The stress of the letters on the deity and incarnation of Christ, their teaching on Christ's appearance in the "flesh," their presentation of the total sufficiency of the saving work of Christ, the importance given to the event of the cross, their teachings regarding the resurrection, and their instruction in Christian ethics with an emphasis upon love for others as the chief practice of the Christian life all point to a proto-gnostic heresy as being the source of trouble in the Christian congregation(s) at Ephesus and Crete. The presence of early

---

72. Gospel of Thomas 27, 28; Apocryphon of John 22:10–20; 24:26–31.

73. Epiphanius, *Panarion* 26:8:2–3. Epiphanius refers to a gnostic source that he calls the "Greater Questions of Mary"; a translation is given in Hennecke et al., *New Testament Apocrypha*, 1:339.

74. Gospel of Thomas 49.

75. Gospel of Philip 57:29—58:10; Gospel of Truth 31:1–9; see the translation and commentary in Rudolph, *Gnosis*, 160.

76. Gospel of Truth 20:15–34; Acts of John 97–101; Second Treatise of the Great Seth 55:9—56:19.

77. Gospel of Thomas 51; Exegesis on the Soul 134:6–15.

78. *Pistis Sophia* 2–6; Gospel of Thomas 50; Gospel of Truth 16:31—17:4.

Gnosticism in Asia Minor (where Timothy was conducting his ministry) when John wrote his Gospel and letters also make this identification likely.[79]

A teaching of a "gnostic" type would not be incompatible with the Jewish elements in the heresy that Paul combats in these letters. While the mention of circumcision (Titus 1:10) goes beyond anything attested in gnostic writings, there is ample evidence of the presence of Semitic terminology within gnostic systems.[80] Thus, when we describe this heresy as "Jewish-gnostic," this does not suggest the amalgamation of two worlds of thought that did not already have certain points of contact.[81]

There is certainly no consensus among scholars as to the origins of Gnosticism. Nevertheless, it seems probable that this heresy arose when the teachings or at least the terminology of Christianity (including its Semitic [Old Testament] elements) were reinterpreted in light of Greek philosophy—especially that of (Neo-) Platonism.[82]

This harmonization of Christian concepts and/or vocabulary with Greek philosophy points to the attractiveness of early Gnosticism, especially for some within the outward association of the first-century Christian church. Gnostic writings give evidence of a high level of intellectual achievement by at least some of its leaders,[83] so that to follow after "Gnosticism" was to associate with the educated elite. The false teachers against whom the Pastoral Letters are written appear to have been "clever in specious reasoning, fluent in words, and confident in their own powers."[84] "Gnosticism" surely struck many as a more sophisticated or intellectually mature version of the faith. "Gnosticism" seemed to offer one the best of Greek philosophy as well as of the church; it gave one the air of sophistication and appealed to the modern and "trendy." "Gnosticism" had all the outward attraction of a theology of glory over against Christianity's theology of the cross.[85] Hence, the apostle points to the

---

79. Refer to the discussion in n46.

80. Rudolph, *Gnosis*, 73–74.

81. See also Kelly, *Pastoral Epistles*, 10–12; Debelius and Conzelmann, *Pastoral Epistles*, 16–17.

82. Hennecke et al., *New Testament Apocrypha*, 1:275; see also Grant, *Gnosticism*, 16; Towner, *Letters*, 42–43; *DPL* 71, 714.

83. Rudolph, *Gnosis*, 210.

84. Ramsey, *Historical Commentary*, 36.

85. On the theology of the cross, see Luther's Heidelberg Disputation (AE 31:35–70) and Forde, *Theologian of the Cross*.

ultimate (eschatological) advantage of his gospel of an incarnate, crucified, and risen Christ followed by a faith active in obedience over against the tenets of the false teachers.

SALUTATIONS IN PAUL'S LETTERS

Letters in the ancient world normally began with the name of the writer, followed by the name of the recipient(s), followed by the word "greetings" (Acts 15:23; 23:26). In his letters Paul adapts this format. He adds descriptive statements to his name and/or that of the recipient(s). Moreover, he changes "greetings" (χαίρειν) to the similarly sounding "grace" (χάρις) and adds the word "peace" (an important concept in Old Testament thought and a greeting used in Jewish letters of the time).[86]

The descriptions of himself and of the recipients that the apostle makes in these salutations are significant. They say something about Paul's ministry and gospel and often point toward some theme of the letter in question. See the commentary on the salutation of each of the letters treated in this volume for the use that Paul makes of each one.

MATTERS OF INTERPRETATION

How ought we read and regard these letters? Do they record the opinions of some ancient author, which we are free to follow or disregard at our discretion? Should we think of them as principles that may have been valid for another time and place but which no longer pertain to us today? Do these continue to have validity and authority for future generations? To resolve this matter we need to see how the author of these letters himself regarded them.

It should be noted that the matter of the authorship of the Pastorals, discussed above, is related to their interpretation. Those who deny the Pauline authorship of these letters often pit them against those letters that they regard as authentic works of the apostle. The teachings of the Pastorals are then judged to be inferior to those of the "authentic Paul." Thus, the decision made regarding the authorship of the Pastorals will have an effect on how one interprets them.[87]

---

86. See, for example, 2 Macc 1:1.
87. Towner, *Letters*, 227, gives an example of such an approach to these letters.

In the salutation of each of these missives Paul identifies himself as an "apostle of Christ Jesus/Jesus Christ." The term "apostle" is a weighty and significant one; the chief characteristic of an apostle is that he is one who is sent with authority. By identifying himself at the outset of each letter as an apostle of Christ Paul indicates that in these epistles he is speaking with all the authority of the Lord of the church himself (see further the entry "Apostle" in the Extended Notes).

That this is the case may be seen most clearly in that portion of 1 Timothy where the apostle begins a section by indicating that it sets forth what "the Spirit explicitly says" (1 Tim 4:1). Thus, Paul clearly regarded this letter as more than fatherly advice; as an apostle of Jesus Christ he was serving as a mouthpiece for God the Holy Spirit (cf. John 15:13–15).

Paul's apostolic authority is reflected in the forceful directives he gives throughout the Pastoral Letters. He writes: "I desire" (1 Tim 2:8); "I do not permit" (1 Tim 2:12); "It is necessary" (1 Tim 3:2, 15); "I adjure you before God and Christ Jesus and the elect angels, that you keep these things without prejudice" (1 Tim 5:21); "Before God, who gives life to all things, and Christ Jesus, who bore witness to Pontius Pilate about the good confession, I direct you to keep the commandment spotless and irreproachable until the appearing of our Lord Jesus Christ" (1 Tim 6:13–14); "I adjure [you] before God and Christ Jesus, who is about to judge the living and the dead, and by his appearing and his kingdom, preach the word" (2 Tim 4:1); "I left you in Crete, in order that you would set right the things that are lacking and appoint elders town by town, just as I commanded you" (Titus 1:5). He directs his coworkers not to teach any other doctrine (1 Tim 1:3) but rather to "command and teach these things" (1 Tim 4:11; 5:7; cf. 6:2) and to hold to the "standard of sound words which you heard from me" (2 Tim 1:13). These are all similar to the apostle's words to the Corinthians: "If anyone thinks he is a prophet or spiritual, let him acknowledge that the things which I am writing to you are a command of the Lord" (1 Cor 14:37). These statements clearly attest that what is written in the Pastorals consists of more than one man's private opinions.

Paul concludes two of his letters with the instruction that they be "read" (1 Thess 5:27; Col 4:16). In this way he is indicating that these epistles are to be regarded on the same level as the Hebrew Scriptures, which God's people had long been reading as part of their public worship (Luke 4:16–21; Acts 13:14–15). At the end of each of the Pastoral Letters the apostle offers the blessing "grace be with you," the word "you" in the Greek (ὑμῶν) being plural in number; this demonstrates that Paul intended these letters to be read in the worship services of the congregations in the same way as they read from the Torah and the Prophets.

In connection with this it may be helpful to refer to the apostle's instruction to the church at Thessalonica (2 Thess 2:15). After speaking of how the Thessalonians were called by the gospel to salvation through faith in Jesus Christ, he continues: "Therefore brothers, stand firm and hold to the traditions which you were taught, whether by word or by our letter."

The context of any use of the term "tradition" (παράδοσις) will determine whether or not it is to be understood in a positive or a negative light. The New Testament plainly rejects the validity of the Pharisaic "traditions of the elders."[88] However, the Scriptures also use the "tradition" word family in a very positive sense.

The Greek word for "tradition" derives from a verb (παραδίδωμι) that means "hand over." Thus, a "tradition" is something that is handed over; the source from which the "tradition" is handed over will determine the character of that particular "tradition." If it is handed over from humans, it is something indifferent or perhaps even corrupted by sin. However, it is quite a different matter if it is handed over from God.

The "tradition" of 2 Thess 2 has been taught/handed over by Paul. The use of the verb "taught" (ἐδιδάχθητε) here demonstrates that in this context "tradition" is the equivalent of "teaching," a word which encompasses the entirety of Christian doctrine.[89] Thus, tradition that comes from God, such as through an apostle like Paul, is authoritative and saving, and so is to be believed and followed.[90]

This is further indicated by the apostle's use of the cognate verb "handed on" (παραδίδωμι) and its complementary verb "received" (παραλαμβάνω). The apostle informs the Corinthians that he handed on to them what they received, namely, the gospel facts with regard to the death and resurrection of Jesus Christ (1 Cor 15:1–4). Similarly, Paul relates that he himself received from the Lord the truth about the Lord's Supper, which he in turn handed on to the church at Corinth (1 Cor 11:23–26). He wrote to the Romans that they were given

---

88. See Matt 15:1–20; Mark 7:1–23; Gal 1:11–17; Col 2:8.
89. See the entry "Teaching/Doctrine" in the Extended Notes.
90. See also 1 Cor 11:2; 2 Thess 3:6.

(παρεδόθητε) the pattern (τύπον) of teaching that had set them free from their slavery to sin (Rom 6:17).

All of this leads to the conclusion that the Letters to Timothy and to Titus are to be regarded in the same way as the Hebrew Scriptures. Within these letters the apostle indicates how he regarded those ancient writings.

When Paul writes about "the holy Scriptures" that Timothy has known "from infancy" (2 Tim 3:15), the writings that make up the New Testament had not yet been gathered together into a collection; at that point some of them might not even have been written. Therefore, the reference here to "the holy Scriptures" is to those sacred writings that we commonly call the Old Testament. The fact that the apostle regards his letters as being on a par with the Hebrew Scriptures demonstrates that what he writes about the Old Testament applies also to his own letters (and, for that matter, to the rest of the New Testament).

Paul speaks of the Scriptures as being "breathed into by God" (θεόπνευστος, 2 Tim 3:16). This recollection of Gen 2:7 points to the Scriptures as being alive in a way in which no other writing is alive. As another apostle attributes this activity to the Holy Spirit (2 Pet 1:21), as Paul speaks of the Spirit speaking explicitly through his own writing (1 Tim 4:1), and as the Spirit is associated with the breath of God (Job 33:4; John 20:22), it may be concluded that the one who breathed into the Scriptures is God the Holy Spirit.

The apostle spells out in further detail what being breathed into by God means. He writes that the Scriptures "are able to make you wise unto salvation through faith, which is in Christ Jesus" (2 Tim 3:15). He adds that they are "profitable for teaching, for rebuke, for improvement, for instruction in righteousness, in order that the man of God might be complete, completely equipped for every good work" (2 Tim 3:16–17).

This attitude toward Scripture is equivalent to that of Jesus himself, who used both "Scripture" and "the word of God" to identify a portion of the Hebrew Scriptures (John 10:35). Paul regarded Scripture as being breathed into by him "who does not lie" (Titus 1:2).

As we read the Scriptures, including the Pastoral Letters, we need to distinguish the contingent from the constant. Some portions of the Bible are descriptive of circumstances that pertained at the time of writing but which are not mandatory for all times, while other parts have to do with circumstances that are binding on all believers, at least until the parousia. For example, in the case of the Pastorals there is no requirement that churches have an order of widows,[91] while it is clear that it is the will of God that his people be served by pastors (Titus 1:5). That being said, the distinction that the Scriptures themselves indicate between the contingent and constant is not the same as readers of the Bible deciding which portions of them are to be followed and which may be ignored or even rejected.

In light of all of this we must treat these letters as coming from God himself. They express God's eternal word to his church and the world and his abiding will for his people.

In connection with this I would call your attention to a type of shorthand that I use in this volume. When I write "Paul" or "the apostle" as the subject of a verb denoting proclamation—such as "Paul writes," "the apostle indicates," "Paul states," "the apostle demonstrates"—you should realize that such phrases are an abridgment for "God the Holy Spirit through the apostle Paul."

---

91. See the commentary on 1 Tim 5:3–16.

Appendix

Parallels Between the Pastoral Letters and the Other Letters of Paul

	1 Tim	2 Tim	Titus	Rom	1 Cor	2 Cor	Gal	Eph	Phil	Col	1 Th	2 Th	Phm
"Christ Jesus"	1:1 (2x), 2, 4, 12, 14, 15; 2:5; 3:13; 4:6; 5:21; 6:13	1:1 (2x), 2, 9, 10, 13; 2:1, 3, 10; 3:12, 15; 4:1	1:4	1:1; 2:16; 3:24; 6:3, 11, 23; 8:1, 2, 34, 39; 15:5, 16, 17; 16:3	1:1, 2, 4, 30; 4:15; 15:31; 16:24	1:1	2:4, 16 (2x); 3:14, 26, 28; 4:14; 5:6, 24	1:1 (2x); 2:6, 7, 10, 13, 20; 3:1, 6, 11, 21	1:1 (2x), 8, 26; 2:5; 3:3, 8, 12, 14; 4:7, 18, 21	1:1, 4; 2:6; 4:12	2:14; 5:18		1, 9, 23
Justification/ Righteousness	6:11	2:22; 3:16; 4:8	3:5–7	1:17; 3:20–30; 4:3–13; 5:1, 9, 17, 21; 6:7; 8:10, 30, 33; 9:30; 10:6	1:30; 6:11	3:9; 5:21; 6:7; 9:9, 10	2:16, 17, 21; 3:8, 11, 21, 24; 5:4–5	4:24; 5:9; 6:14	1:11; 3:9				
God as Savior	1:1; 2:3–4; 4:10	1:9	2:10–11; 3:4–5	1:16	1:21	6:2		2:5, 8	1:28		5:9		
Christ as Savior	1:15	1:10; 2:10; 3:15; 4:18	1:4; 2:13; 3:6	5:9–10	5:5; 15:2	7:10		1:13; 5:23	3:20		5:9	2:13	
Mercy	1:2	1:2	3:5	9:23; 11:31; 15:9			6:16	2:4					

	1 Tim	2 Tim	Titus	Rom	1 Cor	2 Cor	Gal	Eph	Phil	Col	1 Th	2 Th	Phm
Holy Spirit	(3:16) 4:1	(1:7); 1:14	3:5	1:4; 2:29; 5:5; 8:2, 4–6, 9, 11, 13–15, 23, 26–27; 9:1; 14:17; 15:13, 16, 19, 30	2:4, 10–14; 3:16; 6:11; 7:40; 12:3–4; 7–9, 11, 13	1:22; 3:3, 6, 8, 17–18; 6:6; 13:13	3:2–3, 5, 14; 4:6, 29; 5:5, 16–17, 22, 25; 6:8	1:13–14; 2:18, 22; 3:5, 16; 4:3–4; 5:18; 6:17–18	1:19; 2:1; 3:3	1:8	1:5–6; 4:8; 5:19	2:13	
Good works follow faith	2:10; 3:1; 5:10, 25; 6:18	2:21; 3:17	1:16; 2:14; 3:1, 8, 14	13:3, 12		9:8		2:10		1:10	1:3	2:16–17	
Similar catalogues of vices	1:9–10; 6:4–5	3:2–5	3:2–4	1:29–30			5:19–21	5:3–5					
Need for rebuke	5:20	4:2	1:9, 13					5:11					
Epiphaneia for Parousia	6:14	4:1, 8	2:13									2:8	
In(to) Christ; in the Lord, etc.	1:1, 4; 3:13	1:1, 9, 13; 2:1, 10; 3:12, 15		3:24; 6:3,11, 23; 8:1, 2, 39; 9:1; 12:5; 14:14; 15:17; 16:2, 3, 7–13, 22	1:2, 4, 5, 30, 31; 3:1; 4:10, 15, 17; 7:22, 39; 9:1; 2; 11:11; 15:18, 22, 31, 58;16:19, 24	1:19–21; 2:12, 14, 17; 5:17, 19, 21; 10:17; 12:2, 19; 13:4	1:22; 2:4, 16, 17; 3:14, 26–28; 5:6, 10	1:1, 3, 4, 6, 7, 9–13, 20; 2:6, 7, 10, 13, 15, 21, 22; 3:6, 11, 12, 21; 4:1, 15, 17, 21, 32; 5:8; 6:1, 10, 21	1:1, 14, 26; 2:1, 5, 19, 24, 29; 3:1, 3, 9, 14; 4:1, 2, 4, 7, 10, 19, 21	1:2, 4, 14, 16, 17, 19, 20, 28; 2:3, 6, 7, 9–11, 15; 3:18; 4:7, 17	1:1; 2:14; 3:3; 4:1, 16; 5:12, 18	1:1, 12; 3:4, 12	8, 16, 20, 23

	1 Tim	2 Tim	Titus	Rom	1 Cor	2 Cor	Gal	Eph	Phil	Col	1 Th	2 Th	Phm
Hope (noun)	1:1		1:2; 2:13; 3:7	4:18; 5:2, 4, 5; 8:20, 24; 12:12; 15:4, 13	13:13	3:12	5:5	1:18; 4:4	1:20	1:5, 23, 27	1:3; 5:8	2:16	
Hope (verb)	4:10; 5:5; 6:17			8:25		1:10							
"Labor" in ministry	4:10; 5:17				15:10; 16:16		4:11		2:16	1:29	5:12		
Instruction to slaves	6:1–2		2:9–10					6:5–8		3:22–25			
Transformation of master/slave relationship	6:1–2		2:9–10					6:5–8		3:22–25			16
Paul entrusted with gospel	1:11		1:3				2:7						
Timothy Paul's true child	1:2	1:2			4:17				2:20, 22		2:4		
Christ as God	1:17		2:13										
Glory forever Amen	1:17	4:18		16:27			1:5	3:21	4:20	1:15; 2:9			
Christ gave himself	2:6		2:14				1:4; 2:20	5:2, 25					
To the Gentiles	2:7	4:17		11:13; 15:16, 18			2:7–9	3:1, 8			2:16		

	1 Tim	2 Tim	Titus	Rom	1 Cor	2 Cor	Gal	Eph	Phil	Col	1 Th	2 Th	Phm
Overseers	3:1–7		1:5–9						1:1				
Example (*typos*) to believers	4:12		2:7						3:17		1:7	3:9	
Lists of virtues	4:12; 6:11	2:22					6:6	5:22–23					
Showing "hospitality"	3:2; 5:10		1:8	12:13									
Christians as soldiers	1:18	2:3–4			9:7	10:3–4		6:11–17	2:25				
Christinas as athletes	(6:12)	2:5; 4:7			9:25								
Avoid certain people		3:5	3:10–11	16:17	5:9, 11			3:21				3:6, 14	
Doxologies	1:17	4:18		16:27			1:5		4:20				
Grace be with you	6:21	4:22								4:18			
Not by works		1:9	3:5	3:20, 27; 4:2, 6; 9:12, 32; 11:6			2:16; 3:2, 10	2:9					
With Christ		2:11–12		6:4–6, 8; 8:17, 32		4:14; 13:4	2:20	2:5, 6	1:23; 3:10, 21	2:12, 13, 20; 3:1, 3, 4	4:14, 17; 5:10		
Trinitarian expressions			3:4–6		12:4–6			4:4–6					

	1 Tim	2 Tim	Titus	Rom	1 Cor	2 Cor	Gal	Eph	Phil	Col	1 Th	2 Th	Phm
Kerygma to the nations	3:16			1:5; 16:26			2:2						
Saving others	4:16			11:14	9:22								
Churchly Leadership	5:17			12:8							5:12		
Apostle through the will of God		1:1			1:1	1:1		1:1		1:1			
God's plan		1:9		8:28				1:11; 3:11					
Resurrection of Christ	3:16	2:8		1:4; 4:24–25; 6:4, 9; 8:11, 34; 10:9	6:14; 15:4, 12–20	4:14; 5:15	1:1	1:20		2:12	1:10		
God/Christ faithful		2:13			1:9; 10:13	1:18					5:24		
The word of truth		2:15				6:7		1:13		1:5			
Christ provides strength		4:17				12:9–10			4:17				
Heirs Inheritance			3:7	4:13–14; 8:17	6:9–10; 15:50		3:18, 29; 4:7; 5:21	1:14, 18; 5:5		3:24		3:3	
Paul the least or worst	1:15–16				15:9			3:8					
Pray regularly	2:1			12:12				6:18	4:6	4:2	5:17		

	1 Tim	2 Tim	Titus	Rom	1 Cor	2 Cor	Gal	Eph	Phil	Col	1 Th	2 Th	Phm
Quiet undisturbed life	2:2										5:11	3:12	
One God	2:5			3:30	8:4, 6			4:6					
Quietness a virtue	2:11–12										4:11	3:12	
All foods received with thanksgiving	4:3–4			14:6	10:30–31								
Make mention in prayer		1:3		1:9							1:2		
Paul afflicted for others		2:10						(3:13)		1:24			
Warning of deception			1:10	16:18			6:3	5:6		2:4			
"Of the circumcision"			1:10				2:12			4:11			
All things pure to the pure			1:15	14:14, 20	10:25–27								
Awaiting the Parousia			2:13		1:7				3:20				
Past sinful life			3:3					2:2; 5:6		3:7			
Christ our hope	1:1									1:27			

	1 Tim	2 Tim	Titus	Rom	1 Cor	2 Cor	Gal	Eph	Phil	Col	1 Th	2 Th	Phm
Christ empowers Paul	1:12								4:13				
Lord regards Paul faithful	1:13				7:25								
Paul shown mercy	1:13				7:25								
Superabundant grace	1:14			5:20									
God wants all saved	2:4			11:32									
Man Christ Jesus	2:5			5:15									
For all	2:6					5:15							
Speaking the truth, not lying	2:7			9:1									
Incarnation as "flesh"	3:16			1:3									
Rising by "S/spirit"	3:16			1:4									
Kerygma to the cosmos	3:16									1:6, 23			
Progress in faith and ministry	4:15								1:12, 25				
Teaching	4:13			12:7									

	1 Tim	2 Tim	Titus	Rom	1 Cor	2 Cor	Gal	Eph	Phil	Col	1 Th	2 Th	Phm
S/spirit of power		1:7			2:4								
Eternal now made known		1:9–10		16:25–26									
Salvation as incorruption		1:10			15:42, 53–54								
Dwelling of the Holy Spirit		1:14		8:11									
Christ of the seed of David		2:8		1:3									
We unfaithful; God faithful		2:13		3:3									
Scripture for teaching		3:16		15:4									
Rescue		4:17–18				1:10							
"with your spirit"		4:22					6:18		4:23				
Greetings from "all"			3:15		16:20	13:12			4:22				25
"washing" for baptism			3:5					5:26					
Law is good	1:8			7:12, 16									
Paul formerly a persecutor	1:13						1:13						

	1 Tim	2 Tim	Titus	Rom	1 Cor	2 Cor	Gal	Eph	Phil	Col	1 Th	2 Th	Phm
Give over to Satan	1:20				5:5								
Without disputing	2:8								2:14				
Order of the sexes in the church	2:11–12				11:3, 33–35								
Adam created before Eve	2:13				11:8–9								
Deception of Eve	2:13					11:3							
Deacons	3:8–13								1:1				
End times apostasy	4:1–3	3:1–9										2:3	
No one is to despise Timothy	4:12				16:11								
Reproof of busybodies	5:13											3:11	
Need for some to marry	5:11–15				7:9								
Citation of Deut 25:4	5:18				9:9								
Contentment	6:6								4:11				
Paul a drink offering		4:6							2:17				

	1 Tim	2 Tim	Titus	Rom	1 Cor	2 Cor	Gal	Eph	Phil	Col	1 Th	2 Th	Phm
Pastor as a steward			1:7		4:1								
Order of the sexes in marriage			2:5					5:22–24					
Shaming the opposition			2:8									3:14	
Subject to the governing authorities			3:1	13:1–7									
Be kind to others			3:2						4:5				
Having the form		3:5		2:20									

Introduction to 1 Timothy

RECIPIENT

During his first missionary journey (Acts 13–14) Paul had brought the gospel to the city of Lystra in Asia Minor (Acts 14:6–23). Opponents of his from other cities had followed him there and had stirred up "the crowds" against the apostle, so that he was stoned and left for dead (14:19). Paul survived this assault, and after carrying out ministry in the town of Derbe, he returned to Lystra, strengthening the believers and appointing one or more "elders" (pastors and perhaps other church leaders) for the church there (14:23).[1]

The apostle began his second missionary journey (Acts 15:36—18:22) intending to revisit the churches started during the previous journey (Acts 15:36). The first cities revisited were Derbe and Lystra (Acts 16:1). Timothy was one of the disciples at Lystra. His father was a Greek, that is, a gentile, and as the son of a mixed marriage of a Greek and a Jewess, Timothy had not received the Old Testament rite of circumcision (Acts 16:1–3). Nevertheless, he had been taught the faith of the Old Testament Scriptures by his grandmother Lois and his mother Eunice (2 Tim 1:5). Since he had a Greek father, he might have had a Greek style of education as well.[2]

Paul wanted Timothy to join him in his missionary endeavors. He had this half-Jewish coworker circumcised, so that his lack of that Old Testament rite would not be a hindrance to their outreach to Jews (Acts 16:3).

When the apostle wrote his First Letter to Timothy, he could still refer to his coworker as a youth (4:12). Paul himself was a "young man" at the time of the death of Stephen (Acts 7:58), some thirty-plus years

---

1. See the textual note on πρεσβύτεροι at 1 Tim 5:17, including the footnote.
2. Johnson, *Letters*, 94.

prior to the writing of this letter, and so he was probably about thirty years old at that time.³ When the apostle wrote to Timothy, it had been about fifteen years since he had first added the young man to his missionary troupe.⁴ From all of this we gather that when he first became Paul's coworker, Timothy may have still been a teenager.

For all his youth, Timothy must have nevertheless been comparatively mature in his faith. The book of Acts reports that he was well spoken of by the Christians at both Lystra and Iconium (Acts 16:2), and Paul himself testifies that the Philippians were acquainted with the worthwhile ministry in the gospel that Timothy carried out among them (Phil 2:22).

When the apostle writes of the "good confession" that Timothy confessed before many witnesses (1 Tim 6:12), this likely refers to his baptism.⁵ As Paul had first brought the Christian gospel to Lystra, it is likely that Timothy came to the Christian faith at that time. That the apostle here displays familiarity with the circumstances of Timothy's reception of "the washing of rebirth and of renewal of the Holy Spirit" (Titus 3:5) strongly suggests that he was the one who had administered baptism to this new convert.⁶

Having joined the apostle near the beginning of his second missionary journey, Timothy was a trusted coworker during much of Paul's ministerial career; he is mentioned in all of the apostle's letters save for Galatians, Ephesians, and Titus.⁷ On the second missionary journey he was with Paul (and Silas) at Berea, and he and Silas remained there, when the apostle, under duress from troublemakers who had come from nearby Thessalonica, departed for Athens, but not before he had left instructions that Timothy and Silas were to join him as soon as possible (Acts 17:13–15). From Athens Paul went to Corinth, where Timothy and Silas rejoined him (Acts 18:5) for his eighteen-month ministry in that city (Acts 18:5, 11). During his time there Timothy was also engaged in proclaiming Christ to the people of that city (2 Cor 1:19).

---

3. See the "Chronology of Paul's Life" in the Introduction to the Pastoral Letters.

4. See "The Date of This Letter" elsewhere in this introduction.

5. See the section "Timothy's Good Confession" in the commentary on 1 Tim 6:11–16.

6. See the section "Timothy's Good Confession" in the commentary on 1 Tim 6:11–16.

7. Rom 16:21; 1 Cor 4:17; 16:10; 2 Cor 1:1, 19; Phil 1:1; 2:19, 22; Col 1:1; 1 Thess 1:1; 3:2, 6; 2 Thess 1:1; 1 Tim 1:2, 18; 6:20; Phlm 1.

It was while Paul, Silas (Silvanus), and Timothy were in Corinth that the apostle sent Timothy to Thessalonica to encourage the Christians there in their faith (1 Thess 3:2).[8] Not long after that Paul penned his First Letter to the Thessalonians, with Timothy having recently arrived with good news about the faith and love displayed by the Christians in that city (1 Thess 1:1; 3:6).[9] Timothy and Silas are also with the apostle in Corinth, when he wrote his Second Letter to the Thessalonians (2 Thess 1:1).[10]

During his third missionary journey Paul spent some three years in Ephesus (Acts 19:8–10; 28:31), from which he wrote the letter we know as 1 Corinthians.[11] During that time he sent Timothy, well known to the church in Corinth from his earlier time there, to the church in that city to bring them reassurance (1 Cor 4:17; 16:10–11).[12] The instruction that the Corinthian Christians were to put Timothy at ease and that no one should despise him (1 Cor 16:10–11)—along with the apostle's directive to Timothy himself to "let no one despise your youth" (1 Tim 4:12)—might suggest that by nature Timothy may have been somewhat reserved.[13] On the other hand, the fact that Paul selected him for ministry at a young age, entrusted him with ministry in the relatively hostile environment at Berea (Acts 17:13–15), and sent him to minister in another difficult situation (1 Thess 3:1–3) would suggest that despite any quietness of personality Timothy was nevertheless a capable and trusted coworker.[14]

From Ephesus the apostle continued his third missionary journey by revisiting the churches of Macedonia, during which time he wrote his letter we know as 2 Corinthians.[15] Timothy's presence with him when he writes that letter (2 Cor 1:1) is evidence that he had continued to work alongside Paul.

From Macedonia the apostle traveled to Corinth. Timothy was with him at this time, as is evident from his greeting, sent in Paul's Letter to the

---

8. See Bruce, *1 & 2 Thessalonians*, xxxv, 61–62; Morris, *Epistles to the Thessalonians*, 25.
9. See Bruce, *1 & 2 Thessalonians*, 66–67.
10. Bruce, *1 & 2 Thessalonians*, xxxiv–xxxv; Morris, *Epistles to the Thessalonians*, 24–26.
11. See Lockwood, *1 Corinthians*, 15.
12. See Lockwood, *1 Corinthians*, 155, 617–18.
13. Kelly, *Pastoral Epistles*, 103.
14. Mounce, *Pastoral Epistles*, xlix–l.
15. Kummel, *Introduction to the New Testament*, 293.

GRACE AND LIFE

Romans (16:21), which was written from Corinth during that particular visit.[16]

As the third missionary journey was winding down, Timothy and a number of Paul's other associates accompanied him on his travels from Greece to Macedonia. From there the apostle sent this group ahead of him to Troas, where Paul rejoined them (Acts 20:3–6).

It seems likely that the apostle's "prison letters" to the Philippians, to the Colossians, and to Philemon were all written during his two-year imprisonment in Rome (Acts 28:30–31).[17] Timothy's presence with Paul at that time[18] strongly suggests that he had remained with the apostle from the end of the third missionary journey through the time of his incarceration in Caesarea and subsequent sea voyage to Rome (Acts 21:27—28:31).

The salutation and thanksgiving reports of Paul's Letters to the Thessalonians and especially to the Colossians suggest that Timothy was an especially close associate of the apostle's. Paul ordinarily begins the thanksgiving reports in his letters with the first-person singular,[19] even in those letters in which others are named alongside of him in the salutation.[20] However, in 1 and 2 Thessalonians, where Silas and Timothy are named as co-senders with the apostle, and in Colossians, where the apostle names Timothy as sending the letter with him, Paul begins those thanksgiving reports with "'we' give thanks."[21] In the case of the Letter to the Colossians this suggests that the apostle acknowledged Timothy as contributing, at least in some limited sense, to the content of the letter;[22] perhaps this was also the case with the two Letters to the Thessalonians. This would indicate that Paul had an exceptionally high regard for Timothy.

SETTING AND DATE

See further the "Chronology of Paul's Life" in the Introduction to the Pastoral Letters.

---

16. See Middendorf, *Romans 1—8*, 5–7.
17. Guthrie summarizes the evidence; *New Testament Introduction*, 526–36, 555–58, 639.
18. Phil 1:1; 2:19, 22; Col 1:1; Phlm 1.
19. Rom 1:1, 8; 2 Tim 1:1, 3.
20. 1 Cor 1, 4; Phil 1:1, 3; Phlm 1, 4.
21. Col 1:1, 3; 1 Thess 1:1, 2; 2 Thess 1, 3.
22. See Deterding, *Colossians*, 20.

The book of Acts concludes with the note that Paul's imprisonment in Rome lasted two years. Since the narrative of the book emphasizes that the charges against him were without merit,[23] the implication is that the imprisonment came to an end with his vindication and release.[24]

As indicated in the Introduction to the Pastoral Letters, from Rome the apostle may well have traveled to Spain, from Spain to Crete, from Crete to Ephesus, and from Ephesus to Macedonia. His First Letter to Timothy indicates that Paul left Timothy in Ephesus as he moved on to Macedonia.

In this scenario Paul would have been released from his first Roman imprisonment in AD 61. The present Letter to Timothy would have been composed in the neighborhood of AD 64.

PURPOSE

As we survey the contents of this letter (see "Outline" below), nearly every sentence has to do with the life of the church. The apostle writes about the pastoral ministry and about other positions of ministerial service within the church. He speaks of various groups whom pastors and others serve. He writes of the essentials of the Christian faith, and of various false teachings that threaten the faith and therefore the salvation of believers.

Thus, it may not be going too far to think of the letter as a manual for the life of the church. Paul is concerned with the ongoing life of faith of believers. He writes here in order to equip the church and its ministers for the tasks before them, that they may save themselves and their hearers (1 Tim 4:16).

---

23. The charges were not true (21:27–29); not even the members of the Jewish Sanhedrin could agree on his guilt (22:30—23:9); the tribune Claudius Lysias attested that Paul had done "nothing worthy of death or imprisonment" (23:26–29); his two-year imprisonment in Caesarea was due to his unwillingness or inability to pay a bribe to the Roman governor Felix (24:26–27); the governor Festus and king Herod Agrippa, after hearing him, agreed that he could have been freed, had he not appealed his case to Caesar (26:30–32).

24. See further the subsection "The Historical Setting" of the section "Authenticity and Integrity" in the Introduction to the Pastoral Letters.

OUTLINE

The first seventeen verses of the letter serve as a sort of "overture" to the work.[25] As the overture of an opera[26] introduces themes that will have a prominent role in the remainder of the work, so these verses first touch on themes that will be expounded upon in greater depth in the remainder of the letter.[27]

This epistle sets forth the gospel and the ministry of that gospel that is to be carried out by and within the church. In the overture Paul speaks of Timothy's ministry in the gospel (1:3–11) and of the saving gospel itself (1:12–17).

From this understanding the following outline emerges:

I. Overture

    A. Salutation (1:1–2)

    B. Timothy's Task (1:3–11)

    C. Paul as a Preeminent Example (1:12–17)

II. The Life of the Church

    A. Timothy's Responsibilities (1:18–20)

    B. Life in God's Church (2:1–7)

    C. Various Roles in the Church

        1. Men and Women (2:8–10)

        2. The Pastoral Office (2:11—3:7)

        3. Deacons and Deaconesses (3:8–13)

    D. The Mystery of Godliness (3:14–16)

III. Those Who Minister and Those to Whom They Minister

---

25. See the table on page 46–47.

26. Such as the rock opera "Tommy" by The Who. The tracks "I Am The Sea" and "Quadrophenia" from the band's album *Quadrophenia* serve the same purpose.

27. I would also consider that 2 Tim 1:3–18 and Titus 1:1–4 function as "overtures" to those letters; see "Outline" in the Introduction to 2 Timothy and "One Servant of the Word to Another: Titus 1:1–4 in Context" in the commentary on Titus 1:1–4. In a similar way Col 1:3–20 serves as an overture to that letter; see Deterding, *Colossians*, 26–27. Likewise, Eph 1:3–14 functions in the same way in that epistle (Scharlemann, "Secret of God's Plan," 538–39).

INTRODUCTION TO 1 TIMOTHY

A. Ministry in the Last Times (4:1–5)
B. A Good Minister (4:6–16)
C. Age Groups (5:1–2)
D. Widows and the Office of Widows (5:3–16)
E. Elders (5:17–25)
F. Slaves and Masters (6:1–2a)
G. Timothy's Obligation to Teach the Truth (6:2b–5)
H. True Profit (6:6–10)
I. Timothy's Obligation to Irreproachable Ministry (6:11–16)
J. True Riches for the Rich (6:17–19)
K. Concluding Exhortation to Timothy (6:20–21)

Commentary on 1 Timothy

1:1–17: Overture

The first seventeen verses of this epistle form a sort of "overture" to the letter. As the overture of a symphony introduces certain musical themes that will be explored more thoroughly in the remainder of the piece, these opening verses do likewise.[28] The doxology of verse 17 of this chapter serves as the conclusion to these verses and marks them as a major unit of the letter (see the commentary on 1:17). In this "overture" Paul sketches out both the work of ministry in the gospel and the saving and life-transforming power of the gospel. In the remainder of the letter he will present these topics more thoroughly.

Themes introduced by the overture include the following:

Theme	Overture	Other References
Christ	1:1, 2, 12, 14–17	2:5–6; 3:13, 16; 4:6; 5:21; 6:3, 13–16
Savior/Salvation	1:1, 2, 13–16	2:3–4; 4:10
Ministry	1:1, 3, 11, 12	1:18; 2:7; 2:11—3:13; 3:16; 4:6, 11, 13–16; 5:17–25; 6:2, 11–14, 20
Proclamation	1:3, 8, 11	2:7; 3:16; 4:11, 13
Truth Versus Error	1:4	1:19–20; 2:4, 7; 3:15; 4:1–3; 6:5, 6–10, 21
Faith/Believe	1:2, 4, 5, 14, 16	1:19; 2:7, 15; 3:9, 13, 16; 4:1, 3, 6, 10, 12; 5:8, 12; 6:10, 11, 12, 21

---

28. I would also consider that 2 Tim 1:3–18 and Titus 1:1–4 function as "overtures" to those letters; see "Outline" in the Introduction to 2 Timothy and "One Servant of the Word to Another: Titus 1:1–4 in Context" in the commentary on Titus 1:1–4. In a similar way Colossians 1:3–20 serves as an overture to that letter; see Deterding, *Colossians*, 26–27. Likewise, Ephesians 1:3–14 functions in the same way in that epistle (Scharlemann, "The Secret of God's Plan, 538–539).

Godly Life Versus Ungodly Life	1:9–10	2:1–2, 8–10; 5:1–16; 6:1–10, 17–19
Conscience	1:5	1:19; 3:9; 4:2
Eternal Life	1:1, 16	4:8; 6:12–13, 19

1:1–2: Salutation

On the salutations in Paul's letters see the section "Salutations in Paul's Letters" in the Introduction to the Pastoral Letters.

TRANSLATION

¹ Paul, apostle of Christ Jesus according to the authority of God our savior and Christ Jesus our hope, ² to Timothy, [my] genuine child in the faith: Grace, mercy, and peace from God the Father and Christ Jesus our Lord.

TEXTUAL NOTES

1:1 ἀπόστολος—See the entry on "Apostle" in the Extended Notes.

κατ' ἐπιταγήν—This term often refers to a "command" or "order."[29] However, in Titus 2:15 it means "authority."[30] The author here uses this terminology to describe the source of his apostleship; in five of his other letters[31] he does the same thing with the phrase "through the will of God" (διὰ θελήματος θεοῦ). This suggests that in the present verse ἐπιταγήν is better rendered "authority"; Paul's apostolic ministry is carried out not on his own authority but by the authority of God himself.

σωτῆρος ἡμῶν—The term here refers to God [the Father, cf. 1:2]. That being the case, "savior" here denotes the Father as the one who sent the Son to carry out the plan of salvation. See further the entry "Save, Savior, Salvation" in the Extended Notes and the essay "He Saved Us: The Pastoral Letters on the Way of Salvation" elsewhere in this commentary.

---

29. Rom 16:26; 1 Cor 7:6, 25; 2 Cor 8:8; 1 Tim 1:1; Titus 1:3.
30. BDAG 383.
31. 1 Cor 1:1; 2 Cor 1:1; Eph 1:1; Col 1:1; 2 Tim 1:1.

ἐλπίδος ἡμῶν—This phrase designates Christ Jesus as the object of the Christian's act of hoping and also the one who gives hope to the believer's life. See further the entry on "Hope" in the Extended Notes.

1:2 γνησίῳ τέκνῳ—Timothy had been raised by his mother and grandmother in the faith of the Old Testament (2 Tim 1:5). Timothy was from Lystra, a town to which Paul himself had first brought the Christian gospel (Acts 14:6–23; 16:1–3), so that the apostle could rightly claim him as his "child" both as a Christian believer and as one whom he mentored to be a fellow laborer in the gospel.[32] See further "Timothy's Good Confession" in the commentary on 6:11–16.

ἐν πίστει—The Greek word πίστις ("faith") can refer either to the act of believing (*fides qua creditur*) or to the content of what is believed (*fides quae creditur*). The close association in this letter of faith and truth[33] suggests that the reference here is to the apostle's "genuine child" sharing with him in the ministry of setting forth the true faith (*fides quae creditur*); hence, I have rendered the term here as "*the* faith." See further the entry on "Faith" in the Extended Notes.

τοῦ κυρίου ἡμῶν—As the customary translation in the LXX for the name of God, κύριος is the usual way in which the NT authors identify Jesus Christ as the one true God.[34] See also the essay "Our Great God and Savior: The Christology of the Pastoral Letters" elsewhere in this commentary.

χάρις . . . ἡμῶν—A phrase similar to this is found at the end of the salutations of all of the Pauline Letters—in the two Letters to Timothy the usual phrase "grace and peace" becomes "grace, mercy, and peace." In Paul's letters these are always lacking a verb. Similar phrases in the salutations of other NT letters (1 Pet 1:2; 2 Pet 1:2; Jude 2; 2 John 3) always supply a verb. This suggests the possibility that this style of phrase originated with Paul, and that in "copying" him other authors felt the need to add a verb.[35] In the Pauline phrases some verbal action is clearly implied, something along the lines of "may there be." With these phrases the apostle is pronouncing a blessing on his readers, one that actually delivers the "grace, mercy, and peace" that is spoken of. On the meaning of each of these terms, see the entries on them in the Extended Notes.

---

32. Knight, *Pastoral Epistles*, 365.
33. 1 Tim 2:4, 7; 4:3.
34. BDAG 577 (under 2 b, α) and 577–78 (under 2 b, γ; ב ,א, and ג).
35. Wallace, *Greek Grammar*, 51.

That these blessings come from "God our savior and Christ Jesus our hope" points to the unity of the Father and Christ Jesus and so hints at the deity of Christ.[36] See further "Our Great God and Savior: The Christology of the Pastoral Letters" elsewhere in this commentary.

COMMENTARY

Paul begins this letter in a manner similar to the way in which he begins all his letters: with a salutation that is a modification of the way in which writers of letters in the first-century Greco-Roman world would begin their letters (see "Salutations in Paul's Letters" in the Introduction to the Pastoral Letters). More than simply identifying himself and his recipients, his words touch on some of the truths that will be proclaimed in his letter. Moreover, as a message that comes with the authority of God himself, this greeting actually bestows the blessings with which the apostle concludes this salutation.

As is his usual practice Paul points to the apostolic authority with which he writes. His consciousness of this authority is seen elsewhere in this letter. He does not permit a woman to exercise certain authority in the church (2:12); he writes so that Timothy will know how one ought to behave (3:15); he indicates what the Holy Spirit expressly says (4:1); he gives Timothy a number of imperatives as to how he is to conduct his ministry (4:6, 11; 5:1, 2b, 9, 17; 6:1, 2c, 11, 20).[37]

In this salutation the apostle also refers to the eternal salvation that is the heart and center of the ministry that both he and Timothy carry out. In this way he begins to introduce the substance of the letter that follows.

---

36. Mounce, *Pastoral Epistles*, 9.

37. The authority of Paul's writings is seen also in his directives that his letters are to be "read," that is, to be read aloud in public worship, as God's people had been reading the Torah and the Prophets for centuries (1 Thess 5:27; Col 4:16); see further Deterding, *Colossians*, 192–94.

1:3–11: Timothy's Task

TRANSLATION

³ As I directed you when I was going to Macedonia, remain in Ephesus, in order that you might instruct certain people not to teach any other doctrine ⁴ nor to hold to myths and endless genealogies, which bring about useless speculations rather than to the carrying out of God's plan in faith. ⁵ The goal of this instruction is love from a pure heart and from a good conscience and from an unhypocritical faith. ⁶ By deviating from these things some have turned away into futile talk; ⁷ they desire to be teachers of the law, although they know neither what things they say nor the things about which they insist.

⁸ We know that the law is good, if anyone uses it lawfully, ⁹ knowing this, that the law was not set down for the righteous individual but for the lawless and undisciplined, for the ungodly and sinners, for the unholy and profane, for those who kill father and mother, for murderers, ¹⁰ for fornicators, for homosexuals, for slave dealers, for liars, for perjurers, and for whatever else is contrary to sound teaching, ¹¹ in accordance with the gospel of the glory of the blessed God, with which I was entrusted.

TEXTUAL NOTES

1:3 προσμεῖναι ἐν Ἐφέσῳ . . . Μακεδονίαν—After release from his first Roman imprisonment (Acts 28:30–31), Paul likely travels to Spain (Rom 15:28) and then Crete, where he leaves Titus in charge (Titus 1:5). He then would have traveled to Ephesus, whose ministry he entrusted to Timothy,³⁸ and then to Macedonia, from which he writes the pres-

---

38. As suggested by Eusebius, *Ecclesiastical History* 3.4, in FC 19:142.

ent letter. See further "The Chronology of Paul's Life" and the subsection "The Historical Setting" in the section "Authenticity and Integrity" in the Introduction to the Pastoral Letters.

ἵνα παραγγείλης—The use of ἵνα with the subjunctive here introduces a purpose clause.[39] See further the note on παραγγελίας at 1:5.

ἑτεροδιδασκαλεῖν—This term for "teach any other doctrine," which occurs only here and in 6:3, seems to have been coined by Paul.[40] In his ministry to the Galatians (1:6–9) and to the Corinthians (2 Cor 11:4) he had had to deal with those who taught other doctrines.

1:4 μύθοις καὶ γενεαλογίαις ἀπεράντοις . . . ἐκζητήσεις—The word "myths" indicates what is contrary to the truth;[41] the phrase "endless genealogies" likely has to do with the many beings that the false teachers maintained were intermediaries between God and mankind. Paul regards the false teaching as "useless speculations"; this is another way of saying that the false teachers are "always learning but never able to come to the knowledge of the truth" (2 Tim 3:7). See further "The Nature of the Heresy" in the Introduction to the Pastoral Letters.

οἰκονομίαν θεοῦ—Elsewhere the term οἰκονομίαν refers to management (Luke 16:2–4), to a commission (1 Cor 9:17; Col 1:25; Eph 3:2), or to God's plan of salvation (Eph 1:10; 3:9). In that light "carrying out God's plan" seems to capture the apostle's meaning. Christians are to give their attention to this by putting their faith in what God has done in carrying out that plan. Ministers like Paul and Timothy are to attend to their commission to set forth the word regarding God's plan of salvation.

πίστει—This term can denote the act of believing (*fides qua creditur*) or to the content of faith (*fides quae creditur*). Either designation is possible here: individuals receive salvation through believing; the plan of salvation is to be the content of the saving message that is proclaimed. In the present context the act of believing (*fides qua creditur*) seems to be the primary reference. See further the entry "Faith" in the Extended Notes.

1:5 παραγγελίας—While this noun and the cognate verb παραγγέλλω (see 1:3) can mean "command,"[42] here the translations "instruct," "instruction" are more appropriate. This instruction has authority, as it is in accord with the "gospel . . . of the blessed God" (1:11).

ἀγάπη—See the entry "Love" in the Extended Notes.

39. Wallace, *Greek Grammar*, 471–72.
40. Knight, *Pastoral Epistles*, 72.
41. BDAG 660.
42. BDAG 760.

καθαρᾶς καρδίας καὶ συνειδήσεως ἀγαθῆς—See the entry "Heart and Conscience" in the Extended Notes.

πίστεως ἀνυποκρίτου—"Faith" here refers to the act of believing (*fides qua creditur*). This faith needs to be sincere (not hypocritical).

1:6 ματαιολογίαν—The term means "futile, meaningless talk"; this was also a problem in Crete where Titus was ministering (Titus 1:10).

ἀστοχήσαντες—Paul uses a form of this verb at 6:21 with the meaning "miss the mark." This twofold use serves as a sort of *inclusio* for the entire letter.

1:7 νομοδιδάσκαλοι—Elsewhere in the New Testament the term "teachers of the law" clearly refers to Pharisaic teachers of the law (Luke 5:17; Acts 5:34). As in this section Paul also describes these "teachers of the law" as those who teach another doctrine (1:3), at this time in Ephesus there may have been teachers of Judaism (or perhaps extreme Judaizers, along the lines of those whom the apostle had to oppose in Galatians), after whom the people there were being enticed to follow (see further Acts 19:8–9). As there was a "Jewish" element to the gnostic false teaching plaguing the Christians in Ephesus, "teachers of the law" could also be descriptive of them (see "The Nature of the Heresy" in the Introduction to the Pastoral Letters). In either case, the religion of these false teachers was one of law, not of gospel, and of a mistaken view of the law as well.

1:8 νόμος—In this context "law" is being used in its narrower sense of the commands and threats of God rather than in its broader sense of the whole word of God.

1:9 ὅτι—This introduces a clause in apposition to τοῦτο; the clause explains what it is that Paul and his readers are "knowing."[43]

δικαίῳ—This refers to one who has been justified by grace apart from the works of the law (Titus 3:5–7); hence the term here is a synonym for "believer," "Christian."

ἀνόμοις δὲ καὶ ἀνυποτάκτοις—This is the first of four pairs of nouns, each connected by καί; the four pairs are followed by six individual nouns. This indicates that Paul intends for the paired nouns to be understood as paired synonyms. This first pair would refer to those who are in rebellion against *God's* law (hence their god is not the true God).

ἀσεβέσι καὶ ἁμαρτωλοῖς—Insofar as this pair can be distinguished from the previous one, it seems to bring out an element of dishonor and

---

43. Wallace, *Greek Grammar*, 459.

disrespect toward God (this might be described as "failing to give honor to his name").

ἀνοσίοις καὶ βεβήλοις—This pair might be defined as "those in opposition to what is holy" and those who "have no interest in transcendental matters."[44] This seems to add to the previous pairs of nouns the idea of failing to acknowledge God, failing to give him the worship that he is owed.

πατρολῴαις καὶ μητρολῴαις—When this pair of terms is immediately followed by the more general term "murderers" (ἀνδροφόνοις), it raises the question as to the purpose of the former terms. It seems plausible that the apostle may want these terms in this order to cause his readers to think of how the commandment to honor father and mother is immediately followed by the commandment against murder (see further the commentary). That, in turn, would suggest that Paul intends, in the manner of Christ's Sermon on the Mount (Matt 5:21–24), to point to all manner of violations of these commandments and not simply to actual homicide. Along these lines the ESV renders this phrase "those who strike their fathers and mothers."

1:10 πόρνοις—Although this term can be used in distinction from adulterers (1 Cor 6:9; Heb 13:4), here, as elsewhere,[45] it is used in a general sense to refer to sexual sin in general.

ἀρσενοκοίταις—This is a term compounded with the words for "male" and "bed," meaning "one who beds (has coitus with) a male." In the list given in 1 Cor 6:9 of sins from which baptism has cleansed the readers the term is paired with μαλακοί, "soft" (see Matt 11:8; Luke 7:25), so that the pair of terms designate those who take the passive as well as the active roles in male homosexual activity. Here the term is used by itself to denote all homosexual conduct as contrary to the creator's design as set forth in Gen 2:24 and affirmed by Jesus (Matt 19:5; Mark 10:7).[46]

ἀνδραποδισταῖς—The term could mean "kidnapper," but in this context the reference seems more to one who engages in the slave trade,[47] perhaps then also connoting any unethical business or monetary transaction.

---

44. See BDAG 86, 173.
45. 1 Cor 5:9–11; 6:9; Eph 5:5; Heb 12:16.
46. On the Bible and homosexuality see also Lev 18:22; 20:13; Deut 22:5; Rom 1:26–27; 1 Cor 6:9–11; Jude 7; as well as Lockwood, *1 Corinthians*, 204–9.
47. BDAG 76.

ψεύσταις ἐπιόρκοις—Both terms ("liars," "perjurers") call to mind violations against the commandment prohibiting false witness.

εἴ τι ἕτερον—Perhaps with this phrase the apostle intends for his readers to think of the commandments prohibiting coveting, that is, proscribing sinful desires; see the commentary.

ὑγιαινούσῃ διδασκαλίᾳ—In the Pastorals Paul regularly uses some form of "sound/healthy" (ὑγιαίνω/ὑγιής) to refer to the entirety of Christian teaching/doctrine (διδασκαλίᾳ) to which Christians in general and pastors in particular are to hold.[48] In the present passage the participle ὑγιαινούσῃ serves as an adjective.[49]

1:11 τὸ εὐαγγέλιον τῆς δόξης τοῦ μακαρίου θεοῦ—In this context the term εὐαγγέλιον ("gospel") is used in its wider sense, referring to the entire word of God, whose central message is the good news of salvation through Christ. Elsewhere in the Pastorals (2 Tim 2:10; Titus 2:13) the apostle uses "glory" to describe salvation as sharing in the exalted glory of Christ (1 Tim 3:16); that evidently is the meaning here as well. Only through the gospel of Christ will anyone attain to this glory. See further the entry "Glory" in the Extended Notes.

ἐπιστεύθην—Paul often speaks of himself or of other proclaimers of the word being "entrusted" with the word that they proclaim.[50] Thus, the message is not theirs but God's. This indicates both that they must proclaim it in faithful adherence to that word and also that by speaking God's word their proclamation has the authority and power of God himself.

COMMENTARY

No Other Doctrine

As one who was left by Paul as pastoral leader of the church in Ephesus, Timothy is to promote the right teaching of God's word. The task of setting forth the truth of God's word includes also refuting and opposing error. That is a task that lies before Timothy in Ephesus, for it is plain from these opening words that in Ephesus there were those who not merely held to some false teaching but who were actively promoting it.[51]

---

48. 1 Tim 1:10; 6:3; 2 Tim 1:13; 4:3; Titus 1:9, 13; 2:1, 2, 8.
49. Wallace, *Greek Grammar*, 618.
50. 1 Cor 9:17; Gal 2:7; 1 Thess 2:4; 1 Tim 1:11; 6:20; 2 Tim 1:12, 14; Titus 1:3.
51. *DPL* 448.

When the apostle instructs Timothy to see to it that those at Ephesus are "not to teach any other doctrine," he makes it plain that there is a standard of true teaching to which Christ's church is to hold and which it is to set forth.[52] In his Second Letter to Timothy Paul will explicitly spell out what that standard is: the Scriptures that were breathed into by God (2 Tim 3:14–17).

Here the apostle specifically identifies some of the other doctrines that were being bandied about in Ephesus. The phrases "myths and endless genealogies" and "speculations" most likely refer to an early form of Gnosticism that was prevalent in Ephesus at that time (see "The Nature of the Heresy" in the Introduction to the Pastoral Letters). The false teachers were setting forth what they claimed was a superior "knowledge." These heretics taught that there were various deities (alluded to here by the term "genealogies") and that in order to achieve salvation one had to give these deities their due.

Paul dismisses all of these as "useless" and "futile talk." Those who promoted these ideas claimed to be "teachers of the law," but in fact they knew "neither what things they say nor the things about which they insist." This phrase probably indicates that they both set forth false doctrines and also tried to impose on others various practices that they claimed were necessary for eternal salvation (they were teachers of both a false soteriology and incorrect ethics).[53]

The apostle contrasts all of this with "the gospel of the glory of the blessed God, with which I was entrusted." With these words Paul draws a contrast between himself and the false teachers. For one thing, he has the truth to proclaim over against the false teaching of the heretics. By describing the message he promotes as "the gospel of the glory of the blessed God," he points to his teaching as the saving good news; the teaching of those whom Timothy must oppose was not the saving gospel (nor even the correct teaching of the law). Furthermore, he had been "entrusted" with the truth (see 2:7); as those who set forth their own "speculations" the false teachers could not claim a legitimate, godly calling to be "teachers of the law."

---

52. Luther (AE 28:221): With this expression he means the arrogance of the false apostles, because they cannot be content. They cannot stay in the pattern. They cannot, as Jude says (v. 3), "contend for the faith which was once . . . delivered." For wicked men will come, and they will not persevere. They always have this fault of teaching something different and new. A wicked spirit, not rooted in solid doctrine, causes this. It always looks for something new and a better doctrine.

53. As noted by John of Damascus, *On Divine Images*, 1.21 (ACCS, NT 9:140.)

The Goal of Instruction

The apostle states that the goal of genuine instruction in the truth of God's word is "love from a pure heart and from a good conscience and from an unhypocritical faith." The order of the terms is significant. The source of all this is faith in Christ. That faith must, of course, be genuine; it must be "unhypocritical." Through faith in Christ one has a "pure heart" and a "good conscience" (on both of these terms see further "Heart and Conscience" in the Extended Notes). When through faith in Christ one's heart is pure and his conscience is good, then love (for God and for others) will follow (Gal 5:6).[54]

The Right Use of the Law

Paul writes that the law is good, if it is used lawfully, and that it was not set down for the righteous but for the unrighteous. For insight into what the apostle means here, it is helpful if we briefly survey what he has to say about the law.

Although the law is good (Rom 2:18–20; 7:12), it cannot save (Rom 3:20; Gal 2:16). The law shows our sin for what it is (Rom 7:7): that which brings eternal death (Rom 7:8; 8:2). The law curses those who attempt to acquire salvation by works (Gal 3:10–13; Rom 9:31–32) and makes the whole world accountable to God (Rom 3:19). Christ was born under the law (Gal 4:4), fulfilled the law (Rom 8:3–4), and redeemed mankind from the curse of the law (Gal 3:13). Thus, the righteousness of God is revealed apart from the law (Rom 3:21). Christ is thereby the end of the law (Rom 10:4), so that those in Christ are no longer under the condemnation of the law (Rom 6:14) and are free from it (Rom 6:20—7:6), so that they no longer live by the law but by the Spirit (Rom 7:6).

From this we can see that using the law rightly includes not seeking salvation through the law.[55] In that sense the law was not set down for the righteous, for they are righteous/justified through faith in the redemptive work of Christ—apart from the works of the law (Rom 3:24–25, 28). The godly way of life that follows from their salvation is motivated and empowered not by the law but by the Spirit (Rom 7:6). That is how they live a life of love, which is the fulfillment of the law (Rom 13:8–10).

---

54. Similarly Towner, *Letters*, 115–17.

55. Luther (AE 28:231): "Only keep this use away from [the law], that you credit it with the remission of sins and righteousness."

Those who desired to be "teachers of the law" understood none of this: "They know neither what things they say nor the things about which they insist." Their assertions amounted to a seeking of salvation by way of the law; their doctrines were "futile talk" and "useless speculations" that were inimical to "sound teaching," destructive of "unhypocritical faith," and hence ruinous of eternal salvation.[56]

The law was not set down for the righteous but for the unrighteous. The law shows them their sin and its eternal consequences (Rom 7:7–8; 8:2).

Paul gives various examples of the sort of unrighteous people for whom the law is set down. His categories seem to be based, at least in a general sort of way, upon the Ten Commandments.[57] Those who are "lawless and undisciplined" would be those whose lawlessness amounts to a rejection of God himself. Those who are "ungodly and sinners" are those who fail to give God the honor required in the commandment concerning his name. Failing to give God the worship required by the commandment regarding the Sabbath day would make one "unholy and profane." Certainly, anyone who killed father or mother (either literally or in the manner that Jesus himself indicated in his Sermon on the Mount, Matt 5:21–24) would not give them the honor required in the Decalogue. Of course, the Ten Commandments proscribe murder. The commandment against adultery is violated by sex being used outside of marriage as well as by any nonheterosexual activity. Slave trading would be an egregious violation of the commandment against stealing. Lying and perjury are both ways of violating the prohibition of false witness, and the apostle's concluding "whatever else" might be a nod to the Decalogue's proscription of coveting. Even if there is not this sort of one-to-one correspondence to the individual injunctions of the Ten Commandments, the list here certainly is intended to include any and every violation of the law of God.

In dogmatic terminology the apostle's comments on the law correspond most closely to the second use of the law.[58] The law does not

---

56. On the false teaching opposed by the Pastorals see further "The Nature of the Heresy" in the Introduction to the Pastoral Letters.

57. This is also noted by Kelly, *Pastoral Epistles*, 49–50; Knight, *Pastoral Epistles*, 83–85; Easton, *Pastoral Epistles*, 110–11; and Johnson, *Letters*, 169–71.

58. On the uses of the law, see the Formula of Concord, Articles V and VI (Epitome and Solid Declaration); Pieper, *Christian Dogmatics*, 3:239–40; and Walther, *Proper Distinction*.

provide the way of salvation; instead, it exposes sin, calling to repentance and preparing the way for the proclamation of the saving message about Christ, to which Paul turns in the portion of this letter that follows.

Timothy's Task: 1 Timothy 1:3–11 in Context

This is one of four Pauline Letters in the New Testament addressed to an individual.[59] In it Paul is giving specific instruction to his younger co-worker about fulfilling his obligations as a minister of the gospel. In the following section of this letter he will focus on the message of the gospel itself and will speak of himself as a preeminent example of the power of that message. After that he will turn to more detailed instruction about carrying out the ministry in that message.

---

59. However, see the commentary on 1 Tim 6:21.

1:12–17: Paul as a Preeminent Example

TRANSLATION

¹² I give thanks to him who empowered me, Christ Jesus our Lord, because he accounted me faithful, having appointed me for ministry, ¹³ even though I was formerly a blasphemer, a persecutor, and an arrogant man, but I obtained mercy, because being ignorant I acted in unbelief. ¹⁴ However, the grace of our Lord was more than abundant with faithfulness and love that are in Christ Jesus. ¹⁵ The saying is trustworthy and worthy of full acceptance: Christ Jesus came into the world to save sinners, of whom I am the foremost. ¹⁶ However, I was shown mercy for this reason, in order than in me as the foremost Christ Jesus might demonstrate the utmost long-suffering for an example for those about to believe in him for eternal life. ¹⁷ To the king of the ages; imperishable, unseen, the only God, be honor and glory for ages of ages. Amen.

TEXTUAL NOTES

1:12 ἐνδυναμώσαντί—The aorist participle refers to action prior to the main verb; here it refers to the apostle's calling on the road to Damascus (Gal 1:13–17; Acts 9:1–20).

Χριστῷ Ἰησοῦ—The order of the names here (as in 14, 15, and 16) shows that by this time Χριστός has morphed from being a title (the Greek equivalent of "Messiah") into a name. That being the case, the authors of the New Testament sometimes refer to Jesus as "Christ" or "Jesus Christ." Paul also uses these names for our Lord. However, in addition to these he also identifies him as "Christ Jesus," and he is the only biblical author to do so.⁶⁰

κυρίῳ—As in 1:2 (and throughout the NT) this stands for the name of God from the Old Testament;⁶¹ compare this with Θεῷ in 1:17.

πιστόν με ἡγήσατο—The aorist tense can denote one-time action in the past;⁶² here it refers to the Damascus road experience as a calling not only to faith but also to ministry. Therefore, the meaning here is not that God appointed Paul for ministry because he saw that he was trustworthy; instead, it was Christ's merciful call that changed this persecutor into one who was a faithful, trustworthy minister of his word (cf. 1 Cor 7:25).⁶³ In an attempt to bring this out I have rendered ἡγήσατο as "accounted" rather than "considered."

διακονίαν—This word can be rendered "service," but in this context "ministry" seems to be more suitable.⁶⁴

1:13 ὄντα βλάσφημον καὶ διώκτην καὶ ὑβριστήν—The participle ὄντα introduces a concessive clause.⁶⁵

βλάσφημον—Blasphemy can refer to putting something ordinary on the level of God (Luke 5:21; John 10:33) or to treating God as though he were ordinary (Matt 27:39; Mark 15:29; Luke 22:65). Prior to his calling Paul regarded Jesus as someone (far less) than God; hence, he (Paul) was a blasphemer.

διώκτην—As illustrated in Acts 8:3; 9:1.

ὑβριστήν—The apostle includes this term in his list in Romans (1:30) of those who do not acknowledge God.

ἠλεήθην—The aorist tense can denote one-time action in the past (see footnote 62); like the previous aorist tense verbs that Paul uses in this section it refers to his apostolic calling on the road to Damascus. See further the entry "Mercy" in the Extended Notes.

---

60. The only "exception" to this is found in Acts 24:24, but since this reports Paul's own testimony, it is not really an exception. The use of "Christ Jesus" is found in Rom 1:1; 2:16; 3:24; 6:3, 11, 13; 8:1, 2, 34, 39; 15:5, 16, 17; 16:3; 1 Cor 1:1, 2, 4, 30; 4:15; 15:31; 16:24; 2 Cor 1:1; Gal 2:4, 16 (2x); 3:14, 26, 28; 4:14; 5:6, 24; Eph 1:1 (2x); 2:6, 7, 10, 13, 20; 3:1, 6, 11, 21; Phil 1:1 (2x), 8, 26; 2:5; 3:3, 8, 12, 14; 4:7, 19, 21; Col 1:1, 4; 2:6; 4:12; 1 Thess 2:14; 5:18; 1 Tim 1:1 (2x), 2, 12, 14, 15; 2:5; 3:13; 4:6; 5:21; 6:13; 2 Tim 1:1 (2x), 2, 9, 10, 13; 2:1, 3, 10; 3:12, 15; 4:1; Titus 1:4; Phlm 1, 9, 23.

61. BDAG 577 (under 2 b, α) and 577–78 (under 2 b, γ; ב ,א, and ג).

62. BDF 166 [§ 318 (1)].

63. Knight, *Pastoral Epistles*, 94.

64. Cf. Rom 11:13; 2 Cor 3:7, 8, 9; 4:1; 5:18; 6:3; 11:8; Acts 1:17; 6:4; 20:24; 21:19.

65. Wallace, *Greek Grammar*, 634–35.

ἀγνοῶν ἐποίησα—The participle ἀγνοῶν, "being ignorant," is a circumstantial participle;[66] it describes the circumstances under which Paul, before the Damascus road experience, acted in unbelief.[67] Note the similar use of the concept of ignorance to describe unbelief in Rom 10:3.

ἀπιστίᾳ—The use of "unbelief" here demonstrates that it is the root of all sin.

1:14 ὑπερεπλεόνασεν—This word is compounded of a preposition that can mean "beyond," "more than," and a verb that means to "increase," "be in abundance."[68] In an effort to capture the import of both parts of this compound word I have rendered it "was more than abundant." Like the previous aorist tense verbs that the apostle uses in this section, this one refers to his calling on the road to Damascus.

χάρις—See the entry on "Grace" in the Extended Notes.

πίστεως—Here in conjunction with "love" (ἀγάπης) the term denotes divine "faithfulness."

ἐν Χριστῷ Ἰησοῦ—See the entry on "In Christ" in the Extended Notes.

1:15 πιστὸς ὁ λόγος καὶ πάσης ἀποδοχῆς ἄξιος—See the excursus "The Trustworthy Sayings of the Pastoral Letters" at the end of this section.

ἦλθεν—As noted above, the aorist tense can refer to one-time action in the past; in connection with the term "world" (κόσμον) ἦλθεν here and in 1:16 denotes the past event of the incarnation as the beginning of Christ's saving ministry.

σῶσαι—See the entry on "Save, Savior, Salvation" in the Extended Notes as well as the essay "He Saved Us: The Pastoral Letters on the Way of Salvation" elsewhere in this commentary. The infinitive here denotes purpose.[69]

πρῶτός—Encapsulates his life as a blasphemer, persecutor, and arrogant man. Similarly, in 1 Cor 15:10 he calls himself the least of the apostles.

1:16 ἠλεήθην—Like the aorist tense verbs in verses 13 and 14 this refers to his calling on the road to Damascus.[70]

---

66. BDF 215 (§ 417).
67. See also 1 Cor 15:9; Gal 1:13, 23; Phil 3:6; Acts 9:21; 22:4, 19; 26:10–11.
68. BDAG 824, 1030–31, 1034.
69. Wallace, *Greek Grammar*, 664.
70. As noted also in *DPL* 49–50.

ἵνα . . . ὑποτύπωσιν—Here ἵνα plus a subjunctive verb constitutes a purpose clause;[71] a purpose of the calling of this foremost of sinners was to be an example for others who did not yet have faith.

ἅπασαν μακροθυμίαν—This unusual construction means "the utmost long-suffering."[72]

ἐπ' αὐτῷ—This prepositional phrase denotes the object of the verb "believe"; in English we generally use the phrase "*in him*."

1:17 Τῷ δὲ βασιλεῖ τῶν αἰώνων—"Ages" can refer to time (Luke 1:70) or to the created world (Heb 11:3); probably both are in view here. The genitive τῶν αἰώνων is not attributive but a genitive of subordination; the meaning is not that he is an eternal king (although that is, of course, true) but that he is king over the "ages."[73] The only other reference to a transcendent king in the Pauline Letters is the ascription of Jesus Christ as "the king of those who are having kingship" in 1 Tim 6:15. See further the commentary.

ἀφθάρτῳ—Is he "immortal" because he is not subject to death, or "imperishable" because of the resurrection from the dead? Romans 1:23 might suggest the former; 1 Cor 9:25 and especially 15:52 would argue for the latter. See the commentary.

ἀοράτῳ—Should this be rendered "invisible" because he cannot be seen, and hence referring to God the Father, or "unseen" because he cannot be seen at this time, referring to Christ, who retains his resurrected and hence visible body (Col 2:9)? See the commentary.

μόνῳ θεῷ—Although in the New Testament θεός usually refers to God the Father, the present passage and John 1:18 (and likely Rom 9:5[74]) each use it with reference to Christ; see the commentary. See also the commentary on Titus 2:13.

τιμὴ καὶ δόξα εἰς τοὺς αἰῶνας τῶν αἰώνων, ἀμήν.—In the Pauline Letters ascriptions of praise like these are not uncommon. They often come at or near the end of a letter (Rom 16:27; Phil 4:20; 2 Tim 4:18) or to conclude a major section of a letter (Rom 11:36; Eph 3:21). Here (and in Gal 1:5) it concludes an introductory portion of the letter, before the apostle plunges into the "nuts and bolts" of the letter.

---

71. Wallace, *Greek Grammar*, 664.
72. BDF 144 [§ 275 (7)].
73. Wallace, *Greek Grammar*, 86–88, 103–4.
74. Middendorf, *Romans 9—16*, 842–48.

Grace and Life

COMMENTARY

Paul's Salvation as an Example

These verses center around the teaching of the salvation of sinners. "Sin" and "sinner" are broad words referring to being out of a right relationship with God. In this section Paul elaborates on what it means to be a sinner.

At the outset we ought to note the apostle's use of the present tense verb, "I *am* foremost." Paul is a forgiven sinner, but he is still a sinner. The believer in Christ is a forgiven sinner, but he is still a sinner. Until the consummation of all things at the parousia, repentance and Christ's gift of forgiveness are ongoing needs in the life of every believer.[75]

The apostle notes that he acted in unbelief. Unbelief is the root of all sin; all sins of any description spring from a lack of (or at least a weakness of) faith.

As a result of this Paul was "ignorant." As faith is the way to wisdom (Job 28:28; 1 Cor 1:21), that is, to being in harmony with the creator, as faith is the "knowledge of the truth,"[76] so unbelief brings ignorance, that is, being alienated from the Almighty.

The apostle notes that in his case his sin was especially heinous (he was the foremost of sinners). His sin was a form of hubris which showed itself in a blasphemous attitude toward Christ, which resulted in him persecuting Christ through the persecution of his believers (Acts 9:4, "Why are you persecuting *me*?").

It should be noted that in the present passage, as well as in other instances in Paul's letters where he speaks of his passing from unbelief and opposition to the gospel to faith in Christ (1 Cor 15:9–10; Gal 1:13–16), there is no attempt to explain it in terms of a psychological process. Instead, the apostle describes the experience as his having been shown grace/mercy for the sake of Christ.[77]

As great as his sin against Christ was, the salvation of Christ for him was even greater ("more than abundant"). Paul describes this salvation in a number of ways. Christ showed him "grace," meaning that he received salvation as a gift without any cost to him. He was shown "mercy," which refers to an attitude of compassion shown to another. The grace of salvation was due to the "faithfulness of Christ"; although the apostle had been

---

75. See Kelly, *Pastoral Epistles*, 55.
76. 1 Tim 2:4; 2 Tim 2:25; 3:7; Titus 1:1.
77. Debelius and Conzelmann, *Pastoral Epistles*, 27.

faithless toward Christ, Christ remained faithful to him (cf. 2 Tim 2:13a). All this was a demonstration of undeserved "love" and "long-suffering," for Jesus had endured Paul's former arrogant and blasphemous attitudes for a long time and had not given up on him.

The more-than-abundant grace shown to this foremost of sinners made him an ideal example for others. The apostle's message here is easily seen: if Christ's grace is enough for a sinner like me, then it is enough for anyone else.[78]

This message is "trustworthy"; it is worth believing. Hence, it is a message that works faith in those who would come to faith after Paul did.

This faith in Christ brings blessing; believing in Christ means eternal life. Hence, the apostle is moved to the grand doxology that closes this section of his letter.

Paul in Ministry

The mercy shown to Paul had made another remarkable transformation in his life. He had been changed from a blasphemer and persecutor not only to a believer but even beyond that to one appointed for ministry and who would carry out that ministry faithfully (see textual note on πιστόν με ἡγήσατο above).

With the verb "appointed" the apostle refers to what happened to him on the road to Damascus. There he received his gospel through a revelation of Jesus Christ (Gal 1:11–12), and he was appointed as Christ's chosen vessel to carry his name before others (Acts 9:15).

By noting that Christ is the one who "empowered" him for ministry, Paul points to the source of power in the ministry carried out by him and all faithful proclaimers of the word. The power for ministry lies in the teaching/doctrine of Christ.

To have the divine power of Christ in one's ministry he must not "teach any different doctrine" (1:3). Hence, the qualification for ministry is that Christ regard the minister to be "faithful." In 3:1–7 Paul will spell out in greater detail what it means to be a faithful minister.

---

78. Note the comments of Luther, AE 28:240–49.

GRACE AND LIFE

The Only God

Of whom is the apostle speaking in 1:17? Several factors point to the answer to that question.

Throughout this section Paul mentions Jesus Christ: "Him who empowered me, Christ Jesus our Lord . . . the grace of our Lord . . . in Christ Jesus . . . Christ Jesus came into the world . . . Christ Jesus might demonstrate . . . believe in him for eternal life."

In the sixth chapter of this same letter the apostle refers to "the king of those who are having kingship." This also occurs in a context in which Paul has been speaking of Christ.

If 1:17 is speaking of Christ, what is the meaning of ἀφθάρτῳ? The somewhat time-honored translation "immortal" might suggest a being that did never and could never die; hence, God the Father. However, in 1 Corinthians (9:25; 15:52) the apostle uses this adjective with reference to an eternal existence that results from the resurrection from the dead that Christ brings about. Therefore, the rendering "imperishable" would capture that thought.

If 1:17 is speaking of Christ, what would be the meaning of ἀοράτῳ? The somewhat traditional rendering "invisible" might cause us to think of the Father, who has never been seen, rather than of the incarnate Christ, who definitely was seen. However, although Jesus Christ is not invisible (Rev 1:7), he is at present unseen (cf. John 14:19).

Pauline doxologies often refer to God the Father (Rom 11:36; 16:27; Gal 1:5; Eph 3:21; Phil 4:20) However, the doxology of 2 Tim 4:18 is addressed to "the Lord," which is the usual way of identifying Jesus, by way of the LXX, as Yahweh, the one true God of the Old Testament (see footnote 61).

In the New Testament θεός is usually reserved for God the Father. However, the term is occasionally used of Christ the Son, as in John 1:18 (probably Rom 9:5) and Titus 2:13 (for which see the commentary on that passage).

Weighing all of this in the balance, the preponderance of the evidence would argue for "the only God" here being a reference to Jesus Christ. The passage would therefore be one of the Bible's most explicit references to the deity of Jesus of Nazareth.[79]

---

79. Along these lines it is to be noted that the verb "came" (ἦλθεν) in 1:15 implies the divine preexistence of Jesus Christ; Towner, *Letters*, 146.

Paul as a Preeminent Example: 1 Timothy 1:12–17 in Context

Paul had been Timothy's teacher in the faith, meaning especially preparing him for the work of the pastoral ministry (2 Tim 1:13; 2:2). That being the case, he can have no better example for ministry and the power of the gospel to set forth to his younger coworker than himself.

The message of salvation for the sake of Jesus Christ is to be at the heart of any pastor's ministry. In the life of Paul we can see what that gospel is and its power to change lives.

So grand is the wonder of this gospel that the apostle begins with a word of thanksgiving to Christ Jesus and concludes by breaking into a doxology; as with the thanksgiving Christ is also the object of this praise. In this way Paul models the praise and thanksgiving that is to characterize the life of every believer.

As with other doxologies in the apostle's letters this one marks the end of a major section of the letter. Paul has completed the "overture" of this opus (see the commentary on 1:1–17). He will now turn to expounding in great detail on the ministry that he and Timothy share.

EXCURSUS: THE TRUSTWORTHY SAYINGS OF THE PASTORAL LETTERS

At five places in the Pastoral Letters[80] there occurs the statement πιστὸς ὁ λόγος ("the saying is trustworthy/faithful"), a turn of phrase that occurs nowhere else in Scripture.[81] Since this wording is characteristic of this particular portion of the New Testament, the question arises as to whether these phrases might have some connection other than common vocabulary.

Some variety between the expressions is to be noted. Twice (1 Tim 1:15; 4:9) there is the added note that the saying is "worthy of full acceptance" (πάσης ἀποδοχῆς ἄξιος). In two of the remaining instances (2 Tim 2:11; Titus 3:8) the statement is worded in the first person (singular or plural), which in and of itself indicates full acceptance of what is stated. The other statement (1 Tim 3:1) has to do with the pastoral office; since not every Christian will meet the qualifications for this office, what

---

80. 1 Tim 1:15; 3:1; 4:9; 2 Tim 2:11; Titus 3:8.
81. The phrase "these words are trustworthy/faithful and true" occurs in Rev 22:6.

is said there, while certainly true, does not pertain to all believers; this seems to account for the absence of "worthy of full acceptance" there.[82]

In two cases (1 Tim 1:15; 2 Tim 2:11) the saying clearly precedes that which is trustworthy;[83] once it follows (Titus 3:8), and twice (1 Tim 3:1; 4:9) the phrase seems to tie together what proceeds with what follows. Although it is admittedly a judgment call, in the last two mentioned passages it seems that what follows is "weightier" and hence more deserving of being designated as a trustworthy saying; it is on that basis that we will proceed.

The statements of three of the passages (1 Tim 1:15; 2 Tim 2:11; Titus 3:8) have to do with the central articles of the Christian faith; indeed, they have the nature of early Christian creeds.[84] The saying of 1 Tim 3:1 introduces that letter's catalogue of qualifications for holding the pastoral office, while the remaining passage (1 Tim 4:9–10) has elements of both as follows: creedal—"Godliness has the utmost benefit, having promise . . . for the life to come. . . . We have hoped in the living God, who is the savior of all people, especially of believers," and pastoral—"For this we labor and struggle."

These letters are concerned both with the heart and soul of the saving message and with the need for the proclaimers of that message to set it forth in all its truth. With that in mind it is perhaps to be expected that the apostle would lay both of these teachings before his audience as being "trustworthy/faithful."

Support for this interpretation is found in other uses of the adjective "trustworthy/faithful" in the Pastorals. Paul uses it to describe himself as one accounted "faithful" and hence qualified to be entrusted with ministry (1 Tim 1:12). Twice (1 Tim 3:11; 2 Tim 2:2) he uses the term to describe the kind of person worthy to be entrusted with some responsibility. He speaks of Christ himself as one who remains faithful even in the face of the faithlessness of others (2 Tim 2:13). He refers to the faithfulness as well as the grace and love that were shown to him by Christ (1 Tim 1:14). Finally, the apostle's assertion that one who would be a pastor must hold to the trustworthy/faithful word as taught (Titus 1:9) shows the importance of faithfully teaching the message into which people are to put their faith for eternal salvation.

---

82. Knight, *Pastoral Epistles*, 100.
83. Kelly, *Pastoral Epistles*, 54, 179.
84. *DNTB* 232.

We ought not imagine that these are the only teachings that Paul would regard as "worthy of full acceptance." Rather, they are highlighted in this way because the circumstances under which the apostle was writing called for them to be given special emphasis.

What might be the source of the faithful sayings? There are some who suggest that the apostle here is citing traditional material passed down from earlier sources.[85] However, it is entirely possible that each of these is an original statement by Paul, who uses this formula to emphasize both the truth and the importance of what he writes.[86]

---

85. For example, Debelius-Conzelmann, *Pastoral Epistles*, 28–29.

86. For example, Mounce, *Pastoral Epistles*, 437, notes that the faithful saying of Titus 3:4–7 "is so replete with Paul's terminology that it is difficult to believe it is a citation."

1:18–20: Timothy's Responsibilities

TRANSLATION

¹⁸ I am entrusting this instruction to you, Timothy, [my] child, in accord with the prophecies made previously about you, in order that with them you may fight the good fight, ¹⁹ having faith and a good conscience. By rejecting this some have suffered shipwreck with regard to the faith. ²⁰ Among these are Hymenaeus and Alexander, whom I gave over to Satan, in order that they may be taught not to blaspheme.

TEXTUAL NOTES

1:18 Ταύτην τὴν παραγγελίαν παρατίθεμαί σοι—The noun παραγγελίαν is the same word as that which occurs in 1:5 and which is cognate to the verb used in 1:3. Hence, "this instruction" encompasses all the apostle's directives given in the letter's "overture" (1:1–17), instruction that serves as the basis for the remainder of the letter. The instruction that Paul is giving Timothy serves as the foundation for the responsibilities that he is to carry out.

τέκνον—When used as a term of address to one other than a biological child, this word expresses affection (Matt 9:2; Mark 2:5). It is a term of address from teacher/master to student;[87] it is used this way several times in the Pastoral Letters.[88]

προφητείας—In 4:14 (whose commentary see) the term also occurs, again in a context of speaking of the ministry Timothy is to carry out. "By and large the NT understands by the prophet the biblical proclaimer of

---

87. BDAG 994–95.
88. See also 1 Tim 1:2; 2 Tim 1:2; 2:1; Titus 1:4.

the divine, inspired message";[89] "prophecy is not only the telling of things future but also of the present."[90] Thus, it is best to understand the term in the 1 Timothy passages as referring to all the instruction in God's word that Timothy received to prepare him for ministry. See also 2 Tim 1:6 and the commentary there.

ἵνα στρατεύῃ—ἵνα plus a subjunctive verb here forms a purpose clause.[91]

στρατεύῃ ἐν αὐταῖς τὴν καλὴν στρατείαν—This cognate-accusative construction depicts the ministry as a war. This is similar to the message of Paul's discourse on the whole armor of God (Eph 6:10–17), which indicates that the battle with the devil is to be waged with the word of God (the "prophecies" spoken of earlier and referred to by the prepositional phrase ἐν αὐταῖς).

1:19 πίστιν καὶ ἀγαθὴν συνείδησιν—Faith in Christ is the way to a good conscience. See further the entries on "Faith" and "Heart and Conscience" in the Extended Notes.

The word "faith" (πίστιν) occurs twice in this verse. The first instance refers to the personal act of believing (*fides qua creditur*); the second is to the content of what is to be believed (*fides quae creditur*).

ἀπωσάμενοι—From ἀπωθέω, this word can be used of physical rejection (Acts 7:27) or of rejection by unbelief (Acts 7:39; 13:46).

ἐναυάγησαν—Paul himself had suffered shipwreck three times (2 Cor 11:25) before the episode of Acts 27. That personal experience may well have suggested this metaphor and made it a particularly vivid one for him. The reference to "the faith" (*fides quae creditur*) indicates not simply the personal falling away from the faith of these individuals (πίστιν καὶ ἀγαθὴν συνείδησιν . . . ἀπωσάμενοι) but also that by their error they have caused damage to the message of the gospel.[92]

1:20 Ὑμέναιος καὶ Ἀλέξανδρος—Hymenaeus is mentioned in 2 Tim 2:17–18 (along with Philetas) as one who has departed from the truth by holding to the false teaching that the resurrection has already taken place (on this false teaching see "The Nature of the Heresy" in the Introduction to the Pastoral Letters). In 2 Tim 4:14 the apostle mentions "Alexander the metalworker" (see further the commentary there). Regardless of whether or not that Alexander is the same individual as

---

89. *TDNT* 6:828.
90. Chrysostom, *Homilies on 1 Timothy* 5; *NPNF*[1] 13:423 (ACCS, NT 9:148).
91. Wallace, *Greek Grammar*, 471–72.
92. *DPL* 44; similarly Mounce, *Pastoral Epistles*, 67.

the one mentioned here, Paul indicates that this Alexander was a false teacher who strongly opposed his message. Despite the fact that the apostle had seen to it that Hymenaeus and Alexander had been removed from the Christian community, several years later at least the former was still troubling Timothy's churches with false teaching.

The early church father John Chrysostom counted those aforementioned individuals among the adversaries of the word, whom he identified as the "messenger of Satan" of which the apostle speaks in 2 Cor 12. Thus, the thorn in the flesh/messenger of Satan would be opposition to his ministry by false teachers; this is what kept Paul from being too elated.[93] As the verses that both precede and follow this section of 2 Cor 12 (1–10) have to do with "super-apostles" (11:5; 12:11) who were a trouble to him at Corinth, such an understanding of this passage has as much to commend it as does any other.[94]

οὓς παρέδωκα τῷ σατανᾷ—Compare 1 Cor 5:5; in contemporary ecclesiastical parlance this would be called excommunication, "so that penitence may follow."[95] If these two individuals were indeed a part of the "messenger of Satan" of 2 Corinthians, the punishment would certainly be most appropriate to the crime.

ἵνα παιδευθῶσιν—ἵνα plus a subjunctive verb here forms a purpose clause.[96]

βλασφημεῖν—Paul had used a cognate of this word (1:13) to describe himself before he was called to saving faith. The two individuals in question, therefore, have departed from saving faith altogether and need to be restored to it.

---

93. Hughes, *Second Epistle*, 443–44; Plummer, *Second Epistle*, 141.

94. Penner, *In the Shadow of the Cross*, 160; Tertullian, *On Modesty* 13, in *ANF* 4:87.

95. Theodore of Mopsuestia, *Commentary on 1 Timothy* (*Theodori episcopi Mopsuesteni: In epistolas b. Pauli commentarii*, 2:84 (ACCS, NT 9:150). Knight, *Pastoral Epistles*, 111, comes to a similar conclusion. Basil the Great in *Letters*, 288 (FC 28:276) also identifies handing over to Satan with the steps given by Jesus in Matt 18. So also Mounce, *Pastoral Epistles*, 69–70.

96. Wallace, *Greek Grammar*, 471–72.

COMMENTARY

Timothy's Ministry

Timothy has a pastoral responsibility for those in his care. He has been entrusted with this responsibility by the "prophecies" made about him. This would refer to all the instruction in God's word that prepared him for ministry. Although a bit of an anachronism, we might think of this as involving his seminary education, his call, and his ordination (see further the section "A Good Minister" in the commentary on 1 Tim 4:6–16). Paul's address of Timothy as his "child" might well indicate that the apostle himself had supplied all this instruction in God's word.

These "prophecies" have equipped Timothy for the task. Nevertheless, he himself must persevere in the faith, as is the case with any minister of the word (as will be indicated in 3:1–7). Through such faith he will have a good conscience; therefore, he will be able to deal with the false teaching that is troubling those for whom he has responsibility.

Paul instructs his coworker to "fight the good fight." Jude probably speaks for most ministers of the word when he writes that while he would have preferred to write about salvation, he found it necessary to ask his readers to join him in contending for the faith (Jude 3). The ministry involves proclaiming the saving truths of God's word; it also includes refuting and opposing false teachings. The similarity of 1 Tim 1:18 with Eph 6:10–17 would point to Satan and his hosts being the ultimate source of all false teaching as well as indicating that this "fight" is to be fought by setting forth the word of God in all its truth.

Dealing with the Danger of False Teaching

This passage shows the real and serious danger of false teaching. The apostle states that the false teachers whom he has in mind have suffered shipwreck with regard to the faith, that is, they have lost the saving faith altogether. They do not have the good conscience that comes only through faith in Christ, and which is necessary to be acceptable before almighty God. Thus, false teaching runs the risk of the loss of salvation altogether.

Paul has dealt with these false teachers by seeing to it that they have been removed from the fellowship of the church ("whom I gave over to Satan"); the first-person singular ("I gave over") points to his apostolic authority.[97] A comparison with 2 Cor 5 demonstrates the purpose of this discipline. The removal of false teachers (or of anyone who is impenitent) has as its ultimate goal the coming of the impenitent to repentance and faith. The apostle indicates this here by saying that the purpose of his removing these false teachers is that they may be taught not to blaspheme (cf. 2 Tim 2:25–26). "Blasphemy" here (as in 1:13) designates teaching and belief that is antithetical to Christianity and its saving truth. Thus, Paul wants even his opponents to come to repentance and faith.[98]

The apostle's instruction offers a model for the church of all ages. In carrying out church discipline God's people in general and pastors in particular need to "maintain the balance between firmness and proper motivation."[99]

Timothy's Responsibilities: 1 Timothy 1:18–20 in Context

Timothy is to be a good and faithful minister of the word. Fidelity in the ministry involves not only setting forth the truth but also refuting and opposing error.

Thus, it may even be necessary for a pastor to take the lead in removing false believers and especially false teachers from the fellowship of the Christian church. One purpose of this is to keep such false teachers from upsetting the faith of others (2 Tim 2:18). Like any act of "excommunication" it also is done with the hopeful intent that those removed will be moved to repentance and faith.

See further the essay "An Excellent Task: The Pastoral Ministry According to the Pastoral Letters" elsewhere in this commentary.

---

97. Towner, *Letters*, 160–61.
98. *DPL* 44.
99. Mounce, *Pastoral Epistles*, 72.

2:1–7: Life in God's Church

TRANSLATION

¹ First of all, then, I urge that requests, prayers, petitions, and thanksgivings be made for all people, ² for kings and all those who are in authority, in order that we may lead a tranquil and undisturbed life in all godliness and reverence. ³ This is good and acceptable to God our savior, ⁴ who desires all people to be saved and to come to the knowledge of the truth. ⁵ For there is one God and one mediator between God and mankind, the man Christ Jesus, ⁶ who gave himself as a ransom for all, as a testimony at the right time, ⁷ for which I was appointed a proclaimer and an apostle—I am speaking the truth, I am not lying, a teacher of the nations[a] in faith and truth.

[a]Or *the gentiles*

TEXTUAL NOTES

2:1 Παρακαλῶ—This is a gnomic rather than an exhortational present. It does not mean "right now, but not later"; instead, it refers to matters that are always in effect.[100]

δεήσεις προσευχὰς ἐντεύξεις εὐχαριστίας—There seems to be some slight distinctions between these terms. While προσευχὰς is a general word for prayer, the others denote a particular type of prayer. Since δεήσεις frequently occurs with some designation of the party for whom the prayer is offered,[101] and since a cognate of ἐντεύξεις is used to refer to Christ's intercession for his people (Rom 8:34; Heb 7:25), these terms

---

100. Wallace, *Greek Grammar*, 526.
101. Rom 10:1; 2 Cor 1:11; 9:14; Eph 6:18; Phil 1:4, 19.

seem to denote supplications, that is, prayers for others. While δεήσεις and ἐντεύξεις indicate requests, εὐχαριστίας has to do with giving thanks. Even if Paul is not using these terms with such precise distinctions of meaning, he surely must intend this group of four to designate all manner of prayer.

ὑπὲρ πάντων ἀνθρώπων—The term ἀνθρώπων is used here (and in verses 4 and 5) to designate all people. See the textual notes on 2:5 for the significance of the use of the singular of this word there. The apostle will use a different term in 2:8 and 3:2 when he wants to distinguish males from females.

2:2 βασιλέων—In 1 Pet 2:13 the singular of this term is used for the Roman emperor. In conjunction with "all those who are in authority" the plural here refers to all manner of governing authorities.

ἵνα ... διάγωμεν—In this instance ἵνα plus a subjunctive verb forms a purpose clause.[102]

ἤρεμον καὶ ἡσύχιον—These two Greek adjectives begin with the same letter (although they begin with different breathing marks); this play on words suggests that they are to be understood as virtual synonyms. "Undisturbed" seems to be the meaning of ἡσύχιον; note the use of the cognate noun ἡσυχία in Acts 21:40 D; 22:2; 2 Thess 3:12. Together these two adjectives describe the way of life of one who does not trouble others as he himself is left untroubled.

βίον—Whereas Paul often uses ζωή to refer to eternal salvation (as in 1:16), here he uses βίος to designate this-worldly existence (as also 2 Tim 2:4).[103]

εὐσεβείᾳ καὶ σεμνότητι—The word εὐσεβείᾳ encapsulates the entirety of the Christian faith and life; see the entry "Godliness" in the Extended Notes. Both the noun σεμνότης (1 Tim 2:2; 3:4; Titus 2:7) and the cognate adjective σεμνός (1 Tim 3:8, 11; Titus 2:2) are used in the Pastorals to describe godly living. Together the two terms encompass the entirety of genuine Christian piety.

2:3 τοῦ σωτῆρος ἡμῶν θεοῦ—In the Pastoral Letters Paul sometimes applies the title "savior" to God (the Father).[104] In other instances he uses it for Jesus Christ.[105] There is also the interesting (and highly significant) designation of Jesus Christ as "our great God and savior" (Titus 2:13;

---

102. Wallace, *Greek Grammar*, 471-72.
103. DPL 553-54.
104. 1 Tim 1:1; 2:3; 4:10; Titus 1:3; 2:10; 3:4.
105. 2 Tim 1:10; Titus 1:4; 3:6.

see the commentary on that verse). God the Father and God the Son together worked out the salvation of mankind. See further the entry on "Save, Savior, Salvation" in the Extended Notes and also the essay "He Saved Us: The Pastoral Letters on the Way of Salvation" elsewhere in this commentary.

2:4 σωθῆναι—See the entry on "Save, Savior; Salvation" in the Extended Notes.

ἐπίγνωσιν—See the entry on "Know, Knowledge" in the Extended Notes.

ἀληθείας—See the entry on "Truth" in the Extended Notes.

2:5 Εἷς γὰρ θεός—That there is only one true God is foundational to the teaching of the entire Scripture (Deut 6:4).

εἷς καὶ μεσίτης θεοῦ καὶ ἀνθρώπων—Elsewhere in the NT Moses is called the mediator through whom God gave the law (Gal 3:19–20), while Jesus is termed the mediator of the new covenant (Heb 9:15; 12:24). The term, therefore, implies that without such a go-between, God and mankind are irreparably alienated from one another. The paired genitives θεοῦ καὶ ἀνθρώπων mean that there is one mediator *between* God and people.[106] The plural ἀνθρώπων here refers not to males but to people in general; however, in order to preserve the play on words between ἀνθρώπων and ἄνθρωπος, I have translated it "mankind."

ἄνθρωπος Χριστὸς Ἰησοῦς—Paul uses ἄνθρωπος here rather than ἀνήρ to make a connection with the previous phrase; the man Christ Jesus is the mediator between God and all people. The phrase points to the necessity of Christ being incarnate in order that he might be the one mediator between God and mankind.

2:6 ὁ δοὺς ἑαυτὸν—The aorist tense of the verb can refer to a one-time action in the past;[107] here it refers to Christ's death on the cross.

ἑαυτὸν ἀντίλυτρον—These two words serve as a double accusative.[108] See the entry on "Redeem, Redemption/Ransom" in the Extended Notes.

ὑπὲρ πάντων—The preposition ὑπέρ in conjunction with the prefix ἀντί on the compound word ἀντίλυτρον indicates substitution.[109] This combination might mean "in place of" as well as "on behalf of"; in an attempt to cover both meanings I have used the translation "for." The self-giving of Jesus on the cross was not limited; it was "for all." The use

---

106. Wallace, *Greek Grammar*, 135.
107. BDF 166 [§ 318 (1)].
108. Wallace, *Greek Grammar*, 187.
109. Wallace, *Greek Grammar*, 388; BDAG 87–88; Guthrie, *Pastoral Epistles*, 82.

of πάντων here and in 2:1 is probably intended to make a definite contrast between the universal scope of Christianity and the exclusivist character of the heresy troubling these churches,[110] on which see "The Nature of the Heresy" in the Introduction to the Pastoral Letters.

τὸ μαρτύριον καιροῖς ἰδίοις—The term μαρτύριον often refers to the speaking of the word as a "witness" or "testimony" to what God/Christ has done.[111] However, there are also instances when an action is said to be a testimony (Matt 8:4; Mark 6:11). Thus, the apostle here describes Christ's self-giving itself as a "testimony."

That being said, in what sense is the Lord's death a testimony "at the right time?" The vocable καιρός rather than χρόνος is used here; whereas the latter term tends to denote time in general, the former has more of a connotation of a particular point in or era of time[112] (a comparison with 1 Tim 6:15 and Titus 1:3 demonstrates that the plural form καιροῖς ἰδίοις does not point to multiple times in history). The phrase "the right time" points to the biblical truth that God planned out mankind's salvation. Christ's sacrifice accomplished God's plan and did so at the right time.[113] Compare Gal 4:4 and see Titus 1:3 and the commentary there.

2:7 ἐτέθην—The aorist tense of the verb can refer to a one-time action in the past;[114] here it refers to Paul's calling on the road to Damascus.

κῆρυξ—The secular Greek background to this word is instructive. A "herald/proclaimer" held a significant place at a royal court. He might be sent on diplomatic missions; heralds were often honored for their service.[115] It was required of heralds "that they deliver their message as it is given to them. The essential point about the report which they give is that it does not originate with them."[116]

A proclaimer (κῆρυξ) is one who proclaims (κηρύσσω) a proclamation (κήρυγμα); the content of the proclamation determines the significance of the proclaimer and of his act of proclaiming. In his directions

---

110. Kelly, *Pastoral Epistles*, 60.
111. Acts 4:33; 1 Cor 1:6; 2 Thess 1:10; 2 Tim 1:8.
112. Cf. BDAG 497–98 (καιρός) with BDAG 1092 (χρόνος).
113. Wallace, *Greek Grammar*, 157. A comparison of the present passage, 1 Tim 6:15, and Titus 1:3, all of which use the plural (καιροῖς ἰδίοις) with Gal 6:9, where the singular form of the phrase is used (καιρῷ γὰρ ἰδίῳ), indicates that there is no difference in meaning between the singular and the plural; Knight, *Pastoral Epistles*, 123–24.
114. BDF 166 [§ 318 (1)].
115. *TDNT* 3:683–85.
116. *TDNT* 3:687–88.

to Timothy in his Second Letter to him Paul makes it plain that the proclaimer is to proclaim the entire word of God;[117] other passages emphasize that the central message of the word is the death and resurrection of Jesus Christ.[118]

As a message that originates not with the proclaimer but with almighty God this proclamation has power. This power is not that of human wisdom but of the Holy Spirit (1 Cor 2:4). Elsewhere the apostle indicates that the proclamation of Christ is like the word of God at creation (2 Cor 4:3-6). As the word of creation brought into being everything in creation, so the proclamation of Christ brings into being the faith that receives the glory of eternal salvation.

ἀπόστολος—See the entry "Apostle" in the Extended Notes.

διδάσκαλος ἐθνῶν—This phrase could be rendered "teacher of the nations" or "teacher of the gentiles." In this section Paul notes that God desires "all people" to be saved, which would argue for the translation "teacher of the nations." On the other hand, in the "division of labor" referred to in Gal 2:7-9 it was agreed that Paul (along with Barnabas) would concentrate his ministry on the gentiles, while Peter, James, and John would devote the majority of their attention to their fellow Jews. Moreover, in his Letter to the Romans he describes himself as an "apostle of the gentiles" (11:13) and "a minister of Christ Jesus to the gentiles" (15:16; see also verse 18).

In the Pastoral Epistles in general and in the present letter in particular there is little evidence of the friction between Jewish and gentile believers that was such a contentious issue at some times in the history of the early church.[119] In view of this, while either rendering could be defended, the translation "teacher of the nations" seems called for here.

πίστει—See the entry "Faith, Believe" in the Extended Notes. Here "faith" denotes the content of what is taught (*fides quae creditur*).

ἀληθείᾳ—See the entry "Truth" in the Extended Notes.

---

117. 2 Tim 4:2; see the notes and commentary on that passage for the connection between what Paul says there concerning preaching "the word" and what he indicates about the purpose/profitability of "all Scripture" (2 Tim 3:16-17).

118. 1 Cor 1:21, 23; 15:11, 14; 1 Tim 3:16.

119. In Titus 1:14 there is a criticism of those who devote themselves "to Jewish myths and the commands of people who turn away from the truth."

COMMENTARY

The Church at Worship

Central to the life of the people of God is their gathering together for worship. That worship has two major elements: the sacramental (God to people) and the sacrificial (people to God).[120]

In the present section of this letter Paul speaks to both of these. A major element of the church's sacrificial worship involves prayer; here he gives some rather explicit instruction about prayer. The apostle also teaches about the sacramental focus of worship with his words about the church's proclamation of the saving truth and about those called to labor in that message.

Prayer

As Paul begins his instruction regarding the life and ministry of Christ's church, he first takes note of the church's life of prayer. The terms he uses point to petitions for self, supplications for others, and thanksgivings for all as being part of the church's worship of prayer.

The apostle singles out one particular type of prayer for special mention: prayers for the governing authorities. In his Letter to the Romans (13:1–7) he had spoken of both the institution of government and the individual governments themselves as having been established by God to suppress evil and to promote good in this world. In the present letter he speaks of the benefit that God gives to his people through his creation of government.[121] When government does what the Almighty has created it to do and keeps at least a degree of justice, order, and peace in the world, this creates a favorable environment for Christians to live "a tranquil and undisturbed life in all godliness and reverence." Paul writes these words fully aware of the reality that government may become corrupted and do other than what God established it to do (1 Tim 6:13; 2 Tim 4:6),[122] which can be one source of Christians being persecuted (2 Tim 3:12).

---

120. On worship see further the essay "Honor and Glory Forever Amen: The Pastoral Letters on Worship" elsewhere in this commentary as well as Deterding, *Colossians*, 157–59.

121. First Peter 2:13 specifically uses the term κτίσει ("creation," "thing created") to refer to the governing authorities.

122. As noted by Johnson, *Letters*, 308.

Nevertheless, when the enemies of the church are hindered in their efforts to oppress Christians and suppress godly conduct, this is an aide to godly living.

We should note a precedent for this practice in the Hebrew Scriptures. The prophet Jeremiah was as forceful as anyone in his condemnations of the pagan empire of Babylon (Jer 50 and 51). Yet he instructed the exiles in Babylon to "seek the welfare of the city where I have sent you into exile, and pray to Yahweh on its behalf, for in its welfare you will find your welfare" (29:7).[123]

Hence, Christians have both a responsibility and a vested interest in praying for those in authority. There is a long-standing precedent for congregational prayers to include petitions for government; individual Christians would do well to make this a part of their own personal lives of prayer as well.

Paul's directive that the church is to offer prayers for *all* people and *all* those in authority reflects the truth that God wants *all* to be saved and that Christ Jesus gave himself as a ransom for *all*. The emphasis that the apostle gives to the universal scope of God's saving grace and to the

---

123. Luther (AE 28:256, 259) offers this observation: "The first fruit of love is to be that you Christians respect every public officer in the world and that you pray for them, because you hear what it means to keep the realm in peace. When a good magistrate fails or is upset, then nothing good is left in this life. Then you will be unable to come to love, to obey parents, rear children, or support the wretched. We must forget about all fruits of love if public offices do not stand firm in peace. In time of war you must anticipate your death at every moment; the inviolacy of virgin, wife, and all property is in peril. . . . If we pray for public officials, this is the fruit: to lead a placid, quiet, peaceful life." Note also the following comments from early church fathers: "The soul of some Christians might be slow at hearing this and may resist this exhortation. For at the celebration of the holy mysteries it may be necessary to offer prayers for a heathen king. Paul shows them the advantage of fulfilling this duty at least to reconcile them to the advice, 'that we may lead a peaceable and quiet life.' . . . For God has appointed government for the public good. When therefore they use force for the common good and stand on guard for our security, isn't it reasonable that we should offer prayers for their safety in wars and dangers?" (Chrysostom, *Homilies on 1 Timothy* 6, in *NPNF*² 1.13:426). "It is to our advantage that there be such peace in this life. For, as long as the two cities are mingled together, we can make use of the peace of Babylon. Faith can assure our exodus from Babylon, but our pilgrim status, for the time being, makes us neighbors. All of this was in St. Paul's mind when he advised the church to pray for this world's kings and high authorities—in order that 'we may lead a quiet and peaceful life in all piety and worthy behavior.' Jeremiah, too, predicting the Babylonian captivity to the Old Testament Jews, gave them orders from God to go submissively and to serve their God by such sufferings, and meanwhile to pray for Babylon. 'For in the peace thereof,' he said, 'shall be your peace'—referring, of course, to the peace of this world, which the good and bad share in common." (Augustine, *City of God* 19.26, in FC 24:245–46).

objects of the church's prayers may well be due to the heretics' contention that only a select number, namely, those who followed them and their teachings, would be the recipients of salvation.[124]

See further the essay "Honor and Glory Forever Amen: The Pastoral Letters on Worship" elsewhere in this commentary.

The Saving Truth

Paul's opening words of this portion of the letter call attention to God's (first article of the creed) work of caring for the this-worldly needs of his people, and indeed of all humanity (the kingdom of God's left hand). Nevertheless, the God who provides for good in this world is the same one who provides for eternal good in the life to come (second and third articles of the creed, the kingdom of God's right hand),[125] to which the apostle quickly turns his attention.

Paul's instruction here takes us to the heart of the majesty and mystery of the Triune nature of God. He affirms the biblical teaching that there is one God. He names the one mediator between God and mankind: Christ Jesus, the one whom he had earlier called the only God (1:17),[126] and whom he here identifies as a man. This can only be understood in light of what the Scriptures assert regarding the incarnation of the Son of God.[127]

This passage, as much as any in the Scriptures, points to the significance of the incarnation for the salvation of mankind. Only one who was fully God and fully man could bridge the gap between God and humanity that was caused by the latter's fall into sin.[128]

What, therefore, is the significance of speaking of Christ as the "mediator" between God and mankind? In Romans (8:34) the apostle states that Christ Jesus intercedes for us before God; that may well be

---

124. Mounce, *Pastoral Epistles*, 78.

125. Helpful resources among the vast literature on the distinction of God's right- and left-hand kingdoms, in addition to volumes 44–47 of the American edition of *Luther's Works*, include the following: Scharlemann, "Theology of Freedom," 103–8; Huegli, *Church and State*; Neuhaus, "Ambiguities," 285–95; Althaus, *Ethics*.

126. Refer to the section "The Only God" in the commentary on 1:12–17.

127. For further reading on the Incarnation consult Formula of Concord Epi and SD, article VIII; Luther, *Confession Concerning Christ's Supper* (AE 37:161–372); Pieper, *Christian Dogmatics*, 2:55–394; and Nafzger et al., *Confessing the Gospel*, 380–96.

128. See, for example, *DPL* 110–11; Nafzger et al., *Confessing the Gospel*, 459–80.

included in the present passage's designation of Jesus as mediator.[129] In the immediate context Paul speaks of Christ as one who gave himself as a ransom for all; this recalls his teaching that God made the Christ who knew no sin to be sin for us, that in him we might become righteous before God (2 Cor 5:21). Either or both of these might be included in the identification of Christ Jesus as the mediator between God and mankind.

The identification of Christ Jesus as the "one" mediator between God and mankind is emphatic. The heresy afflicting Timothy's churches envisioned many such mediators.[130]

Christ's self-giving was a testimony at the right time. This is similar to the apostle's assertion that Christ came in the fullness of time (Gal 4:4; Eph 1:10). The work of Jesus Christ accomplished God's eternal plan for mankind's salvation, and he did so at just the right time.

Even as God desires all to be saved, so Christ gave himself as a ransom for all. This is in harmony with other statements in the Pauline corpus[131] to the effect that Christ's redemptive work was for all. These assertions are direct refutations of the gnostic contention that salvation was limited to those who were privy to their secret "knowledge" (γνῶσις).[132]

There is a sense in which salvation is for those with knowledge, but this "knowledge" is very different from that set forth by the heretics. The salvation acquired by Christ was for all, but individuals receive it when they come to the knowledge of the truth (2:4).[133] In biblical vocabulary "knowledge" has to do with more than intellectual activity; "knowledge" designates an intimate relationship with someone or something (Gen 4:1); hence, "knowledge" often serves as a synonym of saving faith.[134]

---

129. "For he still pleads even now as man for my salvation. He continues to wear the body which he assumed, until he makes me divine by the power of his incarnation; although he is no longer known after the flesh—the same as ours, except for sin." Gregory of Nazianzus, *Theological Orations* 4.30.14, in LCC 3:187.

130. Kelly, *Pastoral Epistles*, 63; see further "The Nature of the Heresy" in the Introduction to the Pastoral Letters.

131. Rom 5:18; 6:10; 2 Cor 5:14–15; Titus 2:14.

132. Mounce, *Pastoral Epistles*, 85.

133. In systematic theology this has to do with the distinction between objective and subjective justification; see Nafzger et al., *Confessing the Gospel*, 475–77, 570–72, and *Theses on Justification*, numbers 1–23.

134. See the entry on "Know, Knowledge" in the Extended Notes.

Grace and Life

The object of this knowledge/faith is "the truth." Paul frequently insists that the content of his teaching and therefore the object of saving faith is the truth.[135] The knowledge of faith does not save because of anything in itself; faith saves because of its object, which is the truth and therefore the one and only true way to salvation.

Proclamation

Faith in Christ saves; the proclamation of the truth about Christ creates this faith.[136] The apostle asserts this truth in the present passage by speaking of himself as a teacher "in faith and truth" (2:7).

In this section Paul speaks of his role in this in several ways. He identifies himself as a "proclaimer"; this term connotes that the message is not his, so that it is imperative that he speak the message in complete fidelity to how it was given to him. He reaffirms that he is an "apostle"; this title points to the authority given him by Christ himself to transmit his word to the world (see the essay "Apostle" in the Extended Notes). He also describes himself as a "teacher of the nations (or gentiles)"; even as Christ gave himself as a ransom for all, so the word about Christ is to be proclaimed to all.

Paul asserts that he did not presume to take these roles by his own initiative; he was "appointed" to these. In his case this points to his calling on the road to Damascus.[137] As the high priest of the first covenant did not take that office upon himself (Heb 5:4), so Paul was not an apostle "from men nor through man" (Gal 1:1). Instead, it was God himself who set him apart for this task (Gal 1:15–16).

The apostle puts great emphasis on his status with the assertion, "I am speaking the truth, I am not lying." As the intended audience for this letter included the church at large (note the plural "you" at 1 Tim 6:21), and as there was the need to combat false teachers at Ephesus, there was a need to stress the authenticity of the ministry of Paul, and by extension that of Timothy.[138] As at the beginning of the letter he had proclaimed

---

135. 2 Cor 4:2; 13:8; Gal 2:5; 4:16; Eph 1:13; 4:15, 21; Col 1:5-6; 2 Thess 2:13; 1 Tim 2:7; 2 Tim 2:15, 18; 3:7; 4:4; Titus 1:1

136. Rom 10:17; 2 Thess 2:13-14; also compare 2 Cor 4:2 and 4:6 in the context of the entire passage.

137. Acts 9:1-22; 22:3-21; 26:4-23; see also Gal 1:11-17.

138. Guthrie, *Pastoral Epistles*, 83.

his apostleship "through the will of God," he does the same here with this assurance that he is not lying.

Life in God's Church: 1 Timothy 2:1–7 in Context

Paul begins this section by speaking of a matter of central importance to the life of God's people: their assembling together for worship. The church's worship involves both the sacrificial (prayer) and the sacramental (proclamation).

In the context of the church at worship the apostle speaks of his own role as a proclaimer of God's word. He shows the necessity of proclaiming the word in complete harmony with the truth. In so doing he sets his ministry as a model for Timothy and for those whom Timothy has prepared or will prepare for the ministry.

This section, therefore, serves as normative instruction to all who would proclaim Christ's word. The ministry does not belong to the pastor; it belongs to Christ. The word to be proclaimed does not belong to the proclaimer; it belongs to Christ. For that reason, it is incumbent upon any pastor (or any other proclaimer of the word) to set it forth in full conformity to the word of God.

2:8–10: Various Roles in the Church: Men and Women

TRANSLATION

⁸ Therefore, I desire the men in every place to pray, lifting up holy hands without anger and disputing, ⁹ and the women, likewise, to adorn themselves in terms of appropriate attire with respect and prudence as opposed to the braiding of hair and gold or pearls or costly clothing, ¹⁰ but rather, as is fitting for women who profess godliness, through good works.

TEXTUAL NOTES

2:8 Βούλομαι—First singular verbs in this letter (see also 2:12) reflect that Paul writes here as an apostle (1:1; 2:7). This means that he is not merely voicing an opinion but is speaking with the authority of Christ himself (see the entry "Apostle" in the Extended Notes).[139]

ἄνδρας—Paul uses this term rather than a form of ἄνθρωπος as he is specifying males and not persons in general.

ἐν παντὶ τόπῳ—This phrase points to what is said here having to do not merely with local or temporal circumstances but being directed to Christ's *church* in every time and place (cf. 3:15: "You might know how it is necessary to conduct yourself in the household of God, which is the church of the living God"). This fits in well with the apostolic authority with which Paul writes here.

---

139. As recognized also by Mounce, *Pastoral Epistles*, 106.

ἐπαίροντας ὁσίους χεῖρας—This is a well-attested posture for prayer in Bible times.[140] Historically, this practice has been preserved in the Lutheran church by the way a pastor customarily positions his hands during the proper preface of the communion liturgy.

χωρὶς ὀργῆς καὶ διαλογισμοῦ—Conflicts between Christians are incompatible with their shared oneness in Christ (1 Cor 1:10-13), particularly when they are gathered together for worship (1 Cor 11:17-22). Therefore, the biblical writers exhort believers to steer clear of such behavior (see also Phil 2:14; 1 Pet 4:9). "This is his explanation of the meaning of purity of hands. What is it? There should be peace and love between brothers. If there is anger and quarreling, then prayer is hindered and the hands are impure. Therefore take care that everywhere there be peace, love, purity."[141]

2:9 αἰδοῦς καὶ σωφροσύνης—The term αἰδοῦς is used in a variant reading of Heb 12:28 to denote the attitude that a believer is to have toward God; in 1 Tim 2:15 σωφροσύνης is paired with "faith, love, and holiness." Thus, Christian women are to live every aspect of their lives as an act of reverence toward God.

μὴ ἐν πλέγμασιν ... πολυτελεῖ—"Costly" (πολυτελεῖ) is the adjective used in Mark 14:3 (πολυτελοῦς) of the ointment worth a year's wages (14:5) with which Mary anointed the feet of Jesus. In John's account of this episode (12:3) he uses the adjective πολύτιμος, the same word that Matthew uses to describe the pearl that was so valuable that it was worth the merchant selling all he had to buy it (13:46). In the present passage the vocable πολυτελεῖ therefore carries the connotation of being extraordinarily costly.

Even as gold, pearls, and costly clothing would be characteristic of upper-class women, so would uncovered, braided hair.[142] The literature of the time associates these things with those who expend an inordinate amount of expense and time on such things and often connects them with courtesans and prostitutes.[143] Compare what is written here with Isa 3:16-26.

---

140. Exod 9:29, 33; 1 Kgs 8:22, 38, 54; 2 Chr 6:29; Ezra 9:5; Neh 8:6; Job 11:13; Pss 28:2; 63:4; 68:31; 88:9; 134:2; 141:2; 143:6; Isa 1:15; Lam 2:19; 3:41. The posture is illustrated by fresco paintings in the Roman catacombs (Kelly, *Pastoral Epistles*, 66).

141. Luther, AE 28:272.

142. *DNTB* 446; *DPL* 590.

143. References are given in Knight, *Pastoral Epistles*, 135-36; Towner, *Letters*, 205-9.

"Dialectical negation" is the sophisticated term for what Paul does here; more simply stated this means that the speaker/writer uses "not" for "not only."[144] This is not a blanket prohibition of any and every sort of outward adornment.[145] Instead, the apostle's meaning is that Christian women are to adorn themselves not merely with respect to their appearance but especially by the way in which they live their lives—with "modesty and prudence" and "through good works" (2:10).

These words, along with the instruction to "those who are rich in this age" in 6:17–19, demonstrates something about the social class of early Christians. While slaves[146] and poor people[147] were numbered among the early believers, not all first-century Christians were from the lower classes. Believers could also be found among the wealthy and slave owners (Eph 6:9; Col 4:1; 1 Tim 6:2).

2:10 ὃ πρέπει—The use of this verb in Matt 3:15 and Heb 2:10 and 7:26 indicates that what is "fitting" is not simply what is in accord with custom or human preferences but rather what is the will of almighty God.

ἐπαγγελλομέναις θεοσέβειαν—In other contexts ἐπαγγέλλομαι means "promise";[148] thus, to "profess" (as here and in 1 Tim 6:21) is to make a public profession. "Godliness" encompasses matters of faith as well as of practice.[149] Christian women (and for that matter Christians in general) are to confess/profess their Christian faith by their lifestyle as well as by their spoken words.

δι᾽ ἔργων ἀγαθῶν—All Christians are to display the life of good works (Matt 5:16; Titus 3:8, 14) for which Christ has redeemed them (Eph 2:10; Titus 2:14); hence, good works are to be seen in the lives of Christian

---

144. See Bartelt, "Dialectical Negation."

145. The Scriptures contain various references to outward adornment without any implication of disapproval: Abraham's servant gives jewelry and comparable clothing to Rebekah when she is to become Isaac's wife (Gen 24:53); the friends of the beloved of the Song of Songs promise to make for her "ornaments of gold, studded with silver" (Song 1:11); gold is presented to the Christ child (Matt 2:11) and is used favorably in a metaphorical sense (1 Cor 3:12; Rev 3:18; 21:18); the best robe and a ring are given to the prodigal son upon his restoration (Luke 15:22); pearls are spoken of favorably (Matt 7:6; 13:46; Rev 21:21); Lydia was a seller of purple goods (Acts 16:14); a woman's long hair is said to be her "glory" (1 Cor 11:15). Knight, *Pastoral Epistles*, 136, makes similar observations; note also the comment of Luther, AE 28:273–74.

146. 1 Cor 7:21–22; Eph 6:5, 8; Col 3:22; 1 Tim 6:1; Titus 2:9; Phlm 16.

147. Rom 15:26; Gal 2:10; Jas 2:2–6, 15.

148. Mark 14:11; Acts 7:5, 17; Rom 4:21; Gal 3:19; Titus 1:2; Heb 6:13; 10:23; 11:11; 12:26; Jas 1:2; 2:5; 2 Pet 2:19; 1 John 2:25.

149. BDAG 452; see also the entry "Godliness" in the Extended Notes.

women (Acts 9:36; 1 Tim 5:10), wealthy Christians (1 Tim 6:18), and especially Christian pastors (Titus 2:7).

COMMENTARY

Paul continues his exposition of the life of Christ's church. Here he focuses both on the church's service of worship and its worship of service.

The apostle had spoken of the worship of God's people in prayer and proclamation and of his own role as a proclaimer of God's word (2:1–7). He then continues by returning to the matter of prayer in worship (2:8).

The worship of God's people as they gather together for a service is to be matched by the worship they offer him in the manner in which they conduct their lives. Anger and disputes are incompatible not only with formal worship but with any and every aspect of the believer's life. The Christian worships God with "psalms, hymns, and spiritual songs" (Col 3:16) but also with a life that displays the good works for which he/she has been created in Christ (Eph 2:10). Respect and prudence are to characterize not only formal times of worship but also the believer's entire conduct.

Paul also notes that men and women each have distinct roles to play in their worship and service. In many cultures the temptation to focus on outward appearance rather than the greater significance of being a genuine person of integrity has been greater for women than for men. Therefore, the apostle issues a special warning about this to the women of the church.

Paul also indicates that worship is not "women's work"; the men are to lead the people of God in worship. The leading role that men are to play in the life of Christ's church will be noted in the following section of the letter as Paul turns to the qualifications for the pastoral office.

2:11—3:7: Various Roles in the Church: The Pastoral Office

TRANSLATION

¹¹ Let a woman receive instruction in quietness with all orderliness. ¹² I do not permit a woman to teach or to exercise authority over a man, but to be in quietness, ¹³ for Adam was formed first, then Eve. ¹⁴ Adam was not deceived (first), but the woman, having been deceived, became a transgressor. ¹⁵ Yet she will be saved through childbearing, if they continue in faithfulness, love, and holiness with prudence.

³:¹ The saying is trustworthy: If anyone aspires to the office of overseer, he desires an excellent task. ² It is necessary for an overseer to be beyond reproach, the husband of one wife, self-controlled, sensible, respectable, a lover of traveling missionaries, able to teach, ³ not a drunkard, not a bully, but kind, not quarrelsome, not a lover of wealth, ⁴ having his own household in order, having well-behaved children who demonstrate sensibleness ⁵ (for if anyone does not know how to order his own household, how will he care for the church of God?), ⁶ not a recent convert, lest being conceited he fall into the judgment prepared for the devil. ⁷ It is necessary for him to have a good witness from those on the outside, lest he fall into disgrace and the snare of the devil.

TEXTUAL NOTES

2:11 Γυνή—This term here and in the following verse is a generic noun, referring not to a particular woman but to any woman.[150] The use of both

---

150. Wallace, *Greek Grammar*, 253–54.

a singular (σωθήσεται) and a plural (μείνωσιν) verb in 2:15 makes this understanding certain.

ἡσυχία—This term is used in 2 Thess 3:12 of a demeanor in contrast to being a busybody; its use in Acts 22:2 implies respectful attention.[151] Other uses of this word group demonstrate that the term does not indicate complete silence;[152] hence I have translated as "quietness." In 2:12 the word is used in distinction from teaching and exercising authority.

μανθανέτω—To receive instruction as a disciple from a teacher (1 Cor 14:31; 2 Tim 3:7).[153]

ὑποταγῇ—See also 3:4. The typical English translations of "subjection" or "submission" carry demeaning connotations that the Greek word does not have. The cognate verb is used of the child Jesus being subject to Mary and Joseph (Luke 2:51) and even to refer to the risen and exalted Christ being subject in eternity to God the Father (1 Cor 15:28). To avoid the demeaning connotations of "submission" and "subjection" I have opted for the translation "orderliness." See further the commentary below.

2:12 διδάσκειν—This term often has the implication of formal, authoritative teaching; moreover, in the Pastorals the nouns "teacher" (διδάσκαλος) and "teaching" (διδασκαλία, διδαχή) and the verb "teach" (διδάσκω) often denote the activity of an official position of ministry.[154] In the NT this verb and the cognate noun διδαχή often refer to all of Christian doctrine as contained in the Scriptures (Matt 28:20; Rom 16:17; 2 Thess 2:15).

ἐπιτρέπω—First singular verbs in this letter (as in 2:8) reflect that Paul writes here as an apostle (1:1; 2:7). This means that he is not merely voicing an opinion but is speaking with the authority of Christ himself (see the entry "Apostle" in the Extended Notes).[155] The verb here is a gnomic present; it refers not simply to the present but to what pertains at all times.[156]

---

151. BDAG 440.

152. Luke 23:56; Acts 11:18; 21:14; 1 Tim 2:2; 1 Pet 3:4.

153. BDAG 615.

154. Matt 4:23; Mark 1:21; John 7:14; 1 Cor 4:17; 1 Tim 4:11; 6:2; BDAG 241; in the Pastorals: διδάσκαλος (1 Tim 2:7; 2 Tim 1:11); διδασκαλία (1 Tim 4:13, 16; 5:17; 2 Tim 4:3; Titus 1:9; 2:7); διδαχή (2 Tim 4:2); διδάσκω (1 Tim 4:11; 6:2; 2 Tim 2:2; Titus 1:11).

155. As noted also by Kleinig, "Scripture," 8.

156. Wallace, *Greek Grammar*, 525. Wallace notes that in this passage: (1) there is no indication of a time to which this imperative might be limited; (2) a comparison with a passage such as Eph 5:18 ("do not be filled with wine, but be filled by the Spirit") shows the absurdity of taking these imperatives as limited to the present situation; (3)

διδάσκειν... αὐθεντεῖν... εἶναι—These three infinitives are complementary (supplementary) to the main verb, ἐπιτρέπω.[157] Thus, διδάσκειν and αὐθεντεῖν are essentially synonyms, while the adversative ἀλλ' makes εἶναι ἐν ἡσυχίᾳ an antonym of the other two. "To exercise authority" is to function as a master.[158] The nature of this "authority" must be determined from the context, in particular its being paired here with "teach," yielding the sense to teach with authority.[159] On ἡσυχίᾳ see the note on the previous verse. See further the commentary below.

2:13 πρῶτος—This superlative functions here as a comparative.[160]

ἐπλάσθη—This verb occurs in Rom 9:20–21 to describe the action of a potter shaping a lump of clay. The use here is a clear reflection of the creation of Adam as described in Gen 2:7. With this statement Paul, with the authority of an apostle of Jesus Christ, roots his directives about the roles of the sexes in the church in God's creation of man and woman.

2:14 ἠπατήθη... ἐξαπατηθεῖσα—The apostle uses this same word group in 2 Cor 11:3 with reference to the serpent's deception of Eve; it is the verb used in the LXX at Gen 3:13. For clarity I have added the word "first" to the translation; it is absurd to think that Paul would have maintained that only Eve and not Adam had been deceived (Rom 5:12–21; 1 Cor 15:21–22, 45–49).

παραβάσει—This word for sin, "transgression," implies the willful violation of a known boundary or norm (Rom 5:14).[161]

2:15 σωθήσεται—See the commentary.

τεκνογονίας—See the commentary.

ἐὰν μείνωσιν ἐν πίστει καὶ ἀγάπῃ καὶ ἁγιασμῷ μετὰ σωφροσύνης—In connection with other virtues of the Christian life πίστει means "faithfulness," a virtue which, like all Christian ethics, is possible only for one who has saving faith (Rom 14:23). "Love" (ἀγάπη) is a foundational virtue of

---

in this and the previous verse the nouns γυνή and γυναικί are used in a generic sense, not a specific sense; and (4) the rooting of the entire section in creation (2:13) demonstrates the omnitemporality of this directive.

Similarly, Knight, *Pastoral Epistles*, 140, makes note of the apostle's appeal to creation and demonstrates that Paul frequently uses the first-person singular present indicative to give "universal and authoritative instruction or exhortation" (Rom 12:1, 3; 1 Cor 4:16; 2 Cor 5:20; Gal 5:2, 3; Eph 4:1; 1 Thess 4:1; 5:14; 2 Thess 3:6; 1 Tim 2:1, 8).

157. Wallace, *Greek Grammar*, 599.
158. BDAG 150.
159. As noted also by Kleinig, "Scripture," 7.
160. Wallace, *Greek Grammar*, 303.
161. BDAG 758.

the Christian life (1 Cor 13). The noun "holiness" is a cognate of an adjective (ἅγιος) that is used of God himself,[162] thus designating the Christian life as one that endeavors to pattern itself after the very character of the Almighty (Eph 4:30). "Prudence" (σωφροσύνης) is paired in 2:9 with "respect"; the life of those (women) who believe is to be one in which the mind is also placed in service to God.

3:1 Εἴ τις—The indefinite particle τις makes this a general condition.[163]

ἐπίσκοπος (also verse 2)—This word is genitive, as the verb ὀρέγεται always takes its objects in that case.[164] The word here is ἐπισκοπή, designating the office of overseer; the noun ἐπίσκοπον, meaning one who holds that office, occurs in 3:2. The latter term is one of several used in the NT for the pastoral office (Acts 20:28; Phil 1:1; Titus 1:7; see further "The Pastoral Office: Qualifications and Ministry" in the commentary that follows). That the same word is used of Christ (1 Pet 2:25) indicates that the Lord himself sets the pattern for ministry/service that those called to be pastors are to follow.

ὀρέγεται—This term can be used in a negative (1 Tim 6:10) or positive (Heb 11:16) sense; this indicates that to "aspire" to something is to desire it as one of the main things in one's life. The context (καλοῦ ἔργου ἐπιθυμεῖ) indicates that here the word is being used with a most wholesome meaning. Since the verb ἐπιθυμεῖ always takes its objects in the genitive case, the phrase καλοῦ ἔργου occurs in that case here.[165]

3:2 τὸν ἐπίσκοπον—The article is generic (any ἐπίσκοπος), as in 2:8, 9, 10, 11, 12.[166]

εἶναι—The entire infinitive phrase is the subject of the verb δεῖ.[167]

ἀνεπίλημπτον—In light of all of Scripture (e.g., Rom 7) this does not mean "without sin" but "irreproachable," along the lines of not being able to be charged with any overt violations of God's law. The same term is used with the same meaning in 6:14.

μιᾶς γυναικὸς ἄνδρα—As polygamy was largely unknown in the first-century Roman world, at least among the masses,[168] a stipulation regarding polygamy would not be needed. As Paul himself experienced

---

162. Luke 1:29; John 17:11; 1 Pet 1:16; Rev 4:8; 6:10.
163. Wallace, *Greek Grammar*, 706.
164. BDAG 72.
165. Wallace, *Greek Grammar*, 132.
166. Wallace, *Greek Grammar*, 229.
167. Wallace, *Greek Grammar*, 601.
168. Scheidel, "Population and Demography," 7.

the value of service by those who are single (1 Cor 7:6–8, 32–40), the notion that this means that unmarried men may not be pastors can also be dismissed. Since the apostle permitted (and even directed) younger widows to remarry (1 Tim 5:11–14), this also demonstrates that his meaning here is not that a pastor whose wife had died might not continue in office if he would remarry. Instead, these words prohibit the pastoral office to those divorced (for other than biblically valid reasons) and remarried.[169] The scriptural teaching regarding divorce and remarriage is found in Matt 19:1–12 (Mark 10:1–12) and 1 Cor 7:12–16. The present passage along with 1 Cor 9:5 also demonstrates that prohibitions of pastors marrying is contrary to Scripture. That one who would be a pastor is to be "the husband of one wife" also indicates that the pastoral office is to be reserved to men. See further the essay "An Excellent Task: The Pastoral Ministry According to the Pastoral Letters" elsewhere in this commentary.

νηφάλιον—As excessive drinking is prohibited in verse 3 (μὴ πάροινον; see the note there), the term here would be more than a prohibition of drunkenness but would denote demonstrating self-control and being well balanced[170] in all areas of his conduct.

σώφρονα—Also mentioned in the qualifications for the pastoral office given in Titus (1:8), this denotes "prudence," what is characteristic of genuine maturity (Titus 2:2, 5). The use of the cognate verb (σωφρονοῦντα) for the Gerasene demoniac after Jesus had cast the demons out of him (Mark 5:15; Luke 8:35) further illuminates the meaning of this noun. The pastor is to use the God-given gift of reason free of the corruption of sin and evil.

κόσμιον—Inspiring genuine respect from others as opposed to merely appearing good (cf. 2:9).

φιλόξενον—While "hospitable" would suffice as a one-word translation of this term, the typical connotation of that English word suggests sociability. While that may be a worthwhile trait for a pastor, it hardly seems to qualify as a necessary qualification for the pastoral office. It seems rather that the term here points to support for traveling Christian pastors/missionaries in their work of proclaiming the gospel, as set forth elsewhere in Scripture (Matt 25:31–46; 3 John 5–8);[171] therefore, I

---

169. Knight, *Pastoral Epistles*, 157–59, comes to a similar conclusion.

170. BDAG 672.

171. For a missionary-encouragement understanding of these passages, see Gibbs, *Matthew 21:1—28:20*, 1348–62; Schuchard, *1–3 John*, 675–80. This type of "hospitality"

have rendered/paraphrased it "a lover of traveling missionaries." Such a missionary-encouragement understanding of "hospitality" would point to support for spreading the gospel far as well as near as a requirement for one who would be a pastor. See also Titus 3:13.

διδακτικόν—As setting forth the teaching of God's word is an essential part of the work of pastors,[172] it is to be expected that a pastor must be able to teach.

3:3 μὴ πάροινον—As the Bible speaks of wine as a gift of God for mankind's benefit (Ps 104:14-14; John 2:1-11), this is a prohibition of excessive drinking (drunkenness) and not of any and every use of beverage alcohol (see also 1 Tim 5:23).

μὴ πλήκτην—This noun describes one who is likely to strike others,[173] as a bully might well do. The blows/plagues (πληγή) with which one strikes another might be other than physical; note the use of πληγή in the book of Revelation (15:1, 6, 8; 16:9). A pastor might certainly be tempted to "strike out" in various ways at people who are less than fully cooperative.

ἐπιεικῆ—This describes one who displays "the quality of making allowances despite facts that might suggest reason for a different reaction."[174] The model for this aptitude and attitude is Christ himself (2 Cor 10:1). See further the entry "Gentle, Kind" in the Extended Notes.

ἄμαχον—As being "not quarrelsome" is a virtue that is expected of Christians in general (Titus 3:2), it should certainly be displayed by those who would hold the pastoral office.

ἀφιλάργυρον—The love of money can potentially result in a straying from the faith altogether (1 Tim 6:10). This points to the importance of a pastor not being "a lover of wealth."

3:4 τοῦ ἰδίου . . . προϊστάμενον—The verb implies both devotion to (Titus 3:8, 14) and leadership of (Rom 12:8) one's household; it is used of the pastoral office here and in 5:17 as well as in 1 Thess 5:12.

τέκνα . . . ὑποταγῇ—The last word implies that the pastor's household, including his children, will display the orderliness that God intends for a family.

---

was necessitated by the reality that ancient inns were little better than houses of prostitution; Ramsey, *Pauline and Other Studies*, 384–85.

172. 1 Tim 4:11, 13, 16; 5:17; 6:2–3; 2 Tim 1:11; 2:2, 24; 3:16; 4:2–3; Titus 2:1, 7.
173. πλήκτης and πληγή are both related etymologically to πλήσσω, "to strike."
174. BDAG 371.

σεμνότητος—Refers to showing the respect that is fitting toward another person, especially in view of that person's vocation (as in 2:2).

3:5 ἐκκλησίας θεοῦ—Here and in 3:15 Paul speaks of the "church of God" as a household.

ἐπιμελήσεται—The other use of this verb in the NT, Luke 10:34, shows that this "care" is an expression of genuine "compassion" (Luke 10:33).

3:6 νεόφυτον—This word refers to one "newly planted" in the Christian faith.[175]

τυφωθείς—The other uses of this verb (6:4; 2 Tim 3:4) indicate that "conceit" here means falling into "a different (non-Christian) doctrine" (6:3). A new convert assuming the pastoral office puts him in danger of falling from the faith altogether and so falling into "the judgment prepared for the devil"; see the following note.

εἰς κρίμα ἐμπέσῃ τοῦ διαβόλου—The genitive διαβόλου is an objective genitive, "the judgment prepared for the devil."[176] This is another way of speaking of "the eternal fire prepared for the devil and his angels," "eternal punishment" (Matt 25:41, 46).

3:7 μαρτυρίαν καλὴν ἔχειν ἀπὸ τῶν ἔξωθεν—With these words the apostle shows that a pastor cannot be concerned only with his own "flock," for he also has a responsibility for outreach toward those outside the faith. The preposition ἀπό here denotes agency.[177]

ἵνα μὴ ... ἐμπέσῃ—The word ἵνα plus the subjective here introduces a purpose clause;[178] here it is negated by μή.

ὀνειδισμόν—This word group can refer to persecutions that are borne by Christ (Rom 15:3) and believers (Heb 10:33). However, in this context the meaning seems more along the lines of the cognate verb used by Jesus to "reproach" the cities of Chorazin and Bethsaida (Matt 11:20), as he told them that they would be "brought down to Hades" (11:23) and that their lot on the day of judgment would be worse than that of Tyre, Sidon, and Sodom (11:22, 24).

παγίδα τοῦ διαβόλου—This potentially could lead to a loss of saving faith altogether (1 Tim 6:9–10), although through the ministry of the word God can provide escape through repentance and the "knowledge of the truth," that is, faith (2 Tim 2:25–26).

---

175. BDAG 669.
176. On the objective genitive see Wallace, *Greek Grammar*, 116–19.
177. Wallace, *Greek Grammar*, 432–33.
178. Wallace, *Greek Grammar*, 664.

COMMENTARY

The Significance of the Context

Chapter and verse divisions were not originally a part of any biblical manuscript but were added later.[179] These are an aid to our use of the Scriptures; unfortunately, these sometimes can place a division between portions of a biblical book that ought to be read together. One such instance is the chapter division that separates 1 Tim 2:11–15 from 3:1–7.

When read divorced from the apostle's words on the office of pastor in chapter 3, the closing verses of chapter 2 are susceptible to confusion if not misunderstanding. In these verses Paul is not giving directions about society in general or even about life in the church in general. Instead, he is speaking specifically about God-given qualifications for holding the pastoral office.[180]

The presence here of the phrase "this is a trustworthy saying" also demonstrates that 2:11–15 and 3:1–7 belong together. A comparison of these verses with 1 Tim 4:8–10 suggests that Paul can use a "trustworthy saying" to tie together two related thoughts. Thus, although in the present passage what the apostle deems a "trustworthy" saying consists of the verses that follow, the preceding section ought to be read in conjunction with it. (See further the excursus "The Trustworthy Sayings of the Pastoral Letters" at the end of the commentary on 1:12–17.)

The Authority of an Apostle

As readers of the Scriptures approach this portion of the Bible, it is important to recognize that this is not merely the private correspondence (and opinions) of one individual. Instead, Paul speaks here as an apostle of the Lord (see the entry "Apostle" in the Extended Notes). This means that even though he writes here in the first-person singular,[181] what he writes is not simply his personal point of view. As an apostle Paul writes here as one who is used by the Lord of the church himself to give his

---

179. Stephen Langton, Archbishop of Canterbury (1228), was the first to add chapter divisions to the Scriptures; Rabbi Isaac Nathan (1488) added verse divisions to the Hebrew Scriptures; Robert Estienne (Stephanus) provided verse divisions to the books of the New Testament (1551). Wegener, *6000 Years of the Bible*, 214–15; Dowley, *Eerdman's Handbook*, 366–67.

180. As noted also by Luther, AE 28:276–77.

181. See the second paragraph of n156.

instruction to his people for their life as the church until he comes again in glory.

It is also to be noted that Paul grounds his instruction here in the reality of creation. Male and female are not random categories, as though they were the accidental result of an evolutionary development controlled by no one. Even less are these mere social constructs between which an individual can make a choice for himself/herself. God created humanity male and female, and as creator of the sexes he has assigned different roles to each. Each sex is to receive the role given by the creator. That is indicated when the apostle instructs a woman to learn with all "orderliness" (the translation I have chosen here for ὑποταγῇ); this is in keeping with the order that God has given to his creation.

The apostle's reference to the deception of Adam and Eve (Gen 3) is to be read in this light. The creator had given distinct roles to the man and to the woman. God created man as the head of the woman (1 Cor 11:3). That this implies no rank or inferiority is borne out when in the same verse of 1 Cor 11 it is said that the head of Christ is God (the Father).[182] Thus, headship and "subjection" (ὑποταγῇ) is not a matter of value but of order. When there were only two people on earth, the man was the head of the woman also in a spiritual sense. The fall occurred, in part, because the woman took the role of leading the pair into disobeying the command of God. Therefore, this supports the teaching that the creator reserves the role of spiritual "authority" to men. Thus, the authority that Paul refers to in these verses is the authority that is found in God's word,[183] the word that is the heart and soul of the pastoral ministry ("able to teach," "not a recent convert").

The reference to the woman's deception also serves to support the grounding in creation of the limiting of the pastoral office to men. The apostle reminds women who might have been enticed to assume the pastoral office that Eve was also culpable in the fall; in point of fact, she had even been the first one who was "deceived."[184]

---

182. Mounce, *Pastoral Epistles*, 148: "The equating of worth and role is a nonbiblical, secular view of reality. Nowhere in Scripture are role and ultimate worth ever equated."

183. Matt 7:29; 8:8–9; Mark 1:22, 27; Luke 7:7–8; John 12:49; 14:10; 16:13; Titus 2:15; 3 John 9.

184. Towner, *Letters*, 232.

The Pastoral Office: Qualifications and Ministry

The church office that Paul here designates with the term "overseer" is elsewhere referred to with other language: "elder," "shepherd/pastor," "leader," "those over you in the Lord."[185] In this passage as well as some others, in particular Titus 1:5–9 (which see), the Scriptures set forth God's qualifications for one who would hold this office. In broad terms we can identify two general categories of qualifications for one who would hold this position in Christ's church: solid grounding in God's word and an exemplary life of Christian piety.

We note that the apostle indicates that one who would hold this office must be "able to teach." Related to this is the qualification that he must not be a recent convert (not a neophyte). This presupposes that a pastor's main task is to be setting forth God's word. Such ability to teach involves "holding fast to the faithful word as taught, in order that he might be able both to encourage in the sound teaching and to convince (or reprove) those who speak against it" (Titus 1:9).[186] This proclamation of the word is not limited to formal preaching in worship or formal teaching in classes; in a variety of encounters with others (such as calls, meetings, visitation, and all manner of interaction with others) a pastor must be well equipped to convey God's word.[187] This means that one who would aspire to the pastoral office must be well acquainted with and well grounded in the Scriptures. Many Christian denominations have developed institutions and programs (such as seminary education) to assure that those who would serve as pastors among them will have this solid foundation in God's word. This is important for those to whom the pastor will minister; it is also important for the pastor himself. There will be many spiritual challenges to a pastor's faith during the course of his ministry (including "the reproach and snare of the devil"); a solid foundation in the word of God will equip him to respond to these, "lest he fall into the judgment prepared for the devil" (see, for example, Eph 6:10–17).

---

185. "Overseer" (Acts 20:28; Phil 1:1; 1 Tim 3:1, 2; Titus 1:7); "elder" (Acts 14:23; 15:2, 4, 6, 22, 23; 16:4; 20:17; 21:8); "pastor" (Eph 4:11; 1 Pet 5:2); "leader" (Heb 13:7, 17); "over you in the Lord" (1 Thess 5:12). Without using any specific title the following passages also imply the presence of this office within the churches of the Corinthians and the Galatians: 1 Cor 6:1–6; 12:28; 16:15–18; Gal 6:6.

186. Ramsey, *Historical Commentary*, 71.

187. On the qualification of being "able to teach" Guthrie (*Pastoral Epistles*, 92) notes, "The church has been at its weakest when this basic requirement has been absent in its leaders."

Grace and Life

The apostle also speaks of the personal piety that is necessary for one who would serve as a pastor. The Bible directs all Christians to godly living, but this is especially impressed upon pastors. The pastor's life is to be an example to those to whom he ministers. It is also important for the church's mission to those outside (3:7), for those outside often form opinions (at least initially) about Christianity from the conduct of its ministers.[188]

From all this it is clear that simply an ardent desire to be a pastor is not sufficient for holding the office. That being said, it is nevertheless true that an ardent desire to be a pastor *is* a qualification for the office (3:1). Although the pastoral office may indeed be one's occupation (1 Cor 9:1–7, 12–14), it is not merely a "job." (In recognition of this it is customary to speak of "calling" a pastor rather than of "hiring" one.) That one "aspires" (3:1) to the pastoral office implies that he has a wholehearted, all-consuming desire to serve the Lord of the church in this way.

See further the essay "An Excellent Task: The Pastoral Ministry According to the Pastoral Letters" elsewhere in this commentary.

"She Will be Saved"

The last verse of chapter 2 is quite an exegetical conundrum.[189] In order to suggest a plausible interpretation of this statement, we must answer four questions: (1) Who is the subject of the verb? (2) What is the meaning of the verb σωθήσεται? (3) What is the precise nuance of the preposition διά? (4) To what does the noun τεκνογονίας, "childbearing," refer?

Is the subject of the verb "Eve" or "a woman" (understood to represent all Christian women)? Since the apostle closes his statement with the note that she will be saved "if *they* continue in faithfulness, love, and holiness with prudence," the use of the plural would seem to exclude any reference to Eve and point to "a woman" (understood generically) as the subject.

What does it mean that she "will be saved" (σωθήσεται)? Certainly "save" is a word used often of eternal salvation (Rom 5:9, 10; Eph 2:8).

---

188. 1 Cor 10:32; Phil 2:15; Col 4:5; 1 Thess 4:12; 1 Tim 6:1; Titus 2:5.

189. In Ancient Christian Commentary on Scripture (NT 9:167) there are listed five different understandings by ancient church fathers of this passage. Knight, *Pastoral Epistles*, surveys five different categories of interpretations of this verse.

On the other hand, it can also have the meaning "deliver from temporal death."[190]

The preposition διά, "through," often denotes the agent or means through which something is done (e.g., John 3:17; Eph 2:8). However, it can have the meaning of passing "through" something (also in a non-spatial sense).[191] It can also have a temporal sense, "during."[192]

Philology and syntax, while important, will not be sufficient to establish a position on the meaning of this passage. Other factors must be taken into consideration.

The references to Eve, the fall into sin, and to childbearing call to mind one such factor. One consequence of the fall into sin was that there would be pain in childbearing (Gen 3:16). To those with a biblical worldview labor pains serve as a reminder of the fall into sin and of humanity's need for a savior.

One suggestion, therefore, for the reference to "childbearing" in this passage is that it refers to the birth of the Messiah, who brought salvation.[193] In this case the point of reference for "childbearing" would be different than what is the case elsewhere in this letter (5:14), where Paul uses the cognate verb "bear children" (τεκνογονεῖν) in what is plainly a reference to Christian women giving birth to children.

Another opinion is to understand the verb "save" as meaning "deliver from temporal death," and to see the passage as a promise of God's providential care for a Christian woman in labor.[194] While the Almighty certainly promises to care for the earthly needs of his people (e.g., Matt 6:33), to understand the passage, including the concluding conditional clause ("if they continue in faithfulness, love, and holiness with prudence"), in this way would seem to require that any woman dying in labor would be proven to be an unbeliever; this hardly comports with the biblical witness (Gen 35:16–20; 1 Sam 4:19–22). Also to be noted in this regard is that the apostle never uses the vocable "save" with this meaning anywhere else in his letters.[195]

Reading the verse in light of the entire section and of its background in Gen 3 suggests another option. In this entire portion of the letter Paul

---

190. Matt 8:25; 27:42, 49; Mark 3:4; Luke 7:50; Acts 27:20, 43.
191. 1 Cor 10:1; 2 Cor 6:8; 11:33; Eph 4:6; Col 2:19.
192. Wallace, *Greek Grammar*, 369.
193. Knight, *Pastoral Epistles*, 146.
194. Knight, *Pastoral Epistles*, 145.
195. BDAG 982–83.

is dealing with the matter of different vocations that Christians hold.[196] The Lord of the church is also the creator, which means that he is the creator of us as men and women. While both sexes are called to many vocations, the Almighty has reserved some vocations for one sex or the other. One vocation that women but not men may be called to is that of childbearing and motherhood. In that light the apostle may well be saying that for Christian women, who have Christ's gift of salvation, part of their continuing "in faithfulness, love, and holiness with prudence" may include childbearing, a topic on which he will touch again later in this letter (5:14).

While it is certainly true that the birth of the Messiah led to salvation for believing women (and men), the present passage hardly seems to be a clear reference to that teaching. It is the position of this commentary that the last option offered above, with its reference to Christian vocation, is the most likely one.[197] However, any interpretation of this verse will have to be considered tentative.

The Pastoral Office: 1 Timothy 2:11—3:7 in Context

Paul is in the midst of giving instruction regarding various roles in the church. Because of the importance of the word of God for God's people, the role of pastor is of special importance. Therefore, the apostle devotes considerable attention to the qualifications for the pastoral office. He speaks here with the authority of an apostle of the Lord Jesus Christ. Having given instruction about the office of pastor, he will continue with instruction regarding other offices in the early church.

---

196. A good, succinct presentation of the biblical teaching on vocation is contained in Veith, *Spirituality*, 89–114.

197. Luther (AE 28:279–80) advocates for the same understanding.

3:8–13: Various Roles in the Church: Deacons and Deaconesses

TRANSLATION

⁸ In the same way deacons are to be worthy of respect, not insincere, not indulging in much wine, not seeking shameful gain, ⁹ holding the mystery of the faith with a pure conscience. ¹⁰ Let them be examined first, then let those who are deemed irreproachable serve (as deacons). ¹¹ In the same way deaconesses are to be respectable, not slanderers, sober-minded, trustworthy in all things. ¹² Let deacons be husbands of one wife, having their children and their own households in good order, ¹³ for those who served well obtain for themselves a good standing and much courage in faith, which is in Christ Jesus.

TEXTUAL NOTES

3:8 Διακόνους—This noun is a cognate of the verb διακονέω, "to serve," and the noun διακονία, "service." In some contexts (John 2:5) it refers to a domestic servant. The cognate verb and noun are used in Acts 6:1–7 of the charitable service that was entrusted to seven men other than the twelve. The group of seven would tend to charitable service, while the twelve would continue to be devoted to the ministry/service (διακονία) of the word. This would be the case even though the seven men of Acts 6 are not called "deacons."

In the present passage this position is distinguished from that of overseer, who must be "able to teach" and "not a recent convert." That being the case, a διάκονος would seem to be one who was responsible not for teaching the word but for acts of human care.

This Greek word is the source of the English word "deacon." In various Christian denominations this word is used for different positions which may or may not have responsibilities that correspond precisely to those of the διακόνους of 1 Timothy. While "servant" would be a possible translation of the word here, the fact that Paul is referring to a particular office/position within the church means that "servant" does not capture the particular responsibilities of a διάκονος. Thus, I have chosen to use the translation "deacon" here (and "deaconess" in 3:11; see the note there) with the caveat that the rendering here must be understood as it is described here without any of the associations that the contemporary use of the term might have.

ὡσαύτως—The use of this term here (and in 3:11) indicates that the apostle is here describing two offices/positions in the church distinct from that of "overseer" (ἐπίσκοπος).

σεμνούς—This is also a requirement of the γυναῖκας (3:11); both the διακόνους and the γυναῖκας should live in a manner than commands respect (see also Titus 2:2 regarding Christian older men in general).

μὴ διλόγους—They are to be sincere; the etymology of the word indicates that they are not to be guilty of "double-talk," not guilty of saying different things to different people.[198]

μὴ οἴνῳ πολλῷ προσέχοντας—The Bible speaks of wine as a gift of God for mankind's benefit (Ps 104:14-14; John 2:1-11; 1 Tim 5:23). Therefore, like πάροινον in 3:3 this is a prohibition of *excessive* consumption of alcohol.

μὴ αἰσχροκερδεῖς—As someone who would be entrusted with the proper management of worldly goods (see the commentary), mismanagement and embezzlement would be a very real danger for a deacon. Thus, it would be especially important for such a one not to be seeking shameful gain.

3:9 μυστήριον—See the commentary on 3:14-16 and also the entry "Mystery" in the Extended Notes. Here the term serves as a summary of the entire Christian faith.

τῆς πίστεως—Here the term refers to the content of faith, the doctrines of Christian teaching (*fides quae creditur*). See the entry "Faith" in the Extended Notes.

καθαρᾷ συνειδήσει—A comparison with 1 Tim 1:5, 19, and 2 Tim 1:3 demonstrates that having a "pure conscience" means living out one's

---

198. BDAG 250; Kelly *Pastoral Epistles*, 81.

saving faith, for it is only through saving faith that one's conscience is "pure" or "good" (1 Tim 1:5, 19). For this reason, I have chosen to translate this phrase as "pure conscience" rather than "clear conscience," as in English this latter rendering might give the (erroneous) implication that the meaning is something along the lines of "my conscience is clear" because I haven't done anything that I consider wrong. See also the entry "Heart and Conscience" in the Extended Notes.

3:10 δοκιμαζέσθωσαν—Having been examined, they will show themselves to be proven genuine.[199]

ἀνέγκλητοι—"Irreproachable" is a necessary qualification also for pastors (elders, overseers) according to Titus 1:6–7. Hence, the term is a synonym of ἀνεπίλημπτον, as used in the present letter in the qualifications for overseers (1 Tim 3:2).

3:11 Γυναῖκας—What does this word mean here? This term can refer to biological women in general (Luke 8:2); it can also have the meaning "wives" (Eph 5:22–25).

The meaning "wives," meaning the wives of the deacons, does not seem to fit here. While this chapter requires that both an overseer and a deacon is to be "the husband of one wife" (3:2, 12), nothing is said regarding the wives of overseers. That being the case, there seems to be no reason why the apostle would need to say anything about the wives of deacons. Moreover, the mention of these "women" before the requirement of deacons being the husband of one wife suggests that these "women" are not the wives of the deacons.

Furthermore, the use of ὡσαύτως ("likewise") at the beginning of the instruction regarding "deacons" (3:8) and these "women" (3:11) would also indicate that what is said here about "women" would have to do with women who are taking up the same (or at least similar) tasks as the "deacons." Consequently, I have adopted the translation "deaconesses."[200]

As with the term "deacon," it is the case that the term "deaconess" is used among various groups within Christianity for a position with activities that may differ from group to group and from what was entrusted to the "deaconesses" of Timothy's churches. Again, I ask the reader not to

---

199. BDAG 255–56.

200. That is also the position taken by these church fathers: Chrysostom, Theodoret of Cyrrhus, Theodore of Mopsuestia, and Pelagius (ACCS, NT 9:174). More recent commentators holding this position include Kelly, *Pastoral Epistles*, 83–84, and Towner, *Letters*, 265–67.

associate the use of "deaconess" (and "deacon") here with anything other than what can be gleaned from Paul's letters themselves.

μὴ διαβόλους—The nature of the work of these women (see the commentary) would make slanderous talk an especially grave temptation. Therefore, one who would hold this position in the church must be someone able to resist such enticements.

νηφαλίους—As with pastors (3:2–3) and "deacons" (3:8) so with anyone engaged in church work it is important to have self-control, also with respect to the use of alcohol. In the culture in which Paul and Timothy labored some diversions were not available to women; however, wine was one that was.[201] Therefore, the temptation to excessive drinking would have been especially strong for them (cf. Titus 2:3). In 3:2 the term νηφαλίους is used in addition to the prohibition of drunkenness in 3:3; hence, it has a range of meaning beyond not being a drunkard; it can refer to being "self-controlled" overall. To try to capture both nuances of the term here, I have rendered it "sober-minded."

πιστὰς ἐν πᾶσιν—Women who would hold this position in the church must be "trustworthy/faithful"; they must be women of integrity in all things.

3:12 μιᾶς γυναικὸς ἄνδρες—See the textual note on 3:2; as with overseers/pastors the issue is not polygamy but unbiblical divorce and remarriage.

τέκνων καλῶς προϊστάμενοι καὶ τῶν ἰδίων οἴκων—This qualification is the same as what is required of overseers/pastors (1 Tim 3:4–5; see the notes and commentary there).

3:13 βαθμὸν ἑαυτοῖς καλὸν περιποιοῦνται—"Standing" (βαθμόν) may have been a semi-technical term of the mystery religions for the last stages of the soul in its heavenward journey; it may have had a similar use in various schools of philosophy for the attaining of wisdom.[202] That being the case, the apostle's point is that the only "standing" that has any true worth comes from service to Christ (see the textual note that follows).

παρρησίαν—"Courage" in the Pauline Letters can denote confidence before others (2 Cor 7:4; Phil 1:20; 1 Thess 2:2) or the confidence of faith before God (Eph 3:12). The emphasis in the present passage seems to be that the deacon's faith active in love (see following note) will give him courage before others as he carries out his work.

---

201. *DNTB* 1277.
202. BDAG 162.

πολλὴν παρρησίαν ἐν πίστει—This phrase would indicate that those who have "served well" (καλῶς διακονήσαντες) do so by living out their saving faith; their faith is "active in love" (Gal 5:6).

ἐν Χριστῷ Ἰησοῦ—See the entry "In Christ Jesus" in the Extended Notes. As indicated there, the phrase here probably does not designate the object of faith but rather the relationship with Christ that is given through faith.

COMMENTARY

The Nature and Responsibilities of These Positions

Paul continues by speaking of those whom he calls διακόνους, "servants." In a churchly context this is a term that can be used of those in the pastoral office (1 Tim 4:6; Acts 6:4). However, the introductory word "likewise" (ὡσαύτως—3:8, 11) demonstrates that the apostle is here speaking of an office/position distinct from that of overseer/pastor.

For reasons indicated in the textual notes I have chosen to render the terms here as "deacon" and "deaconess." As positions distinct from the pastoral office those of deacon and deaconess have responsibilities that differ from those of a pastor.

The use of the cognate verb and a cognate noun in Acts 6 offers insight into what those responsibilities would have been. There the apostles determine that they should devote themselves to prayer and the service/ministry of the word (6:4) rather than abandoning the word of God to serve tables (διακονεῖν) and to attend to the daily service (διακονία) for widows (6:1–2). That being the case, they call upon the early church to appoint seven faithful/trustworthy individuals to attend to this task (6:3).

This sort of charitable, eleemosynary work, therefore, would be the type of work with which deacons and deaconesses would have been entrusted. The pastors are to concern themselves with prayer and the word: with worship, proclamation, teaching, and outreach (refer to 1 Tim 4:13 and the commentary there). Deacons and deaconesses, while not ignoring the service in God's word that is incumbent upon every believer, attend to other needs: providing for the needy, the sick, and others with the needs of this life.

Requirements for These Positions

It is to be noted that while deacons and deaconesses concern themselves with the needs that pertain to this world, their service is not "worldly" in the sense that it is not connected to matters of faith and eternal salvation. The work of these other "servants" of the church is to be a service of "faith active in love" (Gal 5:6). Hence, it is imperative that deacons and deaconesses be those who hold "the mystery of the faith with a pure conscience" (see the textual notes above).

Moreover, they are also to be exemplary in their Christian sanctification. As they deal with the needs of others, they will face many temptations to misuse money, to be busybodies, to gossip, to take advantage of others, and to fail to mind their own business (see also 5:13; 2 Thess 3:11–12). Therefore, they need to conduct themselves in a way that commands respect from others.

Deacons and Deaconesses: 1 Timothy 3:8–13 in Context

Paul has been giving instruction regarding life within Christ's church. He has outlined roles for men and women, and he has given qualifications for the pastoral office. There are other positions of service within the church that need attention. Here he sketches out the qualifications and duties of "deacons" and "deaconesses."

The apostle indicates that a deacon must hold "the mystery of the faith with a pure conscience." Although he does not use this precise terminology with reference to overseers and deaconesses, the overall context of this entire letter would indicate that this is something that might be said of any worker in the church (and, for that matter, would be applicable to any believer). Having referred to the faith with the word "mystery" (3:9), Paul will continue by drawing this section of the letter (1:18—3:16) to a close with a creedal, almost doxological statement (3:14–16) about the "mystery of godliness," which centers in Jesus Christ.

3:14–16: The Mystery of Godliness

TRANSLATION

¹⁴ Although I am hoping to come to you soon, I am writing these things to you, ¹⁵ in order that, even if I am delayed, you might know how it is necessary to conduct yourself in the household of God, which is the church of the living God, the pillar and foundation of the truth. ¹⁶ Undeniably great is the mystery of godliness,
> who was manifested in the flesh,
> vindicated in the spirit,
> seen by angels,
> proclaimed among the nations,
> believed on in the world,
> taken up in glory.

TEXTUAL NOTES

3:14 Ταῦτά σοι γράφω—There is no obvious neuter plural noun that would serve as the antecedent to the neuter plural demonstrative pronoun ταῦτα. The apostle uses a present tense verb (γράφω) rather than the epistolary aorist that he might have used here (1 Cor 9:15; Gal 6:11).[203] Taken together, this indicates that "these things" (ταῦτά) refers to all of the instruction contained in this letter.[204]

ἐλπίζων ἐλθεῖν—The participle ἐλπίζων here is used in a concessive sense ("although . . ."").[205] Paul uses "hope" (ἐλπίζων) here in the secular

---

203. On the epistolary aorist, see Wallace, *Greek Grammar*, 562–63.
204. Towner, *Letters*, 271; Marshall, *Pastoral Epistles*, 498, 505.
205. Wallace, *Greek Grammar*, 634–35.

sense of "wish" or "desire" rather than with the Bible's usual, theological meaning of the believer's certain expectation regarding his eternal future[206] (on the theological meaning see the entry "Hope" in the Extended Notes). On the apostle's future plans at this point see also 4:13.

3:15 εἰδῇς πῶς δεῖ ἐν οἴκῳ θεοῦ ἀναστρέφεσθαι—In this letter Paul is not simply giving his personal opinions. He is writing with the authority of an apostle of Christ Jesus (see the entry "Apostle" in the Extended Notes). With the word "necessary" (δεῖ) he indicates that this letter is instruction for Christ's church for every place and time throughout its earthly existence.

ἐκκλησία—This is a significant term for the followers of Jesus Christ. In the LXX it is the regular translation of one of the two Hebrew terms for God's people Israel (קָהָל). In this way this term denotes that believers in Jesus Christ, and not the adherents of Judaism, are the continuation of God's people of the Old Testament. (The other Hebrew term for Old Testament Israel, עֵדָה, is usually translated in the LXX by συναγωγή, "synagogue"; since that became the customary term for a place of worship within Judaism, it quickly lost its usefulness for referring to followers of Christ.)

In ordinary Greek discourse ἐκκλησία referred to a public assembly (Acts 19:32, 40). Thus, the use of ἐκκλησία for a Christian assembly indicated that Christianity was open to all races, social classes, and sexes (Gal 3:28) and thereby distinguished it from the mystery religions and any other religion whose membership was limited by categories such as these.

τῆς ἀληθείας—See the entry "Truth" in the Extended Notes. "The truth" has to do with the truth from and about God (Rom 1:25; 3:7), made known through the word of God (2 Tim 2:15, 18), which centers in the gospel of salvation (Eph 1:13; Col 1:5–6) but also includes the law of God that rebukes sin (Gal 4:16) and his law that directs the believer to godly living (Eph 4:21). Thus, the church is the "pillar and foundation of the truth" as it sets forth the truth of God's entire word.

3:16 εὐσεβείας—This is a word attested in the Pastorals and 2 Peter.[207] It serves as a summary of Christianity: faith that is active in godly living. See further the entry "Godliness" in the Extended Notes.

μυστήριον—See further the entry "Mystery" in the Extended Notes.

ὅς—A number of manuscripts replace this with θεός, "God." While this is certainly in harmony with biblical teaching (see the commentary

---

206. As in 1:1; 4:10; 5:5; 6:17; Titus 1:2; 2:13; 3:7.
207. 1 Tim 3:16; 4:7, 8; 5:4; 6:3, 5, 6, 11; 2 Tim 3:5; Titus 1:1; 2 Pet 1:3, 6, 7; 3:11.

on 1:17 and Titus 2:13), it is not the original reading here. Older and more reliable NT manuscripts, before being subjected to the hand of a later editor, preserve the reading ὅς. It is possible that ὅς was misread as θς, the abbreviation for θεός,[208] although there is no manuscript support for the reading θς. Moreover, it is understandable why a later editor or copyist would have changed ὅς to θεός; had θεός been what the apostle had originally written, it is unimaginable that later hands would have changed it to ὅς. The gender of the pronoun is masculine, even though it stands in apposition to the neuter noun μυστήριον; this is a construction according to sense, as the pronoun clearly refers to Christ.[209]

ἐφανερώθη ἐν σαρκί—The verb refers to being made known, especially by becoming visible (John 21:1, 14; 1 Pet 1:20); its use here implies Christ's existence prior to his appearing.[210] The noun σάρξ has a wide range of meanings; here it denotes what is material, physical, tangible (Luke 24:39; John 1:14; 1 Cor 15:39). The reference here is to the incarnation.

ἐδικαιώθη—While δικαιόω is an important word to describe our being "justified" by grace through faith (Rom 3:24, 28; 4:2; 5:1, 9), it can mean to prove someone to be right, to vindicate (Rom 3:4), which is the meaning here.

ἐν πνεύματι—This refers to Christ's resurrection, regardless of whether πνεύματι refers to God the Holy Spirit (Rom 1:4; 8:11) or to the human spirit, that is, the force of life (1 Cor 15:44–46). In the latter case (the option I have chosen) this refers to the human spirit, which departs from the body at death (Luke 23:46; John 19:30), but which causes the body to rise from the dead upon returning to the body (Luke 8:55).

ὤφθη ἀγγέλοις—Angels were present to announce the birth of Christ and to offer praises for it (Luke 2:8–14), to minister to him after the temptation in the wilderness (Matt 4:11; Mark 1:13), to strengthen him in Gethsemane (Luke 23:43), at his resurrection (Matt 28:2–7; Mark 16:5–7; Luke 24:4–7; John 20:12–13), and at his ascension into heaven (Acts 1:10). Since the phrase occurs right after the reference to the resurrection, either Christ's rising or his ascension would seem mostly likely to come to mind. Perhaps the clause here is intended to recall both events.[211]

---

208. Metzger, *Text*, 187.
209. As noted by Marshall, *Pastoral Epistles*, 523.
210. Mounce, *Pastoral Epistles*, 227.
211. Knight, *Pastoral Epistles*, 185, comes to a similar conclusion.

The Greek term ἄγγελος means "messenger," and while in the NT it usually is a name for heavenly messengers, it sometimes refers to human messengers.[212] If that would be the meaning here, the phrase would speak of those to whom the risen Christ appeared (as in 1 Cor 15:1–11), who then became messengers of his redemptive work, which would include the apostles of our Lord (Acts 1:21–22), also Paul himself (1 Cor 9:1). In that case this line of the hymn/creed would be naturally followed by the reference to Christ being proclaimed (by such messengers) to the nations.

This letter, as the other two Pastoral Letters, certainly contains much regarding the message of Christ and those who proclaim it. However, this passage seems to be structured around three contrasting pairs: "flesh" and "spirit"; "angels (spiritual beings) and nations (material beings)"; and "world (this life) and glory (the life to come)." This would point to ἀγγέλοις designating angelic and not human messengers.[213] Furthermore, the only other reference to "angels" in these letters (1 Tim 5:21) plainly refers to heavenly angels. While a designation of human messengers cannot be ruled out, the other use of the word in this letter and the overwhelming usage of the term throughout the NT argues in favor of a reference to heavenly angels. Moreover, that the proclaimers of the risen Christ included more than eyewitnesses of the resurrection, among them the addressee of this letter, would also argue against this being a mention of human messengers.

Could "angels" here be a reference to fallen angels, making the phrase a reference to Christ's victorious descent into hell by which he proclaimed his victory over Satan and his hosts, as in 1 Pet 3:18–22?[214] In those passages of the NT that use ἄγγελος to refer to the hosts of Satan[215] something in the context always gives indication that fallen angels are in view.[216] The lack of such a pointer in the present passage, the otherwise exclusive use in these letters of ἄγγελος for heavenly beings, and the use

212. Matt 11:10; Mark 1:2; Luke 7:24, 27; 9:52; Jas 2:25. Other instances where ἄγγελος might refer to a human messenger include Matt 24:31 (Mark 13:27); Rev 2:1, 8, 12, 18; 3:1, 7, 14.

213. Debelius and Conzelmann, *Pastoral Epistles*, 61–62.

214. Origen *(Homilies on Luke* 6:9–10) suggests that it may refer to Christ being seen by the fallen angels during his descent into the "nether world" (FC 94:27).

215. Matt 25:41; 2 Cor 12:7; Col 2:18; 2 Pet 2:4; Jude 6; Rev 9:11; 12:9.

216. The one possible exception is 1 Cor 6:3. However, that reference might include good as well as evil angels (Lockwood, *1 Corinthians*, 191–92); moreover, the passage is too enigmatic to establish ἄγγελοι standing alone as a designation of fallen angels.

of other terms in this letter for the devil's minions (πνεύμασιν πλάνοις, δαιμονίων, 1 Tim 4:1) tells decisively against this phrase speaking of the *descensus* of Christ.

ἐκηρύχθη ἐν ἔθνεσιν—The term ἔθνη can mean "gentiles" or "nations." Paul had a special obligation for ministry to the gentiles (Rom 11:13; Gal 2:6–10); nevertheless, since there is nothing in the context that calls to mind the friction between Jews and gentiles, the rendering "nations" is to be preferred here. In any event the phrase points to the reality that the "mystery of godliness" is to be proclaimed to all.

ἐπιστεύθη ἐν κόσμῳ—While κόσμος can refer to creation (1 Tim 6:7) or to fallen humanity in rebellion against God (2 Tim 4:10), here it refers to all manner of humanity. As Christ came to save the world (1:15), that is, all people, so all manner and classes of people have come to faith in this one proclaimed to them. Thus, ἔθνεσιν in the previous phrase and κόσμῳ here function as synonyms.

ἀνελήμφθη ἐν δόξῃ—The verb "taken up" (ἀνελήμφθη) is used elsewhere in the NT of Christ's ascension (Acts 1:2, 11, 22). The term δόξα, "glory," is one that is used of eternal blessedness.[217] The phrase here, therefore, refers to Christ's ascension and exaltation (e.g., Eph 1:20–23). See further the entry "Glory" in the Extended Notes.

COMMENTARY

Timothy as Paul's Agent

This letter opens with the observation that the apostle had left Timothy in Ephesus to have pastoral oversight of the church(es) there. In the present passage as well as elsewhere in this letter (4:13) he expresses the intention to come to Ephesus himself. This fits in with what we know of Paul's ministerial practice elsewhere.

The apostle had sent Timothy to serve the church at Thessalonica (1 Thess 3:2). Nevertheless, he had every intention of returning to the church there (1 Thess 3:6), and the evidence of the book of Acts suggests he did just that (Acts 20:1–6). Similarly, Paul dispatches his younger coworker to Corinth (1 Cor 4:17), all the while intending to go there himself (1 Cor 4:19; 16:10–11). In the same way he intended to send

---

217. Rom 8:18; 1 Cor 15:43; Phil 3:21; Col 3:4; 2 Thess 1:9.

Timothy to Philippi (Phil 2:19, 23), all the while with the thought that he himself could come to see the Christians there (Phil 2:24).

Thus, the picture of the apostle sending Timothy as his representative in Ephesus is just what these other letters (all of which are commonly counted among the "undisputed" Pauline Letters) would lead us to expect. This serves as one more apologetic argument for the authenticity of 1 Timothy.[218]

Conduct in the Church

At the time when he wrote 1 Timothy Paul was still a free man. Therefore, he had reason to think that he would be able to come to see Timothy. He may have felt no need at this point to put his directives in writing. Nevertheless, he penned this letter of instruction regarding the church, its life, and its ministry. In this we can see the providence of God. The Holy Spirit moved the apostle to put his directives in writing (2 Tim 3:16; 2 Pet 1:20–21) for the good of the church of all ages.

Paul indicates that he writes (γράφω) here about what is necessary (δεῖ) in the church of God. He writes as an apostle (1:1; 2:7); these are not merely his private opinions, for he writes as an authoritative spokesman for Christ himself (refer to the entry "Apostle" in the Extended Notes). Basic to what is necessary is the authoritative word of God (1:18–20; 2:7). This word centers in the redemptive ministry of Jesus Christ (2:3–6; 3:16). That Christ-centered word is central to the church's worship (2:1–2, 8–10)

There are various functions in the church's ministry, and these are carried out by various individuals. To men God has entrusted the work of the pastoral office and therefore also to leadership in worship (2:8; 2:11–3:7). Men and women are called to works of love and service within the household of God (3:8–13).

The church of God is "the pillar and foundation of the truth." The church functions in this role, as it sets forth "the word of truth" (2 Tim 2:15); see the textual note above. That being the case, it is essential that those who proclaim the truth of God's word be qualified.[219]

---

218. As argued by Johnson, *Letters*, 230–31.
219. As noted by Mounce, *Pastoral Epistles*, 222.

The Mystery of Godliness

The false teachers that the apostle combats in these letters put an emphasis on "knowledge"[220] and evidently put themselves forward as the exclusive arbiters of such knowledge.[221] That being the case, they may have used the term "mystery" with reference to this knowledge that they claimed was hidden from all who did not follow their teachings. Thus, even though Paul had already made rich use of this term in his letters, he may have intentionally chosen to employ it here as a way of saying that his teaching and not that of the heretics was the revelation of the mystery of salvation.

As the apostle uses the term "mystery," it has a plentiful kerygmatic content (see the entry "Mystery" in the Extended Notes). The plan of salvation, which was a mystery hidden in times past, was only revealed in the ministry of Jesus Christ.[222]

In this creedal[223] passage Paul spells out the details of that ministry. It begins with the coming of Jesus Christ in the flesh. In view of the presence of "gnostic" elements in the false teaching bedeviling the churches at this point in history,[224] the apostle emphasizes the reality of the human nature of Jesus. He was born a man with a true and full human nature of flesh and blood.

The true humanity of Jesus was part and parcel of his work of salvation. In his true human body he died a real death on the cross, and that same human body was raised from the dead on the third day by the return of his human "spirit" (the force of life) to his body. By his resurrection he was "vindicated." He had made remarkable claims during his ministry: being the fulfillment of the Old Testament, the Messiah, the savior, and indeed God himself. His death seemed to give the lie to all these claims (e.g., Matt 27:39–44), but his resurrection vindicated him;

---

220. 1 Tim 4:3; 6:20; 2 Tim 2:25; 3:7; Titus 1:1, 16.

221. See "The Nature of the Heresy" in the Introduction to the Pastoral Letters.

222. Theodoret of Cyr, *Interpretation of the First Letter to Timothy*, Patrologia Graeca, 82:809D/810D (ACCS, NT 9:179). Leo the Great, in an allusion to Eph 1:4 (Sermons 23.4), speaks of the mystery as being laid down from the foundation of the world (FC 93:90–91). See also 1 Pet 1:10–12.

223. *DNTB* 235–36; *DPL* 988. The common ending of each of the six verbs here (each ends in "θη") supports the idea that these lines are a creed or a hymn (or a credal hymn); BDF 258 [§ 488 (3)].

224. See "The Nature of the Heresy" in the Introduction to the Pastoral Letters.

his rising from the dead proved that everything he had claimed was true and that his death had accomplished the work of salvation.

The risen Christ was "seen by angels." Whether this phrase has reference to the resurrection, the ascension, or both, it serves as a confirmation of the reality and sufficiency of the saving work of Jesus.

The content of the mystery of salvation is to be proclaimed to all. This proclamation serves to reveal the salvation that remains a mystery apart from its proclamation. That proclamation is the work of the church and especially of those like Paul and Timothy who have been called to the office of the ministry.

The proclamation of this mystery is the power that brings hearers to believe it (1 Cor 12:3; Rom 10:17). Since this mystery is to be proclaimed to all, it has found believers throughout the world, that is, among any and all races and classes of people. Hence, the Christian church is a public assembly (ἐκκλησία); its membership is open to all who put their faith in the Christ it proclaims.

Jesus Christ was taken up in glory. He reigns over all creation (Eph 1:20–23), so that he is able to care for his church. He will come again in glory to take his believers to eternal glory (Col 3:4).

The Mystery of Godliness: 1 Timothy 3:14–16 in Context

The closing phrases of this section are creedal, almost doxological. Therefore, they mark the conclusion of this section (1:18—3:16) on the life of the church.

In writing about the life of Christ's church Paul has been giving instruction regarding various roles that are carried out in the church. Central to the life of the church and of all the roles of service within it is its message. That message can be summarized as a "mystery," as it was hidden for long ages but has now been revealed in the ministry of Jesus Christ. It can be summarized as "godliness," for Christ gives believers godliness before the Almighty and empowers them to demonstrate godliness in the way in which they live. That being the case, it is fitting that he concludes this section with this exposition of "the mystery of godliness," referencing those things that Christ has done to bring godliness (in all senses of that term) to his church.

4:1–5: Ministry in the Last Times

TRANSLATION

¹ The Spirit explicitly says that in the last times some will turn away from the faith, holding to deceptive spirits and teachings of demons, ² in the subversion of those who speak falsehood, who are seared in their own conscience, ³ who forbid marrying, who require abstaining from [certain] foods, which God created to be received with thanksgiving by those who believe and know the truth. ⁴ Every creation of God is good, and none is to be rejected, if it is received with thanksgiving, ⁵ for it is sanctified by the word of God and prayer.

TEXTUAL NOTES

4:1 Τὸ δὲ πνεῦμα ῥητῶς λέγει—What follows is the teaching of God the Holy Spirit; see further the commentary.

ὑστέροις καιροῖς—In this context ὑστέροις means "last (of all)" as in Matt 21:37; 26:60; Luke 20:32.[225] See further the commentary.

ἀποστήσονταί—This verb means to "turn away," to "depart."[226] It is a tragic reality that some will hold the faith for a while, but in time they will fall away.

τῆς πίστεως—As "faith" is contrasted with demonic "teachings" (διδασκαλίαις), the term here denotes the content of faith (*fides quae creditur*); thus, in translation the article should be included ("*the* faith"). See further the entry "Faith" in the Extended Notes.

---

225. BDAG 1044; Wallace, *Greek Grammar*, 299; BDF 34 [§ 62].
226. Luke 8:13; Acts 12:10; 15:38; 19:9; Heb 3:12.

πνεύμασιν πλάνοις . . . δαιμονίων—Here these two terms are equivalent.

διδασκαλίαις—The Christian faith involves holding to divine teaching. Thus, holding to the teachings of demons rather than the teachings of God results in turning away from the faith.

4:2 ὑποκρίσει—The word "hypocrisy" derives from this Greek word. However, the English word usually connotes someone pretending to be something he is not or advocating for others something that he does not apply to himself. The Greek word does not necessarily carry those connotations. For example, Jesus rebukes the scribes and Pharisees for being hypocrites,[227] not because they were insincere (many of them were very sincere about what they believed and did), but because their beliefs were wrong. Similarly, the "hypocrisy" of the scribes and Herodians who asked Jesus about paying taxes to Caesar (Mark 12:15) had to do not with insincerity but with their evil intent (Matt 22:18), for they were very earnest in their desire to entrap him in his words (Matt 22:15; Mark 12:13; Luke 20:26), that they might get him in trouble with the Roman authorities (Luke 20:20). For this reason, I have opted for the translation "subversion" here. See also the following note.

ψευδολόγων—While "liar" is the normal rendering of this word, adhering closely to its etymology, I have chosen to translate it "one who speaks falsehood." "Liar" might tend to suggest those who intentionally speak what they know to be false. While that might be true of some of those about whom Paul writes here, the overall context of the Pastorals would indicate that many of the apostle's opponents were sincere about their teachings. The issue is rather than they are sincerely wrong; their teachings, however sincerely held, are false, and because they are false, they are inimical to the saving faith.

κεκαυστηριασμένων τὴν ἰδίαν συνείδησιν—The background to "sear" may be of a crime whose perpetrator is punished by being branded with a red-hot iron.[228] On "conscience" (συνείδησιν) see the entry "Heart and Conscience" in the Extended Notes.

4:3 κωλυόντων γαμεῖν, ἀπέχεσθαι βρωμάτων—This is a situation in which the idea is not fully expressed grammatically, so that the hearer/reader is left to supply what is not expressed, since what is not stated is self-evident (this figure of speech is known as zeugma). In this verse

---

227. Matt 23:13, 15, 23, 25, 27, 28, 29.
228. BDAG 536; Mounce, *Pastoral Epistles*, 237–38.

the participle κωλυόντων, "who forbid," grammatically governs the infinitives γαμεῖν, "marry," and ἀπέχεσθαι, "abstain"; however, the participle only suits γαμεῖν.[229] The sense is that the "liars" forbid marrying and the eating of certain foods. For the translation above I have rendered the phrases in question "forbid marrying . . . require abstaining."

γαμεῖν—In NT times this word covers both "marrying" (used of a man) and "be given in marriage" (used of a woman).[230]

ἃ ὁ θεὸς ἔκτισεν—The neuter plural antecedent to which the neuter plural relative pronoun ἃ refers is βρωμάτων ("foods"); however, this is a *constructio ad sensum* ("construction according to sense"); the pronoun refers to marriage as well as to foods as things that God created. With ἔκτισεν here and κτίσμα in 4:4 Paul roots his instruction in the biblical doctrine of creation. See further the note on ἐντεύξεως in 4:5.

εὐχαριστίας—The apostle again uses this term in 4:4; this is a case of repetition for emphasis.

τοῖς πιστοῖς καὶ ἐπεγνωκόσι τὴν ἀλήθειαν—To "know the truth" means the same thing as to "believe"; Paul uses both expressions here to emphasize the essential nature of faith for Christian living.

4:4 πᾶν κτίσμα θεοῦ καλὸν—This is a direct reference to God's verdict of "good" pronounced over everything that he created.[231]

λαμβανόμενον—This adverbial participle is used here to indicate condition ("if").[232]

4:5 ἁγιάζεται—The verb "sanctify" and its cognates have several different (although related) denotations. To be sanctified could mean to have all one's unholiness forgiven, so that he is now holy before God (Acts 20:32; 1 Cor 1:2; 6:11). The same verb could refer to being empowered by that forgiveness to do those things that are holy before God (Rom 15:16; 1 Cor 7:14; 2 Tim 2:21).

The root meaning of this verb is to "set apart." Thus, when Jesus says that the Father has "sanctified" him and sent him into the world (John 10:36) or states that he "sanctified" himself (John 17:19), he is not referring to being removed from sin but to being set apart for the task set before him.

It is in this light that we should understand the apostle's words here regarding the things God has created being "sanctified" by the word of

---

229. BDF 253 [§ 479 (2)].
230. Wallace, *Greek Grammar*, 415.
231. Gen 1:4, 10, 12, 18, 21, 25, 31.
232. Wallace, *Greek Grammar*, 633.

God and prayer. It is through these (see the notes that follow) that the believer can make acceptable use of all the things that God has provided for our use.

λόγου θεοῦ—One is sanctified through faith (2 Thess 2:13). The faith that sanctifies is worked by the word of God (Rom 10:17; 2 Thess 2:14; the word that sanctifies would also include the sacraments of baptism and the Lord's Supper: 1 Cor 6:11). This same faith produces "sanctification" in the sense of godly living (Gal 5:6; Eph 2:8–10). This sanctifying power of God's word sanctifies the believer's entire life and conduct (Phil 4:8; Col 3:17). Hence, the believer's life in word and worship (see the following note) is what sanctifies his eating of any food.

ἐντεύξεως—This term ("prayer") and the references to "thanksgiving" in 4:3 and 4:4 might well be a reference to the practice of prayer at mealtime.[233] On the basis of this verse many Christians have adopted the custom of praying before (and offering thanksgiving after) meals.[234] However, here "prayer" probably serves as a synecdoche (part for the whole); as one part of Christian worship and the Christian life prayer denotes the entirety of the believer's sanctified living.

COMMENTARY

The Spirit Explicitly Says

Twice in this letter Paul has identified himself as an "apostle" (1:1; 2:7), a self-identification he makes in many of the New Testament letters from his pen.[235] In this way he indicates that he writes not by his own authority but by that of Jesus Christ (see the entry "Apostle" in the Extended Notes).

Therefore, when he writes "I urge" (2:1), "I desire" (2:8), and "I do not permit" (2:12), he is not giving his own opinion; his words have all the authority of Christ himself. Similarly, when he tells Timothy that it is "necessary" to conduct oneself in the church of God as he instructs in this letter (3:15), he can make such an assertion, because in this letter he is a spokesman for God himself.

---

233. Kelly, *Pastoral Epistles*, 96; Guthrie, *Pastoral Epistles*, 105; note Rom 14:6; 1 Cor 10:30; Phil 4:6 and compare Mark 8:6.

234. See, for example, Luther's suggested prayers for before and after meals in the Small Catechism (LSB 327–28) and the musical setting of another common table prayer in LSB 776.

235. Rom 1:1; 1 Cor 1:1; 2 Cor 1:1; Gal 1:1; Eph 1:1; Col 1:1; 2 Tim 1:1; Titus 1:1.

This authoritative character of the letter is confirmed by the opening words of this chapter. What Paul writes here is what "the [Holy] Spirit explicitly says." A comparison of this passage with 2 Pet 1:20–21, which speaks of the authors of the Scriptures being carried along by God the Holy Spirit, demonstrates that the apostle's words here are a direct affirmation of the inspiration, and therefore also of the authority, of this letter as a portion of Scripture. The apostle will write about the inspiration of the Scriptures in his Second Letter to Timothy (3:14–17); that passage and the present one complement one another in teaching about the inspiration of the Bible.

Elsewhere Paul sets forth the same view of the inspiration, authority, and therefore of the "canonicity" of his letters. In both 1 Thessalonians (5:27) and Colossians (4:16) he gives instruction that his letters be "read." In these instances, the fact that the letters are to be "read" means that they are to be read in the context of the recipients being gathered together for worship, just as they and their ancestors in the faith had been accustomed to reading the Hebrew Scriptures in public worship (Luke 4:16–20; Acts 13:14–15).[236]

The apostle points to the authority of his letters in other ways. He instructs the Thessalonians to hold to what he taught in his letter to them (2 Thess 2:15). In 1 Corinthians he states that what he is writing is "a command of the Lord" (1 Cor 14:37). He directs the Philippians to do what they "learned and received and heard and saw in" him (Phil 4:9). He instructs Timothy to hold to what he had taught him (2 Tim 1:13; 2:2; 3:14).[237]

In view of all this what the apostle writes in this letter (and all of his other epistles) must not be dismissed as merely his own opinions, as the antiquated culture of the times, or in any other way. Instead, we must read his letters as he (and the Holy Spirit) intended them to be read: as the authoritative word of God alongside the Scriptures of the Old Testament.

The Last Times

Paul writes here about what will take place in "the last times"; similarly, he speaks in 2 Timothy (3:1) concerning activity in "the last days." A comparison of 4:1 with 4:7 ("reject . . . myths") indicates that "the last times"

---

236. See further Deterding, *Colossians*, 192–94.

237. Note also 2 Pet 3:16, where that apostle speaks of the letters of Paul as equal to "the other Scriptures."

describes the time when the apostle and Timothy were living. Again, a comparison of 2 Tim 3:1 with 3:5 ("avoid these people") demonstrates that "the last days" refers to the time when the letter was written. These passages are examples of the biblical view of time and history.

Paul expresses a similar understanding of time in 1 Corinthians. There (10:11) he speaks of what was written for the "instruction of us, on whom the end of the ages has come."

The apostle, like all the authors of the New Testament, viewed time and history in light of the history of salvation. The time before Christ was a time of promises of salvation that were as yet unfulfilled. God performed many saving acts for mankind, but always there remained something else that needed to be accomplished. That necessary work of salvation was carried out by Jesus Christ, by his death for forgiveness and his resurrection for mankind's justification (Rom 4:25). With the completion of this work by Christ, God's plan of salvation was finally accomplished. Nothing remained to be done for the world's salvation, save for Christ to return in glory to take his redeemed to the full realization of that salvation. From that perspective the apostle could say that the time is short (1 Cor 7:29) and that the Lord is near (Phil 4:5), for since the work of salvation had been completed, the Lord might return at any time.

This view of time and history is one that Paul shared with other authors of the New Testament. The apostle Peter asserts that Christ was manifested as savior "at the last times" (1 Pet 1:20). On the day of Pentecost the same apostle proclaimed that what his hearers were witnessing was what the prophet Joel had foretold would take place "in the last days" (Acts 2:17). The author of Hebrews declares that after the time of the Old Testament prophets God spoke to us by his Son "in these last days" (1:2). That same author asserts that Jesus offered his once-for-all sacrifice "at the end of the ages" (9:26). Both Peter (2 Pet 3:3) and Jude (18) give their readers warnings about temptations taking place about them "in the last days/times." The apostle John writes, "It is the last hour" (1 John 2:18). James warns that the coming of the Lord is near and that the judge is standing at the door (Jas 5:8–9).

This view of time and history had its origin in the teaching of the Lord himself. Jesus proclaimed that with his coming "the saving rule of God [ἡ βασιλεία τοῦ θεοῦ] had come" (e.g., Matt 12:28; Luke 11:20). He said that the hour of the resurrection "is coming and is now here" (John 5:25).

Jesus Christ has completed the work of salvation; hence, he could return for the final judgment at any time. This gives a sense of urgency to the instruction that the authors of the New Testament give to their readers and hearers (such as in this letter). It is of utmost importance that we follow the biblical instruction about holding to the faith (especially in view of temptations to abandon it) and concerning the type of living that will follow faith.[238]

Teachings of Demons

In the present letter Paul declares that "in the last times some will turn away from the faith, holding to deceptive spirits and teachings of demons." Elsewhere the apostle had also proclaimed that there would be false teachings and false teachers that would draw people away from the truth and to heresy and therefore into eternal punishment (Acts 20:29–30; 2 Thess 2:1–12).

On the false teaching combated by the Pastorals, see "The Nature of the Heresy" in the Introduction to the Pastoral Letters. In the present passage Paul characterizes it as "teachings [or doctrines] of demons" that come from "deceptive spirits." With these words the apostle indicates that the ultimate source of non-Christian teaching is Satan and his hosts.

As would be expected, deceptive spirits (πνεύμασιν πλάνοις) speak falsehood (ψευδολόγων). As something that is false, this teaching is the opposite of the truth, and because it is not the truth (1 Tim 4:3), it does not save (1 Tim 2:4); those who hold to it by definition have turned away from the only faith (knowledge of the truth) that saves.

Because their teaching does not save, those who hold to this teaching do not have salvation. Paul expresses this in the present passage by saying that these false teachers have a conscience that is seared. This is the very opposite of the good conscience that comes from holding to the true faith (1 Tim 1:5, 19). As the only way to a good conscience is genuine faith in Christ, the only deliverance from a seared conscience is the truth about Christ.

The apostle notes here that the false teachers present among those churches served by Timothy forbid marrying and require abstaining from certain foods (see the textual notes above). These prohibitions arose from the negative view that the heretics took toward all things material.

---

238. See further Deterding, "New Testament View," 385–99.

Grace and Life

They took the attitude that only the spiritual was good and acceptable; all things material by definition were inherently evil. That being the case, they held that the only way to escape the evil control of the material and to find fellowship with God, whom they considered to be pure spirit, was to avoid all things material. Since marriage involved contact with what was "flesh" rather than "spirit," the false teachers judged it to be unacceptable for anyone who would find fellowship with God. Apparently, they also classified certain foods as also involving the flesh and therefore being unacceptable.

Paul refutes this heresy by noting that God created these things good and created them to be received. While grammatically the antecedent of the phrase "which God created to be received" is "foods," theologically the phrase also refers to marriage.[239] The creation of man and woman in the image of God was a part of what the creator pronounced to be very good (Gen 1), and marriage was also instituted in creation before the fall (Gen 2). Therefore, those who are a new creation in Christ (2 Cor 5:17) are able to make use of those things that God created for mankind's use.

Ancient Gnosticism has not been the only falsehood that has been the basis for forbidding marrying and requiring abstaining from certain foods. Some Christians do possess the gift for living as an unmarried person (1 Cor 7:1, 6–9). Some Christians may choose to abstain from certain foods (Rom 14:3, 6). Nevertheless, these verses from 1 Timothy demonstrate that any religious teacher who prohibits marriage or the eating of certain foods is speaking falsehood (4:2).[240]

Sanctified by the Word of God and Prayer

The apostle speaks of those who have faith (knowledge of the truth) as being able to receive the good things of God's creation such as marriage and foods. These things are "sanctified," that is, acceptable for use, because those who receive them have themselves been sanctified through faith in Christ.

The word of God works that faith in Christ by which one is sanctified in the sight of God. This faith sanctifies the believer's entire existence so that he is able to live a godly life. That godly life includes worship ("prayer"). Since sanctifying faith embraces the believer's entire existence,

---

239. Knight, *Pastoral Epistles*, 190, comes to the same conclusion.
240. See also Mark 7:15; Acts 10:1–23; Rom 14; 1 Cor 7 and 8.

his use of such things as marriage and food is also sanctified by that faith worked by the word of God.

Twice Paul states that these good things of God's creation are to be received "with thanksgiving." As gifts of God the only appropriate way to make use of them is with thanksgiving.

Ministry in the Last Times: 1 Timothy 4:1–5 in Context

Paul has been writing extensively about life and ministry within the church. He now turns to dealing with the reality that the ministry and the beliefs of Christ's people are always under attack from the outside.

The attacks on the church have their ultimate origin in Satan and his hosts. These are not trivial matters, for they endanger the very faith that saves. That being the case, it is necessary that Christians in general and their pastors in particular be on guard against them.

Here the apostle exposes the false teaching that needs to be rejected. In the following section he will instruct Timothy regarding the type of ministry necessary to provide care for God's people over against these false teachers.

4:6–16: A Good Minister

TRANSLATION

⁶ By setting these things before the brothers you will be a good minister of Christ Jesus, being instructed[a] in the words of the faith and of the good teaching,[b] after which you have followed, ⁷ but reject worldly and senseless myths. Train yourself for godliness, ⁸ for bodily training has a little benefit, but godliness has the utmost benefit, having promise both for the present life and for the life to come. ⁹ The saying is trustworthy and worthy of full acceptance, ¹⁰ for we labor and struggle for this, because we have hoped in the living God, who is the savior of all people, especially of believers.

¹¹ Command and teach these things. ¹² Let no one despise your youth, but be an example for the believers in speech, in conduct, in love, in faith, in purity. ¹³ Until I come, devote yourself to the public reading [of Scripture], to preaching, to teaching. ¹⁴ Do not neglect your gift, which was given to you through prophecy with the laying on of the hands of the elders. ¹⁵ Put these things into practice, live in them, in order that your progress might be evident to everyone. ¹⁶ Pay attention to yourself and to your teaching; continue in these things, for by doing this you will save yourself and your hearers.

[a] Or *being nourished*
[b] Or *doctrine*

COMMENTARY ON 1 TIMOTHY

TEXTUAL NOTES

4:6 Ταῦτα—There is no obvious antecedent to this neuter plural pronoun. That being the case, it most likely refers to all the teachings that Paul has set forth in this letter—in other words, to all the teachings of God's word.

ὑποτιθέμενος—This present tense participle has an active sense here and designates "setting these things before" as the "means" by which (or the condition in which) Timothy will carry out the work of being a good minister of Christ.[241]

ἀδελφοῖς—This is a common NT term for fellow Christians; see, for example, 1 Tim 6:2; hence, some English translations render it "brothers and sisters."

διάκονος—This is a term that can mean "(household) servant" (e.g., John 2:5, 9). It occurs in 3:8, 12 for those who served as "deacons" in Timothy's churches (see the commentary on 3:8–13). However, in the present context, speaking of Timothy as one who labors in the word of God, "minister" is the preferred translation.[242]

ἐντρεφόμενος—The participle here is in the passive voice; by being instructed in the teaching of the faith (*fides quae creditur*) Timothy is equipped to be a good minister of Christ. The translation "nourished" takes this word as a compound of the preposition ἐν and the term τρέφω; this rendering would provide a slightly different word picture, but the overall meaning of the phrase would be the same.

τῆς πίστεως—This refers to the content of what is believed (*fides quae creditur*); hence the article should be translated "*the* faith." See further the entry "Faith" in the Extended Notes.

καλῆς διδασκαλίας—That this teaching (doctrine) is "good" indicates that it is from God,[243] which is why Timothy and other believers are to "follow" it. The use of the word "teaching" and of verbs cognate to it points to a body of authoritative and normative teaching,[244] which in time will have been put into writing (2 Thess 2:15), that is, in the holy Scriptures (see further the section "The Spirit Explicitly Says" in the commentary on 1 Tim 4:1–5).

---

241. Wallace, *Greek Grammar*, 633.
242. Cf. 2 Cor 3:6; 11:23; Eph 3:7; Col 1:7, 23, 25.
243. Gen 1:4, 8, 10, 12, 18, 21, 25, 31 LXX.
244. Eph 4:14; 1 Tim 1:10; 6:3; Titus 1:9; 2:1, 10.

Grace and Life

παρηκολούθηκας—The perfect tense of this verb indicates that Timothy began to hold to "the good teaching" in the past and has continued to hold to it up unto the present.[245]

4:7 βεβήλους—This adjective can mean "worldly" (in the sense of belonging to this fallen, corrupted world: 1 Tim 1:9; Heb 12:16) or "corrupt," "worthless" (1 Tim 6:20; 2 Tim 2:16). Anything belonging to this corrupted world is worthless in matters of eternal importance.

γραώδεις—Literally "what is characteristic of an elderly woman";[246] compare the phrase "old wives' tales." Philosophic polemics from that era also used this kind of terminology.[247] These would be the type of women who would become idlers, gossips, and busybodies (5:13; 2 Thess 3:11). On the apostle's actual attitude toward older women, see 1 Tim 5:2.

μύθους—Except for 2 Pet 1:16 this is a word that in the NT is found only in the Pastorals.[248] Paul distinguishes "myths" from the "truth" (2 Tim 4:4; Titus 1:14); hence, things that are "myths" are by definition false.

παραιτοῦ—Rejecting false teaching (1 Tim 4:7; 2 Tim 2:23) will involve also rejecting those who teach it (Titus 3:10, whose commentary see).

Γύμναζε—The apostle uses bodily training as an illustration of the intensity and dedication with which the Christian in general and the minister/pastor in particular is to approach matters of faith and godly living.

εὐσέβειαν—This is a term ("godliness") that encapsulates the entirety of Christian faith and living.[249]

4:8 πρὸς ὀλίγον ἐστὶν ὠφέλιμος—Paul does not deny that there is some benefit to bodily training; he demonstrates an interest in athletic performance (1 Cor 9:24–27; Phil 4:1; 2 Tim 4:7–8); perhaps he even participated in bodily training and/or athletics himself. His point here is the far greater benefit from "godliness."

πρὸς πάντα ὠφέλιμος—The term πάντα here means not "entire" but "utmost."[250]

---

245. On the perfect tense see Wallace, *Greek Grammar*, 572–74.
246. BDAG 207.
247. Debelius and Conzelmann, *Pastoral Epistles*, 68, and Marshall, *Pastoral Epistles*, 550, provide examples from Cleomedes, Epictetus, Galen, Lucian, Plato, and Strabo.
248. 1 Tim 1:4; 4:7; 2 Tim 4:4; Titus 1:14.
249. See further the entry "Godliness" in the Extended Notes.
250. BDAG 783 (section 3, "marker of the highest degree").

ζωῆς τῆς νῦν καὶ τῆς μελλούσης—Jesus and Paul both indicate that God promises to provide his people what they need in this life as well as in the life to come (Matt 6:25–34; Rom 8:31–32).

4:9 πιστὸς ὁ λόγος καὶ πάσης ἀποδοχῆς ἄξιος—See the excursus "The Trustworthy Sayings of the Pastoral Letters" at the conclusion of the commentary on 1 Tim 1:12–17. Here the phrase seems to tie together what precedes and what follows. See further the commentary below.

4:10 κοπιῶμεν καὶ ἀγωνιζόμεθα—"Labor" (κοπιῶμεν) can be used of physical work (Luke 5:5 12:27). "Struggle" (ἀγωνιζόμεθα) can refer to athletic competition (1 Cor 9:25; 2 Tim 4:7), such as boxing (1 Cor 9:25 in light of 9:27); it can also be used of combat (John 18:36). The two terms are used here as synonyms to give concrete illustrations of great exertion being put forth in the work of ministry. Both terms here are present tense verbs that describe the ongoing activity of the ministry. Because of the hope that is theirs (see following note) those in ministry are motivated to put forth great effort in the work of ministry.

ἠλπίκαμεν—A perfect tense verb, it describes what took place in the past and whose results continue to the present.[251] One's having hope precedes his being active in ministry. On the meaning of "hope" see the entry by that name in the Extended Notes.

θεῷ ζῶντι—One of the ways in which Paul contrasts his God with all other gods is by saying that while other gods are lifeless, his is the living God.[252]

σωτὴρ πάντων ἀνθρώπων—God the Father sent Christ to acquire salvation for all;[253] in dogmatic terminology this is known as "objective justification."[254] As the Greek word ἀνθρώπων often accents humanity rather than maleness, I have chosen to render it "people."

μάλιστα πιστῶν—Christ acquired salvation for all. Nevertheless, that salvation is only received through believing in Christ.[255] In dogmatic terminology this is known as "subjective justification."[256]

---

251. On the perfect tense see Wallace, *Greek Grammar*, 572–74.

252. Acts 14:15; Rom 9:26; 2 Cor 3:3; 6:16; 1 Thess 1:9; 1 Tim 3:15; 4:10.

253. John 3:14–16; Cor 5:5; 1 Tim 2:6.

254. On objective justification see Nafzger et al., *Confessing the Gospel*, 475–77, 501–3, 572–74; *Theses on Justification*, numbers 1–12.

255. John 3:16; Acts 16:30–31; Rom 3:25; Gal 2:15–16.

256. On subjective justification see Nafzger et al., *Confessing the Gospel*, 475–77, 570–72, 574–75; *Theses on Justification*, numbers 13–23.

4:11 Παράγγελλε... δίδασκε—"Command" (παράγγελλε) is a strong word.[257] This is another indication that the apostle writes with authority (see the entry "Apostle" in the Extended Notes). "Teach" (δίδασκε) often denotes instruction in a (semi-) formal setting;[258] it also carries an implication that what is taught has authority (Matt 28:15, 20). Together the two verbs portray an important aspect of Timothy's ministry: he is to give instruction in these matters, which carry the weight of ultimately coming from God himself. The present tense of each of these imperatives indicates that such activity is to be a regular part of Timothy's labor.

ταῦτα—As in 4:6 there is no obvious antecedent to this neuter plural pronoun. That being the case, it most likely refers to all the teachings that Paul has set forth in this letter—in other words, to all the teachings of God's word.

4:12 νεότητος—How old would this "youth," Timothy, have been at this time? This same Greek word is used in the account of the apostle's defense before Festus and Herod Agrippa II, where he speaks of his manner of life in Judaism from his "youth" (Acts 26:4). In Acts (7:58) Luke uses a cognate noun (νεανίου) to refer to Saul/Paul as a "young man" at the time of the stoning of Stephen in AD 30.[259] Paul refers to himself as an "old man" when he writes his Letter to Philemon (verse 9), perhaps in the neighborhood of AD 60. In view of all of this we could conjecture the apostle's birth to have been about AD 1 and his calling on the road to Damascus around AD 30. Therefore, Paul's reference to his "youth" (Acts 26:4) would include his life prior to his being thirty years old.

The apostle first encounters Timothy and adds him to his missionary team at the beginning of his second missionary journey (Acts 16:1), which would have been about AD 49. In the Introduction to 1 Timothy I have suggested a date of around AD 64 for this letter; thus, fifteen years after Paul and Timothy first joined together in ministry. The apostle notes that Timothy first learned the faith of the Scriptures from his mother and grandmother (2 Tim 1:5), as his father had not been of God's Old Testament people (Acts 16:1, 3).

From all of this we might hazard a guess that Timothy would have been about fifteen when he first joined up with the apostle, which would

---

257. See 1 Tim 5:7; 6:13, 17; 2 Thess 3:4, 6, 10, 12.

258. BDAG 241; Towner, *Letters*, 313.

259. On this and other dates in this note see the section "The Chronology of Paul's Life" in the Introduction to the Pastoral Letters.

make him thirty at the time of the writing of this letter.[260] If Paul has already passed his sixtieth birthday, he would probably have considered a thirty-year-old to be a "youth" in comparison with himself and in view of the great responsibilities that this letter asserts are his.

Among those for whom Timothy labored in ministry were those who were older than he was, while younger people would have been his peers (1 Tim 5:1–2). The present passage makes it clear that among the people for whom Timothy labored in ministry were those who would have considered him a "youth."

There is room for debate over Timothy's age at this time. However, what the description of Timothy as a "youth" points to is that the authority of the pastoral ministry rests not on age or experience (however valuable those indeed might prove to be for carrying out the ministry; see the commentary below) but on the word of God (on the authority in the word of God see also the entry "Apostle" in the Extended Notes).

καταφρονείτω—Although this word can be used in a positive sense (Heb 12:2), it usually denotes not giving to others the respect/regard that ought to be given them.[261] This third person imperative indicates that the meaning is the same as if the apostle had written, "I command others not to despise your youth"[262] (that others besides Timothy would read this letter is indicated in 6:21, whose commentary see). Timothy is owed such respect because of the office that he holds. This verse, along with the instruction of 1 Cor 16:10–11 that the Corinthian Christians were to put Timothy at ease and that no one should despise him, might suggest that Timothy was by nature more quiet than assertive.[263]

τύπος γίνου τῶν πιστῶν—This letter (and the entire NT) emphasizes that the work of the ministry centers in the proclamation of God's word. Here Paul indicates that the pastor is also to minister to others by the example that he sets.

λόγῳ—This term can be used for the word of God, as it is in verse 5 of the present chapter; in such a case this would be an exhortation to be an example of diligently studying the Scriptures.[264] However, all the other items in this list of things of which Timothy is to be an example have to

---

260. Kelly, *Pastoral Epistles*, 2, 104, and Knight, *Pastoral Epistles*, 205, as well as Ramsey, *Historical Commentary*, 117–18, come to a similar conclusion.

261. 1 Tim 6:2; see also Matt 6:24; 18:10; Luke 16:13; Rom 2:4; 1 Cor 11:22; 2 Pet 2:10.

262. Wallace, *Greek Grammar*, 486.

263. Kelly, *Pastoral Epistles*, 103.

264. Luther (AE 28:327–28) suggests this as the meaning.

Grace and Life

do with virtues of the Christian life. That would suggest that the term "word" here refers to being an example of godly speech.

ἀναστροφῇ—This term denotes an individual's entire way of life.[265] Accompanying adjectives will indicate whether the conduct at issue is either good or bad. Here the noun occurs by itself; however, its use here with other terms designating various virtues for which Timothy is to be an example denotes that Paul is instructing Timothy to exemplary conduct.

ἀγάπῃ—"Love" is the chief virtue of the Christian life (1 Cor 13:13; Col 3:14). Therefore, it is not surprising that the apostle should single out this virtue for special mention.

πίστει—See the entry "Faith" in the Extended Notes. Here the term refers to the act of believing, *fides qua creditur*. Perhaps it should be translated "faithfulness," referring to a virtue of the Christian life. Biblically one can be faithful only as a fruit of genuine saving faith.

ἁγνείᾳ—This word denotes moral purity.[266] The use of a cognate word elsewhere in the NT (1 John 3:3) would suggest the idea of Christ as the epitome of such purity and of Christ's gift of salvation supplying the power to live with such purity.

4:13 ἀναγνώσει—This word refers to the public reading of Scripture in worship, a practice that the early Christian church inherited from Old Testament Israel (Deut 31:10–13; Neh 8:1–8) and from the synagogue service (Luke 4:16; Acts 13:15; 2 Cor 3:14). Here it serves as a synecdoche (part for the whole) and designates the entirety of public worship.

παρακλήσει—This word has a wide scope of meaning. However, what does it mean here?

As the term follows immediately after a word denoting public worship, it is significant that this vocable and its cognates are used to refer to the act of preaching. Paul delivers his synagogue sermon in Pisidian Antioch in response to the invitation to give a "word of exhortation [λόγος παρακλήσεως]" (Acts 13:15). Luke follows his record of the preaching on the day of Pentecost with the note that with many other words Peter "exhorted" (παρεκάλει) his hearers (Acts 2:40). In his Second Letter to Timothy the apostle instructs his younger coworker, "Preach the word . . . exhort [παρακάλεσον]" (2 Tim 4:2). Luke concludes his account of the preaching of John the baptist by saying that John was exhorting (παρακαλῶν) as he "evangelized" (εὐηγγελίζετο) the people

---

265. Gal 1:13; Eph 4:22; Jas 3:13; 1 Pet 1:15, 18; 2:7; 2 Pet 2:7; Heb 13:7.
266. *TDNT* 1:123.

(Luke 3:18). Both Peter and the author of Hebrews describe their entire letters with some form of this word group (Heb 13:22: παρακαλῶ, λόγου τῆς παρακλήσεως; 1 Pet 5:12: παρακαλῶν).

In the NT the use of "exhort"/"exhortation" is not confined to preaching in worship. Nevertheless, the context would point to that as being the reference here.[267]

Further insight into this word is the use of the cognate noun παράκλητος to refer both to Christ (1 John 2:1) and to God the Holy Spirit (John 14;16; 15:26; 16:7). Christian "exhortation" is something more than a pep talk. The task of Christian exhortation involves speaking of the work of Jesus Christ for the forgiveness of our sins. Furthermore, unlike any type of worldly exhortation, which depends on the persuasive power of the speaker, the Holy Spirit himself works with power when Christ is proclaimed as our advocate.

διδασκαλίᾳ—Here the emphasis is more on the act of teaching; in 4:1 and perhaps 4:16 it lies more on the content of what is taught, but the two emphases are never divorced from one another. One of Timothy's chief tasks is the teaching of the faith, and it is essential that he teach the correct and true substance of God's word.

4:14 χαρίσματος—In both this passage and 2 Tim 1:6 Paul speaks of a χάρισμα, "gift," that Timothy received. This is one of the terms that the apostle uses in his exposition of the gifts of the Spirit (Rom 12; 1 Cor 12). In both of these lists he includes gifts of speaking the word of God. In his Letter to the Romans he mentions prophecy and teaching (12:6–7). When writing to the Corinthians, he lists "first apostles, second prophets, third teachers" (12:28); this being the case, his exhortation that his readers seek the greater gifts (12:31) would point to these gifts of the word as the greater gifts.

In both of his Letters to Timothy Paul is giving instruction about the responsibilities of one entrusted with the word of God. In this light the "gift" that the apostle references here must be Timothy being entrusted with the office of overseer/elder (3:1; 5:17), that is, of pastor. See also the following two notes and the commentary.

προφητείας—The English words "prophecy," "prophesy," and "prophet" are often assumed to have to do with foretelling the future. While this word group certainly does include prediction, that does not

---

267. DPL 985–86; Kelly, *Pastoral Epistles*, 105.

exhaust the scope of its meaning.[268] These terms refer to the proclamation of God's word, whether or not any foretelling of the future is involved.

Even a cursory look at the writings of the OT prophets makes it plain that they were often speaking God's word without necessarily making any forecasts about the future. In the New Testament the word group is used to designate the entirety of Scripture (Rom 16:26; 2 Pet 1:20–21); this is especially evident in the designation "the law [of Moses] and the prophets."[269] On the day of Pentecost Peter indicates that the proclamation of God's word carried out by him and his fellow disciples was the fulfillment of the prediction of Joel that those on whom God would pour out his Spirit would prophesy (Acts 2:17, 18).

As a term associated with the whole of the biblical revelation, "prophecy" here would point to Timothy's instruction in the word of God that prepared him for taking up the task of the pastoral ministry (2 Tim 2:2; 3:14). Thus, prophecy would be the first-century equivalent of what we would think of as seminary education, and the laying on of hands (see the following note) would be the occasion when he formally entered into the office of pastor.

ἐπιθέσεως τῶν χειρῶν τοῦ πρεσβυτερίου—While the word group from the root πρεσβυτερ- can refer to older persons (1 Tim 5:1–2) or to leaders within Judaism (Matt 16:21), the term here refers to those who hold the pastoral office.[270]

In the New Testament the laying on of hands has a number of different results. Both Jesus (e.g., Mark 6:5) and various apostles (Acts 5:12; 14:3) laid hands on someone to perform a miracle. At certain times the Holy Spirit was imparted by the laying on of hands (Acts 8:17; 19:6) in order to designate a groundbreaking event in the history of the early church.[271]

---

268. "By and large the NT understands by the prophet the biblical proclaimer of the divine, inspired message" (*TDNT* 6:828); "Prophecy is not only the telling of things future but also of the present" (Chrysostom, *Homilies on 1 Timothy* 5, in *NPNF*² 1.13:423).

269. Matt 7:12; 11:13; 22:40; Luke 16:16; 24:27, 44; John 1:45; Acts 13:15; 24:14; 28:23; Rom 3:21.

270. Acts 14:23; 20:17 (in light of 20:28); 1 Tim 5:17; Titus 1:5 (in light of 1:7); 1 Pet 5:1.

271. It is always the work of the Holy Spirit when anyone comes to saving faith (1 Cor 12:3). However, in the book of Acts a special manifestation of the Holy Spirit occurs at four significant events in the history of the spread of the gospel through the church's witness "in Jerusalem, in Judea and Samaria, and to the ends of the earth" (Acts 1:8). Special signs of the coming of the Holy Spirit take place first of all on the day of Pentecost, which is the beginning of the disciples' witness to their fellow Jews

Nevertheless, the laying on of hands does not always involve observable miracles. The seven men entrusted with supervising the distribution of poor relief to the church's widows are set aside for this task by the laying on of hands (Acts 6:6). Similarly, by the laying on of hands Barnabas and Saul/Paul are set apart to be sent forth on the latter's first missionary journey (Acts 13:2–3).

These two episodes are closest to the laying on of hands that is mentioned in the Pastoral Letters. The present passage speaks of Timothy having received a gift when elders (pastors) laid their hands on him. In 2 Timothy (1:6) Paul states that he himself laid hands on Timothy so that he received a gift. The apostle also directs Timothy not to be hasty in laying hands on others (1 Tim 5:22).

A comparison of these events with those of Acts 6 and 13 suggests that these are all similar episodes, namely the setting aside of persons for a special position in the church; in the case of the Pastorals the task would be the office of the pastoral ministry. The laying on of hands, therefore, should not be thought of as a supernatural imposition of the Holy Spirit or of any of his gifts apart from the usual work and ministry of Christ's people (the present passage also makes explicit mention of "prophecy" [see the previous textual note] as being a part of this "setting aside.") See further the commentary below.

4:15 ταῦτα—As in 4:11 the word here probably refers to everything that Paul has set forth in this letter, the whole word of God.

μελέτα—This verb denotes study and meditation but also putting into practice what has been studied.[272]

ἴσθι—This is a form of the verb "to be."[273] As a minister of the word Timothy's very existence is to be bound up with the teachings of the

---

(Acts 2:1–4, 17). A second such episode occurs at the "Samaritan Pentecost" (Acts 8:14–17), which is the beginning of the outreach of Christ's gospel to the Samaritans, who were descendants of Jewish-gentile intermarriage. A third instance takes place at the "Gentile Pentecost" (Acts 10:44–48), which marks the first outreach of the gospel to gentiles. There are also special signs of the coming of the Holy Spirit on some who knew only of the baptism of John the Baptist (Acts 19:1–6) to show that Christ's gospel was for them as well. The events of Acts 8:17 and 19:6 do not prescribe the laying on of hands as a special means to receiving the Holy Spirit (such laying on of hands is absent from the episodes of Acts 2 and 10). Rather, in each case there are out-of-the-ordinary manifestations of the Holy Spirit to indicate some special episode in the expansion of Christ's church.

272. BDAG 627.
273. BDAG 284.

Scriptures. In an attempt to bring this out, I have offered the translation "live in them."

ἵνα ... ᾖ—Here ἵνα plus a subjunctive verb serves as a purpose-result clause.[274]

προκοπὴ—A cognate verb is used to describe the maturing of the twelve-year-old Jesus (Luke 2:52) and of Paul's stellar advancing in following the traditions of Judaism (Gal 1:14).

φανερὰ ᾖ πᾶσιν—In the context of 4:12 this probably means "evident to all believers."

4:16 ἔπεχε σεαυτῷ καὶ τῇ διδασκαλίᾳ—In this sentence the verb ἔπεχε plainly has a different connotation of meaning between the two direct objects that it takes. Timothy is to pay attention to his spiritual wellbeing in that he is to keep hold of his Christian faith (contrast those referred to in 1:19 and 4:1). He is to diligently study and follow the teaching (doctrine) of the word of God. By giving this attention to the word of God he will keep hold of his own faith.

ἐπίμενε αὐτοῖς—There is no obvious, close-by, plural antecedent to the plural pronoun αὐτοῖς. Hence, it is probable that the apostle's meaning is that his younger coworker is to continue in everything that he has been setting before him in this letter.

ποιῶν—The participle here indicates means ("by doing this");[275] by means of giving attention to the teaching of God's word Timothy will save himself and others.

σώσεις—It is common for Paul to speak of God/Christ saving others.[276] In the present passage and in a few other places in his letters (Rom 11:14; 1 Cor 9:22; 10:33) he speaks of himself saving others. The gospel of Christ works saving faith, and in that way it brings the salvation that Christ acquired by his work.[277] Therefore, when one, such as Paul or Timothy, brings the gospel that works saving faith to another, he may be said to "save" that person.

σεαυτὸν ... καὶ τοὺς ἀκούοντάς σου—When someone speaks the saving gospel, he does so for his own eternal welfare as well as that of others to whom he brings that gospel. He will save his hearers, for saving faith comes by hearing the word of Christ (Rom 10:17).

---

274. Wallace, *Greek Grammar*, 473–74.
275. Wallace, *Greek Grammar*, 630.
276. 1 Tim 1:15; 2:3–4; 4:10; 2 Tim 1:9; Titus 3:5.
277. 1 Cor 1:21; 15:2; 1 Thess 2:16; 2 Thess 2:13–14.

COMMENTARY

A Good Minister

What makes a man a good minister? Answers to that question will be many and varied. But how do we answer that question biblically? The passage before us provides some guidance toward that answer.

We note that here Paul speaks of the preparation that goes into making a man qualified to hold this office. He indicates that Timothy has been "instructed in the words of the faith and of the good teaching, after which you have followed" (4:6). It is probable that the word "prophecy" in 4:14 also refers to the instruction in the word that Timothy received in preparation for entering into the office of the ministry. When elsewhere the apostle speaks of those things that his younger coworker has "heard" from him (2 Tim 1:13; 2:2), this also points to preparation that made him equipped to take up the ministry. Timothy himself is instructed to pass these things along to others (2 Tim 2:2); this again highlights the necessity of proper preparation for one who would hold the pastoral office.

When Paul further instructs Timothy to "reject worldly and senseless myths" (4:7), this indicates that there is a definite standard of teaching to which a pastor and one who would be a pastor must hold. This is also brought out by the apostle's instruction that Timothy is to "pay attention . . . to your teaching/doctrine" (4:16).

A program of seminary education, such as those that have been adopted by many Christian churches, is a way by which they endeavor to be faithful to these instructions of the Scriptures. There are definite, biblical requirements for one who would hold the pastoral office (1 Tim 3:1–7; Titus 1:5–9); preparation by grounding in the word of God is how a man is equipped to meet these requirements.

No one takes this office for himself; instead, he must be called to it (Heb 5:4). Ultimately that call comes from God himself (Rom 1:1; 1 Cor 1:1). Nevertheless, the Lord of the church often makes that call through the members of his church.[278]

In that light we can understand the reference to the gift Timothy received by the laying on of hands of the elders (4:14). Although we are in the dark with respect to particulars, this must have been a public

---

278. Note, for example, how at the end of Paul's first missionary journey he and Barnabas appoint elders (pastors and perhaps other church leaders) for each of the churches that they had founded (Acts 14:23).

recognition of Timothy's being called for his ministry. This would have been similar to what is described in Acts 13, where, by the laying on of hands, Barnabas and Saul/Paul are set apart to be sent on the first missionary journey.

The apostle instructs Timothy to "let no one despise your youth." We see here the respect that Christians are to have for their pastor on the basis of the office to which he has been called. This in no way belittles the value of a pastor's years of experience in the ministry. As someone grows, develops, and improves at anything with practice and experience, the same is true of pastors (see the paragraph that follows).[279] A veteran pastor will have grown through his years of ministry experience; nevertheless, the respect due a pastor is not contingent on a certain amount of experience. Christians are to respect their pastor because of the office of God's word to which he has been called. The respect we owe the word of God should be reflected in the respect we show to those who labor in that word.

Preparation that precedes a call to the ministry qualifies a man to receive such a call, but one's preparation in the word is not to cease with the call. Paul instructs Timothy to train himself for godliness, to put into practice what he has learned—indeed, to live in these things so that his progress might be evident to all. No pastor will ever be so saturated with the word and so competent in the ministry that he will have no room to grow.

Many Christian denominations provide programs of ongoing education for their clergy. Even if a pastor is not involved in any type of formal continuing education, it is vital that he continue to train himself in "godliness," that is, in faith and in the living out of that faith.

Like people in general, many pastors experience benefits from "bodily training," for the Lord of the church is also the creator; hence, there is benefit from caring for the physical life that he has given us. Without belittling the advantages of such training, the apostle notes that training for godliness has "the utmost benefit . . . both for the present and for the life to come." Godliness brings its blessings: the kingdom of God and all the things that God will add to it (Matt 6:33). These blessings are for the pastor himself and for those whom he serves through God's word.

---

279. As with anything there may be exceptions. I think back to a mentor of mine, a veteran pastor, sharing an insight from the career of a certain pastor of his acquaintance. His comment went something like this: "He had had one year of pastoral ministry experience fifteen times." This is certainly the exception rather than the rule.

Also to be noted in this section is the emphasis on the work of proclaiming God's word. Timothy is to "set these things before the brothers" (4:6); he is to "command and teach these things" (4:11). He is to devote himself to preaching (exhortation) and teaching (4:13); he is to "pay attention to [his] teaching" (4:16). The task of ministry is primarily the task of setting forth the word of God.

That does not mean that proclamation refers exclusively to occasions of formal preaching and teaching. The word is the pastor's primary tool in whatever facet of ministry he may be engaged.[280]

That being said, times of public worship and teaching are certainly to be a major focus of the pastor's ministry. Hence, Timothy is instructed, "Devote yourself to the public reading [of Scripture], to preaching, to teaching" (4:13). As a prime part of the worship of the synagogue and subsequently of the early Christian church "the public reading [of Scripture]" refers to the entirety of such services of worship (see textual notes on 4:13 above).[281] Formal occasions for worship, preaching, and teaching are not the sum total of a pastor's ministry, but they do comprise a most significant part of it.

The pastor is to speak the word, but not just any word. Paul instructs his coworker to "reject worldly and senseless myths" (4:7). Instead, he is to be devoted to "the words of the faith and of the good teaching" (4:6) and to "pay attention to . . . [his] teaching/doctrine" (4:16). In his Second Letter to Timothy (3:14–16) the apostle will point explicitly to the Scriptures as the source and norm of that teaching.

These words from the apostle also point to the saving gospel as the center of the word that Timothy is to proclaim, namely, the word of him "who is the savior of all people" (4:10). In doing so he "will save [himself] and [his] hearers" (4:16). The pastor proclaims the entirety of the Scriptures (2 Thess 2:15; 2 Tim 4:2, whose commentary see), but his proclamation focuses primarily on the message of salvation.

---

280. I recall the occasion when a fellow pastor said that he saw himself primarily as a teacher; then he quickly added that he was not thinking only of "classroom" occasions. He was a teacher, he went on to say, when making shut-in or other types of calls, in meetings, indeed, anytime that he had the opportunity to provide some insight, comfort, or guidance from the word.

281. At the same time, it is perhaps worthwhile to consider that Paul singles out for mention the public reading of Scripture. We ought not overlook the importance of that particular portion of our worship. I recall as a young pastor hearing a veteran pastor pass along some sage guidance from one of his mentors. As to the reading of the Scripture lessons in the worship service he counseled, "Read the lessons in such a way that people will come to your church just because of the way you read the Scriptures."

GRACE AND LIFE

This emphasis on the reading and proclamation of the word points to the power of the word. Since this word is the word of God, it has the power of God. Therefore, as one sets forth the word of God, he presents a word that has the power of him who is the savior of all; it is the word that has the power to save through working faith in the savior.[282]

This seems to be the emphasis of the "trustworthy saying" of this section (4:9). This particular occurrence of this expression appears to tie together what proceeds and what follows; hence, the work of the ministry is to be pursued energetically ("we labor and struggle for this") for the purpose of bringing salvation ("godliness has the utmost benefit, having promise... for the life to come.... We have hoped in the living God, who is the savior of all people, especially of believers").

The word is the heart and center of the pastor's ministry, but it is not the totality of it. A pastor like Timothy is also to be an example to others. He is to be an example of faith and of the godly living that flows from faith.

Among those things that Paul mentions here is "speech." This is similar to what he writes in Col 4:6. There he instructs all his readers to "let your speech always be with graciousness, seasoned with salt."[283] What is apropos for Christians in general certainly applies to their pastors. Some speech is out-and-out sinful (Col 3:8-9; Jas 3:2-12): profanity, vulgarity, gossip, and the sort of animosity that Jesus condemns in the Sermon on the Mount (Matt 5:22). Other sorts of speech are also unbecoming for those who hold the pastoral office. Pastors certainly are subject to temptations to be verbose or pretentious in the way they speak. On the other hand, clear disregard for the conventions of language, especially by a pastor, who is likely in a position to know better, does nothing to commend the faith to others (including those outside the faith).

The apostle also instructs Timothy to provide an example in his "conduct" (4:12). This is a broad term for one's entire way of life. Even the world resents someone whose actions do not live up to what he says; that was as true in the New Testament era as it is in our own.[284] Christians

---

282. See the comments of Luther (AE 28:328-30).

283. For translation and commentary see Deterding, *Colossians*, 177-80.

284. Johnson (*First and Second Letters to Timothy*, 252) notes examples from Plutarch, Seneca, and Philo Judaeus, all roughly contemporaneous with Paul. He also observes "the widespread unwillingness in contemporary Western culture to provide direct and unambiguous moral instruction or to assume responsibility for acting in a manner that can be exemplary for others would have been unintelligible in antiquity" (255).

are to live in such a way that their conduct testifies to what they believe (Matt 5:16); how much more is that to be true of their pastors.

The chief virtue, "love," is singled out for special mention. A Christian's faith is to be active in love (Gal 5:6), and a pastor is to provide an example of this for others (see further the entry "Love" in the Extended Notes).

The pastor is to be an example of living faith. In Greek as well as in English the words (and concepts) of "faith" and "faithfulness" are related. Faith is not truly faith unless it is faithful, and genuine faithfulness is impossible without a living and active faith in Jesus Christ. A pastor needs to be an example of genuine faith; after all, others might well ask, "If he doesn't seem to believe it, why should I?"[285]

The last item in this list is "purity," referring to moral purity. The standard of what is or is not pure must be the word of God as recorded in the Scriptures. Various times and places in world history have had a particular need for examples of such purity. The condition of the Roman Empire at the time of Paul and Timothy was such a time. As of this writing our own point in history would also be such a time.

In all of this the pastor is to put forth great effort. He is to "labor and struggle" (4:10). The life of a Christian in general and of a pastor in particular often involves hardship (see 2 Tim 3:12 and the commentary there). Nevertheless, God provides the strength for the pastor to endure such hardship and even in the face of it to work mightily in the task to which the Lord of the church has called him.

The Savior of All

At its most basic level the word group "save/savior/salvation" refers to rescue, such as from a disease or from death (e.g., Matt 9:22; 14:30). In the New Testament it is a standard term for rescue from the eternal wrath

---

285. I am mindful of a quote from C. S. Lewis. Writing from the perspective of the Church of England, where the local parish pastor is called the vicar, Lewis had this to say to the clergy and theologians of his time and place: "Such are the reactions of one bleating layman to Modern Theology. It is right you should hear them. You will not perhaps hear them very often again. Your parishioners will not often speak to you quite frankly. Once the layman was anxious to hide the fact that he believed so much less than the Vicar: he now tends to hide the fact that he believes so much more. Missionary to the priests of one's own church is an embarrassing role; though I have a horrid feeling that if such mission work is not soon undertaken the future history of the Church of England is likely to be short." Lewis, "Modern Theology," 166.

of God (Rom 5:9). Paul uses it with a number of points of reference, so that it encompasses a rich tapestry of salvation.

At times the apostle will name God [the Father] as savior.[286] In other places he applies that title to Christ.[287] In the salutation to the Letter to Titus he does both (Titus 1:3–4).

As savior God the Father sent Christ to be the savior (2 Tim 1:9). Hence, Paul speaks of Christ coming into the world to save sinners (1 Tim 1:15) and of the grace of God appearing and bringing salvation (Titus 2:11) when Christ came as savior (Titus 2:13).

When applied to Christ the term "savior" encompasses all his redemptive work. He saved us by giving himself (to death) in order to redeem us (Titus 2:13–14).

God desires all people to be saved (1 Tim 2:3–4). As the work of salvation was carried out for all, God is therefore the savior of all (1 Tim 4:10).

That salvation is received only through faith (Eph 2:8–9); hence, God is the savior especially of those who believe/have faith (1 Tim 4:10). That faith is created by God through his word (Rom 10:17; 1 Cor 12:3). God calls us to such faith (1 Cor 12:3) through his word (Rom 10:17); hence, the Scriptures make one wise to salvation through faith (2 Tim 3:15). That word joined to the water of baptism is also a way by which God saves people through calling them to faith in Christ (Titus 3:5; cf. 1 Pet 3:21).

It is in this light that Paul can speak of Timothy saving himself and his hearers (1 Tim 4:16). As one who labors in the word of God, Timothy sets forth the word (and administers baptism and the Lord's Supper) through which people are called to faith and thereby have salvation.

A Good Minister: 1 Timothy 4:6–16 in Context

This rather long discourse on the office of the ministry follows Paul's exposition on the "teachings of demons" that precedes it. The defense against teachings of demons is the word of God, and the Lord of the church provides his church with pastors to proclaim that word.

This accounts for the length of the present section. The threat from false teaching is real and the consequences of succumbing to it are most severe. Pastors are called upon to wage war against false teaching and to

---

286. 1 Tim 1:1; 2:3–4; 4:10; Titus 1:3; 2:10; 3:4.
287. 2 Tim 2:10; Titus 1:4; 2:13; 3:6.

do so for the eternal, spiritual wellbeing of those in their care. The pastor who is well grounded in God's word will be a great blessing to the people of God whom he serves.

5:1–2: Groups in the Church 1: Age Groups

After the "Overture" of 1:1–17 Paul begins speaking about life in the church. He writes about various roles of ministry in the church, particularly that of the pastoral ministry (1:18—3:16). Having established that, he speaks of the work of pastors with special reference to dealing with false teaching (4:1–16).

At this point in the letter he turns to directing Timothy about his dealings with various groups within the churches. These groups include age groups (5:1–2), widows (5:3–16), elders/pastors (5:17–25), and slaves and masters (6:1–2a).

TRANSLATION

¹ Do not rebuke an older man, but encourage him as a father, younger men as brothers, ² older women as mothers, younger women as sisters in all purity.

TEXTUAL NOTES

5:1 Πρεσβυτέρῳ—In some contexts (4:14; Titus 1:5) this is a term for one who holds the pastoral office. Here in conjunction with νεωτέρους, πρεσβυτέρας, and νεωτέρας, it plainly means an older man.

ἐπιπλήξῃς—This verb is a compound of the preposition ἐπί and the verb πλήσσω, meaning "strike" (Rev 8:12). Thus, it denotes a sharp, forceful rebuke. It takes as its object the dative πρεσβυτέρῳ; here the word μὴ negates it.

παρακάλει—This verb is a cognate of the noun παρακλήσει in 4:13; there I have rendered the term "preaching," as it has reference to the pastor's task of the public proclamation of God's word (see further the textual note on that verse). Here in contradistinction to ἐπιπλήξῃς the implication is that a pastor such as Timothy is to relate to others in a pastoral manner as opposed to doing so in a harsh fashion.

5:2 ἁγνείᾳ—This word denotes moral purity.[288] The use of a cognate word elsewhere in the NT (1 John 3:3) would suggest the idea of Christ as the epitome of such purity and of Christ's gift of salvation supplying the power to live with such purity.

COMMENTARY

Here Timothy is instructed about being pastoral in his approach to others. The importance of properly distinguishing law and gospel lies at the heart of this directive.[289]

Although Paul here explicitly forbids rebuking only older men, the fact that the positive injunction "encourage" also speaks to Timothy's interaction with the other three groups mentioned here indicates that the prohibition of rebuking applies to Timothy's dealings with all in his care.

This passage is certainly not a blanket constraint on any and every sort of rebuke. The Scriptures record countless examples of Jesus, Paul, and many others rebuking some individual or group on account of sin and/or unbelief. In that light, Timothy may be called upon to rebuke those with whom he deals as well as to encourage them.

This prohibition of rebuking must be seen in connection with the positive instruction to "encourage." "Rebuke" is a law word; "encourage" is more a gospel term. To encourage is to proclaim the fullness of God's salvation in Christ, which is both the way to salvation and the power and motivation for godly living.[290] As Timothy deals with those in his care, he may need to give words of rebuke (law) as well as those of encouragement (gospel). The point here is that as he does so, his ministry is to be characterized by a greater preponderance of gospel rather than law.[291]

Furthermore, Timothy's ministry is to be characterized by respect for those to whom he ministers (older men as fathers, younger men as

---

288. *TDNT* 1:123.

289. On the proper distinction between law and gospel refer to Formula of Concord, Epitome and Solid Declaration, Article V. Further insight is given in the classic treatment by Walther, *Proper Distinction*.

290. On "encourage" see 1 Tim 4:14 and the commentary there.

291. See Walther's twenty-fifth thesis in *Proper Distinction*. This topic is presented in the form of a novel in Giertz, *Hammer of God*.

brothers, etc.) Every pastor faces the temptation to look down on his parishioners. His education, experience, and call might indeed put him in a position "over" others.[292] Nevertheless, arrogance and lording it over others are usually resented in every area of life. As we appreciate and even expect a certain degree of dignified humility in any leader, such an attitude is especially needed by those in the pastoral ministry.

Paul's instruction to Timothy to act "in all purity" is certainly applicable to his dealings with all, but here it is appended to his instruction about the pastor's dealings with younger women. Sadly, improper dealings by a pastor with a woman not his wife, even to the point of fornication/adultery, is a scandal not unknown in the church. The call to the ministry does not exempt a man from temptations to sin, including sins against the commandment prohibiting adultery. A pastor, perhaps especially a young pastor such as Timothy, must be on guard against such enticements. He would do well to avoid letting himself be found in situations that might lend themselves to these types of temptations. Yes, there is forgiveness for sin, but forgiveness of sin is not an excuse to sin (Rom 3:8; 6:1–2).

In the course of their ministry pastors will have to deal with troubles, conflicts, and issues of one sort or another. There will always be the temptation to deal with these curtly and even harshly. Paul's instruction to Timothy here is a reminder to Christians in general and to pastors in particular that the solution to dealing with any sin is both law and gospel, with the gospel having predominance. While our initial inclination might be to "rebuke," the apostle wisely instructs us to "encourage" instead.

---

292. Hence, pastors are described as "those who are over you in the Lord" (1 Thess 5:12).

5:3–16: Groups in the Church 2: Widows and the Office of Widows

TRANSLATION

³ Honor widows who are actual widows. ⁴ If any widow has children or grandchildren, let them learn first to display godliness to their own household and to give back to their parents; this is pleasing before God. ⁵ An actual widow is one who is left alone and who has hoped in God and continued in requests and prayers night and day, ⁶ but one who has lived luxuriously is as good as dead, even while alive. ⁷ Command these things, in order that they might be beyond reproach. ⁸ If anyone does not provide for his own [relatives], especially those of his own household, he has denied the faith and is worse than an unbeliever.

⁹ Let a widow be enrolled, if she is not less than sixty years old, having been the wife of one husband, ¹⁰ having a reputation for good works, if she raised children, if she has been a lover of traveling missionaries, if she washed the feet of the saints, if she helped those afflicted, if she followed after every good work. ¹¹ Refuse to enroll younger widows, for whenever they are enticed away from Christ, they wish to marry, ¹² bringing judgment [on themselves], having broken their first pledge. ¹³ Being idle, they learn to go from house to house; they become not only idle but also gossips and busybodies, saying what ought not be said. ¹⁴ Therefore, I desire younger women to marry, to have children, to manage their households, to give the adversary[a] no opportunity for reviling, ¹⁵ for some have already turned away after Satan. ¹⁶ If any believing woman has widows, let her help them, and do not let the church be burdened, in order that it may help those who are actual widows.

[a] Or *an adversary*

TEXTUAL NOTES

5:3 τίμα—Other uses of this verb (Matt 27:9) and the cognate noun τιμή (1 Pet 2:7) suggest the idea of "(monetary) value." We might paraphrase the present verse "consider worthy of financial support [by the church] only those widows who are actual widows."

τὰς ὄντως χήρας—The singular of this expression occurs in 5:5; Paul uses the plural (although in a different grammatical case) in 5:16.

5:4 τέκνα ἢ ἔκγονα—While ἔκγονα can refer to descendants in general, this context calls for the translation "grandchildren."[293]

εὐσεβεῖν—The cognate noun εὐσέβεια is usually translated "godliness" and denotes "awesome respect accorded to God."[294] That and Paul's use of this verb to refer to the worship of "an unknown God" by the Athenians (Acts 17:23) indicates that respect owed to parents is part and parcel of the worship that we owe to him who commands that we honor father and mother.

ἀμοιβὰς ἀποδιδόναι—The noun ἀμοιβή designates what is appropriate to do to "repay" someone for the good done for you.[295] The use of the plural here might suggest that parents have done many good things for their children, for which "repayment" is proper.

5:5 ἤλπικεν ἐπὶ θεὸν—This is a way of saying that they have had genuine faith. On "hope" see the entry by the name in the Extended Notes.

προσμένει ταῖς δεήσεσιν καὶ ταῖς προσευχαῖς—Genuine worship is an example of the kinds of good works that always result from genuine faith (Gal 5:6; Eph 2:8–10). Both of these terms for prayer also occur in 2:1; here, as there, they are intended to designate all manner of prayers.

5:6 σπαταλῶσα ζῶσα τέθνηκεν—Compare Jas 5:5 and Luke 12:16–21. In contrast to the blessed paradox of 2 Cor 6:9 ("dying and behold we live"), here is a tragic one: "One who has lived luxuriously is as good as dead, even while alive." Later in this letter the apostle will give instructions for wealthy Christians (6:17–19) and will indicate that it is the *love* of money, not money itself, that is a root of evil (6:10); therefore, he is not condemning wealth in and of itself. Therefore, living "luxuriously" is the opposite of "hoping in God," hence, without saving faith.

5:7 παράγγελλε—This is an emphatic command; Paul uses it also in 1:3; 4:11; 5:7; 6:13, 17.

---

293. BDAG 300; Knight, *Pastoral Epistles*, 217.
294. BDAG 412–13. See further the entry "Godliness" in the Extended Notes.
295. MM 27.

ἵνα ἀνεπίλημπτοι ὦσιν—Here ἵνα plus a subjunctive verb denotes purpose.[296] The term ἀνεπίλημπτοι occurs in 3:1 to indicate the type of conduct expected of pastors: behavior that is "beyond reproach."

5:8 προνοεῖ—The use of the cognate noun πρόνοια (Acts 24:2; Rom 13:14) suggests that advance planning is an element of "providing for" others.

τὴν πίστιν ἤρνηαι καὶ ἔστιν ἀπίστου χείρων—This is as strong a statement as is the better known "faith without works is dead" (Jas 2:17, 26). One who fails in this regard is worse than an unbeliever, for the right conduct in such a matter is something that even an unbeliever would understand from the law written on his heart (Rom 2:14–15; cf. 1 Cor 5:1).[297] "Faith" (πίστιν) here denotes the content of Christian teaching (*the* faith; *fides quae creditur*); however, such a denial of the faith would involve a cessation of the act of believing (*fides qua creditur*) as well.

5:9 καταλεγέσθω—This verb can be used as a technical term for being enrolled in a designated group;[298] see further the commentary.

ἑνὸς ἀνδρὸς γυνή—This is similar to one of the qualifications for a man to hold the pastoral office (3:2, whose commentary see), so the meaning here would be that she has not had an unscriptural divorce. This and the verb καταλεγέσθω would both indicate that beginning with this verse Paul is writing about acceptance to a particular position or office within the early church. See further the commentary.

5:10 ἐν ἔργοις καλοῖς μαρτυρουμένη—She has a well-known reputation as someone whose life is characterized by good works. The following phrases give specific examples of the types of good works for which she would be known.

ἐτεκνοτρόφησεν—This would be essential work of any parent; the term may imply spiritual as well as physical nourishment.[299] While the aptitude for such parental care would be a requirement for such a position, it would be "absurd" to think that with this requirement Paul means to prohibit from enrollment childless widows who otherwise would be qualified.[300]

ἐξενοδόχησεν—While hospitality was a significant part of Hebrew culture (Gen 18:1–8; Luke 7:36, 44–46), the term here has more

---

296. Wallace, *Greek Grammar*, 471–73.
297. Knight, *Pastoral Epistles*, 221.
298. BDAG 520; Kelly, *Pastoral Epistles*, 115.
299. BDAG 995.
300. Such is the judgment of Kelly, *Pastoral Epistles*, 116.

of a distinctly churchly application. As ancient inns were often places of questionable character, Christians who traveled often depended on the hospitality of fellow believers. This was particularly true of traveling Christian preachers.[301] This qualification, therefore, would have to do with a woman's support of the church and particularly of its mission.[302] To bring this out I have rendered it "has been a lover of traveling missionaries."

ἁγίων πόδας ἔνιψεν—Foot washing was a standard part of ancient Oriental hospitality.[303] Therefore, this would be another mention of the way these women would have supported the mission of the church;[304] it would also be a mark of a lack of sinful pride and the presence of humility. Godly humility would be an essential attribute of anyone who would aspire to serve in the church of him who humbled himself to death on a cross (Phil 2:1–11), particularly for the type of work for which these women were to be enrolled; see the commentary below.

θλιβομένοις ἐπήρκεσεν—The verb θλίβω and the cognate noun θλῖψις have a rather broad range of meaning.[305] However, it is interesting to note those places where this word group is used synonymously with "persecute/persecution."[306] In view of the mission encouragement significance of the previous two qualifications, it may be that the apostle is here pointing to widows who have supported those being persecuted for their Christian faith. This may well have been what Jesus was speaking of when he commended the sheep for visiting him when he was in prison by doing so to "one of the least of these my brothers" (Matt 25:39–40).[307]

παντὶ ἔργῳ ἀγαθῷ ἐπηκολούθησεν—The use of "all" (παντί) in this concluding qualification makes this a "catch-all" qualification; eligible widows are those who have overall put their Christian faith into practice with a life of good works.

---

301. Matt 25:35, 38; Acts 15:4; 18:27; Col 4:10; 3 John 10. That Matt 25:31–46 has to do with missionary encouragement rather than social ministry, see Gibbs, *Matthew 21:1—28:20*, 1342–64.

302. See also Schuchard, *1–3 John*, 631–34.

303. Gen 18:4; 19:2; 24:32; Judg 19:21; Luke 7:44.

304. Kelly, *Pastoral Epistles*, 117, comes to the same conclusion.

305. Matt 13:21 (par Mark 4:17); Rom 8:35; 2 Thess 1:4.

306. Acts 7:10, 11; 2 Cor 1:4; 7:4; BDAG 457.

307. That Matt 25:31–46 has to do with missionary encouragement rather than social ministry, see Gibbs, *Matthew 21:1—28:20*, 1342–64.

5:11 νεωτέρας δὲ χήρας παραιτοῦ—The verb παραιτοῦ is a rather emphatic one.[308] In this context it seems best to render it "refuse to enroll." Nevertheless, it should be noted that these are the same type of women whom Timothy is to treat like sisters (5:2).

καταστρηνιάσωσιν τοῦ Χριστοῦ—This is a strong verb that denotes wantonness or strong physical desire;[309] to bring this out I have opted for translating it here as "are enticed away from." As the material in verses 12 and 13 indicate, this would involve falling away from the faith altogether. The younger women are not to be enrolled in this office, because doing so would expose them to such serious dangers to their faith.

γαμεῖν θέλουσιν—As a comparison with verse 14 indicates, in this verse the desire to marry is an expression of a "wanton" desire that leads her away from Christ to giving to someone or something else a devotion that belongs to Christ alone.

5:12 ἔχουσαι κρίμα—The noun κρίμα often refers to divine condemnation and punishment;[310] this is another indication that what is spoken of in these verses has to do with the danger of falling from the faith altogether.

ὅτι τὴν πρώτην πίστιν ἠθέτησαν—The phrase πρώτην πίστιν might have the meaning "first pledge" (of faithfulness to Christ). In whatever way one might render it, the phrase is an additional demonstration that the danger to be avoided by not enrolling younger women is their falling away from faith altogether.

5:13 περιερχόμεναι . . . περίεργοι—The similar initial sound of these two words helps to emphasize the concurrence of these two activities; we might paraphrase "busy going from house to house, they become . . . busybodies." Note the similar play on words in 2 Thess 3:11: μηδὲν ἐργαζομένους ἀλλὰ περιεραζομένους, "not busy working but busybodies."

φλύαροι—Note the use of the cognate verb in 3 John 10. Other Pauline rebukes of the sin of gossip (Rom 1:29; 2 Cor 12:20) use a different Greek word.

λαλοῦσαι τὰ μὴ δέοντα—"Saying what ought not be said" is an apt, concise description of the sins of both gossips and busybodies.

5:14 Βούλομαι οὖν νεωτέρας γαμεῖν, τεκνογονεῖν, οἰκοδεσποτεῖν—Note the different verb from that of 2:12, ἐπιτέπω ("I do not permit").

308. 1 Tim 4:7; 2 Tim 2:23; Titus 3:10; Heb 12:25 (2x).
309. BDF 97 (§ 181).
310. BDAG 567.

It is not as though every younger widow is under obligation to remarry. Rather, the vocation of marriage (and of the potential concomitant vocations of motherhood and managing a household) is preferable to attempting to assume a vocation for which one is not (yet) prepared.[311]

μηδεμίαν ἀφορμὴν διδόναι . . . λοιδορίας χάριν—The use of the verb λοιδορέω, "revile, abuse," cognate to the noun λοιδορίας, "reviling," often occurs in contexts that imply that the abuse is undeserved.[312] Christians, including younger widows, are to live in such a way that deprives their opponents of the opportunity to heap any kind of abuse on them (cf. 1 Pet 3:16).

τῷ ἀντικειμένῳ—What is the significance of the article τῷ on this noun? The article could be generic, meaning "do not give *any* adversary opportunity to revile the faith." On the other hand, the article might be specific, referring to *the* adversary, that is, Satan.[313] The fact that Satan is mentioned by name just a few words later might argue in favor of that understanding. Nevertheless, Paul had indicated earlier that it is necessary for an overseer/pastor "to have a good witness from those on the outside, lest he fall into disgrace and the snare of the devil" (3:7). This would suggest the understanding that *any* occasion for *any* adversary to speak ill of the church and its faith leads to such a human adversary doing the work of *the* adversary, Satan. Thus, the apostle's words here may well be deliberately ambiguous.[314]

5:15 ἤδη γάρ τινες ἐξετράπησαν ὀπίσω τοῦ σατανᾶ—This phrase, "for some have already turned away after Satan," is one more indication that the conduct warned against in verses 11 and 12 is a falling away from saving faith altogether.

5:16 πιστὴ—This is a feminine form, "believing woman." A believing woman has a calling/vocation to care for any widows in her family, so that the church's resources may be reserved for those who have no such support, "actual widows." Presumably this would point to women in a position to provide this sort of care, women such as Lydia (Acts 16:14-15, 40), Phoebe (Rom 16:1-3), Chloe (1 Cor 1:11), Prisca/Priscilla (1 Cor 16:19), or Nympha (Col 4:15).

---

311. A good, concise introduction to the doctrine of vocation is found in Veith, *Spirituality*, 89-114. See also Luther, *The Judgment of Martin Luther on Monastic Vows* (AE 44:243-400) and *Whether Soldiers, Too, Can Be Saved* (AE 46:87-137).

312. John 9:28; Acts 23:4; 1 Cor 4:12; 5:11; 6:10; 1 Pet 2:23; 3:9.

313. DPL 864, 865.

314. Kelly, *Pastoral Epistles*, 119.

βαρείσθω—This is the equivalent of "they must not burden the church."[315]

ἐπαρκείτω ... ἐπαρκέσῃ—The same verb was used in verse 10. Here it refers to tending to a widow's needs in general.

COMMENTARY

Two Groups

It is important to realize that the apostle is speaking of two distinct groups in this section, even though he uses the term χήρα, "widow," for both. There are several indications that he distinguishes the widows of 5:3–8 from those of 5:9–16.

For one thing, it is only with the second group that Paul speaks of being "enrolled" (καταλεγέσθω, 5:9; see the textual note on that verb). The first group consists of widows in general; it is the second group that is to be enrolled for a special task.[316]

Furthermore, the necessary qualifications for being a part of the respective groups are different. Those in the first group are those who have no family to care for them and who have demonstrated genuine faith ("hoped in God") and worship ("continued in requests and prayers"). While living faith is presupposed in the second group, it is further necessary that they have been active in supporting the mission of the church (see the details in the textual notes).

In short, the first part of this section of the letter deals with widows who *need* care. In contrast, the second section is about widows who qualify for a position in the church in which they *give* care to others.

Actual Widows

Three times (5:3, 5, 16) Paul speaks of "actual [ὄντως] widows." He is quite emphatic that when there is a widow with a family that has the

---

315. Wallace, *Greek Grammar*, 487

316. In spite of differences in detail between them, this is essentially the position of Chrysostom, *On Virginity* 39:2 (*On Virginity, Against Remarriage*, 58), Theodore of Mopsuestia, *Commentary on 1 Timothy* (*Theodori episcopi Mopsuesteni: In epistolas b. Pauli commentarii*, 2:158–159), Tertullian, *To His Wife* 1.7 (*ANF* 4:73), and Pelagius, *Pelagius's Commentary on the First Letter to Timothy* (*Pelagius's Expositions of Thirteen Epistles of St. Paul*, 494) [see ACCS NT 9:200].

wherewithal to provide for her, the family should do so, and the church should not be burdened with providing care for her. The church's care ought to be reserved for those widows who have no such means of support.

Why does the apostle lay down other requirements for those widows who would receive aid from the church? Why does he say that they need to have "hoped in God" and have been constant in prayer? It seems unlikely that Paul is here suggesting that the church turn away a needy widow unless she has met these conditions; after all, he does direct the Galatians to "do good to all" (6:10). But in that same directive he adds "especially to those of the household of faith." That seems to be the point here as well. It is not that Christians are to refuse to help anyone; it is simply a matter of their prime responsibility being for their fellow believers.

The Office of Widow

When the apostle speaks of enrolling a widow, he turns his attention to a particular role of service within the church. Earlier in this letter he outlines responsibilities for an overseer (3:1–7), deacons (3:8–10, 12–13), and deaconesses (3:11), and later he includes further instruction regarding the obligations of elders, "elder" being, as the Letter to Titus (1:5–7) demonstrates, another term for "overseer," that is, "pastor" (5:17–22).[317] Here he gives the qualifications and responsibilities for another group: widows.

"Overseer" (ἐπίσκοπος) and "elder" (πρεσβύτερος) are often interchangeable terms in the New Testament (Titus 1:5, 7) for the pastoral office. "Pastor/shepherd" (ποιμήν) is another term used in the Scriptures to refer to this office (Acts 20:17, 28; Eph 4:11; 1 Pet 5:2). As the New Testament speaks of this position, it becomes evident that Christ intended it to be a permanent office of ministry in his church.

In this letter Paul mentions other offices for the church. As these are not generally mentioned in the rest of the New Testament, they must have been created for specific needs in some congregations rather than being envisioned as permanent offices in the church. An example of such offices would be the seven men of Acts 6:1–7, who, even though they

---

317. See the commentary on each of these sections. For the possibility that "elders" in 5:17 might designate a larger group than only the pastors ("overseers"), see the textual notes on that verse.

are not named "deacons," do seem to be charged with the same sort of responsibilities as are the deacons of 1 Tim 3.

The churches served by Timothy must have had needs that were served by those appointed to be deacons and deaconesses. Apparently, there was a need for another kind of service, one which could be served by widows who had certain qualifications. Thus, within these churches there had been established another position. While recognizing that the term might be a bit anachronistic, I have decided to speak of the "office" of widow.[318]

As we look at the qualifications for this office, it seems that it was established to provide support to other Christians. The concluding verse of this section would suggest that those who held the office of widow had as their responsibility providing for those who were "actual widows," that is, those for whom the church took responsibility, because they had no one of their own to provide for them.

Thus, their areas of responsibility would have involved them in what the church of our own time generally refers to as "human care." The church's ministry of human care differs from that of government programs and secular agencies in a number of ways.[319] Among these would be that the church administers human care as a reflection of the love of Christ for humanity. Thus, the church's ministry of human care would often open avenues for sharing the saving gospel of Christ. In that light we can understand why a widow who would hold this office must have already demonstrated an involvement in the mission of Christ's church.

To qualify for this office a widow had to have demonstrated Christian faith and living. Moreover, she must have previously taken a role in the mission of the church (see the textual notes for details).[320] She must also be a Christian of great integrity, someone who would not be a gossip or a busybody; some of the apostle's other letters (1 Thess 4:11;

318. Similarly, Kaveny speaks of the "order" of widows in 1 Timothy; "Order of Widows," 16. Second-century church authors speak of such an office/order current in their day: Ignatius (*To the Smyrnaeans* 13:1; *To Polycarp* 4:1), Polycarp (*To the Philippians* 4:3), Tertullian (*De Virginibus Velandis* 5:9).

319. Alvin Schmidt mentions the following: (1) Government programs are coerced; Christian charity is voluntary and motivated by love. (2) Government programs create a class of people whom politicians exploit as a voting block for their reelection. (3) Government programs create a permanent welfare class, who are in a type of slavery. Schmidt, *How Christianity Changed the World*, 146–47.

320. Johnson, *Letters*, 264, points out that the qualifications enumerated here have to do with a woman's past activity rather than any perceived aptitude for future participation.

Grace and Life

2 Thess 3:11–12) demonstrate that this certainly could have been a problem in first-century churches.[321]

While such integrity is here required for the office of widow, it is certainly a trait that is desirable if not essential for Christians in general and church workers in particular. Readers of this commentary may perhaps have unhappy memories of a church worker (or church worker's spouse) whose habits of gossip or of failing to mind their own business were a blot on the mission of the church. Especially those who are closest to the work of the church need to take this portion of this letter to heart.[322]

What are we to make of the requirement that she be "not less than sixty years old?" Paul himself would have been about sixty years of age when in his Letter to Philemon he described himself as "an old man" (Phlm 9). The apostle prohibits "younger" widows who might well "wish to marry" from entering this office, for he does not want to discourage them from remarrying (5:14). Therefore, restricting this office to those who were no longer "young" would assure that those enrolled would not be attracted to the idea of leaving this office in order to marry.[323] Thus, the age requirement seems to be laid down to ensure that a woman

---

321. The following observation from Jerome (*Letters* 22.29) may be helpful: "Paul speaks of idle persons and busybodies, whether virgins or widows, such as go from house to house calling on married women. They display an unblushing effrontery greater than that of a stage parasite. . . . Women like these care for nothing but their lowest appetites. They will often urge you, saying, 'My dear creature, make the best of your advantages, and live while life is yours,' and, 'Surely you are not laying up money for your children.' Given to wine and wantonness, they instill all manner of mischief into people's minds and induce even the most austere to indulge in enervating pleasures" (*NPNF*[2] 2.6:35* and *NPNF*[2] 6:168 [ACCS, NT 9:202–3]).

I am put in mind of a passage near the conclusion of the first installment of the *Chronicles of Narnia* series (usually numbered book 2 in collections of the volumes). In what we might call the epilogue of the story, the narrator reports on the beneficial rule of the Pevensie siblings over Narnia. We are told that "these two Kings and two Queens governed Narnia well, and long and happy was their reign. . . . And they made good laws and kept the peace and . . . generally stopped busybodies and interferers and encouraged ordinary people who wanted to live and let live." It seems that Lewis regarded the crime of being a busybody as especially reprehensible. I suspect that I am not the only one who is inclined to agree with him. Lewis, *Lion, the Witch, and the Wardrobe*, 183.

322. Kaveny ("Order of Widows," 17) speaks of the functions of the office of widows being taken over by deaconesses.

323. Kelly, *Pastoral Epistles*, 115; Knight, *Pastoral Epistles*, 223.

entering this office would have the necessary Christian maturity to carry it out properly.[324]

The witness of the New Testament demonstrates that the office of overseer/elder/pastor is one that Christ has established for his church from Pentecost to the parousia. The present letter indicates that the church of every age, from New Testament times until the end, has the freedom to establish other offices of ministry to assist its mission. Positions such as schoolteacher, director of Christian education, and deaconess are some that are in use in our time. The qualifications given in this letter for the office of deacon, deaconess, and widow would suggest similar qualifications for these offices as well.

The office of widow as described in 1 Timothy seems to correspond a great deal to the position of a deaconess, as that is being carried out in the twenty-first century.[325] Like the work of the widows of the present letter, the human care ministry carried out by a deaconess does more than provide for this-worldly needs. Human care ministry often involves also bringing the message of Christ's saving love to its recipients. Thus, the work of the widows of 1 Tim 5:9–16 provides a suitable model for contemporary deaconesses in their important work in Christ's church.

Widows and the Office of Widows: 1 Timothy 5:3–16 in Context

Paul continues writing about various groups within the church and about Timothy's responsibilities toward them. He now turns to the topic of widows.

The apostle speaks of two distinct groups of widows within the church. The first are "actual widows" who are in need of help. The church is to show the love of Christ to them by caring for them.

The second group of widows are those who qualify for an office of ministry/service within the church. Widows who are capable and

---

324. The fact that life expectancy in the first-century Mediterranean world was not what it is today would also suggest that there might not have been a large number of women who were ever enrolled in the order of widows; Johnson, *Letters*, 274.

325. For example, the website of Concordia Seminary, St. Louis, describes deaconess ministry as follows: "Deaconesses are called by congregations and into foreign missions, employed by hospitals, nursing homes and social service organizations. Through her theological training, skills and practical experience, a deaconess serves the church by sharing the Gospel of Jesus Christ through works of mercy, spiritual care and teaching the Christian faith" (Concordia Seminary, St. Louis, "Master of Arts").

qualified for these sorts of works of love are to be enrolled in such an office. This office gives the church of later ages insight and guidance as to how to carry out its own eleemosynary work.

5:17–25: Groups in the Church 3: Elders (Pastors)

TRANSLATION

¹⁷ Let elders who give good care and leadership, that is, those who labor in preaching and teaching,ᵃ be considered worthy of twofold honor, ¹⁸ for the Scripture says, "You will not muzzle an ox that is threshing," and "The worker is worthy of his wages." ¹⁹ Do not accept an accusation against an elder, except on the basis of two or three witnesses. ²⁰ Rebuke those who persist in sin before all, in order that the rest might have fear. ²¹ I adjure you before God and Christ Jesus and the elect angels, that you keep these things without prejudice, doing nothing with partiality. ²² Do not be hasty in laying hands on anyone, lest you have fellowship in the sins of others; keep yourself pure. ²³ No longer drink [only] water but use a little wine for your stomach and for your frequent infirmities. ²⁴ The sins of some people are evident, preceding them into judgment, but for others they follow after them. ²⁵ Similarly, good works are evident, and those that are otherwise are not able to be kept hidden.

ᵃ Or *Let elders who give good care and leadership, especially those who labor in preaching and teaching*

TEXTUAL NOTES

5:17 προεστῶτες—The same verb is used in 3:4–5, 12, of how overseers/pastors (and deacons) are to guide their own families. In 1 Thess 5:12 it is used along with "labor among you" and "admonish/instruct you" (νουθετοῦντς) to describe the work of those who do so "in the Lord." Thus, the "leadership" here has to do with leading others by and to the word of God. In the Letter to Titus (3:8, 14) the word has the meaning "be devoted to," "give attention to." While admittedly it is a bit of a paraphrase, I have rendered it here as "give good care and leadership" to try to capture both senses of προΐστημι.

πρεσβύτεροι—Titus 1:5, 7, and Acts 20:17, 28, use this term as a synonym of "overseer" (ἐπίσκοπος) and therefore as another biblical term for the pastoral office. Another possibility is that "elder" here is used in a broader sense to embrace both "overseer" (ἐπίσκοπος, 3:2) and "deacons" (διάκονοι, 3:8, 12), and perhaps other church leaders.[326] See further the note on μάλιστα below and also the commentary.

διπλῆς τιμῆς ἀξιούσθωσον—The third person imperative here (ἀξιούσθωσον) is the equivalent of "the church must consider them worthy."[327] The word τιμή can mean "value, price [in money],"[328] and certainly that pastors should be adequately paid is a topic that is addressed in the following verse and elsewhere in Paul's letters (1 Cor 9:3–12; Gal 6:6; 2 Thess 3:8–9). However, talk about *comparable* salaries seems out of place in this passage. Instead, the OT stipulation that the firstborn son would receive a double portion of the father's inheritance in comparison to that given to any of the other sons (Deut 21:17) seems to be in the background here.[329] A pastor who carries out the work of his office well ought to have preeminent honor; he is to be regarded as the "firstborn" within the family of God.

μάλιστα—While this word often means "especially," the sense "that is" or "namely" is also possible.[330] As Paul uses the terms "elder" and "overseer" interchangeably (Titus 1:5–7), and as a requirement for an overseer given earlier in this letter (3:2) is that he be "able to teach," the meaning "that is" for μάλιστα seems to be required here. Hence, those elders/pastors who "give good care and leadership" are those who "labor in preaching and teaching." See further the commentary below.

326. The use of the term in Acts 11:30; 14:23; 15:2, 4, 6, 22–23; 16:4 perhaps encompasses such a broader reference. In some passages the LXX uses πρεσβύτεροι to translate the Hebrew זְקֵנִים; in some instances (Deut 31:9; Josh 8:33 [LXX 9:2d]; Ezek 7:26) this appears to refer to those other than priests or prophets, i.e., other than those who were antecedents of the pastors of the NT. When referring to members of the Jewish Sanhedrin (e.g., Matt 16:21) πρεσβύτεροι certainly denotes lay members of that body.

327. Wallace, *Greek Grammar*, 486.

328. Matt 27:9; Acts 4:34; 5:2–3; 7:16; 19:19 (used metaphorically: 1 Cor 6:20; 7:23).

329. This is also the background to the request of Elisha to Elijah for a double portion of the Spirit that he had (2 Kgs 2:9). Thus, the ministries of Elijah and Elisha would serve as paradigms for that of any pastor.

330. Knight, *Pastoral Epistles*, 232; Marshall, *Pastoral Epistles*, 612. See also BDAG 613–14 (μάλα, μάλιστα, μᾶλλον); MM 387.

κοπιῶντες ἐν λόγῳ καὶ διδασκαλίᾳ—"Labor" (κοπιάω) is used elsewhere in the apostle's letters (1 Cor 16:16; 1 Thess 5:12-13) for the work of ministry. This statement agrees with earlier portions of this letter (3:1-7; 4:6-16, whose commentaries see), which point to the dissemination of God's word as the chief task of the pastoral ministry.

5:18 λέγει—The present tense verb here indicates the ongoing significance of something from the past.[331]

γραφή—This term occurs frequently in the NT to refer to the Scriptures (i.e., the OT). The first citation here is from the Hebrew Scriptures (Deut 25:4), but in what sense does Paul consider the second citation to be part of "the Scripture?"

This citation is found word for word on the lips of Jesus in Luke 10:7 (the only difference in the parallel in Matt 10:10 is a different term being used for "hire, wages"). Why would the apostle regard this logion as Scripture? There would seem to be at least two possible explanations.

I have suggested a date for this letter of about AD 64.[332] It is not unthinkable that Luke and/or Matthew might have already written his Gospel by this time,[333] and that Paul, a figure of significant importance in the early church, could have been aware of it. As the apostle considered his own letters to be on a par with the writings of the Old Testament,[334] and as the Gospels according to Luke and to Matthew record the words and deeds of the Messiah/Christ himself, it is possible that already at this time Paul (and others) regarded the work of Luke and/or Matthew also to be on the same level as the Hebrew Scriptures.

If we (at least hypothetically) discount the possibility that Luke and/or Matthew had already put pen to paper by this time, nevertheless, the words (and deeds) of Jesus would have been remembered and treasured

---

331. Wallace, *Greek Grammar*, 532-33.

332. See "The Date of This Letter" in the Introduction to 1 Timothy.

333. Just, *Luke 1:1—9:50*, 3-7, 15-16, suggests that Luke may have written his Gospel during the years when Paul was imprisoned in Rome (about AD 60-61). As Luke had accompanied Paul on his sea voyage from Caesarea to Rome (Acts 27:1—28:16 is the last of the "we sections" of Acts), it is entirely possible that he remained with the apostle during his Roman imprisonment. If all of this took place, Paul would have had firsthand knowledge of the content of Luke's Gospel. For indications that the Gospel according to Matthew might have been written as early as the mid-to-late fifties, see Gibbs, *Matthew 1:1—11:1*, 64-66.

334. Col 4:16; 1 Thess 5:27. See also 1 Tim 1:1; 2:12; 4:1, the commentary on those verses, and the entry on "Apostle" in the Extended Notes.

even before any of the evangelists put them into writing.³³⁵ It is certainly believable that even under this scenario, Christians like Paul would have regarded such words of Jesus as having the authority of God's written word in the OT, for, after all, unlike the scribes, Jesus had taught with (divine) authority (Matt 7:29; 9:6; Luke 4:32).³³⁶

5:19 κατηγορίαν μὴ παραδέχου—The list of qualifications for an overseer/elder in Titus includes that there be no "accusation" (κατηγορία) of debauchery or lack of discipline against his children (1:6). Most of the uses of this noun and its cognate verb κατηγορέω have to do with formal charges, as in a court of law.³³⁷ As one in a position of oversight over other pastors Timothy would be one to whom accusations against one of the pastors in his care might be brought. Our own experience would suggest that anyone might bring any charge against anyone else. This can be as true in the church as it is in the world in general, and the first-century world may not have been any different (note that in the previous section of this letter Paul had had to speak to the issues of gossips and busybodies). In that light the apostle's instruction that such accusations should not be given a hearing unless substantiated by the Old Testament's own standards (see following note) is perfectly understandable.

ἐκτὸς εἰ μὴ—Two different ways of saying "except" are used here: ἐκτὸς and εἰ μή.³³⁸ Perhaps this is done for emphasis. One's reputation, once sullied, is difficult to restore; hence, it is of the utmost importance not to countenance any unsubstantiated accusations against a pastor.

δύο ἢ τριῶν μαρτύρων—This standard is set down in Deut 19:15 and is the background to Christ's directive in Matt 18:16.

5:20 ἁμαρτάνοντας ... ἔλεγχε—The present tense of the participle as well as the overall context makes it plain that this has to do with *impenitent* sinners (or at least someone who has not yet been confronted and who therefore has not yet given evidence of repentance). The verb ἔλεγχε is a strong one that is used of excoriating (and correcting) those who have fallen into doctrinal and/or moral error;³³⁹ the context in which this word is used in the Pastorals often points to the authority with which the pastor can issue such rebukes.³⁴⁰

---

335. As in Acts 20:35.
336. Knight, *Pastoral Epistles*, 233–34, offers similar views on this matter.
337. BDAG 533.
338. ἐκτός: BDAG 311 (3, a); εἰ μή: BDAG 278 (6, i); BDF 221 [§ 428 (3)].
339. *DPL* 216.
340. 1 Tim 5:20; 2 Tim 4:2; Titus 1:9, 13; 2:15.

ἐνώπιον πάντων ... οἱ λοιποὶ—The context both before and after the instruction of this verse offers a key to its interpretation. As Paul is giving instructions in this section regarding the pastoral office, "those who persist in sin" and the "rest" must all be pastors; while the "all" might mean before all the pastors, it could also refer to all the members of the church (as in Matt 18:17, "the church").[341]

The sin here must be either ongoing (again note the present tense of the participle) promotion of false doctrine or persistent ungodly living contrary to the standards that the apostle set forth in 3:1–7 (or both). "Those who persist in sin" must be engaging in false teaching and/or false living in such a way that it is public knowledge. These must be sins of such a nature as to call for a public accusation (κατηγορίαν). The public nature of the sin would make this a situation comparable to that of Gal 2:11–14, which called for public rebuke (note there that Paul speaks to Peter "before all"). Matthew 18 would not be applicable since this would not be a sin against only one person but a public transgression.[342]

Sins of this nature must be dealt with; they cannot be swept under the rug. As the sin is open to all, so the rebuke must be before all.

ἵνα ... ἔχωσιν—The word ἵνα followed by a subjunctive verb here designates purpose.[343] Part of the reason for public rebuke is to serve as a corrective, rebuke, and/or warning to other pastors, lest they also succumb to sins of this sort.

5:21 Διαμαρτύρομαι ἐνώπιον τοῦ θεοῦ καὶ Χριστοῦ Ἰησοῦ καὶ τῶν ἐκλεκτῶν ἀγγέλων—The threefold witness to what Paul has to say here (God [the Father], Christ, the angels) makes this a most solemn charge. This verb has a connotation of what is said under oath.[344] It is as though the apostle is binding Timothy by an oath (διαμαρτύρομαι, "adjure") to do what he is instructed to do here. God, Christ, and the angels will all be witnesses as to whether or not Timothy does as he is charged here. The adjective "elect" on "angels" here seems simply to designate them as the angels who are not numbered among those who rebelled against God (2 Pet 2:4; Jude 6).[345] The inclusion of angels alongside the Father and the Son seems due to the fact that the angels will also be witnesses of this, as

---

341. Towner, *Letters*, 371; Mounce, *Pastoral Epistles*, 313–14; Kelly, *Pastoral Epistles*, 127; Marshall, *Pastoral Epistles*, 618–19.

342. Gibbs, "'Following' Matthew 18," 15–20; Luther, AE 28:350–53.

343. Wallace, *Greek Grammar*, 472.

344. BDAG 233.

345. *DPL* 226; Kelly, *Pastoral Epistles*, 127; Knight, *Pastoral Epistles*, 238.

they will accompany Christ when he comes again in judgment.[346] This is in keeping with the fact that the rebuke must be before all.

ἵνα . . . πρόσκλισιν—This clause is the direct object of the verb διαμαρτύρομαι; it tells Timothy what he is charged to do.[347]

χωρὶς προκρίματος, μηδὲν ποιῶν κατὰ πρόσκλισιν—Even more than the English words "prejudice" and "partiality" the Greek terms used here sound a bit alike. This rhetorical flourish serves the purpose of emphasizing that Timothy (and others in the church who serve in similar positions of oversight) must carry out their tasks on the basis of fact, not allowing themselves to be swayed by any inner preferences or outside influences.[348]

Paul sets this solemn exhortation in between his preceding comments on considering accusations against and carrying out discipline toward pastors in his charge and his following directive regarding authorizing new candidates to enter the office of the ministry. This positioning suggests that the apostle aims this solemn directive for impartiality at both circumstances.

5:22 χεῖρας ταχέως μηδενὶ ἐπιτίθει—On the meaning of "laying on hands," see the commentary on 4:14. Here as there this has to do with setting men apart for the office of overseer/elder/pastor. This is not to be done in a "hasty" manner. In view of the high qualifications for the office (3:1–7) and the need for "prophecy," that is, instruction in the faith (see the commentary on 4:14) before one is qualified to assume the duties and responsibilities of being a pastor, there will need to be some extensive and therefore time-consuming preparation.

κοινώνει ἁμαρτίαις ἀλλοτρίαις—That this follows immediately after the instruction about bringing others into the ministry suggests that a too-hasty or inadequate preparation for the ministry will make one in a position like Timothy's responsible for the ministerial malpractice ("sins") committed by his ill-equipped students.

ἁγνὸν—Earlier in this letter Paul uses the noun (ἁγνεία) cognate to this adjective (4:12; 5:2). Timothy's responsibilities for preparing future pastors are just as much a part of his responsibilities as his example and his personal piety.

---

346. As noted also by Johnson, *Letters*, 280, and Marshall, *Pastoral Epistles*, 619; see Matt 25:31; Mark 8:38; Luke 9:26; 2 Thess 1:7.

347. Wallace, *Greek Grammar*, 475.

348. Luther, AE 28:353–54.

5:23 Μηκέτι ὑδροπότει—That Timothy is "no longer" to "drink [only] water" indicates that at present he has been drinking only water.[349] This could well indicate that he has been doing so to disassociate himself from those (perhaps some of the false teachers) who were drinking to excess.[350] While restraining one's Christian freedom is certainly called for in certain circumstances (1 Cor 8:13; Rom 14:15, 21) the younger pastor's practice here was being detrimental to him, hence the apostle's instruction that his coworker should feel free to drink wine.

οἴνῳ—Drunkenness is certainly forbidden to Christians in general (Eph 5:18) and those in ministry in particular (1 Tim 3:8); there are some who are especially in need of taking heed of those warnings. That being said, this passage certainly gives the lie to any notion that the Christian may not partake of alcoholic beverages at all.

διὰ τὸν στόμαχον καὶ τὰς πυκνάς σου ἀσθενίας—The Bible itself recognizes that not only is temperate consumption of alcohol not a sin; it can even provide some benefits to one's health.[351]

5:24 Τινῶν . . . προάγουσαι εἰς κρίσιν—Some people's sins are open and obvious; hence, it is no surprise when they suffer the consequences in this life as well as in the life to come.

τισὶν δὲ καὶ ἐπακολουθοῦσιν—Others commit sins that are less obvious, even hidden to all others. Nevertheless, while their sins may be hidden in this life, God will bring his judgment upon them, if not here and now, then certainly in the hereafter.

5:25 ὡσαύτως καὶ—Paul draws a comparison between evil and good works. Ultimately neither escapes the notice of the Almighty.

τὰ ἔργα τὰ καλὰ πρόδηλα, καὶ τὰ ἄλλως ἔχοντα κρυβῆναι οὐ δύνανται—Some good works are evident to human sight. Those that are not recognized by people are known to God, and he will acknowledge them in his way and according to his timetable.

---

349. BDAG 1023.

350. Mounce, *Pastoral Epistles*, 318–19.

351. See also Prov 31:6. Kelly, *Pastoral Epistles*, 129, calls attention to similar evaluations from Hippocrates (*De med. antiq* 13) and Plutarch (*De sanit. praec.* 19).

COMMENTARY

The Honor Due Pastors

Paul had written about the qualifications and responsibilities of the pastoral office earlier in this letter (3:1–7; 4:6–16). Here he takes up certain other issues pertaining to that office, beginning with the matter of the honor that is due to pastors.

How 1 Tim 5:17 is to be translated (and understood) depends upon two factors: what is included here in the noun "elders" (πρεσβύτεροι) and the meaning here of the term μάλιστα. There are two ways in which the verse can be interpreted. If the noun includes the offices of both "overseer" (pastor) and "deacon" (and perhaps others), and if μάλιστα has its usual meaning of "especially," the apostle is here directing that "honor" be shown to all church leaders and especially to pastors. If "elder" here is a synonym of "overseer/pastor," and if μάλιστα has the meaning "that is," then Paul is directing his comments specifically to the "honor" to be shown to pastors. In terms of what is said of the office of overseer/pastor there is no real difference between these two understandings; either would be in harmony with what the Scriptures say elsewhere about the pastoral office.

The phrase "twofold honor" (διπλῆς τιμῆς) here has a twofold reference (no pun intended). In the context it certainly includes the idea that a pastor is entitled to be able to make a living from his pastoral work. The apostle himself had often declined to accept such compensation so as not to be a financial burden on those he was serving,[352] as his ministry was largely one of starting new churches consisting of new Christian converts; these infant congregations might well have struggled to support a pastor on their own. Nevertheless, he makes it clear here and elsewhere (1 Cor 9:3–14[353]) that the church needs to give adequate financial support to its pastors.

That being said, the term here embraces more than just financial considerations. A pastor ought to be honored for the work of the office that he holds. Christians should give respect to their pastor(s), not so much to the man himself but in recognition of the eternally significant work he does in bringing the word ("preaching and teaching") of salvation to others (1 Cor 4:1).

---

352. 1 Cor 9:6, 11–15, 18; 2 Cor 11:7–9; 1 Thess 2:9; 2 Thess 3:7–9.
353. Note that the apostle also quotes Deut 25:4 in 1 Cor 9:9.

The "honor" due a pastor should then be appropriate to the ministry to which he has been called. The background of the phrase "twofold honor" points to the double portion of inheritance given to a firstborn son in Old Testament Israel. The honor given a pastor, both of respect and of compensation, should reflect the respect due the word of God. While clergy who abuse the office of pastor to enrich themselves often bring reproach upon the ministry, the opposite situation, a pastor being inadequately respected and supported, should not be acceptable in the church of God.

By describing pastors as those who "labor in preaching and teaching" Paul reaffirms what he says elsewhere about the pastoral office. The apostle notes that a pastor must be "able to teach" (διδακτικόν—1 Tim 3:2; 2 Tim 2:24), that he "be able both to encourage in the sound teaching and to convince/reprove those who speak against it" (Titus 1:9), and that he adhere to the sound teaching that he has learned (2 Tim 1:13; 3:10–11; Titus 1:9). All this is necessary for him to be able properly to "labor in preaching and teaching."

Timothy's Role as Supervisor: Dealing with Sin

From the way in which Paul addresses Timothy throughout this letter we gather that the younger man was exercising oversight over a number of churches and their pastors. If we would speak of Timothy's situation in the language of current ecclesiastical life, we could think of the churches for which he was responsible as a denomination or church body. In this body of Christians Timothy functioned both as its spiritual head and as a one-man seminary. As the spiritual head he might be called its president or bishop, and as such he was the one responsible to promote orthodox ministry by its other pastors.

One task before him as the spiritual head of these churches would be to consider accusations of misconduct or other improper ministry by the pastors.[354] The apostle must have been aware of how easy it would have been for anyone to make any manner of charges against a pastor.[355]

---

354. That would seem to be the type of charges that are under consideration here. Matters pertaining to the public teaching of false doctrine would be a somewhat different matter; if it is matter of *public* preaching/teaching, the matter would be evident to all.

355. Paul himself had, after all, been present when false witnesses had made the accusations against Stephen that had led to his martyrdom (Acts 22:20; 6:8—8:3; see especially the "false witnesses" of 6:13). He had also himself been the victim of false

To guard the pastors against unjust and unfounded accusations Paul directs his younger associate that he must not consider any accusation that cannot be substantiated by the biblical minimum of two or three witnesses.[356]

That being said, it could be that some pastor under Timothy's supervision had indeed been guilty of something of which he had been accused. Misconduct (i.e., sin) by a pastor dare not be "swept under the rug." When sin had been demonstrated, it was incumbent on someone in Timothy's position to deal with it. The apostle directs Timothy that the rebuke of the offending pastor must be known to all the church or perhaps to all the other pastors (see the textual notes). The purpose of this was that the others would "have fear" (5:20). The rebuke of sin through the law serves to call others to examine their own lives, to repent of their own failings, and to attend to themselves, lest they too fall into sin and endanger the spiritual wellbeing of both themselves and those whom they serve.

That would seem to be the upshot of the closing observations of this section about sin. The church and its leaders are to deal with those sins that are known; they, of course, cannot deal with sins known only to God. On the other hand, one might be able to keep his sins hidden from others, but he can never hide them from the Lord. Even if he were to keep his wrongdoings hidden from all others, God will deal with such a one in his own, omniscient way.

Sin and malfeasance constitute a potential problem in the church on earth; another difficulty is the failure to acknowledge faithful service. Some good works of ministry are easily seen (5:25a), but others may be overlooked (5:25b).[357] It can be discouraging to a pastor who has served faithfully to have his ministry overlooked, taken for granted, or even met with hostility. In a fallen world godly ministry will never be acknowledged as it should. However, such ministry will be known to the Lord of the church. In his love and omniscience, he will speak his "well done good and faithful servant" (Matt 25:21, 23; Luke 19:17) in ways and times that he knows are best.

---

accusations (Acts 16:19–21, 35–37; 21:27–29; 26:30–32). Readers of this commentary might have in mind some instance either within the church or in the world at large where a charge of wrongdoing against someone had, after thorough investigation, turned out to be false.

356. Note the textual note on ἐκτὸς εἰ μὴ in verse 19. Note that Paul cites the same OT passage in 2 Cor 13:1.

357. Note the comments of Kelly (*Pastoral Epistles*, 129–30) and Guthrie (*Pastoral Epistles*, 120–21).

Timothy's Role as Supervisor: Providing Future Pastors

One in Timothy's position is not only to deal with the pastors under his supervision; he is also to take the lead in supplying additional pastors for the church. That too is a great responsibility. Timothy is not to be hasty in promoting men to the pastoral office, lest ill-prepared and hence unqualified men be put in that position of responsibility.

I have argued earlier in this commentary[358] that when Paul speaks of his coworker receiving a gift through "prophecy and the laying on of hands" (4:14), the word "prophecy" refers to the instruction in God's word that Timothy received to prepare him for entering into the ministry. In that light the instruction here presupposes that as head of the churches in and around Ephesus Timothy would take the lead in preparing men to become pastors for the church.[359] If he were to promote men to the ministry without a thorough grounding in the word, he would be at least partially responsible for the consequences of ministerial malpractice ("sins") by which such individuals would inflict harm upon the church and its ministry.

The Church's Responsibility

The apostle's instruction in these verses is apropos to anyone in the church today with similar responsibilities for the supervision and/or preparation

---

358. See the textual notes and commentary on 4:14.

359. I have argued elsewhere (Deterding, *Colossians*, 2) that at an earlier time in his ministry Paul himself had undertaken this very role in Ephesus. The congregation at Colossae was not founded directly by Paul, for, a few exceptions to the contrary, the recipients had never met him (Col 2:1). The book of Acts indicates that Paul's three-year [AD 53–55] ministry (Acts 19:8, 10; 20:31) in Ephesus (Acts 19) had as a result that "all who dwelt in Asia, Jews and Greeks, heard the word of the Lord" (Acts 19:10). The founding of the congregation in Colossae—as well as those in Laodicea and Hierapolis—would seem to be the result of this period of the apostle's life (Col 2:1; 4:13, 15, 16). This would point to Paul not only doing mission work himself but also preparing others for mission outreach and pastoral ministry in outlying areas of the province of Asia. The description of Epaphras in Col 1:7–8 and 4:12–13 strongly suggests that he was the founding missionary (Dunn, *Epistles*, 22) of the congregations at Colossae, Laodicea, and Hierapolis (located within about fifteen miles of one another and about one hundred miles east of Ephesus), and that he carried out his work there under the supervision of Paul himself [I would read Col 1:7 as "faithful servant of Christ on *our* behalf"]. This would account for the pastoral concern and responsibility that the apostle demonstrates toward the recipients of this letter (1:24, 25; 2:1, 5); their coming to faith had come about under the supervision and auspices of Paul.

of pastors. Church discipline must be administered for the good of the church, yet it must never be hasty or based upon unfounded accusations. The formation of future pastors for the church is also a serious responsibility. The people of God need the best in the way of pastoral leadership that can be had. Thus, the preparation of the church's future shepherds must also be the best that those in the church are able to achieve.

Physical and Spiritual Self-Care

When Paul instructs Timothy to "drink . . . a little wine for your stomach and for your frequent infirmities," he displays a practical concern for the wellbeing of his fellow pastor. With this single sentence the apostle shows the need for a pastor not to neglect his physical welfare.

In the church's history pastors have sometimes so emphasized their role as servants of Christ and servants of his people that they have overlooked that they do have a need to care for themselves. Pastors have suffered from failing to attend to their needs as creatures of God; consequently, their ministry to their parishioners has suffered as well.

In recent years denominations have taken deliberate steps to assure pastors that self-care is also a part of their ministry. Good practices with regard to diet, exercise,[360] recreation, lifestyle, and medical care are important for a pastor as a creature of flesh and blood, and such self-care will in turn equip him better to serve those in his care. While Paul's words here hardly cover the whole gamut of self-care, they certainly point in that direction and serve to indicate that this also has to do with the pastor's ability to carry out his ministry.

Physical self-care needs to be matched by spiritual self-care. Timothy is entrusted with supervision of other pastors, but each pastor needs to exercise such oversight over himself. Thus, the closing words of this section about sins and good works also serve to call pastors to self-oversight. Pastors are tempted to sin and unbelief just as are other Christians. By virtue of their grounding in the word of God pastors have tools at their disposal for dealing with such temptations that other Christians might not necessarily have. This being the case, it is incumbent upon pastors to make use of these resources to guard themselves against succumbing to temptations that would lead them into open sin, impenitence, and/or unbelief.

---

360. In this very letter the apostle notes that "bodily training has a little benefit" (4:8).

Elders (Pastors): 1 Timothy 5:17–25 in Context

Paul is in the midst of speaking about ministry to various groups within the church. At this point he turns his attention to the topic of elders/pastors.

The apostle had previously set out the qualifications for the pastoral office (3:1–7), and he had described for Timothy how he ought to carry out his own ministry (4:6–16). Now he takes up two related issues: Timothy's supervision of other pastors and his preparation of future pastors.

In the ongoing life of the church its pastors sometimes fail and are sometimes in need of correction. Those called to supervise their fellow pastors are engaged in one of the most delicate tasks that a minister of the gospel can ever face. The word of God will guide them in this task.

As long as the Lord of the church tarries, there will be a need to prepare men to take up the pastoral office for the good of the church. Those engaged in this task are also involved in a most high and holy calling. In these verses Paul gives guidance to the church of all ages for this important work.

6:1–2a: Groups in the Church
4: Slaves and Masters

TRANSLATION

¹ Let any who are under a yoke as slaves consider their own masters worthy of all honor, lest the name of God be blasphemed, and the teaching be brought into reproach. ² Let those who have believing masters not despise them because they are brothers [in the faith]; instead, let them serve all the more, because those who benefit from [their] goodness are believers and beloved.

TEXTUAL NOTES

6:1 ζυγὸν—As "yoke of slavery" was a somewhat customary way of speaking,[361] there seems to be no distinction between "slaves" and "slaves under a yoke."

τιμῆς—The word here would imply not merely the feeling of honor but also the display of honor toward another.[362]

ἵνα μὴ ... βλασφημῆται—Here ἵνα followed by the subjunctive verb βλασφημῆται introduces a (negative) purpose clause.[363]

τὸ ὄνομα τοῦ θεοῦ καὶ ἡ διδασκαλία βλασφημῆται—The verb βλασφημῆται would have a slightly different shade of meaning with reference to each of the subjects of this passive verb. A slave's failure to properly honor his master would be an act of rebellion against the will

---

361. BDAG 429.
362. BDAG 1005.
363. Wallace, *Greek Grammar*, 472.

of God; hence, God and his name would be treated with reproach, i.e., would be "blasphemed." This would also bring the teaching of Christianity into reproach. In order to bring this distinction out I have chosen the somewhat expanded translation above.

6:2 καταφρονείτωσαν—Paul uses this verb in 4:12 with reference to treatment that Timothy is not to have to tolerate from others. As older people might be tempted to treat those younger with scorn, so a believing slave might be tempted to do the same toward his master, if the latter were also a believer. Neither is an attitude or action that is befitting Christians.

μᾶλλον—The term might be rendered "to a greater degree" or "for a better reason."[364] The translation "all the more" tries to capture both nuances.

οἱ τῆς εὐεργεσίας ἀντιλαμβανόμενοι—The phrase could mean "those who devote themselves to goodness," referring to the slaves, or "those who benefit from the/their goodness," referring to the masters.[365] The context seems to favor the latter.[366] The participle ἀντιλαμβανόμενοι is a verb that takes its object (τῆς εὐεργεσίας) in the genitive case.[367]

COMMENTARY

Here and in four of his other letters[368] Paul gives instruction to Christian slaves as to how they are to live in their particular station in life. The slave-master relationship was a part of the economy of the first-century Roman world. The Scriptures present economy (1 Pet 2:18–25) along with governmental authority (1 Pet 2:13–17) and the family (1 Pet 3:1–7) as largely making up the created orders[369] that the Almighty has established for the wellbeing of people in this life, even as he has given his word (and sacraments) for our eternal good. Understanding these matters in light of what Lutheran theology has historically spoken of as the distinction

---

364. BDAG 613–14.

365. BDAG 89, 405.

366. Knight, *Pastoral Epistles*, 247; Johnson, *Letters*, 288–90; Towner, *Letters*, 387–90.

367. BDF 94 [§ 170 (3)].

368. 1 Cor 7:20–22; Eph 6:5–8; Col 3:22–25; Titus 2:9–10. Although not addressed to a slave, the letter to Philemon also gives insight into the apostle's instruction concerning slaves and slavery.

369. Note that 1 Pet 2:13 speaks of "everything created for humanity" (πάσῃ ἀνθρωπίνῃ κτίσει).

between the kingdom of God's left hand and the kingdom of God's right hand will inform us of our obligations in each area.[370]

In the present passage the apostle indicates that it is the will of God that slaves show their masters the honor that is due them as their masters. As citizens have obligations to the office of the governing authorities, even if the individuals in those offices are not personally particularly honorable (Rom 13:1–7; Titus 3:1–2; 1 Pet 2:13–17), so a slave has an obligation to the office held by his/her master, regardless of the personal "worthiness" of said master.[371]

This is the case even for those whose masters are fellow believers. The fact that both slave and master are equally free in Christ and equally bound to Christ (1 Cor 7:22) does not negate the duties and responsibilities that the slave has toward his master. Furthermore, the fact that a Christian slave has a fellow Christian as his master should move him to be all the more willing to serve (see the last textual note on 6:2), for although believers are to serve all, they have a special calling to serve their fellow members of the household of faith (Gal 6:10).[372]

Moreover, the way in which a Christian slave serves his master will have an evangelistic purpose. Good service by him will commend the faith he holds; a failure to serve in this way may well bring reproach upon the church and its message.

See further the entry "Slavery in the New Testament World" in the Extended Notes.

Slaves and Masters: 1 Timothy 6:1–2a in Context

With these words Paul concludes the section of his letter devoted to Timothy's responsibilities toward various groups within the church. In his words regarding slaves and masters he notes that improper conduct in this area might have a negative effect on the mission and ministry of the church.

---

370. Helpful resources among the vast literature on the distinction of God's right- and left-hand kingdoms, in addition to volumes 44 through 47 of the American edition of *Luther's Works*, include the following: Scharlemann, "Theology of Freedom," 103–8; Huegli, *Church and State*; Neuhaus, "Ambiguities," 285–95; Althaus, *Ethics*.

371. Knight, *Pastoral Epistles*, 245.

372. Luther (AE 28:362): "If slaves must honor unbelieving masters who are not their brothers, they must honor even more those who are believers and brothers."

From this the apostle segues into his next topic. The mission and ministry of the church requires adherence to the truth of Christian doctrine. This leads Paul to take up the topic of contrasting true versus false teaching and therefore true versus false ministry.

6:2b–5: Timothy's Obligation to Teach the Truth

TRANSLATION

² Teach and proclaim these things. ³ If anyone teaches otherwise, and does not devote himself to the sound words of our Lord Jesus Christ and to the teaching that is in accord with godliness, ⁴ he has become conceited, understanding nothing; instead, he has a morbid craving for controversies and disputes about words, from which come envy, strife, slanders,ᵃ evil conjectures, ⁵ and arguing of people who are depraved in mind and who have been robbed of the truth, who consider godliness to be a way of profiteering.

ᵃ Or *blasphemies*

TEXTUAL NOTES

6:2 Ταῦτα—Since there is no obvious neuter plural antecedent, this neuter plural looks back to everything that Paul has instructed, at least everything since the last similar imperatives of 4:11.

δίδασκε καί παρακάλει—"Teach" (δίδασκε) is a readily understood activity. The usual English renderings of παρακάλει ("exhort," "encourage") might suggest the notion of a mere suggestion (pun intended). The fact that this verb is cognate to a name for God the Holy Spirit, παράκλητος (John 14:16, 26; 15:26; 16:7), helps to fill in its meaning here. One who sets forth the things that Paul articulates in this letter is setting forth the word of the Holy Spirit himself (see the references at ὑγιαίνουσιν λόγοις . . . διδασκαλίᾳ below). The two activities indicated by these two words are the activities to which Timothy has previously been instructed to devote himself (4:13). Thus, Timothy is to set forth "these things" as those things that his hearers are to take to heart. Recognizing that no English translation of παρακάλει is fully adequate, I have chosen to render it here as "proclaim." Both δίδασκε and παρακάλει are present tense imperatives, indicating that such teaching/proclaiming is to be a regular and ongoing part of a pastor's ministry.

6:3 ἑτεροδιδασκαλεῖ—This is another indication of the authority with which Paul writes in this letter. Any different teaching is not the sound words of Christ or godliness; instead, it is heterodoxy.

προσέρχεται—Many other uses of this verb in the NT have the meaning "approach."[373] This gives an image of devotion and rapt attention.

ὑγιαίνουσιν λόγοις . . . διδασκαλίᾳ—The teaching/doctrine that Paul sets forth is "sound," "healthy," good for you. That the apostle identifies his teaching as the "words of our Lord Jesus Christ" indicates the authority in his teaching; these are not his ideas; they come, by way of inspiration (cf. 2 Tim 3:16), from Christ himself.[374] That the apostle had familiarity with the "sound words of our Lord Jesus Christ" is demonstrated by 1 Cor 11:23–25.

τοῦ κυρίου ἡμῶν Ἰησοῦ Χριστοῦ—The genitive "of our Lord Jesus Christ" could be objective (teaching about Christ) or subjective (teaching that comes from Christ). Here it is likely that the phrase is intended to be deliberately ambiguous; one teaches the truth as he teaches the truth *about* Christ, a truth that ultimately comes *from* Christ.

εὐσέβειαν—This word can serve as shorthand for true faith/religion and so a right standing before God (1 Tim 3:16).[375]

6:4 τετύφωται—Here "conceited" means holding to "a different [non-Christian] doctrine" (6:3).

μηδὲν ἐπιστάμενος—"Knowledge" was an important concept for the false teachers; see "The Nature of the Heresy" in the Introduction to the Pastoral Letters. Here Paul asserts that in reality these heretics do not have any genuine knowledge.

---

373. BDAG 878.

374. Paul indicates the same thing in other ways. As an apostle he was one sent by Christ with authority, for through apostles such as Paul the Lord communicated his authoritative and saving word to the church and to the world; see the entry "Apostle" in the Extended Notes. When he instructed his addressees to "read" the letters he had sent to them (1 Thess 5:27; Col 4:16), he was indicating that what he wrote was to be regarded on the same level as the Hebrew Scriptures, which believers had for centuries been reading in their public worship services (see Deterding, *Colossians*, 192–94). In this very letter he indicates that what he is writing is what "the Spirit expressly says" (4:1).

375. BDAG 412–13. See further the entry "Godliness" in the Extended Notes.

νοσῶν περὶ ζητήσεις καὶ λογομαχίας—The literal meaning of νοσῶν refers to physical ailments.³⁷⁶ In English we may speak of something depraved in this way ("That's sick"); the word has the same figurative meaning here. The false teachers want to have arguments (ζητήσεις) over the meaning of words (λογομαχίας); this may well have made them look learned and sophisticated, but in reality, they and their religious opinions were not healthy (the meaning of "sound" in "sound words")—for them or for anyone else.

φθόνος ἔρις—"Envy" (φθόνος) and "strife" (ἔρις) are commonly mentioned among the vices condemned in the NT.³⁷⁷

βλασφημίαι—It is difficult to decide whether "slanders" or "blasphemies" would be the better translation. The context has to do with disruptions between people that some make by their false words; that would argue for the rendering "slanders." But since this is in a context of theological teaching, it could also denote that all of this is an abomination to God and thus favor the translation "blasphemies." Perchance the apostle himself might have intended his readers to think of both possibilities.

ὑπόνοιαι πονηραί—The use of the cognate verb ὑπονοέω in the book of Acts (13:25; 25:18; 27:27) serves to illustrate the meaning of ὑπόνοιαι, "conjectures." These are assumptions or guesses that have no basis in fact; the adjective πονηραί, "evil," makes it clear that the opponents' conjectures are wrong. This is an apt, searing critique of the false teachers and their teachings; they teach nothing more than wild (and erroneous) speculations.

6:5 διαπαρατριβαὶ—As a heightened form of the noun παρατριβή, "dispute," this compound word implies constant disputations.³⁷⁸ Paul elsewhere describes the people who engage in such things as those "who are always learning but never able to come to the knowledge of the truth" (2 Tim 3:7).

διεφθαρμένων ἀνθρώπων τὸν νοῦν—The verb διαφθείρω can be used of wasting away and destruction (Luke 12;33; Rom 8:9), even of the destruction of the final judgment (Rev 11:18). Hence, this passive participle indicates that for all their high-sounding arguments and claims of knowledge, the "minds" of these false teachers are actually corrupted and therefore headed for (eternal) destruction. As the object of the action

---

376. BDAG 678. See also the cognate noun νόσος; BDAG 679.
377. BDAG 392, 1054.
378. BDF 63 [§ 116 (4)].

of the verb "depraved" (διεφθαρμένων) the noun "mind" (νοῦν) is in the accusative case, even though the verb is in the passive voice.[379]

ἀπεστερημένων τῆς ἀληθείας—The verb ἀποστερέω means "to steal" or "defraud."[380] The teachings to which the false teachers have given themselves actually rob them of the truth.

πορισμὸν—The word "profiteering" is used here in a negative sense. With a play on words the apostle uses it again in the following verse in a positive sense. One of the errors of the false teachers was to treat religious teaching as a means for monetary gain. In the culture of the time teachers of religion or philosophy might well be suspected of having a desire for financial gain,[381] and Paul himself had to defend himself against possible accusations of the same (Acts 20:33; 1 Thess 2:5). The apostle will point to a gain of a much different and greater kind in true godliness (1 Tim 6:6).

τὴν εὐσέβειαν—The article (τὴν) on this noun indicates that it is the subject of the phrase πορισμὸν εἶναι τὴν εὐσέβειαν.[382]

COMMENTARY

Teaching with Authority

In this section we see another example of the authority with which the apostle writes in this letter. He instructs Timothy to set forth what he has taught here; the present tense imperatives indicate that this is to be the regular practice of his coworker's ministry. As we examine this section, it is evident that Paul's teaching is the correct teaching. It is "the truth," the "teaching that is in accord with godliness," and the "sound words of our Lord Jesus Christ." Those who teach otherwise "understand nothing" (see further "The Opponents and Their Teaching" below).

This is not the first place in this letter that demonstrates that Paul is teaching with divine authority. Already in the salutation (and in 2:7) he identifies himself as an "apostle," a term which shows that he is speaking with the authority of the Christ who commissioned him.[383] When he uses language such as "I do not permit" (2:12), "the Spirit expressly says" (4:1), "command and teach these things" (4:11), as well as "teach and proclaim

---

379. BDF 87 [§ 159 (3)].
380. BDAG 121.
381. Marshall, *Pastoral Epistles*, 198.
382. Wallace, *Greek Grammar*, 194, 243.
383. See the entry "Apostle" in the Extended Notes.

these things" (6:2b), he indicates that the things that he writes in this letter are not his own ideas or opinions; rather, he is serving as a spokesman for God himself.[384]

It is worth noting that what the apostle instructs Timothy to teach includes more than just the essentials of the Christian faith. His instruction in the previous sections regarding the responsibilities incumbent upon Christians in their various vocations is also something that his fellow pastor is to teach and to proclaim.

The Opponents and Their Teaching

In this section Paul is emphatic in his negative characterization of the false teachers. The detailed description that he gives of them suggests that he has specific individuals in mind.

The apostle's description of the false teachers as "understanding nothing" is particularly pointed. Characteristic of the false teachers against whom the Pastoral Letters are written is their claim that they possessed a special religious knowledge that others did not have.[385] Paul vigorously insisted that the contrary is the case; the false teachers do not have the right understanding of things spiritual and eternal.

Related to this is the apostle's assertion that the false teachers are "depraved in mind." The term "mind" (νοῦς) designates one's real, inner self, especially the activity that controls his entire being and actions (Rom 7:23, 25; 12:2). The mind may be subject to the corrupting influence of sin (Rom 1:28; Eph 4:17; Col 2:18) or to the control of the "spirit" (πνεῦμα, Eph 4:23) that has been set in a right relationship with almighty God (by the Holy Spirit; Rom 8:16). The former is clearly the case with respect to these false teachers.

It appears that at least a part of the appeal of the false teaching that Paul combats in this letter was its high-sounding terminology. To some the false teaching seemed to provide a more sophisticated and learned version of Christianity than what the apostle and his coworkers set forth.[386] Here Paul gives the true evaluation of this heresy. It was nothing

---

384. See the commentary on those verses.

385. See "The Nature of the Heresy" in the Introduction to the Pastoral Letters.

386. Again, see "The Nature of the Heresy" in the Introduction to the Pastoral Letters.

more than a lot of debates and disputes over the meanings of words, but it had nothing of real, saving substance to offer.

The false teaching had other negative effects on the churches. With the words "envy, strife, slanders [or blasphemies], evil conjectures, and arguing" the apostle indicates that the false teaching created hostility and conflict among Christians. Of course, in and of itself false teaching is evil; it may well bring further harm by dividing Christians from one another.

Almost as a concluding thought Paul also notes that at least some of these false teachers "consider godliness to be a way of profiteering." Unbiblical teaching is an evil in and of itself; it is even worse when it becomes a pretext for using religious matters as a way to profit over trusting or perhaps gullible people (on pastors' legitimate right to be able to make a living from ministry, see the commentary on 5:17–18).

The above might bring to mind examples of those who in the name of religion and even of the Christian faith have enriched themselves off those seeking authentic religious faith. Such conduct is contrary to the requirements set forth in this letter that an overseer/pastor is to be "beyond reproach" (3:2) and be well thought of by those outside the church (3:7). It may also be noted that this would bring reproach upon the church and its message, quite contrary to how Christians are to live.[387]

Timothy's Obligation to Teach the Truth: 1 Timothy 6:2b–5 in Context

Paul turns from dealing with various groups in the church to Timothy's own obligation for ministry to them all. The instructions of the previous sections are a part of the "sound words of our Lord Jesus Christ" and "the teaching that is in accord with godliness."

Teaching the truth involves also rejecting and refuting error. The teaching of this letter, like that of all of Scripture, has the authority of God himself. Thus, any teaching that is in conflict with it is false and must be opposed.

The apostle will return to his instructions to Timothy a bit later in this letter. However, the mention of the false teachers' attempts at "profiteering" leads Paul to digress for a bit in order to give some instruction regarding true profit. It is with that instruction that the letter continues.

---

387. 1 Tim 5:14; 6:1; see further Titus 2:5, 8.

6:6–10: True Profit

TRANSLATION

⁶ However, godliness with contentment has great profit, ⁷ for we have brought nothing into the world; furthermore, we are not able to bring anything out, ⁸ but if we have nourishment and covering, we will be content with these. ⁹ However, those who desire to be rich fall into temptation and a snare and many foolish and harmful desires, which plunge people into ruin and destruction. ¹⁰ For the love of money is a root of all [kinds of] evils; some by desiring these things have been led away from the faith and pierced themselves through with many pangs.

TEXTUAL NOTES

6:6 πορισμὸς—The same noun was used in 6:5 in a negative sense. With a play on words Paul uses it here in a positive sense: the real profit is in godliness with contentment.

εὐσέβεια—This is a term that is found frequently in the Pastorals.[388] It is shorthand for the Christian faith being authentically held and lived out. See further the entry "Godliness" in the Extended Notes.

αὐταρκείας—The apostle uses the cognate adjective (αὐτάρκης) to describe his having learned (from God) to be content (Phil 4:11). The same noun occurs in 2 Cor 9:8 to speak of God providing what is sufficient for the Corinthians to fulfill the task before them.[389]

6:7 εἰσηνέγκαμεν . . . ἐξενγκεῖν—These verbs ("brought . . . into," "bring . . . out") have the same root; the prefixes used with each are the

---

388. 1 Tim 2:10; 3:16; 4:7, 8; 6:3, 5, 6, 11; 2 Tim 3:5; Titus 1:1.
389. Barrett, *Second Epistle*, 236–37.

exact opposite of one another; hence, the verbs stand in stark contrast to one another. Note the similar sentiment expressed in Job 1:21 and Eccl 5:11–15.

κόσμον—We could paraphrase the meaning here as "this life."

6:8 ἔχοντες—This is a conditional participle: "if we have nourishment and covering."[390]

διατροφὰς—This is a slightly different form of the term for "food" (τροφή) more commonly used in the NT.[391] Therefore, I have chosen to render it with a less common English word.

σκεπάσματα—This word refers to "clothing" but can also designate shelter, "house."[392] Hence, I have used the translation "covering."[393]

ἀρκεσθησόμεθα—This verb is cognate to the noun used in 6:6 (αὐταρκείας, "contentment"). In the passive voice (as here) it means "be content."[394] The use of the future tense indicative here ("we will be content") rather than a cohortative ("let us be content") makes the apostle's assertion all that more emphatic.

6:9 πειρασμὸν—This is a commonly used word in the NT for temptations to sin and unbelief;[395] for example, it occurs in the petition of the Lord's Prayer concerning not being lead into temptation (Matt 6:13; Luke 11:4).

παγίδα—Paul uses this term elsewhere in the Pastorals of the snare of the devil (1 Tim 3:7; 2 Tim 2:26). Its use elsewhere in the NT (Luke 21:35; Rom 11:9) suggests that this "snare" ultimately means eternal punishment from God on account of unbelief.

ἀνοήτους—This adjective denotes what is the opposite of "wise" (σοφός, Rom 1:14) is synonymous with being hardhearted (Luke 24:25), describes the Galatians who are toying with the notion of trying to be saved by works (Gal 3:1, 3), and designates one's condition before being saved by the grace of God (Titus 3:3).[396]

βλαβεράς—These desires are not merely foolish; this folly is actually "harmful."

---

390. Wallace, *Greek Grammar*, 633.
391. Compare BDAG 238 with BDAG 1017.
392. BDAG 927.
393. Knight, *Pastoral Epistles*, 255, offers a similar understanding of the passage.
394. BDAG 131–32.
395. BDAG 793.
396. BDAG 84.

βυθίζουσιν—The same verb is used in Luke 5:7 of Peter's boat beginning to sink; this shows the vividness of the metaphor that Paul uses here.

ὄλεθρον—The same noun is used of the punishment of eternal damnation that is to be meted out at the last day (1 Thess 5:3; 2 Thess 1:9).

ἀπώλειαν—A number of passages[397] use this noun to refer to eternal damnation.

6:10 ἀπεπλανήθησαν—The passive voice here means that these people have been led away by their own desire/love of money.

τῆς πίστεως—Is this the content of faith (*fides quae creditur*) or the act of believing (*fides qua creditur*)? In this case both are applicable. See further the entry "Faith" in the Extended Notes.

περιέπειραν—This verb can denote literal, physical piercing[398] and hence makes this figure of speech quite vivid.

ὀδύναις—This is another word that can refer to physical pain, such as from a wound or fracture.[399] Thus, it adds to the graphicness of Paul's language here.

COMMENTARY

Great Profit

With a play on words Paul turns his attention for the moment away from warning against false teachers. There is great profit—not in striving to get the things of this world but in holding to the Christian faith.

This "profit" is found in "godliness" (εὐσέβεια), a word whose usage throughout the Pastoral Letters demonstrates that it refers to genuine believing in the authentic Christian gospel and in living it out in one's life.[400] When one has godliness through faith in Christ, he is taught by God to be content (Phil 4:10–13, esp. verse 11; see also 2 Cor 12:10). When one is content with what he has, he is far richer than anyone who may have much more in the way of worldly riches but who is not content with it.

When one has authentic faith, he knows that all he really needs in the way of worldly goods is food, clothing, and shelter (see textual notes). Most, if not all, readers of this commentary will realize that they have far

---

397. Matt 7:13; John 17:12; Rom 9:22; Phil 1:28; 3:19; 2 Thess 2:3; Heb 10:39; 2 Pet 2:1, 3; 3:7; Rev 17:8, 11.

398. BDAG 803.

399. *TDNT* 5:115.

400. See the entry "Godliness" in the Extended Notes.

more than the absolute necessities of life, especially when compared with most of the people who have lived throughout the history of the world. The Lord has blessed many of us with things that even the wealthiest people in earlier eras of history could not have imagined, much less possessed. As if our eternal salvation for the sake of Christ were not enough, this is an additional motivation for Christians to be content.

For the most part even worldly people understand that "you can't take it with you."[401] In these verses the apostle gives his own version of that sentiment. We brought nothing into the world; we can bring nothing out. Thus, our contentment is found not so much in the worldly blessings that we have from the Almighty but especially from his gift of unending life.

Godliness comes from faith worked by the word of God (1 Tim 3:16; 6:3; Titus 1:1); through that same word God teaches us to be content (2 Cor 12:10; Phil 4:11). Thus, contentment is seen to be worked by the word rather than something that we individuals achieve for ourselves.

The Love of Money

It appears that 1 Tim 6:10 will be perpetually misquoted ("money is the root of all evil"), so apparently it will be perpetually necessary to point out what this passage actually says. It is not money but the *love* of money that is the culprit. It is not *the* root but *a* root; there are other causes of evil.[402] Furthermore, the use of the plural ("evils") would indicate that the love of money is a root not of all evil but of many different kinds of evil (all without distinction, not all without exclusion).[403]

There is nothing inherently wrong with money and possessions. In this very letter Paul points out that it is proper, even necessary, for a pastor to be able to make a living from the work of ministry (5:17–18;

---

401. Sentiments similar to the one that concludes this section ("the love of money is a root of all [kinds of] evils") are attested elsewhere in the world of the New Testament. Debelius and Conzelmann, *Pastoral Epistles*, 85–86, cite the following examples: "Love of money is the mother-city of all evil" (Stobaeus, *Eclogae* 3); "But you have named what is pretty much the chief of all evils: they are all included in love of money" (Apollodorus Comicus, *Philodelph Fragmenta* 4); "Love of money is the mother of all wickedness" (Pseudo-Phocyclides 42).

402. Even though according to Colwell's rule (definite predicate nominatives that precede the verb are usually anarthrous) ῥίζα could be considered definite, this would yield the meaning that the love of money is the exclusive cause of all evil(s), which would not be biblical. See Wallace, *Greek Grammar*, 265; also 5–6, 256–62.

403. See Wallace, *Greek Grammar*, 265.

see further the commentary on those verses). There is not even anything inherently wrong with riches. Abraham possessed a household of 318 men able to go to battle (Gen 14:14). A group of women provided for Jesus and the Twelve out of their means (Luke 8:2–3); they would have had to have had considerable means to do this. One of the apostle's converts at Philippi was Lydia, a seller of purple goods; selling that sort of expensive wares would have made her a woman of considerable means herself; that would explain why she was able to give Paul and Silas lodging in her home while they were in Philippi (Acts 16:14–15). Since Philemon owned at least one slave (Onesimus) and was able to have the church at Colossae meet in his house, he would have had to have been a man of at least some means (Phlm 1, 9, 16). Later in this very letter Paul will have occasion to direct instruction to those who are "rich in this age" (6:17).

Thus, when the apostle speaks of the love of money and the desire to be rich, it is plain that he is speaking of a desire to have things beyond what God, in his love and providence, gives to us. Paul's rebuke of the Thessalonians regarding their idleness and their being busybodies rather than being busy with work (2 Thess 3:6–12) should make it plain that there is nothing inherently sinful about working hard (and in an honest way) to earn the goods of this world, even those things that are beyond the absolute essentials needed for life.

There is a real danger to one's eternal wellbeing in the love of money/desire for riches. The terms that the apostle uses here indicate that the consequences may be eternal (see textual notes above); perhaps he uses two terms (ὄλεθρον, ἀπώλειαν) to suggest the possibility of both temporal and eternal judgment.[404] The love of money can turn one away entirely from the saving faith and into the power of Satan. This would mean the penalty of eternal damnation.

In view of the previous section, where Paul had excoriated those who think that Christianity is a means to profiteering, the disgrace of high-profile religious leaders who have accumulated great wealth might come to mind—especially those who appear to carry out ministry in a manner not wholly in keeping with God's word. Upon reading these verses one might be inclined to think of others who are or at least seem to be guilty of such a love of money. Of more pressing urgency, however, is the need to take these words to heart ourselves. Even though we have a standard of living that is higher than most of the rest of the world and

---

404. Knight, *Pastoral Epistles*, 256–57.

most of the rest of human history, we are not exempt from the temptations to "desire to be rich" in an ungodly way.

Much to be preferred for Christians in general and for pastors in particular is occupying ourselves with godliness (1 Tim 4:7–8). As we attend to "the sound words of our Lord Jesus Christ and to the teaching that is in accord with godliness" (1 Tim 6:3), God himself will empower us to live our lives with contentment.

True Profit: 1 Timothy 6:6–10 in Context

Paul had been instructing Timothy about teaching the truth over against the false teachers who were troubling his churches—a topic to which he will return shortly (6:11–16). The reference to those regarding godliness as a means to profiteering leads him to take up the topic of the proper role of money and wealth in the life of Christians—a topic to which he will return before long (6:17–19).

With these words the apostle points to godliness *with contentment* as the true profit/wealth. His words here have ongoing relevance, for both relative poverty and relative wealth can be a grave temptation and dangerous to one's faith (Prov 30:7–9). The fact that he places these instructions in between directives to Timothy regarding the conduct of his ministry suggests that they have special relevance and applicability to pastors in every age of church history.

6:11–16: Timothy's Obligation to Irreproachable Ministry

TRANSLATION

¹¹ But you, O man of God, flee these things; pursue righteousness, godliness, faith,ᵃ love, endurance, gentleness. ¹² Fight the good fight of the faith; lay hold of eternal life, to which you were called, having confessed the good confession before many witnesses. ¹³ Before God, who gives life to all things, and Christ Jesus, who bore witness to Pontius Pilate about the good confession, I direct ¹⁴ you to keep the commandment spotless and irreproachable until the appearing of our Lord Jesus Christ, ¹⁵ which he will show at the right time, he who is the blessed and only sovereign, the king of those who are having kingship and lord of those who are having lordship,¹⁶ the only one who has immortality, who dwells in unapproachable light, whom no one among men has seen nor is able to see, to whom be honor and might forever, Amen.

ᵃ Or *faithfulness*

TEXTUAL NOTES

6:11 ὦ ἄνθρωπε θεοῦ—Whenever Paul uses this particular grammatical form, the vocative introduced with an omega,[405] he speaks with great emphasis and passion, more so than when he uses the simple vocative

---

405. In addition to the present passage, Rom 2:1, 3; 9:20; Gal 3:1; 1 Tim 6:20; see also Acts 13:10. In all of these passages he is addressing some person or persons. In Rom 11:33, another emphatic, emotional declaration, the apostle uses an omega (Ὦ) without any accompanying vocative simply as an exclamation (in English typically rendered "Oh" rather than "O"), without addressing any particular person.

case.⁴⁰⁶ In this way he here emphasizes the importance of what he is about to say. The phrase "man of God" has a rich OT history as a designation for those who led God's people with the word of God.⁴⁰⁷

ταῦτα—At the end of 6:2 Paul uses this same neuter pronoun to refer to all that he had said up to that point (see textual notes on 6:2b–5). As there so here there is no obvious neuter plural noun to which this pronoun might refer. That being the case the apostle uses the neuter plural to point back to all of the ungodly things he had mentioned since 6:3, as he instructs Timothy to flee all of these.

δικαιοσύνην—See the entry "Righteousness/Justification" in the Extended Notes. In close proximity to "godliness" and "faith" the term here denotes seeking the righteousness that Christ gives through faith in him, with the result that this will produce righteous works in the life of the believer.

εὐσέβειαν—Shorthand for the entire Christian faith and life, received by faith in Christ. See further the entry "Godliness" in the Extended Notes.

πίστιν—See the entry "Faith" in the Extended Notes. Here the term lacks the article and is mentioned in conjunction with various virtues of the Christian life. That being the case, here it probably denotes the act of believing (*fides qua creditur*) that expresses itself through "faithfulness" in believing and in displaying the works that faith produces in the life of the believer (Gal 5:6; Eph 2:8–10).

ἀγάπην—See the entry "Love" in the Extended Notes.

ὑπομονὴν—The word here denotes patience and endurance, perhaps with a sense of expectation.⁴⁰⁸

πραϋπαθίαν—"Hesychius [fifth century AD] explains it by using the words ἡσυχία [quietness] and πραΰτης [humility] as synonyms, hence the opp[osite] of an overbearing attitude."⁴⁰⁹

6:12 ἀγωνίζου . . . ἀγῶνα—This verb and noun can be used with a martial (John 18:36) or athletic reference (1 Cor 9:25; 2 Tim 4:7; Heb 12:1), but most often it denotes any general kind of struggle.⁴¹⁰ Since the apostle uses the identical phrase in his Second Letter to Timothy (4:7)

---

406. See, for example, 1 Cor 7:16 and Phlm 20.
407. Deut 33:1; Josh 14:6 (Moses); 1 Sam 9:6–7 (Samuel); 1 Kgs 17:18 (Elijah); 2 Kgs 4:7 (Elisha); 2 Chr 8:14 (David).
408. BDAG 1039–40.
409. BDAG 861.
410. Luke 13:24; Col 1:29; 2:1; 4:12; 1 Thess 2:2; 1 Tim 4:10.

as a comparison to athletic endeavor, it would seem that if he intends any particular sort of metaphorical meaning here, it would be one of sport.

τῆς πίστεως—The use of the article as well as the overall emphasis of this letter to holding to true doctrine might suggest that "faith" here means the content of what is taught and believed (*fides quae creditur*), meaning that Timothy is to fight on behalf of true doctrine. That being said, the following context might suggest rather a reference to Timothy's personal faith (*fides qua creditur*). Since there are arguments in favor of either one, and since the two are closely related to one another, it could well be that the term here embraces both meanings of the word.

ἐπιλαβοῦ τῆς αἰωνίου ζωῆς—One lays hold of eternal life by pursuing faith (6:11), by fighting the good fight of the faith (6:12).

εἰς ἣν ἐκλήθης—The passive voice of the verb ("called") implies the action of God.

ὡμολόγησα . . . ὁμολογίαν—Wherever Paul uses some form of this word group in his letters,[411] it is in a context of making a profession of the saving truth. See further the commentary below.

ἐνώπιον πολλῶν μαρτύρων—This implies a public confession/profession.

6:13 παραγγέλλω—This is a verb that Paul uses frequently in this letter (1:3; 4:11; 5:7; 6:13, 17), often as an imperative.

ἐνώπιον . . . Ἰησοῦ—Note the repetition of the preposition ἐνώπιον from the previous sentence. This is a solemn oath formula,[412] calling upon God the Father, as the creator and preserver, and God the Son, as the redeemer and savior, to witness to the truth of what is being said.

μαρτυρήσαντος . . . ὁμολογίαν—Jesus confessed before Pilate that he was the king of the Jews and also bore witness to what sort of king he was. See Matt 27:11; Mark 15:2; Luke 23:3; John 18:36–37. John 19:11 contains the only other record of Jesus saying anything to Pilate.

6:14 τηρῆσαί σε τὴν ἐντολὴν ἄσπιλον ἀνεπίλημπτον—The word ἐντολὴν refers to Timothy's responsibilities as a "man of God" (6:11); he is to carry out the duties of his calling as a pastor in a manner that is "spotless" and "irreproachable" (ἀνεπίλημπτον, the same adjective as is used in 3:2).[413] The adjective "spotless" (ἄσπιλον) recalls that in Old Tes-

---

411. Rom 10:9, 10; 14:11; 2 Cor 9:13; Phil 2:11; 1 Tim 3:16; 6:13. In Titus 1:16 he uses it in the sense of someone making the claim of professing the truth, when in reality it is a false claim.

412. BDAG 342.

413. The understanding of the passage is the same, whether one (with Kelly,

tament Israel only unblemished animals were permitted to be offered as a sacrifice to God (as in 1 Pet 1:19, although used there in a metaphorical sense of Christ's moral perfection; see also Lev 22:17–25).

ἐπιφανείας—The word here refers to the parousia, as in 2 Thess 2:8; 2 Tim 4:1, 8; Titus 2:13.

6:15 καιροῖς ἰδίοις—This is a dative of time (at the right time).[414] Christ's coming in glory and judgment will take place according to his own timetable (1 Thess 5:1–2), one which is unknown to mere humans.[415]

ἥν . . . δείξει . . . δυνάστης—The accusative feminine singular relative pronoun "which" (ἥν) refers back to the feminine singular noun "epiphany" (ἐπιφανείας) and is the direct object of the verb "show" (δείξει). The closest antecedent that can serve as subject of this verb is "our Lord Jesus Christ"; that and the overall context (who would accomplish the "epiphany" of our Lord Jesus Christ except Christ himself) indicate that δυνάστης must be a reference to Jesus Christ.

ὁ βασιλεὺς τῶν βασιλευόντων καὶ κύριος τῶν κυριευόντων—The genitive plurals here are participles: "king of those reigning and lord of those having dominion." In order to bring out the play on words I given the somewhat clumsy rendering "the king of those who are having kingship and lord of those who are having lordship." In the only other places in the NT where the equivalent of either of these phrases are used (Rev 17:14; 19:16) the reference is clearly to Jesus Christ.[416]

6:16 ἀθανασίαν—The apostle uses the same term in 1 Cor 15:53 to refer to immortality as a result of the resurrection from the dead. So also

---

Pastoral Epistles, 144–45) takes the adjectives ἄσπιλον ("spotless") and ἀνεπίλημπτον ("irreproachable") as modifying the noun ἐντολήν ("commandment") or (with Knight, *Pastoral Epistles*, 268) as modifying the entire expression τηρῆσαί σε τὴν ἐντολήν ("you to keep the commandment").

414. Wallace, *Greek Grammar*, 157; BDF 107 [§ 200 (4)].

415. Matt 24:36 records Jesus saying that as the Son he did not know the time of the parousia. This is to be understood in light of the two natures in Christ, divine and human, and in view of the two states of his incarnation: the state of humiliation and the state of exaltation. During the state of humiliation (from his conception up until his death and burial) Jesus did not make full use of his divine power and glory; he does do so during his state of exaltation (from his resurrection forward). According to his human nature in the state of humiliation Jesus did not know the time of the second coming. According to his divine nature he did/does know, and during the time of his state of exaltation he does know. On the interpretation of Matt 24:36 see Gibbs, *Matthew 21:1—28:20*, 1294–97. On the two natures in the person of Christ and the two states of his incarnation see Nafzger et al., *Confessing the Gospel*, 381–96, 460–70.

416. On the translation "king of those who are reigning and lord of those who are having dominion" see Wallace, *Greek Grammar*, 621.

here, Christ alone has immortality because he was the first to rise from the dead, never to die again.

φῶς οἰκῶν ἀπρόσιτον—Light here serves as a designation of the presence of God. Christ dwells in "unapproachable light" (φῶς ... ἀπρόσιτον); mankind cannot approach him because humanity's sin cuts them off from the presence of the holy God (e.g., 2 Cor 6:14). This is another attestation to the deity of Christ.

ὃν εἶδεν οὐδεὶς ἀνθρώπων οὐδὲ ἰδεῖν δύναται—In light of Exod 33:20 the point here is that Christ cannot be seen, not because he is invisible, but because it would be fatal for sinful humanity to look upon this holy one. He cannot be seen now, not because he is invisible (immaterial), but because although he is visible (risen from the dead) he is at present hidden (but not absent).[417]

ᾧ τιμὴ καὶ κράτος αἰώνιον, ἀμήν—This is similar to doxologies that Paul directs to God the Father (Rom 1:25; 11:36; Gal 1:5; Phil 4:20), to the Father through Christ (Rom 16:27; Eph 3:21), or to Christ himself (Rom 9:5; 1 Tim 1:17; 2 Tim 4:18). Doxologies like these are another way in which the apostle confesses the deity of Jesus Christ.

In the Pauline Letters ascriptions of praise like these are not uncommon. They often come at or near the end of a letter (Rom 16:27; Phil 4:20; 2 Tim 4:18) or, as here, to conclude a major section of a letter (Rom 11:36; Eph 3:21).

COMMENTARY

"From the solemn opening phrase, '[O] man of God,' to the closing doxology, this section brings the commissioning and instructing of Timothy to a climax."[418] This portion of the letter highlights the responsibilities of the pastoral office and also places Jesus Christ at the center of it all to provide the pastor with the motivation and power for his ministry.

Flee—Pursue

Paul begins this exhortation with a look backwards. He instructs Timothy to flee "these things." With these words he tells his young coworker to

---

417. On the difference between God being hidden rather than absent see Veith, *Spirituality*, 69–86.

418. Towner, *Letters*, 406.

turn away from all the vices against which he had warned in the preceding portion of this letter.

But beyond simply issuing a warning against wrongful behavior the apostle also directs Timothy to godly, beneficial activity. Each of these objects that Timothy is to pursue is a window on the Christian faith and life.

He begins by directing his younger coworker to "righteousness" (see the entry "Righteousness/Justification" in the Extended Notes). This largely Pauline term is virtually a microcosm of the Christian faith and life. Righteousness is something that God demands of us, but which we cannot achieve on our own. Instead, righteousness before God is a gift from God for the sake of Jesus Christ, that is, because of his death and resurrection. The gospel message of Christ is the means by which God reveals and gives his righteousness to humanity. This righteousness is received by the individual through faith without any works on his part (note the close proximity of "faith[fulness]" in this section). When one has righteousness/is righteous through faith in Christ, then he is empowered to do those things that are righteous in the sight of God.

Paul continues by telling Timothy to pursue "godliness." Like "righteousness," "godliness" encompasses all the main features of Christianity (see the entry by that name in the Extended Notes). Godliness is received by us through faith as it is given in the word of God. While people can put on an outward show of godliness that is anything except true godliness, the genuine article will display itself in the way in which one lives.

Thirdly the apostle exhorts his younger coworker to "faith" or "faithfulness." The context suggests that here Paul is referring to the act of believing (see the entry on "Faith" in the Extended Notes). As righteousness and godliness are ours through faith, the apostle is directing Timothy to that genuine trust of the heart in Christ that is created, maintained, and strengthened through the word of God and which in turn will show itself in faithfully producing the fruit of good works in the believer's life.

Paul follows his directive to faith/faithfulness with one to love, the chief virtue of the Christian life (1 Cor 13:13; Col 3:14; see also the entry "Love" in the Extended Notes). The apostle is the great champion of faith active in love (Gal 5:6). As a mere show of godliness is not true godliness (2 Tim 3:5, contrast 1 Tim 2:10), so faith is more than a mere intellectual assent to some propositions. Genuine faith will always produce acts of love in the believer's life, and so Paul places faith/faithfulness and love side by side in this exhortation to Timothy.

There are challenges to faith that might cause it to die out;[419] in this very letter the apostle has provided some examples of this sad reality (1:19–20; 5:12; see also 2 Tim 2:17–18). Therefore, he also directs Timothy to endurance. The word implies steadfastness even in the face of difficulty; if the etymology of the word has any significance,[420] it suggests one who "remains [firm] under difficulty." In a couple of places in his letters Paul associates endurance with hope (Rom 5:4; 15:4). The believer's certain hope of eternal salvation gives him the strength to endure trials.

Finally, the apostle exhorts Timothy to gentleness. The Greek word suggests the quiet strength to face any and all circumstances with humility rather than displaying an overbearing attitude, which might be a cover for doubts arising from a misplaced confidence in oneself (see textual note above).

Through pursuing all of these, one will "lay hold of eternal life." Genuine faith—which shows itself in godliness, love, endurance, and gentleness—is the way to the righteousness before God that brings eternal life (Rom 5:17–21).

This catalogue of objects for the Christian's attention are certainly applicable to any believer. However, since Paul introduces these by addressing Timothy as a "man of God," this suggests that the apostle highlights these while thinking especially of his coworker's role as a pastor. While a pastor has a responsibility for the spiritual condition of others, he dare never neglect the nurture of his own life of faith. Moreover, such spiritual "self-care" is part and parcel of his work as a "man of God."

Man of God

In this section Paul addresses Timothy as a "man of God." As a man of God, he certainly needs to tend to his own spiritual wellbeing and to the genuineness of his saving faith. But as a "man of God" he also has additional responsibilities. These are highlighted twice in the space of these verses.

The apostle instructs Timothy to "fight the good fight of the faith." The article on the word "faith" suggests that Paul here is directing Timothy to the same activity to which Jude in his letter directed his readers,

---

419. Note the comments of Luther (AE 28:373–76).

420. This noun is cognate to the verb ὑπομένω, a compound of ὑπό, "under," and μένω, "remain"; BDAG 630–31, 1035–36, 1039–40.

namely, to "contend for the faith" (Jude 3). In several places in the present letter the apostle has warned his coworker about false teachers and has directed him to set forth the true faith in contradistinction to the teachings of such heretics.[421] Fighting the good fight of the faith is another way of speaking about this task.

When Paul tells Timothy to "keep the commandment spotless and irreproachable," this recalls the instruction that one who would be an overseer/pastor must be "irreproachable" (3:2). The pastor is called to teach the truth of the Scriptures without error and to be able to rebuke contrary teachings (see Titus 1:9).

The seriousness of all this is seen in the apostle directing Timothy "before God . . . and Christ Jesus." These words put Timothy under a solemn obligation to carry out this ministry in an irreproachable way. Earlier in this letter Paul had made mention of the "laying on of the hands of the elders" that had taken place in Timothy's past (4:14), which must have referred to some public recognition of his call to and placement in ministry.[422] At that time Timothy may well have been called upon to make some type of pledge of faithfulness to the word of God and to faithfulness in carrying out his ministry. The apostle's directive here "before God . . . and Christ Jesus" may well recall the promise Timothy made at that time and hence be a directive to him to act in accord with it.

Holding to the truth of the Scriptures and refuting error is important and beneficial for all Christians. However, it is especially incumbent on those with responsibility for the spiritual wellbeing of others.

Timothy's Good Confession

The general sense of Paul's exhortation to Timothy to "fight the good fight of the faith; lay hold of eternal life, to which you were called, having confessed the good confession before many witnesses" is clear enough. However, an identification of the "good confession" that the apostle's younger coworker "confessed" will add to our understanding of Paul's instruction.

Timothy had been taught the faith of the Old Testament Scriptures by his grandmother Lois and his mother Eunice (2 Tim 1:5). His hometown was Lystra, a city to which Paul had first brought the Christian

---

421. 1 Tim 1:18–20; 4:1–7; 5:20; 6:3–5.
422. See the commentary on 4:6–16.

gospel during his first missionary journey (Acts 14:5–19). When the apostle revisited that town on his second missionary journey, he added Timothy to his missionary troupe (Acts 16:1–3). Timothy is identified as a "disciple" (16:1), that is, a believer in Christ. From this it is possible, even likely, that Timothy's coming to the Christian faith had been due to the evangelistic work of Paul, possibly (if not probably) already during the apostle's first missionary journey to Lystra.[423]

Timothy's coming to saving faith through the ministry of the word would have been confirmed by his subsequent baptism. Later church history indicates that adult baptisms would have involved some type of confession of the Christian faith[424] by those being baptized into that faith.[425] Thus, Timothy's "good confession" most likely refers to his making a profession of his faith in Christ at his baptism before other Christians gathered together for the occasion.[426] That the apostle would show such familiarity with the particulars of this event would suggest that he himself had administered baptism to Timothy.

Timothy (like all Christians) is not to take the attitude that since he has been baptized, he is guaranteed to have eternal life. He needs to remain in the faith and to exert great effort in doing so. That said, he also (like all Christians) is not to overlook the significance of his baptism.[427] His baptism was one of the ways by which God called him to faith. Now, by means of the word of God, he is to lay hold of and pursue eternal salvation by nurturing that faith, so that he holds it to the end.

---

423. Kelly, *Pastoral Epistles*, 1, and Knight, *Pastoral Epistles*, 63–64, come to a similar conclusion.

424. Perhaps like verses 15 and 16 of the present chapter. Other possibilities might include 1 Tim 1:15; 3:16; 2 Tim 2:8, 11–13; or Titus 3:8.

425. Kelly, *Early Christian Creeds*, 6–61.

426. See Kelly, *Pastoral Epistles*, 142. The book of Acts (16:1–3) reports that Timothy was the son of a Greek (non-Jewish) father and a Jewish mother. As such he had never received the Old Testament rite of circumcision. In order not to create an obstacle to ministry to his fellow Jews Paul saw to it that this half-Jew Timothy received circumcision before he joined the apostle's missionary endeavor.

In his Letter to the Colossians (2:11–12) Paul draws a comparison between the Old Testament act of circumcision and Christian baptism. The connection between the Old Testament rite and the Christian sacrament makes it certain that Timothy would have received baptism, very possibly by the hands of Paul himself. Thus, the apostle would have been in a ready position to remind his younger coworker of what had taken place at the time of his baptism.

427. On Paul's teaching regarding baptism see Deterding, "Baptism," 93–100.

Our Lord Jesus Christ

Paul directs Timothy to faithfulness in his work of ministry "before God, who gives life to all things, and Christ Jesus, who bore witness to Pontius Pilate about the good confession." The vocable "God" here, being distinguished from "Christ Jesus," is a reference to God the Father. Describing him as the one "who gives life to all things" refers to his work of creation and preservation. This gives an increased sense of grandeur and solemnity to the apostle's words here.

As Paul uses the same phrase to describe the "good confession" confessed by Timothy and "the good confession" borne witness to by Christ Jesus, this shows that he intends there to be some connection between the two. The faith that Timothy confessed at his baptism is a necessary part of his keeping his ministry ("the commandment") spotless and irreproachable. Strength for that faith comes from the good confession that Jesus made before Pontius Pilate.

Other than the record of a prayer and a couple of speeches in the book of Acts[428] this is the only reference to Pilate in the New Testament outside the Gospels, and it is one of only three places in the Scriptures that mention the name "*Pontius* Pilate."[429] During his tenure as "prefect" (governor) of Judea Pilate dedicated a theater in Caesarea on the Mediterranean; the fragment of an inscription on the dedicatory stone of that edifice preserves his name.[430]

In the commentary on 5:18 (which see) we examined the evidence for the possibility that the Gospel according to Luke and/or the Gospel according to Matthew might have been written by this time and so been known to Paul. However, even if we consider the possibility that none of the Gospels had been written when the apostle penned the present letter, it is unthinkable that Paul would not have been familiar with this fact from our Lord's passion. Both the Jewish historian Josephus[431] and the Roman historian Tacitus[432] knew that Jesus had been executed under the supervision of (Pontius) Pilate; this puts it beyond the realm of believability that such a major figure in the early church as Paul would not have known this. As one who came to the Christian faith after the conclusion

---

428. Acts 3:13; 4:27; 13:28.
429. The others are Luke 3:1 and Acts 4:27.
430. *DNTB* 804.
431. *Antiquities of the Jews* 18:3:3.
432. *Annals* 15:44.

of the earthly ministry of Jesus, the apostle would not have had firsthand information about all the details of the ministry of his Lord; nevertheless, this mention of the name of the one who ordered the crucifixion of Jesus demonstrates that he had at a minimum a basic knowledge of the particulars of Christ's passion and death.[433]

The four Gospels record very little of what Jesus may have said to Pilate.[434] However, since they all indicate that Christ was largely silent throughout his appearance before both the Roman governor and Herod Antipas,[435] it may be that Jesus said nothing more to Pilate than what we have in the Gospels.

"The good confession" that Christ made before Pilate, therefore, would refer to him acknowledging his being "the king of the Jews," although, as the fuller account in John makes plain, what it meant that he was a king was very different from what a Roman official might have imagined. This confession helped lead to his eventual death to save sinners (1 Tim 1:15).

Christ's good confession in the face of hostility and opposition was a part of his work for Timothy's salvation. That moves and empowers Timothy to devote himself to faithful ministry, even in the face of hostility and opposition.

There is a word of encouragement for all pastors in that. As they focus on what Christ did for their salvation, they will be strengthened for the tasks of ministry that face them.

The apostle's mention of the "appearing" (ἐπιφανείας) that Christ will show "at the right time" (his second coming) serves two purposes. On the one hand it adds solemnity to Paul's charge to Timothy to tend to his ministry: as Christ the judge is coming, taking care of one's responsibilities is serious business. But that he will accomplish this "at the right time" points to the benefit of the parousia: Christ is coming to take his people to the full enjoyment of their salvation, which he accomplished according to God's eternal plan (2 Tim 1:9–10). Thus, all of God's plan of salvation, including the second coming of Christ, was and will be accomplished at just the right time. This allusion to the work of salvation being accomplished just as it needed to be will further encourage Timothy (and all pastors) in their work of ministry.

---

433. *DPL* 202.
434. Matt 27:11; Mark 15:2; Luke 23:3; John 18:36–37; 19:11.
435. Matt 27:12–14; Mark 15:4–5; Luke 23:9; John 19:9.

As he draws near to the end of this letter and with these thoughts of the work of Jesus fresh in his mind, the apostle is led into an ascription of the praiseworthy attributes of Christ. The phrases "blessed and only sovereign," "king of those who are having kingship," and "lord of those who are having lordship" are essentially synonymous. Each designates Christ Jesus as the one and only head over all things.

The phrase "who alone has immortality" is not only about who Christ is but also about what he has done. The term "immortality" points to his resurrection from the dead. His resurrection not only exalts him above all creation (Eph 1:20–23) but also is his victory over death for the benefit of mankind (1 Cor 15:19–21).

Paul says of Christ that he dwells in "unapproachable light." This is another of the attestations of the deity of Christ found in the Pastoral Letters.[436]

The apostle adds that the only sovereign is one "whom no one among men has seen nor is able to see." Mere mortals cannot see Jesus Christ risen from the dead in his body, not because he is invisible but because he at present is not visibly present; he is hidden but not absent.[437]

Paul draws this ascription of praiseworthy attributes and deeds of Christ to a close by noting that he is worthy of honor and might, two terms that are found in other doxologies in the New Testament (Rev 5:12–13). The apostle concludes with an "amen," a term he uses at the end of doxologies addressed to God the Father as well as to Jesus Christ (see textual notes). Such a doxology addressed to Christ is another attestation of his deity.

Timothy's Obligation to Irreproachable Ministry: 1 Timothy 6:11–16 in Context

Paul had stepped away from his exhortation to Timothy to teach the truth (6:2b–5) in order to give some instruction regarding true profit (6:6–10). In the present section he resumes his directives to his coworker, after which he will again have something to say about wealth and its proper use (6:17–19).

The apostle instructs Timothy to flee what is harmful to his salvation and to his ministry and to pursue those things that will benefit him.

---

436. See the commentary at 1 Tim 1:17 and Titus 2:13.
437. Refer to n417.

In this way his coworker will lay hold of eternal salvation and will keep his ministry irreproachable.

To this end Paul reminds Timothy of the good confession of faith made at his own baptism and of the good confession made by his Lord before Pontius Pilate. This leads the apostle to conclude with a glorious proclamation of the person and the works of the "king of those who are having kingship and lord of those who are having lordship."

6:17–19: True Riches for the Rich

TRANSLATION

¹⁷ Direct those who are rich in this age not to be high-minded nor to put their hope in the uncertainty of riches but in God, who richly bestows all things to us for our enjoyment, ¹⁸ to do what is good, to be rich in good works, to be generous, and to share, ¹⁹ thereby storing up for themselves a good foundation for the future, in order that they might lay hold of what is really life.

TEXTUAL NOTES

6:17 παράγγελλε—"Direct" (παράγγελλε) is a strong word.[438] It is a verb that Paul uses frequently in this letter (1:3; 4:11; 5:7; 6:13), often as an imperative.

παρέχοντι—This is not the customary NT term for "give" (δίδωμι) but one much less often used.[439] Therefore, I have rendered it with a less common synonym for give: "bestow."

πλούτου ἀδηλότητι—The genitive πλούτου is a genitive of quality; thus, "in riches, which are uncertain."[440]

6:17–18 πλουσίοις . . . πλούτου . . . πλουσίως . . . πλουτεῖν—Paul uses two different cognate nouns, a cognate adverb, and a cognate verb ("rich . . . riches . . . richly . . . to be rich"), making an extended play on words.

---

438. See 1 Tim 5:7; 6:13, 17; 2 Thess 3:4, 6, 10, 12.
439. Note the respective number of uses of each verb: BDAG 242–43, 776–77.
440. BDF 91 [§ 165].

6:18 εὐμεταδότους ... κοινωνικούς—The apostle uses two different words for "generous"; that being the case, I have chosen to translate them with two different English phrases ("to be generous, and to share").

6:19 ἐπιλάβωνται τῆς ὄντως ζωῆς—Paul uses very similar language in his directive to Timothy in 6:12.

COMMENTARY

Paul has not lost his train of thought. From 5:1 to 6:2a he has dealt with the responsibilities of Christians in their various vocations. In the section that runs from 6:2b to 6:5 he directs his comments to Timothy's responsibilities in his vocation as a pastor. In that section he contrasts true teaching with false, one of the features of false teaching being the attitude that godliness is a means to profit. That leads him into a section of the letter (6:6–10) in which he expounds upon the true profit of true godliness, contrasting that with the love of money. From there he returns to a consideration of true ministry. Upon concluding that he takes up the present section, where he returns to the subject of riches with his instruction to those who are rich in the things of this world as to their responsibilities in their "vocation" of managing the wealth with which God has blessed them.

In connection with the previous section on money (6:6–10) it was noted that there is nothing inherently sinful about being well-to-do and that there are examples of believers in the Scriptures who were wealthy. The fact that the apostle has occasion here to address those "who are rich in this age" demonstrates also that the early Christians did not come exclusively from the lower classes of ancient society. The Christian faith did not appeal only to societal outcasts; its message was for all and had a benefit for all.

Pride and the love of money, of course, are special temptations for those who are wealthy. Hence, Paul appeals to them to display the humility of setting their hope on God (6:17; cf. 4:10; 5:5). "Hope" is a word about the future (see the entry by that name in the Extended Notes). By setting their hope on God, they, like all believers, will "store up for themselves a good foundation for the future" and will, like Timothy (6:12), "lay hold of what is really life."

Wealthy Christians, because of their wealth, are in a position to accomplish good things for the ministry of Christ's church, hence the apostle's exhortation to them to be generous and to share. Readers of this commentary will probably be able to think of at least one instance in which a Christian of means enhanced the mission and ministry of the church with a substantial monetary gift.[441]

The service of the rich to Christ's church is not to be confined to their monetary gifts to Christ's mission. Paul also directs them to be rich in good works. Wealthy believers serve their savior not only with their funds but with every aspect of their lives.

We ought not pass by Paul's observation that God is the one "who richly bestows all things to us for our enjoyment." All good things come from the creator. Christians are able to *enjoy* these things, recognizing them as gifts from God.

True Riches for the Rich: 1 Timothy 6:17–19 in Context

As he draws nearer to the end of his letter, Paul has occasion to alternate between discussions of ministry and directives about this-worldly matters. After speaking about the role and responsibilities of various age groups (5:1–2), of widows and those in the order of widows (5:3–16), and of elders (pastors) in the church (5:17–25), he gives instruction about the relations between slaves and masters (6:1–2a). He follows with teaching to Timothy about his obligation to teach the truth over against error (6:2b–5); mention of one particular vice of the errorists leads him to comment on earthly wealth and the Christian's responsibilities toward it (6:6–10). Returning to concerns about the ministry he exhorts Timothy regarding irreproachable ministry (6:11–16) before offering some final directives about earthly wealth to those Christians who have been blessed with a great deal of it (6:17–19).

---

441. One such example is noted in the editor's preface to Deterding, *Colossians*, x.

6:20–21: Concluding Exhortation to Timothy

TRANSLATION

²⁰ O Timothy, guard what has been entrusted [to you], turning away from the corrupt, meaningless talk and the contradictions of what is falsely named knowledge; ²¹ by professing this some [have] missed the mark concerning the faith.

Grace be with [all of] you.

TEXTUAL NOTES

6:20 Ὦ Τιμόθεε—Whenever Paul uses this particular grammatical form, an omega with or without a vocative,[442] he speaks with great emphasis and emotion,[443] more so than when he uses the simple vocative case.[444] In this way he here emphasizes the importance of what he is about to say.

παραθήκην—The apostle has used the cognate verb in this letter (1:18) and will do so again in his next Letter to Timothy (2:2) to speak of entrusting the work (and office) of the ministry. That work and office is what his younger coworker is to guard.

φύλαξον—This verb can mean "protect" (2 Tim 1:14), "watch out for" (2 Tim 4:15), or "observe, follow" (1 Tim 5:21). While the first meaning is certainly the prime connotation here, in the context of the entire

---

442. In addition to the present passage, Rom 2:1, 3; 9:20; Gal 3:1; 1 Tim 6:11; see also Acts 13:10. In all of these passages he is addressing some person or persons. In Rom 11:33, another emphatic, emotional declaration, the apostle uses an omega (Ὦ) without any accompanying vocative simply as an exclamation (in English typically rendered "Oh" rather than "O"), without addressing any particular person.

443. BDF 81 [§ 146 (1)].

444. See, for example, 1 Cor 7:16 and Phlm 20.

letter, the latter two definitions seem to be involved as well. Timothy is to protect his ministry by watching out for threats to it from false teaching and by observing and following the truth of God's word.

ἐκτρεπόμενος—Paul uses this verb elsewhere (1 Tim 1:6; 5:15; 2 Tim 4:4) of turning away from the truth to follow heresy and Satan. Here he uses it to denote turning away from error to follow the truth. In order to hold to the truth one must turn away from error.

βεβήλους κενοφνίας—The apostle uses the same phrase in 2 Tim 2:16.

βεβήλους—Other uses of this adjective (1 Tim 1:9; 2 Tim 2:16) and its cognate verb (Matt 12:5; Acts 24:6) suggest that this talk is not merely "worthless" but is "corrupt, desecrated"; beyond being worthless, it is actually harmful.

κενοφνίας—Etymologically this word means "empty sound." The false teaching is all sound but no substance, at least no substance that is beneficial.

ἀντιθέσεις—The English word derived from this term implies the refutation and rejection of contrary teaching. The implication here is that this teaching is something that is contrary to the truth. The term here is singular, but it would pertain to all the false teachings of the heretics.

ψευδωνύμου γνώσεως—The heretics gave the name "knowledge" to their teaching, or they at least described it as such; however, that claim was false. See further "The Nature of the Heresy" in the Introduction to the Pastoral Letters.

6:21 τινες ἐπαγγελλόμενοι—The term "professing" (ἐπαγγελλόμενοι) indicates that those referred to here are not simply holding to some error; they are actively *promoting* it.

περὶ τὴν πίστιν ἠστόχησαν—The phrase "the faith" refers to the content of the Christian faith (*fides quae creditur*), but the implication here is also that the false teachers are also lacking in saving faith (*fides qua creditur*). See further the entry "Faith" in the Extended Notes. The translation "missed the mark" for ἠστόχησαν attempts to capture the nuance of the verb used. That these false teachers have missed the mark concerning "the faith" means that they are outside the saving faith altogether. Paul also uses a form of the verb ἠστόχησαν in 1:6; therefore, these two occurrences serve as a sort of *inclusio* for the entire letter.

χάρις—On this significant NT term see the entry "Grace" in the Extended Notes.

ὑμῶν—This is the second person plural pronoun—in Southern American slang "all y'all." This indicates that Paul intends for this letter to be read publicly within and to the congregations. See further the commentary.

COMMENTARY

Timothy's Further Instruction

Paul begins this concluding section of his letter by addressing Timothy directly. The vocative case introduced by an omega is relatively rare in the apostle's letters (see the textual notes); its use here helps to emphasize the importance he places on this concluding exhortation.

From Paul's letters we learn that he used a scribe (an amanuensis) for the actual writing of his epistles (Rom 16:22) but would write something in his own hand near the letter's conclusion.[445] That practice and the great emotion that he displays here makes it all but certain that he wrote this in his own hand.[446]

Paul has both a positive directive that Timothy is to follow and a warning about something that he is to avoid. What has been "entrusted" to him is the office of the ministry. He is to "guard" this by carrying it out in accord with God's word—as he has been instructed to do at a number of places in this letter. In light of the participle that follows (ἐκτρεπόμενος), he is also to "guard" his ministry by protecting it from contamination by false teaching.[447]

It is necessary for a pastor to proclaim the truth. However, to be a true pastor, he must also avoid (and refute) false teaching (Titus 1:9).

An Evaluation of the Heresy

This is perhaps the most direct and explicit description in this letter of the heresy troubling Timothy's churches. The apostle characterizes it in several ways.

He states that it is talk that is both meaningless and corrupt. The teachings of the heretics may have sounded appealing and profound, but

---

445. 1 Cor 16:21; Gal 6:11; Col 4:18; Phlm 19; and especially 2 Thess 3:17.
446. Kelly, *Pastoral Epistles*, 150, comes to the same conclusion.
447. As noted by Luther (AE 28:381–82).

these were actually meaningless.[448] Even worse, because they were false, they were corrupt; they actually did harm to those who would follow them.

Paul also dubs the heresy "contradictions." This noun designates the false teaching as contrary to the truth.

The apostle finishes his evaluation by saying that it is falsely named "knowledge." This points to the false teaching being an earlier form of the heresy of Gnosticism, against which a number of early church fathers had to do battle. When Paul terms it "falsely named," the language that he uses here suggests that the false teachers themselves actually used the term "knowledge" (γνῶσις) to designate their philosophy/theology. By calling it "contradictions" of his teaching, the apostle shows that the only true theological teaching is that which is in harmony with what he, as an apostle of the Lord Jesus Christ, sets forth in this letter. See further the entry "Apostle" in the Extended Notes and "The Nature of the Heresy" in the Introduction to the Pastoral Letters.

A Final Word

Paul concludes this letter with a blessing of "grace" (on which see the entry by that name in the Extended Notes). It is significant that in this letter addressed to one of his fellow ministers, he offers it to all the believers, as indicated by his use of the second person *plural* pronoun.

This would indicate that the apostle intended for this letter to be read publicly, as part of congregational worship, as was the case with other of his letters.[449] What is written in this letter concerns matters of the pastoral ministry, but these are matters with which also lay Christians may and should be interested and involved.

In many cases pastors have had the opportunity for an in-depth theological education.[450] In many cases they are able to make their living by the gospel,[451] and so are able to devote "work time" rather than only "their own time" to the study of God's word. This means that all other

---

448. Kelly, *Pastoral Epistles*, 150, describes it as "pseudo-theological jargon."

449. Kelly, *Pastoral Epistles*, 42 ("He expects it to be read out publicly... and then to be preserved in the church's archives"). See, for example, Col 4:16 and 1 Thess 5:27; see also "The Authority of the Pauline Letters" in Deterding, *Colossians*, 192–94.

450. See the commentary on 1 Tim 4:14.

451. See the commentary on 1 Tim 5:17–18.

things being equal, a pastor is in a better position to comprehend and to judge doctrine than the lay Christian.

That being said, the learning and discerning of Christian doctrine is not the exclusive purview of the clergy. This is also of interest and concern to the laity; also their religious and spiritual wellbeing is at stake; it is benefited by true teaching and endangered by falsehood. In the current twenty-first-century context lay Christians are far more likely to be well educated than was perhaps the case in some times past.

Thus, also the laity have the privilege and the obligation to be well informed about the Scriptures, that they may be able to judge between truth and error. It is their privilege and obligation to search out churches and pastors who teach the whole truth of the Scriptures and to "turn away from" those who do not. In some cases it might even be incumbent upon them to correct pastors who are not proclaiming the whole truth of God's word. For all of these reasons Paul offers a blessing of "grace" to all those in the churches served by Timothy.

That word "grace," therefore, forms an *inclusio* to this letter. As the apostle began this epistle with a blessing of grace (1:2), he ends it in the same way (6:21), as he does in all of his letters.[452] He lets the grace of God have the first and the last word, for the grace of God is the source of our salvation.[453]

Concluding Exhortation to Timothy: 1 Timothy 6:20–21 in Context

Paul offers a two-part conclusion to this letter. He offers a final exhortation to Timothy to be committed to a ministry that is faithful to the truth. He also sends a final blessing of "grace" to all the members of all of Timothy's churches. That pastors carry out a faithful, orthodox ministry is not only their personal concern; all Christians, for their own spiritual wellbeing, have a right and an obligation to know that their pastors are teaching the truth.

---

452. Salutations: Rom 1:7; 1 Cor 1:3; 2 Cor 1:2; Gal 1:3; Eph 1:2; Phil 1:2; Col 1:2; 1 Thess 1:1; 2 Thess 1:2; 1 Tim 1:2; 2 Tim 1:2; Titus 1:4; Phlm 3. Farewell blessings: Rom 16:20; 1 Cor 16:23; 2 Cor 13:14; Gal 6:18; Eph 6:24; Phil 4:23; Col 4:18; 1 Thess 5:28; 2 Thess 3:18; 1 Tim 6:21; 2 Tim 4:22; Titus 3:15; Phlm 25.

453. *DPL* 374.

Introduction to Titus

RECIPIENT

The present letter is addressed "to Titus," whom Paul identifies as "my genuine child in accord with a common faith" (1:4). Our knowledge of him from the New Testament comes entirely from the apostle's letters.

Chronologically the earliest interactions of Paul and Titus that are referred to in the Scriptures occurred in connection with the apostle's second (famine) visit to Jerusalem (AD 46).[1] Of that visit Paul writes that fourteen years after his calling on the road to Damascus he and Barnabas went up to Jerusalem, taking Titus along with them (Gal 2:1).[2]

Titus is identified as a Greek (Gal 2:3), that is, unlike Timothy, he had no Jewish ancestry.[3] That being the case, in spite of some pressure to the contrary, the apostle refused to have Titus, a gentile, submit to the rite of circumcision, as he had done in the case of Timothy.[4]

Paul speaks of this Greek as "my genuine child in accord with a common faith." This would indicate that it was through the ministry of the apostle that Titus was brought to the Christian faith.[5] That and his having come with Paul from Antioch (Gal 2:1) would point to Titus being among those who had come to the Christian faith through the apostle's time in ministry there (Acts 11:25–26; 13:1) and perhaps to

---

1. See the "Chronology of Paul's Life" in the Introduction to the Pastoral Letters.

2. On the identity of the visit of Gal 2 with the famine visit of Acts 11:27–30; 12:25, see Hoerber, "Galatians 2:1–10," 482–91.

3. On the ethnic heritage of Timothy, see Acts 16:1.

4. On the rationale for the circumcision of Timothy, see "Recipient" in the Introduction to Timothy in this commentary.

5. Kelly, *Pastoral Epistles*, 228, comes to a similar conclusion.

his being among the Greeks of Antioch to whom the gospel had been proclaimed (Acts 11:20).[6]

Unlike its record of the presence of Timothy, the book of Acts tells us nothing about any ministerial work of Titus alongside of Paul. Nevertheless, 2 Corinthians does contain several references to him (see the following). These include one (8:23) in which the apostle speaks of Titus as "my partner and fellow worker" and another (8:16) in which Paul states that this coworker has the same concern for the Christians at Corinth that he himself had. That and the witness of the Letter to Titus that the apostle entrusted Titus with supervision of ministry in Crete (see below) strongly suggests that Titus was involved with Paul in mission and ministry during much of the latter's career.

From the apostle's two letters to the Corinthians and the book of Acts we can piece together the contacts of Titus with the Christians of Corinth. From the second of the letters to Corinth we learn that Titus was also involved with Paul in his interactions with that church.

During his three-year ministry in Ephesus (Acts 19:1–10) during his third missionary journey (Acts 18:23—21:16) the apostle penned the letter we know as 1 Corinthians, likely in AD 54.[7] At the conclusion of his time in Ephesus he made his way to Macedonia by way of Troas, a city in the northwest corner of the Roman province of Asia. The fact that he did not find Titus in Troas (2 Cor 2:13) must have been due to the latter being occupied with ministry elsewhere.

---

6. The textual evidence at Acts 11:20 is divided between Ἕλληνας, "Greeks," and Ἑλληνιστάς, "Hellenists," that is, Jews who used Greek as their language, probably as their language in worship. However, the context calls for "Greeks," that is, gentiles. Hellenists had been present in the church since the earliest days (Acts 6:1), when its witness was still confined to "Jerusalem," that is, to their fellow Jews (Acts 1:1—6:7 in light of 1:8). By chapter 11 the narrative of Acts has moved beyond the witness to the Jews (1:1—6:7) and even beyond that to the Samaritans (6:8—9:31 in light of 1:8). With 9:32 the record moves beyond those to the outreach to the end of the earth, that is, to the gentiles (Acts 9:32—28:31 in light of 1:8). By the time of the events recounted in Acts 11 it would not have been noteworthy that there were some who were speaking the gospel of the Lord Jesus to Greek-speaking Jews. Instead, the contrast is between those who were speaking the word only to their fellow Jews (Acts 11:19) and those who began to evangelize Greeks, that is, gentiles. Acts 11:20 is a part of the record of the spread of the gospel beyond the Jews and even beyond the "half-Jews," that is, the Samaritans, to the gentiles, to all nations, to the end of the earth (1:8).

7. Lockwood, *1 Corinthians*, 15, prefers AD 55 but notes that some opt for 54. Barrett, *First Corinthians*, 5, puts the letter in 54 or possibly late 53.

INTRODUCTION TO TITUS

While in Macedonia Paul wrote the letter we known as 2 Corinthians.[8] From that letter we learn that the apostle had sent Titus to Corinth (8:16–17; 12:18); among the reasons for this mission was to give encouragement to the Corinthians in participating in the collection of funds for the church at Jerusalem.[9] This same letter indicates that the Corinthians had refreshed the spirit of Titus, suggesting that his ministry there had been graciously received (7:13; see also 12:18). News of this, in turn, brought encouragement to Paul himself, when Titus returned to report on his activities there (7:6, 13).

Near the end of his Second Letter to Timothy (4:10), Paul reports that Titus had gone to Dalmatia. The context of this statement would indicate that unlike Demas, who had deserted the apostle, Titus had gone to Dalmatia for ministry (see the commentary on 2 Tim 4:9–15).

SETTING AND DATE

See further the "Chronology of Paul's Life" in the Introduction to the Pastoral Letters.

The book of Acts concludes with the note that Paul's imprisonment in Rome lasted two years. Since the narrative of the book emphasizes that the charges against him were without merit, the implication is that the imprisonment came to an end with his vindication and release.[10]

As indicated in the Introduction to the Pastoral Letters, from Rome the apostle may well have traveled to Spain, from Spain to Crete, from Crete to Ephesus, and from Ephesus to Macedonia. His Letter to Titus indicates that Paul left Titus in Crete as he moved on to Ephesus.

The island of Crete was an important link for seagoing trade in the Mediterranean. Consequently, it would also be exposed to a variety of religious and philosophical beliefs. For both of these reasons it is understandable that the apostle would have been interested in bringing the gospel of Jesus Christ to that place.[11]

---

8. Bruce, *New Testament History*, 326, 330–31; Bruce, *Paul*, 317–18.

9. 2 Cor 8:6 in light of the entire chapter. On the collection organized by Paul for the Christians at Jerusalem, see Bruce, *Paul*, 319–24.

10. See the subsection "The Historical Setting" of the section "Authenticity and Integrity" in the Introduction to the Pastoral Letters.

11. Towner, *Letters*, 678.

In this scenario Paul would have been released from his first Roman imprisonment in AD 61. The present Letter to Titus would have been composed in the neighborhood of AD 65.

PURPOSE

Titus 1:5 indicates the purpose of this letter: "For this reason I left you in Crete, in order that you would set right the things that are lacking and appoint elders town by town, just as I commanded you." The apostle lays out qualifications for the pastoral office (1:5–9). Paul notes that the circumstances of life in Crete provide special challenges for ministry there (1:10–16).

The apostle follows this with sketches of standards of conduct for various vocations among Christians (2:1–10). Other directives for Christian living are interspersed in the remainder of the letter (3:1–3, 8–11).

Related to this are two significant kerygmatic sections of the epistle (2:11–15; 3:4–7). These offer both powerful proclamation of the way of salvation and also provide power and motivation for living according to the ethical directives given in the letter.

From all of this we can see two related purposes to this epistle. Titus is to supervise a ministry faithful to the word of God and centered in the justifying and sanctifying message of the gospel. As a part of this he is to see to it that pastors able to minister in this way are provided for the churches in Crete.[12]

OUTLINE

The salutation of this letter (1:1–4) serves as a sort of "overture" to the work.[13] As the overture of an opera[14] introduces themes that will have a

---

12. Luther (AE 29:3) holds a similar view: "The Epistle to Titus is short, but it is a kind of epitome and summary of other, wordier epistles. . . . Paul is the sort of teacher who is engaged most of all in these two topics, either teaching or exhorting. Moreover, he never exhorts in such a way that he fails to mingle didactic, that is, doctrinal, instruction with it. . . . By his teaching he sets down what is to be believed by faith, and by his exhortation he sets down what is to be done. Thus by doctrine he builds up faith, by exhortation he builds up life."

13. Refer to the table on page 214 and the segment "One Servant of the Word to Another: Titus 1:1–4 in Context" at the end of the next section.

14. Such as the rock opera "Tommy" by The Who. The tracks "I Am The Sea" and "Quadrophenia" from the band's album *Quadrophenia* serve the same purpose.

prominent role in the remainder of the work, so these verses first touch on themes that will be expounded upon in greater depth in the remainder of the letter.[15]

This salutation/overture leads into the body of the work. From this understanding the following outline emerges:

I. Salutation/Overture: One Servant of the Word to Another (1:1–4)

II. Life in the Church (1:5—3:11)

    A. Requirements for Pastors (1:5–9)

    B. Dealing with False Teaching (1:10–16)

    C. Life in Vocation (2:1–10)

    D. The Power for Godly Living (2:11–15)

    E. The Life of the Justified (3:1–11)

III. Concluding Matters (3:12–15)

---

15. I would also consider that 1 Tim 1:1–17 and 2 Tim 1:3–18 function as "overtures" to those letters; see "Outline" in the Introduction to 1 Timothy and "Outline" in the Introduction to 2 Timothy. In a similar way Col 1:3–20 serves as an overture to that letter; see Deterding, *Colossians*, 26–27. Similarly, Eph 1:3–14 functions in the same way in that epistle (Scharlemann, "Secret of God's Plan," 538–39).

Commentary on Titus

1:1–4: One Servant of the Word to Another

On the salutations in Paul's letters see the section "Salutations in Paul's Letters" in the Introduction to the Pastoral Letters. As noted in the "Introduction to Titus" above, this salutation serves as a sort of "overture" to the rest of the letter. Refer to the table below and also to the segment "One Servant of the Word to Another: Titus 1:1–4 in Context" at the end of this section.

Theme	Salutation/Overture	Other References
Savior/Salvation	1:3, 4	2:10, 11, 13–14; 3:4–7
Proclamation/Ministry	1:1, 3	1:5–9, 13–14; 2:1, 7–8, 15
Truth Versus Error	1:1	1:9, 10–11, 14; 2:1, 7; 3:9–11
Faith	1:1, 4	1:6, 13; 2:2, 10; 3:8
Godliness	1:1	1:15–16; 2:1–10, 12; 3:1–2, 8, 14
Time and History	1:2, 3	2:11; 3:4
Hope/Eternal Life	1:2	2:13; 3:7

TRANSLATION

[1] Paul, slave of God, apostle of Jesus Christ for the faith of God's elect ones and the knowledge of the truth that is in accord with godliness, [2] for the hope of eternal life, which God, who does not lie, promised before eternal times, [3] and made known at just the right time by the proclamation of his word, with which I was entrusted according to the authority of God our savior, [4] to Titus, my genuine child in accord with a common faith, grace and peace from God the Father and Christ Jesus our savior.

COMMENTARY ON TITUS

TEXTUAL NOTES

1:1 δοῦλος θεοῦ—The institution of slavery in the first-century Roman world was complex and in significant ways different from its practice in the antebellum United States.[16] Here the term is plainly used in a metaphorical sense (cf. Rom 1:1; Phil 1:1). The use here recalls the designation "my servants [δοῦλοι] the prophets" for God's OT spokesman.[17] That Paul is a "slave" of God means that he is entirely dependent on God, which is a good thing. Its pairing here with "apostle" means that the term here is to be understood with reference to his ministry.

ἀπόστολος—See the entry on "Apostle" in the Extended Notes.

κατὰ πίστιν ἐκλεκτῶν θεοῦ καὶ ἐπίγνωσιν ἀληθείας—The preposition κατά here has the meaning "for"; cf. John 2:6.[18] In this context πίστιν ("faith") and ἐπίγνωσιν ("knowledge") are synonyms. The apostle uses two terms here to denote two different aspects of saving faith; see the commentary. The term "faith" here refers to the act of believing (*fides qua creditur*); see further the entry "Faith" in the Extended Notes. The term ἐκλεκτῶν ("elect ones") is a subjective genitive[19] (the elect ones are those who believe/have faith); ἀληθείας ("truth") is an objective genitive[20] (the truth is what God's elect ones know/believe). Thus, "knowledge of the truth" is the same as "faith" as the content of faith (*fides quae creditur*).

τῆς κατ' εὐσέβειαν—Faith/knowledge will show itself in the believer's present existence by a life of εὐσέβειαν ("godliness"); see further the entry "Godliness" in the Extended Notes.

1:2 ἐπ' ἐλπίδι ζωῆς αἰωνίου—As faith/knowledge produces "godliness" in the believer's present life, so the future outcome of faith/knowledge is eternal life. This, in turn, means that the believer's existence in this life is also characterized by hope, on which see further the entry "Hope" in the Extended Notes.

ὁ ἀψευδὴς θεός—For the assertion that "God ... does not lie" see also Num 23:19; Rom 3:4; Heb 6:18.

---

16. For a brief survey, see "Slavery in Bible Times" in Harstad, *Deuteronomy*, 448–51. See further the entry "Slavery in the New Testament World" in the Extended Notes.

17. See 2 Kgs (LXX 4 Kingdoms) 9:7; 17:13; Jer 7:25; 26:5 (LXX 33:5); 29:19 (missing from the LXX); 35:15 (LXX 42:15); 44:4 (LXX 51:4); Ezek 38:17; Zech 1:6.

18. Knight, *Pastoral Epistles*, 283.

19. Wallace, *Greek Grammar*, 113n3.

20. Wallace, *Greek Grammar*, 116–17.

πρὸ χρόνων αἰωνίων—In ordinary conversation we would say simply "from eternity." Cf. Rom 16:25; 2 Tim 1:9.

1:3 ἐφανέρωσεν ... τὸν λόγον αὐτοῦ ἐν κηρύγματι—Although the grammar is rough,[21] the sense is clear. Both the relative pronoun ἥν (1:2), "which," referring to the "hope of eternal life," and τὸν λόγον αὐτοῦ, "his word," are objects of the verb ἐφανέρωσεν, "made known." The hope of eternal life is made known by the proclamation of God's word.

καιροῖς ἰδίοις—A different word for "time" is used here than what occurred in the previous verse; it emphasizes that God acted according to his own timetable, at his own "right time."[22]

κηρύγματι—This word for the content of what is proclaimed is cognate to the noun κῆρυξ ("herald," "proclaimer") and the verb κηρύσσω ("proclaim"). Even in the use of this word group in secular Greek there is an emphasis on the message being faithfully delivered as given to the proclaimer, for the message does not originate with the proclaimer but with the one who sent/authorized him.[23] The word group can be used in a general sense of some message other than the gospel of salvation, as in Luke 12:3[24] and 1 Pet 3:19 (contrast the use of εὐηγγελίσθη in 4:6), also by Paul (Rom 2:21; Gal 5:11). However, for the most part, as here, the apostle uses the word group to refer to the proclamation of the message of salvation.[25]

ἐπιστεύθην—Paul often speaks of himself or of other proclaimers of the word being "entrusted" with the word that they proclaim.[26] Thus, the message is not theirs but God's. This indicates both that they must proclaim it in faithful adherence to that word and also that by speaking God's word their proclamation has the authority (see following note) and power of God himself.

κατ' ἐπιταγὴν—This term often refers to a "command" or "order."[27] However, in Titus 2:15 it means "authority."[28] This suggests that in the

---

21. BDF 246 (§ 469).
22. Wallace, *Greek Grammar*, 157.
23. *TDNT* 3:687-88.
24. *TDNT* 3:705.
25. κήρυγμα: Rom 16:25; 1 Cor 1:21; 2:4; 15:4; 2 Tim 4:17; κῆρυξ: 1 Tim 2:7; 2 Tim 1:11; κηρύσσω: Rom 10:8, 14, 15; 1 Cor 1:23; 9:27; 15:11; 2 Cor 1:19; 4:5; Gal 2:2; Col 1:23; 1 Thess 2:9; 1 Tim 3:16; 2 Tim 4:2.
26. 1 Cor 9:17; Gal 2:7; 1 Thess 2:4; 1 Tim 1:11; 6:20; 2 Tim 1:12, 14; Titus 1:3.
27. See BDAG 383 on ἐπιταγή and ἐπιτάσσω.
28. BDAG 383.

present verse it is better rendered "authority"; Paul's proclamation is carried out not on his own but by the authority of God our savior himself.[29]

τοῦ σωτῆρος ἡμῶν—This term is used here of God [the Father] and in the next verse of Christ Jesus. This points to the mutual involvement of both the Father and the Son in the work of salvation and also gives a Trinitarian cast to the entire letter (the Holy Spirit is explicitly mentioned in 3:5). See also the entry "Save, Savior, Salvation" in the Extended Notes and also the essay "He Saved Us: The Pastoral Letters on the Way of Salvation" elsewhere in this commentary.

1:4 Τίτῳ—See "Recipient" in the Introduction to Titus.

γνησίῳ τέκνῳ—The apostle describes Timothy with the same term (1 Tim 1:2). Timothy had been raised by his mother and grandmother in the faith of the Old Testament (2 Tim 1:5). Timothy was from Lystra, a town to which Paul himself had first brought the Christian gospel (Acts 14:6–23; 16:1–3), so that the apostle could rightly claim him as his "child" both as a Christian believer and as a laborer in the gospel.[30] As Titus was a Greek and not a Jew (Gal 2:1–3) this reference to him as Paul's "genuine child" would denote him as one brought by the apostle both to saving faith and to ministry in the gospel.

When used as a term of address to one other than a biological child, this word expresses affection (Matt 9:2; Mark 2:5). It is a term of address from teacher/master to student;[31] it is used this way several times in the Pastoral Letters.[32]

κοινὴν πίστιν—On the possible referents of both "common" and "faith" see the commentary.

χάρις . . . ἡμῶν—A phrase similar to this is found at the end of the salutations of all of the Pauline Letters. In Paul's letters these are always lacking a verb. Similar phrases in the salutations of other NT letters (1 Pet 1:2; 2 Pet 1:2; Jude 2; 2 John 3) always supply a verb. This suggests the possibility that this style of phrase originated with Paul, and that in

---

29. Similarly Luther (AE 29:13): "By delegation, something with which he has been commissioned. He wants to say that every herald ought to bring a mandate, a command, an order that is issued; there must be a mandate, an authority, or a right to instruct and teach, as the lawyers say. 'I have a mandate to preach. God the Savior has given me this mandate.'"

30. Kelly (*Pastoral Epistles*, 228) comes to a similar conclusion. See the commentary on 1 Tim 4:14 and 6:12.

31. BDAG 994-95.

32. See also 1 Tim 1:2, 18; 2 Tim 1:2; 2:1.

"copying" him other authors felt the need to add a verb.[33] In the Pauline phrases some verbal action is clearly implied, something along the lines of "may there be." With these phrases the apostle is pronouncing a blessing on his readers, one that actually delivers the "grace and peace" that is spoken of. On the meaning of each of these terms, see the entries on them in the Extended Notes.

COMMENTARY

Slave and Apostle

In this salutation Paul identifies himself as a "slave of God" and an "apostle of Jesus Christ," and he speaks of being entrusted with God's word by the "authority of God our savior." At first blush the notion of his being a slave seems incompatible with the authority of an apostle, but on closer inspection we see that they are in perfect harmony with one another.

The distinguishing characteristic of an apostle is the authority with which he speaks (see the entry on "Apostle" in the Extended Notes). However, this authority is not the individual's own; rather, it is a derived authority. The authority wielded by an apostle is the authority of the one whom he represents; in Paul's case this is Jesus Christ. In order to speak with the authority of the one who sent him, an ἀπόστολος had to subordinate his will completely to that of the sender, which is precisely what Paul indicates in this salutation, when he identifies himself as a slave of God. Paul's slavery to God was the source of the authority with which he speaks.

Paul's apostolic ministry, therefore, provides a paradigm for all who hold the pastoral office. A pastor will carry out his preaching and ministry only as he subordinates his ministry entirely to the authority of God, which is to be found in the apostolic word of the Scriptures (see also the commentary on 2 Tim 3:14–17).

Time and Salvation

In this salutation the apostle uses three designations of time. These are "before eternal times," "at his own right times," and "the hope of eternal life."

---

33. Wallace, *Greek Grammar*, 51.

The phrase "before eternal times" indicates that the God who does not lie promised salvation from eternity. This assertion is in harmony with many similar statements in the Scriptures concerning the eternal origin of salvation.[34] Eternal salvation was no afterthought or "Plan B" on God's part; he planned it from before the creation of time. From eternity God chose individuals to be saved through faith in Christ; that is the "faith of God's elect ones" of which Paul speaks in 1:1.

This salvation was made known "at the right times." The plural form of this phrase suggests that the apostle is referring to multiple instances of God's plan of salvation being made known. This would include various prophecies, typologies, and other adumbrations of Christ and his saving work that are dispersed throughout the Hebrew Scriptures, culminating in the saving work of Jesus Christ.

The expression "at the right times" is somewhat reminiscent of the apostle's assertion that God sent his Son "in the fullness of time" (Gal 4:4), and that God's saving work in Christ was in accord with his plan for the fullness of the times (Eph 1:10). Thus, the ministry of Christ was when the time was fulfilled (Mark 1:15) and when the hour for accomplishing the plan of salvation had come (John 12:23; 13:1; 17:1).

Paul continues with the note that at God's own right times the Almighty made known the promise of eternal life "by the proclamation of his word." God's gift of salvation remains hidden and unattainable until he makes it known through his word (Eph 3:8–10; Col 1:25–27), the word with which the apostle himself had been entrusted and which he proclaimed.

Thus, God's eternal plan of salvation remained unknown until it was made known through the incarnation of Christ and through the proclamation about Christ. Paul sets forth this same idea elsewhere in his letters, when he writes of the "mystery" that has been revealed, on which refer to "The Mystery of Godliness" in the commentary on 1 Tim 3:14–16.

The salvation that God promised before eternal times and which was made known in his own right times is the gift of eternal life. This means that the believer's future is secure and is a source of hope for the future.

Thus, the promise of salvation spans past, present, and future. It was planned and promised before the creation of time. It was revealed at a point in time, namely, the ministry of Christ. It continues to be made

---

34. Rom 8:29–30; 9:23; Eph 1:3–6; 2 Tim 1:9.

known whenever God's word is proclaimed. Because it is a promise of eternal life, the believer has a glorious and endless future.

Along these same lines see the section "Time and History" in the commentary on Titus 2:11–15.[35]

Proclamation and Ministry

It is significant that in this letter to a fellow pastor regarding his ministry the apostle speaks of his own ministry. In this way he offers himself as a paradigm of ministry to his younger coworker (and to all who would hold the pastoral office).

In speaking of his being "entrusted" with the proclamation of the word, Paul shows that this is a task that mankind neither creates nor enters by human means. The ways in which men enter into the office of the ministry vary from place to place, from age to age, and in many other particulars. However, ultimately no man takes this task on himself; rather, it is God who entrusts a pastor with the task of proclaiming his word.

This salutation emphasizes the truth of the word that is proclaimed. The apostle identifies the message as "the truth," emphasizing this by stating that God "does not lie."[36] This assertion stands in dramatic contrast both to the sad reality that "Cretans are always liars" (1:12) and the universally accepted fact that Greek gods regularly lied.[37]

God's word is the truth. This means that it can be believed and trusted. It also means that it is essential that anyone proclaiming that word does so in full harmony with the revelation of that word in the Scriptures.[38]

Paul's apostleship is "in accord with the faith of God's elect ones and the knowledge of the truth." The truth of God's word is what creates saving faith. Thus, those who speak the word of God do so in order that saving faith might be created and sustained. They are able to accomplish this because the word they proclaim has the power to do so.

---

35. See further Deterding, "New Testament View," 385–99.

36. This is a corollary of God being the possessor and source of all wisdom (Rom 11:33; 1 Cor 1:20, 30; 2:7; Eph 3:10); *DPL* 362.

37. Towner, *Letters*, 670–71.

38. On the Scriptures see further the commentary on 2 Tim 3:10–17.

The Faith of God's Elect Ones

In this salutation Paul uses the terms "faith" and "knowledge" as synonyms. As is often the case in the Scriptures, "knowledge" denotes more than intellectual assent; it rather refers to a relationship (Gen 4:1: "Adam knew Eve, his wife, and she conceived and gave birth"). This knowledge, this relationship, is one of faith.

This faith/knowledge is held by the "elect ones." The biblical teaching of election/predestination must be understood in connection with what the Scriptures have to say about the redemptive work of Jesus Christ.

By his death and resurrection Christ acquired salvation for all (Rom 5:18; 2 Cor 5:14–15). The word of Christ's work dispenses this salvation and creates the faith that receives it (2 Cor 5:18; Rom 10:17). Through faith in Christ, apart from works, one receives God's gift of salvation (Eph 2:8–9). The faith in Christ that saves without works moves and empowers the believer to produce good works in his/her life (Eph 2:10). Through the word that brought one to faith God continues to nourish and so to preserve that faith until the end (Phil 1:6; 4:7), when those who died in the faith will be resurrected and those believers still alive will be glorified (1 Thess 4:16–17; Rom 8:17–18). When all of this is kept in mind, then the individual believer, focusing on the person and work of Jesus Christ, will be able to see that God chose him/her from eternity for this salvation (Rom 8:29–30).[39]

The apostle states that this faith is in "accord with godliness." As noted above, saving faith always produces godliness, that is, good works, in the life of the believer (Eph 2:10). Genuine faith will always show itself by godly living, by genuine piety.

Paul states here that the object of this faith is "the truth." The mere act of believing that one will be saved will not save. The act of believing does not save unless it has the right object, namely, the truth about Jesus Christ. When one's faith is directed to the truth about Jesus Christ,

---

39. It must be asserted that the Scriptures teach about the eternal election of those saved; it does not teach that there was any election by God of anyone to damnation. Note that in Rom 9:22–23 Paul speaks of God in advance (προ-) preparing vessels of mercy for glory (σκεύη ἐλέους ἃ προητοίμασεν εἰς δόξαν); however, when he refers to vessels of wrath, he states that they were prepared for destruction (σκεύη ὀργῆς κατηρισμένα εἰς ἀπώλειαν); nothing is said about this being done in advance, and God is *not* identified as the one who prepared them for this. On the scriptural teaching regarding the election of grace see further the Formula of Concord, Article XI (Epitome and Solid Declaration), and Nafzger et al., *Confessing the Gospel*, 1195–261.

crucified and risen, the believer's faith receives the benefits of Christ's redemptive work. It is in this sense that faith saves.

One Servant of the Word to Another: Titus 1:1–4 in Context

Other than Romans (1:1–7) and Galatians (1:1–5) Paul's Letter to Titus contains the longest salutation in the Pauline corpus, and like those other greetings this one is "most carefully and theologically constructed."[40] As in those other letters[41] here the apostle uses his salutation as a sort of "overture," introducing themes on which he will expand in the body of the letter.[42]

Among the themes that Paul mentions in this salutation is the saving work of Christ that is received through faith. He applies the title "our savior" both to God the Father and to Christ Jesus, and he refers to eternal life. The apostle will apply this title twice more to both the Father (2:10; 3:4) and the Son (2:13; 3:6); he will make mention of saving faith (1:13; 2:2, 10; 3:15); and he will speak of salvation, including the hope of eternal life, in two of the most significant sections of this epistle (2:11–14; 3:4–7).

Related to this is his mention of the "eternal times" from which God promised salvation and the "right times" when he made this known. He will later refer to the times when "the grace of God appeared, bringing salvation" (2:11) and "when the goodness and philanthropy of God our savior appeared" (3:4).

Paul identifies himself as an apostle of Jesus Christ, and he speaks of the authoritative word with which he was entrusted. In the body of the letter he gives qualifications for the office of the ministry (1:5–9), instructs Titus about the tasks of the ministry of word and sacrament (2:1, 15; 3:5), and gives instruction about the support of the ministry of others (3:12–13); see the commentary on those verses.

---

40. Towner, *Letters*, 75.

41. That Rom 1:1–7 functions in this way, see Middendorf, *Romans 1—8*, 61. Similarly, Das, *Galatians*, 72, notes that this is a purpose of the salutation to the Letter to the Galatians.

42. Similarly Luther (AE 29:13): "This is a very beautiful salutation in which the sum total of the Christian doctrine has been made known in very few words."

I would also consider that 1 Tim 1:1–17 and 2 Tim 1:3–18 function as "overtures" to those letters; see "Outline" in the Introduction to 1 Timothy and "Outline" in the Introduction to 2 Timothy. In a similar way Col 1:3–20 serves as an overture to that letter; see Deterding, *Colossians*, 26–27. Similarly, Eph 1:3–14 functions in the same way in that epistle (Scharlemann, "Secret of God's Plan," 538–39).

In the salutation the apostle describes saving faith and the knowledge of the *truth*, and he notes that God does not lie. One of the emphases of this letter is that the word that he proclaims (and that Titus is to proclaim) is the truth, is sound doctrine, and is trustworthy. This is in contrast to the "Jewish myths and commandments of men who have turned away from the truth" (1:14) and to the "foolish controversies and genealogies and disputes and arguments about the law" (3:9).

Paul notes that the saving truth is in accord with godliness. By both exhorting to good behavior (2:1–10) and warning about ungodly conduct (3:1–3, 10–11) he gives instruction as to just what that godliness involves.

The apostle considers Titus, his "genuine child," as a colleague in ministry. With the salutation of this letter he sketches out the instruction that he will give his coworker in how the ministry is to be carried out.

1:5–9: Requirements for Pastors

TRANSLATION

⁵ For this reason I left you in Crete, in order that you would set right the things that are lacking and appoint elders town by town, just as I commanded you, ⁶ if anyone is beyond reproach, the husband of one wife, has believing children who are not liable to an accusation of wild living or rebellion. ⁷ For it is necessary that an overseer be beyond reproach as a steward of God, not arrogant, not quick-tempered, not a drunkard, not a bully, not guilty of shameful gain, ⁸ but a lover of traveling missionaries, a lover of good, sensible, righteous, pious, self-controlled; ⁹ holding fast to the faithful word as taught, in order that he might be able both to encourage in the sound teaching and to convince[a] those who speak against it.

[a] Or *reprove*

TEXTUAL NOTES

1:5 ἐν Κρήτῃ—Paul left Titus in charge of the churches on the island of Crete, even as he had left Timothy as the head of the churches in Ephesus (1 Tim 1:3). See further the Introduction to Titus.

ἵνα . . . ἐπιδιορθώσῃ καὶ καταστήσῃς—The use of ἵνα here with verbs in the subjunctive mood introduces a purpose clause.[43]

τὰ λείποντα ἐπιδιορθώσῃ—There are things that are "lacking" (τὰ λείποντα; cf. Luke 18:22; Titus 3:13) in the churches on Crete. These will be "set right" (ἐπιδιορθώσῃ) by Titus appointing elders/pastors for the churches in the various towns. See further the commentary.

---

43. Wallace, *Greek Grammar*, 472–73.

πρεσβυτέρους—The use of ἐπίσκοπος in this same section (1:7) as a synonym of πρεσβύτερος indicates that here both terms refer to the pastoral office, as in Acts 20:17, 28. The book of Acts notes that at the end of the first missionary journey Paul and Barnabas concluded their work by "appointing elders" (χειροτονήσαντες . . . πρεσβυτέρους) in the churches they had started (14:23); Titus is to do likewise for the churches of Crete. On the possibility that "elders" in 1 Tim 5:17 has a slightly different meaning, see the textual notes on that passage.

Unlike in 1 Timothy there is nothing said here regarding "deacons" (διάκονοι). Paul had brought the gospel to Ephesus during his approximately three-year stay in that city (53–55) in the course of his third missionary journey (Acts 19:1, 8–10). His evangelization at Crete would have occurred after his release from his first Roman imprisonment (60–61); hence, this would have taken place in about AD 63, roughly a decade after the founding of the church in Ephesus (see "The Chronology of Paul's Life" in the Introduction to the Pastoral Letters). As the present letter was written no more than a year or two later, the churches in Crete would not have been as fully organized at this point as were Timothy's churches in Ephesus; this would perhaps account for the lack of references to deacons in this letter.[44]

ὡς ἐγώ σοι διεταξάμην—Paul speaks here with his authority as an apostle of Jesus Christ (see the entry "Apostle" in the Extended Notes). Thus, with his instruction that elders/pastors need to be provided he is not simply giving directives for a particular situation; he is expressing the will of the Lord of the church that his churches of every time and place be served by pastors. See further the commentary.

1:6 ἀνέγκλητος—In 1 Tim 3:2 the apostle uses a different Greek work (ἀνεπίλημπτον) for the requirement for one who would hold the office of overseer/pastor. He uses the same word as here (and in verse 7) in 1 Tim 3:10 of the requirements for "deacons." This shows that the two words are synonyms.

μιᾶς γυναικὸς ἀνήρ—As polygamy was largely unknown in the first-century Roman world, at least among the masses,[45] a stipulation regarding polygamy would not be needed. An understanding of these words as requiring a pastor to be married is ruled out by Paul's own practice and commendation of the single estate (1 Cor 7:7). Similarly,

---

44. Knight, *Pastoral Epistles*, 175; Marshall, *Pastoral Epistles*, 488.
45. Scheidel, "Population and Demography," 7.

the apostle's permission for younger widows to remarry (1 Tim 5:14) would refute the notion this passage means that a widowed pastor could never remarry. Instead, these words prohibit those divorced (for other than biblically valid reasons) and remarried from holding the pastoral office. The scriptural teaching regarding divorce and remarriage is found in Matt 19:1–12 (Mark 10:1–12) and 1 Cor 7:1–16. The present passage along with 1 Cor 9:5 also demonstrates that prohibitions for clergy marrying are contrary to Scripture.

τέκνα ἔχων πιστά, μὴ ἐν κατηγορίᾳ ἀσωτίας ἢ ἀνυπότακτα—This is similar to the requirements delineated in 1 Tim 3:4–5. In that other passage the rationale for this provision is set forth: if one cannot manage his own household, how can he be entrusted with the care of God's church?

ἀσωτίας—Luke 15:13 uses the cognate adverb ἀσώτως to refer to the immoral living by which the prodigal son squandered his share of the inheritance. Elsewhere it characterizes drunkenness (Eph 5:18); summarizes conduct that includes drunkenness, orgies, and idolatry (1 Pet 4:4); and makes explicit reference to sexual immorality (2 Macc 6:4).

1:7 οἰκονόμον—This term is used of a financial manager of a household or an estate[46] or of the public treasurer of a city,[47] a position of great responsibility.[48] In a spiritual sense it is used of Christians in general (1 Pet 4:10) and, as here, of those called to the office of preaching the word (1 Cor 4:1); the chief responsibility for these is to be faithful to Christ (1 Cor 4:2).

μὴ αὐθάδη—The vice of being "arrogant" is illustrated by the use of this word in 2 Pet 2:10 ("Bold, arrogant people; they do not tremble [with fear] as they slander/blaspheme the glorious ones [angels]").

μὴ ὀργίλον—Another translation of this phrase might be "not hotheaded."[49]

μὴ πάροινον—Passages such as Ps 104:14–15 ("You cause ... plants [to grow] for man to cultivate, that he may bring forth ... wine to gladden the heart") and 1 Tim 5:23 ("No longer drink [only] water but use a little wine for your stomach and for your frequent infirmities") make it plain that the present passage prohibits excessive drinking and not all consumption of alcoholic beverages.

---

46. Luke 12:42; 16:1, 3, 8; 1 Cor 4:2.
47. Rom 16:23; see BDAG 698.
48. Spicq, *Theological Lexicon*, 572–73.
49. BDAG 721.

μὴ πλήκτην—This noun describes one who is likely to strike others.[50] The blows/plagues (πληγή) with which one strikes another might be other than physical (note the use of πληγή in Rev 15 and 16 [15:1, 6, 8; 16:9]). A pastor might certainly be tempted to "strike out" in various ways at people who are less than fully cooperative.

μὴ αἰσχροκερδῆ—"Avaricious" would be a good one-word translation of αἰσχροκερδῆ; however, I have opted for the rendering above to bring out the element of the etymology of the word, "shameful gain."

1:8 φιλόξενον—While hospitality was a significant part of Hebrew culture (Gen 18:1–8; Luke 7:36, 44–46), the term here has more of a distinctly churchly application. As ancient inns were often places of questionable character, Christians who traveled often depended on the hospitality of fellow believers. This was particularly true of traveling Christian preachers (see Titus 3:13).[51] This qualification, therefore, would have to do with a pastor's support of the church and particularly of its mission.[52]

φιλάγαθον—A lover of "good" is a lover of the way that the creator intends all things to be; see the repeated "good" in Gen 1.

σώφρονα—This virtue, implying avoidance of extremes,[53] is to be displayed by Christians in general,[54] as well as by pastors (see also 1 Tim 3:2). Being "sensible" is to display "common sense." If this is expected of Christians in general, then surely a pastor ought to display it in his life.

The use of the cognate verb for the Gerasene demoniac after Jesus cast the demons out of him (Mark 5:15; Luke 8:35) illuminates the meaning of this noun. Having this virtue means using the God-given gift of reason free of the corruption of sin and evil.

δίκαιον—This adjective, "righteous," is part of the word group that describes justification by grace through faith as the means to righteousness before God and therefore also the means to the renewal of conduct that enables the believer to perform righteous deeds. All of that is in the

---

50. πλήκτης and πληγή are both related etymologically to πλήσσω, "to strike."

51. Matt 25:35, 38; Acts 15:4; 18:27; Col 4:10; 3 John 10. Ramsey, *Pauline and Other Studies*, 384–85. That Matt 25:31–46 has to do with missionary encouragement rather than social ministry, see Gibbs, *Matthew 21:1—28:20*, 1342–64.

52. Schuchard, *1–3 John*, 631–34; *DNTB* 1246; Quinn, *Titus*, 90–91.

53. BDAG 987.

54. Titus 2:2, 5; also note the use of the cognate adverb in Titus 2:12.

background here. See further the entry "Righteousness/Justification" in the Extended Notes.

ὅσιον—This term for "pious," "holy" is even used of God (Rev 15:4) and of Christ (Acts 2:27; 13:35; Heb 7:26). The holiness of God is the model for how a pastor, or for that matter, any Christian (1 Tim 2:8), should live.

ἐγκρατῆ—The etymology of this adjective, "self-controlled," from κράτος, "strength," would suggest that "self-control" involves the strength to control oneself.[55] Elsewhere Paul uses the cognate verb to refer to the ability to control one's sexual desires (1 Cor 7:9) and to the control that characterizes an athlete's training (1 Cor 9:25). Since the word is used here without reference to any particular example of self-control, it refers to one's exercise of self-discipline overall.

1:9 ἀντεχόμενον—The use of a form of this verb in the logion of Jesus (Luke 16:13) regarding two masters, God and "mammon," "hate the one and love the other, hold fast to [ἀνθέξεται] the one and despise the other," illustrates the meaning of "holding fast to" here.

τοῦ κατὰ τὴν διδαχὴν πιστοῦ λόγου—There is a standard of teaching/doctrine to which the pastor must hold: the faithful word as taught by the authority of Christ (cf. Rom 16:17). See the entries "Apostle" and "Teaching/Doctrine" in the Extended Notes. See also the commentary below.

ἵνα δυνατὸς ᾖ—Here the use of ἵνα with a verb in the subjunctive mood introduces a purpose clause.[56] See further the commentary below.

παρακαλεῖν ἐν τῇ διδασκαλίᾳ τῇ ὑγιαινούσῃ—"Sound/healthy teaching/doctrine" is a special emphasis in the Pastorals.[57] The pastor needs to be well grounded in "the faithful word as taught"; hence, his doctrine must be "correct."[58] This is necessary in order to be able to give others genuine encouragement through it. On encouraging (παρακαλεῖν) see also the commentary on 1 Tim 4:13; see also the entry "Paraklesis" in the Extended Notes.

καὶ τοὺς ἀντιλέγοντας ἐλέγχειν—The pastor's responsibility is not only setting forth the truth but also refuting and correcting error. See 1 Tim 6:2b–5 and the commentary there. The verb ἐλέγχω is a strong one that is used of excoriating (and correcting) those who have fallen

---

55. *TDNT* 2:339; MM 180.
56. Wallace, *Greek Grammar*, 472–73.
57. 1 Tim 1:10; 2 Tim 4:3; Titus 1:13; 2:1, 2, 8, as well as in the present passage.
58. Knight, *Pastoral Epistles*, 294.

into doctrinal and/or moral error;[59] "convince" seems to capture the meaning here most fully. The context in which this word is used in the Pastorals often points to the authority with which the pastor can issue such rebukes.[60]

COMMENTARY

The Historical Setting

"For this reason I left you in Crete." With these words Paul indicates the purpose of this letter. As with Timothy in Ephesus, so in Crete the apostle has entrusted care of the churches on the island to one of his coworkers: Titus.

The island of Crete was a significant link for seagoing trade in the Mediterranean. As such it would also be exposed to a variety of philosophical and religious beliefs. For both of these reasons it is understandable that Paul would have been interested in bringing the gospel of Jesus Christ to that place.[61]

From the contents of this letter we can discern two tasks that lay before Titus. He was to provide guidance to the churches to ensure that the people of God would be taught the whole truth of God's word. Related to that is his responsibility to take the initiative to seeing to it that the churches would be supplied with pastors to bring them the saving truths of God's word.

The directive about appointing elders flows without interruption into a list of qualifications for that office. This would indicate that Paul here, as Luke in Acts 14, mentions only the "last act" in this undertaking.[62] Before men are placed in the pastoral office, it is necessary that they be properly prepared, that they indeed meet the qualifications that are given in this letter. Thus, the task before Titus is to include also the first-century equivalent of seminary education.[63]

---

59. *DPL* 216; Matt 18:15; Luke 3:19; John 3:20; 8:48; 15:8; 1 Cor 14:24; Eph 5:11, 13; 1 Tim 5:20; 2 Tim 4:2; Titus 1:9, 13; 2:15; Heb 12:5; Jas 2:9; Jude 15; Rev 3:19.

60. 1 Tim 5:20; 2 Tim 4:2; Titus 1:9, 13; 2:15.

61. Towner, *Letters*, 678.

62. Knight, *Pastoral Epistles*, 288.

63. This was also a task assigned to Timothy at Ephesus; see the section "Timothy's Role as Supervisor: Providing Future Pastors" in the commentary on 1 Tim 5:17-25. I have argued elsewhere (*Colossians*, 2) that at an earlier time in his ministry Paul himself had undertaken this very role in Ephesus. The congregation at Colossae was not

The Scriptures do not prescribe any particular form of church governance. Nevertheless, one thing is clear from the Pastorals: for its own good the church of Christ is to hold fast to the whole word of God, to the "faithful word as taught."

The Pastoral Office

One of the main tasks that Paul set before Titus was to provide pastors for the churches of Crete. It is significant that he states that providing pastors is how his coworker will "set right the things that are lacking."

From this it is clear that the pastoral office is not optional for Christ's church on earth. The pastoral office has been created by God himself. This is evident from the apostle's address to the elders/pastors of the church in Ephesus, as recorded in the book of Acts (20:17–35). There he directs them to give attention to "all the flock, in which the Holy Spirit has set you as overseers, to shepherd the church of God" (20:28).

From this it is evident that the church must never overlook the importance of the pastoral office and of taking steps to provide pastors for the future. Guidance for that is provided in these verses from Titus as well as from the similar section in the First Letter to Timothy (5:17–25).

As with the list of qualifications in 1 Timothy, those given in the present letter may be grouped into two categories. On the one hand the pastor must live an exemplary life ("beyond reproach"). In addition, he must be capable of setting forth the "faithful word as taught" and of reproving and/or convincing those who speak against it. This last

---

founded directly by the apostle, for, a few exceptions to the contrary, the recipients of the letter to that church had never met him (Col 2:1). The book of Acts indicates that Paul's three-year [AD 53–55] ministry (Acts 19:8, 10; 20:31) in Ephesus (Acts 19) had as a result that "all who dwelt in [the Roman province of] Asia, Jews and Greeks, heard the word of the Lord" (Acts 19:10). The founding of the congregation in Colossae—as well as those in Laodicea and Hierapolis—would seem to be the result of this period of the apostle's life (Col 2:1; 4:13, 15, 16). This would point to Paul during his time in Ephesus not only doing mission work himself but also preparing others for mission outreach in outlying areas of the province of Asia. The description of Epaphras in Col 1:7–8 and 4:12–13 strongly suggests that he was the founding missionary (Dunn, *Epistles*, 22) of the congregations at Colossae, Laodicea, and Hierapolis (located within about fifteen miles of one another and about one hundred miles east of Ephesus), and that he carried out his work there under the supervision of Paul himself [I would read Col 1:7 as "faithful servant of Christ on *our* behalf"]. This would account for the pastoral concern and responsibility that the apostle demonstrates toward the recipients of his Letter to the Colossians (1:24, 25; 2:1, 5); their coming to faith had come about under the supervision and auspices of Paul.

requirement corresponds to the prerequisite given in 1 Timothy that the pastor be "able to teach" (3:2)[64]

Beyond Reproach

As in 1 Timothy so here, the requirements given for holding the pastoral office presuppose that only men are to hold that position in Christ's church.[65] Going forward, the apostle gives as the basic qualification for holding the pastoral office that a man be beyond reproach. Of course, Paul does not teach perfectionism (Rom 7:15–25), but he does indicate that one who would be a pastor must be exemplary in his life of Christian sanctification. Each of the qualifications that he lists further in this section serves as a kind of a window on the conduct that a pastor must demonstrate.

The pastor's conduct with regard to his personal, family life is emphasized by being placed at the head of the specific qualifications. As "the husband of one wife" he has not divorced and remarried other than for reasons recognized in the Scriptures. If he is married, and if his marriage has been blessed with children, he is to demonstrate that he is fit to be a father to a congregation of believers by having raised his own children to be well behaved.

In his personal conduct he is not to be "arrogant" (as befits one who is a "slave of God," 1:1). He must not be "quick-tempered" (hotheaded); any pastor will face many situations that will tempt him to respond with anger, a response he might well regret later. He must be "self-controlled," which would include not being enslaved to drink. He must not be a "bully"; the ministry involves dealing with people by the power and motivation of the gospel and not by manipulating them, either by force or by any other stratagems (or gimmicks).

Money brings its temptations also to those who hold the pastoral office. Thus, a pastor must not be "guilty of shameful gain." Sadly, in the history of the church there have been believers—and more than one "man of the cloth"—who have been guilty of greed and/or mismanagement of church funds.[66]

---

64. Knight, *Pastoral Epistles*, 294.

65. See further the section on "Women and the Pastoral Office" in the essay "An Excellent Task: The Pastoral Ministry According to the Pastoral Letters" elsewhere in this commentary.

66. Just from the Scriptures consider Achan (Josh 7), Judas (John 12:5–6), Ananias

To say that he is to be "righteous" and "pious" means that his sincere faith will show itself in how he lives; his faith will be active in love (Gal 5:6). He is to be a "lover of good"; he is to conform his life to how the creator intends all things to be. God created all things with wisdom (Ps 104:24; Prov 3:19–20), and wisdom includes those things that characterize the virtue of "common sense."[67] Thus, a pastor also ought to be able to be described as "sensible" (σώφρονα). This is important in view of the reality that some will hold a preconceived notion of Christians in general and their pastors in particular as being out of touch with the real world.

Holding Fast to the Faithful Word

That a pastor be beyond reproach is necessary, as he is a "steward of God." This term implies a position of great responsibility. The pastor is responsible for those in his care, and he is responsible for caring for them by the word of God. Hence, his management involves properly serving others through the word of God.

Thus, it is essential that a pastor be "holding fast to the faithful word as taught." The only way in which he is able to serve those in his care is through the word of God. He is able to serve them, for the word through which he serves is "faithful." The pastor can be confident that with the word of God he will be able to care for those for whom he is responsible.

He will be able to "encourage" with this teaching. That the verb "encourage" (παρακαλεῖν) is cognate to a word that designates Christ (1 John 2:1) and especially the Holy Spirit (John 14:16, 26; 15:26; 16:7) shows why this is so. None of this depends on anything in the pastor himself. With the word of God he has the power of God himself, who works through that word to bring all the blessings of salvation to the hearers.

And the word through which he serves must be the word "as taught." This phrase points to a specific body of doctrine that he has been taught. This body of doctrine is the standard that he must follow. This body of doctrine also has the power to enable him to minister to others. In the Second Letter to Timothy Paul will spell out specifically the source of this teaching: the Scriptures (2 Tim 3:14–17). That he "hold fast" to what has

---

and Saphira (Acts 5:1–11), and Paul's warning about those "who consider godliness to be a way of profiteering" (1 Tim 6:5).

67. This is evident from the seemingly mundane matters that are covered in the proverbs of the book of Proverbs.

been "taught" indicates that he is to be well versed in the body of doctrine that is taught. To do so he must have an in-depth grasp of the Scriptures, one that has been acquired through rigorous study of the same.[68]

The Pastoral Letters were written to encourage Paul's fellow workers in the face of a false teaching that was bedeviling their churches.[69] False teaching, of course, is a constant threat to ministry and to the church of Christ. Therefore, in addition to encouraging in sound teaching, the pastor must also be prepared by the word to reprove those who speak against it in the hope that they might be won over to the truth.[70]

Related to all of this is that the pastor is to be a "lover of traveling missionaries" (on the translation, see the textual notes). A pastor is not a "lone ranger"; he is one of many whom the Lord of the church calls to the task of speaking the word. Thus, it is also incumbent upon the pastor to be supportive of the mission and ministry of those who take the word elsewhere.

It is a sad state of affairs when a pastor (and/or a congregation) takes the attitude of "taking care of our own," and so of supporting missions only if there is anything left over. Paul himself was the great missionary whose work is highlighted in the New Testament. Thus, it is to be expected that he would call the attention of his fellow workers to this responsibility. The church of all ages would do well to give heed to these words of the apostle.

Requirements for Pastors: Titus 1:5–9 in Context

The first item of business for this letter is to deal with the task of providing pastors for the churches. As the gift of salvation comes through the proclaimed word, it is to be expected that this would be a high priority.

Therefore, Paul instructs Titus to see to it that pastors are provided for the churches in his care. This would indicate also that he is entrusted with the task of preparing men to become pastors.[71] The qualifications

---

68. Chrysostom speaks in this way of the need for being well grounded in the Scriptures: "If it is permissible to welcome such inexperience in the episcopacy, then why should any church leader bother to read books and study the Scriptures? This is all just a pretense and excuse and a pretext for carelessness and indolence" (*Six Books on the Priesthood*, 124; ACCS NT 9:288).

69. See "The Nature of the Heresy" in the Introduction to the Pastoral Letters.

70. Luther (AE 29:33): "If a [pastor] is unable to convert and to restrain the gainsayers, he should merely declare that they are in error."

71. See also the instruction to Timothy in 1 Tim 5:17–25 and the commentary on those verses.

for the pastoral ministry are set out here. He who would be a pastor must be exemplary in godly living and also be well equipped to minister to others with the word of God.

See further the essay "An Excellent Task: The Pastoral Ministry According to the Pastoral Letters" elsewhere in this commentary.

1:10–16: Dealing with False Teaching

TRANSLATION

¹⁰ For there are many disorderly persons, who say worthless things, and who are deceivers, especially those of the circumcision, ¹¹ whom it is necessary to silence, who for the sake of shameful gain ruin entire households by teaching things that they ought not [teach]. ¹² A certain prophet of theirs has said of them, "Cretans are always liars, wicked beasts, lazy gluttons." ¹³ This witness is true, for which reason reprove them severely, in order that they might be sound in the faith, ¹⁴ not holding to Jewish myths and commandments of people who have turned away from the truth. ¹⁵ All things are pure to the pure; to the defiled and the unbelieving nothing is pure, but their mind and conscience have been defiled. ¹⁶ Confessing to know God, they deny him by their works, being loathsome and disobedient and unproven by any good work.

TEXTUAL NOTES

1:10 ἀνυπότακτοι—Paul uses the same adjective ("disorderly") in 1:6 to describe the type of children that a pastor should not have. It is paired with ἀνοσίοις ("lawless") in 1 Tim 1:9 at the head of a list of practitioners of various kinds of vices.

ματαιολόγοι—The apostle uses a cognate noun in 1 Tim 1:6 to describe whatever does not come from "a pure heart and a good conscience and an unhypocritical faith."

φρεναπάται—This is compounded from a word for "understanding" (φρήν) and a term for deception (ἀπάτη).[72] The compound seems espe-

---

72. See BDAG 99, 1065.

cially appropriate for these circumstances, as the false teachers presented their philosophy as a more sophisticated, learned version of religion. See "The Nature of the Heresy" in the Introduction to the Pastoral Letters.

οἱ ἐκ τῆς περιτομῆς—On the possible Jewish element to the heresy combated by these letters see "The Nature of the Heresy" in the Introduction to the Pastoral Letters.

1:11 ἐπιστομίζειν—While this term can mean "bridle," in this context "silence" seems more appropriate.[73] See further the commentary below.

ἀνατρέπουσιν—This verb ("ruin," "overturn") occurs in a similar context in 2 Tim 2:18. It is used in John 2:15 to refer to Jesus overturning the tables of the money changers in the temple.

διδάσκοντες—Those against whom Paul is writing here are those who not merely hold to erroneous beliefs but who actively promote them. This participle designates the means by which the action of the main verb (ἀνατρέπουσιν) is carried out.[74]

ἃ μὴ δεῖ—The expression refers to doctrines that must not be taught because they are false.

αἰσχροῦ κέρδους χάριν—A similar critique of false teachers is made in 1 Tim 6:5. In the culture of the time teachers of religion or philosophy might well be suspected of having a desire for financial gain,[75] and Paul himself had to defend himself against possible accusations of the same (Acts 20:33; 1 Thess 2:5). Apparently, Titus and Timothy both had to deal with similar if not identical heretical sects, although different proponents of the heresy may have been present in Crete than were at work in Ephesus.

1:12 τις ἐξ αὐτῶν ἴδιος αὐτῶν προφήτης—By calling this individual, Epimenides, a "prophet," the apostle is indicating that this man's evaluation of his fellow countrymen is accurate; he is a prophet in the same sense as was the Jewish high priest Caiaphas, who "prophesied" the death of Jesus for others (John 11:51). For similar instances of Paul citing pagan sources to make a point see Acts 17:28; 1 Cor 15:33; the former passage includes an allusion to this same work of Epimenides (see following note).

Κρῆτες ἀεὶ ψεῦσται, κακὰ θηρία, γαστέρες ἀργαί—The quotation is from Περὶ Χρησμῶν, "Concerning Oracles," by Epimenides.[76] As the

---

73. BDAG 382.

74. Wallace, *Greek Grammar*, 630.

75. Marshall, *Pastoral Epistles*, 198.

76. The quotation also occurs partially in Callimachus's third-century BC *Hymn to Zeus*; DNTB 759, 762. It is not necessary for the apostle to have read the works of Epimenides to be able to cite this quotation. It had acquired the status of a Cretan

quotation lacks any verb and is a bit of poetry, Quinn offers the following translation to imitate its poetic nature: "Liars ever, men of Crete, Nasty brutes that live to eat."[77] By citing a Cretan author the apostle is able to fend off objections to this unflattering characterization ("These aren't my words; one of your own said this").

1:13 ἡ μαρτυρία αὕτη ἐστὶν ἀληθής—Paul gives approval to this statement, as he did by implication when he referred to the author as a "prophet."

ἔλεγχε—The apostle uses this same verb in 1:9 with the meaning of "convince" and/or "reprove" and in 2:15 as a synonym of "speak" (λάλει) and "encourage, exhort" (παρακάλει). Titus is to bring these matters into the light[78] for the purpose (ἵνα plus a verb in the subjunctive)[79] of opposing and correcting those who advocate them. The verb ἔλεγχε is a strong one that is used of excoriating (and correcting) those who have fallen into doctrinal and/or moral error;[80] the context in which this word is used in the Pastorals often points to the authority with which the pastor can issue such rebukes.[81] See further the commentary below.

ἀποτόμως—In Rom 11:22 Paul uses a noun (ἀποτομίαν) cognate to this adverb to refer to the severity of God in contrast to his kindness.

ἵνα ὑγιαίνωσιν—Here the use of ἵνα with a subjunctive verb would indicate purpose.[82] The apostle uses the verb ὑγιαίνωσιν, "be sound," and its cognates in a number of places in the Pastorals[83] to denote sound doctrine, healthy faith.

Τῇ πίστει—Although not excluding the act of believing (*fides qua creditur*), the word here refers to the (orthodox) content of what is believed (*fides quae creditur*). See further the entry "Faith" in the Extended Notes.

1:14 μὴ προσέχοντες—This verb, "holding to," occurs several times in 1 Timothy[84] in connection with what the devout Christian should (or should not) be devoted to.

---

proverb; Quinn, *Titus*, 107–8. Paul could assume that it would be the sort of thing that would be common knowledge among his readers (Titus 3:15 shows that he intended for this letter to be read to the Cretan church at large).

77. Quinn, *Titus*, 26.
78. BDAG 315.
79. Wallace, *Greek Grammar*, 472.
80. *DPL* 216.
81. 1 Tim 5:20; 2 Tim 4:2; Titus 1:9, 13; 2:15.
82. Wallace, *Greek Grammar*, 472.
83. 1 Tim 1:10; 6:3; 2 Tim 1:13; 4:3; Titus 1:9, 13; 2:1, 2, 8.
84. 1:4, 14; 3:8; 4:1, 13.

Ἰουδαϊκοῖς μύθοις—The adjective "Jewish" points to a non-Christian Jewish aspect to the false teaching, while the noun "myths" indicates a pagan (gentile) component. However, these seemingly dichotomous elements were, in fact, combined in at least some forms of early Gnosticism.[85]

In 1 Timothy Paul speaks of "myths" and "genealogies" together (1:4). While here he describes the tenants of the false teaching as "myths," he uses "genealogies" in the similar section at the end of this letter (3:9). This suggests that "myths" and "genealogies" are both ways of referring to the erroneous speculations of the heretics.[86] See "The Nature of the Heresy" in the Introduction to the Pastoral Letters.

ἐντολαῖς ἀνθρώπων—The word ἐντολαῖς, "commandments," shows that the false teaching was based on law, not gospel; while the term ἀνθρώπων, "of people," demonstrates that the heresy had its origin in man, not in God. As ἀνθρώπων does not necessarily refer to males, I have rendered it as "people"; there may have been women among the false teachers troubling those in the care of Titus (as in Rev 2:20).

ἀποστρεφομένων τὴν ἀλήθειαν—The perfect tense of this participle demonstrates that these are individuals who have already "turned away" from the truth. The use of this verb form elsewhere (Matt 5:42; 2 Tim 1:15; Heb 12:25) indicates that the verb here means that they have rejected the truth; the verb may well also indicate that they are apostate Christians or at least make the claim that they are Christians.[87] This turning away from the truth has come about because they are following human teachings rather than the truth; this indicates that the heresy demanded certain rules and regulations of its followers in order to be "pure" (cf. 1:15). On "truth" see the entry by that name in the Extended Notes.

1:15 πάντα καθαρὰ τοῖς καθαροῖς . . . οὐδὲν καθαρόν—The word "pure" here denotes moral purity, free from guilt (1 Tim 1:5; 3:9; 2 Tim 2:22).[88] There is a bit of a play on words here; when one is morally pure, then all things are pure for him. This statement is to be understood in light of Paul's teaching in Rom 14. See further the following textual note and the commentary below.

μεμιαμμένοις καὶ ἀπίστοις . . . μεμίανται—Here "defiled" stands in contrast to "pure." That "unbelieving" is used here as a synonym of "defiled" demonstrates that "purity" before God comes through faith and

---

85. Rudolph, *Gnosis*, 73–74.
86. Knight, *Pastoral Epistles*, 300.
87. Knight, *Pastoral Epistles*, 295, 304.
88. BDAG 489.

not through following "commandments of people." See further the commentary below.

ὁ νοῦς καὶ ἡ συνείδησις—The two words "mind" and "conscience" (νοῦς, συνείδησις) are used here as synonyms. See the entry "Heart and Conscience" in the Extended Notes.

1:16 θεὸν ὁμολογοῦσιν εἰδέναι—In describing the false teachers as those who "confess" (ὁμολογοῦσιν) to know God, Paul indicates that these heretics set forth some sort of a "confession" of their teaching. This was therefore a group that could be recognized by their doctrines. There is a bit of irony in the characterization of them as claiming to "know" (εἰδέναι) God, for they claimed that they had a knowledge that others did not have, and that their "knowledge" was the way to God. Elsewhere Paul says explicitly what he implies here, namely, that these false teachers do not have a genuine knowledge of the truth (1 Tim 6:20; 2 Tim 3:7). See further "The Nature of the Heresy" in the Introduction to the Pastoral Letters.

τοῖς δὲ ἔργοις ἀρνοῦνται—For all the claims of their "confession," the reality of the false teachers' theology was a denial of the one true God. This is not an assertion that they were merely hypocrites in the sense that they did not live up to what they taught; see further the commentary below.

βδελυκτοί—The use of this word group in the LXX for polytheistic cults[89] and in the Synoptics (Matt 24:15; Mark 13:14) of the "abomination of desolation" indicates that because of their false teaching the heretics are "loathsome" (βδελυκτοί) to God.

ἀπειθεῖς—This term "disobedient" can be used of those who are disobedient to parents (Rom 1:30; 2 Tim 3:2). The bare use of the term (here and in 3:3) carries the implication of being disobedient to God. Note that in Luke 1:17 it stands in contrast to the "righteous" (δικαίων), on which see the entry "Righteousness/Justification" in the Extended Notes.

πρὸς πᾶν ἔργον ἀγαθὸν ἀδόκιμοι—The falseness of the heretics' theology meant that they could not actually do anything that was a good work in the sight of God; see further the commentary below.

---

89. Deut 29:16; 3 Kgdms (= 1 Kgs) 11:5, 33; 4 Kgdms (= 2 Kgs) 23:13; 2 Chr 28:3.

Grace and Life

COMMENTARY

Disorderly Persons and Deceivers

This section indicates that Titus is dealing with false teachers who are present within the communities of the churches for which he has responsibility. While it is unclear whether these heretics are present within the churches themselves, Paul makes it clear that his fellow pastor is to oppose this false teaching.

The apostle characterizes these false teachers as those who "confess" to "know" God. With this language he makes it plain that there is a definite group within the communities and/or the congregations, and that they hold to and promote certain doctrines; the language here suggests that they might even have had some sort of "confession" of faith. At the heart of this "confession," whether formally or informally held, was the contention that they were able to "know" God.

This and other indications in the Pastoral Letters demonstrate that the heresy with which Titus was dealing was an early form of "Gnosticism." The false teachers claimed that they had a special—and perhaps secret—knowledge of God, and that it was through this "knowledge" which was theirs to impart (and only through this knowledge) that one could find his way to acceptance with God.[90]

Paul refutes the claims of these false teachers. He states that in fact they have "turned away from the truth" and that by their works they "deny" the God whom they claim to know. With the phrase "confessing to know God, they deny him by their works" the apostle does not necessarily mean that the errorists say one thing but practice another. Like the Pharisees whom Jesus repeatedly excoriated as "hypocrites" (Matt 23:13, 15, 23, 25, 27, 29), these false teachers may very well have been very sincere about what they believed and taught. The issue is not that they were insincere but that they were sincerely wrong, for what they advocated was not the "truth" of God's word (see further the entry "Truth" in the Extended Notes).

These errorists were not simply guilty of holding to wrong beliefs; they actively promoted them. The apostle describes them as those who "say worthless things" and who are "teaching things which they ought not [teach]." Thus, as advocates for these heresies they were a special danger to Titus' churches.

---

90. See further "The Nature of the Heresy" in the Introduction to the Pastoral Letters.

Paul warns Titus about the presence of false teachers, "especially those of the circumcision," and he warns that their promulgation of their teachings might lead some to hold to "Jewish myths." When the authors of the New Testament warn against things "Jewish," the danger is often the teaching that keeping the various prescriptions of the law (particularly those of the Old Testament and Jewish ceremonial law) was necessary for salvation (the apostle's Letter to the Galatians was written to prevent its readers from being drawn to such teachings). However, the description of the false teaching as Jewish "myths" suggests something beyond the heresy that was endangering the Galatians. The teachings of Gnosticism certainly included things that could accurately be described as "myths." Although Gnosticism has much in common with (neo-)Platonic philosophy, as noted elsewhere in this commentary there were also Jewish elements to it, so that "Jewish myths" would certainly not be an inaccurate description of it (again, see further "The Nature of the Heresy" in the Introduction to the Pastoral Letters).

The apostle further characterizes the teachings of the heretics as the "commandments of people." In the overall context of this section, it seems that the claim about such commandments was that they would make one "pure" (see further the section "The Pure and the Defiled" below). By styling these as commandments *of people* Paul indicates their insufficiency. Since they are human in origin, they are not divine, and since they are not divine, they cannot provide the salvation that they claim to offer.

The apostle also names the false teachers "deceivers." As with the use of the term "hypocrites" by Jesus (see above), the use of this term should not be interpreted as a charge that the heretics were teaching things that they knew to be false (in order to enrich themselves; see below). They may well have been convinced of the truth of what they were advocating. The issue is not that they were necessarily insincere but that what they were setting forth was falsehood and not the "truth."

Paul also calls them "disorderly persons." As this is a general term for religious vice (see textual note above), this does not amount to an accusation that they were religious anarchists. Rather, disorder is one of the consequences when false teaching is promoted, held, or tolerated.

The result of the "worthless things" that the errorists say and their "teaching things that they ought not [teach]" is that they "ruin entire households." The apostle's critique is religious rather than sociological. He is not *necessarily* claiming interpersonal or financial ruin in the homes of those holding to these errors. Even if all is sweetness and light in these families, they are ruined theologically, for this false teaching does not bring God's salvation but rather his judgment, just as our Lord brought the judgment of God upon the tables of the money changers in the temple (John 2:15).

Paul notes that the heretics do this "for the sake of shameful gain." A similar charge is made against the false teachers troubling the churches served by Timothy (1 Tim 6:5). Are these errorists simply "in it for the money?" Perhaps. On the other hand, they might have sincerely held their beliefs and sincerely went about advocating for them. But even if that were the case, their gain was still shameful.[91] Teachings that depart from the truth, even if held and promulgated sincerely, are still something other than the saving truth. Whatever gain they make from it, even if outwardly done honestly, is still shameful, for it is a gain from something that, since it is contrary to the truth, brings divine judgment and not salvation.

Cretans

In the midst of this section dealing with false teaching, the apostle inserts a quotation from the Cretan author Epimenides, a highly regarded Cretan author from about the sixth century BC.[92] What is his purpose in doing so?

At the outset we should take note of the fact that this letter is not a confidential message to Titus. The closing blessing of this missive, being addressed to "all of you" (πάντων ὑμῶν), indicates that Paul intended this letter to be read to all the congregation(s) as a part of their public worship.[93] The apostle has some hard truths to say to and about the people to whom Titus ministers. That being the case, quoting one of their own authors will serve to head off (at least some of) their resentment at what he has to say, making it easier for them to give a listening ear to it.

The apostle describes Epimenides as "a certain prophet of theirs." By dubbing him a "prophet" Paul indicates that at least in this instance what this Cretan author has to say should be heeded.

---

91. That it is entirely proper for those who speak the truth of God's word to make a living by speaking the word, see the section "The Honor Due Pastors" in the commentary on 1 Tim 5:17–25.

92. *DNTB* 759, 762, 1282.

93. See further the commentary on 3:15.

The apostle evaluates this quotation by saying "this witness is true." Readers of the Scriptures are used to New Testament authors citing quotations from the Hebrew Scriptures in such a way that they show that they regard these words from the Old Testament as the word of God and therefore "true" (John 10:34–35; 17:17) and "profitable for teaching, for reproof, for correction, and for training in righteousness" (2 Tim 3:16). That Paul regards this quotation from this pagan author as "true" does not mean that he holds the works of Epimenides on the same level as the Hebrew Scriptures. Instead, he simply attests that in this instance what this Cretan author says is true, and since he has this to say about his own people, this should mean that they ought to accept what he has to say—even though it is less than flattering.[94]

Paul (like Epimenides) regards Cretans in general as being liars, wicked, lazy, and gluttons; the Greek verb κρητίζειν took on the meaning "to lie."[95] Even in their outward conduct they leave much to be desired; they show that they are far from the kingdom of God. The apostle warns Titus that his ministry in Crete will be challenging. He will need to be firm and emphatic in his teaching.

Therefore, he instructs his younger coworker to "reprove them severely." When someone's outward conduct lies far afield from Christian sanctification, one ministering to him must be forceful in his instruction regarding Christian living as well as regarding the gospel of salvation. Thus, it is not surprising that Paul follows this section with instruction regarding the virtues that need to characterize Christians in their various stations in life (2:1–10).

The ultimate purpose[96] of this instruction is that the pastor's hearers be "sound in the faith." "The faith" involves acceptance of and trust in correct doctrine, but it is not limited to that. Being sound in the faith also involves the believer's faith bearing the fruit of godly living.[97] The apostle takes up that topic at the end of this section and in the following one.

---

94. Luther (AE 29:38): "Truth comes from the Holy Spirit, regardless of who says it, especially the true sayings of the poets, when they show us our sins. The cause and the origin of this statement is always in Him; it is an emphatic statement."

95. References in Marshall, *Pastoral Epistles*, 201.

96. See the textual note on ἵνα ὑγιαίνωσιν above.

97. For example, the words on salvation by faith in Eph 2:8–9 are followed immediately by the instruction in 2:10 on the saved being created for good works.

Grace and Life

The Pure and the Defiled

As he brings this section to a close, the apostle draws a contrast between the "pure" and the "defiled." Seeing what he means by these terms opens up the meaning of his instruction here.

Later in this letter Paul will speak of Christ's redemptive work and of how through it he purified "for himself a chosen people, who are zealous for good works" (2:14). In his First Letter to Timothy (1:5) he refers to what comes "from a pure heart and from a good conscience and from an unhypocritical faith"; this demonstrates that "the pure" are those who have received Christ's purifying work through faith in him.[98]

In contrast "the defiled" are "the unbelieving." Unlike the believing, who have a good conscience, those who do not believe have a "mind and conscience" that "has been defiled." As a result, for them "nothing is pure."

The apostle also describes the unbelieving as "loathsome and disobedient." They lack the genuine "good works" that those who believe in Christ are able to do; this lack of any true good works proves that they are defiled and disproves any claim of theirs to know God.

From the First Letter to Timothy (4:3) we learn that at least some of the heretics were those "who forbid marrying, who require abstaining from [certain] foods, which God created to be received with thanksgiving by those who believe and know the truth." At least some among the false teachers put forth the claim that to be acceptable to God ("pure") one had to abstain from marriage and from certain foods. Apparently, this was the same sort of heresy that troubled the churches served by Titus.

When one is "pure" before God through faith in Jesus Christ, then the things of this creation, such as marriage and foods, are pure for him and acceptable for him to enjoy.[99] In contrast, for those who do not have this faith, nothing that they can do will make them "pure" before God; in fact, since they are defiled by sin, everything they do is defiled.

Silence, Reprove

Paul uses two different imperatives (ἐπιστομίζειν, "silence," ἔλεγχε "reprove") when instructing Titus as to how to deal with the false teaching

---

98. Knight, *Pastoral Epistles*, 301–2 comes to a similar conclusion.
99. See further Mark 7:14–19; Acts 10:9–16; Rom 14:1–23.

that is plaguing his churches. The context indicates that each verb has its own direct object.

Those whom the apostle tells Titus to "silence" are the false teachers. They are teaching falsehood that is inimical to the Christian faith and potentially destructive of even the faintest remnants of the saving faith. He is to silence these; their heresies must not be allowed to have a place in his churches.

Those whom Titus is to "reprove" may well include those within his churches. These are Christians who err "in the simplicity of their hearts";[100] they are not actively promoting false teachings but are victims of it. The task before Titus (and his fellow pastors) is to correct these "with gentleness" in the hope that "perhaps God will give them repentance unto the knowledge of the truth, and they will come to their senses and escape from the snare of the devil" (2 Tim 2:25–26; see further the commentary on those verses).

Many pastors no doubt feel about ministry as did the biblical author Jude; they are eager to teach about "our common salvation" but find it necessary to "contend for the faith" by opposing "certain people . . . who pervert the grace of our God" (Jude 1–4). It is the pastor's responsibility to set forth the truth, but doing so also involves refuting error.

Nevertheless, the pastor must avoid doing so in a bombastic, self-righteous manner. Instead, as the apostle instructed Timothy (2 Tim 2:25), he must do so "with gentleness," so that these may come to "a knowledge of the truth." The purpose of opposing and refuting error is never merely to win "debating points." The pastor is always concerned with the religious and spiritual wellbeing of others, even his opponents. Every pastor needs to pray for the courage, the wisdom, the love, and the tact necessary to deal with error in such a way as to win those in error (whether as deceivers or in simplicity of heart) to the truth.

Dealing with False Teaching: Titus 1:10–16 in Context

In these verses Paul takes up the challenges of the false teaching that Titus and his churches are facing. These are twofold: the false teachers that are present in the community (if not, in fact, the congregations themselves) and the nature and culture of the peoples among whom Titus ministers.

---

100. This turn of expression comes from the Preface to the *Book of Concord*, para. 20.

There is a close connection between this section and the preceding one. In view of the situation in Crete it is significant that when the apostle sets out qualifications for the pastoral office, he puts emphasis upon the pastor "holding fast to the faithful word as taught, in order that he might be able both to encourage in the sound teaching and to reprove/convince those who speak against it" (Titus 1:9).

The situation in which any given pastor serves may or may not have a great deal in common with the one that Titus faced. Nevertheless, the instruction offered here is pertinent to the ministry of any pastor. We see from Paul's Letter to Titus that all pastors need to be well grounded in the word of God. We see that all pastors need to be prepared to give sound teaching to those in their care and also to refute false teaching.

2:1–10: Life in Vocation

TRANSLATION

¹ You, however, be speaking those things that are in accord with sound teaching. ² [Tell] older men to be self-controlled, honorable, sensible, sound in the faith, in love, and in endurance. ³ Likewise, [tell] older women to be reverent in [their] behavior, not slanderers, not enslaved to much wine, teaching what is good, ⁴ in order that they might instruct younger women to love [their] husbands, to love [their] children, ⁵ to be sensible, pure, carrying out [their] household responsibilities well,[a] to be subject to their own husbands, in order that the word of God might not be slandered.[b] ⁶ Likewise, proclaim to younger men to be sensible ⁷ concerning all things,[c] while you present yourself as a model of good works, as one who is sound in the teaching, as one who is worthy of dignity, ⁸ as one who speaks soundly and without reproach, in order that one from the opposition might be put to shame, having nothing foul to say about us. ⁹ [Proclaim to] slaves to be subject to their own masters in all things, to be well pleasing, not to be speaking against [them], ¹⁰ not to be holding back, but demonstrating all good faith[fullness], in order that they may adorn the teaching of God our savior in all things.

    [a] Or *tending to household responsibilities, to be kind*
    [b] Or *blasphemed*
    [c] Or *sensible, while you present yourself in all things*

TEXTUAL NOTES

2:1 Σὺ δέ—Paul turns to directing Titus to instruct his people in a life that differs dramatically from that he has just finished describing; thus, the conjunction δέ should be translated as an adversative, such as "however."

λάλει—Note the present tense of the imperative, suggesting regular, ongoing activity.[101] It is the implied verb that governs the accusatives "older men" in 2:2 and "older women" in 2:3.

ὑγιαινούσῃ διδασκαλίᾳ—On "teaching" (διδασκαλίᾳ) as the whole of Christian doctrine, see the entry by that name in the Extended Notes. "Sound" (ὑγιαινούσῃ) here means "correct," "orthodox."[102] The idea of "healthy" also points to correct teaching as bringing the benefits of salvation.[103]

2:2 νηφαλίους ... σεμνούς, σώφρονας, ὑγιαίνοντας—These accusative adjectives all stand in predicate relation to the accusative noun πρεσβύτας.[104]

νηφαλίους—In 1 Timothy this virtue ("self-controlled") is required of "overseers" (3:2) and of "deaconesses" (3:11). As it can have the specific nuance of "moderate in the use of alcohol,"[105] it is matched by a similar virtue required of older women (2:3). In the ancient world excessive drinking was a vice particularly associated with older men and women;[106] hence, there was a special need to direct older believers to the virtue of all manner of self-control, including sobriety.

σεμνούς—This same virtue ("honorable") is required of "deacons" (1 Tim 3:8) and "deaconesses" (1 Tim 3:11).

σώφρονας—The same virtue is required of pastors (Titus 1:8; 1 Tim 3:2). The use of the cognate verb for the Gerasene demoniac after Jesus cast the demons out of him (Mark 5:15; Luke 8:35) illuminates the meaning of this noun: using the God-given gift of reason free of the corruption of sin and evil. That this is a virtue expected of *older* men (and is to be taught by older women to younger women; see 2:5 below) indicates that mature Christians should be able to display the wisdom learned through faith and life experiences.

---

101. Wallace, *Greek Grammar*, 485, 525.
102. 1 Tim 1:10; 6:3; 2 Tim 1:13; 4:3; Titus 1:9, 13; 2:2.
103. Luke 5:31; 7:10; 15:27; 2 John 2.
104. Wallace, *Greek Grammar*, 190–92.
105. BDAG 672.
106. References in Quinn, *Titus*, 130–31.

ὑγιαίνοντας τῇ πίστει—See also the note on ὑγιαινούσῃ διδασκαλίᾳ above. Although not excluding the act of believing (*fides qua creditur*), the term τῇ πίστει, "the faith," here denotes the content of faith (*fides quae creditur*); older men are to be "healthy" by holding to correct (orthodox) teaching. See further the entry "Faith" in the Extended Notes.

ἀγάπῃ—As genuine faith is always active in love (Gal 5:6), the faith of those who are sound/healthy in the faith will always show itself in works of love toward others. See further the entry "Love" in the Extended Notes.

ὑπομονῇ—Faith and its accompanying virtues must have "the capacity to hold out or bear up in the face of difficulty";[107] cf. 2 Tim 4:7.

2:3 καταστήματι ἱεροπρεπεῖς—In some contexts ἱεροπρεπεῖς means "priestlike."[108] A believer is to perform all of his/her conduct as an act of worship to God.

μὴ διαβόλους—The devil (ὁ διάβολος) is the chief "slanderer." The term here should not be narrowly restricted to the specific sin of slander; rather, "slander" here represents all sins of the tongue. Older Christian women should not be guilty of any of these.

μὴ οἴνῳ πολλῷ δεδουλωμένας—Here is another passage that indicates that the sin is not drinking but drunkenness (1 Tim 3:8; 5:23). In the culture of the first-century Mediterranean world some amusements were not available to women, but alcohol was one that was.[109] Therefore, the temptation to excessive drinking would have been a special danger for them.

καλοδιδασκάλους—This is tied to the phrase that follows, and so does not conflict with the prohibition of 1 Tim 2:12 that women not hold the pastoral office.[110] Older women are ideally equipped to be teachers of the younger of their sex.

2:4 ἵνα σωφρονίζωσιν τὰς νέας—Here ἵνα plus a verb in the subjunctive mood introduces a purpose clause;[111] older women are to use their abilities to teach younger women. Here the adjective νέας serves in place of a noun: "young [women]."[112]

---

107. BDAG 1039.
108. BDAG 470.
109. *DNTB* 1277.
110. Knight, *Pastoral Epistles*, 307; Mounce, *Pastoral Epistles*, 410: "Context shows that this refers not to an official teaching position in the church (1 Tim 2:11–12) but rather to informal, one-on-one encouragement." See also the section "Women and the Pastoral Office" in the essay "An Excellent Task: The Pastoral Ministry According to the Pastoral Letters" elsewhere in this commentary.
111. Wallace, *Greek Grammar*, 472.
112. Wallace, *Greek Grammar*, 233.

φιλάνδρους εἶναι—In this context φιλάνδρους means "to be those who love [their] husbands."

φιλοτέκνους—Biblically motherhood is a high and holy calling.[113] Paul's other younger coworker, Timothy, benefited from having a godly mother (2 Tim 1:5)

2:5 σώφρονας—The same virtue is required of older men; see note on 2:2.

ἁγνάς—The word has associations of cultic purity;[114] the apostle directs Timothy to display the same virtue by neither sharing in the sins of others nor being too quick to bring others into the ministry (1 Tim 5:22, whose commentary see).

οἰκουργούς—This type of conduct stands in contrast to that condemned in 1 Tim 5:13, which see.[115] The household would be the typical area of responsibility for a woman in the first century, although there would be exceptions, such as Lydia, a seller of purple goods (Acts 16:14), Priscilla, a tentmaker (Acts 18:2–3), and the women who out of their means provided for Jesus and the Twelve (Luke 8:1–3). A Christian, man or woman, serves God by carrying out the responsibilities of his/her vocation in the best possible manner (on vocation see further the commentary below).

ἀγαθάς—If this word is to be joined together with οἰκουργούς, the meaning would be that the younger women are exhorted to being those who carry out their household responsibilities well.[116] If the two words are meant to stand independent of one another, the term ἀγαθάς here perhaps means "kind."[117]

ὑποτασσομένας τοῖς ἰδίοις ἀνδράσιν—However the verb ὑποτάσσω is translated, it is liable to be misunderstood. "Subjection" (or "submission") in the Bible's ethical exhortations has to do with order, not value. This may be seen from the youthful Jesus being subject to Mary and Joseph (Luke 2:51) and from the exalted Christ being subject to the Father in eternity (1 Cor 15:28).

Subjection does not mean that the wife is inferior to her husband, nor that the husband may be domineering over his wife (see, for example, 1 Pet 3:7). It does mean that Christian women and men are to

---

113. Prov 1:8; 6:20; 30:7; 31:1.
114. BDAG 13.
115. Kelly, *Pastoral Epistles*, 241.
116. Debelius and Conzelmann, *Pastoral Epistles*, 140–41.
117. BDAG 4.

recognize the order established by the one who has made us male or female (Gen 1:26–27; 2:18–24) and to act accordingly.

ἵνα μὴ—A verb in the subjunctive mood (βλασφημῆται) following ἵνα μὴ here denotes a negative purpose clause.[118]

ὁ λόγος τοῦ θεοῦ βλασφημῆται—Ungodly living on the part of those who follow the word of God will bring reproach on that word; godly living removes an occasion for such reproach.

2:6 παρακάλει—On the various nuances of this verb see the entry "Paraklesis" in the Extended Notes. It is the implied verb that governs the accusative "slaves" in 2:9.

2:6–7 σωφρονεῖν περὶ πάντα—See the textual note on σώφρονας at 2:2. Younger men are to strive to attain the spiritual and ethical maturity that one might expect of older Christian men and women.

Should περὶ πάντα be joined to the preceding (the younger men are to be sensible in all things) or the following (Titus is to be an example to others in all things)? The phrase σωφρονεῖν περὶ πάντα seems to be complementary to ἐν τῇ διδασκαλίᾳ ἀφθορίαν, σεμνότητα, which clearly refers to Titus; hence, in the translation above I have joined it to the preceding. The overall meaning is not changed, regardless of the decision made.[119]

2:7 σεαυτὸν παρεχόμενος—The use of a middle participle (παρεχόμενος) instead of the expected active (παρέχων)[120] brings out the personal involvement of Titus in leading by example.

τύπον καλῶν ἔργων—At this point Paul turns to instructing Titus himself. Part of living with Christian maturity (see note on σωφρονεῖν περὶ πάντα above) is living one's life in such a way that it is an example of Christian living to others.

ἐν τῇ διδασκαλίᾳ ἀφθορίαν—Right faith (doctrine) and right living are not to be set in opposition to one another. Both are important.

σεμνότητα—The same virtue is expected of older men (2:2) and of pastors (1 Tim 3:4).

2:8 λόγον ὑγιῆ ἀκατάγνωστον—Christianity is often judged as much by how things are said as by what is said.[121] Titus is to take care about his manner of speaking as well as about speaking right doctrine.

---

118. Wallace, *Greek Grammar*, 472.
119. Knight, *Pastoral Epistles*, 311.
120. BDF 165 (§ 316).
121. See the similar instruction in Col 4:6; see Deterding, *Colossians*, 177–80.

ἵνα—This word with a subjunctive verb (ἐντραπῇ) here introduces a purpose clause.[122]

ἐξ ἐναντίας—This phrase denotes unbelievers (the singular is generic, so I have rendered it "one from the opposition").

ἐντραπῇ—In other contexts this verb ("put to shame") can mean "have regard for."[123] Thus, the idea is perhaps that they are put to shame by being "put in their place."

μηδὲν ἔχων λέγειν περὶ ἡμῶν φαῦλον—As φαῦλον is the opposite of "good" (Rom 9:11; 2 Cor 5:10), the term means "bad"; however, since this Greek word is the origin of the English word "foul," that is how I have chosen to render it here. Slander, gossip, and bad "public relations" are always a potential problem for Christ's church; conduct, in this case speech, that would minimize such problems is certainly to be desired.

2:9 Δούλους ἰδίοις δεσπόταις ὑποτάσσεσθαι ἐν πᾶσιν—See the comparable directive in Col 3:22 and the comparable syntactical construction in Eph 5:24. On being "subject" see the note at 2:5 above. On slavery see the entry by that title in the Extended Notes.

εὐαρέστους εἶναι—All the other uses of this word group in the NT have to do with what is well pleasing to God.[124] That being the case, its use here may perhaps indicate that in rendering good service to one's master a Christian slave is actually performing a well-pleasing service to God.[125] This would certainly be in harmony with what the Scriptures teach on vocation; on that topic see the commentary below.

μὴ ἀντιλέγοντας—In this context the prohibition is against back talk and insubordination.

2:10 μὴ νοσφιζομένους—It would be self-evident that a Christian slave ought not steal (from his master); hence, the directive here seems more nuanced. In Acts 5:2–3 this term is used of Ananias and Sapphira holding back some of the proceeds of the sale of some property and claiming it was the entire amount. While a slave might conceivably be entrusted with managing his owner's money (Luke 16:1–9; 19:11–27; Matt 25:14–30), and while Christians in such a role certainly are not to be guilty of any form of mismanagement or fraud, the reference here

---

122. Wallace, *Greek Grammar*, 472.

123. Matt 21:37; Mark 12:6; Luke 18:2, 4; 20:13; Heb 12:9.

124. Rom 12:1, 2; 14:18; 2 Cor 5:9; Eph 5:10; Phil 4:18; Col 3:20; Heb 11:5, 6; 13:16, 21.

125. BDAG 403.

seems more general. Slaves are not to be guilty of withholding their best efforts in serving their own masters.

πᾶσαν πίστιν ἐνδεικνυμένους ἀγαθήν—In contrast to "holding back," Christian slaves are to display all good faithfulness in all that they do (and in this way demonstrate their faith being active in love).

ἵνα ... κοσμῶσιν—With a verb in the subjunctive mood (κοσμῶσιν, "adorn") ἵνα here introduces a purpose clause.[126]

τὴν διδασκαλίαν—Here the term indicates the whole of Christian doctrine; see further the entry "Teaching" in the Extended Notes.

τοῦ σωτῆρος ἡμῶν θεοῦ—In the NT the vocable "God" (θεός) usually refers to God the Father;[127] he is the savior in that he sent Christ for his redemptive work. However, see also 2:13 and the commentary on that verse. See also the entry "Save, Savior, Salvation" in the Extended Notes.

κοσμῶσιν ἐν πᾶσιν—Christians (in general as well as those who are slaves) are to live in a manner that corresponds to the magnificence of the teaching of God himself, especially to his teaching regarding the way of salvation. Their living in this way may also serve to commend the faith to others.

COMMENTARY

The Service of Various Vocations

Having spoken of the need for Christians to demonstrate their faith in lives of good works (1:13–16), Paul continues by directing Titus to instruct those in his care as to the good works that they are to perform. In this section he offers guidance as to how various groups within the church are to do good by carrying out the responsibilities of their various vocations.[128]

Older Men

In the instruction for older men the first three adjectives have similar meanings. All suggest that these older men are to have all their behavior under control, so that they live in a way that is acceptable to God.

---

126. Wallace, *Greek Grammar*, 472.
127. BDAG 450–51.
128. On vocation see Veith, *Spirituality*, 89–114, and Veith, *God at Work*.

This entire section was introduced with the directive that Titus was to instruct all people in a manner of life that would be in accord with "sound/healthy" doctrine. These older men are to be instructed to be "sound" in three interrelated areas: faith, love, and endurance.

"Sound" faith means a faith that is orthodox; it is to be in accord with the teachings of God's word, for example, as set forth in this letter. As genuine faith will always be active in love (Gal 5:6), "sound" faith is to show itself in "sound" love. Love is "sound" when it is in accord with the will of God as expressed in his law; that is how love is the fulfilling of the law (Rom 13:8–10).

Because of the challenges to both faith and love, each of these requires endurance. Hence, the apostle indicates that older men are also to be instructed to be "sound" in that virtue.

The section of instructions regarding older men is shorter than those addressed to any of the other groups. One can only speculate as to the reason for this. Perhaps it is because the "overseers/elders" are likely to have come from this group, so that it is taken for granted that the older men who are not overseers/elders will model their behavior after that of those who are.

Older Women

The instructions to older women may be divided into two categories. On the one hand there are directives regarding their own personal behavior. This, then, is matched by their responsibility to teach the younger women.

Slander—which might include gossip (1 Tim 5:13–14)—and excessive drinking (1 Tim 3:8) are the very opposite of the reverent behavior that ought to characterize the life of older Christian women. These might be thought of as sins that would be a particularly strong temptation for older women.

Titus is also directed to instruct older women in the church to be "teaching what is good in order that they might instruct younger women." While teaching the faith is certainly one of the responsibilities of a pastor,[129] some things, particularly with respect to living in vocation, are best taught by those who share said vocation. Thus, it is incumbent upon older Christian women to teach their younger sisters in the faith the truths about living life as a Christian woman.

---

129. 1 Tim 3:2; 5:17; 2 Tim 2:2, 24; 4:2; Titus 2:7.

Younger Women

The apostle continues by naming the type of things that older women are to teach to their younger peers. In addition to showing virtues such as all Christians are to display, younger women have special responsibilities toward family and home.

Some of the virtues that younger women are to demonstrate are those that are shared with other groups of Christians (see textual notes above). We might think of the two items that Paul mentions here as being one first article and one third article virtue. Being "sensible" (σώφρονας) means using the gift of reason bestowed by the creator and using it as he intended. Being "pure" (ἁγνάς) is a more distinctively Christian ethic. Purity would mean living in a way that is in keeping with the will of the savior.

The apostle also mentions desirable characteristics that pertain more directly to younger women. As those less likely to be widowed than their older sisters in the faith, younger women are to be instructed to love their own husbands. As those of child-bearing age, they are directed to love their children. For both of these reasons they are likely to be in charge of a household with more than one or two persons; hence, they are especially exhorted to be those who do well in carrying out their responsibilities in the household (οἰκουργούς).

Younger women are also to be taught "to be subject to their own husbands." Sadly, English translations of the Greek word ὑποτάσσω and its cognates carry connotations that the Greek term, at least as it is used in the New Testament, does not have.

This concept is often misunderstood as being demeaning and indicating that one who is made subject to another is inferior to the other. While such an implication is applicable to some uses of this verb (1 Cor 15:24–28a), it is not inherent in the concept itself: Jesus was subject to Mary and Joseph (Luke 2:51), and Paul himself writes that in the eschaton the risen and exalted Christ will be made subject to God the Father (1 Cor 15:28b). As little as the glorified Christ is inferior to his heavenly Father,[130] so little does a wife's being made subject to her husband denote any inferiority of her to him.

The concept of subjection has to do not with value but with order. This concept denotes that there must be an order of rank among a group of people if they are to be united and work together (see also 1 Cor 14:33).

---

130. See the essay "There Is One God: The Pastoral Letters on the Identity of God" elsewhere in this commentary.

The quarterback of a football team[131] may not be the strongest, fastest, smartest, or most athletic member of the team, yet for the sake of the united effort and success of the team it is necessary for the other players on the offense to be made subject to him, so that they follow his signals and the plays he calls (the latter of which may even be called by the head coach). For the united effort toward a "successful" marriage relationship, the Scriptures direct the wife to be made subject to the husband; this does not imply any inferiority of her to him; that the subjection of the wife to the husband is no grounds for any kind of domineering or inconsideration on the part of the husband is seen in the instruction to husbands to love their wives (as Christ loved the church and gave himself—to death—for her).[132]

Further light on the meaning of ὑποτάσσω may be cast by the status in ancient society and the early church of the two groups to whom this imperative is directed, wives (Eph 5:24; Col 3:18) and slaves (Titus 2:9; 1 Pet 2:18). The social, political, educational, economic, and religious opportunities available to women in the New Testament world varied greatly from time to time and place to place, but the fact that freedoms and opportunities in these areas were enjoyed by some of the women of the New Testament world demonstrates that the New Testament's directives to wives to "be subject" were not reflective of a culture that universally degraded or abased women.[133] Moreover, the large numbers of women and slaves who joined themselves to the early church[134] indicate that they did not understand their instruction to "be subject" to be demeaning.

If the etymology of the word has any significance (ὑπό—"under" plus τάσσω—"arrange"), a rendering like "be put under arrangement to" another, while infelicitous as a readable translation, might well paraphrase the idea of the verb. A Christian wife is to stand in the appropriate arrangement or order toward her husband.[135]

---

131. The reference here, of course, is to the American and Canadian versions of the game of "football."

132. Eph 5:25, 28, 29; Col 3:19.

133. Meeks, *First Urban Christians*, 23–25; *DPL* 587. From the New Testament itself we note that Lydia was a seller of purple (Acts 16:14) and hence a merchant of "upper-class" wares, and that Mary, the mother of John Mark, had a house large enough to serve as a meeting place for the early Jerusalem church (Acts 12:12). Furthermore, that there were women who were able to provide for Jesus and the twelve out of their possessions (Luke 8:1–3) indicates that at least some of these women had sufficient freedom, authority, and possessions to do so.

134. Meeks, *First Urban Christians*, 50–55, 72–73.

135. Theodoret of Cyr notes that the apostle's instruction here has particular applicability to Christian women who are married to unbelieving men (PG 82:621A/622A).

To be made subject to another means putting your own desires beneath those of the other. A comparison with what is said of the virtues of love (1 Cor 13:5) and humility (Phil 2:3–4) indicates that being made subject and being humble are expressions of the supreme virtue of love. Christ himself is the premier example of subjection (1 Cor 15:28), humility (Phil 2:5–11), and love (Eph 5:25). Thus, both husbands and wives have Christ as the ultimate example to guide their conduct toward their spouse.[136]

Older women are likely to already have had experience in these areas. Thus, they are ideally suited to teach these things to their younger sisters in the faith.

There is an element of mission/witness involved in these directives. Younger women are to display this behavior "in order that the word of God might not be slandered." The conduct of Christians will often serve to commend (or, sadly, to besmirch) their faith to the outside world. This, however, does not mean that the apostle's directives are merely reflective of culturally acceptable norms. The foundation of these is God's creation of humanity as male and female, a truth that even the pagan world understands from the law of God written in their hearts (Rom 2:15).[137]

Younger Men

Paul gives Titus very few things to say to younger men. Perhaps this is because Titus, as a young man himself, is to lead the younger men by example as he carries out his obligations as a pastor.

The apostle instructs Titus that his message to younger men is that they be "sensible" (σωφρονεῖν) in all things. As being sensible is mentioned also in the instruction to older men and younger women, it is a virtue that is required of Christians in general. Thus, it is to be understood as

---

136. Chrysostom takes note of this element of mutuality (or "reciprocity") in the obligations of husband and wives to one another: "Observe again that Paul has exhorted husbands and wives to reciprocity. As with wives toward husbands, here too he enjoins fear and love. For it is possible for one who loves to be bitter. What Paul says then is this. Don't fight; for nothing is more bitter than fighting in marriage, when it takes place on the part of the husband toward the wife. For disputes between people who love another are bitter. These arise from great bitterness, when, Paul says, any one disagrees with his own member. To love, therefore, is the husband's part, to yield pertains to the other side. If then, each one contributes his own part, all stand firm. From being loved, the wife too becomes loving; and from her being submissive, the husband learns to yield" (*NPNF*[1] 13:304 [ACCS, NT 9:51]).

137. Knight, *Pastoral Epistles*, 309–10, 318.

an umbrella term covering all manner of conduct that younger Christian men are to display in their lives of sanctification.

Titus, the Pastor, Himself

Paul's instruction regarding younger men segues naturally into directives to Titus himself. As the instruction to younger men was general in tone, so the apostle continues by enjoining his coworker to be a model of good works. The pastor teaches especially his fellow younger men not only by words but also by the example of godly living that he himself sets forth.

Hence, Titus is to conduct his ministry in such a way as to be worthy of dignity. He is to do so by being sound/healthy in his teaching/doctrine. His speech in general as well as his teaching the faith is to be done "soundly and without reproach" (ὑγιῆ ἀκατάγνωστον).

Slaves

On the institution of slavery in the first-century Greco-Roman world, the early church's response to it, and the applicability to the church of every age of what the Scriptures say about it, see the entry "Slavery in the New Testament World" in the Extended Notes.

The number of places in the apostle's letters where he speaks to or about slaves[138] demonstrates that there were a considerable number of slaves among the early Christian congregations. Here as elsewhere Paul gives instruction as to how Christian slaves are to live out their faith.

Rather than being rebellious, Christian slaves were to continue to serve their masters in "subjection/orderliness" (on this concept, see the above commentary on the instruction to younger women). The apostle specifies that slaves were to be well pleasing. The prohibition against speaking against their masters probably encompasses both back talk and slander/gossip. Christian slaves were not to hold back on their effort in their service (see the textual note above). In everything they were to demonstrate their faith, which would include being faithful in all that they did.

---

138. 1 Cor 7:21–22; 12:13; Gal 3:28; Eph 6:5, 8; Col 3:11, 22; 4:1; 1 Tim 6:1; Titus 2:9; Phlm 16.

Life in Vocation

This entire section is significant for illustrating the importance of vocation for godly living. The good works that a Christian is to perform in thanksgiving for his salvation and to the glory of God involves distinctively religious activity: corporate and individual worship, support of and involvement in the church's ministry and mission, avoiding vices, and displaying the virtues of the Christian life (e.g., Gal 5:18–23) in his/her conduct.

Nevertheless, one's new life of sanctification is not limited to deeds such as these. As the believer carries out the duties of his/her vocation, this is also an act of service to God which is pleasing to him. One's vocations might well be many and varied and may change from time to time throughout one's life. Such vocations might be that of son or daughter, husband or wife, father or mother, employer or employee, supervisor or subordinate, citizen, friend, neighbor, and many others. The present verses point to the truth that as believers in Jesus Christ we serve him also by carrying out our vocations with integrity, to the best of our ability, and to his glory and honor. Thus, even rather ordinary, seemingly banal activities take on dignity and value when done for one's Lord and savior.[139]

Further Purposes

Godly living by Christians has a value all its own as a service done in thanksgiving for their salvation and to the glory of God. In addition, Paul here indicates that a life of Christian virtue has other purposes as well.

---

139. Martin Luther—not the civil rights leader but the Reformer—said it well: "If this could be impressed on the . . . people, a servant girl would dance for joy and praise and thank God; and with her careful work, for which she receives sustenance and wages, she would obtain a treasure such as those who are regarded as the greatest saints do not have. Is it not a tremendous honor to know this and to say, 'If you do your daily household chores, that is better than the holiness and austere life of all the monks'? . . . How could you be more blessed or lead a holier life, as far as works are concerned? . . . You are a true nobleman if you are simply upright and obedient." Large Catechism, 145–48; translation in Kolb and Wengert, *Book of Concord*, 406–7.

Martin Luther King Jr.—not the Reformer but the civil rights leader—also said it well: "If a man is called to be a street sweeper, he should sweep streets even as Michelangelo painted, or Beethoven composed music, or Shakespeare wrote poetry. He should sweep streets so well that all the hosts of heaven and earth will pause to say, 'Here lived a great street sweeper who did his job well.'" From a speech ("What Is Your Life's Blueprint") to a group of students at Barratt Junior High School in Philadelphia on October 26, 1967; Goodreads, "Martin Luther King Jr."; Eisenstein, "MLK," 00:00–00:40.

Godly living is important for preventing reproach from the outside world on the word of God and on those who follow it. Some of the virtues listed here were expectations of any respectable person in the ancient world;[140] it ought to be taken for granted that Christians should meet the culture's minimal presumptions for noble conduct. Younger women are to live as directed here "in order that the word of God might not be slandered" (2:5). Titus himself is to conduct his ministry "in order that one from the opposition might be put to shame, having nothing foul to say about us" (2:8). Unbecoming conduct on the part of Christians and especially on the part of their pastors provides fodder for the unbelieving world, often all too eager to think ill of Christians and Christianity, to reject Christ and even to actively speak against the faith. While up until the eschaton there will be those who will badmouth Christianity and its adherents, godly living by believers will at least lessen the opportunities for its opponents to do so.

On the other hand, godly living not only prevents evil but can also promote good. Titus is to instruct Christian slaves as to how they are to live "in order that they may adorn the teaching of our savior in all things" (2:10).[141] What is said here of slaves in particular holds true for Christians in general. Godly living is to be done to the glory of God, and it may even commend the saving word of God to others.

Life in Vocation: Titus 2:1–10 in Context

Paul had concluded the previous section of this letter by referring to those who claim to know God but who "deny him by their works, being loathsome and disobedient and unproven by any good work." He moves on from there by giving this instruction in how the Christian lives a life of good works.

The apostle directs how various groups of Christians are to serve God in their various stations and callings in life. This teaching regarding the Christian life sets the stage for the following portion of the letter,

---

140. Marshall, *Pastoral Epistles*, 238, 260–61.

141. Chrysostom makes this observation: "For if [a Christian slave] restrains not his hand or his unruly tongue, how shall the Gentile admire the doctrine that is among us? But if they see their slave, who has been taught the philosophy of Christ, displaying more self-command than their own philosophers and serving with all meekness and good will, he will in every way admire the power of the gospel. For the Greeks judge not of doctrines by the doctrine itself but make the life and the conduct the test of the doctrines" (*NPNF*[1] 13:533* [ACCS, NT 9:296–97]).

where Paul proclaims the gracious work of God in Christ that makes it possible for one to be "zealous for good works" (2:14).

2:11–15: The Power for Godly Living

TRANSLATION

¹¹ For the grace of God appeared, bringing salvation to all people, ¹² schooling us, in order that having denied irreverence and worldly desires, we might live sensibly, righteously, and reverently in this age, ¹³ while awaiting the blessed hope and the appearing of the glory of our great God and savior Jesus Christ, ¹⁴ who gave himself for us, in order that he might redeem us from all lawlessness and might purify for himself a chosen people, who are zealous for good works. ¹⁵ Speak, exhort, and convince of these things with all authority; let no one despise you.

TEXTUAL NOTES

2:11 Ἐπεφάνη—This verb ("appeared") is in the aorist tense, the tense that can denote one-time action in the past.[142] Here it refers to the appearance of God's grace in the incarnation, in the birth of Jesus Christ at a point in history.

γάρ—This conjunction connects this section to the preceding.[143] In this section Paul describes that which provides the motivation and ability for living as he directed in the previous portion of the letter. See further the commentary.

χάρις—See the entry "Grace" in the Extended Notes.

---

142. BDF 166 [§ 318 (1)].
143. BDAG 189.

σωτήριος—Here the term serves as an adjective ("bringing salvation") modifying χάρις ("grace"); the same form serves for both masculine and feminine.[144]

πᾶσιν ἀνθρώποις—Here ἀνθρώποις refers not to males but to all people; hence, that is how I have translated it. The apostle's reference to Jesus as savior "of all" (objective justification) may well be made in deliberate contrast to the heretics' notion that salvation was restricted to a sufficiently knowledgeable elite.[145]

2:12 παιδεύουσα—This participle functions here as an adjective modifying χάρις. Depending on the context this verb can mean "educate" (Acts 7:22; 22:3) or "discipline," "punish."[146] In this context "schooling" seems to capture the right nuance of the verb. The grace that appeared in the past continually schools us (present tense participle) for godly living.

ἵνα … ζήσωμεν—Here ἵνα plus a verb in the subjunctive mood serves to introduce a purpose-result clause.[147] The present tense verb (ζήσωμεν) denotes the ongoing nature of the new life of godly living.

ἀρνησάμενοι—This participle indicates the means by which the action of the main verb (ζήσωμεν) is carried out.[148] The aorist tense of the verb means that this action precedes the action of the main verb; it precedes it (theo)logically, not chronologically, for theologically the new way of living commences at the same moment as this denying.

This is a strong verb; it is used of Peter's denial of Jesus,[149] of those who deny him by failing to confess him,[150] and of unbelief.[151] To preserve this strong sense of the verb I have opted for the translation "deny" over against something like "disdain" or "disregard."

ἀσέβειαν καὶ τὰς κοσμικὰς ἐπιθυμίας—I have rendered ἀσέβειαν "irreverence" to preserve the play on words with εὐσεβῶς, "reverently," later in the verse. Here "worldly" (κοσμικάς) plainly has the sense of what pertains to the fallen world, "sinful."

---

144. BDAG 986.

145. *DPL* 959–60. On objective justification see Nafzger et al., *Confessing the Gospel*, 475–77, 570–72, 574–75 and *Theses on Justification*, 1–12.

146. Luke 23:16, 22; 1 Cor 11:32; 2 Cor 6:9; 1 Tim 1:20; 2 Tim 2:25; Heb 12:6, 7, 10 (2x); Rev 3:19.

147. Wallace, *Greek Grammar*, 473–74.

148. Wallace, *Greek Grammar*, 628–30.

149. Matt 26:70, 72; Mark 14:68, 70; Luke 22:57; John 13:38; 18:25, 27.

150. Matt 10:33; Luke 12:9.

151. 1 Tim 5:8; 2 Tim 2:12; 2 Pet 2:1; Jude 4.

GRACE AND LIFE

σωφρόνως—This adverb is a cognate of a virtue that Paul variously enjoins on pastors (1 Tim 3:2; Titus 1:8), older men (Titus 2:2), older women (1 Tim 2:9, 15; Titus 2:4), younger men (Titus 2:6), and younger women (Titus 2:5). In that light it is a good, broadly applicable word to use to describe the kind of life that all Christians are to live (1 Tim 1:7). All Christians are to live in a sensible, self-controlled way.[152]

δικαίως—See the entry "Righteousness/Justification" in the Extended Notes.

εὐσεβῶς—There is a play on words and a contrast with ἀσέβειαν earlier in the verse. As a cognate of εὐσέβεια this word denotes the kind of conduct that is owed to God himself.[153] The noun εὐσέβεια is sometimes rendered "godliness." "Godliness" has to do with the right standing that is given for the sake of Christ and through faith in him; therefore, it is only faith in Christ that empowers one for living in a reverent or godly manner. See further the entry "Godliness" in the Extended Notes.

τῷ νῦν αἰῶνι—"This age" is contrasted with the life to come. See further the commentary.

2:13 προσδεχόμενοι—The present age is marked by both ongoing godly living and continual anticipation of the life to come, the latter indicated by the present tense of this participle. The object for which one is waiting will determine the character of the waiting (e.g., expectation, dread); this verb is often used, as here, of believers waiting for salvation.[154]

τὴν μακαρίαν ἐλπίδα—This is the content of the Christian's future hope (*spes quae speratur*) rather than the act of hoping (*spes qua speratur*).[155] It is a "blessed" (μακαρίαν) hope, for it is the hope of eternal salvation (Rom 4:7–8). See also the entry "Hope" in the Extended Notes.

ἐπιφάνειαν τῆς δόξης—On "glory" see the entry by that name in the Extended Notes. The noun ἐπιφάνειαν is cognate to the verb ἐπεφάνη in verse 11, referring to the incarnation. As Jesus came in human flesh for his earthly ministry, he will do likewise at his second coming.

τοῦ μεγάλου θεοῦ καὶ σωτῆρος ἡμῶν Ἰησοῦ Χριστοῦ—The "Granville Sharp Rule" states that in the NT in the construction article-substantive-καί-substantive (the article not being used with the second substantive), when neither substantive is impersonal, plural, nor a proper name, the

---

152. BDAG 986–87.
153. BDAG 412–13.
154. Mark 15:43 (Luke 23:51); Luke 2:25, 38; 12:36; 24:15; Jude 21.
155. Also noted by Knight, *Pastoral Epistles*, 321.

two substantives are equivalent.[156] This would mean that in the present passage "the great God" and "our savior Jesus Christ" would be two references to the same person. For further argumentation in support of this translation and identification, see "Time and History" in the commentary that follows.

2:14 ἔδωκεν ἑαυτόν—The verb "gave" (ἔδωκεν) is in the aorist tense, which can refer to one-time action in the past.[157] Here it refers to Christ's death on the cross.

ὑπὲρ ἡμῶν—As with 1 Tim 2:6, the close association of the preposition ὑπέρ with the concept of "redeem/ransom" (λυτρώσηται, ἀντίλυτρον) demonstrates a substitutionary meaning to the preposition,[158] "in place of" and "on behalf of."

ἵνα λυτρώσηται—Here ἵνα plus a verb in the subjunctive mood serves to introduce a purpose-result clause.[159]

λυτρώσηται ἡμᾶς—The use of λυτρόω elsewhere in the Greek Scriptures (e.g., Isa 52:3; 1 Pet 1:18) indicates that this verb includes the idea of a payment by which ransom/redemption is accomplished, as also in Matt 20:28 (Mark 10:45).[160]

ἀπὸ πάσης ἀνομίας—The law is good, if anyone uses it lawfully (1 Tim 1:8); however, no one can (Matt 5:48), so all are in a state of "lawlessness" (ἀνομίας), from which they must be redeemed. The adjective "all" (πάσης) points to the work of Christ as being fully sufficient for the redemption of all people from all their wrong.

καθαρίσῃ—This subjunctive mood verb is also connected to the word ἵνα earlier in the verse and is part of the same purpose-result clause. The verb "cleanse," "purify" (καθαρίσῃ) can refer to physical washing (Matt 23:25–26; Luke 11:39) or, as here, to purification from sin (also Eph 5:26). Physical cleansing thus serves as an illustration of redemptive cleansing. A bit later in this letter Paul will refer to salvation through a physical washing (3:5).

λαὸν περιούσιον—The LXX uses this very phrase of Israel as the chosen people of God (Exod 19:5; Deut 7:6; 14:2). Christ has acquired this blessed

---

156. Wallace, *Greek Grammar*, 270–77; Mounce, *Pastoral Epistles*, 426–27, offers examples of this rule from the NT. See also Harris, "Titus 2:13," 267, with reference to Greek grammars by Zerwick and Robertson.
157. BDF 166 [§ 318 (1)].
158. BDAG 1030–31; Wallace, *Greek Grammar*, 388.
159. Wallace, *Greek Grammar*, 473–74.
160. *TDNT* 4:350–51.

status for all people (2:12). Hence, it is those who follow him (2:12–13) and not the ethnic people of Israel who belong to God himself (ἑαυτῷ).[161]

ζηλωτὴν καλῶν ἔργων—The word ζηλωτήν, literally a "zealot," and its cognate ζῆλος can have positive (1 Pet 3:13; 2 Cor 9:2) or negative (Luke 6:15; Rom 13:13) connotations; in every instance only the context will indicate which. In the present passage "good works" plainly makes for a positive association.

2:15 Ταῦτα—Although ἔργων as a neuter plural noun could hypothetically be the antecedent of this neuter plural pronoun, that hardly makes sense here. Instead, ταῦτα refers back to all that Paul has been saying up to this point, at least to 2:1 if not all the way to 1:10.

λάλει—Note the present tense of the imperative, suggesting regular, ongoing activity.[162]

παρακάλει—Another present tense imperative. See also the entry "Paraklesis" in the Extended Notes.

ἔλεγχε—Another present imperative; it is also used in 1:9, 13. This verb and its cognates are forceful; the word family can have meanings such as "reproof" (2 Pet 2:16), "proof" (Heb 11:1), and "convince" (Titus 1:9, 13). The word is used of excoriating (and correcting) those who have fallen into doctrinal and/or moral error;[163] the context in which this word is used in the Pastorals often points to the authority with which the pastor can issue such rebukes.[164]

μετὰ πάσης ἐπιταγῆς—This is another forceful term; the word ἐπιταγῆς often means "command";[165] here the translation "authority" fits better.[166]

περιφρονείτω—The apostle uses a word from the same root (καταφρονέω) in instructing Timothy not to let others "despise" his youth (1 Tim 4:12). Like Timothy Titus was a younger man (2:6–8), but Christians are to respect the ministry of the word regardless of the relative age of those called to carry it out. As both that Letter to Timothy and the present one to Titus were intended to be read before the entire Christian community (1 Tim 6:21; Titus 3:15), these amount to directives to the entire community not to despise either of these men of God (see the commentary on each of those verses).

---

161. Knight, *Pastoral Epistles*, 328, comes to a similar conclusion.
162. Wallace, *Greek Grammar*, 485.
163. DPL 216.
164. 1 Tim 5:20; 2 Tim 4:2; Titus 1:9, 13; 2:15.
165. Rom 16:26; 1 Cor 7:6, 25; 2 Cor 8:8; 1 Tim 1:1; Titus 1:3.
166. BDAG 383.

COMMENTARY

The Power for Godly Living

Paul has been giving instruction regarding godly living within one's vocation. With the conjunction with which this section begins (γάρ) he indicates that the things that he sets forth here provide both the motivation and the power by which the Christian is able to do good works.

The grace of God that appeared in the past is not only bringing salvation; it is also "schooling" us for a life of good works. The verb that the apostle uses here (παιδεύουσα) denotes more than the supplying of information. God's grace "schools" us also in that it enables us to live in a godly manner. Paul here describes godly living as denying "irreverence [or ungodliness] and worldly desires," as living in a sensible, righteous, and reverent (or godly) manner, and as being zealous for good works.

Each of these terms or phrases provides a glimpse at what godly living involves (see the textual notes). The instruction about denying irreverence (or ungodliness) indicates that part of godly living is turning away from what is contrary to the will of God. Sensible living means acting in a sensible, self-controlled way. Righteous living is possible only by those who have the righteousness of Christ through faith in him. Reverent or godly living is the type of conduct that is appropriate to offer to almighty God; only faith in Christ will empower one to live in this way. "Good works" is a general term for what constitutes godly living, and one who is schooled by the grace of God will have zeal for living as God would have him live.

The apostle states that Christ gave himself both to redeem us and also that he might "purify" (καθαρίσῃ) us for good works. If someone or something is purified, it means that he, she, or it was formerly in a state of impurity. Those who are impure cannot do what is pure (good works). Also in this way Paul indicates that it is only the work of Christ that enables us to do those things that are good and pure in the sight of God.

Time and History

Paul notes that sensible, righteous, and reverent/godly conduct is to characterize the believer's living "in this age." His reference to "this age" helps to alert us to the significance of time for his proclamation here.

It is to be noted that in this section the apostle refers to past, present, and future. Two past (aorist) tense verbs (ἐπεφάνη, ἔδωκεν) have to do to the work of Christ in history that provides for our salvation and empowers our godly living. The pairing of the phrase "in this age" with a present tense verb (ζήσωμεν) refers to the believer's present response to Christ's past saving acts. The references to "hope" and to Christ's "appearing" point the readers to the future. Each of these epochs of time has significance for this section.

Past

Two aorist verbs in this section each designate particular past events of salvation history. When Paul writes that the grace of God "appeared," he points to the incarnation, the birth of Jesus in Bethlehem. For the apostle grace was no abstract concept; it manifested itself in a particular place and time. That being the case, it is little wonder that Titus 2:11–14 has historically been appointed as an epistle lesson for Christmas Eve.[167]

Christ appeared in order to bring salvation. His work to bring about salvation is designated by the other aorist verb in this pericope, "gave." Jesus "gave himself" to death on a cross. The intended result of this[168] was twofold: to redeem for himself a people and to purify them. The word "redeem" carries with it the idea of the payment of a necessary price; the death of Christ on the cross was the price that needed to be paid that mankind might be delivered from sin and its consequences. The word "purify" here has two related senses. On the one hand "purify" here serves as a synonym for "redeem"; it speaks of the removal of sin, so that we might have salvation. A further consequence of this is that one who is purified will in turn be able to bring forth good works.

Present

Christ's past redemptive work also has a wholesome effect on the believer's present existence "in this age." During this age believers await the age to come.[169] They do so by being zealous for good works, that is, by living

---

167. See, for example, LSB xiv, xvi, xviii, xx.

168. In verse 14 both of the subjunctive mood verbs λυτρώσηται and καθαρίσῃ are connected with ἵνα as part of a purpose-result clause; Wallace, *Greek Grammar*, 473–74.

169. On Paul's use of "this age" and "the age to come" in setting forth the significance

sensibly, righteously, and reverently. They also await the age to come by living in hope. That their lives are lives of hope points to the significance of the future for Christian faith.

Future

As the past and the present are significant for the Christian's faith and life, so is the future. The believer's present existence is characterized by hope. "Hope" is a word about the future. Christians have hope because their future salvation is assured. This salvation will be consummated at the appearance of Christ, and so believers await the coming of Christ with hope.

Paul describes the second coming as the appearance of "our great God and savior, Jesus Christ." The textual notes indicate that the "Granville Sharp Rule" supports this translation. The overall context also sanctions this rendering. If we would suppose for the moment that "the great God" (τοῦ μεγάλου θεοῦ) and "our savior Jesus Christ" (σωτῆρος ἡμῶν Ἰησοῦ Χριστοῦ) were distinct individuals, we would be at a loss to identify what the appearance of "the great God" as someone other than Jesus Christ would be. Thus, for both of these reasons this verse stands as one of the Bible's most explicit identifications of the full deity of Jesus Christ.[170]

This profession of the deity of Christ makes explicit what is implicit elsewhere in the Pastorals. The deity of Jesus Christ is indicated when the title "savior" (σωτήρ) is used of Christ[171] as well as of God the Father.[172] The vocable "Lord" (κύριος), standing for the name of the one true God of the

---

of time and history for the proclamation of the gospel see Deterding, "New Testament View," 390–92.

170. Knight, *Pastoral Epistles*, 323, argues for the same conclusion. Towner, *Letters*, 750–58, opts for seeing "Jesus Christ" as being in apposition to "glory," similar to the way in which "Christ" stands in apposition to "mystery" in Col 2:2, resulting in a translation along these lines: ". . . the appearing of our great God and Savior's glory, that is, Jesus Christ . . ." However, this would involve a most unusual use of the vocable "glory" by Paul (contrast 2 Cor 4:4, 6; Col 1:27). Furthermore, even if we accept the possibility of this less-than-certain understanding (Marshall, *Pastoral Epistles*, 279, notes that whereas "Christ" being in apposition in Col 2:2 is quite clear, in Titus 2:13 "it is anything but obvious"), the fact that "glory" (δόξα) often denotes (the appearance of) the being of God (cf. John 1:14) means that this would still amount to an assertion of the identify of Jesus Christ as God (θεός). See the entry "Glory" in the Extended Notes.

171. 2 Tim 1:10; Titus 1:4; 3:6.

172. 1 Tim 1:1; 2:3; 4:10; Titus 1:3; 2:10; 3:4.

Hebrew Scriptures, in some places clearly refers to Jesus.[173] In addition these letters contain doxologies that are addressed to Christ (1 Tim 1:17; 6:14–16; 2 Tim 4:18).

Already/Not Yet

The presence of past, present, and future elements in this text with respect to the gift of salvation points to the already/not-yet character of that salvation. The grace of God "appeared" in the past; Christ "gave" himself in the past. In that respect salvation is already accomplished.

On the other hand, we are "awaiting . . . the appearing of the glory of our great God and savior Jesus Christ." His coming will bring the full realization of the salvation that he acquired by his past redemptive work.

Hence, the believer's life is one of hope. What Christ did in the past has made our future salvation secure. Therefore, we live with a sure and certain hope.

The Obligation of Titus

The apostle has written about the service of Christians in their various vocations (2:1–10) and the work of Christ as both the power and the motivation for such godly living (2:11–14). He continues (2:15) by impressing upon Titus the importance of his proclaiming all of this (see ταῦτα in the Textual Notes).

With three related present tense imperatives Paul instructs his younger fellow pastor to proclaim this message. He impresses upon him the authority (ἔλεγχε μετὰ πάσης ἐπιταγῆς) with which he is to set this forth. Because he has a message with divine authority to proclaim, no one should despise him.

Pastors (and parishioners) of every age have a lesson to be learned from this verse. The message can be proclaimed with authority, for it is God's message. When a pastor sets forth that message (and not merely his own opinions), it can be proclaimed with authority. When a pastor carries out his ministry in that way, he is not to be despised but rather held in high regard as a messenger of God.

---

173. 1 Tim 1:2, 12; 6:3, 4; 2 Tim 1:2, 8; 4:8.

The Power for Godly Living: Titus 2:11–15 in Context

We might think of this section as the "keystone" that ties the entire letter together. After the salutation/overture (1:1–4) Paul launched into the body of his missive. He began with sketching qualifications for the pastoral office (1:5–9). He continued by showing the need among the readers of this letter for the type of pastoral ministry that he had described (1:10–16). That led him to outline how Christians are to live within their various vocations (2:1–10). The present section then proclaims the gracious work of God in Christ that makes such godly living possible. Titus is directed to proclaim all of this (2:15).

The section that follows the present one serves somewhat to reiterate the truths proclaimed here. The apostle will again give some instruction in Christian living (3:1–3, 10–11) that will envelop another section in which he proclaims the significance of the saving work of Christ (3:4–7). Having finished that, it remains only for him to bring the letter to a close.

Thus, the present section's proclamation of the present and future significance of the past work of Christ encapsulates the entire epistle. The work of the ministry is to proclaim the redemptive work of Christ that gives salvation and moves the believer to upright living.

3:1–11: The Life of the Justified

TRANSLATION

¹ Remind them to be subject to rulers and authorities, to be obedient, to be prepared for every good work, ² to slander no one, not to be combative, to be kind, showing compete gentleness to all people. ³ For we ourselves were at one time foolish, disobedient, deceived, being slaves to various lusts and desires, living in wickedness and envy, loathsome, hating one another. ⁴ But when the goodness and love for mankind of God our savior appeared, ⁵ he saved us, not by works in righteousness which we had done, but according to his mercy, through the washing of rebirth and of renewal of the Holy Spirit, ⁶ whom he poured out on us richly through Jesus Christ our savior, ⁷ in order that having been justified through his grace, we might become heirs according to the hope of eternal life. ⁸ The saying is trustworthy, and I want you to insist on these things, in order that those who have believed in God might be intent on good works. These things are good and profitable for people. ⁹ But avoid foolish controversies and genealogies and disputes and arguments about the law, for these are unprofitable and futile. ¹⁰ After a first or a second admonition reject a heretic, ¹¹ knowing that such a one has become perverted and is sinful, being self-condemned.

TEXTUAL NOTES

3:1 Ὑπομίμνῃσκε—The present tense of the imperative suggests that this reminding is to be an ongoing activity.[174]

---

174. Wallace, *Greek Grammar*, 485.

ἀρχαῖς ἐξουσίαις ὑποτάσσεσθαι—Nearly identical terminology is used in the similar instruction of Rom 13:1–7.

πειθαρχεῖν—It is interesting that this word, seldom used in the NT, occurs in the well-known passage in Acts (5:29; cf. 5:32) concerning the necessity to obey God rather than men; see further the commentary.

ἔργον ἀγαθὸν—This connects this directive with the instruction of 2:14 (which see).

3:2 μηδένα βλασφημεῖν—In this context "slander" rather than "blaspheme" is the preferred translation. In view of the reference to ἀνθρώπους at the end of the verse (whose note see), the meaning here is not limited to "slander no rulers or authorities" but prohibits slander of anyone.[175]

ἀμάχους—This word is formed by an alpha privative attached to a root that denotes fighting (2 Cor 7:5; 2 Tim 2:23; Jas 4:1), even physical fighting (Acts 7:26). To bring this out I have opted for the translation "not to be combative."

ἐπιεικεῖς . . . πραΰτητα—These two words are virtual synonyms (2 Cor 10:1). See further the entry "Gentle, Kind" in the Extended Notes.

ἀνθρώπους—Here the term means "people" not "males."

3:3 Ἦμεν γάρ ποτε—This phrase indicates that all the various vices mentioned in this verse characterized the past of all people.[176] This is another way of saying that "anyone who keeps the entire law but stumbles in one [tenet] has become guilty of all of them" (Jas 2:10).[177] Thus, the conjunction δέ in 3:4 draws a sharp contrast between our former state and what has been accomplished by the "goodness and love for mankind of God our savior."

ἀνόητοι—"Foolish" in this sense means lacking in faith (Luke 24:25) and therefore lacking in that saving wisdom (Rom 1:14) that comes from faith (2 Tim 3:15).

ἀπειθεῖς—Those who are "disobedient" are those who are unable to do good works, because they are not sound in the faith (1:16 in light of 1:13).

πλανώμενοι—Another name for the unbelieving is those who are "deceived" (2 Tim 3:10–15).

δουλεύοντες ἐπιθυμίαις καὶ ἡδοναῖς ποικίλαις—"Being enslaved" (δουλεύοντες) takes the dative of that to which one is enslaved.[178] Those

---

175. Knight, *Pastoral Epistles*, 333.
176. *DNTB* 1255.
177. Translation in Giese, *James*, 199.
178. BDAG 259.

who do not believe are truly enslaved; they cannot free themselves from the "various lusts and desires" that enslave them. Everyone is enslaved to someone or something; if he is not a slave of God (Titus 1:1), a slavery which is the only true freedom (Rom 6:18, 22), then he will be enslaved to someone or something from which he cannot free himself.

ἐν κακίᾳ καὶ φθόνῳ διάγοντες—The verb "living" (διάγοντες) is the same verb used in 1 Tim 2:2 of Christians being able to live "in all godliness and reverence" when government performs its duties as God intends it to do. Thus, we see the great contrast in living that takes place because God "saved us" (3:5). Prior to salvation we live "in wickedness and envy"; after salvation we are empowered to live a godly life.

στυγητοί—A passage in Philo (*De Decalogo* 131) pairs this word with θεομίσητον, "hated by God,"[179] suggesting that the apostle's meaning here is that apart from salvation we make ourselves hateful to God (and we hate others; see next note).

μισοῦντες ἀλλήλους—A reflexive pronoun is used here; we hate "one another."

3:4 χρηστότης—This term can refer to the goodness of people[180] as well as the goodness of God.[181]

φιλανθρωπία—This is the root of the English word "philanthropy." Since the English term usually refers to human philanthropy, I have chosen to translate it here as "love for mankind."

ἐπεφάνη—This verb ("appeared") is in the aorist tense (as it is in 2:11), the tense that can denote one-time action in the past.[182] Here it refers to the appearance of God's grace in the incarnation, in the birth of Jesus Christ at a point in history.

τοῦ σωτῆρος ἡμῶν θεοῦ—Note that the appellation "our savior," used here of God (the Father), occurs in 3:6 with reference to "Jesus Christ" (God the Son). See further the commentary. For references to the deity of Jesus Christ see the commentary on 1 Tim 1:17 and Titus 2:13. See also the essay "There Is One God: The Pastoral Letters on the Identity of God" elsewhere in this commentary.

3:5 οὐκ ἐξ ἔργων τῶν ἐν δικαιοσύνῃ ἃ ἐποιήσαμεν ἡμεῖς—Compare "works" in the present passage with that in 2:14. Good works are not the cause of salvation but rather the result of it. "Righteousness" (δικαιοσύνη)

---

179. MM 594.
180. Rom 3:12; 2 Cor 6:6; Gal 5:22; Col 3:12.
181. Rom 2:4; 11:22 (3x); Eph 2:7.
182. BDF 166 [§ 318 (1)].

here has the same meaning as it does in Phil 3:9: "My own righteousness from the law."

κατὰ τὸ αὐτοῦ ἔλεος—See the entry "Mercy" in the Extended Notes.

ἔσωσεν ἡμᾶς—See the entry "Save, Savior, Salvation" in the Extended Notes and also the essay "He Saved Us: The Pastoral Letters on the Way of Salvation" elsewhere in this commentary. As the aorist tense of a verb can refer to one-time action in the past, the aorist tense of the verb ἔσωσεν points to the unique place in history of the death and resurrection of Jesus Christ as well as to the one-time event of baptism[183] (see also the following note).

διὰ λουτροῦ παλιγγενεσίας καὶ ἀνακαινώσεως πνεύματος ἁγίου—Each of these terms contributes something to the meaning of this phrase. The preposition διά with an object in the genitive case regularly indicates instrumentality,[184] "through." The only other use of λουτροῦ in the NT, Eph 5:26, "the washing of water in the word," is strong evidence that "washing" in the present passage refers to baptism.[185] Likewise, in this context Paul mentions "God [the Father]" (3:4), "Jesus Christ," the Son (3:6), and the "Holy Spirit" (3:5); this recollection of the Trinitarian formula for baptism of Matt 28:19 surely "cannot be regarded as accidental."[186]

The only other use of παλιγγενεσίας, "rebirth," in the NT, Matt 19:28, refers to the resurrection; the washing of baptism gives the resurrection to eternal life, as Paul implies in Rom 6:3–11 and explicitly states in Col 2:12. In the only other use of ἀνακαινώσεως in the NT, Rom 12:2, "renewal" stands in contrast to "this age"; hence, "renewal" is another way of describing the life of the resurrection. It is certainly no surprise that the apostle would attribute all of this to the working of God the Holy Spirit.[187]

3:6 οὗ ἐξέχεεν ἐφ' ἡμᾶς πλουσίως—Does the neuter relative pronoun οὗ refer to "washing" (λουτροῦ) or to "the Holy Spirit" (πνεύματος ἁγίου)? Grammatically either is possible. Perhaps Paul would assert that the ambiguity is fortuitous; since the Holy Spirit works through this washing, both can be true. However, since it seems pedantic to speak of the water being poured out "richly," I have opted to translate "whom." In baptism the Holy Spirit is poured out richly.

---

183. Koeberle, *Quest for Holiness*, 62–63.

184. BDAG 224–25.

185. Kelly, *Pastoral Epistles*, 251–52.

186. DPL 367.

187. Rom 5:5; 15:13; 1 Cor 12:3; Eph 1:13; 4:30; 1 Thess 1:5. Towner, *Letters*, 783, shows how the grammar and syntax points to the Holy Spirit as the one who accomplishes "the washing of rebirth and of renewal."

διὰ Ἰησοῦ Χριστοῦ τοῦ σωτῆρος ἡμῶν—In a previous verse (3:4) the apostle identifies God (the Father) as "our savior." On the significance of this see the commentary below.

3:7 ἵνα . . . γενηθῶμεν—Here ἵνα plus a verb in the subjunctive mood express purpose and result.[188]

δικαιωθέντες—See the entry "Righteousness/Justification" in the Extended Notes.

χάριτι—See the entry "Grace" in the Extended Notes.

κληρονόμοι—"Inheritance" is a rather common biblical expression for obtaining eternal salvation.[189] The very concept of inheritance indicates that salvation is received entirely as a gift of "grace," without merit.

κατ᾽ ἐλπίδα ζωῆς αἰωνίου—See the entry "Hope" in the Extended Notes. The term here denotes the object of hope, *spes quae speratur*.

3:8 Πιστὸς ὁ λόγος—See the excursus "The Trustworthy Sayings of the Pastoral Letters" at the end of the commentary on 1 Tim 1:12–17. In this instance the trustworthy saying precedes this notation. See further the commentary.

περὶ τούτων—The apostle gave a similar directive in 2:15. Therefore by "these things" in this passage he refers to everything that he has written since that previous imperative.[190] To accomplish the goal of those in his care being "intent on good works" Titus needs to "insist" on the guidance for good works given in 3:1–3 and the work of Christ sketched out in 3:4–7 as the motivation and power for doing good works.

βούλομαί—Paul writes as an apostle (1:1); therefore, he writes with the authority of Christ (see the entry "Apostle" in the Extended Notes). These are not just his ideas; these are the directives of Christ himself.

διαβεβαιοῦσθαι—That this is a strong word ("insist") is seen in its being a cognate of the verb βεβαιόω, "confirm" (Rom 15:8; 1 Cor 1:6; Heb 2:3), and of the noun βεβαίωσις, "confirmation" (Phil 1:7; Heb 6:16).

ἵνα φροντίζωσιν—Here ἵνα plus a verb in the subjunctive mood introduces a purpose clause.[191]

καλῶν ἔργων προΐστασθαι—This is a verb (προΐστασθαι, "be intent") that in other contexts refers to leadership.[192] Its use here indicates that the

---

188. Wallace, *Greek Grammar*, 473–74.

189. Matt 19:29; 25:34; Mark 10:17; Luke 10:25; 18:18; 1 Cor 6:9, 10; 15:50; Gal 5:21; Heb 1:14; 6:12; Rev 21:7.

190. Knight, *Pastoral Epistles*, 352, comes to the same conclusion.

191. Wallace, *Greek Grammar*, 471–72.

192. Rom 12:8; 1 Thess 5:12; 1 Tim 3:4, 5, 12; 5:17.

Christian life involves being intentional about bringing forth the good works that God directs in his word.

οἱ πεπιστευκότες θεῷ—Faith receives justification before God for the sake of Jesus Christ (3:7); this gift of justification empowers one to do good works (3:1). See further the commentary.

καλὰ καὶ ὠφέλιμα τοῖς ἀνθρώποις—The good works of the Christian life benefit others as well as pleasing God. The term "people" (ἀνθρώποις) is a broad, general term. The Christian has a special responsibility toward his fellow believers (Gal 6:10); nevertheless, he is to do good to all. His life of being "intent on good works" that "are good and profitable to people" would include his life of Christian citizenship (3:1).

3:9 μωρὰς δὲ ζητήσεις—Compare 1 Tim 6:4; 2 Tim 2:23. The false teachers engaged in debates to try to win adherents by presenting themselves as learned and sophisticated. In reality, because these are lacking in the wisdom of God that saves (2 Tim 3:15), they are "foolish." See further "The Nature of the Heresy" in the Introduction to the Pastoral Letters.

γενεαλογίας—This may well have to do with proto-gnostic speculations about intermediary beings between God and mankind. See further "The Nature of the Heresy" in the Introduction to the Pastoral Letters.

ἔρεις—This may be a general word about the "disputes" in which the heretics engaged; this would include "arguments about the law" (see the following note).

μάχας νομικὰς—This points to a Jewish element in the false teaching afflicting the churches served by Titus. See further "The Nature of the Heresy" in the Introduction to the Pastoral Letters.

περιΐστασο—Compare 2 Tim 2:16. The literal meaning of this verb, "stand around, stand by" (John 11:42; Acts 25:7) suggests the idea of "keep your distance," hence "avoid."

ἀνωφελεῖς καὶ μάταιοι—The apostle uses two synonyms ("useless and futile") to emphasize his point about the uselessness of such controversies.

3:10 αἱρετικὸν ἄνθρωπον—The adjective is, of course, the source of the English term "heretical." A cognate noun, αἵρεσις, refers neutrally to a group (Acts 26:5) or negatively to divisions (1 Cor 11:19; Gal 5:20). That same noun takes on a negative connotation in referring to a religious group that is deemed to be heretical (Acts 24:5, 14; 28:22); it can even be used of false teachings (2 Pet 2:1). Furthermore, Paul has just given instructions about avoiding "foolish controversies and genealogies and disputes and arguments about the law," language that describes the false teaching afflicting the churches for which Titus is to care. In light of all this a rendering like "one who causes divisions" seems inadequate—after all, to "reject" (παραιτοῦ) such a one would itself create a division; rather, the translation "a heretic" appears justified. See further the commentary.

μετὰ μίαν καὶ δευτέραν νουθεσίαν—Being a heretic would involve a public sin, along the lines of Gal 2:11–14 and 1 Tim 5:20. Therefore, this would be outside the scope of the instruction of Jesus recorded in Matt 18:15–17, which deals with private sins.[193] Hence, there is no conflict between the three steps of that passage and the one or two admonitions of the present verse.

A verb cognate to the noun νουθεσίαν ("admonition") is used in 2 Thess 3:15 of warning a fellow Christian ("brother"); 2 Tim 2:25–26 speaks of approaching an opponent so as to bring him to repentance and faith. This would point to admonitions such as the one referred to here being intended to bring a "heretic" to repentance and faith.[194]

παραιτοῦ—Compare this imperative ("reject") with its use in 1 Tim 4:7; 5:11; 2 Tim 2:23. Although different terminology is used, this instruction is similar to that of Rom 16:17; 1 Cor 5:9–11; 2 Thess 3:6, 14–15; 2 Tim 3:5. The references in 1 Corinthians and 2 Thessalonians demonstrate that these directives would not be limited to unbelievers; they could also apply even to those whose error might not involve loss of saving faith altogether, that is, erring Christians. See further the commentary.

3:11 εἰδὼς—This present tense participle designates action contemporaneous with the main verb (παραιτοῦ).[195]

ἐξέστραπται—This is a perfect passive form of the verb ἐκστέφω, hence "has become perverted."

ἁμαρτάνει—To bring out the significance of the present tense of this verb, I have chosen to render it "is sinful."

ὢν αὐτοκατάκριτος—In this context the verbal root from which this word is formed (κρίνω) has the meaning "condemn."[196]

---

193. On the Matthean passage see Gibbs, "'Following' Matthew 18," 6–25.
194. Knight, *Pastoral Epistles*, 355.
195. Wallace, *Greek Grammar*, 625–26.
196. Rom 2:1, 3; 14:3, 4, 10, 13; Col 2:16; Jas 4:11, 12.

COMMENTARY

At One Time

The heart and center of this section is its kerygmatic presentation of the work of "our savior." But to set the stage for this proclamation of salvation Paul writes about the human condition "at one time" (ποτε, 3:3).

It is significant that when he does this, the apostle uses the first-person plural, and he employs the plural form of all the nouns, verbs, and adjectives that he uses here.[197] He is speaking of the condition of all humanity apart from the saving work of Christ. Thus, there is no homiletical license needed to apply these words to any and every group of hearers. These words of law and rebuke are true of everyone.

The various terms and phrases that Paul employs supply a variety of windows through which to view the human condition (see the textual notes). "Foolish" denotes a lack of that faith which is the only way to the "wisdom" that saves; such people are "deceived." Apart from faith we are "disobedient," as we can do nothing that is truly in keeping with the will and law of God. The unbelieving are truly "slaves to various lusts and desires," for they cannot free themselves from evil, so that they cannot do anything that is not contaminated by sin. This means that their entire life is characterized by "wickedness and envy." This means that they are "loathsome" to God. Moreover, their evil nature is seen in that they are "hating one another." This is how all people are, until and unless God makes his saving change in their life (pointed to by the adversative δέ, "but," in 3:4).

Our Savior Appeared

The adversative δέ introduces the "trustworthy saying" of 3:4–7, which speaks of the way of salvation (on the trustworthy sayings of the Pastoral Letters see the excursus by that name at the end of the commentary on 1 Tim 1:12–17). In this section Paul writes both of what God did in history for humanity's salvation and also of the way in which he gives that salvation to individuals.

Initially we note that in this section the apostle identifies both "God" and "Jesus Christ" as "our savior." A mere six verses prior to this section

---

197. The "inclusive we"; Wallace, *Greek Grammar*, 398.

Paul had spoken of "our great God and savior, Jesus Christ" (2:13).[198] That fact might argue for understanding "God" and "Jesus Christ" in the present verse to be two names for the same person. However, in the Pauline correspondence, as well as in the New Testament generally, the vocable "God" (θεός) is usually reserved for God the Father, while the deity of Jesus Christ is indicated with the word "Lord" (κύριος), standing for the name of God from the Hebrew Scriptures (יהוה).[199] That being the case, it is most likely that in the present passage "God" refers to God the Father.

What, therefore, is the meaning behind identifying both the Father and Christ the Son as "our savior?" God the Father saved us in that he made his eternal plan of salvation and sent his Son, Jesus Christ, to carry out that plan.[200] Jesus Christ saved us by completing the plan of salvation through his death on the cross (and subsequent resurrection).[201] Thus, it is fitting to apply the appellation "our savior" to both God the Father and God the Son, Jesus Christ.[202]

Paul uses four different terms in this section to describe what moved God to act for humanity's salvation. "Goodness" (χρηστότης) is a relatively rare word in the Pauline corpus (see the textual notes); human goodness, therefore, serves as an (albeit not fully adequate) illustration of the goodness of God. The vocable φιλανθρωπία is an even less common Pauline term; its etymology, "love for mankind," aptly indicates its meaning. Both "mercy" (ἔλεος) and "grace" (χάριτι) are terms of major significance in the apostle's letters; each designates that it is God's favorable attitude toward us rather than anything, such as "works in righteousness" of our own doing, that saves us.[203]

When the apostle writes that God's goodness and love for mankind "appeared," he uses this aorist tense verb to refer to a particular point in history: the coming of Jesus Christ into the world.[204] Hence, Titus 3:4–7

---

198. For the rationale for and defense of this translation see the commentary on 2:13.

199. For example, in the salutations of both 1 Timothy (1:2) and 2 Timothy (1:2). See also the essay "There Is One God: The Pastoral Letters on the Identity of God" elsewhere in this commentary.

200. Eph 2:5; 2 Thess 2:13; 1 Tim 1:1; 2:3–4; 4:10; 2 Tim 2:8–9; Titus 1:3; 2:10; 3:5.

201. Eph 5:23; Phil 3:20; 1 Tim 1:15; 2 Tim 1:10; 2:10; Titus 1:4; 2:13; 3:6.

202. Since God saves through sanctification by the Spirit (2 Thess 2:13) and calls to this through the gospel (2 Thess 2;14), which is the folly of what is preached (1 Cor 1:21), God the Holy Spirit also plays a role in saving people.

203. See the entries "Mercy" and "Grace" in the Extended Notes.

204. See the textual note on ἐπεφάνη (3:4) above.

has historically been appointed for reading in public worship during the Christmas season.²⁰⁵ However, since Christ came into the world to carry out the work of salvation (1 Tim 1:15), the verb here points not merely to the incarnation but also to its purpose: the death and resurrection of Jesus Christ for mankind's salvation.

A complementary term that Paul often uses for "save" is "justify."²⁰⁶ In the present passage he employs it while speaking of how God gives the salvation that Christ acquired for all to persons individually.

Here the apostle designates the "washing of rebirth and of renewal of the Holy Spirit" as a means by which God saves us, so that we are justified; that this entire phrase is attached to a single preposition (διά, "through") indicates that "rebirth and renewal" denote one action rather than two.²⁰⁷ The similar vocabulary that Paul uses elsewhere of baptism shows that this is also his reference here. The apostle speaks of God (the Father) pouring out this washing of the Holy Spirit through Jesus Christ; the Trinitarian nature of this description echoes the Trinitarian formula given by Jesus after his resurrection (Matt 28:19). This instruction about baptism should be read in connection with all the other places in the Pauline corpus that speak of baptism.²⁰⁸

Grammatically either the washing or the Holy Spirit could be what God the Father poured out richly. Although we have argued above that "the Holy Spirit" is the better alternative, Paul might well maintain that there is no real difference between these options. When the water of baptism is poured out, God the Holy Spirit is also being poured out to accomplish the work of salvation for the one baptized.

The result of all of this is eternal life. That we receive eternal life as "heirs" reemphasizes that salvation is received by grace as a gift.

"Hope" here is no mere wish. Hope has its usual, theological meaning in the Scriptures of something sure and certain for which believers can confidently wait.²⁰⁹

The apostle speaks in these verses of salvation as an accomplished reality. The goodness of God "appeared"; God "saved" us; we have "been justified through his grace." Paul balances these references to the historical reality of salvation with mention of the future "hope of eternal life."

---

205. For example, LSB xiv, xvi, xviii, xx.
206. See the entry "Righteousness/Justification" in the Extended Notes.
207. As Marshall, *Pastoral Epistles*, 321, acknowledges.
208. See Deterding, "Baptism," 93–100.
209. See the entry "Hope" in the Extended Notes.

This partnering of past and future elements points to the already/not-yet character of our salvation: Christ has already acquired our salvation. Nevertheless, the full realization of it awaits the future.

This makes the believer's life one of hope. What Christ did in the past has made our future salvation secure. Therefore, we live with a sure and certain hope.

The reference to the "hope of eternal life" forms a bit of an inclusion for the letter. Already in the salutation of this missive the apostle had spoken of the hope of eternal life (1:2). Paul gives the hope of eternal life the first and last word in this letter, emphasizing its importance for the church's proclamation.

Good Works

This section of the Letter to Titus gives a succinct exposition of the place of good works in the life of the Christian. In the language of systematic theology, he shows that good works are excluded from the doctrine of justification but are included in the believer's life of sanctification.[210]

Paul writes that God saved us "not by works in righteousness which we had done, but according to his [God's] mercy." Salvation/justification is entirely the work of God. Christ acquired salvation through his redemptive work (death and resurrection); moreover, it is entirely the work of God that salvation is given to each one personally, for example, through baptism as the washing of rebirth and of renewal. The individual receives that salvation through faith/believing.

That being said, it is also true that those "who have believed in God" are to be "intent on good works." Hence, Titus is to remind them "to be prepared for every good work." Having been saved without works, believers are to busy themselves with doing good works. In the present section the apostle speaks both of positive virtues that the believer is to display and of negative vices that he or she is to avoid.

With a variety of examples Paul illustrates what it means to be prepared for and to be intent on every good work. He writes that believers are to be subject to rulers and authorities. This is a briefer version of the instruction that the apostle gives at greater length in Rom 13 (1–7). Perhaps it is more than coincidence that in the present passage he follows

---

210. An outstanding work on the distinction between and interrelation of justification and sanctification is Koeberle, *Quest for Holiness*, the English translation of his work *Rechtfertigung und Heiligung* ("Justification and Sanctification").

those words with a directive about being "obedient," using the same rare word that occurs in the statement about obeying God rather than men (Acts 5:29). Perchance this was all that was necessary to indicate that obedience to government is limited to what does not involve disobedience to God.[211] Paul continues with other positive directives regarding the Christian life. In addition to being obedient, being kind and showing gentleness are general virtues that describe the entirety of the Christian life (see the textual notes).

The apostle notes that the virtues of the Christian life "are good and profitable to people." As God himself is the standard of all good (1 Tim 2:3) these words indicate the scope of those whom Christians are to serve. They serve God by doing those things that he desires and commands. In so doing they also serve other people; doing what is good in the eyes of God is beneficial to our fellow human beings.

Doing good also involves avoiding evil. In his description of the pre-Christian state Paul sets forth vices that those who have come to saving faith are to avoid (see the section "At One Time" above). He adds slander and being combative as further evils to be shunned.

Another class of evil that the Christian is to flee has to do with false teaching. In mentioning "controversies and genealogies and disputes and arguments about the law" the apostle refers to the false teaching that is endangering the churches served by Titus (see further "The Nature of the Heresy" in the Introduction to the Pastoral Letters). Just as the virtues of the Christian life are "profitable to people," so false teaching is "unprofitable and futile." As spiritual leader of the churches of Crete, Titus has a special obligation with respect to such matters.

The Responsibility of Titus

Titus had a pastoral responsibility toward the Christians in his care. As such he is to teach the truth about matters of faith and life.

Paul's coworker is both to "remind" his people about these matters and to "insist" on them. Thus, the pastoral ministry, such as that of Titus,

---

211. A detailed study of the relationship of the Christian to God and to government (the kingdoms of God's right hand and his left hand) is beyond the scope of the present commentary. Helpful resources among the vast literature on this subject, in addition to volumes 44–47 of the American edition of *Luther's Works*, include the following: Scharlemann, "Theology of Freedom"; Huegli, *Church and State*; Neuhaus, "Ambiguities"; Althaus, *Ethics*.

includes teaching how believers should live as well as proclaiming the way of salvation.

In telling Titus to "avoid" the false teachings, Paul is indicating that Titus is to steer those in his charge away from error and to the truth. Related to that is the directive to "reject" a heretic. As this comes immediately after the description of the false teachings, and as the heretic is described as "perverted," "sinful," and "self-condemned," it is evident that the apostle is speaking of adherents of the false teaching. This supports the translation "heretic" and indicates that the instruction here has to do with dealing with false teaching within the outward association of the church. Similar instruction elsewhere in the Pauline corpus (1 Cor 5:9–11; 2 Thess 3:14–15) demonstrates that the present passage also applies to dealing with error on the part of those who still are part of the Christian church ("brother").

The Life of the Justified: Titus 3:1–11 in Context

The previous kerygmatic section of this letter (2:11–14) had followed a section of instruction in Christian living that gave specific directives to individuals in their particular vocations. The first part of the present section speaks in more general terms of the kind of life that God's people are to lead.

Paul sets forth examples of virtues to be practiced and of vices to be avoided. He follows these by noting that all people (himself included) were at one time enslaved to sin and vice. From there he segues into a proclamation of the way of salvation, including baptism as a means by which God the Holy Trinity grants the gift of justification/salvation.

This section of gospel proclamation is sandwiched in between the previous portion of instruction in Christian living and the one that follows. In this latter hortatory section the apostle directs his readers to Christian living, which includes rejecting heresy and also those who persist in teaching false doctrine.

3:12–15: Concluding Matters

TRANSLATION

¹² Whenever I send Artemas to you (or Tychicus), come speedily to me in Nicopolis, for I have decided to spend the winter there. ¹³ Speedily send ahead Zenas the lawyer and Apollos, in order that nothing might be lacking for them. ¹⁴ Let our people learn to be intent for good works for pressing needs, in order that they might not be unfruitful. ¹⁵ All who are with me greet you. Greet those who love us in the faith. Grace be with all of you.

TEXTUAL NOTES

3:12 Ἀρτεμᾶν—This is Artemas (Ἀρτεμᾶς), a friend of Paul's, not to be confused with Artemis (Ἀρτεμις), a pagan goddess (Acts 19:24, 27–28, 34–35).

Τύχικον—Tychicus was a man from the province of Asia who accompanied Paul when the latter was taking the money for the collection to Jerusalem (Acts 20:4). In Eph 6:21 (and Col 4:7) the apostle identifies him as "the beloved brother and faithful minster/servant (and fellow slave) in the Lord." In 2 Tim 4:12 Paul reports that he is sending/had sent (depending on whether we read the verb as a regular or an epistolary aorist) him to Ephesus.

The position of "or Tychicus" after "to you" perhaps suggests that the apostle writes this almost as an afterthought; his first inclination is to send Artemas, but he may end up sending Tychicus instead. It appears that the one sent will at least temporarily take over the responsibilities that Titus currently shoulders; that being the case, Paul must have regarded both Artemas and Tychicus as capable and trustworthy ministers of the word.

σπούδασον ἐλθεῖν πρός με—"Come to me as soon as you can." In order to preserve the play on words with σπουδαίως in 3:13 I have used the translation "come speedily to me."

Νικόπολιν—A number of cities in the NT world bore this name; this one is probably the one on the western shore of Greece.[212] Epictetus, a near contemporary of the apostle (AD 50–120) residing in Nicopolis, refers to "Galileans" in the area (*Discourses* 4.7); this would have been his way of referring to Christians.[213] The presence of Christians in this region at a relatively short time after Paul had spent the winter there suggests at least the possibility that the apostle (and his coworker Titus; see the following note) had spent time there active in the ministry of the gospel. It would certainly have been characteristic of Paul to have done so. As Nicopolis was a port city where travelers might well have wintered before continuing their journeys, the city might have provided the apostle with a wide variety of people with whom he might have shared the gospel.[214]

παραχειμάσαι—In this instance of indirect discourse the aorist infinitive stands in place of a future indicative in direct discourse: "I have decided that I will spend the winter there."[215] Winter was not a favorable time for travel, especially by ship (Acts 27:12; 28:11). Hence, the apostle instructs Titus to "come speedily to me." At this point Paul is still free to travel in the service of the gospel, so long as conditions are favorable.

3:13 Ζηνᾶν τὸν νομικὸν καὶ Ἀπολλῶν—Nothing more is known of the former; the latter is known for his ministerial work in Corinth and Ephesus.[216] What is said of them here would suggest that they were the bearers of this letter.[217]

σπουδαίως πρόπεμψον—They are to be sent "speedily" (without delay), as the coming winter will make travel more difficult. In order to preserve the play on words with σπούδασον in 3:12 I have used the translation "speedily."

ἵνα μηδὲν αὐτοῖς λείπῃ—The use of a purpose clause[218] as well as the similarity of the language of this clause to comparable passages in the

---

212. BDAG 673.
213. *DNTB* 322–23; Marshall, *Pastoral Epistles*, 341–42.
214. Quinn, *Titus*, 264–65.
215. Wallace, *Greek Grammar*, 604.
216. Acts 18:24; 19:1; 1 Cor 1:12; 3:4–6, 22; 4:6; 16:12.
217. Kelly, *Pastoral Epistles*, 258.
218. Wallace, *Greek Grammar*, 471–72 (ἵνα plus a verb in the subjunctive mood).

NT[219] would suggest that the two are being sent for ministering purposes. This would be an example of Titus being "a lover of traveling missionaries" (φιλόξενον, 1:8; cf. 1 Tim 3:2).

3:14 μανθανέτωσαν—As a cognate of the noun μαθητής, "disciple,"[220] this verb would imply intentional, religious teaching. This *plural* imperative anticipates the final words of the letter, which indicate that Paul intended for this to be read to the entire church. Hence, the apostle directs the people to learn to live as a disciple is supposed to live. This directive would also imply that Titus is to see to it that such (catechetical) instruction takes place.

καλῶν ἔργων προΐστασθαι—Christian instruction involves both matters pertaining to salvation and also directives concerning the Christian's life of sanctification.

τὰς ἀναγκαίας χρείας—The Christian life is one of service; good works are done to meet the needs of others (as well as of self). The adjective ἀναγκαίας is cognate to the noun ἀνάγκη, which can mean "pressure,"[221] so "pressing" is a good translation here.

ἵνα μὴ ὦσιν—Here ἵνα plus a verb in the subjunctive mood introduces a (negative) purpose clause.[222]

ἄκαρποι—"Fruitless" is the opposite of bearing fruit, which is a Pauline way of speaking of sanctified living,[223] and one which goes back to Jesus himself (John 15:2, 4, 5, 8, 16).

3:15 Ἀσπάζονταί ... ἄσπασαι—The sending of greetings by the apostle from "all who are with me" (or a similar turn of phrase) is attested in some of his other letters (1 Cor 16:20; 2 Cor 13:12; Phil 4:22). The greetings of Paul's letters serve to express unity and love between Christian brothers and sisters. See further the commentary below.

ἐν πίστει—Christians are not unconcerned for those outside the faith, but they have a special love for and obligation to their fellow believers (Gal 6:10). That Titus is to "greet all who love us in the faith" indicates that the false teachers are excluded from these greetings, since by their false teaching they have excluded themselves from the blessings of

---

219. Kelly, *Pastoral Epistles*, 358; cf. Acts 15:3; Rom 15:24; 1 Cor 16:6, 11; 2 Cor 1:16; 3 John 6.

220. BDAG 609, 615.

221. BDAG 60–61.

222. Wallace, *Greek Grammar*, 471–72.

223. Rom 7:4; Gal 5:22–23; Eph 5:9; Col 1:10.

salvation.²²⁴ "Faith" (πίστει) here refers to the content of what is believed (*fides quae creditur*). The word for "love" here (φιλοῦντας), as often in the NT, is used as a synonym of the ἀγάπη word group; see the entry "Love" in the Extended Notes.

χάρις—See the entry "Grace" in the Extended Notes.

πάντων ὑμῶν—The use of the plural and of the word "all" makes it plain that this letter is not merely private correspondence between two individuals; rather, this is to be read to the entire church. See further the commentary below.

COMMENTARY

From Paul's letters we learn that he used a scribe (an amanuensis) for the actual writing of his epistles (Rom 16:22) but would write something in his own hand near the letter's conclusion.²²⁵ This practice would make it all but certain that the apostle wrote these last few sentences himself.

Paul's Plans for Ministry

Paul is perhaps in his mid-sixties when he writes this letter,²²⁶ having already at an earlier point in his life described himself as "an old man" (Phlm 9). Yet he is still active in ministry (in modern parlance, if not working "full time," he is at least still active in "semi-retirement").

His plans to send either Artemas or Tychicus to Titus seem designed to provide coverage for the latter while he is away visiting the apostle, likely to report on ministry in Crete or otherwise to provide some assistance to Paul for ministry. In the same way the wording of the instruction about Titus sending Zenas and Apollos must surely have to do with those two being about some work of ministry.

Many pastors have looked to the apostle as a role model for their own ministry. Many factors, health and family responsibilities among them, go into a pastor's decision to retire from ministry. For some that may mean completely stepping away from the tasks of the pastoral ministry. Others might continue in some type of ministry in "semi-retirement." Whatever the particulars, since a pastor recognizes the ministry

---

224. Kelly, *Pastoral Epistles*, 259.
225. 1 Cor 16:21; Gal 6:11; Col 4:18; Phlm 19; and especially 2 Thess 3:17.
226. See the Introduction to Titus in this commentary.

as a vocation and not merely an occupation, even a retired pastor will likely seek to serve the Lord of the church as best he can. For a pastor in such a situation, the author of the Letter to Titus can continue to serve as a role model.

Discipleship

Paul has nearly come to the end of this letter. Nevertheless, he adds one last imperative. With a view to the fact that this letter is to be read to all the churches as an authoritative word of God (3:15),[227] he calls on "our people" to learn to be intent for doing good deeds. The implication is that Titus and other pastors will teach the same.

The church is to teach the saving truth of Jesus Christ. The church is also to teach and to promote godly living. The church's main task is to teach the saving truth, so that people may come to saving faith, but that faith will also show itself by the fruit of good works (John 15:4–5; Gal 5:22–23).

There is certainly a danger that ministry will wander into moralism. That being said, it is nevertheless true that the church of all ages needs to follow the apostle's instruction here and also teach its people how to be about godly living.

Greetings and Grace

In many of his letters Paul includes greetings from himself, from fellow proclaimers of the gospel, and/or from entire churches.[228] In the present letter Paul and those with him send greetings to Titus; then the apostle sends greetings to all the believers in the churches served by his coworker. The fact that Paul intends for the letter to be read in the churches means that this sending of greetings is not merely a courtesy or formality; the parishioners will hear these greetings as the apostle's letter is read to them in their worship services.[229] This sending of greetings reflects the unity in the faith that is shared by Paul, Titus, and all those in his care.

---

227. See the textual notes on 3:15 above.

228. In addition to the present letter, note Rom 16:3–16, 21–23; 1 Cor 16:19, 21; 2 Cor 13:12–13; Phil 4:21–22; Col 4:10–15; 1 Thess 5:26; 2 Tim 4:19, 21; Phlm 23–24.

229. See the section "The Spirit Explicitly Says" in the commentary on 1 Tim 4:1–5.

Grace and Life

The final "greeting" in this letter, as in all the Pauline Letters, is "grace."[230] As the apostle always includes that word in the salutations of his letters,[231] so he always gives grace the final word in them. "Grace" therefore forms an *inclusio* for his letters, showing that if there is a word that can encapsulate all that he has to say, it is "grace." Like the greetings of his letters, so this word "grace" is full of meaning. Paul always closed with the blessing of grace, pointing his readers (including us today) to the grace of God in Christ that is our salvation and hope.

---

230. Rom 16:20; 1 Cor 16:23; 2 Cor 13:14; Gal 6:18; Eph 6:24; Phil 4:23; Col 4:18; 1 Thess 5:28; 2 Thess 3:18; 1 Tim 6:21; 2 Tim 4:22; Titus 3:15; Phlm 25.

231. Rom 1:7; 1 Cor 1:3; 2 Cor 1:2; Gal 1:3; Eph 1:2; Phil 1:2; Col 1:2; 1 Thess 1:1; 2 Thess 1:2; 1 Tim 1:2; 2 Tim 1:2; Titus 1:4; Phlm 3.

Introduction to 2 Timothy

RECIPIENT

See the section by this title in the commentary on 1 Timothy.

SETTING AND DATE

See further the "Chronology of Paul's Life" and "Authenticity and Integrity" in the Introduction to the Pastoral Letters.

Paul is in prison when he writes this letter (1:16). This imprisonment is very different from that of Ephesians, Philippians, Colossians, and Philemon. Those letters have a very positive tone; the apostle has good reason to think that he will be acquitted (Phil 1:21–26; Phlm 22). When he writes 2 Timothy, it is with a sense of resignation; he knows that his life's work is drawing to a close and that this imprisonment will end with his martyrdom (4:6–8).[1]

Paul had been free to move about when he wrote 1 Timothy (1:3) and again when he wrote Titus (3:12). His imprisonment has changed all of that. This points to the apostle writing 2 Timothy at a later date than either of the other two Pastoral Letters.

The Letter to Titus indicates that Paul had left him as head of the churches in Crete in order to supply the churches with pastors (1:5). By the time of the writing of 2 Timothy, Titus was no longer at Crete but had moved on to Dalmatia (4:10). This also places the writing of 2 Timothy after that of Titus (as well as of 1 Timothy).

The chronology of the apostle's life from the book of Acts suggests that he would have been freed from his first Roman imprisonment in

---

1. As recognized by Johnson, *Letters*, 450–51.

AD 61. If he then traveled to Spain (Rom 15:24, 28) as well as to Crete (Titus 1:5), to the home of Philemon in Colossae² (Phlm 22), to Ephesus and Macedonia (1 Tim 1:3), to Miletus (2 Tim 4:20) and to Nicopolis (Titus 3:12), these travels and accompanying periods of ministry would have taken several years.

As 2 Timothy postdates the other two Pastoral Letters, the dates assigned to those two epistles would help determine the date of this letter. In light of the travel presupposed by these letters between the end of Acts and the writing of 2 Timothy we can reasonably conjecture that Paul wrote 1 Timothy around 63 or 64, Titus in perhaps 65, and 2 Timothy in 67 or 68, shortly before his martyrdom.

Timothy was in Ephesus at the time of the writing of 1 Timothy (1:3). There are indications that he was still there when Paul penned the present letter. Onesiphorus is associated with Ephesus (1:18), and in this letter the apostle sends greetings to his household (4:19). The wording of 4:12 in light of 4:9, 21, would appear to indicate that Paul was sending Tychicus to Ephesus to take over Timothy's responsibilities there.³ Thus, it is reasonable to conjecture that Timothy was still carrying out ministry in Ephesus when the apostle wrote this letter to him.

PURPOSE

The character of 1 Timothy and Titus as "pastoral epistles" is well known due to the list of qualifications for the pastoral office ("overseer," "elder") given in each of those letters (1 Tim 3:1–7; Titus 1:5–9). On the other hand, 2 Timothy may be thought of as Paul's "last will and testament," as he writes a very heartfelt Letter to Timothy, seeing that his martyrdom is imminent and asking that, if possible, he might be able to see his younger coworker one last time.

Without discounting any of that, it should be noted that this letter also has the character of a *pastoral* epistle. Throughout much of the letter the apostle is concerned with matters pertaining to faithful ministry in the truth and especially with such ministry by those who will hold the

---

2. That Philemon dwelt in Colossae can be seen from the many individuals who are named in both Colossians and Philemon: Onesimus (Col 4:9; Phlm 10–12), Aristarchus (Col 4:10; Phlm 24), Mark (Col 4:10; Phlm 25), Demas (Col 4:14; Phlm 24), and Archippus (Col 4:17; Phlm 2).

3. See the textual note on 4:12.

office of the pastoral ministry. It is in light of this understanding that the letter can be outlined.

OUTLINE

As we read this letter, it appears that the part of it that consists of 1:3–18 serves as an "overture" to the letter.[4] As the overture of an opera[5] introduces themes that will have a prominent role in the remainder of the work, so these verses first touch on themes that will be expounded upon in greater depth in the remainder of this epistle.[6] These themes include (1) the need for pastors in particular and Christians in general to hold to and to proclaim the truth of God's word; (2) the consequential need to proclaim that truth over against error; (3) the resulting reality that holding to and proclaiming this truth will subject one to various forms of suffering and persecution. In the remainder of the letter Paul develops all of these themes in greater detail.

From this understanding of the purpose of the letter we can develop the following outline:

I. Salutation (1:1–2)

II. Overture

    A. The Cross, Ministry, and the Office of the Ministry (1:3–14)

    B. Adversaries and Supporters; Suffering and Faithfulness (1:15–18)

III. The Main Body of the Letter

    A. The Ministry—and the Suffering That It Entails (2:1–7)

    B. Suffering and Endurance for the Gospel (2:8–13)

    C. The Minister and His Ministry; the Truth and Its Opponents (2:14–26)

---

4. See the table on page 298.

5. Such as the rock opera "Tommy" by The Who. The tracks "I Am The Sea" and "Quadrophenia" from the band's album *Quadrophenia* serve the same purpose.

6. I would also consider that 1 Tim 1:1–17 and Titus 1:1–4 function as "overtures" to those letters; see "Outline" in the Introduction to 1 Timothy and "One Servant of the Word to Another: Titus 1:1–4 in Context" in the commentary on Titus 1:1–4. In a comparable way Col 1:3–20 serves as an overture to that letter; see Deterding, *Colossians*, 26–27. Similarly, Eph 1:3–14 functions in the same way in that epistle (Scharlemann, "Secret of God's Plan," 538–39).

D. The Truth and Its Opponents in the Last Days (3:1–9)

E. Suffering for Faithfulness to the Scriptures (3:10–17)

F. Opposition to the Truth Brings Suffering (4:1–5)

G. Suffering for the Truth: Paul's Impending Martyrdom (4:6–8)

H. Ministry in the Truth and Those Who Oppose It (4:9–18)

IV. Concluding Greetings and Blessings (4:19–22)

Commentary on 2 Timothy

1:1–2: Salutation

On the salutations in Paul's letters see the section "Salutations in Paul's Letters" in the Introduction to the Pastoral Letters.

TRANSLATION

¹ Paul, apostle of Christ Jesus through the will of God in accord with the promise of life, which is in Christ Jesus, ² to Timothy, my beloved child: grace, mercy, and peace from God the Father and Christ Jesus our Lord.

TEXTUAL NOTES

1:1 ἀπόστολος—See the entry "Apostle" in the Extended Notes.

διὰ θελήματος θεοῦ—This is a phrase that Paul uses seven times in his letters; five of the seven occur in the salutation of the respective letters to designate that he is an apostle "by the will of God."[7] This emphasizes what is inherent in the concept of "apostle." A man does not appoint himself as an apostle; he is called to it by God himself. Furthermore, the authority that one exercises as an apostle is not his own; rather, it comes from God.

κατ' ἐπαγγελίαν ζωῆς—One serves as an apostle for an ultimate purpose, namely, to bring the gift of eternal life to others.

ἐν Χριστῷ Ἰησοῦ—See the entry "In Christ" in the Extended Notes.

1:2 Τιμοθέῳ ἀγαπητῷ τέκνῳ—Timothy had been raised by his mother and grandmother in the faith of the Old Testament (2 Tim 1:5).

---

7. Rom 15:32; 1 Cor 1:1; 2 Cor 1:1; 8:5; Eph 1:1; Col 1:1; 2 Tim 1:1.

Timothy was from Lystra, a town to which Paul himself had first brought the Christian gospel (Acts 14:6–23; 16:1–3), so that the apostle could rightly claim him as his "child" both as a Christian believer and as one whom he mentored to be a fellow laborer in the gospel.[8] He uses the word "child" with this same meaning elsewhere in the Pastorals.[9]

χάρις . . . ἡμῶν—A phrase similar to this is found at the end of the salutations of all of the Pauline Letters. In Paul's letters these are always lacking a verb. Similar phrases in the salutations of other NT letters (1 Pet 1:2; 2 Pet 1:2; Jude 2; 2 John 3) always supply a verb. This suggests the possibility that this style of phrase originated with Paul, and that in "copying" him other authors felt the need to add a verb.[10] In the Pauline phrases some verbal action is clearly implied, something along the lines of "may there be." With these phrases the apostle is pronouncing a blessing on his readers, one that actually delivers the "grace, mercy, and peace" that is spoken of. On the meaning of each of these terms, see the entries on them in the Extended Notes.

COMMENTARY

This is one of the shorter salutations in the Pauline corpus.[11] Nevertheless, Paul does fill it with some significant theological points.

As is his usual custom, at the beginning of this letter's salutation Paul identifies himself as an "apostle."[12] Here he notes that he has this status "through the will of God." One did not make himself as apostle; only God's call put a man in this office.

He further states that is "in accord with the promise of life, which is in Christ Jesus." The purpose of an apostle is to speak the word that gives the life that Christ acquired for all.

---

8. Knight, *Pastoral Epistles*, 365.
9. 1 Tim 1:2, 18; 2 Tim 2:1; Titus 1:4.
10. Wallace, *Greek Grammar*, 51.

11. In terms of the number of Greek words used, Romans, 1 and 2 Corinthians, Galatians, Philippians, 1 Timothy, Titus, and Philemon are longer, while Colossians and the two Letters to the Thessalonians are shorter. The place for Ephesians depends on whether or not one counts ἐν Ἐφέσῳ as an original part of that letter.

12. In the four epistles where he does not do this (Philippians, 1 and 2 Thessalonians, and Philemon) Paul names at least one other individual (either "Timothy" or "Silvanus and Timothy") as a "co-sender" of the letter. Since his co-senders were not apostles, it would not be suitable for him to use the appellation "apostle" in these instances.

The words "grace, mercy, and peace from God the Father and Christ Jesus our Lord" are more than a pious wish. Through such a word of God these blessings are actually given.

With this benevolent salutation the apostle moves into the substance of his letter.

1:3–14: The Cross, Ministry, and the Office of the Ministry

As noted in the Introduction to 2 Timothy, verses 3 through 18 of chapter 1 seem to serve as an "overture" to this epistle, introducing themes and topics that Paul will explore in more detail in the remainder of the letter.[13] In the main, these are (1) the need for the proclamation of the truth of God's word by Christians in general and pastors in particular; (2) the need to oppose error; (3) the need to endure suffering and persecution that will come upon those who believe and proclaim this truth.

Themes introduced by the overture include the following:

Theme	Overture	Other References
Truth Versus Error	1:3, 5, 13	2:2, 8, 12, 14–16, 18, 25; 3:7–8, 14–17; 4:3–4, 7
Ministry/Proclamation	1:6, 8, 10, 11, 13	2:2, 8, 15, 24–25; 3:14, 17; 4:2, 5, 11, 17
Suffering	1:9–10	1:15; 2:3, 9–10; 3:11, 12; 4:6, 16
Salvation	1:9–10	2:8, 10–12, 25–26; 3:15; 4:8, 18
Christ	1:1, 2, 9, 10, 13	1:16, 18; 2:1, 3, 7, 8, 10, 19, 22, 24; 3:11, 12, 15; 4:1, 8, 14, 17, 18, 22

TRANSLATION

³ I give thanks to God, whom I worship, as my ancestors did, with a pure conscience, as without ceasing I remember you in my prayers night and

---

13. See further the section "Outline" in the Introduction to 2 Timothy. I would also consider that 1 Tim 1:1–17 and Titus 1:1–4 function as "overtures" to those letters; see "Outline" in the Introduction to 1 Timothy and "One Servant of the Word to Another: Titus 1:1–4 in Context" in the commentary on Titus 1:1–4. In a similar way Col 1:3–20 serves as an overture to that letter; see Deterding, *Colossians*, 26–27. Similarly, Eph 1:3–14 functions in the same way in that epistle (Scharlemann, "Secret of God's Plan," 538–39).

day, ⁴ longing to see you, remembering your tears, in order that I might be filled with joy, ⁵ remembering your sincere faith that dwelt first in your grandmother Lois and your mother Eunice, and, I am certain, does also in you.

⁶ For this reason I am reminding you to rekindle the gift of God, which is in you through the laying on of my hands, ⁷ for God did not give us a spirit of cowardice but of power and love and prudence. ⁸ Therefore, do not be ashamed of the witness of our Lord nor of me his prisoner, but join in suffering for the gospel by the power of God,

⁹ who saved us
and called us by a holy calling,
not according to our works
but according to his own plan and grace,
which was given to us in Christ Jesus
before eternal times,
¹⁰ but now has been made known
through the appearing of our savior Christ Jesus,
who abolished death
and brought to light life and incorruption through the gospel,

¹¹ for which I was appointed a proclaimer and apostle and teacher, ¹² for which reason I suffer these things; however, I am not put to shame, for I know in whom I have believed, and I have been persuaded that he is able to guard my deposit until that day. ¹³ Hold to the standard of sound words which you heard from me in faith and love which are in Christ Jesus. ¹⁴ Guard the good deposit through the Holy Spirit who dwells among us.

TEXTUAL NOTES

1:3 Χάριν ἔχω τῷ θεῷ—Just as the salutations of Paul's letters follow the pattern of those of contemporary Greek letters, the same is true of the section immediately following. It was not uncommon for the salutation of a Greek letter to be followed by a section in which the author tells his reader(s) why he has been praying to his gods on his/their behalf.[14]

---

14. Deissmann, *Light*, offers the following examples:
Apion to Epimachus his father and lord many greetings. Before all things I pray that thou art in health, and that thou dost prosper and fare well continually together with my sister and her daughter and my brother. I thank the lord Serapis that, when I was in peril in the sea, he saved me immediately (180).
Antonius Maximus to Sabina his sister many greetings. Before all things I pray that

The apostle has a similar, although distinctly Christian, section of thanksgiving to God in all of his letters except Galatians, 1 Timothy, and Titus.[15] These are not thanksgiving prayers as such but report the reasons why Paul gives thanks to God.[16] The absence of a thanksgiving report in 1 Timothy and Titus seems to be due to the apostle's desire to "get down to business" by turning to the urgent task of ministry and church supervision that he is entrusting to his younger coworkers (1 Tim 1:3–11; Titus 1:5–9).[17] The lack of such a thanksgiving in Galatians reflects the potentially tragic circumstances among those Christians that occasioned that letter.[18]

Although the situation of the present letter was every bit as grim as that which Paul faced when writing to the Galatians (see the Introduction to 2 Timothy), it was of a different character. In Galatians the apostle wrote to deal with a serious breach of faith. When he authored this letter, he was facing his imminent death. In these circumstances, as his thoughts turned to Timothy, he was encouraged by the faith and life of his colleague. That moved him to thanksgiving for the faith of Timothy and his family and to report to Timothy that he was giving thanks.

ᾧ λατρεύω ἀπὸ προγόνων—Paul here connects faith in Christ with the faith of genuine believers in Old Testament times. This is similar to what he writes in Rom 9:3–5. See further the note on 1:5 and the commentary below.

ἐν καθαρᾷ συνειδήσει—See the entry "Heart and Conscience" in the Extended Notes.

---

thou art in health, for I myself also am in health. Making mention of thee before the gods here I received a little letter from Antoninus our fellow-citizen. And when I knew that thou farest well, I rejoiced greatly (184).

15. The precise wording differs from letter to letter: εὐχαριστῶ τῷ θεῷ (Rom 1:8; 1 Cor 1:4; Phil 1:3; Col 1:3; Phlm 4); εὐλογητὸς ὁ θεός (2 Cor 1:3; Eph 1:3); εὐχαριστοῦμεν τῷ θεῷ (1 Thess 1:2); εὐχαριστεῖν ὀφείλομεν τῷ θεῷ (2 Thess 1:3); χάριν ἔχω τῷ θεῷ (2 Tim 1:3).

16. Marshall, *Pastoral Epistles*, 689, comes to a similar conclusion.

17. Knight, *Pastoral Epistles*, 287, comes to a similar conclusion. The section in 1 Timothy that begins "I give thanks" (χάριν ἔχω, 1:12) is not a real parallel to the thanksgiving reports of the other letters, not only because it does not occur right after the salutation but also due to its being a thanksgiving for what has taken place in Paul's life rather than in the lives of his addressees.

18. See Das, *Galatians*, 80, 99, 630.

ἀδιάλειπτον ... νυκτὸς καὶ ἡμέρας—"Night and day" is a common biblical expression for speaking of something that was taking place regularly.[19]

1:4 ἐπιποθῶν σε ἰδεῖν ... ἵνα χαρᾶς πληρωθῶ—In his present circumstances the apostle was longing for the joy of person-to-person contact with a beloved coworker.

μεμνημένος σου τῶν δακρύων—This somewhat cryptic reference to sadness on Timothy's part points to his being separated from Paul. This might have been when the apostle left his coworker in Ephesus; another possibility is that Paul is referring to the time when he himself was taken captive for his present imprisonment.[20]

1:5 ἐν σοὶ ἀνυποκρίτου πίστεως—Genuine faith is "unhypocritical"; it is not feigned by simply going through the motions. "Faith" here is the act of believing, *fides qua creditur*. See further the entry "Faith" in the Extended Notes.

τῇ μάμμῃ σου Λωΐδι καὶ τῇ μητρί σου Εὐνίκῃ—The book of Acts (16:1) reports that although Timothy's father was a Greek (in that context meaning a nonbeliever), his mother was Jewish and a believer. This and the present passage combine to inform us that Timothy's mother and grandmother had been practitioners of the faith of the Old Testament people of God, and that they had imparted this Old Testament faith to Timothy. The likelihood that Paul had been the one to bring Timothy, and presumably his mother and grandmother as well, to the faith as fully revealed in the ministry of Christ is set forth in the section "Timothy's Good Confession" in the commentary on 1 Tim 6:11–16.

πέπεισμαι δὲ ὅτι καὶ ἐν σοί—This indicates that the Christian faith, of which Timothy's faith is an example, is the continuation of the authentic faith of Old Testament believers. See further "Timothy's Good Confession" in the commentary on 1 Tim 6:11–16.

1:6 ἀναμιμνῄσκω σε ἀναζωπυρεῖν—Paul calls on Timothy to "rekindle" (ἀναζωπυρεῖν) the gift of God that he had received. As this gift is ultimately a gift from God the Holy Spirit (see following textual note),

---

19. Mark 4:27; 5:5; Luke 2:37; 18:7 ("day and night"); Acts 26:7; 1 Thess 2:9; 3:10; 2 Thess 3:8. The order "night and day" may reflect the practice of regarding the day as beginning at sunset. With the exception of Luke 18:7 the order "day and night" (Acts 9:24; Rev 4:8; 7:15; 20:10) may, in contrast, denote nonstop, around the clock, activity.

20. Knight, *Pastoral Epistles*, 368, opts for the former, while Kelly, *Pastoral Epistles*, 156, argues for the latter.

and as fire is associated with the Holy Spirit and with his gifts of speaking the word (Acts 2:3), "rekindle" is an apt turn of phrase here.

τὸ χάρισμα τοῦ θεοῦ—In both this passage and 1 Tim 4:14 Paul speaks of a χάρισμα, "gift," that Timothy received. This is one of the terms that the apostle uses in his expositions of the gifts of the Spirit (Rom 12:6; 1 Cor 12:4, 9, 28, 30, 31). In both of these lists he includes gifts of speaking the word of God. In his Letter to the Romans he mentions prophecy and teaching (12:6–7). When writing to the Corinthians, he lists "first apostles, second prophets, third teachers" (12:28). This being the case, his exhortation that his readers seek the greater gifts (12:31) would point to these gifts of the word as the greater gifts.

In both of his Letters to Timothy Paul is giving instruction about the responsibilities of one entrusted with the word of God. In this light the "gift" that the apostle references here must be Timothy being entrusted with the office of overseer/elder (3:1; 5:17), that is, of pastor.[21]

ὅ ἐστιν ἐν σοὶ διὰ τῆς ἐπιθέσεως τῶν χειρῶν μου—In the New Testament the laying on of hands has a number of different results. Both Jesus (e.g., Mark 6:5) and various apostles (Acts 5:12; 14:3) laid hands on someone to perform a miracle. At certain times the Holy Spirit was imparted by the laying on of hands (Acts 8:17; 19:6) in order to designate a groundbreaking event in the history of the early church.[22]

Nevertheless, the laying on of hands does not always involve observable miracles. The seven men entrusted with supervising the distribution

---

21. Gordon Fee comes to the same conclusion; DPL 341.

22. It is always the work of the Holy Spirit when anyone comes to saving faith (1 Cor 12:3). However, in the book of Acts a special manifestation of the Holy Spirit occurs at four significant events in the history of the spread of the gospel through the church's witness "in Jerusalem, in Judea and Samaria, and to the end of the earth" (Acts 1:8). Special signs of the coming of the Holy Spirit take place on the day of Pentecost (Acts 2:1–4)—the beginning of the witness to their fellow Jews ("in Jerusalem"), at the "Samaritan Pentecost" (Acts 8:14–17)—the beginning of the outreach of Christ's gospel to the Samaritans, those descendants of Jewish-Gentile intermarriage ("in Judea and Samaria"), and at the "Gentile Pentecost" (Acts 10:44–48)—the first outreach of the gospel to Gentiles ("to the end of the earth"). There are also special signs of the coming of the Holy Spirit on some who knew only of the baptism of John the Baptist (Acts 19:1–6); this takes place to point to Jesus as the one who fulfilled John's promise of the coming of one who would baptize with the Holy Spirit (Matt 3:11; Mark 1:8; Luke 3:16) and to show that Christ's gospel was for these disciples as well. The events of Acts 8:17 and 19:6 do not prescribe the laying on of hands as a special means to receiving the Holy Spirit (such laying on of hands is absent from the episodes of Acts 2 and 10). Rather, in each case these are out-of-the-ordinary manifestations of the Holy Spirit to indicate some special episode in the expansion of Christ's church.

of poor relief to the church's widows are set aside for this task by the laying on of hands (Acts 6:6). Similarly, by the laying on of hands Barnabas and Saul/Paul are set apart to be sent forth on the latter's first missionary journey (Acts 13:2–3).

These two episodes are closest to the laying on of hands that is mentioned in the Pastoral Letters. In the present passage Paul states that he laid hands on Timothy, so that he received a gift. The reference in 1 Tim 4:14 is to Timothy having received a gift when elders (pastors) laid their hands on him. The apostle also directs Timothy not to be hasty in laying hands on others (1 Tim 5:22).

A comparison of these events with those of Acts 6 and 13 suggests that these are all similar episodes, namely the setting aside of persons for a special position in the church; in the case of the Pastorals the task would be the office of the pastoral ministry. The laying on of hands, therefore, should not be thought of as a supernatural imposition of the Holy Spirit or of any of his gifts apart from the usual work and ministry of Christ's people—referenced in 1 Tim 4:14 by the mention of "prophecy" as being a part of this "setting aside," "prophecy" referring to Timothy's instruction in the word of God that prepared him for taking up the task of the pastoral ministry (see the textual note on "prophecy" at 1 Tim 4:14).

1:7 πνεῦμα—This word can refer to God the Holy Spirit (Rom 8:16a), to the human spirit (Rom 8:16b), or to demonic spirits (Acts 19:12). In that light, it serves multiple purposes here, depending on the genitive attached to it (see the following notes). "Cowardice" (δειλίας) is plainly a defect of the fallen human spirit; perhaps there is even the hint that the demonic is behind it or at least makes use of it. "Power" (δυνάμεως), "love" (ἀγάπης), and "prudence" (σωφρονισμοῦ) are all virtues given by God the Holy Spirit (see below).

δειλίας—Paul contrasts this word with "power" (δυνάμεως), and Jesus contrasts the cognate verb with the otherworldly peace that he gives (John 14:27). Thus, this word denotes a "lack of mental or moral strength."[23]

δυνάμεως—Power is often linked with God the Holy Spirit.[24] Noteworthy is the association of such power with terms for the word of God (μαρύριον, "witness," here; εὐαγγέλιον, "gospel," in 1 Thess 1:5).

ἀγάπης—"Love" is, of course, a word of major importance in the Scriptures (see the entry by that name in the Extended Notes), but what

---

23. BDAG 215.
24. Luke 1:35; 4:14; Acts 1:8; 10:38; Rom 15:13, 19; Eph 3:16; 1 Thess 1:5.

is its precise nuance here? Both the love that God shows to us (Rom 5:5; 15:30) and the love that we in turn are to show to others (2 Cor 6:6; Gal 5:22; Col 1:8) are associated with the Holy Spirit. That being the case, this reference to a spirit of love would point to the truth that the love of God for us empowers us to show love to others.

σωφρονισμοῦ—Paul uses a cognate of this word ("prudence") in Rom 12:3 in speaking of the gifts that God gives to his people. The similarity of that section of Romans with his recitation of gifts of the Spirit in 1 Corinthians (12:1-11) would suggest that he would identify prudence as a gift of the Spirit; the present verse would support such a conclusion. The opposite of cowardice is power, but power is not the same thing as arrogance or harshness. Thus "prudence" (σωφρονισμοῦ) along with love has a wholesome modifying effect on power to keep it from becoming corrupted into arrogance or harshness.

1:8 ἐπαισχυνθῇς—The use of this word in verse 16 clarifies its meaning here: do not be ashamed of me even in view of the fact that I am in prison.[25]

μαρτύριον—Here the word "witness" refers to the entirety of the Christian message.[26]

δέσμιον αὐτοῦ—This phrase shows that the apostle is in prison, that his imprisonment is persecution for his Christian faith and witness, and that nevertheless Christ ("our Lord") has not abandoned him. Paul speaks of himself in a similar way also in Eph 3:1; 4:1; Phlm 1, 9.

συγκακοπάθησον τῷ εὐαγγελίῳ—The prefix σύν (which becomes σύγ before the guttural κ in κακοπάθησον) roots this entire discussion in baptism (Rom 6:3-4; Col 2:11-12). All Christians suffer with Christ (3:12), but this is especially the burden/calling of those who speak the gospel (2:3; 4:5). See further the commentary.

---

25. It is worth noting here that "from a human point of view, there was much in the gospel of which to be ashamed. It was the message of a failed prophet, rejected by his people, executed by the world's power, and preached by a collection of fishermen and other undesirables. The message they proclaimed was foolishness in the world's eyes (1 Cor 1:23), based on assumptions that ran counter to the generally accepted norms of Greek philosophy (Acts 17:32). And there was, on the surface, much to be ashamed about in reference to Paul, a man who met constant opposition (2 Cor 11:23-27) and was imprisoned in Rome. But Timothy was called not to be ashamed; in fact, he was called to share in suffering for this very gospel with Paul. The gospel is the power of God for salvation (Rom 1:16), and regardless of opposition, suffering, and shame, it is nothing to be ashamed of; rather it invites participation. One is reminded of Jesus' words, that 'whoever is ashamed of me and of my words in this adulterous and sinful generation, of him will the Son of man also be ashamed, when he comes in the glory of his Father with the holy angels' (Mark 8:38)." Mounce, *Pastoral Epistles*, 480.

26. BDAG (619) cites also 1 Cor 1:6; 2:1; and 2 Thess 1:10 as having this meaning.

κατὰ δύναμιν θεοῦ—The power of God gives those who suffer with Christ more than sufficient (Rom 8:37) strength to bear their sufferings.[27]

1:9 σώσαντος—This is a soteriological word of major importance in the NT; see the entry "Save, Savior, Salvation" in the Extended Notes and also the essay "He Saved Us: The Pastoral Letters on the Way of Salvation" elsewhere in this commentary.

καλέσαντος κλήσει ἁγίᾳ—God's call is unlike any other; God's call enables one to respond to that call with saving faith (1 Cor 1:9; Eph 4:1; 1 Tim 6:12).

οὐ κατὰ τὰ ἔργα ἡμῶν—Paul is the great proclaimer of the truth that no one is justified by works.[28]

πρόθεσιν—The apostle uses this term to refer to God's plan of salvation (Rom 8:28; 9:11; Eph 1:11); Eph 3:11 and the present passage indicate that God made this plan from eternity (πρὸ χρόνων αἰωνίων; cf. Rom 16:25; Titus 1:2).

χάριν—This is a term of major importance for the NT teaching on the way of salvation; see the entry "Grace" in the Extended Notes.

ἐν Χριστῷ Ἰησοῦ—See the entry "In Christ" in the Extended Notes.

1:10 φανερωθεῖσαν δὲ νῦν—The eternal plan was made known in history at the coming of Christ (see following note), so that Paul could write that it "now" has been made known.

ἐπιφανείας—Here the term refers to the incarnation and subsequent ministry (including the death and resurrection) of Christ Jesus. It is worth noting that in non-Christian Greek this term had a background of referring to the appearance of a god.[29] On the teaching of the Pastorals on the deity of Jesus Christ see the essays "Our Great God and Savior: The Christology of the Pastoral Letters" and "There Is One God: The Pastoral Letters on the Identity of God" elsewhere in this commentary.

---

27. In Phil 3 Paul speaks of knowing not only "the fellowship of [Christ's] sufferings" but also "the power of his resurrection" (10). Since in the following verse the apostle uses a compound form of the word "resurrection" (ἐξανάστασιν) to emphasize that he is there speaking of the resurrection *from* the dead at the last day, his use of the simple form of the noun in verse 10 (ἀναστάσεως) indicates that he is speaking there of the power that the resurrected Christ gives to his people to enable them to endure suffering in the present life.

28. In addition to the present passage see Rom 3:20; 4:2; 9:11, 32; Gal 2:16; 3:10; Eph 2:9; Titus 3:5.

29. Debelius and Conzelmann, *Pastoral Epistles*, 104; Easton, *Pastoral Epistles*, 41.

σωτῆρος—See the entry "Save, Savior, Salvation" in the Extended Notes and also the essay "He Saved Us: The Pastoral Letters on the Way of Salvation" elsewhere in this commentary.

καταργήσαντος—Here the term means "abolish" as in "take away the power of"; cf. Heb 2:14.

τόν θάνατον—Of course Christians still die, but Christ has taken the power away from death (1 Cor 15:54–57).

φωτίσαντος—Light is a common biblical metaphor for life and salvation.[30]

ζωὴν καὶ ἀφθαρσίαν—The joining together of these two terms points to *eternal* life.

διὰ τοῦ εὐαγγελίου—The gospel gives the salvation that Christ acquired; cf. Rom 1:16–17.

1:11 εἰς ὃ ἐτέθην—This verb can have the force of "appoint for a task or function."[31]

κῆρυξ—The secular Greek background to this word is instructive. A "herald/proclaimer" held a significant place at a royal court. He might be sent on diplomatic missions; heralds were often honored for their service.[32] It was required of heralds "that they deliver their message as it is given to them. The essential point about the report which they give is that it does not originate with them."[33]

A proclaimer (κῆρυξ) is one who proclaims (κηρύσσω) a proclamation (κήρυγμα); the content of the proclamation determines the significance of the proclaimer and of his act of proclaiming. In his directions to Timothy elsewhere in this letter Paul makes it plain that the proclaimer is to proclaim the entire word of God;[34] other passages emphasize that the central message of the word is the death and resurrection of Jesus Christ.[35]

Especially in conjunction with the terms ἀπόστολος and διδάσκαλος, κῆρυξ gives a sense of transcendent majesty to Paul's message, as it comes from one higher, in his case the most majestic one of all, God. As a

---

30. BDAG 1072–74; see the entries at φῶς (1, b, α, β, and γ), φωτίζω (3, a and b), and φωτισμός (a and b).

31. John 15:16; Acts 13:47; 1 Tim 2:7; 2 Tim 1:11; BDAG 1004.

32. *TDNT* 3:683–85.

33. *TDNT* 3:687–88.

34. 2 Tim 4:2; see the notes and commentary on that passage for the connection between what Paul says there concerning preaching "the word" and what he indicates about the purpose/profitability of "all Scripture" (2 Tim 3:16–17).

35. 1 Cor 1:21, 23; 15:11, 14; 1 Tim 3:16.

message that originates not with the proclaimer but with almighty God this proclamation has power. This power is not that of human wisdom but of the Holy Spirit (1 Cor 2:4; 1 Thess 1:5). Elsewhere (2 Cor 4:3–6) the apostle indicates that the proclamation of Christ is like the word of God at creation. As the word of creation brought into being everything in creation, so the proclamation of Christ brings into being the faith that receives the glory of eternal salvation.

ἀπόστολος—See the entry "Apostle" in the Extended Notes.

διδάσκαλος—See the entry "Teaching/Doctrine" in the Extended Notes.

1:12 δι' ἣν αἰτίαν καὶ ταῦτα πάσχω—Paul is not speaking here of things that afflict humanity in general (sickness, injury, death). Instead, his reference is to those things that he suffers on account of his Christian faith, witness, and way of life. See further the commentary.

ἀλλ' οὐκ ἐπαισχύνομαι—In biblical thought "shame" is not merely a negative feeling, as though it simply meant embarrassment. Shame is a reality; the word group is sometimes used with reference to God's eternal displeasure.[36]

οἶδα γὰρ ᾧ πεπίστευκα καὶ πέπεισμαι—"Have believed" (πεπίστευκα) is cognate to "faith" (πίστις); see the entry "Faith" in the Extended Notes. Faith in Christ is the way to overcome shame; faith also brings conviction (πέπεισμαι) regarding the matter Paul raises next.

δυνατός ἐστιν τὴν παραθήκην μου φυλάξαι—The apostle has saving faith, and his faith also gives him confidence regarding the "deposit" of ministry to which God has called him. On "deposit" see also the note on 1:14.

εἰς ἐκείνην τὴν ἡμέραν—This would refer either to the last day or to the day of Paul's death.

1:13 Ὑποτύπωσιν ἔχε ὑγιαινόντων λόγων ὧν παρ' ἐμοῦ ἤκουσας— "Sound" (the adjective ὑγιής or a form of the verb ὑγιαίνω) as a description of doctrine, words, and faith is common in the Pastorals to refer to correct doctrine in all aspects;[37] here the noun ὑποτύπωσιν denotes the correct "standard" of doctrine that Timothy has in Paul.[38] That the author of this letter is a standard of such soundness for Timothy is due to his being (1) the younger pastor's teacher and especially to his being (2) an apostle; see the entry by that title in the Extended Notes. The verb

---

36. Mark 8:38; Rom 5:5; 9:33; 10:11; 1 Cor 1:27–28; Heb 12:2; 1 Pet 2:6; 1 John 2:28.
37. 1 Tim 1:10; 6:3; 2 Tim 1:13; 4:3; Titus 1:9, 13; 2:1, 2, 8.
38. Towner, *Letters*, 477–78.

ἔχε is a present tense with gnomic implications: "Continually hold to the standard of sound words."[39]

πίστει καὶ ἀγάπῃ τῇ ἐν Χριστῷ Ἰησοῦ—Here, in conjunction with the phrase ἐν Χριστῷ Ἰησοῦ, these terms serve as a summary of the entire Christian faith: through faith in Christ we receive the love of God (1 Tim 1:14); that faith is also active in love (Gal 5:6). See the commentary and also the entries "Faith," "Love," and "In Christ" in the Extended Notes.

1:14 τὴν καλὴν παραθήκην—As in 1:12 and 1 Tim 6:20 this term refers to the call to ministry in the word of God.

φύλαξον—This term has a broad range of meanings.[40] Here it means "watch after intently," "protect." See also the following note.

διὰ πνεύματος ἁγίου—Other mentions of the Holy Spirit in the Pastorals make reference to the word of God (1 Tim 4:1, whose commentary see), the office of the ministry of the word (2 Tim 1:7, whose commentary see), and baptism (Titus 3:5, whose commentary see); θεόπνευστος in 2 Tim 3:15 should also be seen as a reference to God the Holy Spirit (see the commentary there), so that that passage also connects the Holy Spirit with the word of God; the same is true of Rom 15:18–20, 1 Cor 2:4–5, and 1 Thess 1:5–6. Thus, Timothy is to "guard" his ministry (see previous note) by conforming it to the word of God.

τοῦ ἐνοικοῦντος ἐν ἡμῖν—Should ἐν with a plural object, as here, be rendered "within" (the Spirit's indwelling individuals) or "among" (the Spirit's dwelling through his word among those devoted to that word)? Some passages[41] in the Scriptures would point to the former; others[42] would suggest the latter. Perhaps Paul intends for us to think of both.

COMMENTARY

Faith in the Family

From this section, the book of Acts, and 1 Timothy we can piece together the history of Timothy's religious faith. Similar to Simeon and Anna (Luke 2:22–40) Lois and Eunice had held to faith in the God of

---

39. Wallace, *Greek Grammar*, 525.
40. BDAG 1068–69; 1 Tim 5:21; 6:20; 2 Tim 1:12, 14; 4:15.
41. 2 Cor 1:22; Gal 4:6; Eph 3:17 (although this last passage speaks of Christ, not the Spirit).
42. John 14:17; Rom 8:9, 11; 1 Cor 3:16; 2 Tim 1:14.

the Hebrew Scriptures and to his promise of salvation. They had, in turn, passed this faith along to Timothy.

Paul had brought the Christian gospel to Lystra (Acts 14:5–20), the home of these three (Acts 16:1–5). Through his ministry they had been brought to believe that the promises of salvation had been fulfilled in the redemptive work of Jesus Christ (1 Tim 1:2, 18; 2 Tim 1:2; 2:1). That faith had been confirmed by their reception of Christian baptism, most likely at the apostle's hand (1 Tim 6:12).

Paul's words here draw a connection between the faith of the Old Testament and the Christian faith (see also Rom 9:4–5). He demonstrates that the Pharisaic Judaism and devotion to the tradition of the elders that he had followed at a certain point in his life is not the continuation of what was set forth in the Hebrew Scriptures (Acts 26:5; Gal 1:13–14; Phil 3:4–7). Rather, the message and faith of the Old Testament continued in the messianic ministry of Jesus Christ, as the apostle himself had often proclaimed (see Acts 17:1–3; 1 Cor 10:1–13). It is the work of Christ and not any deeds of one's own, Pharisaic or otherwise, that gives one a "pure conscience" with which he can worship God.

The Call and the Cross

Paul is giving thanks for the coming to faith within the family and for the work of the ministry that brings people to faith. In the midst of this discourse, he turns to speak of the saving work of Christ. Although this proclamation has the appearance of a creed,[43] its grammatically subordinate position in the sentence (an extended subordinate clause introduced by an articular participle) and its distinctively Pauline vocabulary (as seen in a comparison with other letters of the apostle)[44] indicate that this is his original composition.[45]

What Paul has to say here reveals the reality that God's salvation is rooted in history. The aorist participles that he uses here demonstrate that these saving actions are antecedent to the present time.[46]

---

43. *DNTB* 233.
44. See the appendix "Parallels Between the Pastoral Letters and the Other Letters of Paul" at the end of the Introduction to the Pastoral Letters elsewhere in this commentary.
45. As noted by Kelly, *Pastoral Epistles*, 161–62, and Knight, *Pastoral Epistles*, 377.
46. Wallace, *Greek Grammar*, 614.

The apostle identifies God (the Father) as the one "who saved us." Later in the clause he speaks of Christ Jesus as "our savior." The verb "saved" here, therefore, serves as an introduction to and a summary of the entire clause. As Paul continues, he spells out various details of how it is that God "saved us."

This salvation is in accord with God's "plan and grace," which are from eternity ("before eternal times"). The phrase "plan and grace" is a hendiadys;[47] we might translate this as God's "gracious plan." Our salvation was no afterthought or "Plan B" on God's part; it had its origin in eternity.

God's eternal plan was "in Christ Jesus." From eternity God resolved to save through the work of Jesus Christ (see further the entry "In Christ" in the Extended Notes).

God's saving plan from before time was "made known" in time. At a given point in history God's plan was made known "through the appearing of our savior Christ Jesus." The use of the cognate noun "savior" to refer to Christ as the one who carried out God's plan shows that it was through his work that God the Father "saved" us.

Christ came into the world, and he "abolished death and brought to light life and incorruption." In this way the apostle refers to Christ's death on the cross and his subsequent resurrection from the dead.

Through the work of Christ God saved all people (1 Tim 2:4, 6; Titus 2:11).[48] He has made that salvation the personal possession of individuals as he "called" them to faith (1 Tim 6:12).[49] God made this call through the gospel. This reference to the saving gospel links these lines about salvation to the ministry of the gospel, in which Paul and Timothy share.

The Ministry of the Gospel

The reference to the saving power of the gospel leads the apostle to speak of his own ministry in the gospel. Paul here designates his ministry with three terms: "proclaimer," "apostle," and "teacher."

---

47. Easton, *Pastoral Epistles*, 41; on this figure of speech see BDF 228 [§ 442 (16)].

48. In dogmatic terminology this is known as objective justification, on which see Nafzger et al., *Confessing the Gospel*, 475-77, 501-3, 572-74; *Theses on Justification*, numbers 1-12.

49. In dogmatic terminology this is known as subjective justification, on which see Nafzger et al., *Confessing the Gospel*, 475-77, 570-72, 574-75; *Theses on Justification*, numbers 13-23.

The gospel is the saving message, the power of God for salvation (Rom 1:16). God appoints certain individuals, Paul among them, to be proclaimers of the gospel. Through their proclamation God calls individuals to salvation through faith in Christ.

Paul was among those whom Christ called to be one of his apostles. The apostles were those whom the risen Christ used to bring his word to the church and to the world; see the entry "Apostle" in the Extended Notes.

Paul also writes that he was appointed to be a teacher of the gospel. The cognate noun "teaching" often implies the entirety of the biblical revelation; see the entry "Teaching/Doctrine" in the Extended Notes.

The apostle's coworker Timothy, while not himself being an apostle, nevertheless also was one who was called to set forth God's word. When Paul speaks of the "gift" that Timothy had received, this refers to his younger associate's also being set apart to speak God's word. As observed in the Textual Notes as well as in the commentary on 1 Tim 4:6–16 (which see), the apostle's reference to the "laying on of my hands" denotes the final step in the procedure by which Timothy was brought into the ministry. As other references in the Pastoral Letters indicate,[50] Timothy would have received preparation for the ministry by Paul himself, so that he would meet the qualifications for the pastoral office, such as are set out in 1 Timothy (3:1–7) and Titus (1:5–9).

The apostle states that he was "appointed" to be a proclaimer, apostle, and teacher. No one takes the office of the ministry for himself. Whatever the particulars of how one is brought into the ministry, whether directly by the Lord of the church himself, as was Paul (Acts 9:1–31; Gal 1:10–17), or through the instrumentality of others, as was Timothy (see the notes and commentary on 1 Tim 4:14), it is ultimately God who appoints a man to be a pastor.

The Pastoral Letters prescribe certain qualifications for holding the pastoral office (1 Tim 3:1–7; Titus 1:5–9). The apostle alludes to these, when he speaks to Timothy of the "standard of sound words which you heard from me in faith and love which are in Christ Jesus." As an apostle Paul was called and commissioned by Christ to bring his word to the world. The "standard of sound words" would denote the teachings of

---

50. A comparison of 2:2 ("those things which you heard from me through many witnesses") with 1:13 ("Hold to the standard of sound words which you heard from me") and 3:14 ("the things which you learned and believed, knowing from whom you learned [them]") indicates that these passages are referring to the preparation that Timothy received from Paul that prepared him to hold the pastoral office. See further the commentary on those verses.

God's word, communicated also through the teachings and writings of Paul, contained in the Scriptures.⁵¹

With the terms "gift" and "deposit" the apostle refers to the office of the ministry as held respectively by Timothy and himself. As with the verb "appointed," so with these nouns Paul indicates that the ministry is not something that is self-appointed or self-achieved; ultimately God puts a man in the office of the ministry.

The apostle tells Timothy to "rekindle" his gift of ministry, and he speaks of God guarding his own deposit of this office. Taken together these terms denote the ongoing responsibility that a pastor has with respect to his office. As a fire must have a continuous supply of fuel and oxygen or it will burn out, so a pastor's ministry must be continually "fueled." The pastoral office is an office of God's word. Thus, the pastor preserves and promotes his office, as he "rekindles" it through his ongoing involvement with the word of God.⁵² That being the case, it is not really the pastor who does this, for since the word of God has the power of God himself (Rom 1:16; 2 Cor 4:3–6; 1 Thess 1:5), when a pastor makes use of the word of God, through that word God himself preserves him in his faith and therefore also in his office.

In speaking of this office that the two of them share Paul notes that they have not received "a spirit of cowardice" but rather one "of power and love and prudence." The adaptability of the Greek word πνεῦμα to refer to the human spirit or to evil spirits as well as to God the Holy Spirit sheds light on the apostle's meaning here. If a pastor's word depended solely on him, he might well be afflicted with cowardice, perhaps even with such cowardice being a tool of Satan to disrupt and even corrupt his ministry. But the ministry and its power come from God the Holy Spirit. Through his word he empowers the pastor to speak with the power of God (1 Thess 1:5) and to minister with love and prudence (1 Cor 13).

The apostle states that he suffers on account of his ministry, and he encourages Timothy to "join in suffering for the gospel by the power of God." While all Christians are called upon to take up the cross

---

51. On the scriptural authority of the letters of Paul, see "The Spirit Explicitly Says" in the commentary on 1 Tim 4:1–5 as well as the entry "Apostle" in the Extended Notes. See also "The Authority of the Pauline Letters" in Deterding, *Colossians*, 192–94.

52. As Timothy had been a trusted coworker of Paul's for many years, the verb "rekindle" should not be construed as though the younger man had been negligent or indifferent in faith or in ministry (Mounce, *Pastoral Epistles*, 475–76). Instead, this reflects the reality that the believer in general and the pastor in particular needs ongoing nurture via the word of God.

(e.g., Matt 16:24) and to suffer with Christ (2 Tim 3:12), since this suffering comes largely on account of one's witness to the gospel, it is the special burden of those who are called to the office of the ministry to bear suffering. Nevertheless, this burden of suffering is more than offset by the power that God provides (through his word) in order to be able to bear that suffering (Phil 3:10).[53] See further "Suffering with Christ" in the commentary on 2 Tim 2:8–13.

The Cross, Ministry, and the Office of the Ministry: 2 Timothy 1:3–14 in Context

As is his usual custom, Paul follows the salutation of this letter with a thanksgiving report. This statement that he (Paul) is giving thanks for his (Timothy's) faith leads him (Paul) to several related topics.

The mention of his coworker's faith reminds the apostle of how Timothy came to faith through the witness of his mother and grandmother, a faith confirmed by the ministry of Paul himself. The reference to this intrafamilial ministry of teaching the faith causes the apostle to think of the ministry that Timothy shares with him.

Nevertheless, before expounding on the ministry of the gospel that he and Timothy share, Paul elaborates on the gospel itself. He notes that God's plan of salvation was formed in eternity and carried out by Christ within history. The Lord not only planned our salvation and carried it out; he also calls us to salvation through the gospel.

This exposition of the gospel causes the apostle to return to speaking of the office of the ministry that he and Timothy both occupy. He calls on Timothy to hold to the standard of truth that he learned from Paul himself. Since this standard is apostolic, the church and its pastors of all ages have this standard in the Scriptures. By holding fast to this standard, a pastor, like Timothy, can fan into flame the gift he has received, and, like the apostle, he will have his ministry guarded by God himself. In this way the pastor will also be able to carry on his ministry with the power that the Holy Spirit gives.

---

53. Note that in Phil 3:10–11 the apostle uses a slightly different form of the word for "resurrection" in each of these verses. In 3:11 he uses the compound term ἐξανάστασιν, emphasizing that he is speaking of the resurrection *from* the dead at the last day. That being the case, his use of the simple form ἀναστάσεως indicates that his reference in 3:10 is to the *power* of Christ's resurrection in the daily life of the believer that enables him to endure the "fellowship of his sufferings."

An earlier version of this section appeared in Deterding, *Colossians*, 75–79.

1:15–18: Adversaries and Supporters; Suffering and Faithfulness

On these verses being a portion of the "Overture" of this letter, see the commentary on 1:3–14.

TRANSLATION

¹⁵ You know that all those in Asia turned away from me, among whom are Phygelus and Hermogenes. ¹⁶ May the Lord give mercy to the household of Onesiphorus, because he often refreshed me and was not ashamed of my being chained, ¹⁷ but when he was in Rome, he eagerly sought me and found me. ¹⁸ May the Lord grant him to find mercy from the Lord on that day. You well know how many services he rendered in Ephesus.

TEXTUAL NOTES

1:15 Οἶδας τοῦτο—There is no indication as to how Timothy knows this. It must have been communicated either by a letter, now lost to us, or by a personal messenger.

ὅτι ἀπεστράφησάν με πάντες οἱ ἐν τῇ Ἀσίᾳ—As Paul uses the verb ἀπεστράφησάν ("turn away from") in the Pastorals of turning away from the truth (2 Tim 4:4; Titus 1:14), it would seem that he uses it here to indicate that the abandonment of him by "all those in [the Roman province of] Asia" involved also a departure from true teaching, if not, in fact, from the faith altogether. Theodoret of Cyr suggested that the apostle might have made mention of this abandonment by those "in Asia" because they might prove to be a problem for Timothy, who at the time was in Asia (2 Tim 4:12–13).[54]

ὧν εστιν Φύγελος καὶ Ἑρμογένης—This is all we know about these two; that Paul identifies them by name among those in Asia who deserted him suggests that their abandonment must have been particularly distressing to him.[55] The apostle will refer elsewhere in this letter to a former coworker who deserted him (2 Tim 4:10; cf. Col 4:14; Phlm 24).

1:16 δῴη ἔλεος ὁ κύριος—Wallace dubs this verb form as the optative of polite request, as also in 1:18.[56] Hunter calls them "wish prayers."[57] The "Lord" (κύριος) in the Greek NT, by way of the LXX, generally refers to the name of God from the Hebrew Scriptures (יהוה);[58] typically in the NT it refers to Jesus Christ.[59] For ἔλεος see the entry "Mercy" in the Extended Notes.

τῷ Ὀνησιφόρου οἴκῳ—Paul greets this household (along with Priscilla and Aquila) at the end of this letter (4:19).

ὅτι πολλάκις με ἀνέψυξεν—Etymologically the verb ἀνέψυξεν means to give someone a breathing space, hence, "refresh."[60] The cognate noun is used in Acts 3:21 to refer to forgiveness as a result of the suffering of the Messiah. Thus, the reference might be to physical and/or spiritual "refreshment." The following reference to the apostle's "chain" demonstrates that Onesiphorus sought Paul while he was imprisoned.

τὴν ἅλυσίν μου οὐκ ἐπαισχύνθη—Does the noun "chain" (ἅλυσίν) here refer to a literal chain or to a prisoner's state of being chained? Either is possible. Acts 21:33 clearly refers to literal "chains," as would appear to be the case in 28:20. Ephesians 6:20 seems more likely to be denoting the state of imprisonment.[61] The overall meaning of the passage is not affected either way. For "not ashamed" see the notes on 1:8 and 1:12.

1:17 ἀλλὰ γενόμενος ἐν Ῥώμῃ σπουδαίως ἐζήτησέν με καὶ εὗρεν—As the circumstances of Paul's present imprisonment seem much harsher

---

54. PG 82:837A/838A.
55. Kelly, *Pastoral Epistles*, 169.
56. Wallace, *Greek Grammar*, 483.
57. *DPL* 727.
58. BDAG 577 (under 2 b, α).
59. BDAG 577–78 (under 2 b, γ; ב ,א, and ג).
60. BDAG 75–76.
61. BDAG 48 and *DPL* 753 opt for "imprisonment," while Knight, *Pastoral Epistles*, 385–86, argues for a literal chain.

than the Roman imprisonment described in Acts 28:16–31, this verse apparently refers to his current incarceration.[62]

1:18 δῴη αὐτῷ ὁ κύριος εὑρεῖν ἔλεος παρὰ κυρίου—See the first textual note on 1:16.

ἐν ἐκείνῃ τῇ ἡμέρᾳ—This refers to the day of the final judgment (1:12; 4:8).

In verses 17 and 18 there is a play on words. Onesiphorus "found" Paul, who in turn offers the "wish prayer" that Onesiphorus will "find" mercy from the Lord at the final judgment.

Some point to the reference to the "household" of Onesiphorus as evidence that he had died and therefore conclude that verse 18 amounts to prayer for the dead.[63] However, in 1 Cor 1:16 Paul speaks about a man's household while that individual is still alive, as demonstrated by 1 Cor 16:17. Moreover, the apostle references what he himself will experience on "that day," even though he obviously is still alive (4:8).[64]

ὅσα ἐν Ἐφέσῳ διηκόνησεν—Timothy had been ministering in Ephesus (1 Tim 1:3), so he would have been familiar with the activity of Onesiphorus. As διηκόνησεν can refer to physical "service" or to religious "ministry,"[65] the activity of Onesiphorus might have involved either or both of these; see the note above on "refreshed" (ἀνέψυξεν).

βέλτιον σὺ γινώσκεις—The comparative (βέλτιον) is used here for the positive, not "better" but "well."[66]

COMMENTARY

Paul here contrasts two groups: those who have abandoned him and those who have supported him. The purpose of this is more than information; Timothy himself is aware of these circumstances already.

Instead, this brief section points to other portions of this letter in which the apostle deals with suffering in the Christian life and especially by those who are called to the ministry of the word.[67] Suffering for the

---

62. Kelly, *Pastoral Epistles*, 169, and Knight, *Pastoral Epistles*, 385, come to a similar conclusion.

63. So argued by Kelly, *Pastoral Epistles*, 169–71.

64. Knight, *Pastoral Epistles*, 386; Guthrie, *Pastoral Epistles*, 148–49; Debelius and Conzelmann, *Pastoral Epistles*, 106.

65. BDAG 229–30 on διακονέω and the cognate διακονία.

66. BDF 127 [§ 244 (2)].

67. See, for example, 1:8, 12; 2:1–13; 3:12.

Christian faith, life, and witness can indeed be a deterrent to holding the Christian faith and can even be a temptation to abandon it altogether. Through this letter the apostle will equip and encourage his coworker to be faithful in believing, serving, and ministering in the gospel of Jesus Christ.

2:1–7: The Ministry—and the Suffering That It Entails

TRANSLATION

¹ Therefore, you, my child, be strong in the grace which is in Christ Jesus, ² and entrust those things which you heard from me in the presence of many witnesses to faithful men, who will be suited to also teach them to others. ³ Join together in suffering evil as a good soldier of Christ Jesus. ⁴ No one who has become a soldier becomes entangled in matters of ordinary life, in order that he may please the one who enlisted him. ⁵ If anyone competes as an athlete, he is not crowned the victor unless he competes according to the rules. ⁶ It is necessary that the hardworking farmer first receives the fruits. ⁷ Consider what I say, for the Lord will give you understanding in all things.

TEXTUAL NOTES

2:1 τέκνον μου—Paul addresses Timothy in this way as one whom he brought to the Christian faith.[68]

---

68. When the apostle writes of the "good confession" that Timothy confessed before many witnesses (1 Tim 6:12), this likely refers to his baptism. As Paul had first brought the Christian gospel to Lystra, it is likely that Timothy came to the Christian faith at that time. That the apostle here displays familiarity with the circumstances of Timothy's baptism strongly suggests that it was he himself who had administered baptism to this new convert. See further the section "Timothy's Good Confession" in the commentary on 1 Tim 6:11–16.

ἐνδυναμοῦ—Strength comes from God (1:7–8), who strengthens us.[69] Thus, to be strong is to rely on the strength that God provides. This verb is a present tense with gnomic implications: "Always be strong."[70]

τῇ χάριτι—See the entry "Grace" in the Extended Notes.

ἐν Χριστῷ Ἰησοῦ—See the entry "In Christ" in the Extended Notes.

2:2 παρ' ἐμοῦ διὰ πολλῶν μαρτύρων—Compare 1:13 and 3:14. The preposition διά here has the meaning "in the presence of."[71] This refers to Timothy's "seminary education," learned at the feet of the apostle, and not only to his day of "ordination."[72] If the reading "from whom" in 3:14 is in the plural (τίνων rather than τίνος; see the textual notes on 3:14), these "witnesses" would be among those from whom Timothy learned the truths of the Scriptures, suggesting that Paul was not the only one involved in preparing Timothy for the pastoral ministry.

παράθου—Etymologically this verb is related to the noun (παραθήκην) used in 1:12, 14 and also 1 Tim 6:20 to refer to the "deposit" of ministry given to Paul and Timothy. As Timothy was prepared to be a pastor, so he has now been entrusted with the task of preparing other men to be pastors.

πιστοῖς ἀνθρώποις—"Faithful" (πιστοῖς) here would encompass both having saving faith and also being trustworthy to carry out the tasks of ministry.[73] In harmony with 1 Tim 2:11—3:7 ἀνθρώποις here bears the sense of "male," as it does on certain other occasions (Matt 19:5; 1 Cor 7:1; Eph 5:31).

οἵτινες—Here, as elsewhere in the NT, the indefinite relative pronoun ὅστις has no difference in meaning from the definite relative pronoun ὅς.[74]

ἱκανοὶ ἔσονται καὶ ἑτέρους διδάξαι—Being able to teach the word is a requirement for one who would hold the pastoral office (1 Tim 3:2; 2 Tim 2:24; Titus 1:9).

2:3 Συγκακοπάθησον—The prefix σύν (which becomes σύγ before the guttural κ in κακοπάθησον) connects this imperative with baptism (Rom 6:3–4; Col 2:11–12). See the commentary.

στρατώτης Χρισοῦ Ιησοῦ—See verse 4 as well as 1 Cor 9:7 and Phlm 2 for other examples of Paul using military language to describe those who

---

69. Eph 6:10; Phil 4:13; 1 Tim 1:12; 2 Tim 4:17.
70. Wallace, *Greek Grammar*, 525.
71. BDAG 225.
72. Knight, *Pastoral Epistles*, 390, comes to the same conclusion.
73. Knight, *Pastoral Epistles*, 391.
74. Wallace, *Greek Grammar*, 344–45.

Grace and Life

labor in the word of God. Ephesians 6:10–17 uses similar imagery of the faith and life of all Christians.

2:4 στρατευόμενος—This is a participle functioning as a noun:[75] "one who has become a soldier."

ἐμπλέκεται—This verb tends to give the connotation of being caught in something, such as sheep or hares caught in thorns.[76]

ταῖς τοῦ βίου πραγματείαις—In the NT, whereas ζωή can refer to transcendent, eternal life, βίος has more to do with ordinary, earthly life.[77] Hence, it is the more appropriate of the two words to use here.

ἵνα τῷ στρατολογήσανι ἀρέσῃ—This continues the military metaphor of the verse. In this context "the one who enlisted him" refers to Christ calling one to faith and ministry through the gospel.

2:5 οὐ στεφανοῦται—This verb comes from the awarding of a botanical crown to the winner of an athletic contest.[78] Its use here heightens the sense of the metaphor.

ἐάν μὴ νομίμως ἀλήσῃ—Does this imagery have to do with proper training (νομίμως would mean something like "sufficiently") or with competing according to the rules governing the competition (νομίμως would seem to denote "lawfully")? Either might have an application to the work of ministry. In the ancient Olympic games competitors took an oath both that they would compete according to the rules and also that they had trained for the competition for ten straight months,[79] so perhaps both are in view. In an effort to capture something of this ambiguity, I have translated the phrase as "unless he competes according to the rules"; see the commentary below.

2:6 τὸν κοριῶντα γεωργὸν δεῖ πρῶτον τῶν καρπῶν μεταλαμβάνειν—To the military and athletic metaphors Paul now adds an agricultural one; see further the commentary.

2:7 νόει ὃ λέγω—Paul speaks here with his authority as one of Christ's apostles; see the entry "Apostle" in the Extended Notes. On the authority of Paul's writings see the section "The Spirit Explicitly Says" in the commentary on 1 Tim 4:1–5.

---

75. Wallace, *Greek Grammar*, 621.
76. BDAG 324.
77. BDAG 176–77, 430–31.
78. BDAG 943–44.
79. Barrett, *Pastoral Epistles*, 102; see Brown, "Getty Villa Guide."

δώσει γάρ σοι ὁ κύριος σύνεσιν ἐν πᾶσιν—The Lord will give this understanding, for he will do so through the authoritative word such as communicated by Paul, one of his apostles.

COMMENTARY

The First Letter to Timothy and the Letter to Titus are known for their lists of qualifications for the pastoral office (1 Tim 3:1–7; Titus 1:5–9). In addition to them we should note what Paul writes here about the pastoral ministry. He continues the present letter by addressing various aspects of Timothy's life and ministry. He touches on his coworker's existence as a Christian, as a student, as a pastor, and as a teacher of pastors.

Timothy as One in Christ

The apostle points to Timothy as one who has the grace of God since he is "in Christ Jesus." This prepositional phrase refers to the saving relationship that one has with Christ. This relationship is created by God through the gospel and through baptism, and it consists of faith directed toward Christ (see further the entry "In Christ" in the Extended Notes). In this way he has the saving grace of God. When Paul exhorts Timothy to be strong in this grace, he is directing him to those things (God's word and the washing of baptism) by which he has this grace. This will strengthen him in his saving faith, and that faith will in turn empower him for ministry.

Timothy as Student

When the apostle directs Timothy to "those things which you heard from me," and when he exhorts him to "consider what I say," he is pointing to the standard for Timothy's faith and ministry, namely, the authoritative word that he was taught by Paul as an apostle of the Lord.

A comparison of 2:2 ("those things which you heard from me through many witnesses") with 1:13 ("You have a standard of sound words which you heard from me") and 3:14 ("the things which you learned and believed, knowing from whom you learned [them]") indicates that these passages are referring to the preparation that Timothy received from Paul (and perhaps others) that qualified him to hold the pastoral office;

this preparation was the first-century equivalent of seminary education. As an apostle, Paul was one of those whom the risen Christ used to communicate his authoritative word to his church and to the world.[80] The Christian's faith and the pastor's ministry are both founded on the word of Christ as delivered in the apostolic Scriptures. The word imparts salvation through faith in Christ; it also serves as the standard and the power for the ministry of Christ's church and of her pastors.

Timothy as Pastor

In this letter the apostle directs Timothy to serve faithfully as a pastor, as a proclaimer of the word. Related to that is the exhortation that Timothy is to "join together in suffering evil as a good soldier of Christ Jesus." All Christians are called to suffer with Christ (Rom 8:17; 2 Tim 3:12). Nevertheless, since the suffering in question is a consequence of one's Christian faith, life, and witness,[81] the call to suffering falls especially upon pastors. Therefore, these words call upon Timothy to minister faithfully, even in the face of unjust suffering and persecution.

Paul's comment that Timothy needs to suffer "as a good soldier of Christ Jesus" leads into some additional illustrations for the pastoral ministry. As a soldier focuses on his military service to please those to whom he is responsible, so the pastor must be certain to please the one to whom he is responsible: the Lord of the church. The phrase "no one who has become a soldier becomes entangled in matters of ordinary life" does not prohibit Timothy from pursuing a craft or trade; Paul himself had been a tentmaker.[82] So also this does not mean that a pastor should have a monomaniacal preoccupation with the tasks of ministry to the detriment of everyone and everything else, such as family, hobbies, and self-care. If the athletic metaphor in 2:5 has to do with following the rules of competition, the apostle's meaning would be that as an athlete cannot win if he violates the rules of the competition, so also the pastor cannot go contrary to the "rules" of his ministry, namely, ministering through and according to the word of God. If this athletic metaphor has to do with sufficient and proper training, Paul would be impressing upon

---

80. See the entry "Apostle" in the Extended Notes.

81. See the section "Persecution" in the commentary on 2 Tim 3:10–17 and the section "Faithfulness in Suffering" in the commentary on 2 Tim 2:8–13.

82. Easton, *Pastoral Epistles*, 51.

Timothy (and upon all pastors) the importance of diligent preparation and ongoing conscientiousness in the conduct of the ministry. It is possible that both meanings are intended; see the textual note on 2:5. If he has worked diligently, the farmer enjoys the fruits of his labor. In the same way the pastor will receive a harvest of blessing from God for his diligent and faithful service.[83]

Timothy as Teacher of Pastors

Timothy's task of ministry was not limited to his own speaking of the word of God. He was also to "entrust those things which you heard from me in the presence of many witnesses to faithful men, who will be suited to also teach them to others."[84] As the apostle had prepared Timothy to be a pastor, so the younger man was now to carry on the task and prepare others to take up the pastoral office.[85]

The description here of the type of men with whom Timothy is to entrust the ministry is in keeping with the requirement that one who would be a pastor must be a capable teacher of the word.[86] Paul, therefore, entrusts Timothy with the task of identifying such men and of preparing them, so that they also are qualified and equipped to take up the pastoral ministry, especially the ministry of teaching the word. In this way the word would be passed on to future generations.[87]

---

83. "All three [soldier, athlete, farmer]—the first with his detachment, the second with his strict training, the third with his unremitting toil—reflect different aspects of the life of anyone who gives himself to Christ's service"; Kelly, *Pastoral Epistles*, 174. All three are also examples of those who understand the need for enduring suffering; Towner, *Letters*, 492–95. Note also 1 Cor 9:7, 24.

84. Compare also the directive of 1 Tim 5:22. The list of qualifications for the office of overseer/pastor in 1 Tim 3:1–7 also implies that Timothy was to prepare others for the pastoral ministry; cf. the instructions to Paul's other younger coworker in Titus 1:5–9.

85. Hence, we have here early traces of what would develop into theological schools and seminaries; Knight, *Pastoral Epistles*, 392.

86. 1 Tim 3;2; 5:17; 2 Tim 2:24; see also 1 Tim 4:11, 13.

87. *DPL* 604.

The Ministry—and the Suffering That It Entails: 2 Timothy 2:1–7 in Context

The present letter, the last one from the apostle's pen, is the most personal. Nevertheless, he also has much to say about the pastoral ministry—of Timothy and of pastors in general.

Paul lays out the responsibilities incumbent upon Timothy as Christian, student, pastor, and teacher of pastors. In all of these he emphasizes the importance and centrality of the word of God. Timothy is to be a man of the word, for his personal faith, for his learning, for his ministry, and for his teaching. In this way this section reflects one aspect of this letter, namely the contributions it makes to the life and work of the pastoral ministry.

2:8–13: Suffering and Endurance for the Gospel

TRANSLATION

⁸ Remember Jesus Christ, risen from the dead, of the offspring of David, according to my gospel, ⁹ for which I am suffering evil as an evildoer to the point of bonds; however, the word of God is not bound. ¹⁰ For this reason I endure all things for the sake of the elect ones, in order that they also may obtain salvation, which is in Christ Jesus with eternal glory. ¹¹ The saying is trustworthy:

For if we died with him, we will also live with him;
¹² if we endure, we will also reign with him;
if we will deny him, he also will deny us;
¹³ if we are faithless, he remains faithful,
for he is not able to deny himself.

TEXTUAL NOTES

2:8 Μνημόνευε—This word is sometimes used, as here, with the connotation "remember and respond accordingly."[88] This verb is a present tense with gnomic implications: "Always remember."[89] See the commentary.

ἐγηγερμένον ἐκ νεκρῶν—Paul's letters contain many references to the resurrection of Jesus Christ from the dead.[90] Here the resurrection, as the culmination of Christ's redemptive work, encompasses the entirety of that work. The perfect tense of the participle (ἐγηγερμένον) is fitting,

---

88. Matt 16:9; John 15:20; 16:4; Acts 20:35; Eph 2:11; Heb 13:7; Rev 2:5; 3:3.

89. Wallace, *Greek Grammar*, 525.

90. Rom 1:4; 4:24, 25; 6:4, 5, 9; 7:4; 8:11, 34; 10:9; 1 Cor 6:14; 15:4, 12, 20; 2 Cor 4:14; 5:15; Gal 1:1; Eph 1:20; Phil 3:10; Col 1:18; 2:12, 13; 3:1; 1 Thess 1:10.

as Jesus continues to be risen from the dead. This impersonal verb is a divine passive.[91]

ἐκ σπέρματος Δαυίδ—The apostle also asserts this in his Letter to the Romans (1:3). In the NT the descent of Jesus from David is often noted,[92] as it identifies him as the one who would have an eternal rule as promised in God's covenant with David (2 Sam 7:1–17; 1 Chr 17:1–15), that is, as the Messiah. This recognition of Christ's Davidic descent (involving his true humanity) also serves as another refutation of the gnostic heresy troubling the churches served by Timothy.[93]

κατὰ τὸ εὐαγγέλιόν μου—Paul connects the resurrection of Christ and his descent from David with his gospel also in Rom 1:2–4.

2:9 ἐν ᾧ—The relative pronoun ᾧ refers back to the noun εὐαγγέλιον; the apostle's sufferings are specifically on account of his ministry in the gospel; hence, he is suffering with Christ (Rom 8:17).

κακοπαθῶ ... ὡς κακοῦργος—There is a play on words; Paul is suffering *evil* as though he were one who had done *evil*.

μέχρι δεσμῶν ... ἀλλὰ ὁ λόγος τοῦ θεοῦ οὐ δέδεται—There is another play on words here: even though the apostle is bound with *bonds*, the word of God is not *bound*.

2:10—On this entire verse, see the section "For the Sake of the Elect Ones" in the commentary below.

διὰ τοῦτο πάντα ὑπομένω διὰ τοὺς ἐκλεκτούς—The phrase διὰ τοῦτο connects what precedes with what follows; Paul is enduring sufferings, and by doing so he is serving others.

διὰ τοὺς ἐκλεκτούς—"Elect ones" (ἐκλεκτούς) is a synonym for "believers," "Christians," as in Rom 8:33; 16:13; Col 3:12; Titus 1:1.

ἵνα καὶ αὐτοὶ σωτηρίας τύχωσιν—Here ἵνα plus a subjunctive verb (τύχωσιν) is to be understood as a purpose-result clause.[94]

σωτηρίας—See the Entry "Save, Savior, Salvation" in the Extended Notes and also the essay "He Saved Us: The Pastoral Letters on the Way of Salvation" elsewhere in this commentary. As abstract nouns are generally anarthrous,[95] the word here is modified by the phrase τῆς ἐν Χριστῷ

---

91. DPL 265.

92. Matt 1:1; 9:27; 12:23; 15:22; 20:30–31 (par Mark 10:47–48; Luke 18:38–39); 21:9, 15; 22:42, 45 (par Mark 12:35, 37; Luke 20:41, 44); Luke 1:32.

93. Easton, *Pastoral Epistles*, 52.

94. Wallace, *Greek Grammar*, 473–74.

95. Wallace, *Greek Grammar*, 250.

Ἰησοῦ. One has salvation if he has that relationship to God described by the phrase "in Christ Jesus"; see the following note.

ἐν Χριστῷ Ἰησοῦ—See the entry "In Christ" in the Extended Notes.

μετὰ δόξης αἰωνίου—"Glory" (δόξης) is a word often used to describe the character of eternal life. See further the entry by that name in the Extended Notes.

2:11-13: εἰ γὰρ συναπεθάνομεν, καὶ συζήσομεν; εἰ ὑπομένομεν, καὶ συμβασιλεύσομεν; εἰ ἀρνησόμεθα, κἀκεῖνος ἀρνήσεται ἡμᾶς; εἰ ἀπιστοῦμεν, ἐκεῖνος πιστὸς μένει—εἰ with the indicative in the protasis ("if") indicates the assumption of the reality of what is stated (first class condition);[96] the future tense verbs in the apodosis ("then") of the first three clauses give a special emphasis to the certainty of what will subsequently take place.[97]

2:11 πιστὸς ὁ λόγος—See the excursus "The Trustworthy Sayings of the Pastoral Letters" at the end of the commentary on 1 Tim 1:12-17. In the present passage this phrase introduces the lines that follow.

εἰ γὰρ συναπεθάνομεν—A comparison with Rom 6:3 indicates that this is a reference to death with Christ in baptism.

καὶ συζήσομεν—A comparison with Col 2:12; 3:1, 4 demonstrates that one's death, burial, and resurrection with Christ in baptism is an assurance of his/her resurrection with him at the last day.

2:12 εἰ ὑπομένομεν—When one dies with Christ in baptism, he also is called upon to live out that baptismal death by a life of suffering with Christ (Rom 8:17; Phil 3:10-11). One's baptismal resurrection with Christ supplies the power to endure such suffering with Christ (Phil 3:10).[98]

καὶ συμβασιλεύσομεν—The prefix on the verb συμβασιλεύσομεν shows that, like συζήσομεν, this is also a way of speaking of the believer's future life with Christ; one's baptism with Christ will assure of him of sharing in that life.

εἰ ἀρνησόμεθα—This warning uses the same verb used of Peter's denial of Jesus[99] and thereby stresses the seriousness of this sin.

κἀκεῖνος ἀρνήσεται ἡμᾶς—Jesus also spoke of denying one who would deny him (Matt 10:33; Luke 12:9).

2:13 εἰ ἀπιστοῦμεν, ἐκεῖνος πιστὸς μένει—English translation is able to replicate the play on words in the Greek. Even if we are faithless, he remains faithful (cf. Rom 3:3). See further the commentary.

---

96. Wallace, *Greek Grammar*, 663, 689, 762.
97. Wallace, *Greek Grammar*, 566.
98. *DNTB* 703.
99. Matt 26:70, 72; Mark 14:68, 70; Luke 22:57; John 13:38.

ἀρνήσασθαι γὰρ ἑαυτὸν οὐ δύναται—There is a further play on words. Even if we deny him, he will not deny himself, that is, he remains ready to forgive. The middle voice of the verb ἀρνήσασθαι already denotes denying self; hence, the redundant use of ἀρνήσασθαι . . . ἑαυτὸν gives emphasis to the apostle's assertion.[100] See further the commentary.

COMMENTARY

"According to My Gospel"

Paul begins this section with a recounting of those events that make up the content of the gospel. This section is often viewed as confessional and/or liturgical, perhaps used in connection with baptism.[101] It may well be that, but this does not rule out the possibility that it is an original composition by the apostle himself.[102]

Paul starts with the exhortation to "remember" Jesus Christ. As with other uses of this term in the New Testament, here the word implies more than a mere mental recollection.[103] To "remember" Jesus Christ as risen from the dead is not only to recall the fact but also to place one's trust in that historical reality for salvation.

The apostle speaks of Christ as "risen from the dead." That Jesus is risen from the dead presupposes that he died, so that a bit later Paul can speak of Christians both dying and living with Christ. Thus, this phrase encompasses the entirety of Paul's gospel that Jesus was "given over (to death) for our trespasses and raised for our justification" (Rom 4:25).

The apostle further refers to Jesus as being of "the offspring of David." As in the salutation of his Letter to the Romans (1:3-4) so here Paul speaks of Christ's resurrection and his Davidic descent in close proximity. That Jesus was descended from king David was significant, for it was a way of designating him as the one who fulfilled the promises of God's covenant with that king (2 Sam 7:1-17; par 1 Chr 17:1-15),

---

100. Wallace, *Greek Grammar*, 419.

101. *DNTB* 1256; Knight, *Pastoral Epistles*, 408.

102. Commenting on another passage in the Pauline corpus and advocating the greater likelihood of its being an original composition by Paul rather than an adaptation of a preexisting hymn, N. T. Wright ("Poetry and Theology," 445) noted, "Nothing would be more calculated to puzzle a congregation than tampering with a hymn they are in the act of singing."

103. Matt 16:9; John 15:20; 16:4; Acts 20:35; Eph 2:11; Heb 13:7; Rev 2:5; 3:3.

that is, as a way of designating him as the Messiah.[104] In making his covenant with him the Lord had promised that he would raise up a descendant from David's line (2 Sam 7:12), that he, the Lord himself, would be a father to this descendant, so that he would be God's Son (2 Sam 7:14), and that this descendant would have an eternal rule (2 Sam 7:16). As a descendant from David Jesus fulfilled this promise, for he is/was the Son of God (e.g., Rom 1:4), and he established an eternal kingdom (e.g., 1 Tim 1:16; 2 Tim 4:18).

This section alludes to the eternal kingdom of the Davidic Messiah when the apostle speaks of those who will live with Christ (2:11) and reign with him (2:12). This kingdom is the salvation of which Paul also writes here (2:10).

Baptism is one of the ways in which this salvation that Christ acquired by his death and resurrection is given to us. The references in this section to dying with, living with, and reigning with Christ, all of which make use of the baptismal prefix σύν, are a clear echo of the apostle's teaching on baptism, as recorded in Rom 6:3–11 and Col 2:11–12. Through baptism one participates with Christ in his redemptive death and justifying resurrection, in this way receiving all the benefits that Jesus obtained by his saving work.[105]

These blessings are received through faith. If one becomes "faithless," that is, without faith in Christ, such a one forfeits these benefits. Nevertheless, Paul notes that Christ remains faithful. His promises of salvation offered in baptism (and in the word of God) remain available. One will again receive these if he or she resumes believing in the one who for him or her was crucified and raised.

Faithfulness in Suffering

In the midst of the baptismal language concerning dying, living, and reigning with (σύν) Christ occurs the apostle's statement concerning enduring suffering. To die with Christ in baptism is to be conformed to his death (Phil 3:10), which entails the call to suffering with him (Rom 8:17).

Suffering with Christ, like taking up the cross to follow him (Matt 16:24–25; Mark 8:34–35; Luke 9:23–24), does not involve any

---

104. *DNTB* 703.

105. As noted by both Chrysostom (*NPNF*[1] 13:492 [ACCS, NT 9:244]) and Basil the Great (FC 9:370a).

and every type of hardship or affliction that might come the Christian's way. Some hardships are the consequence of sin (so the hangover that would come from drinking too much could be thought of as punishment for the sin of drunkenness). Christians bear other types of affliction simply because these are things that affect all of humanity in this fallen world (Christians and non-Christians alike will experience ill health and inclement weather). When a believer suffers with Christ, he is bearing things that are imposed on him because of his faith, his witness, and/or his way of life. At the time of the writing of this letter Paul himself was experiencing suffering of this type, for his imprisonment had resulted from his faith, witness, and way of life. Persecution, such as the apostle was experiencing at this point, is one form of suffering with Christ; however, the use of the plural here (πάντα, "all things") demonstrates that bearing affliction for Christ's sake involves all manner of suffering and hardship on account of a Christian's faith, manner of life, and/or witness.

The references to denying Christ and to becoming faithless, therefore, imply the need instead to endure such sufferings by remaining faithful, that is, without falling from faith. The power of Christ's resurrection, in which the believer shared in his baptism, will supply the power to endure such sufferings.[106]

"For the Sake of the Elect Ones"[107]

It is in light of the reality of the Christian's suffering with Christ that we can understand the apostle's statement, "For this reason I endure all things for the sake of the elect ones." Paul's reference here is similar to that of his Letter to the Colossians (1:24), where he states, "In my flesh I complete the things lacking of the afflictions of Christ."[108]

All Christians must suffer with Christ (2 Tim 3:12); they share in the sufferings which are endured by proclaimers of God's word such as the apostle himself (2 Cor 1:6–7). This participation in Christ's sufferings is a

---

106. Note that in Phil 3:10–11 the apostle uses a slightly different form of the word for "resurrection" in each of these verses. In 3:11 he uses the compound term ἐξανάστασιν, emphasizing that he is speaking of the resurrection *from* the dead at the last day. That being the case, his use of the simple form ἀναστάσεως indicates that his reference in 3:10 is to the *power* of Christ's resurrection in the daily life of the believer that enables him to endure the "fellowship of his sufferings."

107. An earlier version of this section appeared in Deterding, *Colossians*, 75–79.

108. DPL 19–20; Kelly, *Pastoral Epistles*, 178.

result of the believers' baptismal incorporation into Christ's death. In the present passage this is indicated by several verbs compounded with the baptismal preposition σύν. Here the phrase "if we endure" stands in parallelism with "if we died with him," just as "we will reign with him" does with "we will live with him," indicating that the believers' past death with Christ in baptism (συναπεθάνομεν is an aorist tense verb) involves enduring suffering throughout this life (ὑπομένομεν is a present tense verb).

Thus, by way of baptism Christ so closely identifies himself with his followers that they share both in the forgiveness and salvation that he acquired by his death and also in the sufferings that he endured. Paul speaks of suffering with Christ (Rom 8:17), of being weak in him who was crucified in weakness (2 Cor 13:4), of being conformed to Christ's death and knowing the fellowship of his sufferings (Phil 3:10), and of carrying about the death of Jesus and being given up unto death on his account (2 Cor 4:10-11). Elsewhere he describes believers' sufferings as the afflictions of Christ (Col 1:24) and refers to the scars on his body that he received as a result of persecution and mistreatment as the "stigmas" of Jesus (Gal 6:17).[109] The apostle's teaching corresponds to the word that he heard from the risen Lord on the road to Damascus, "Why are you persecuting *me*?" (Acts 9:4-5; 22:7-8; 26:14-15), for in being persecuted by Saul those Christians were suffering with their Lord.

Even as these sufferings are a result of our baptismal incorporation into him who suffered for us, so our baptism gives us the power to endure them, for with the fellowship in Christ's sufferings and conformity to his death baptism also imparts the power of our Lord's resurrection (Phil 3:10; see also Col 2:12). To reach the consummation of their baptismal resurrection with Christ believers live out their baptismal incorporation into him; this involves suffering.[110]

The sufferings to which Paul refers in these passages are not simply what all people experience as a result of the fall; they are those sufferings which are inflicted upon those who follow Christ precisely on account of their being followers of this one who suffered. In 2 Timothy (3:12) the apostle speaks of persecution on account of a godly way of life in Christ Jesus. Both passages in 2 Corinthians that deal with enduring the sufferings of Christ (4:10-11; 13:3-4) occur in contexts in which Paul is speaking of proclaiming the gospel. Similarly, the reference to the afflictions of

---

109. Rom 8:17; 2 Cor 4:10-11; 13:4; Phil 3:10-11; 2 Tim 2:11-12.
110. Schneider, *Die Passionsmystik des Paulus*, 51.

Christ (Col 1:24) occurs within a section devoted to the author's ministry in the gospel.[111] Likewise, his reference in Ephesians (3:13) to "my afflictions for your sake" comes at the conclusion of a lengthy discourse (3:2–12) on his ministry (3:7) in the gospel.

When the apostle speaks of completing what is lacking of the afflictions of Christ (Col 1:24), there is no thought of anything deficient in our Lord's redemptive work. The term "afflictions" (θλίψεων) is never used in the New Testament of the redemptive work of our Lord. Moreover, the immediate context in Colossians (1:20, 22) speaks of the sufficiency of Christ's atoning work in reconciling all of creation, a sentiment echoed throughout the apostle's letters.[112]

Paul indicates that he is suffering for the sake of the Colossians as the body of Christ, the church; that is, he is suffering on their behalf by suffering in their place.[113] Thus, the deficiency in afflictions/suffering is on the part of the Colossians.[114] Their wavering in faith at being enticed by heresy, a wavering hinted at in 1:23, has meant a neglect on their part of those things (godly living and gospel proclamation) that cause one to suffer with Christ.

By virtue of their common baptismal incorporation into the body of Christ, what affects the Colossians affects the apostle, and what affects him affects them (1 Cor 12:12–27). Therefore, Paul is able to complete what they lack in suffering by suffering for them in his "flesh" (the term in Col 1:24 is synonymous with "body" and is used to distinguish the human body from the church as the body of Christ). This he does by his ministry for them, for their wavering calls for further proclamation on his part to them, and such proclamation is a major element of that godly life which causes one to suffer with Christ. Hence his additional sufferings complete what they lack in afflictions. Those who proclaim the

---

111. Along these lines is the statement of Severian of Gabala: "I fulfill what is lacking in the tribulations of Christ through my suffering, which is on your behalf. How so? Because in order to preach to you, I have had to suffer. Since Christ is the head of the body, tribulations will be generated through the word of truth for those who are in the church. These are naturally called the sufferings of Christ" (Staab, *Pauluskommentare*, 321; translation in ACCS, NT 9:24). Similar is the comment of Theodoret of Cyr: "Paul fills up the sufferings of Christ in the sense that he endures sufferings in order to preach salvation to the nations" (PG 82:603B/604B).

112. Schneider, *Passionsmystik*, 54.

113. The range of meaning for the vocable ὑπέρ (used twice in Col 1:24) includes "on behalf of" and "in place of," and, in fact, the two meanings sometimes merge with one another; BDAG 1030–31 (ὑπέρ, A, 1, a and especially A, 1, c).

114. Schneider, *Passionsmystik*, 55–56.

gospel suffer for it, and their sufferings are another way in which they serve fellow members of the body of Christ.

This is the apostle's meaning when he writes that he "endure[s] all things for the sake of the elect ones, in order that they may obtain salvation" (2 Tim 2:10). His ministry brings him suffering to endure (the same term used in 2:12). His ministry in the gospel brings salvation to those to whom he ministers. As a fellow member of the body of Christ, he aids them in their sufferings, as he himself suffers for the sake of Christ.

On the significance of the reference here to "the elect ones" see the section "The Faith of God's Elect Ones" in the commentary on Titus 1:1–4.

"With Eternal Glory"[115]

The goal of Paul's ministry and of the faith of believers is "salvation... with eternal glory." As a term descriptive of eternal life (Rom 8:18; 2 Thess 1:9) and the resurrection existence (Phil 3:21) the word "glory" (δόξα) is a rich one: "The terminology of glory provides a window on virtually the whole of Paul's theology."[116]

As the equivalent of the Hebrew כָּבוֹד (Exod 40:34–35; 1 Kgs 8:11), δόξα is used to describe the being of God himself, especially as this is revealed to mankind (Rom 1:23; 1 Cor 2:8), so that "glory" is an incarnational term (John 1:14). Hence "glory" is a virtual synonym for the image of God (Rom 3:23; 2 Cor 3:18; Phil 3:21). By referring to the resurrection life with a term associated with God's self-revelation Paul asserts the same truth in Col 3:4 as we find in 2 Peter, where it is said that our future salvation involves becoming partakers of the divine nature (1:4). Such a use of δόξα makes it a highly appropriate term to describe eternal salvation (2 Cor 3:8–11). The association of the word δόξα with the restoration of God's image of righteousness and holiness and with the resurrection life also enriches our appreciation for its use to denote the content of the gospel (2 Cor 4:4; 1 Tim 1:11). As the term is also employed to designate that of which God is worthy for accomplishing humanity's redemption (Eph 1:6, 12, 14), we see that eternity will be characterized by the Lord receiving praise from the redeemed for their salvation.

---

115. An earlier version of this section appeared in Deterding, *Colossians*, 139–40.
116. *DPL* 348.

Suffering and Endurance for the Gospel: 2 Timothy 2:8–13 in Context

Paul had been speaking to Timothy regarding the work of ministry in the gospel. He now turns to the content of that gospel and to the results for the Christian life that come from believing that gospel with endurance.

The messianic identity of Jesus and his death and resurrection are at the center of the gospel. Enduring in faith in that gospel brings one salvation with eternal glory. Sharing in his death and resurrection through baptism is one way in which that glorious salvation becomes our own and by which we are strengthened to endure in the faith.

Baptism into Christ's death and resurrection and faith in this one who suffered for us also means that Christians will also face suffering on account of their faith, witness, and way of life. Such sufferings certainly bring the temptation to deny Christ by withdrawing from faith in him. Therefore, the apostle stresses the importance of the Christian enduring in the faith. But in addition to this exhortation to faithfulness on our part, Paul points to faithfulness on the part of Christ. "He is not able to deny himself," for in his gospel (including our baptism) he is always present with his grace to forgive our sins and to build us up in our saving faith.

2:14–26: The Minister and His Ministry; the Truth and Its Opponents

TRANSLATION

[14] Call to mind these things, adjuring them before God not to dispute about words, which is of no use except for the ruin of the hearers. [15] Be eager to show yourself proven to God, a workman who has no need to be ashamed, correctly setting forth the word of truth. [16] Avoid meaningless, empty words, for they further promote ungodliness. [17] The talk of these people will spread like gangrene. Among these are Hymenaeus and Philetus, [18] who strayed from the truth, saying that the resurrection has already taken place; they are overturning the faith of some. [19] However, the firm foundation of God stands, having this seal: "The Lord knows those who are his," and "Let everyone who names the name of the Lord keep away from injustice." [20] In a great house there are not only gold and silver vessels but also wooden and clay, some for honorable use and some for dishonorable. [21] Therefore, if anyone purifies himself from these things, he will be a vessel for honor, sanctified, useful for the master, equipped for every good work.

[22] Flee youthful lusts. Along with those who call on the name of the Lord from a pure heart pursue righteousness, faithfulness, love, and peace. [23] Avoid[a] foolish and uninformed speculations, knowing that they give birth to disputes. [24] A slave of the Lord must not be combative but gentle toward all, able to teach, able to endure wrong, [25] with gentleness instructing his opponents. God may perhaps give them repentance unto the knowledge of the truth, [26] and they may come to their senses and escape from the snare of the devil, having been [previously] caught by him for his will.

[a] Or *reject*

TEXTUAL NOTES

2:14 Ταῦτα ὑπομίμνησκε—As there is no immediate neuter plural noun to which the pronoun ταῦτα would refer, "these things" refers to the particulars of the gospel that Paul has rehearsed in the previous verses. The verb here (ὑπομίμνησκε) can mean "remind others" (John 14:26) or "remember yourself" (Luke 22:61); both meanings fit in this context.

διαμαρτυρόμενος ἐνώπιον τοῦ θεοῦ—This turn of phrase amounts to Paul instructing Timothy to put others under oath ("adjuring"); they are thereby obligated to follow these directives; hence, there will be dire consequences before God if anyone should act contrary to what is commanded here.[117]

μὴ λογομαχεῖν, ἐπ' οὐδὲν χρήσιμον, ἐπὶ καταστροφῇ τῶν ἀκουόντων— "To dispute about words" (λογομαχεῖν) characterizes the false teaching plaguing the churches served by Timothy (1 Tim 6:4) and perhaps those served by Titus as well (Titus 1:10; 3:9). The false teachers may well have presented their views with sophisticated rhetoric, passing their teachings off as a more learned religion/philosophy than the "simple" gospel proclaimed by Paul and his coworkers. See also "The Nature of the Heresy" in the Introduction to the Pastoral Letters.

2:15 σπούδασον σεαυτὸν δόκιμον παραστῆσαι τῷ θεῷ—The pastor is to seek to be approved/genuine (δόκιμον) before God; it is God's judgment and not that of anyone else that determines the authenticity and value of one's ministry.

ἐργάτην ἀνεπαίσχυντον—Biblically "shame" is something rather different than embarrassment, as though "if it doesn't bother you, it's someone else's problem—not yours." Biblically shame is a reality; the word group is sometimes used with reference to God's eternal displeasure.[118] The apostle is here directing Timothy to conduct his ministry according to God's standards, so as not to be corrupted by sin.[119]

ὀρθοτομοῦντα—The meaning of this fairly rare word is less than obvious. The occurrences of the word in the LXX (Prov 3:6; 11:5) point to the meaning "make straight," that is, make correct. By comparison with the similarly formed verb καινοτομέω ("make a new assertion") the sense

---

117. BDAG 233.
118. Mark 8:38; Rom 5:5; 9:33; 10:11; 1 Cor 1:27–28; Heb 12:2; 1 Pet 2:6; 1 John 2:28.
119. Note Luke 14:9; Rom 5:5; 9:33; 10:11; 1 Cor 15:34; Phil 3:19; Heb 12:2; 1 Pet 2:6; Jude 13.

of this verb seems to have its main stress on ὀρθο.¹²⁰ This seems to call for the rendering "correctly setting forth."

τὸν λόγον τῆς ἀληθείας—See the entry "Truth" in the Extended Notes. The "word of truth" stands in contrast to "empty, pointless words"; see the following notes.

2:16 τὰς δὲ βεβήλους κενοφωνίας περιΐστασο—Paul writes this with a sidelong glance at the assertions of the false teachers. Their pronouncements may sound learned (note 1 Tim 6:20), but they have no real meaning or purpose. They are "worldly and senseless myths," such as a man of God like Timothy is to reject (1 Tim 4:7).

ἐπὶ πλεῖον γὰρ προκόψουσιν ἀσεβείας—Even worse than being meaningless, the teachings of the heretics actually further ungodliness. Perhaps the false teachers regarded themselves as having "progressed" beyond what was taught by Paul and others, so that the apostle notes the irony that the only "progress" they make is toward impiety.¹²¹

2:17 καὶ ὁ λόγος αὐτῶν ὡς γάγγραινα νομὴν ἕξει—"Gangrene" is a medical term known since the time of Hippocrites;¹²² its use here is not to pinpoint any particular disease (such as an ulcer or cancer) but to describe false teaching as a detrimental condition that spreads if left unchecked.¹²³

ὧν ἐστιν Ὑμέναιος καὶ Φίλητος—Hymenaeus is quite likely the same individual mentioned in 1 Tim 1:20 (whose commentary see). Philetus is otherwise unknown to us. The fact that Paul must here warn Timothy about the false teaching of Hymenaeus several years after the apostle expelled him from the Christian community (1 Tim 1:20) indicates that he and his heretical teachings had continued to afflict the churches served by Timothy.¹²⁴

2:18 οἵτινες περὶ τὴν ἀλήθειαν ἠστόχησαν—Here, as elsewhere in the NT, the indefinite relative pronoun ὅστις has no difference in meaning from the definite relative pronoun ὅς.¹²⁵ That they strayed (ἠστόχησαν) with regard to the truth means that they have departed from the saving truth altogether; this phrase also indicates that they teach contrary to the

---

120. MM 456; Towner, *Letters*, 522.
121. Knight, *Pastoral Epistles*, 413.
122. BDAG 186.
123. As noted by Towner, *Letters*, 525.
124. See also Towner, *Letters*, 525; Marshall, *Pastoral Epistles*, 751.
125. Wallace, *Greek Grammar*, 344–45.

word of truth that a man of God, like Timothy, is to set forth correctly (verse 15).

λέγοντες τὴν ἀνάστασιν ἤδη γεγονέναι—Here the accusative ἀνάστασιν functions as the subject of the infinitive γεγονέναι.[126] These words point to a major error of the heresy. Such an assertion arises from regarding the resurrection as a merely spiritual event, having nothing to do with the restoration to life of the body of flesh. Such false teaching has its genesis in the unbiblical presupposition that the material is inherently evil. See further "The Nature of the Heresy" in the Introduction to the Pastoral Letters.[127]

καὶ ἀνατρέπουσιν τήν τινων πίστιν—The aorist tense of this verb (ἀνέτρεψεν) occurs in John 2:15 in stating that Jesus overturned the tables of the money changers. That and the nature of the false teaching (denial of the bodily resurrection) would indicate that the heretics have "upset" the faith of "some" others by undermining it altogether, so that they no longer have saving faith ("faith" here would be *fides qua creditur*).[128] On "faith" see the entry by that name in the Extended Notes.

2:19 ὁ μέντοι στερεὸς θεμέλιος τοῦ θεοῦ ἔστηκεν—Structural metaphors giving assurance of God's salvation are found elsewhere in Scripture,[129] including the letters of Paul.[130]

ἔχων τὴν σφραγῖδα ταύτην—A "seal" (σφραγῖδα) was a signet (Rev 7:2) and/or the mark made by such a signet; hence, this word came to denote any type of attestation.[131]

ἔγνω κύριος τοὺς ὄντας αὐτοῦ—Is this presented as a quotation from the (Hebrew) Scriptures? If so, Num 16:5 would seem to be the source. On the other hand, since there is no introductory formula, such as "it is written," perhaps a general proverbial citation, along the lines of Titus 1:12 and 1 Cor 15:32-33, rather than a scriptural quotation is meant.

---

126. Wallace, *Greek Grammar*, 194-95.

127. While some church fathers agreed with the identification of this heretical teaching with the teachings of the gnostics, others claimed that the false teachers equated the resurrection with the natural procreation of children, whereby the children succeeded their parents. See ACCS NT 9:250-51. A twenty-first-century version of this point of view might be that the only thing that is eternal is nature, so that the only way to "immortality" would be in preserving the environment.

128. Knight, *Pastoral Epistles*, 414.

129. Ps 118:22; Isa 8:14; 28:16; Matt 21:42 (Mark 12:10; Luke 20:17); Acts 4:11; 1 Pet 2:4-8.

130. Rom 9:33; 1 Cor 3:16-17; Eph 2:19-22.

131. BDAG 980-81.

ἀποστήτω ἀπὸ ἀδικίας πᾶς ὁ ὀνομάζων τὸ ὄνομα κυρίου—The formula πᾶς ὁ often occurs in the NT in a generic sense to designate one who belongs to a larger class.[132] If this is intended to be a biblical quotation, it is difficult to identify its source. In view of the possible allusion to Num 16 that precedes, this may be a summary of Num 16:26; at the very least it employs terminology from other OT passages; see the commentary.

2:20 Ἐν μεγάλῃ δὲ οἰκίᾳ—The apostle here introduces a structural analogy.

οὐκ ἔστιν μόνον σκεύη χρυσᾶ καὶ ἀργυρᾶ—These would be valuable, precious objects.

ἀλλὰ καὶ ξύλινα καὶ ὀστράκινα—In contrast to the objects previously mentioned, these would be ordinary vessels.

ἃ μὲν εἰς τιμὴν ἃ δὲ εἰς ἀτιμίαν—Precious vessels might include objects of art; these would be for "honorable" use (τιμήν). Objects for dishonorable (ἀτιμίαν) use might be those for cleaning or personal hygiene. We need not inquire into or speculate about the details to appreciate the point of Paul's analogy.

2:21 ἐὰν οὖν τις ἐκκαθάρῃ ἑαυτὸν ἀπὸ τούτων—The apostle quickly moves from analogy to actuality. Cognates of the verb ἐκκαθάρῃ are used elsewhere with reference to living a sanctified life.[133] "These things" (τούτων) refers to the dishonorable "vessels," which would denote the false teachings of the false teachers; purifying oneself from false teachings involves turning away from the false teachers themselves (3:5). See further the commentary.

ἔσται σκεῦος εἰς τιμήν—A vessel for honorable use illustrates the honorable service that is to be seen in the life (and ministry) of an honorable person.

ἡγιασμένον—God's holy calling (2 Tim 1:9) will be reflected in the holy living of those who are his.

εὔχρηστον τῷ δεσπότῃ—Paul returns for a moment to the analogy. God is the master of the house; those who serve him honorably are vessels that are well pleasing to him.

εἰς πᾶν ἔργον ἀγαθὸν ἡτοιμασμένον—The similarity of this to Eph 2:10 indicates that this instruction is pertinent to the life of every Christian; the similarity to 2 Tim 3:17 indicates that it has special applicability to the work of the pastor. The latter passage also points to the truth that the

---

132. Wallace, *Greek Grammar*, 227–30.
133. Titus 2:14; Heb 9:14; Jas 4:8.

Scriptures provide the motivation and especially the power for one to be able to do what is good in the sight of God.

2:22 Τὰς δὲ νεωτερικὰς ἐπιθυμίας φεῦγε—Context will determine whether the term "desires" (ἐπιθυμίας) refers to something good (e.g., Phil 1:23) or evil (e.g., Col 3:5); here the desires are clearly evil. As Timothy is a "youth" (νεότητος, 1 Tim 4:12, whose commentary see), he would be particularly vulnerable to "youthful" (νεωτερικάς) desires.

φεῦγε, δίωκε—Both of these verbs are present tense with gnomic implications: "Always flee; always pursue."[134] "Flee" (φεῦγε) can mean to "run away" or even "escape";[135] hence, it is a strong, vigorous turn of phrase. As in 1 Tim 6:11 δίωκε is used here as the opposite of "flee." As in some contexts the term can mean "drive away" (Matt 23:34) or even "persecute" (e.g., Gal 1:13, 23) it is another strong, vigorous expression.

δικαιοσύνην—See the entry "Righteousness/Justification" in the Extended Notes.

πίστιν—In this list of virtues that Timothy is to pursue πίστιν would refer to the virtue of "faithfulness," such faithfulness being a fruit of saving faith. See the entry "Faith" in the Extended Notes.

ἀγάπην—See the entry "Love" in the Extended Notes.

εἰρήνην—See the entry "Peace" in the Extended Notes. Believers are to strive[136] to live at peace with all people (Rom 12:18).

μετὰ τῶν ἐπικαλουμένων τὸν κύριον—To "call on the name of the Lord" in both Testaments is a designation for those who have saving faith.[137] Is Paul saying that Timothy is to pursue peace with all believers, or is he telling him that along with believers he needs to pursue righteousness, faith, love, and peace? The fact that Paul elsewhere exhorts to being at peace with all (Rom 12:18) and the use of the preposition μετά elsewhere in 2 Timothy (4:11b, 22) argues in favor of the latter.[138]

ἐκ καθαρᾶς καρδίας—See the entry "Heart and Conscience" in the Extended Notes. The word "pure" (καθαρᾶς) can denote what is physically clean (John 13:10), unspotted (Rev 15:6), or clear (Rev 21:18). Thus, a pure conscience is one that is totally free from sin. Faith in Christ is the only way to such a pure heart (1 Tim 1:5).

---

134. Wallace, *Greek Grammar*, 525.

135. BDAG 1052.

136. In Rom 12:18 Paul gives the directive to live at peace with all "if possible," and "in so far as it is up to you."

137. Gen 4:26; 12:8; Joel 2:32 (MT 3:5); Acts 2:21; Rom 10:13; 1 Cor 1:2.

138. BDF 121 [§ 227 (3)]; *TDNT* 2:416–17.

2:23 τὰς δὲ μωρὰς καὶ ἀπαιδεύτους ζητήσεις παραιτοῦ—The word "avoid" (παραιτοῦ) in other contexts can mean "request,"[139] so it is not as strong a word as "flee" in the previous verse. While Timothy must flee evil (sinful) desires, he should, as far as he is able, "avoid" the speculations referred to here. These are "foolish and uninformed"; with these adjectives Paul may well be referring to the false teaching. Sometimes it is necessary to confront false teaching, but, if possible, the pastor would do well to concentrate on proclaiming the truth (cf. Jude 1–4).

εἰδὼς ὅτι γεννῶσιν μάχας—Allowing foolish and uninformed speculations to have a voice in the church will only produce conflict. The word for "disputes" here (μάχας) is cognate to a portion of the compound verb "dispute about words" (λογομαχεῖν) that occurs in 2:14.

2:24 δοῦλον δὲ κυρίου—Paul speaks of himself as a "slave" (δοῦλος) of God;[140] hence, the term here is used of any servant of God's word, particularly of pastors; hence, the apostle here is giving qualifications for the pastoral office similar to those recorded in 1 Tim 3:1–7 and Titus 1:5–9.

οὐ δεῖ μάχεσθαι—The negated verb "(not) to be combative" (μάχεσθαι) is cognate to "disputes" (μάχας) in the previous verse. Foolish and unlearned speculations only produce combats, but a man of God ought not be combative; hence, he is to avoid such speculations as much as possible.

ἀλλὰ—This connective draws a sharp contrast between the preceding vice and the following virtues.

ἤπιον εἶναι πρὸς πάντας—According to a number of manuscripts of 1 Thess 2:7 Paul uses the adjective "gentle" (ἤπιον) to describe his own demeanor and conduct toward those in the church at Thessalonica. Indeed, the man of God is to have such a demeanor toward all.

διδακτικόν—Both 1 Timothy (3:2) and Titus (1:9) give being apt to teach as a qualification for holding the pastoral office.

ἀνεξίκακον—This word is compounded from ἀνέχω ("I endure") and κακός ("evil"), thus the rendering "able to endure wrong." A one-word translation such as "tolerant," especially in the current cultural climate, seems inadequate if not even misleading.

2:25 ἐν πραΰτητι παιδεύοντα τοὺς ἀντιδιατιθεμένους—Since the opponents (ἀντιδιατιθεμένους) need to come to repentance (see the following note), the opposition spoken of here would include holding to

---

139. Mark 15:6; Heb 12:19; BDAG 764.
140. Rom 1:1; Gal 1:10; Phil 1:1; Titus 1:1.

doctrinal error contrary to the Scriptures.¹⁴¹ Becoming harsh and disagreeable with those with whom one disagrees is an easy temptation. A man of God should deal with such people gently. See further the entry "Gentle, Kind" in the Extended Notes.

μήποτε δώῃ αὐτοῖς ὁ θεὸς μετάνοιαν—Here a reason is given for dealing gently with those who need correction. God may¹⁴² grant them repentance.

εἰς ἐπίγνωιν ἀληθείας—"Knowledge of the truth" is a biblical expression for saving faith.¹⁴³ As the false teachers claimed access to an exclusive religious "knowledge" (1 Tim 6:20; 2 Tim 3:7; Titus 1:16), the choice of words here is deliberate; the errorists need to be instructed in the true saving knowledge. See also "The Nature of the Heresy" in the Introduction to the Pastoral Letters and also the commentary below.

2:26 ἀνανήψωσιν—In a context where saving faith is designated as "the knowledge of the truth," "come to their senses" (ἀνανήψωσιν) is an apt way of describing such faith.

ἐκ τῆς τοῦ διαβόλου παγίδος—Paul used this metaphor in his First Letter to Timothy (3:7). A literal trap or snare is a good illustration of the hold of Satan over those without saving faith.

ἐζωγρημένοι ὑπ' αὐτοῦ—The same verb (ζωγρέω) is used in the Lukan account of the miraculous draught of fish, when Jesus tells Peter "from now on you will be catching people" (Luke 5:10).

εἰς τὸ ἐκείνου θέλημα—This is the very opposite of the will of God, which is the usual biblical referent of the word θέλημα.¹⁴⁴ Because this pronoun (ἐκείνου) is different from the one in the previous clause (αὐτοῦ), it has been suggested that each refers to a different antecedent. However, by NT times the sharp distinction between these two pronouns had disappeared; moreover, trying to find separate antecedents to the two pronouns makes the structure of the sentence too convoluted.¹⁴⁵

---

141. DPL 216.

142. Here μήποτε with the optative expresses possibility, not certainty; BDF 48 [§ 95 (2)], 188 [§ 370 (3)].

143. 1 Tim 2:4; 2 Tim 2:25; 3:7; Titus 1:1; Heb 10:26.

144. Matt 7:21; 12:50; Mark 3:35; John 4:34; 5:30; 6:38; 7:17; 9:31; Acts 13; 22:14; Rom 2:18; 12:2; Eph 5:17; 6:6; Col 1:9; 1 Thess 4:3; 5:18; Heb 10:7, 9, 36; 13:21; 1 Pet 2:15; 4:2; 1 John 2:17.

145. Wallace, *Greek Grammar*, 329; Kelly, *Pastoral Epistles*, 191–92; Debelius and Conzelmann, *Pastoral Epistles*, 114.

COMMENTARY

Having written of the essentials of the Christian message and the Christian life, Paul returns to the topic of ministry in those essentials. While his words here have applicability to any Christian, they are especially relevant to those who, like Timothy, have been called to the office of the ministry.

Dealing with Heresy

In this section the apostle makes some of his most direct statements in any of the Pastorals with respect to the heresy troubling the churches served by Timothy and Titus. On that false teaching see further "The Nature of the Heresy" in the Introduction to the Pastoral Letters.

Paul refers to a particular—and no doubt, the deadliest—tenant of the false teachers, namely, their claim that "the resurrection has already taken place." This points to the heresy as an early form of Gnosticism. With the basic doctrine of Gnosticism being that matter is inherently evil and that only the spiritual is good, the foundational teaching of Christianity concerning the resurrection of Jesus Christ and the consequent resurrection of his believers had to be either denied outright or else explained away. The latter must have been the position of Hymenaeus and Philetus. They would have represented the resurrection as having nothing to do with the reanimation of the body; rather, it was a purely spiritual occurrence, no doubt in connection with the individual coming to the "knowledge" that false teachers such as these claimed to be able to impart (1 Tim 6:20; 2 Tim 3:7; Titus 1:16). Thus, the church's task would be to instruct those who held such opinions that they might come to the true "knowledge of the truth."

This false teaching was such that those who held to it could no longer be considered Christians. The apostle notes that they have "strayed" away from the faith; he identifies their dissemination of their views as a "dishonorable use" of their "vessel," and he indicates that they have fallen into "the snare of the devil."

The threat posed by these false teachers was not merely of academic or theoretical concern. Paul notes that the false teaching "promotes ungodliness," that it is "overturning the faith of some," and that it results in the "ruin of the hearers." He further indicates that the "talk of these people will spread like gangrene"; hence, Timothy needs to take care to deal with it appropriately (see further "The Ministry of the Word" below).

Grace and Life

The Life of the Minister

The apostle has occasion to speak about and to warn against the teachings of the heretics, as he turns to instructing Timothy to "call to mind" the truths of the gospel that he has just articulated. In so doing he speaks not only about the ministry of the man of God but also about such a one's life in general.

Paul directs his younger coworker to "flee youthful lusts." While this indeed will include sexual temptations, to which a young pastor might be especially tempted, the term is broad enough to include any sins in thought, word, or deed (note the instruction of Jesus recorded in Matt 5:21–48) that might confront Timothy. In contrast to this the apostle names a number of virtues after which the pastor is to pursue.

"Righteousness" is a comprehensive term regarding the Christian life (as noted in the entry by that name in the Extended Notes). The righteousness given us through faith in Jesus Christ also moves and empowers the believer to righteous living.

"Faithfulness" is to characterize the life of the Christian, especially the life of the pastor. The vocabulary points to the intimate association of faithfulness and saving faith. It is impossible to have faith in Christ that is not faithful to Christ, and faithfulness in all that one does is a part of the fruit of saving faith as worked by God the Holy Spirit (Gal 5:22).

Love is the supreme virtue of the Christian life (1 Cor 13:13). As such, it unites all the other virtues (Col 3:14).[146]

Ethics related to love are peace and gentleness (Gal 5:22–23). The pastor "must not be combative but gentle toward all" (cf. Rom 12:8).

An important virtue for a pastor is that he be "able to endure wrong." In this fallen world, where sin corrupts everything, including the lives of those who claim allegiance to Christ, the Christian pastor can expect to be mistreated (John 15:20; 2 Tim 3:12), perhaps even by those whom he endeavors to serve. Hence, the pastor must hold firmly to the word of the risen Christ, by which he obtains the power to endure suffering (Phil 3:10).

As a "slave of God" the man of God is to be setting forth God's word and not his own ideas. In giving qualifications for the pastoral office Paul had numbered the ability to teach among them (1 Tim 3:2; Titus 1:9). Thus, being "able to teach" (2 Tim 2:24) is a vital part of the ministry of the word.

---

146. See the comments on Col 3:14 in Deterding, *Colossians*, 145, 157.

The Ministry of the Word

In this section the apostle instructs Timothy about dealing with false teaching. While it is clear that Timothy is to oppose, correct, and even attempt to win over those affected by the heresy, it is also important that his ministry not be completely absorbed by these concerns, lest he be robbed of time for dealing with other responsibilities of ministry. Paul directs him to "avoid pointless, empty words, for they further promote ungodliness," not to "dispute about words," and to avoid "foolish and uninformed speculations" that "give birth to disputes." The pastor needs to oppose false teaching, but he must not become sidetracked from the main task of setting forth the truth of God's word to those in his care.

Hence, Paul begins by exhorting Timothy to "call to mind" the truths of the faith, as he had set them forth in the previous section. He further instructs him to be "correctly setting forth the word of truth." The standard for this, as the apostle will indicate later in this very letter, is the holy Scriptures (3:14–17, whose commentary see).

Just as the pastor is to be "instructing his opponents" "with gentleness" (2:25), the same applies to his entire ministry (2:24). Arrogance and pompousness are ill-fitting any Christian; it is especially unsuited to a man of God. As he ministers to those in his care as well as to opponents, he is to do so with gentleness.

In all of this the pastor will show himself to be a vessel for honorable use, one who is sanctified and who is useful for the owner, namely, the Lord of the church. He will be equipped for every good work and a workman who has no need to be ashamed. By "correctly setting forth the word of truth" (2:15) he will be empowered for this, as it is the holy Scriptures that make one "completely equipped for every good work" (2 Tim 3:17).

Although opposition and even persecution face the man of God, by holding to the word of God he has assurance ("this seal") about his ministry. "The firm foundation of God stands," Paul writes, and then he cites the word of God as proof. The words "the Lord knows those who are his"[147] seem to be a quotation of Num 16:5 LXX.[148] That citation comes from the episode of Korah's rebellion. There was opposition to the ministry of Moses and Aaron, yet their ministry, and not that of the opponents,

---

147. Arndt ("*Egno*," 299–302) argues for understanding the verb ἔγνω not as a gnomic aorist (referring to what is generally true) but as referring to a past act, namely, God's election of grace.

148. Knight, *Pastoral Epistles*, 415–16; Kelly, *Pastoral Epistles*, 186–87.

had God's approval. The remaining citation, "let everyone who names the name of the Lord keep away from injustice," summarizes the content of Num 16:26, making use of language from other portions of the Hebrew Scriptures.[149] The "firm foundation of God," therefore, is the word of God. Paul assured Timothy, and with these words assures every pastor, that if he stands faithful to the word of God, his ministry will belong to God in spite of any opposition that may come against it.

The Minister and His Ministry; the Truth and Its Opponents: 2 Timothy 2:14–26 in Context

After speaking of the gospel of Christ and of the salvation and the suffering that come from this gospel, Paul returns to the topic of the ministry of the gospel. He speaks of both the work of the ministry and of the personal life of the minister.

When dealing with heresy and with its adherents and proponents the pastor must strike a balance between that and his other responsibilities of ministry. While he endeavors to correct opponents to protect those in his care from such falsehood and perhaps even to win the errorists over to the truth, the pastor must focus on setting forth the truth and avoid becoming embroiled in disputes about words.

The pastor must also take care of his own personal ministry and his way of dealing with others. The presentation of the truth in a harsh manner or by one whose personal conduct falls far short of what the Scriptures expect of him may bring reproach upon the truth itself. The pastor must take care that he himself is a fit proclaimer of and ambassador for the truth.

The Lord knows those who are his. If the pastor conducts his ministry according to biblical standards, including "correctly setting forth the word of truth," then he can be sure that the Lord of the church will watch over his ministry and use it for the good of others and to the glory of God.

---

149. Lev 24:16 LXX; Josh 23:7; Isa 26:13; Ps 6:8; Isa 52:11; see also Matt 7:23; Luke 13:27.

3:1–9: The Truth and Its Opponents in the Last Days

TRANSLATION

¹ Know this, that in the last days dangerous times will arrive, ² for there will be men who are lovers of self, lovers of money, braggarts, arrogant people, blasphemers, those who are disobedient to parents, ungrateful, unholy, ³ unfeeling, irreconcilable, slanderers, without self-control, untamed, those who do not love what is good, ⁴ betrayers, reckless, conceited, lovers of pleasure rather than lovers of God, ⁵ those who have the form of godliness while denying its power; turn away from such as these. ⁶ For among these are those who slip into households and who take captive foolish women who are loaded up with sins, who are led about by various desires, ⁷ who are always learning but never able to come to the knowledge of the truth. ⁸ In the way that Jannes and Jambres opposed Moses, so also these [men] oppose the truth, men who are corrupted in mind, who are unproven concerning the faith. ⁹ However, they will not progress further, for their folly will be clear to all, as also was that of those [men].

TEXTUAL NOTES

3:1 Τοῦτο δὲ γίνωσκε, ὅτι—Here ὅτι serves in apposition to τοῦτο; the clause that ὅτι introduces explains what it is that Timothy is to "know," what he needs to be aware of.[150]

---

150. Wallace, *Greek Grammar*, 458–59.

ἐν ἐσχάταις ἡμέραις—This is equivalent to the phrase ἐν ὑστέροις καιροῖς in 1 Tim 4:1; see the notes and commentary on that passage as well as the commentary below.

ἐνστήσονται καιροὶ χαλεποί—The evangelist Matthew uses the term χαλεποί with reference to the Gadarene demoniacs being dangerous, so that no one could pass their way (8:28). The last days are difficult in that they present a danger to faith.

3:2 ἄνθρωποι—In light of 3:6–9, where the vocable ἄνθρωποι has the sense of "male," as it does in some other instances in the NT (Matt 19:5; 1 Cor 7:1; Eph 5:31), I have opted to use the translation "men" here as well as in 3:8.

φίλαυτοι—In this list of vices φίλαυτοι ("lovers of self") occurs first, perhaps because this sin is the root of all the other vices.

φιλάργυροι—Since the *love* of money (φιλαργυρία) is a root of all kinds of evil (1 Tim 6:10), this may be mentioned near the beginning of this list to indicate that it is another vice that produces all other manner of evils.

ἀλαζόνες—"Boasting" would certainly have its origin in love of self.

ὑπερήφανοι—This term is used to designate those whom God opposes on account of their sin and unbelief (Luke 1:51; Jas 4:6; 1 Pet 5:5).

βλάσφημοι—While this word family can refer to the sin of slandering people,[151] since the apostle uses a different term (διάβολοι) in the very next verse to designate that sin, it is probable that the present term refers to the sin of blasphemy against God. Paul uses this word to describe himself before he came to saving faith (1 Tim 1:13). Like all the terms the apostle has used up to this point, this one can also sum up the entire ungodly existence of an unbeliever.

γονεῦσιν ἀπειθεῖς—While the vices named up to this point all have to do with one's status before God, Paul now mentions something that is a sin against another person. In the Decalogue (Exod 20:1–17; Deut 5:1–21) the commandment regarding honoring father and mother is the first of the stipulations relating to one's requirements toward other people, following the commandments concerning our responsibilities toward God. Perchance in a similar way these words introduce the present passage's recounting of precepts that have to do with obligations toward one's fellow human beings.

---

151. BDAG 178.

ἀχάριστοι—In Luke 6:35 this word is lumped with πονηρούς ("evil") as a sort of hendiadys to describe all sinners.

ἀνόσιοι—The apostle uses a form of this word in 1 Tim 1:9 to refer to all those who are not just/righteous before God.

3:3 ἄστοργοι—The alpha privative on this word ("unfeeling") negates a Greek term for love (στοργή), giving the meaning "having no wholesome feelings at all for others."

ἄσπονδοι—The sense of this adjective ("irreconcilable") is that these are people who are not willing to be reconciled to others.[152]

διάβολοι—The usual use of this adjective ("slanderers") as a substantive in the NT is as a name for the devil, "the slanderer." Those who engage in slander are really doing the work of the devil. The Christian life is to be characterized by avoiding this vice (1 Tim 3:11; Titus 2:3).

ἀκρατεῖς ἀνήμεροι—These two words ("without self-control," "untamed") are virtual synonyms. Paul uses both here for emphasis.

ἀφιλάγαθοι—What is good is what corresponds to the way God created things to be (Gen 1:31). Thus, this term ("those who do not love what is good") essentially sums up all that is evil, all that is not in keeping with the creator's design.

3:4 ποδόται—The same term is used for Judas (Luke 6:16) and those who brought about the execution of Jesus (Acts 7:52). Its use here depicts the sin of betrayal as a sign of unbelief and rejection of Christ.

ποπετεῖς—The only other NT occurrence of this term ("reckless") refers to the mob in Ephesus stirred up by the silversmith Demetrius (Acts 19:36). Note also Prov 10:14; 13:3 LXX.

τετυφωμένοι—While the precise meaning of this term is uncertain ("conceited," "blinded," "foolish," "mentally ill"),[153] the general sense is plain: they are unable (or unwilling) to grasp the truth (1 Tim 6:4 in light of verse 3).

φιλήδονοι μᾶλλον ἢ φιλόθεοι—In this context the pleasures that such people love surely refer to illicit pleasures but might also include things that in and of themselves are acceptable but which have supplanted the one true God as the object of one's love.

3:5 ἔχοντες μόρφωσιν εὐσεβείας τὴν δὲ δύναμιν αὐτῆς ἠρνημένοι—Some of the vices that Paul names in this section are quite notorious. However, sinful conduct is not limited to such things. Equally

---

152. BDAG 144.
153. BDAG 1021.

condemnable is the outward façade of piety that is not matched by the true godliness of the inner man.[154]

καὶ τούτους ἀποτρέπου—The verb ἀποτρέπου seems a bit stronger than the one used in 2:16 ("Avoid meaningless, empty words"); hence I have rendered it "turn away from." Those who spread falsehood are not just pointless; they may well pose a real danger to one's faith.

That the apostle tells Timothy to turn way from people such as those who will be present "in the last days" demonstrates that Paul understood the entire time after the completion of the ministry of Christ to be "the last days." See further "The Last Days" below and also "The Last Times" in the commentary on 1 Tim 4:1–5.

3:6 Ἐκ τούτων—Paul now turns his attention to a subgroup of those he has been discussing, as he notes the tactics that some of them will use.

οἱ ἐνδύνοντες εἰς τὰς οἰκίας—The connotation of this verb is to enter by stealth, hence, "slip in." Some false teachers employ less than honest means to achieve their goals.

αἰχμαλωτίζοντες—This verb can be used of the literal taking of prisoners of war (Luke 21:24). Here it serves as a vivid picture of the deadly spiritual harm that false teachers can inflict.

γυναικάρια—This diminutive is used here in a derogatory sense: "foolish women."[155] For Paul's actual regard for women see 1 Tim 5:1–2; 2 Tim 1:5.

σεσωρευμένα ἁμαρτίαις—Grammatically the gender of the plural noun γυναικάρια is neuter. Therefore, the neuter plural participle (σεσωρευμένα) refers to the women taken captive by the false teachers. Paul uses the same verb in instructing believers to "heap" burning coals on the enemy by doing good to him (Rom 12:20). This is a vivid metaphor to describe the overwhelming effect of sin.

ἀγόμενα ἐπιθυμίαις ποικίλαις—Again, the neuter plural participle (ἀγόμενα) refers to the women taken captive by the heretics. One's corrupted (sinful) nature leads him, or in this case her, into further sin.

3:7 πάντοτε μανθάνοντα καὶ μηδέποτε . . . ἐλθεῖν δυνάμενα—Once again, the neuter plural participles (μανθάνοντα, δυνάμενα) refer to the women taken captive by the false teachers. In this context "always learning" clearly has a bad connotation. The false teaching currently troubling Timothy's churches presented itself as learned and sophisticated (see

---

154. See Matt 23:27–28; Rom 7:22; Col 3:9–10; Eph 4:22–24.
155. BDF 60–61 [§ 111 (3)].

further "The Nature of the Heresy" in the Introduction to the Pastoral Letters). The apostle here exposes the heresy for what it is: the "teaching" that its leaders claim to impart never brings those who follow it to the knowledge of the truth, that is, to the true, saving faith.

ἐπίγνωσιν ἀληθείας—This expression occurs elsewhere in the Pastorals to designate saving faith, faith in the truth (1 Tim 2:4; 2 Tim 2:25; Titus 1:1).

3:8 ὃν τρόπον δὲ Ἰάννης καὶ Ἰαμβρῆς ἀντέστησαν Μωϋσεῖ—This is a clear reference to the magicians of Pharaoh who by their secret arts duplicated the miracles of Moses (Exod 7:11–12, 22; 8:7), until they were unable to do so (Exod 8:18–19; 9:11).

The names "Jannes" and "Jambres" are known from Jewish tradition.[156] Paul here adopts these traditional names to refer to these ancient enemies of the truth.

οὕτως καὶ οὗτοι ἀνθίστανται τῇ ἀληθείᾳ—The demonstrative pronoun οὗτοι refers back to the heretics of the apostle's day.[157] Here Paul puts the false teachers that he and Timothy will confront into the same category as the magicians of Pharaoh; they may mimic the truth, but they are in reality opponents of the one true God.

ἄνθρωποι κατεφθαρμένοι τὸν νοῦν—The vocable ἄνθρωποι here has the sense of "male," as it does in certain other instances in the NT (Matt 19:5; 1 Cor 7:1; Eph 5:31). The term νοῦς designates one's real, inner self, especially that which controls his entire being and actions (Rom 7:23, 25; 12:2). This may, as here, be subject to the corrupting influence of sin (Rom 1:28; Eph 4:17–18; Col 2:18) or to the control of one's spirit (πνεῦμα, Eph 4:23) as that is under the control of God the Holy Spirit (Rom 8:15–17).

ἀδόκιμοι περὶ τὴν πίστιν—The alpha privative on the word ἀδόκιμοι makes it the opposite of that status to which Timothy (and all Christian pastors) are to be eager to show themselves to be (δόκιμον, 2 Tim 2:15); hence, "unproven [disapproved] concerning the faith." That being the case, τὴν πίστιν here refers primarily to the *fides quae creditur*, "the faith."[158] See further the entry "Faith" in the Extended Notes.

---

156. BDAG 464–65. For example, these names occur in the Targum of Pseudo-Jonathan at Exod 1:15 and 7:10–12, while the Damascus Document (CD 5:17–19), known from Qumran, mentions the opposition to Moses by Jannes and his brother. The pagan author Pliny in his *Natural History* (book 30, chapter 2) also refers to these with the name Jannes.

157. Wallace, *Greek Grammar*, 325–27.

158. Kelly, *Pastoral Epistles*, 197.

3:9 ἀλλ' οὐ προκόψουσιν ἐπὶ πλεῖον—The conjunction ἀλλά is a strong adversative. In spite of their having "the form of godliness," they actually will not advance before God.

ἡ γὰρ ἄνοια αὐτῶν ἔκδηλος ἔσται πᾶσιν—The false teaching made grand claims of knowledge and wisdom (see further "The Nature of the Heresy" in the Introduction to the Pastoral Letters). However, in the view of the Almighty, whose evaluation is the only one that matters, what the false teachers advocate is actually folly. That their folly will be clear "to all" likely points to the final judgment (Matt 25:31–32; Rev 1:7).

ὡς καὶ ἡ ἐκείνων ἐγένετο—The demonstrative pronoun ἐκείνων refers back to Jannes and Jambres.[159] Ultimately the magicians of Pharaoh could not prevail over Moses (Exod 8:18–19; 9:11). In the same way the heretics afflicting Timothy's churches will not carry the day.

COMMENTARY

The Last Days

Paul begins this section by describing the type of people who will be present in "the last days," and then continues by instructing Timothy to "avoid such people." This clearly indicates that the apostle, like other authors of the New Testament, understood that already in his time world history was in the last days.[160] The climactic event in salvation history—and the New Testament looks at all history in light of the history of salvation—was the redemptive death and resurrection of Jesus Christ. By his passion and rising Christ had completed the work of salvation, so that all that still needed to take place was the Lord's coming at the last day. In that light the world has been in "the last days" ever since the beginning of the church's mission (see Acts 2:17). See also the fuller discussion under "The Last Times" at the commentary on 1 Tim 4:1–5.

The description of the last days in the present letter also agrees with the teaching of Jesus that the end times would be characterized by false teaching and apostasy (Matt 24:9–13, 23–26; Mark 13:11–13, 21–23; Luke 21:12–19).[161] This being the case, it calls for the need to be on guard against such heresies.

159. Wallace, *Greek Grammar*, 327–28.

160. As recognized by Kelly, *Pastoral Epistles*, 193, and Knight, *Pastoral Epistles*, 428–29.

161. Jeffrey Gibbs (*Matthew 21:1—28:20*, 1278–79) argues persuasively that those

Men Opposed to the Truth

Paul describes the heretics with a host of vices. In a number of ways this list of vices is similar to the one found in his Letter to the Romans (1:28–32).[162]

It should be noted that misplaced love both begins ("lovers of self, lovers of money") and concludes ("lovers of pleasure rather than lovers of God") this catalogue of vices, forming an *inclusio* around it. As love is the foundational virtue (1 Cor 13:13; Col 3:14), so misplaced love is central to all vices.[163]

For the details of the various vices see the textual notes. This extensive and varied catalog of wickedness might raise the question as to how the apostle could make such extensive accusations regarding his opponents.

The key to understanding this section is to be found in his descriptions of the false teachers as "those who have the form of godliness while denying its power," and as "men [who] oppose the truth, men who are corrupted in mind, who are unproven concerning the faith." The many vices enumerated here are the product of a lack of saving faith. As genuine faith shows itself in good works of love (Gal 5:6; Eph 2:8–10), so false faith manifests itself in a variety of false works (Matt 7:17–19).[164]

To outward appearances false teachers might seem to live upright lives. But since true good works can only be produced by one with true saving faith (e.g., Eph 2:8–10) the works that arise from false faith, however noble they may appear to human sight, are evil works in the sight of God.

Many false teachers are sincere about their teachings; they are simply, sincerely, wrong. But some also engage in deceptive methods. Hence, Paul also comments on the tactics of some ("among these are those") of the false teachers. These people "slip into houses and . . . take captive"

---

verses in Matthew (and by extension the parallels in Mark and Luke) have reference to the fall of Jerusalem. Even granting that, since in many ways the fall of Jerusalem was an anticipation (a type) of the end of all things (Gibbs, *Matthew 21:1—28:20*, 1284, 1289), the Lord's warnings are still apropos to the days leading up to the final judgment.

162. Noted also by Easton, *Pastoral Epistles*, 64.

163. Knight, *Pastoral Epistles*, 430.

164. The lack of conjunctions in this list denotes that the individuals whom the apostle here condemns are not guilty of each and every one of these vices (BDF 240–41 [§ 460 (2)]), just as not all of them "slip into houses and . . . take captive foolish women" ("among these are those who").

others. History contains many examples of proponents of false faiths using deceptive means to lead others into following their erroneous beliefs.

The apostle shows that the heretics cause real problems for those whom they succeed in leading stray. They are described as being "loaded up with sins" and "led about by various desires." With these words Paul demonstrates that those led astray are also themselves to blame. Rather than resisting their sinful desires, they give in to them. The apostle also notes that those who follow this heresy "are always learning but never able to come to a knowledge of the truth." In his letters Paul sets forth the saving truth. The truth is something that can be grasped by faith and also by the mind that is under the influence of the faith wrought by the Holy Spirit.[165] The false teachers claimed to be able to impart "knowledge";[166] in truth their supposed knowledge is actually an impediment to knowing the truth that saves.

The apostle's comparison of his opponents to Pharaoh's magicians reinforces the identification of these heretics as outside the fellowship of the Christian faith. He further identifies them as "[men who] oppose the truth," as "men who are corrupted in mind," and as those "who are unproven concerning the faith." Each of these are ways of pinpointing them as non-Christians. As the "truth" summarizes the Christian faith,[167] opposing the truth is the activity of unbelievers. Since the term "mind" denotes one's true inner being (see the textual notes), the identification of the heretics being corrupted in mind further identifies them as unbelievers. "The faith" here denotes the whole content of belief; hence, being unproven concerning the faith further points to their being non-Christians.

As noted above, the magicians who opposed Moses ultimately failed. Making a comparison with them, Paul notes of his opponents, "They will not progress further, for their folly will be clear to all." The fact that he feels the need to make this observation demonstrates that the false teachers must have had some success in their endeavors. Indeed, to mere human sight false teaching may seem to prosper; it may well seem that false teachers are far more successful than proponents of the truth. But the apostle, like all the writers of the New Testament, views all things eschatologically. In this life false teaching may seem to get along just fine,

---

165. See the textual notes on πάντοτε μανθάνοντα καὶ μηδέποτε... ἐλθεῖν δυνάμενα, ἐπίγνωσιν ἀληθείας, and ἄνθρωποι κατεφθαρμένοι τὸν νοῦν above.

166. See "The Nature of the Heresy" in the Introduction to the Pastoral Letters.

167. See the entry "Truth" in the Extended Notes.

but in the life to come heresy will fail. Only the Christian truth brings a place in the resurrection to eternal life.

Paul mentions this to encourage Timothy, and indeed all Christians,[168] to hold to the truth and to oppose error. Even though the false teaching seems adequate, even triumphant, those who propound it and who embrace it will not succeed. Hence, it is to the advantage of Timothy, of those whom he serves, and indeed of all people, to hold to the truth of the Christian faith.

The Truth and Its Opponents in the Last Days: 2 Timothy 3:1–9 in Context

Throughout this letter Paul has been treating the topic of ministry by Christians and especially ministry by those called to the pastoral office. In the previous section of the letter, he spoke of the need to combat false teaching and false teachers. In this section he focuses on dealing with heresy in view of the church's existence in the last days.

Since the church and the world is in the last days, it is to be expected that the church and its ministers will have to deal with false teachers. It is a reality that until the parousia it may appear that genuine Christianity is losing the day, as various other teachings seem to prosper. In the present section the apostle instructs his younger coworker about the importance of dealing with heresy. But he has a further purpose. He wishes to assure Timothy and those in his care—and Christians and ministers of every era—that false teaching will not carry the day.

The magicians of Pharaoh seemed to be at least equals to Moses and Aaron (Exod 7:11, 22; 8:7), yet in the end they did not triumph (Exod 8:18–19; 9:11). The ministry of the truth seemed, at best, to be floundering in the days of Elijah the prophet (1 Kgs 19:10, 14). Yet the Lord assured his prophet that false religion would not prevail, and that the truth would survive (1 Kgs 19:15–18). Reading between the lines we gather that the heretics bedeviling the churches in Timothy's care were doing well enough to, at a minimum, be a threat to his people and his ministry. Yet Paul assures Timothy that the false teachers "will not progress further." The word of the Lord endures forever; all other words and ministries will fade and pass away (Isa 40:6–8; 1 Pet 1:22–25).

---

168. Note the plural form of "you" in the farewell blessing of this letter (4:22).

3:10–17: Suffering for Faithfulness to the Scriptures

TRANSLATION

¹⁰ But you closely followed my teaching[a], conduct, purpose, faith, long-suffering, love, endurance, ¹¹ persecutions, sufferings, such as happened to me in Antioch, in Iconium, in Lystra, which persecutions I endured, and the Lord rescued me from all of them. ¹² Indeed, all who desire to live in a godly way in Christ Jesus will be persecuted. ¹³ But evil men and impostors will advance in becoming worse, deceiving and being deceived. ¹⁴ But you continue in the things which you learned and believed, knowing from whom you learned [them], ¹⁵ and that from infancy you have known the holy Scriptures, which are able to make you wise unto salvation through faith, which is in Christ Jesus. ¹⁶ All Scripture is breathed into by God and is profitable for teaching, for rebuke, for improvement, for instruction in righteousness, ¹⁷ in order that the man of God might be complete, completely equipped for every good work.

[a] Or *doctrine*

TEXTUAL NOTES

3:10 Σὺ δὲ παρηκολούθησάς—The verb is a compound of a preposition with a word that by itself can mean to follow as a disciple (Matt 8:19; 9:9; 19:21). The compound form emphasizes the idea of closely, intently following (Luke 1:3).

διδασκαλίᾳ—See the entry "Teach, Teaching" in the Extended Notes. The term here denotes the content of what was taught (another translation would be "doctrine") more than the act of teaching.

ἀγωγῇ—The implication here is that life ("conduct") follows faith ("teaching").

προθέσει—This term has a fairly wide range of meaning: "plan," "purpose," "resolve," even "presentation,"[169] any of which could presumably fit here. Paul's resolve was to fulfill his purpose in God's plan of salvation by presenting the gospel to others. The translation "purpose" seems to fit best here.

πίστει—See the entry "Faith" in the Extended Notes. Following both διδασκαλία ("teaching") and ἀγωγῇ ("conduct"), the word here would encompass both the content of faith (*fides quae creditur*) and the act of believing (*fides qua creditur*).

μακροθυμίᾳ—"Long-suffering" seems to fit best with both the etymology and the use of this word. The person with μακροθυμία has the strength to endure for a long time without displaying wrath.

ἀγάπῃ—See the entry "Love" in the Extended Notes.

ὑπομονῇ—The etymology of the word might suggest the ability of "remaining under" some trial or burden without falling into sin or unbelief.

3:11 τοῖς διωγμοῖς, τοῖς παθήμασιν . . . οἵους διωγμοὺς ὑπήνεγκα—"Sufferings" (παθήμασιν) is a more general term (Rom 8:18), while "persecutions" (διωγμοῖς/διωγμούς) refers specifically to deliberate infliction of harm on someone for religious reasons (Acts 8:1).[170] The apostle uses both terms here for emphasis.

ἐν Ἀντιοχείᾳ, ἐν Ἰκονίῳ, ἐν Λύστροις—These are the cities of Paul's first missionary journey (Acts 13:13—14:23). Timothy was from Lystra (Acts 16:1), so it is to be expected that he would have "followed" the apostle's persecutions endured in that part of his pastoral career.[171]

---

169. BDAG 869.

170. BDAG 253, 747.

171. Those who deny Pauline authorship of the Pastorals point to these references as proof of pseudonymity (e.g., Easton, *Pastoral Epistles*, 10). They claim that the non-Pauline author carelessly and randomly picked out some examples of Paul's sufferings in Acts, not realizing that these took place before Timothy joined up with the apostle, so that the younger man, it is claimed, was unfamiliar with them.

Kelly, *Pastoral Epistles*, 199, offers this rejoinder: "Against this it can be urged that it is precisely a seeming incongruity of this kind that such a [pseudonymous] writer, especially if he belonged to a circle which admired Paul and was acquainted with his life-story, would have been careful to avoid. There were certainly much more obvious examples available (cf., e.g., Acts xvi–xvii), and we should have expected him to choose them. On the other hand, if the Apostle himself is the author, it is easy to conjecture special personal reasons for his preferring to mention these particular incidents. His motive, for example, may well have been to concentrate on sufferings which occurred just before Timothy's conversion, and which he knew had left an indelible impression ἐκ πάντων με ἐρρύσατο ὁ κύριος—Paul "endured" (ὑπήνεγκα) all these persecutions, so clearly his being "rescued" (ἐρρύσατο) does not mean that he was spared having to experience them. Rather, his life was spared—in Lystra he was left for dead by his persecutors (Acts 14:19), and he was able to resume his evangelistic work. As he names "Christ" in the sentence that follows immediately afterwards, "the Lord" here most likely refers to Jesus himself.

3:12 πάντες δὲ οἱ θέλοντες εὐσεβῶς ζῆν—This would refer to all Christians—all who sincerely desire to live out the Christian faith that they confess.[172]

ἐν Χριστῷ Ἰησοῦ—See the entry "In Christ" in the Extended Notes.

διωχθήσονται—This verb is cognate to the noun "persecutions" (διωγμοῖς/διωγμούς) that the apostle uses in the previous verse.

3:13 πονηροὶ δὲ ἄνθρωποι καὶ γόητες—Since ἄνθρωποι in 3:2 and 8 bears the sense of "men" (see the textual notes), I have chosen to use that rendering here as well. Some of the false teachers are imposters (γόητες), pretending to be something that they are not and seeking to entice "to impious action by apparently pious words."[173] Others are sincere, but they are sincerely wrong; their erroneous beliefs and teachings make them evil. With this phrase Paul includes any and all of the heretics.

Another suggestion is that the term γόητες means "magicians."[174] Paul had referred to the Egyptian magicians of Exodus a few verses earlier (3:8), although at this point, he seems to have moved on to a somewhat different topic.

προκόψουσιν ἐπὶ τὸ χεῖρον—The false teachers will not advance (3:9)—except in becoming more evil.

πλανῶντες καὶ πλανώμενοι—The false teachers are deceived into believing falsehood; perhaps Satan is implied as the one doing the deceiving. Being deceived, they themselves deceive others.

---

on the young man's imagination. The verb closely followed, as has been pointed out above, does not necessarily imply that Timothy had been personally present at them."

In addition, we might note that Timothy, being from Lystra (Acts 16:1), may have been evangelized by Paul on the apostle's first visit to that city (Acts 14:8–20; see the section "Timothy's Good Confession" in the commentary on 1 Tim 6:11–16) and subsequently joined his missionary troupe on the second journey (Acts 16:1–5). If that were the case, that would provide even more reason for thinking that Timothy was familiar with the apostle's sufferings at these three cities.

172. Knight, *Pastoral Epistles*, 440–41; *DPL* 920.
173. *TDNT* 1:738.
174. *DPL* 582.

3:14 Σὺ δέ—The particle δέ here is disjunctive: "But you."

μένε ἐν οἷς ἔμαθες καὶ ἐπιστώθης—Timothy believes what he has been taught, and in contrast (δέ) to the heretics what he learned and believes is the truth. The verb μένε is a present tense with gnomic implications: "always continue."[175]

εἰδὼς παρὰ τίνων ἔμαθες—The participle εἰδώς expresses cause. The phrase could be rendered "because you know from whom you have learned [them]."[176]

Is the object of the preposition παρά singular (τίνος) or plural (τίνων)? While the manuscript evidence is divided, the older and more highly regarded sources favor the plural.[177] The immediately following statement about Timothy knowing "from infancy" would also suggest that the apostle's reference here includes his learning the faith from his mother and grandmother (1:3–5); this would also favor the plural. Presumably the singular would refer to the apostle as the one from whom Timothy learned the truth of the sacred Scriptures,[178] but the plural might well include Paul and the many witnesses in whose presence Timothy was taught (2:2).

3:15 ἀπὸ βρέφους . . . οἶδας—This references Timothy's instruction in the Scriptures by his mother and grandmother.[179]

[τὰ] ἱερὰ γράμματα—This would denote the Hebrew Scriptures, the Old Testament, the content of what his mother and grandmother taught him. The textual witnesses are about equally divided between the inclusion or exclusion of the article (τά). Regardless, the noun is definite, as the notion that Paul would be referring to any other "holy Scriptures" is out of the question (cf. Rom 1:2; 16:26).

τὰ δυνάμενά σε σοφίσαι εἰς σωτηρίαν διὰ πίστεως—See the entries "Save, Savior, Salvation" and "Faith" in the Extended Notes as well as the essay "He Saved Us: The Pastoral Letters on the Way of Salvation" elsewhere in this commentary. This statement indicates that the Scriptures have the power to work saving faith (the accusative τὰ δυνάμενά serves as the subject of the infinitive σοφίσαι, while the accusative σε is the object of that

---

175. Wallace, *Greek Grammar*, 525.

176. Wallace, *Greek Grammar*, 631–32.

177. Both Kelly, *Pastoral Epistles*, 200–1, and Knight, *Pastoral Epistles*, 443, agree with this conclusion.

178. On Paul as Timothy's teacher in the faith see the section "Timothy's Good Confession" in the commentary on 1 Tim 6:11–16.

179. As noted also by Johnson, *Letters*, 419.

infinitive verb.)[180] The turn of phrase "make you wise" may be intended to contrast the saving power of the Scriptures with the inability of the tenets of the false teachers to do what they claimed (3:5), for they claimed to be able to impart knowledge and wisdom (1 Tim 6:20; 2 Tim 3:7; Titus 1:16); see "The Nature of the Heresy" in the Introduction to the Pastoral Letters.

ἐν Χριστῷ Ἰησοῦ—See the entry "In Christ" in the Extended Notes. The statement that the (OT) Scriptures "are able to make you wise unto salvation through faith, which is in Christ Jesus" demonstrates that the message of the Hebrew Scriptures can only be comprehended through faith in Christ; one does not have the wisdom to rightly understand the OT Scriptures unless he realizes that they bear witness to Jesus Christ of Nazareth (as in John 5:39–40).

3:16 πᾶσα γραφή—How shall this be translated? "All Scripture" or "every Scripture"? "Every/all Scripture is breathed into by God" or "Every/all Scripture breathed into by God is . . ."? As πᾶς with an anarthrous noun in other passages clearly means "all" (Matt 28:18; Acts 2:36; Rom 11:26), as πᾶσα γραφή refers back to [τὰ] ἱερὰ γράμματα, and as the construction πᾶς + noun + adjective in the LXX and NT overwhelmingly favors the understanding that the adjective is to be understood as predicative rather than attributive, the rendering "all Scripture" seems markedly preferable.[181] As the adjectives θεόπνευστος and ὠφέλιμος both follow πᾶσα γραφή, it seems best to regard θεόπνευστος as predicative rather than attributive and translate "All Scripture is breathed into by God and is profitable"; see the following note.[182] The overall meaning of the verse is not greatly affected if other choices are made.

θεόπνευστος—No single English translation will adequately express the possible meanings of this word,[183] which is a compound of θεός and a form of the verb πνέω, "blow," "breathe out." To say that God "breathed into" the biblical books is to compare the origin of the Scriptures with the creation of man (Gen 2:7). As this creative act gave life to the man of dust, so God's inspiration of Scripture makes it alive (cf. Heb 4:12; 1 Pet 1:23). Therefore, the rendering "breathed into by God," while a bit ungainly, is perhaps as good a translation as any. See further the commentary.

---

180. Wallace, *Greek Grammar*, 195–96.

181. See the further discussion in Knight, *Pastoral Epistles*, and Wallace, *Greek Grammar* (220, 253, 313–14).

182. Knight, *Pastoral Epistles*, 446–47, comes to the same conclusion.

183. As this passage is the first known occurrence of this term (Marshall, *Pastoral Epistles*, 973–74), it is entirely possible that Paul himself coined it.

ὠφέλιμος—The Scriptures have various useful purposes.

πρὸς διδασκαλίαν—See the entry "Teach, Teaching" in the Extended Notes.

πρὸς ἐλεμόν—This word and its various cognates (ἔλεγξις, ἔλεγχος, ἐλέγχω) are used in the NT to express strong rebuke, reproach, exposing, and correcting.[184] The message of the Bible is not all "sweetness and light"; exposing, rebuking, and correcting wrong is also a part of its content. See further the commentary.

πρὸς ἐπανόρθωσιν—This word is used in the LXX to denote the restoration of a city (1 Esd 8:52; 1 Macc 14:34) and so can mean "improvement" in a general sense. The Scripture is useful for growth in faith and in Christian living.

πρὸς παιδείαν τὴν ἐν δικαιοσύνῃ—See the entry "Righteousness" in the Extended Notes.

3:17 ἵνα ... ᾖ—Here ἵνα plus a subjunctive verb indicates a purpose clause;[185] only one's sinful disregard of the Scripture would prevent this purpose from being realized.

ἄρτιος—This adjective meaning "complete" is cognate to the passive participle (ἐξηρτισμένος) with which this sentence ends; see the textual note on that term.

ὁ τοῦ θεοῦ ἄνθρωπος—While this section could be applied to any Christian, in this context "man of God" would be equivalent to "overseer/elder/pastor" (1 Tim 6:11).[186]

πρὸς πᾶν ἔργον ἀγαθόν—While this is applicable to any good work of Christian sanctification (e.g., Eph 2:10), here the reference is particularly to the work of the pastoral ministry.

ἐξηρτισμένος—This is the passive participle of a verb that is cognate to the adjective "complete" (ἄρτιος) earlier in the verse; in an attempt to note this, I have translated it "completely equipped." The use of this participle is somewhat redundant; however, the apostle uses it to emphasize the power of the Scriptures to equip the man of God *completely*.

---

184. BDAG 314–15.

185. Wallace, *Greek Grammar*, 472.

186. See also Deut 33:1; 1 Sam 2:27; 9:6–10; 1 Kgs 12:22; 13:1, 4, 5, 6, 7, 8, 11, 12, 14, 21, 26, 29, 31; 17:18, 24; 20:28; 2 Kgs 1:11–13; 4:7, 9, 16, 21, 22, 25, 27, 40, 42; 5:8, 14; 6:6, 9, 10, 15; 7:2, 17, 18, 19; 8:2, 4, 7, 8, 11; 13:19; 23:16–17; 1 Chr 23:14; 2 Chr 11:2; 25:7, 9; 30:16; Ps 90: superscription.

COMMENTARY

Paul has just devoted considerable space to warning about those opposed to the truth. He follows up with the present sentences regarding how Timothy should carry out his ministry in a different way by being faithful to the Scriptures, even though that will bring him opposition and persecution.

The Holy Scriptures

This section concludes with the apostle's words about the holy Scriptures. This exposition is foundational to everything else that he writes in this portion of the letter.

That God has inspired/breathed into the Scripture means that it is different than any other writing. As God breathed into the man of dust and he became alive, so the Scriptures are alive in a way that no other writing is.

Other portions of the Bible help to fill in what this inspiration means. God the Holy Spirit was the one who inspired the Scriptures (2 Pet 1:20–21). That the Bible was inspired by God means that it is the word of God (John 10:34–36; note that Jesus uses "your law/Torah," "Scripture," and "the word of God" as equivalents in referring to a quotation from the Psalter). Since it is the word of him who does not lie (Titus 1:2), the Scriptures are without error. Through the Scriptures the Holy Spirit produces faith in Christ (1 Cor 12:3; 2 Tim 3:15), through which one has salvation.

"All Scripture is breathed into by God"; this means that there is a divine unity to the Scripture. At the same time, the variety of style, vocabulary, and perspective among the individual books that make up the Scriptures demonstrates that within this unity there is also great diversity. The inspiration of the Scriptures by God did not rob the various authors of their own intellect or personality. Each individual human author wrote as a distinct person, as unique as each one's DNA structure. Nevertheless, the splendor of God inspiring the Scriptures is that these many singular individuals wrote exactly what God would have each one write. The unity and diversity of God's word is reflected in the practice—attested in this very passage—of sometimes speaking of "Scripture" (singular, 3:16) and at other times referring to the "Scriptures" (plural, 3:15).

The inspiration of the Scriptures means that they have a multitude of uses—the absence of any conjunction joining together the four phrases that identify the purposes of the Scriptures (each introduced by the preposition πρὸς) gives a sense of importance and solemnity to the apostle's words here.[187] They teach the truth; they rebuke and correct error; they bring about anything that might rightly be termed spiritual "improvement"; they impart the righteousness/justification that brings eternal life; hence, they also serve as the divine standard for righteous living.[188] On the correspondence between those things for which Scripture is profitable and those things that the pastor is to preach (4:2), see the section "Preach the Word" in the commentary on 4:1–5.

At the time when Paul penned these words, there were probably portions of the Bible that had not been written; certainly, the books that make up our New Testament had not yet been gathered together into a collection. Thus, he is speaking here of those "holy Scriptures" that Timothy had known since infancy, the Hebrew Scriptures, what we today are accustomed to call the Old Testament.

Nevertheless, his words may rightly be applied to the Scriptures of the New Testament. We have noted various indications of Paul's awareness that what he writes is on a par with the Hebrew Scriptures. His identifying himself as an "apostle" of Jesus Christ in many of his letters points to the authority with which he writes.[189] He directs his letters to be "read," that is, to be read aloud in public worship, as God's people had been reading the Torah and the Prophets for centuries (1 Thess 5:27; Col 4:16).[190] He instructs Timothy to hold to and to hand on to others the things that he has learned from him (1:13; 2:2). He introduces a portion of his First Letter to Timothy by noting that what he writes is what "the Spirit expressly says" (1 Tim 4:1).[191]

This concluding exposition on the Scriptures is foundational for the rest of the section. Fidelity to the Scriptures distinguishes the man of God from evil men and imposters. Moreover, fidelity to the Scriptures by the man of God will involve also enduring persecution.

---

187. Wallace, *Greek Grammar*, 658.

188. *DPL* 271; cf. Rom 15:3–4; 1 Cor 9:10; 10:6, 11.

189. Rom 1:1; 1 Cor 1:1; 2 Cor 1:1; Gal 1:1; Eph 1:1; Col 1:1; 1 Tim 1:1; 2 Tim 1:1; Titus 1:1. See further the entry "Apostle" in the Extended Notes.

190. On the Colossians passage see Deterding, *Colossians*, 192–94.

191. See further the section by that title in the commentary on 1 Tim 4:1–5.

From Infancy

The apostle speaks of Timothy learning the holy Scriptures "from infancy." This recalls the thanksgiving report at the beginning of this letter, where Paul gives thanks for the genuine faith that dwelt in his younger colleague's grandmother, Lois, and mother, Eunice, as well as in Timothy himself (1:5). Eunice and Lois had followed the biblical injunction to "consecrate a child according to the way he should go" (Prov 22:6; cf. Eph 6:4; Col 3:21).[192] From that passage and the present one we can conclude that Timothy's mother and grandmother passed along to him the faith of God's ancient people as articulated in the Hebrew Scriptures.

That this had been done from the time that Timothy was an infant shows the significance of one being instructed in the Scriptures *in the home*. Research confirms what pastors know by experience, namely, that parents have a more significant influence on their child's moral and spiritual development than the church does.[193] This is said without in any way diminishing the importance of the church providing instruction in the Christian faith for children.

This also indicates that instruction in the faith needs to begin as early as possible.[194] Reading age-appropriate Christian materials to children and regularly worshiping with them at church and at home are significant ways to build their baptismal faith. It is never too early to begin making a child familiar with the Scriptures, doing so in ways that are appropriate to the youngster's age and development.

---

192. Translation in Steinmann, *Proverbs*, 436; see his comments on this passage on pages 441–42.

193. See, for example, Kuriakose and Shaji, "Parental Influence," and Lumen, "Influences on Moral Development" ("In the formation of children's morals, no outside influence is greater than that of the family. Through punishment, reinforcement, and both direct and indirect teaching, families instill morals in children and help them to develop beliefs that reflect the values of their culture"). Note also that in Luther's Small Catechism each of the major sections is headed with the notation "in a simple way in which the head of a house is to present them to the household"; translation in Kolb and Wengert, *Book of Concord*.

194. "The science is clear. From the time a child is born, he or she is learning every waking moment. In fact, babies and toddlers are either learning or sleeping. And between birth to age five, a child learns at a speed unmatched the rest of his or her life!" (Snow, "Learning Begins at Birth").

Man of God

Paul begins this section by contrasting Timothy's life and ministry with that of the false teachers previously referenced. He concludes this portion of the letter by noting the role that the Scriptures play in the life and ministry of a man of God. Thus, the theme of the pastoral ministry forms an *inclusio* to this section.

Essential to the man of God and his ministry are the Scriptures (see above). In the same way the written word of God equips and empowers the Christian for a life of good works,[195] so it also equips and empowers the pastor for his ministry. When it comes to the work of ministry, the word of God is all that the pastor has, but then, it is all that he needs.

Paul presents his own ministry as a model to be emulated, and Timothy has indeed followed it. The apostle mentions many facets of that ministry (for details see the textual notes), facets which fall into two broad categories.

The word that Paul has taught is in agreement with the sacred Scriptures, and so his teaching is part of the biblical witness to which Timothy has adhered. A pastor such as Timothy is to hold to the biblical, apostolic word. This will lead also to living according to that word (see note on ἀγωγῇ above) and to setting forth that word to others (see note on προθέσει above).[196] For that reason, "teaching/doctrine" heads the list of apostolic exemplars that Timothy has followed.

Holding to the word in faith, living according to it, and proclaiming it to others will bring the opposition of the unbelieving world (and of the demonic) against the Christian (and especially against the Christian pastor). Therefore, in this section the apostle speaks of persecution and of the need for Christians to endure these sufferings (see "Persecution" below).

See further the essay "An Excellent Task: The Pastoral Ministry According to the Pastoral Letters" elsewhere in this commentary.

Evil Men and Imposters

Paul contrasts the man of God with "evil men and imposters" (3:13). He characterizes these in four ways.

---

195. Koeberle, *Quest for Holiness*, 89.
196. Knight, *Pastoral Epistles*, 439, comes to a similar conclusion.

By calling these "imposters" he asserts that they claim to be something that they are not. In the context of all the Pastoral Letters his point is that they claim to be Christians, but in reality, they are not.

The apostle states that the false teachers are "deceived." This passive participle implies that the deception is perpetrated by someone else on them. While people may deceive themselves (Gal 6:7), ultimately deception is the work of Satan (Rev 12:9; 20:3, 8, 10).

The heretics are deceived; in turn they deceive others. Drawn to falsehood, they have now taken up the task of leading others astray. Hence, they are especially dangerous to others, which is why Paul warns Timothy about them.

The apostle had written that—often contrary to appearances—the false teachers would not be successful (3:9). The one area in which they will advance is in becoming worse. Thus, a man of God like Timothy must be on his guard and be firmly devoted to the apostolic word.

Persecution

In the midst of this section on the holy Scriptures and ministry in the word, Paul speaks of persecution. This is to be expected, for the Christian's sufferings are a response by the demonic and the unbelieving world to his faith in the message of the Scriptures, to his witness to that message, and to his life as normed by those Scriptures.

The apostle's statement is clear and unambiguous: "*all* who desire to live in a godly way in Christ Jesus will be persecuted" (3:12). The believer's baptismal death with Christ means sharing in the fellowship of his sufferings (Rom 6:3–4; Phil 3:10).

Such persecutions can take many forms. For some it will mean martyrdom. Others may face imprisonment or other types of formal persecution from governmental authorities. But even if the sufferings that one experiences for his Christianity do not take such extreme forms, all believers will face some form of persecution.

In the present passage Paul offers himself as an example of one who experienced persecution (3:11). Moreover, he also offers himself as an example of the deliverance that God provides for his people: "and the Lord rescued me from all of them."

Clearly "rescued" does not mean being spared from undergoing persecution. When the apostle writes these words, he is very much aware of the fact that he will soon be martyred (4:6). Instead, rescue involves two things. One is the power of Christ's resurrection to endure such persecutions by remaining in the faith (Phil 3:10–11).[197] The other is the "crown of righteousness" that the believer will receive on the last day (2 Tim 4:8), a crown infinitely greater than any hardship that one may experience in this life (Rom 8:17–18).

This gives all Christians—and in particular the man of God—the wherewithal to remain faithful to the apostolic Scriptures. We remain faithful to them by believing all that they teach, by proclaiming them faithfully, and by conforming all our conduct to them.

See also the section "Faithfulness in Suffering" in the commentary on 2 Tim 2:8–13.

Suffering for Faithfulness to the Scriptures: 2 Timothy 3:11–17 in Context

Throughout this letter Paul has urged Timothy on to genuine ministry and therefore also to opposing all heretical teaching. As he continues on that theme in this section, he is led to pointing his younger colleague to the holy Scriptures.

Part of confessing the truth is opposing error. Hence, it is important for the man of God to equip himself with the teaching of the holy Scriptures.

His being equipped with the Scriptures will provide him with what he needs to oppose error. As the word of God the Scriptures provide the pastor with the power of no one less than the God who created all things, including mankind. With that power he can stand up to those in error; by giving instruction in the word of God he may even succeed in bringing them to "repentance unto the knowledge of the truth," so that "they will come to their senses and escape from the snare of the devil" (2:24–26).

The chief purpose of the Scriptures is not one of opposing error but of setting forth the truth for the benefit of those who will receive them

---

197. Note that in Phil 3:10–11 the apostle uses a slightly different form of the word for "resurrection" in each of these verses. In 3:11 he uses the compound term ἐξανάστασιν, emphasizing that he is speaking of the resurrection *from* the dead at the last day. That being the case, his use of the simple form ἀναστάσεως indicates that his reference in 3:10 is to the *power* of Christ's resurrection in the daily life of the believer that enables him to endure the "fellowship of his sufferings."

with faith. The Scriptures bring salvation and empower the believer for progress in godly living.

As the pastor (or, for that matter, any Christian) holds firmly to the Scriptures and opposes error, he will become the target of persecution of one sort or another. Here is another circumstance for which it is important to hold firmly to God's word. The Scriptures supply the persecuted Christian with the power to hold on to his/her faith, even, perchance, in the face of martyrdom (4:6–8).

4:1–5: Opposition to the Truth Brings Suffering

TRANSLATION

¹ I adjure [you] before God and Christ Jesus, who is about to judge the living and the dead, and by his appearing and his kingdom, ² preach the word, be ready at opportune times and at inopportune times, rebuke, correct, encourage with all long-suffering and teaching.ᵃ ³ For there will be a time when they will not tolerate sound teaching,ᵇ but having itching ears they will according to their own desires heap up for themselves teachers, ⁴ and they will turn away from listening to the truth, and they will turn away to myths. ⁵ But you be sober-minded in all things; endure suffering; do the work of an evangelist; fulfill your ministry.

ᵃ Or *doctrine.*
ᵇ Or *doctrine*

TEXTUAL NOTES

4:1 Διαμαρτύρομαι ἐνώπιον τοῦ θεοῦ καὶ Χριστοῦ Ἰησοῦ—In prebiblical Greek the verb "adjure" (διαμαρτύρομαι) had to do with taking an oath,[198] an association that it has in some NT occurrences.[199] The oath character of the present use is also borne out by the use of the accusative in an oath (see textual note below). Here Paul names God (the Father) and Christ Jesus as witnesses of the truth of what he is saying; this denotes the utter seriousness of the subject matter. On the application of the vocable "God" (θεός) to Christ, see Titus 2:13 and the commentary there.

---

198. BDAG 233.
199. Gal 1:20; 1 Tim 5:21; 6:13; see also 2 Tim 2:14.

τοῦ μέλλοντος κρίνειν ζῶντας καὶ νεκρούς—This truth about Christ was a part of early Christian proclamation (Acts 10:42) and is reflected here and elsewhere in the letters of Paul (Rom 2:6–11; 2 Cor 5:10; 2 Thess 1:6–10). It occurs here to add further solemnity to the apostle's charge to Timothy.

τὴν ἐπιφάνειαν αὐτοῦ καὶ τὴν βασιλείαν αὐτοῦ—This is an example of the accusative in an oath, indicating the person or thing by which one swears the oath,[200] "by his appearing and his kingdom."

4:2 κήρυξον τὸν λόγον—The verb κήρυξον and the cognate nouns κήρυγμα and κῆρυξ have the connotation of a one making a *public* proclamation;[201] hence, "preach" seems a suitable translation here; nevertheless, this "preaching" is not limited to formal proclamation within a worshiping assembly (cf. Rom 10:14–15; 1 Cor 1:23). The aorist tense of the verb is constative, not ingressive, not "begin to preach" but with the force of "make this your top priority."[202]

As λόγον has a wider scope of meaning than, say, εὐαγγέλιον, its occurrence here implies the entire word of God, whatever is in accord with "sound teaching," "sound doctrine" (4:3), particularly in view of how near Paul's exposition is on "all Scripture" (3:16) and his directive to Timothy to rebuke, correct, and encourage "with *all* . . . teaching" (4:2).[203] Similarly the object of the verb "preach" (κήρυξον) is not limited to the gospel message but includes the law as well (see Rom 2:21). On the further connections between 3:16 and 4:2 see "Preach the Word" in the commentary below.

ἐπίστηθι εὐκαίρως ἀκαίρως—In some contexts the verb "be ready" (ἐπίστηθι) means "to stand";[204] its use here gives the air of sharp focus, almost of standing at attention. The antithetical adverbs "at opportune times" (εὐκαίρως) and "at inopportune times" (ἀκαίρως) are here paired together[205] to indicate constant readiness, whether or not the circumstances seem advantageous.

ἔλεγξον, ἐπιτίμησον—These two verbs are very similar in meaning. The translation "rebuke, correct" seems to cover the range of what all

---

200. Wallace, *Greek Grammar*, 204–5.
201. BDAG 543–44.
202. Wallace, *Greek Grammar*, 721.
203. Wallace, *Greek Grammar*, 220, 314.
204. BDAG 418.
205. Contrasting pairs such as these generally are not joined together with a connective (asyndeton); BDF 240 [§ 460 (1)].

they denote, which includes rebuking and correcting both doctrinal and moral error.²⁰⁶

παρακάλεσον—See the entry "Paraklesis" in the Extended Notes. In conjunction with the other verbs here "encourage" is perhaps its sense.

ἐν πάσῃ μακροθυμίᾳ καὶ διδαχῇ—"Long-suffering" (μακροθυμίᾳ) indicates the manner in which Timothy is to do these things; "teaching" (διδαχῇ) refers to the content of what is to be set forth. "Doctrine" would certainly be an acceptable translation here, but in order to preserve the play on words with "teachers" in 4:3, I have opted for the rendering "teaching." See the entry "Teaching" in the Extended Notes.

4:3 Ἔσται γὰρ καιρὸς ὅτε—The tense of the verb "will be" (ἔσται) points to the future. However, the similarity of this section with 3:1–9 (and with 1 Tim 4:1–5) makes it plain that this is a situation that had already begun. This will be the case now and hereafter until the parousia. The noun καιρός ("time") echoes the adverbs εὐκαίρως ἀκαίρως ("at opportune times and at inopportune times") in the previous verse; verses 3 and 4 describe an example of "inopportune times" during which Timothy must be prepared to "preach the word."

τῆς ὑγιαινούσης διδασκαλίας—This and similar expressions with this adjective (ὑγιαινούσης) denote the entirety of Christian doctrine. As with διδαχῇ in 4:2, "doctrine" would be a perfectly acceptable rendering here, but in order to preserve the play on words with "teachers" in 4:3, I have opted for the translation "teaching." See further the entry "Teaching" in the Extended Notes.

οὐκ ἀνέξονται—This verb often denotes a Christian (or even Jesus himself) bearing up with someone or something, even if that person or thing might be difficult to bear.²⁰⁷ Certainly sound teaching/doctrine is something that one ought to cherish;²⁰⁸ at the very least he ought to "put up" with it. Sadly, there will be those who will not even "tolerate" sound teaching, such is the depth of their theological depravity.

κατὰ τὰς ἰδίας ἐπιθυμίας—Context will determine whether "desires" (ἐπιθυμίας) refers to something good (e.g., Phil 1:23) or evil (as in 1 Tim 6:9; Titus 2:12; 3:3). Here the desires are those of people who will not tolerate sound teaching (sound doctrine); hence, their desires are contrary to all that is good.

---

206. Matt 17:17 (par Mark 9:19; Luke 9:41); 2 Cor 11:1; Eph 4:2; Heb 13:22; perhaps even 2 Cor 11:4, 19, 20.

207. DPL 216.

208. 1 Tim 1:10; 6:3; 2 Tim 1:13; Titus 1:9; 2:1–2.

ἑαυτοῖς ἐπισωρεύσουσιν διδασκάλους—This verb is compounded with the preposition ἐπι and the verb that the apostle used earlier in this letter to refer to the sins with which certain people are burdened (3:6); the simple form of the verb occurs in Rom 12:20 for "heaping" burning coals on one's enemy by treating him well. The compound form of the verb along with the plural number of its object, "teachers," gives the image of those in error turning to one teacher after another in an attempt to satisfactorily "scratch" their itching ears.

κνηθόμενοι τὴν ἀκοὴν—Although this is an unusual expression, its meaning is not difficult to grasp. Those in question have an unhealthy (ungodly) desire that they want others (teachers) to satisfy.

4:4 ἀπὸ μὲν τῆς ἀληθείας τὴν ἀκοὴν ἀποτρέψουσιν, ἐπὶ δὲ τοὺς μύθους ἐκτραπήσονται—Two different compound verbs meaning "turn away" are used (ἀποτρέψουσιν, ἐκτραπήσονται); they turn away from the truth, and having turned away, they then turn to myths. The words "truth" (ἀληθείας) and "myths" (μύθους) stand in marked contrast to one another. The people in question do not simply turn away from the truth to nothing; having turned from the truth, they turn toward its opposite. Humanly speaking any return to the truth will be that much more difficult. There is no neutral ground; one either holds to the truth, or he is captive to error. See also the entry "Truth" in the Extended Notes.

4:5 Σὺ δὲ—Here the connective δέ denotes a sharp contrast: "But you" do just the opposite.

νῆφε ἐν πᾶσιν—The verb νῆφε can be used of sobriety in contrast to literal drunkenness or actual sleep (1 Thess 5:6–8), but that in turn serves as a vivid illustration of the alertness and control, especially of a spiritual nature, that the Christian is to display (see also 1 Pet 1:13; 4:7; 5:8). As a pastor Timothy is to demonstrate this "in all things."

κακοπάθησον—By virtue of their baptismal incorporation into the death of Christ, all Christians are called to a life of suffering for Christ's sake; see the section "Faithfulness in Suffering" in the commentary on 2 Tim 2:8–13 and the section "Persecution" in the commentary on 2 Tim 3:10–17. Here Paul instructs Timothy to "suffer evil." Christians in general and pastors in particular face the wrath of Satan and the unbelieving world, who may impose all manner of undeserved suffering upon them. See the commentary below.

ἔργον ποίησον εὐαγγελιστοῦ—What does the apostle mean here by the work of an "evangelist"? See the commentary below.

τὴν διακονίαν σου πληροφόρησον—While the noun διακονίαν can refer to other types of service, in this context the rendering "ministry" is to be preferred.[209] It would seem that Timothy (and any pastor) is to "fulfill" his ministry by attitude ("be sober"), suffering ("suffer evil"), and setting forth God's word ("work of an evangelist").

COMMENTARY

Throughout this letter the apostle has been speaking in various ways of the work of ministry. In the previous section he has expounded upon the Scriptures as the foundation of that ministry. In the present section he turns his attention to the need for faithfully carrying out one's ministry, especially in view of the opposition and even persecution that will come his way as a result.

There Will Be a Time

This section has connections with the beginning of chapter 3. A careful reading of those verses demonstrates the way in which Paul—in harmony with the rest of the New Testament—views time and history. The authors of the New Testament understood that they were living in the "last days." The ministry of Jesus Christ was the climactic event in the history of salvation and of the world. Since Christ had carried out God's plan of redemption by his death and resurrection, all that remained to take place for salvation was his "appearing" "to judge the living and the dead" and to take the redeemed to eternal life (his "kingdom"). From that perspective the world has been in the last days ever since the day of Pentecost (Acts 2:17).[210]

In the present passage the apostle describes Jesus as one "who is about [μέλλοντος] to judge the living and the dead," indicating that (in terms of the history of salvation) the end is near. When he further notes that "there *will* be [ἔσται] a time when they *will* not tolerate [οὐκ ἀνέξονται] sound teaching (doctrine)," he characterizes it in such a way to make it plain that Timothy himself is dealing with that time and those circumstances.

---

209. Cf. Rom 11:13; 2 Cor 3:7, 8, 9; 4:1; 5:18; 6:3; 11:8; Acts 1:17; 6:4; 20:24; 21:19.

210. See also the section "The Last Times" in the commentary on 1 Tim 4:1–5 and the section "The Last Days" in the commentary on 2 Tim 3:1–9. See also Deterding, "New Testament View," 385–99.

Paul describes this time in several different ways. He notes that instead of holding to sound *teaching*, people will heap up teachers according to their own (sinful) desires to appeal to their "itching ears." He indicates that this involves a turning away from the truth, "truth" serving as a one-word summary of the entirety of Christian doctrine. Having turned away from the truth, they will turn instead to "myths," a term that sums up the heresy and emphasizes its false character (see further "The Nature of the Heresy" in the Introduction to the Pastoral Letters).

As noted previously, the apostle's description of the last days agrees with the teaching of Jesus that the end times would be characterized by false teaching and apostasy (Matt 24:9–13, 23–26; Mark 13:11–13, 21–23; Luke 21:12–19).[211] In view of all this a pastor such as Timothy must offset such heresies with a ministry of truth and integrity, as described in the surrounding verses and indeed throughout the Pastoral Letters.

Preach the Word

Paul highlights the importance of a godly, faithful ministry by the way in which he begins this section. In essence he places his coworker under an oath to carry out his ministry according to the pattern that he sets forth here.

Timothy is to "preach the word." While the associations of the verb κήρυξον with *public* proclamation would point to formal preaching in a worship setting, this term would not be limited to that circumstance but would encompass all types of setting forth of the word of God. The term "word" is a broad one, indicating the proclamation of the whole counsel of God (Acts 20:27). The apostle's further description of the ministry of speaking the word reinforces the comprehensive nature of what is proclaimed. He instructs Timothy to "rebuke," to "correct," and to "encourage," each word pointing to a different aspect of the proclamation and together demonstrating the all-inclusive character of it. He adds that this is to be done "with all . . . teaching (doctrine)"; also this indicates that the entirety of the biblical revelation is to be included within the pastor's instruction.

There appears to be a certain amount of correspondence between those things for which Scripture is profitable (3:16) and those things that the pastor is to preach. Scripture is profitable for "teaching"

---

211. As noted in the previous footnote; on the teaching of Jesus on this point see Gibbs, *Matthew 21:1—28:20*, 1278–79.

(διδασκαλίαν); the pastor is to proclaim "with all . . . teaching" (διδαχῇ). Scripture is profitable for "rebuke" (ἐλεγμόν); the pastor is to "rebuke" (ἔλεγξον). Scripture is profitable for "improvement" (ἐπανόρθωσιν); the pastor is to "correct" (ἐπιτίμησον). Scripture is profitable for "instruction in righteousness" (παιδείαν τὴν ἐν δικαιοσύνῃ); the pastor is to "encourage" (παρακάλεσον—a word that has associations with exhortation to righteous living).[212] This further points to the pastor's duty to proclaim *all* of God's word in the holy Scriptures.

Timothy is to be ready to do this "at opportune times and at inopportune times." In the words of another apostle, Timothy, like any pastor, is to be "always prepared to give a defense to anyone who asks you for a reason for the hope that is in you" (1 Pet 3:15). The pastoral ministry involves times of preparing one's proclamation; there will also be times when one must be ready to speak "off the cuff" as the occasion arises (Matt 10:19–20; Mark 13:11–12; Luke 21:13–15). There will be times when there will be those eager to hear the message; there will be not so favorable times; there may well be times when speaking the truth of God's word might put the preacher at risk of some sort of harm, perhaps even of death, a possibility of which Paul was keenly aware (4:6). Faithful ministry is not always safe, but there is always the promise of the Lord's deliverance.[213]

The instruction to Timothy to be ready to proclaim God's word "at opportune times and at inopportune times" points to the eternal blessings imparted by that word and to the ongoing need of all Christians for God's word. "It is not enough to have taught or read this just once. It is still loose; it has not yet gone deep enough to be made altogether firm. If some people grow sick of it, let them. We who desire salvation enjoy listening to it and having it repeated every day, lest we do lose faith in a time of trial."[214]

Fulfill Your Ministry

Proclamation of God's word is the chief task of the pastoral ministry. However, there are other matters to which a pastor must give attention.

The apostle concludes these instructions by telling Timothy, "Fulfill your ministry." With these words he implores his younger coworker to attend to everything that pertains to the pastoral ministry.

---

212. 1 Tim 2:1; 5:1; 6:2; Titus 1:9; 2:6, 15.
213. See the section "Persecution" in the commentary on 2 Tim 3:10–17.
214. Luther, AE 29:86–87.

That Timothy is to "be sober-minded in all things" points to the pastor's conduct. Above all, he is to keep himself uncontaminated with the intoxicating effect of heretical teaching.[215] This exhortation recalls that many of the necessary qualifications for the pastoral office given in Paul's previous Letter to Timothy (3:1–7), as well as in his Letter to Titus (1:5–9), have to do with the prospective pastor's character and conduct. Both those inside and outside the church often evaluate the church's message, at least initially, by the conduct of its messengers; thus, this is not a matter to be disregarded.

The apostle also directs his coworker to "endure suffering." The particular word that he uses here (κακοπάθησον) indicates that he is speaking of undeserved suffering, of evil perpetrated on the Christian and particularly on the Christian pastor by the unbelieving world—and, sad to say, sometimes by those within the association of the Christian church[216] at the instigation of Satan. The pastor must be prepared to endure these, and God himself will provide the power for him to do so.[217]

The Work of an Evangelist

Paul instructs Timothy to "do the work of an evangelist." Being cognate to the noun εὐαγγέλιον and the verb εὐαγγελίζω, the term "evangelist" (εὐαγγελιστοῦ) has something to do with the gospel of Jesus Christ. Potentially it could have many different shades of meaning, but what does the apostle mean by it here?

The present passage is one of only three in the New Testament where this word occurs. The Philip of the book of Acts (6:5; 8:4–13, 26–40) is called "Philip the evangelist" (Acts 21:8), but that is of little help in interpreting the use in 2 Timothy.

Somewhat more helpful is the occurrence in Eph 4. There Paul states that the risen and exalted Christ gave to his church "apostles, prophets, evangelists, and pastors who are also teachers."[218]

While there is some distinction between these terms, there is also a certain amount of overlap. The "apostles" were those whom the risen

---

215. Kelly, *Pastoral Epistles*, 207.

216. 1 Tim 1:19–20; 2 Tim 2:17–18; 4:14; 3 John 9–10.

217. See the section "Faithfulness in Suffering" in the commentary on 2 Tim 2:8–13 and the section "Persecution" in the commentary on 2 Tim 3:10–17.

218. For this rendering of this verse see Bruce, *Colossians*, 345–49.

Christ used to communicate his authoritative word to the church and to the world (see the entry "Apostle" in the Extended Notes). The term "prophet" could be used to refer to one who proclaimed and taught the word of God; see the note on προφητείας ("prophecy") in the textual notes on 1 Tim 4:14. Pastors who are also teachers would be equivalent to that office that the Pastoral Letters refer to with the terms ἐπίσκοπος ("overseer") and πρεσβύτερος ("elder").

Thus, it would appear that "evangelist" designated one with a responsibility related to but nevertheless beyond that of a "parish pastor." As Timothy had had (and presumably still had) entrusted to him care for a wider group than a single congregation,[219] the work of an "evangelist" that he was to carry out may have involved supervising other speakers of the gospel.

Thus, it may be that this work of an "evangelist" would have involved preparing and sending others to the task of bringing the gospel to new areas. Thus, we might think of a biblical "evangelist" as combining the work of a seminary professor and a mission executive. While this is certainly a plausible explanation, there are other possibilities,[220] and dogmatism on the matter is to be avoided.

Opposition to the Truth Brings Suffering: 2 Timothy 4:1–5 in Context

Having spoken of the inspiration of the Scriptures by God, Paul now exhorts Timothy to preach the scriptural word. Once again, he contrasts this truth with the myths that some are following and even promoting.

There is a definite need for this instruction and encouragement. Just as "all who desire to live in a godly way in Christ Jesus will be persecuted" (2 Tim 3:12), so a pastor like Timothy must be prepared to "endure suffering" (4:5). The challenges are great, the opposition is real, and so the

---

219. Paul instructed Timothy to "instruct certain people" (1 Tim 1:3); he was given responsibility for those who might "aspire to the office of overseer" (1 Tim 3:1); he was not to "accept an accusation against an elder, except on the basis of two or three witnesses" (1 Tim 5:19); he was instructed to "rebuke those sinning before all" (1 Tim 5:20, referring to disciplining those who were pastors; see the textual notes on that verse); he was told, "Do not be hasty in laying hands on anyone, lest you have fellowship in the sins of others" (1 Tim 5:22).

220. Winger, *Ephesians*, 454–55, notes the suggestion that as an "evangelist" Timothy was to be involved in the work of "preserving and copying the stories and words of Jesus for liturgical and proclamatory need."

temptation to satisfy the "itching ears" of people will be hard to resist. Nevertheless, the pastor must withstand these temptations.

Hence, a pastor like Timothy must take care to conduct his ministry with faithfulness to God's word and with personal integrity. The seriousness of this charge is seen in the apostle virtually putting his younger coworker under oath to do all these things. Nevertheless, there is also power for the younger pastor (and all pastors) to live up to this charge. The "appearing" of Christ and his "kingdom" points to the eternal life given by way of God's word. That in itself is a powerful motivation for living up to the standards that are set out here.

4:6–8: Suffering for the Truth: Paul's Impending Martyrdom

TRANSLATION

⁶ For I am already being poured out as a drink offering, and the time of my departure is near. ⁷ I have fought the good fight; I have finished the race; I have kept the faith. ⁸ Therefore, there is reserved for me the crown of righteousness, which the Lord, the righteous judge, will give me on that day, and not only to me but also to all who have loved his appearing.

TEXTUAL NOTES

4:6 Ἐγὼ γὰρ ἤδη σπένδομαι—The time designation "already" (ἤδη) plus the present tense of the verb σπένδομαι ("being poured out") show that the apostle realizes that his death is imminent. The cultic associations of this verb[221] would suggest that Paul looks upon his martyrdom as a final offering of worship to God.[222] In Phil 2:17 he uses the same verb to present a similar picture of his potential martyrdom.

ὁ καιρὸς τῆς ἀναλύσεώς μου ἐφέστηκεν—This phrase reinforces the nearness of the apostle's execution. The use of "departure" (ἀναλύσεως) for death evidently points to the expectation that Paul is departing this life for the life to come. The verb ἐφέστηκεν is the same word that the apostle used in 4:2 to instruct Timothy to "be ready"; is Paul perhaps

---

221. BDAG 937.

222. Theodore of Mopsuestia states that Paul describes "enduring death in the confession of Christ as a libation of wine is poured out on behalf of honoring God"; see ACCS NT 9:273.

implying that his departure is imminent and that because of the resurrection of Jesus Christ from the dead he is ready for it?

4:7 ἠγώνισμαι . . . τετέλεκα . . . τετήρηκα—The use of the perfect tense denotes past actions that have a continuing effect.²²³

τὸν καλὸν ἀγῶνα ἠγώνισμαι—Although ἀγών and its cognate verb ἀγωνίζομαι can be used of military conflict (John 18:36), in the context of running a race the metaphor here has to do with athletic competition, such as a boxing or wrestling match.

τὸν δρόμον τετέλεκα—Paul uses athletics as an illustration or metaphor elsewhere (1 Cor 9:24–27; Phil 4:1; 1 Tim 6:12); was he something of an athlete or at least a sports fan?

τὴν πίστιν τετέλεκα—Here the apostle moves from metaphorical to literal language. He has kept on believing (*fides qua creditur*), and he has held fast to the true teaching (*fides quae creditur*).²²⁴ See the entry "Faith" in the Extended Notes.

4:8 λοιπὸν—This is an adverbial use of the adjective λοιπός ("remaining," "other"): "henceforth," "therefore."²²⁵

ἀπόκειταί μοι ὁ τῆς δικαιοσύνης στέφανος—On "righteousness" see the entry "Righteousness/Justification" in the Extended Notes. "Crown" (στέφανος) originally referred to a literal crown or wreath (Matt 27:29; Mark 15:17; John 19:2, 5); since such a crown was awarded to the winner of an athletic competition (1 Cor 9:25), the word came to be used, as here, metaphorically of other kinds of awards (Jas 1:12; 1 Pet 5:4; Rev 2:10; 3:11). The context, using actual athletic competition as an image for the life of faith, would make the metaphorical use of a wreath for the award of eternal life an obvious choice.

ὃν ἀποδώσει μοι ὁ κύριος—The verb ἀποδώσει ("give") shows that this righteousness is a gift of grace; the future tense of the verb points to the future ("on that day") as the time of its awarding. The vocable κύριος ("Lord") here refers to Christ; see the note on ὁ δίκαιος κριτής below.

ἐν ἐκείνῃ τῇ ἡμέρᾳ—"That day" (or "the day") is a rather common way of referring to the last day, the day of judgment.²²⁶

ὁ δίκαιος κριτής—This is a reference to Christ, as in 4:1. He is "the righteous" judge, both because he judges according to righteous

---

223. BDF 176 [§ 342 (1)].

224. As recognized by Knight, *Pastoral Epistles*, 460; Towner, *Letters*, 613–14.

225. BDAG 602–3; see, for example, Exod 25:29; 29:40–41; 37:16; Lev 23:13, 18, 37.

226. Matt 24:36; 26:29; Mark 13:32; 14:25; Luke 10:12; 17:31; 21:34; Rom 2:16; 1 Thess 5:4; 2 Thess 1:10; 2 Tim 1:12, 18.

standards and because his judgment is to give the crown of *righteousness* to his believers (see following notes).

οὐ μόνον δὲ ἐμοὶ ἀλλὰ καὶ πᾶσι—Although this letter is addressed to Timothy, it is intended to be read to all (see note on "with you" at 4:22). So also, Paul's example of salvation through faith is intended to be a message of encouragement for all Christians.

τοῖς ἠγαπηκόσι τὴν ἐπιφάνειαν αὐτοῦ—In this context Christ's "appearing" (ἐπιφάνειαν) refers to his coming at the last day. To love Christ's appearing is a way of designating saving faith.

COMMENTARY

All of this talk of ministry and the life of suffering that it brings the minister leads Paul to speak of his imminent martyrdom as the culmination of his own suffering for the gospel. While the apostle has his own afflictions in mind, his circumstances serve as an example for others regarding the assurance Christ gives them in the face of their own suffering.

Paul's Martyrdom

The implication of the ending of the book of Acts is that at the end of two years Paul was acquitted of the charges against him and was released from his house arrest (Acts 28:30–31).[227] At the time of the writing of his Letter to the Philippians, likely written during this imprisonment,[228] while he considered the possibility that he might be martyred (2:17), he was equally if not even more of the opinion that he could be released from his incarceration (Phil 1:19–26).

His current imprisonment is an entirely different matter. He is quite confident that this confinement will end with his execution. That being the case, he gives it a theological interpretation by the ways in which he describes it here.

By speaking of himself as being poured out as a drink offering, the apostle designates his martyrdom as the last episode of his earthly ministry, as a final act of service and devotion to God. By calling his death his

---

227. See the subsection "The Historical Setting" of the section "Authenticity and Integrity" in the Introduction to the Pastoral Letters.

228. Franzmann, *Word of the Lord*, 138–39; Guthrie, *New Testament Introduction*, 526–36.

departure he makes the point that his is departing this life and going to the life to come. His reference to a "crown of righteousness" denotes that the righteousness that he has received through faith in Christ (Rom 1:17; 2 Cor 5:21) will give him a place in eternal blessedness. This will reach its consummation in the resurrection from the dead when Christ comes in glory at the last day.

The apostle notes that this will be given to all believers, to all who have loved Christ's appearing. Thus, Paul's anticipation of his death offers a pattern for every child of God to follow. Not all Christians will experience martyrdom, but all will be persecuted (2 Tim 3:12), and all, save for those still alive at the parousia, will face death. To think of our death in terms of a final act of worship, of a departure from this life with all of its hardships to an existence like that which God first created for mankind, and of receiving God's gift of righteousness will empower the believer to meet death with the confidence borne of faith.

Paul's Faith

The apostle here describes his own faith. The use of the perfect tense of the verbs ἠγώνισμαι ("I have fought"), τετέλεκα ("I have finished"), and τετήρηκα ("I have kept"), denoting the completion of these actions,[229] is fitting in this context, as he considers the nearness of his death. He speaks of it in both literal and metaphorical terms.

When he states, "I have kept the faith," he is not boasting, as though his keeping the faith was a good work by which he had merited salvation from God. Instead, he is noting that he has kept faith in "Jesus Christ, risen from the dead, of the offspring of David, according to my gospel" (2 Tim 2:8), and that having endured in that faith, he will therefore reign with Christ (2 Tim 2:12).

Paul also illustrates the keeping of the faith with the language of athletics. He compares holding the faith with a boxing (or wrestling) competition and with running a race. Holding to faith in Christ often involves struggle, as Satan, the unbelieving world, and our own corrupted nature often entice us to abandon the faith. Holding to faith in Christ requires the endurance of a long-distance runner; it requires being faithful unto death. The apostle's description of eternal life in these verses provides

---

229. Wallace, *Greek Grammar*, 577.

motivation and strength for Timothy and for all his readers (note the plural "you" [ὑμῶν] in 4:22) to do that very thing.

Suffering for the Truth: Paul's Impending Martyrdom: 2 Timothy 4:6–8 in Context

Much of this letter has focused on the ministry of the gospel of Christ. At this point Paul is moved to speak of his own life of ministry.

All Christians will be persecuted (2 Tim 3:12), and all pastors are called upon to "endure suffering" (1 Tim 4:5). The apostle is about to suffer such persecution to the fullest extent by being martyred.

The way in which Paul faced his impending suffering is an example and an inspiration to all Christians (and especially to all pastors) as they face their own suffering and persecution. By speaking of his death as his departure and as the reception of the crown of righteousness, the apostle directs us to the value of the Christian faith, life, and ministry. Being a Christian and especially being a Christian minister will bring persecution of one sort or another, but the rewards far outweigh the cost. Whatever persecutions we may face for our faith, witness, and way of life, these are well worth bearing, for the outcome is eternal, and it is glorious (Rom 8:18). That being the case, we are willing to live out our lives as an act of service and worship to our Lord and savior.

4:9–18: Ministry in the Truth and Those Who Oppose It

TRANSLATION

⁹ Hurry to come to me soon, ¹⁰ for Demas, having loved the present age, abandoned me and went to Thessalonica; Crescens went to Galatia; Titus went to Dalmatia. ¹¹ Only Luke is with me. When you have collected Mark, bring him with you, for he is useful to me for ministry. ¹² I am sending Tychicus to Ephesus. ¹³ When you come, bring the cloak that I left in Troas with Carpus along with the books, especially the parchments. ¹⁴ Alexander the metalworker did me much harm; the Lord will give back to him according to his works. ¹⁵ You also be on your guard against him, for he very much opposed our words. ¹⁶ At my first defense no one stood by me, but all left me; may it not be counted against them. ¹⁷ However, the Lord stood by me and strengthened me, in order that through me the kerygma might be fulfilled, and all the gentiles might hear [it], and I was rescued from the lion's mouth. ¹⁸ The Lord will rescue me from every evil work and will save me for his heavenly kingdom; to him be the glory forever and ever. Amen.

TEXTUAL NOTES

4:9 Σπούδασον ἐλθεῖν πρὸς με ταχέως—While σπούδασον often means "be eager,"²³⁰ here the literal meaning "hurry" is more appropriate. The

---

230. Gal 2:10; Eph 4:3; 1 Thess 2:17; 2 Tim 2:15; Heb 4:11; 2 Pet 1:10, 15; 3:14.

urgency for Timothy to come is heightened by the addition of the adverb ταχέως ("soon").[231] A reason for the urgency is given in 4:21, which see.

4:10 Δημᾶς γάρ με ἐγκατέλιπεν ἀγαπήσας τὸν νῦν αἰῶνα καὶ ἐπορεύθη εἰς Θεσσαλονίκην—Paul sends greetings from Demas in his Letters to the Colossians (4:14) and to Philemon (24); in the latter he is included among the apostle's coworkers. Here we are informed that he forsook Paul and went to Thessalonica, "having loved the present age." That his departure from traveling with the apostle was also a departure from the faith is indicated by his being described as in love with "the present age," an expression which denotes what is evil and set in hostility against God (Gal 1:3–4). As Jesus had his Judas, so Paul also had one whom he counted as a fellow worker for Christ forsake the faith; such may also be the experience of other Christian workers.

Κρήσκης εἰς Γαλατίαν—Nothing more from the Scriptures is known of this individual. We can assume that he went to Galatia on good terms with the apostle and likely to be involved in some type of ministry.

There is some textual evidence, including the codices Sinaiticus (א) and Ephraemi (C), for the reading "Gaul" instead of "Galatia." Moreover, "Galatia" was an earlier name for the region of Gaul; several church fathers advocated the identity of this "Galatia" with Gaul, and there is a tradition associating Crescens with the founding of a Christian church near Lyons in France.[232] That being the case, it is possible that this is the reference here. If so, it would be a further testimony to the gospel expanding westward under the guidance of Paul, who may well have brought the gospel to Spain himself (Rom 15:24, 28).

Τίτος εἰς Δαλματίαν—Titus is known from references to him in Galatians and 2 Corinthians as well from Paul's letter to him. As with Crescens it seems probable that he has gone to carry out some work of ministry.

4:11 Λουκᾶς ἐστιν μόνος μετ' ἐμοῦ—The use of the first-person plural in Acts 27:1—28:16 makes it all but certain that Luke was with the apostle during his first Roman imprisonment; so too he is with Paul now. He is mentioned (along with Demas) in the Letters to the Colossians (4:14) and to Philemon (24), two letters which may well have been

---

231. BDF 127 [§ 244 (1)].

232. That "Galatia" here meant "Gaul" was the opinion of Theodore of Mopsuestia (ACCS NT 9:277). Kelly, *Pastoral Epistles*, 213, mentions corresponding judgments held by Eusebius, Epiphanius, and Theodoret.

written during the apostle's imprisonment in Rome.²³³ All of this is one more bit of evidence that confirms Luke as the author of Luke and Acts.

The presence of Luke with Paul at this time is in direct contrast to the apostle's being abandoned by Demas. As Luke was "the beloved physician" (Col 4:14), it is possible that at this time he might have been providing medical aid to Paul.

Μᾶρκον ἀναλαβὼν ἄγε μετὰ σεαυτοῦ, ἔστιν γάρ μοι εὔχρηστος εἰς διακονίαν—The apostle and Mark had separated due to the former's lack of confidence in the latter's suitability for ministry (Acts 15:36–51). After an interval of nearly twenty years, things have changed. Paul now regards Mark as a useful coworker in ministry (διακονία in other contexts can mean "service" of any sort, but in this context "ministry" seems to be the appropriate translation).²³⁴

4:12 Τύχικον δὲ ἀπέστειλα εἰς Ἔφεσον—Tychicus is mentioned elsewhere in connection with the apostle's work.²³⁵ He is identified as a "faithful minister in the Lord" (Eph 6:21; Col 4:7). It seems likely that the verb ἀπέστειλα is an epistolary aorist (hence the translation "I am sending"). As Tychicus is a "faithful minister in the Lord," and as Paul wants Timothy to come to him soon (4:9, 21), the apostle may well be sending Tychicus to Ephesus to take Timothy's place in ministry.²³⁶

4:13 τὸν φαιλόνην ὃν ἀπέλιπον ἐν Τρῳάδι παρὰ Κάρπῳ ἐρχόμενος φέρε—Ancient prisons were not in any way comfortable. Paul may have wanted his cloak for a covering against the cold (Acts 12:8); after all, winter was coming (4:21).²³⁷

What is the point of mentioning such a trivial matter in the Scriptures?²³⁸ It is all but impossible to imagine a pseudonymous author including such a thing when he was trying to pass off his work as that of a revered apostle. The presence of this comment therefore serves as a mark of authenticity for this letter as the work of Paul himself.

---

233. Deterding, *Colossians*, 13–14; Nordling, *Philemon*, 5–9.

234. Cf. Rom 11:13; 2 Cor 3:7, 8, 9; 4:1; 5:18; 6:3; 11:8; Acts 1:17; 6:4; 20:24; 21:19. Knight, *Pastoral Epistles*, 465–66, reaches the same conclusion.

235. Acts 20:4; Eph 6:21; Col 4:7; Titus 3:12.

236. If that is indeed the case, Tychicus might well be the one carrying the Letter to Timothy. See Knight, *Pastoral Epistles*, 365, 466; Guthrie, *Pastoral Epistles*, 184; Towner, *Letters*, 626–27. Marshall, *Pastoral Epistles*, 817, notes, "One does not summon an experienced missionary simply to be a valet."

237. *DNTB* 828; Knight, *Pastoral Epistles*, 466; Towner, *Letters*, 628–29.

238. On the equating of the books of the NT with the Scriptures, see the section "The Holy Scriptures" in the commentary on 3:10–17.

We know that the apostle had been in Troas several times (Acts 16:8, 11; 22:6; 2 Cor 2:12); it is entirely believable that he would have passed through there again. Troas was in the northwest corner of Asia Minor near where one might cross from Asia into Europe (Acts 16:8–12); thus, Timothy might well be expected to pass through Troas on his way from Ephesus to Rome.

καὶ τὰ βιβλία μάλιστα τὰς μεμβράνας—As the codex form long postdates the NT period, all "books" during that time were in the form of scrolls. References to individuals having personal collections of books and of prisoners passing the time by reading are known as far back as the fifth century BC,[239] so it is not unreasonable to think of the apostle owning some books and of him wanting them for an edifying way to spend his days while incarcerated. The word μάλιστα, commonly rendered "especially," at least sometimes has the meaning "that is"; it is possible that this is the meaning here.[240] For suggestions as to what might have been the content of these books/scrolls see the commentary below.

4:14 Ἀλέξανδρος ὁ χαλκὺς πολλά μοι κακὰ ἐνεδείξατο—This Alexander is identified as "the metalworker," which might indicate that this is a different individual than the Alexander that Paul names in 1 Tim 1:20. On the nature of the harm that he caused the apostle, see the note on verse 15.

ἀποδώσει αὐτῷ ὁ κύριος κατὰ τὰ ἔργα αὐτοῦ—Paul here entrusts vengeance to the Lord God (Rom 12:19). He expresses confidence that the Lord will punish evildoers (2 Thess 1:5–10; see also Rom 2:6; Ps 62:12). A comparison with the 2 Thessalonians passage, the frequent NT use of "the Lord" (ὁ κύριος) to refer to Christ, and the previous references to Christ as judge (4:1, 8) taken together indicate that "the Lord" here refers to Jesus and to his coming on "that day" (2 Tim 4:8) to "judge the living and the dead" (2 Tim 4:1).

There is a contrast between Alexander, whom the Lord will repay, and those who had left the apostle at his first defense, for whom he prays that this will not be held against them (4:16). This indicates that while Alexander is an unbeliever, the others are still within the family of faith.

4:15 ὃν καὶ σὺ φυλάσσου—That Timothy needs to be on his guard against this Alexander demonstrates that the latter continues to be a danger to Christ's church.

---

239. *DNTB* 829, 1283.
240. BDAG 613–14 (μάλα, μάλιστα, μᾶλλον).

Grace and Life

λίαν γὰρ ἀντέστη τοῖς ἡμετέροις λόγοις—Paul here indicates the nature of the danger and harm this Alexander presents. He has been (and continues to be) a vigorous opponent of the word of God as faithfully taught by the apostle.

Acts 19:33–34 mentions a Jew named Alexander whom his fellow (non-Christian) Jews had put forward to speak on their behalf at the time of the riot of the silversmiths in Ephesus (he was shouted down by the crowds). Timothy's laboring in the same city might suggest that this could be the same as the Alexander of 2 Tim 4 and/or 1 Tim 1.[241] While this cannot be ruled out, the riot in Ephesus took place in about AD 54, 1 Timothy was written in the neighborhood of AD 64, and 2 Timothy is to be dated around AD 67; that gap of time between the riot and the two letters would make this identification seem less likely.

4:16 Ἐν τῇ πρώτῃ μου ἀπολογίᾳ—This would refer not to Paul's first imprisonment and trial (Acts 28) but to his first hearing (*primo actio*) as a part of his current incarceration and legal proceedings.[242]

οὐδείς μοι παρεγένετο, ἀλλὰ πάντες με ἐγκατέλιπον—The apostle anticipates that, unlike his first trial, when he could foresee the charges against him being dismissed, this imprisonment will end with his execution (4:6–8). Thus, the danger to any of his associates would have been greater at this time than at the previous one. That might account for none of his friends or coworkers being with him at his initial hearing.

μὴ αὐτοῖς λογισθείη—Paul has used the verb λογίζομαι to speak of sins not being accounted against the believer in Christ (Rom 4:8; 2 Cor 5:19); the use here is equivalent. This would indicate that the apostle is not necessarily excusing the conduct of those who forsook him but rather forgiving them.

4:17 ὁ δὲ κύριός μοι παρέστη καὶ ἐνεδυνάμωσέν με—Paul uses the verb ἐνδυναμόω to denote empowering one for a task, such as enduring hardship (Phil 4:13) or carrying out ministry (1 Tim 1:12). Both of those are in view here.

ἵνα δι' ἐμοῦ τὸ κήρυγμα πληροφορηθῇ—Here ἵνα plus a verb in the subjunctive expresses purpose and result.[243] The apostle uses the noun

---

241. DNTB 829, 1283; Knight, *Pastoral Epistles*, 320.

242. Kelly, *Pastoral Epistles*, 217–18; Towner, *Letters*, 639; Mounce, *Pastoral Epistles*, 595.

243. Wallace, *Greek Grammar*, 473–74.

κήρυγμα as a summary of the entirety of the Christian message.²⁴⁴ On this message being "fulfilled" by Paul, see the commentary below.

καὶ ἀκούσωσιν πάντα τὰ ἔθνη—While "nations" is certainly a valid translation of ἔθνη, in this context the reference is to the "gentiles" hearing the kerygma;²⁴⁵ see the commentary below.

καὶ ἐρρύσθην ἐκ στόματος λέοντος—The metaphorical use of "lion" is well attested in the Scriptures.²⁴⁶ As a Roman citizen Paul's method of execution would have been beheading with a sword;²⁴⁷ moreover, the practice of using lions to persecute Christians is not attested until after the first century.²⁴⁸ The lion, therefore, refers to Rome²⁴⁹ or perhaps to Rome as a tool of Satan (cf. 1 Pet 5:8) in persecuting Christians.

4:18 ῥύσεταί με ὁ κύριος ἀπὸ παντὸς ἔργου πονηροῦ καὶ σώσει εἰς τὴν βασιλείαν αὐτοῦ τὴν ἐπουράνιον—This is perhaps an echo of the Lord's Prayer as recorded in the Gospel according to Matthew (6:10a, 13b). The apostle was very much aware that he would not escape execution (4:6–8). Thus, his words do not refer to his being freed from prison. The future tense of the verbs ῥύσεταί ("will rescue") and σώσει ("will save") as well as the adjective ἐπουράνιον ("heavenly") reveal his meaning: the Lord (Christ) will rescue him from the evil of this life by taking him to eternal life in heaven (Paul uses the word βασιλείαν, "kingdom," with this meaning elsewhere in his letters).²⁵⁰ In this way the apostle will live with Christ even while asleep in death (1 Thess 5:10); he will be "away from the body and at home with the Lord" (2 Cor 5:8); he will "depart and be with Christ" rather than continuing "to live in the flesh" (Phil 1:22–23).²⁵¹

---

244. Rom 16:25; 1 Cor 1:21; 2:4; 15:14; Titus 1:3.

245. Knight, *Pastoral Epistles*, 471.

246. Pss 7:2; 10:9; 17:12; 22:13, 21; 35:17; 57:4; 58:6; 91:13.

247. Knight, *Pastoral Epistles*, 471.

248. Tacitus (*Annals* 15:44) writes of persecution during the time of Nero (the time when Paul would have been martyred): "First, then, the confessed members of the sect were arrested; next, on their disclosures, vast numbers were convicted, not so much on the count of arson as for hatred of the human race. And derision accompanied their end: they were covered with wild beasts' skins and torn to death by dogs; or they were fastened on crosses, and, when daylight failed were burned to serve as lamps by night." Jerome (*On Illustrious Men* 16) refers to Ignatius of Antioch hearing the roar of the lions at the time of his execution, but that took place sometime during the second century AD.

249. Josephus (*Ant* 18:6:10) reports that the death of the emperor Tiberius was announced to Agrippa with the words "The lion is dead."

250. 1 Cor 6:9, 10; 15:50; Gal 5:21; Eph 5:5.

251. Knight, *Pastoral Epistles*, 472–73.

ᾧ ἡ δόξα εἰς τοὺς αἰῶνας τῶν αἰώνων, ἀμήν.—This is similar to other doxologies in the Pauline corpus.[252] Except for Rom 16:27, none of these occur at the very end of the letter, as we perhaps would expect. It is to be noted that the wording of the doxology of Gal 1:5 is identical to the present one. Also worthy of note is that this doxology and that of Rom 9:5 are the sole Pauline doxologies directed to Christ.[253]

As we examine these doxologies, it appears that there is a variety of purposes for their use, but each serves to emphasize some message. In the case of the present letter, it puts a literary "exclamation point" on the totality of this most personal of Paul's letters. Other than some greetings and a final benediction the letter is complete. Timothy is to take the message of this letter to heart.

COMMENTARY

Throughout this letter the apostle has been speaking about the ministry of the word and of the suffering that Satan and the world direct against those who carry it out and who believe it. As he draws this letter to a close, he turns to specific instances of ministry and of suffering.

Paul's Situation

Paul writes this letter knowing that his martyrdom is imminent (4:6). Moreover, he has been largely left alone. He was abandoned at his first hearing; his wish-prayer for those who left him rather implies that by this they did him wrong. Clearly Demas has left the apostle, the work of ministry, and the faith itself. Paul has sent two of his coworkers to other places; apparently the need for them to be about ministry in those locations is greater than the apostle's need for their companionship. Only Luke is with him, perhaps in the role of providing medical help. The wrong done to him by Alexander, which perhaps occurred a number of years earlier, still distresses him.

Nevertheless, Paul is not simply giving vent to his pain. His situation leads him to speak of both Timothy's responsibilities and his own deliverance.

---

252. Rom 1:25; 9:5; 11:36; 16:27; Gal 1:5; Eph 3:21; Phil 4:20; 1 Tim 1:17; 6:15–16.
253. On this understanding of Rom 9:5 see Middendorf, *Romans 9—16*, 842–48.

COMMENTARY ON 2 TIMOTHY

Timothy's Responsibilities

We are unsure of who Alexander the metalworker was and are unaware of the harm that he did to the apostle and his ministry. From Paul's words to Timothy about him, however, we can be certain that he was still a spiritual danger to the church and its members. Therefore, Timothy is to be on his guard against him, which means that he must be ready to oppose his false teaching with the truth (4:15).

It is interesting and reassuring to read the apostle's instructions regarding Mark. Perhaps the "sharp disagreement" (Acts 15:39) over including Mark in their next mission endeavor that caused Barnabas and Paul to separate was simply a recognition that they disagreed and were better off pursuing separate ministries. On the other hand, perhaps there were some hard feelings on the occasion. Whatever the particulars, the apostle now regards Mark as "useful to me for ministry."

Paul also instructs Timothy to bring him "the books" (scrolls) that he left in Troas, "especially the parchments." Although we can only guess as to the content of these, two hypotheses commend themselves.

As noted, ancient references to prisoners being able to read while incarcerated might suggest that the apostle wanted reading material. His circumstances were a matter of life and (especially) death, so that if he wanted reading material, it would be most likely that he would desire books of the Scriptures for that purpose.[254]

There is another, related possibility. We have noted various indications in Paul's letters that he recognized that his writings were on a par with the Hebrew Scriptures (the Old Testament).[255] It was the practice in the ancient world to keep a copy of one's letters both for possible future reference and as a backup in the event of loss or damage in transit.[256] There are instances in Paul's letters when he appears to make reference to his own writings (1 Cor 5:9-10; 2 Cor 7:8; 2 Thess 2:15); furthermore, since he regarded his writings as on a par with the Hebrew Scriptures, it would be possible, even expected, that he would have had copies of his writings which he wanted preserved to serve the church (and the world)

---

254. Knight, *Pastoral Epistles*, 467.

255. In 1 Thess 5:27 and Col 4:16 he directs that his letter be read in worship, just as the Hebrew Scriptures were read. Note also "the things I am writing to you are a command of the Lord" (1 Cor 14:37) and "the Spirit expressly says" (1 Tim 4:1). See further the section "The Spirit Expressly Says" in the commentary on 1 Tim 4:1–5.

256. *DPL* 660, referring to Cicero, *On Friendship* 7.25 and 16.18.

at large. Thus, this might be one small step on the road to the eventual canonization of his letters among the books of the New Testament.[257] Hence, the parchments he refers to here might have been such copies of his letters.

We should take notice of this emphasis on the importance of reading and writing. Christians are people of the Book; hence, they should also be people of books. Reading contributes to being a well-informed, well-rounded individual; reading the Scriptures (and quality materials based upon the Scriptures) contributes to being a well-informed, well-rounded Christian. Given the easy access to reading material that characterizes the present age, there is no excuse for a Christian not to be a reader, at the very least a reader of the Scriptures.[258]

This also points to the importance of writing. God committed his word to writing through people such as Paul. There is no presumption that the writing of Christians since the authorship of the Scriptures is in any way comparable to holy writ. Nevertheless, as God put his word in writing for the benefit of the ages that would follow, so it is important that there be Christian pastors and others to write good material for the church and the world. The written, published word is able to benefit those beyond the author's own circle of acquaintances, even able to benefit generations that come after him. We thank God for his written word, but we also are thankful for those who expound on God's word through the written word.

Paul's Deliverance

When the apostle pens this letter, he is certain that his imprisonment will end with his death (4:8). Perhaps he was even executed before Timothy (and Mark) were able to join him (4:9–11). Thus, when he writes, "I was rescued from the lion's mouth," he is not referring to a mere physical rescue. Moreover, when he adds, "The Lord will rescue me from every evil work and will save me for his heavenly kingdom," we realize what sort of a rescue he has in mind. The power of the mighty Roman Empire can be marshaled to silence him by death, but this harm pales by comparison

---

257. Already Chrysostom made a suggestion along those lines; *NPNF*[1] 13:514 (ACCS, NT 9:277–78).

258. See Veith, *Reading Between the Lines*, 224.

with the deliverance that is his. His enemies can end his earthly life, but his heavenly salvation will be eternal.

As Christians face hardship and even persecution from the unbelieving world, they can draw strength from Paul's words here. Whatever hardship may come our way—even martyrdom—it cannot take away our eternal joy and bliss. That is the church's comfort and encouragement throughout life in this vale of tears.

All the Gentiles Might Hear the Kerygma

In this section the apostle makes the statement that the Lord rescued him "that through me the kerygma might be fulfilled, and all the gentiles might hear [it]" (4:17). This assertion, like others in his letters, reflects his understanding that his ministry was fulfilling Christ's promise that his gospel would come to all nations and to the end of the earth (Matt 24:14; Mark 13:10).[259]

In his Letter to the Romans (15:18-19) Paul asserts that he speaks of Christ to the nations, so that the gospel of Christ might be fulfilled. In writing to the Colossians he stated that the gospel "is bearing fruit and increasing in all the world" (1:6.) Later in the same letter he affirms that the gospel "was proclaimed to every creature under heaven" (1:23) and that according to the will of God he became a minister "to fulfill the word of God" (1:25).[260]

All of this is in harmony with the structure and message of the book of Acts. At the outset of the book Luke announces the outline of his work by quoting the words of Jesus that his followers would be his witnesses "in Jerusalem [that is, to the Jews], and in all Judea and Samaria [that is, to the Samaritans, those people who might be considered half-Jewish], and to the end of the earth [that is, to the gentiles]." This points to the conclusion of this work, where Luke reports that in Rome for two whole years the apostle proclaimed the kingdom (saving reign) of God and taught the things concerning the Lord Jesus Christ with all boldness and without hindrance. In this way the book of Acts presents Paul's bold and unhindered proclamation of Christ's gospel in the capital of the empire as the fulfillment of the proclamation of the gospel to the end of the earth.

---

259. See also Towner, *Letters*, 643–44.
260. On these passages from Colossians see Deterding, *Colossians*, 71–73.

In the book of Acts Paul is preeminently the apostle to the gentiles, as he names himself in his Letter to the Romans (11:13; see also Gal 2:9). The latter portion of the book of Acts, from chapter 13 to the end of the book, is essentially the acts of one apostle, Paul. It is largely through his ministry that the gospel comes to the gentiles.

The apostle's statement in verse 17 of the present chapter fits right in with the presentation of him in the book of Acts. It is chiefly through him that the gospel comes to the end of the earth (to the gentiles). It is largely through him that the church comes to the realization that Christ's gospel is for all—gentiles as well as for his own people, the Jews.

Ministry in the Truth and Those Who Oppose It: 2 Timothy 4:9–18 in Context

This letter is filled with matters pertaining to the gospel and its proclamation, including the hardship that comes upon those who believe the gospel and on those who proclaim it. As he draws near to the end of the letter Paul takes up a number of personal matters with reference to the work of proclamation.

The apostle updates Timothy on several of their mutual acquaintances. These include both those who are fellow workers and their current areas of ministry as well as warnings regarding some who have abandoned the faith and/or are actively working against the proclamation of the truth.

Paul gives Timothy certain responsibilities. These concern both Timothy's work of ministry in general and also some personal ministry for the apostle himself.

Paul comments on the significance of his life of ministry. The apostle has been the tool of the Lord of the church, and it is largely through his ministry that the promise of the gospel coming to all nations has been fulfilled.

Paul's circumstances are grave (pun intended), but he also has reason for hope. Death cannot take away his eternal life, nor will his death be the end of ministry. For all this the apostle is moved to a doxology, praising the Lord Jesus Christ for what he has done to him and through him.

4:19–22: Concluding Greetings and Blessings

TRANSLATION

¹⁹ Greet Prisca and Aquila and the household of Onesiphorus. ²⁰ Erastus remained in Corinth; I left Trophimus ill in Miletus. ²¹ Hurry to come before winter. Eubulus greets you, as do Pudens, Linus, Claudia, and all the brothers. ²² The Lord be with your spirit. Grace be with you.

TEXTUAL NOTES

4:19 Πρίσκαν—This is the form of the name (Prisca) that occurs in the letters of Paul (here and in the better-attested variants of Rom 16:3 and 1 Cor 16:19). The book of Acts (18:2, 18, 26) uses the diminutive Πρίσκιλλα,[261] from which comes the more commonly used English version of the name, Priscilla.

Ἀσπασαι Πρίσκαν καὶ Ἀκύλαν—The contacts that Paul had with this married couple are recounted in various places in the NT. The apostle first encountered them in Corinth during his second missionary journey (around AD 50); they had had to leave Rome due to the edict of Claudius expelling all the Jews from Rome (Acts 18:2). The Roman historian Suetonius refers to this edict (AD 49), saying that it was due to riots among the Jews "at the instigation of *Chrestus*." It is commonly believed that "*Chrestus*" is actually a reference to Jesus (Christus), that the riots were due to disagreements between Jewish Christians and non-Christian Jews over whether or not Jesus of Nazareth was "the Christ," that is, the Messiah. Claudius, being unaware of the nature of the conflict between these two groups, sought to resolve the matter by expelling all Jews from

---

261. Mounce, *Pastoral Epistles*, 599.

Rome.²⁶² Compliance with the edict must have been short-lived, for Paul's Letter to the Romans (AD 56) presupposes a significant number of Jewish Christians present in that church at that time.²⁶³

While in Corinth Paul found lodging with Aquila and Priscilla (Acts 18:3). The three worked at their common trade, for they were all tentmakers (or perhaps leatherworkers).²⁶⁴

From Corinth the couple traveled with Paul to Ephesus (AD 51), where they remained while he continued on to Jerusalem (Acts 18:18–21). While in Ephesus the couple tutored Apollos in a more accurate understanding of the Christian message, after which he went to Corinth and ministered there (Acts 18:24–28).

At the time of the writing of 1 Corinthians Paul sends greetings from the two of them and from the church that meets in their house to the church at Corinth (16:19). The writing of this letter from Ephesus in about AD 54 would mean that they had remained in that city for a few years.²⁶⁵ When writing to the church at Rome in AD 56 Paul sends greetings to them and to the church that meets in their house (Rom 16:3–5); this would indicate that the expulsion of Jews from the city by Claudius was no longer being enforced, so that they could return to the capital city. Aquila and Priscilla must have been a couple of some means if they could move about as they did and were able to have their house used as a meeting place for the church (in not one but two different cities).²⁶⁶

The fact that Priscilla is named before her husband more often than the other way around has given rise to various theories as to why this should be so. However, these are nothing more than guesses, and we should draw no conclusions from them, such as any that would contradict biblical teaching on the respective roles of men and women in Christ's church²⁶⁷ (refer to the essay "The Pastoral Ministry According to the Pastoral Letters" elsewhere in this commentary).

τὸν Ὀνησιφόρου οἶκον—Some point to the reference to the "household" of Onesiphorus as evidence that he had died and therefore conclude

---

262. Bruce, *New Testament History*, 297–99.
263. Middendorf, *Romans 1—8*, 7–14.
264. BDAG 928–29.
265. Lockwood, *1 Corinthians*, 15, prefers AD 55 for the writing of 1 Corinthians but notes that some opt for 54. Barrett, *First Corinthians*, 5, puts the letter in 54 or possibly late 53.
266. See further Lockwood, *1 Corinthians*, 628.
267. Knight, *Pastoral Epistles*, 475–76.

that 2 Tim 1:18 ("May the Lord grant him to find mercy from the Lord on that day") amounts to prayer for the dead.[268] However, in 1 Cor 1:16 Paul speaks about a man's household while that individual is still alive, as demonstrated by 1 Cor 16:17. Moreover, the apostle references what he himself will experience on "that day" (2 Tim 4:8), even though he obviously is still alive.[269]

4:20 Ἔραστος ἔμεινεν ἐν Κορίνθῳ—The apostle states that this Erastus remained in Corinth. In his Letter to the Romans, written from Corinth, he sends greetings from an Erastus, who is identified as the city treasurer (Rom 16:23). Near the end of his third missionary journey Paul sent to Macedonia Timothy and Erastus; they are identified as two of his helpers (Acts 19:22). As Erastus does not appear to be a very common name in that part of the NT world, it is possible that the same person is referred to in all three of these passages. A paving stone from ancient Corinth that bears the inscription "Erastus in return for his aedileship laid [the pavement] at his own expense" may also speak of this individual.[270]

Τρόφιμον δὲ ἀπέλιπον ἐν Μιλήτῳ ἀσθενοῦντα—Trophimus is named as one of those who accompanied Paul to bring the gift he had collected to the church in Jerusalem (Acts 20:1–6). The book of Acts reports that the apostle had been seen with Trophimus in Jerusalem, and that this had led to the bogus accusation that he had brought this gentile into the inner courts of the temple (21:29). It seems likely that this is the man that is mentioned here. In any discussion about gifts of miraculous healing, which Paul certainly recognized (1 Cor 12:9, 28, 30), it should be noted that the apostle, who had himself performed miracles,[271] did not (could not?) on this occasion heal his fellow Christian.

4:21 Σπούδασον πρὸ χειμῶνος ἐλθεῖν—In some contexts σπούδασον can mean "be eager";[272] here the literal meaning "hurry" is more appropriate. Travel during the winter in the Mediterranean world, especially by sea, was difficult, even dangerous,[273] as Paul himself had personally experienced (Acts 27:9–44). The time needed for first-century travel and mail delivery would suggest that this letter was intended to arrive by

---

268. So argued by Kelly, *Pastoral Epistles*, 169–71.
269. Knight, *Pastoral Epistles*, 386.
270. *DNTB* 98–99, 229; Knight, *Pastoral Epistles*, 476.
271. Acts 14:3, 8–10; 16:16–18; 19:11–12; 20:9–12; 28:7–10.
272. BDAG 939.
273. Kelly, *Pastoral Epistles*, 222; Guthrie, *Pastoral Epistles*, 190.

early autumn, which would require it to have been written and sent in the summer or even the spring.²⁷⁴

Ἀσπάζεταί σε Εὔβουλος καὶ Πούδης καὶ Λίνος καὶ Κλαυδία καὶ οἱ ἀδελφοὶ πάντες—Eubulus is the subject of the singular verb ἀσπάζεται; Pudens, Linus, Claudia, and "all the brothers" are the subjects of an implied plural form of the same verb. We know nothing further about any of these individuals. While all had deserted the apostle at his first defense (4:16), it appears that at least a bit of time has passed since then. Of his past associates only Luke is now with him (4:11). The individuals mentioned here are apparently new associates from whom he can send these greetings.²⁷⁵

4:22 Ὁ κύριος μετὰ τοῦ πνεύματός σου—Paul uses a similar blessing ("with your spirit") in his Letters to the Galatians (6:18), to the Philippians (4:23), and to Philemon (25). Here "your" is singular; in the others—including Philemon—it is plural.

ἡ χάρις μεθ' ὑμῶν—As also in 1 Timothy (6:21) and Titus (3:15), the Greek for "you" in the closing of the letter is in the plural (in contemporary English we would have to say "with all of you"). Like the other two Pastoral Letters this one was intended for the entire church; it would be read aloud in worship alongside the books of the Hebrew Scriptures, as the apostle had explicitly directed to be done with some of his other letters (1 Thess 5:27; Col 4:16).

COMMENTARY

Paul's Situation

The apostle is aware that his current imprisonment will end with his execution (4:6–8). The doxology that immediately precedes these verses serves as something of a conclusion, so that the present verses are a sort of epilogue. He has a few very personal matters to tend to before he puts down his pen.²⁷⁶

---

274. Towner, *Letters*, 654.
275. Towner, *Letters*, 620.
276. It is well known that Paul, like many in NT times, made use of an amanuensis (a scribe) in writing his letters (Rom 16:22). But he also would take up the pen himself and write a few concluding lines as a mark of authenticity (Gal 6:11; 2 Thess 3:17).

The Purpose of Greetings

The concluding greetings in the Pauline Letters were more than a mere formality or a customary courtesy. This can be seen most clearly in Paul's Letters to the Romans and to the Colossians.

Romans (15:14—16:27) and Colossians (4:7–18) contain the most extensive lists of greetings in the Pauline corpus. These are also the two letters written by the apostle to congregations he had never visited and therefore whose members, by and large, he did not know personally (Rom 1:10–13; 15:22; Col 2:1).

That being the case, the greetings sent from those who are with Paul and to those among the recipients of a given letter that were personally known to him serve to recognize and to further the unity that exists between fellow members of the body of Christ. More than simply saying "hello," these are an epistolary way of Christians showing love to one another, much as they might have done had they been able to see one another face to face.[277]

Previously the apostle had stated that save for Luke he had been left all alone (4:10–11). Here he sends greetings from "Eubulus . . . Pudens, Linus, Claudia, and all the brothers." There is no contradiction here. Luke was the only member of Paul's missionary group who was still with him. "Eubulus . . . Pudens, Linus, Claudia, and all the brothers" are members of the local Christian community.[278]

Final Blessings

Invariably the apostle begins his letters with a word of grace for his addressees.[279] Just as invariably he concludes each of his epistles with a blessing of grace,[280] so that this term serves as a sort of *inclusio* for each of his missives. He gives grace the first and the last word in each of his letters, for in a word grace encapsulates the entirety of the Christian message (see the entry "Grace" in the Extended Notes).

---

277. Rom 16:16; 1 Cor 16:20; 2 Cor 13:12; 1 Thess 5:26; see also 1 Pet 5:14.

278. Marshall, *Pastoral Epistles*, 827.

279. Rom 1:7; 1 Cor 1:3; 2 Cor 1:2; Gal 1:3; Eph 1:2; Phil 1:2; Col 1:2; 1 Thess 1:1; 2 Thess 1:2; 1 Tim 1:2; 2 Tim 1:2; Titus 1:4; Phlm 3.

280. Rom 16:20; 1 Cor 16:23; 2 Cor 13:14; Gal 6:18; Eph 6:24; Phil 4:23; Col 4:18; 1 Thess 5:28; 2 Thess 3:18; 1 Tim 6:21; 2 Tim 4:22; Titus 3:15; Phlm 25.

Grace and Life

The present letter concludes with a twofold blessing. First of all, Paul extends a blessing from the Lord (Jesus Christ) upon Timothy. As a pastor in the church Timothy has great responsibilities, challenges, burdens, opportunities, and joys. To meet them all requires the empowering presence of the Lord. Therefore, here the apostle offers such a blessing to his younger fellow worker. Such apostolic words of blessing are more than just a pious wish. As is always the case with the word of God, these words of blessing have the power to actually impart the benefits that they proclaim.

As noted above, the apostle's concluding blessing of grace goes out to more than just Timothy. As Timothy was entrusted not only with his own ministry but also with equipping and sending out others to be pastors,[281] there may well have been a number of churches who would have been among the addressees of this letter, which would have been read aloud to the congregations assembled for worship. This points to the authoritative status of this letter as being on a par with the Scriptures of the Hebrew canon.[282] It therefore demonstrates that this letter, like the other two Pastoral Epistles, speaks to God's people of all generations from the time of its composition until the parousia.

This is almost certainly the last thing we have from the pen of Paul. We may therefore think of it as his last will and testament to the church. Hence, all Christians should take it to heart, even as we ought do so with the other Pastorals and indeed all the Scriptures, given by inspiration of God (2 Tim 3:16–17).

---

281. Paul directed Timothy to "instruct certain people" (1 Tim 1:3); he was given responsibility for those who might "aspire to the office of overseer" (1 Tim 3:1); he was not to "accept an accusation against an elder, except on the basis of two or three witnesses" (1 Tim 5:19); he was instructed to "rebuke those sinning before all" (1 Tim 5:20, referring to disciplining those who were pastors; see the textual notes on that verse); he was told, "Do not be hasty in laying hands on anyone, lest you have fellowship in the sins of others" (1 Tim 5:22).

282. See the section "The Spirit Expressly Says" in the commentary on 1 Tim 4:1–5.

ESSAYS

Our Great God and Savior

The Christology of the Pastoral Letters

The Pastoral Letters have been given that designation because of the detailed exposition they give on the ministry of the church, for which they are well known. What is perhaps not as well known is that the letters are rich in their presentation of the person and work of Christ.[1] What follows is a study of the great Christological themes of the Pastoral Letters.

THE PERSON OF CHRIST

A distinctive feature of Pauline Christology is Paul's use of "Christ Jesus" as a name for our Lord. The expression ὁ Χριστός occurs in the New Testament as the Greek equivalent of the Hebrew הַמָּשִׁיחַ and Aramaic מְשִׁיחָא, "the Messiah," the name the Jewish people of the first century were using to refer to the savior promised from the line of David (2 Sam 7:1–17; 1 Chr 17:1–15); in this way the New Testament proclaimed Jesus to be that promised Messiah. In time the title ὁ Χριστός morphed into a name for Jesus, so that the authors of the New Testament might refer to him as "Jesus Christ" or simply as "Christ." The apostle also uses these names for our Lord. However, in addition to these he also identifies him as "Christ Jesus," and he is the only biblical author to do so.[2]

---

1. In introducing his own sketch of the soteriology and Christology of these letters (*Letters*, 59–68) Towner notes that their Christology/soteriology comprises the heart and soul of their theology (*Letters*, 59–60).

2. The only "exception" to this is found in Acts 24:24, but since this reports Paul's own testimony, it is not really an exception. The use of "Christ Jesus" is found in Rom 1:1; 2:16; 3:24; 6:3, 11, 13; 8:1, 2, 34, 39; 15:5, 16, 17; 16:3; 1 Cor 1:1, 2, 4, 30; 4:15; 15:31; 16:24; 2 Cor 1:1; Gal 2:4, 16 (2x); 3:14, 26, 28; 4:14; 5:6, 24; Eph 1:1 (2x); 2:6, 7,

Grace and Life

Like other New Testament authors, and as he does in his other letters, in the Pastorals Paul refers to Jesus as "Lord" (κύριος; 1 Tim 1:2; 2 Tim 1:2). As this Greek word served in the Septuagint as the rendering of the Hebrew name of God (יהוה), identifying Jesus as "Lord" was a way of designating him as the one true God revealed in the Hebrew Scriptures.[3]

In the New Testament the vocable "God" (θεός) is usually reserved for God the Father.[4] However, the Pastoral Letters contain two of the rare instances in the New Testament where that term is applied to Jesus Christ.

In the Letter to Titus (2:13) Paul speaks of "our great God and savior Jesus Christ" (τοῦ μεγάλου θεοῦ καὶ σωτῆρος ἡμῶν Ἰησοῦ Χριστοῦ). The syntax of the sentence argues for this translation, as in the New Testament in the construction article-substantive-*kai*-substantive, when neither substantive is impersonal, plural, nor a proper name, the two substantives are equivalent.[5] Furthermore, the context demonstrates that this is the correct rendering, as it would be meaningless to speak of the appearance of "the great God" as distinct from the appearing of "our savior Jesus Christ." Thus, Titus 2:13 stands as one of the strongest attestations in all of the Scripture to the deity of Jesus of Nazareth.

Furthermore, a comparison of 1 Tim 1:17 with 6:15 of the same letter points in the same direction. The similarity of the language of the passages indicates that these are references to one and the same individual. As verse 14 of chapter 6 makes it plain that verse 15 of that chapter must be a description of Christ, this would point to the person of 1:17, who is identified as "the only God," being Christ as well. Thus, 1 Tim 1:17 joins Titus 2:13 as an explicit identification of Jesus Christ as God.

This provides further insight into the ascription of 1 Tim 6:15, where the apostle identifies Jesus Christ as "the blessed and only sovereign, the king of those who are having kingship and lord of those who are having lordship." While such lofty language could theoretically be used of a king or some other exalted being, in the context of the entirety of the Pastorals this can be understood only in the sense that Christ is worthy of all of these appellations precisely because he is the one and only true God.

10, 13, 20; 3:1, 6, 11, 21; Phil 1:1 (2x), 8, 26; 2:5; 3:3, 8, 12, 14; 4:7, 19, 21; Col 1:1, 4; 2:6; 4:12; 1 Thess 2:14; 5:18; 1 Tim 1:1 (2x), 2, 12, 14, 15; 2:5; 3:13; 4:6; 5:21; 6:13; 2 Tim 1:1 (2x), 2, 9, 10, 13; 2:1, 3, 10; 3:12, 15; 4:1; Titus 1:4; Phlm 1, 9, 23.

3. BDAG 577 (under II. 2 b, α) and 577–78 (under II. 2 b, γ; ב, א, and ג).

4. 1 Tim 1:1; 2 Tim 1:1; Titus 1:1.

5. This is known as the Granville Sharp Rule; Wallace, *Greek Grammar*, 270–77.

In 2 Timothy Paul speaks of God's plan of salvation being given in Christ Jesus "before eternal times," and that it has now been "made known through the appearing of . . . Christ Jesus" (1:9–10). This language clearly indicates that Christ has existed from eternity, a statement that can be made of no one other than God himself.[6]

In all these ways the apostle sets forth the true deity of Jesus Christ. Nevertheless, the Pastorals also profess Christ's true humanity. Paul refers to Christ Jesus as a "man" (1 Tim 2:5). He further states of him that he is "of the offspring of David" (2 Tim 2:8). Thus, by ascribing both deity and humanity to Jesus Christ the Pastorals contribute to the Bible's testimony to the incarnation and to the two natures in the one person of Christ.[7]

The reference to Jesus being "of the offspring of David" has further significance. The Lord God had promised to David that there would be a descendant of his who would have an eternal rule (2 Sam 7:1–17; 1 Chr 17:1–15), a promise of one who came to be known as the Messiah, a promise that was fulfilled in the life and ministry of Jesus (Luke 1:31–33). With the simple statement that Christ was "of the offspring of David" the apostle also sets forth that central biblical truth.

This testimony about the identity of Christ helps to inform our understanding of certain other statements from Paul regarding our Lord. The apostle asserts that he is "imperishable" (1 Tim 1:17) and is "the only one who has immortality" (1 Tim 6:16). While "imperishable" (ἀφθάρτῳ) and "immortality" (ἀθανασίαν) are similar, there is a slight difference in meaning between not being subject to corruption and not being subject to death. That Paul ascribes both of these characteristics to the "man Christ Jesus" who is "the only God" defines just what they mean in this context. The Christ who is imperishable and has immortality is the one who died (1 Tim 2:6; Titus 2:14) but who is now risen from the dead (2 Tim 2:8; 1 Tim 3:16). He did die, but as the risen one he is no longer subject to death; moreover, he is the only source of the resurrection for others (1 Tim 6:15; 2 Tim 1:18).

The apostle also indicates that Christ is unseen (ἀοράτῳ; 1 Tim 1:17) and that he is not able to be seen (1 Tim 6:16). As a man and as one risen from the dead, Christ could certainly be seen (e.g., Luke 24:39). But as the one taken up in glory (1 Tim 3:16) he is not at present able to be seen.

---

6. As also noted by Marshall, *Pastoral Epistles*, 707.

7. On these topics the reader is referred to Nafzger et al., *Confessing the Gospel*, 343–418.

Nevertheless, he will be seen at his "appearing" (1 Tim 6:14), when he appears again at the last day (1 Tim 6:15; 2 Tim 1:18; 4:1).

It is in light of all this that we must understand Paul's assertion that Christ "dwells in unapproachable light" (1 Tim 6:16). Jesus was "taken up in glory" (1 Tim 3:16) at his ascension. Because he is the holy one dwelling in unapproachable light, sinful humans are not able to draw near to him. Instead, it is only through his redemptive work that we will be received into his heavenly kingdom.[8]

THE WORK OF CHRIST

The richness of the Pastoral Letters' portrait of the person of Christ is matched by an equally extravagant presentation of the work of Christ. The letters touch on all the major creedal affirmations concerning our Lord's work and provide a number of edifying details about that work.

In these letters the apostle makes a number of references to the incarnation. He speaks of Christ coming into the world (1 Tim 1:15), and he uses words like "manifested" and "appeared" to point to the time of the eternal Christ taking on human flesh.[9]

The chief work of Christ proclaimed by Paul (and by the rest of the New Testament) is that of redemption/salvation. In the Pastoral Letters the apostle identifies Jesus as the "savior" (2 Tim 1:10; Titus 1:4; 2:13), and he speaks of the salvation that is accomplished through his work (2 Tim 2:10; Titus 2:11). When Paul writes that God our savior saved us (Titus 3:4), this also points to the work of Christ, for when the apostle states that God saved us "when the goodness and love for mankind of God our savior appeared," this denotes the incarnation and so designates the subsequent work of Christ as the way in which God "saved us."

The Pastorals also include specific references to the cross of Christ. When Paul refers to Christ as one "who gave himself as a ransom for all" (1 Tim 2:6), the use of a verb in the aorist tense, the tense that can refer to one-time action in the past,[10] points to the death of our Lord, and the word "ransom" indicates that this death was the sufficient price paid to acquire

---

8. 1 Tim 6:14–15; 2 Tim 1:18; 4:1, 8, 18; Titus 2:13.

9. Manifested (ἐφανερώθη, φανερωθεῖσαν, ἐφανέρωσαν): 1 Tim 3:16; 2 Tim 1:10; Titus 1:3; appeared (ἐπιφάνειαν, ἐπεφάνη): Titus 2:13; 3:4.

10. BDF 166 [§ 318 (1)].

release for all from sin and its punishment.[11] The apostle asserts the same truth in his Letter to Titus (2:14), when he writes that Christ "gave himself for us, in order that he might redeem us from all lawlessness."

The Pastoral Letters speak of the resurrection of Christ as well as of his death. In the creedal-like section of his Second Letter to Timothy (2:8–13) Paul refers to Jesus Christ as "risen from the dead" (2:8). In a similar section of 1 Timothy, when he speaks of Christ as having been "vindicated in the spirit" (3:16), his words denote our Lord's resurrection.[12] In the same verse, his statement that Christ was "seen by angels" most likely refers, at least in part, to the presence of angels at the empty tomb of the risen Lord.[13]

In the Pastorals, in order to capture some of the richness of the saving work of Christ, the apostle uses a number of different concepts to describe the results of our Lord's work. He states that Christ "abolished death and brought to light life and incorruption" (2 Tim 1:10). He notes that Christ gave himself for us to "redeem us from all lawlessness" and to "purify for himself a chosen people" (Titus 2:14). The familiar (and largely distinctively Pauline) concept of justification is also attested in the Pastorals, for Paul states that the work of Christ means that we have been "justified through his grace" (Titus 3:7).[14]

In the Pastoral Letters Paul refers to other events from the earthly life of Jesus. We have noted above that when he states that our Lord was "seen by angels" (1 Tim 3:16), this may be a reference to his resurrection; it could just as well also have to do with his ascension into heaven (Acts 1:10–11). Certainly, the statement later in that same verse that Jesus was "taken up in glory" would speak of the ascension of our Lord. In speaking of the work of salvation the apostle states that there is "one mediator between God and mankind, the man Christ Jesus" (1 Tim 2:5). That Christ is the one mediator between God and mankind may well point to the truth that the risen Lord intercedes for us before God (Rom 8:34).[15] As the words in 1 Timothy that immediately follow speak

---

11. Rom 3:24–25; Eph 1:7; see further the entry "Redeem, Redemption/Ransom" in the Extended Notes.

12. See further the commentary on that verse.

13. Matt 28:2–7; Mark 16:5–7; Luke 24:4–7; John 20:12–13. See further the commentary on that verse.

14. See further the sections "Justification/Righteousness" and "Redeem, Redemption/Ransom" in the Extended Notes.

15. "For he still pleads even now as man for my salvation. He continues to wear the body which he assumed, until he makes me divine by the power of his incarnation;

of Jesus giving himself as a ransom for all (2:6), the designation of our Lord as mediator may denote him as the one who was made sin in our place, that we might become righteous before God (2 Cor 5:21). The identification of the man Christ Jesus as the "one" mediator between God and mankind is emphatic, as the heresy afflicting Timothy's churches envisioned many such mediators.[16]

The Pastorals contain a number of references to Christ's coming again at the last day. The last day itself is referred to as his own "right time" (καιροῖς ἰδίοις, 1 Tim 6:15) and "that day" (2 Tim 1:18; 4:8). Paul speaks of Christ's second coming as his "appearing" (ἐπιφάνεια).[17] Christ's future coming gives us mercy (2 Tim 1:18) and hope (Titus 2:13) and is the way to his heavenly kingdom (2 Tim 4:1, 18).

In the Pastorals the apostle's chief focus in speaking of Christ's parousia consists of the blessings of eternal life. Nevertheless, he also refers to the Lord's coming in judgment. He identifies Christ as the one "who is about to judge the living and the dead" (2 Tim 4:1). Furthermore, he states of one who had done great harm to him that "the Lord will give back to him according to his works" (2 Tim 4:14).

Encompassing all of this is the biblical teaching regarding God's eternal plan of salvation being accomplished by Christ. In the Pastoral Letters Paul speaks of God's gracious plan of salvation being made "before eternal times" (2 Tim 1:9). He adds that the fulfillment of this plan was accomplished "through the appearing of our savior Christ Jesus, who abolished death and brought to light life and incorruption through the gospel" (2 Tim 1:10). When elsewhere he refers to the second coming of Christ taking place at "the right time" (1 Tim 6:15), this indicates that the entirety of God's eternal plan was fulfilled at just the right time.

One of the challenges to Timothy—and therefore also to those in his care and to all Christians everywhere—is that of remaining faithful until the coming of the Lord (1 Tim 6:14). In connection with that the apostle directs Timothy's attention to the good confession that Jesus gave before Pontius Pilate (6:13). Jesus said little before Pilate, but what he said was the truth and ultimately helped lead to his death on the cross.[18] The

---

although he is no longer known after the flesh—the same as ours, except for sin." Gregory of Nazianzus, *Theological Orations* 4.30.14 (LCC 3:187).

16. Kelly, *Pastoral Epistles*, 63; see further "The Nature of the Heresy" in the Introduction to the Pastoral Letters.

17. 1 Tim 6:14; 2 Tim 4:1, 8; Titus 2:13.

18. See further the textual notes and commentary on 1 Tim 6:13.

"good confession" of Christ led to our salvation; that in turn will motivate and empower us to make the good confession of faith in Christ uninterruptedly until the end, as we need to do (see below).

CHRIST AND THE CHURCH'S MISSION AND MINISTRY

The person and work of Christ is at the center of life, the universe, and everything. Thus, it is to be expected that Christ would also be at the center of the church's mission and ministry.

Paul describes Christianity's message as "the witness [μαρτύριον] of our Lord [Jesus Christ]" (2 Tim 1:8). He also states that Christ "gave himself... as a testimony [μαρτύριον] at the right time" (1 Tim 2:6). The heart and soul of the witness/testimony that is to be proclaimed is Christ and his redemptive work.

Furthermore, Christ himself works through that witness. The apostle asserts that Christ "abolished death and brought to light life and incorruption through the gospel" (2 Tim 1:10). He further states that God "saved us... through the washing of rebirth and of renewal of the Holy Spirit whom he poured out on us richly through Jesus Christ our savior" (Titus 3:5–6). The ministry of word and sacrament does not simply communicate *about* Christ and his work; through this ministry God—Father, Son, and Holy Spirit—actually *gives* his gift of eternal, incorruptible salvation.

Related to this is Paul's statement concerning "the sound words of our Lord Jesus Christ and to the teaching that is in accord with godliness" (1 Tim 6:3). The apostle understood that his teaching—and that of Christ's entire church—was not his own. Ultimately it came—by way of inspiration (2 Tim 3:15–16)—from the Lord of the church.[19]

Christ works through his word; he does this also by appointing and empowering those who will speak his word. When Paul identifies himself

---

19. Paul indicates the same thing in other ways. As an apostle he was one sent by Christ with authority, for through apostles such as Paul the Lord communicated his authoritative and saving word to the church and to the world; see the entry "Apostle" in the Extended Notes. When he instructed his addressees to "read" the letters he had sent to them (1 Thess 5:27; Col 4:16), he was indicating that what he wrote was to be regarded on the same level as the Hebrew Scriptures, which believers had for centuries been reading in their public worship services (see Deterding, *Colossians*, 192–94). In his First Letter to Timothy (4:1) he indicates that what he is writing is what "the Spirit expressly says" (4:1).

as apostle of Christ Jesus (or of Jesus Christ),[20] he indicates that Christ has put him in this office of ministry and that he himself works through Paul's apostolic ministry. This can be seen in 1 Tim 1:12, where he states that Christ Jesus both appointed him for ministry and empowered him for that service. In a similar way the apostle tells Timothy that by attending faithfully to his ministry he too will be a good minister of Christ Jesus (1 Tim 4:6) and that by paying attention to and continuing in the teaching of the word of God he would save himself and his hearers (1 Tim 4:16).

Paul's statement to Timothy that "the Lord stood by me and strengthened me, in order that through me the kerygma might be fulfilled, and all the gentiles might hear [it]" (2 Tim 4:17) points to a particular aspect of how this apostle's ministry was used by Christ. Jesus had promised that his gospel would come to all the world (Matt 24:14; Mark 13:10). In his letters Paul notes that through his ministry the gospel of Christ was coming to all.[21] In the book of Acts it is Paul's bold and unhindered proclamation of Christ in Rome, the center of the Mediterranean world, for two whole years that brings to a conclusion the account of this volume that Christ's followers would be his witnesses not just "in Jerusalem" [that is, to the Jews], and not just "in all Judea and Samaria" [that is, to the Samaritans, those people who might be considered half-Jewish], but also "to the end of the earth" [that is, to the gentiles].

In the book of Acts Paul is preeminently the apostle to the gentiles, the very thing he names himself in his Letter to the Romans (11:13; see also Gal 2:9). The latter portion of the book of Acts, from chapter 13 to the end of the book, is essentially the acts of one apostle, Paul. It is largely through his ministry that the gospel comes to the gentiles.

The apostle's statement in 2 Tim 4:17, "the Lord stood by me and strengthened me, in order that through me the kerygma might be fulfilled, and all the gentiles might hear [it]," fits right in with the presentation of him in the book of Acts. It is chiefly through him that the gospel comes to the end of the earth [to the gentiles]. It is largely through him that the church came to the realization that Christ's gospel is for all—gentiles as well as for his own people, the Jews.[22]

---

20. 1 Tim 1:1; 2 Tim 1:1; Titus 1:1.

21. Rom 15:18–19; Col 1:6, 23, 25.

22. See further the section "All the Gentiles Might Hear the Kerygma" in the commentary on 2 Tim 4:9–18.

CHRIST AS THE OBJECT OF FAITH

It should perhaps be self-evident that the apostle would regard Christ to be the object of his faith—and of the faith of all other believers. Self-evident or not, this is a truth that he states explicitly in a number of places in his Letters to Timothy.

In his hymn of Christ in 1 Timothy (3:16) Paul states not only that Jesus was "proclaimed among the nations" but also that he was "believed on in the world." Elsewhere, speaking of his own personal faith, he points to Christ Jesus as the one "in whom I have believed" (2 Tim 1:12 in light of 1:9–10). He also speaks of saving faith in Christ when he refers to those who "call upon the Lord from a pure heart" (2 Tim 2:22) and to "those who have loved his appearing" (2 Tim 4:8).

The apostle also speaks of the source of such faith. When he writes of the holy Scriptures that they are "able to make you wise unto salvation through faith, which is in Christ Jesus," he indicates that through the word of God individuals are brought to saving faith in Jesus Christ.

Related to this is Paul's statement that Christ "is able to guard my deposit until that day" (2 Tim 1:12). The word of God not only initially works faith within the believer. Through that same word God also works with the same power to preserve one in his saving faith until the end.

CHRIST AND THE LIFE TO COME

The Pastoral Letters make up a relatively small portion of the Pauline corpus—and of the Scriptures. Nevertheless, they are rich in their presentation of the Christian's future salvation.

Simply stated, the outcome of saving faith in Christ is the gift of eternal life. In the Pastorals Paul refers to eternal life (1 Tim 1:16; Titus 3:7) and eternal glory (2 Tim 2:10).

The apostle uses other language to describe the believer's future salvation. He speaks of it as "the crown of righteousness" (2 Tim 4:8), for in the resurrection the Christian will be perfectly righteous before God. When he indicates that the result of Christ's justifying work is that we become "heirs" of eternal life (Titus 3:7), this presents eternal salvation as an inheritance (of the most magnificent kind). At almost the very end of his Second Letter to Timothy he states that the Lord will save him "for his heavenly kingdom"; that kind of language is dear to the heart of every believer.

Christ's coming in glory at the last day is the time when he will bestow his eternal salvation on his faithful. In his Second Letter to Timothy Paul refers to the Lord Jesus as "the righteous judge" (4:8), and he twice identifies the time of his coming as "that day" (1:12, 18). When he speaks of Christ's "appearing" (2 Tim 4:8; Titus 2:13), this is another reference to the last day. Christ will appear, and at that time he will give his believers "the crown of righteousness," for to speak of "those who have loved his appearing" (2 Tim 4:8) is another way of identifying those who have put their faith in him.

This future salvation also blesses our present existence. Our future salvation makes our present life one of hope, hope meaning that the goodness of our future gives us something good to look forward to, however dismal our present circumstances might be. In these letters Paul speaks of the sure and certain hope that we have because of Jesus Christ.[23]

In the salutation of his Second Letter to Timothy the apostle refers to "the promise of life which is in Christ Jesus" (1:1). This also is language about the future—and about hope. We have the promise of life, and because this is a promise that comes from him who is "risen from the dead" (2:8), it is a promise that is certain to be fulfilled.

THE REVELATION OF THE MYSTERY

The term "mystery" (μυστήριον) is a significant kerygmatic vocable in the New Testament and one which is used by Paul far more often than by any other New Testament author.[24] By definition a mystery is something hidden; it may be made known through revelation (ἀποκάλυψις).

The apostle uses μυστήριον with reference to God's plan of salvation.[25] This plan is a mystery, because although present during Old Testament times, it was hidden in shadows and types (Col 2:17). Conversely, the mystery has been revealed or made known (ἐφανερώθη) in the New Testament era (the "now" of Col 1:26).[26] The plan itself predates the Old Testament period, for its origin is in eternity ("ages" and "generations") (Col 1:26; see also Rom 16:25–26; 1 Cor 2:7; Eph 3:9).

---

23. 1 Tim 1:1; 4:10; 5:5; 6:17; Titus 1:2; 2:13; 3:7.

24. See Rom 11:25; 16:25–26; 1 Cor 2:7; 4:1; Eph 1:9; 3:3, 4, 9; 6:19; Col 1:26–27; 2:3; 4:3. See also the entry "Mystery" in the Extended Notes.

25. Rom 11:25; 1 Cor 2:7; Eph 1:9; 1 Tim 3:9.

26. See also Rom 16:25–26; 1 Cor 2:7; Eph 1:9; 3:3–6, 9.

Christ himself is the μυστήριον (Col 1:27; 2:2), so that his coming is the revelation of this mystery. This revelation of Christ as savior also for the gentiles (see also Rom 16:26; Eph 3:6) marks another characteristic of the New Testament era; much of the story of Jesus' ministry and of the history of the earliest church was bound up with making known that Christ had come for all and not only for the chosen people of Old Testament times.

This mystery is revealed by the Holy Spirit (Eph 3:5) through both the written word (Rom 16:26) and the oral proclamation of the word.[27] For this reason Paul refers to proclaimers of the gospel as stewards of the mysteries (1 Cor 4:1), for, as he says, the μυστήριον is given them to proclaim (Eph 3:3–4, 6, 8–9; Col 1:28). The μυστήριον is proclaimed to all (Rom 16:26; Eph 3:8–9; 1 Tim 3:16); in fact, its scope involves all of creation (Eph 3:10).

The mystery is known through faith (Rom 16:26; 1 Tim 3:9, 16). Among all nations it is those of saving faith who know the riches of the glory of this mystery, for it was God's desire (Col 1:27), that is, his eternal plan of salvation (οἰκονομία) that this be experienced through saving faith (Eph 3:2, 9).

The apostle's use of this term in 1 Timothy reflects its usage in the rest of his letters. In the Christ hymn of 3:16 ("the mystery of godliness") all six verbs refer to Christ. Mention is made of his being proclaimed, of his being received through faith, and of the mystery being made known to the nations/gentiles.

This use of the term "mystery" in 1 Tim 3:16 to encapsulate the entire Christian message gives light to an earlier passage in the chapter. A requirement for those who would hold the office of "deacon" is that they hold the "mystery of the faith" with a pure conscience (3:9). This designates genuine faith in the Christ-centered kerygma as a requirement for serving in this capacity.

All of this serves to shed light on Paul's statement to Timothy: "Consider what I say, for the Lord will give you understanding in all things" (2 Tim 2:7). As an apostle Paul was being used by Christ to communicate his authoritative, saving word to the church and to the world; through this word the Lord would reveal the mystery of salvation. Timothy would "understand" this (and all the truths of God's word) through "considering" the authoritative, apostolic word, such as was being communicated by Paul through this letter.

---

27. Note that "the mystery" in Col 1:26 is in apposition to "the word of God" in 1:25; see also Col 4:3; Rom 16:25; 1 Cor 2:7; 4:1; Eph 3:3, 6, 8–9; 6:19.

THE FAITHFULNESS OF CHRIST

Of particular note in these letters is an emphasis on the faithfulness of Christ. His faithfulness is a source of reassurance to God's people.

The apostle's statement that "the grace of our Lord was more than abundant with faithfulness and love in Christ Jesus" (1 Tim 1:14) places faithfulness alongside grace and love as benevolent gifts from God. That those "in Christ Jesus" have his faithfulness means that his grace toward them and love for them will never fail.

Moreover, he is faithful to us in spite of any lack of faithfulness on our part. In one of the "trustworthy" sayings of these letters Paul assures all his readers, "If we are faithless, he remains faithful, for he is not able to deny himself" (2 Tim 2:13).

The faithfulness of Christ extends to his provision for the ministry of those who labor in his word. When the apostle writes of Christ that "he is able to guard my deposit until that day" (2 Tim 1:12), this indicates that Christ is watching over Paul and his ministry in the word,[28] and that he will do so until that ministry reaches its conclusion.

This enriches our understanding of the penultimate blessing of 2 Timothy. Before concluding with the benediction "grace be with you [plural]" the apostle writes, "The Lord be with your [singular] spirit." The faithful Lord Jesus Christ will watch over Timothy, both as a believer and as a minister of his word.

CHRIST AND THE BELIEVER'S LIFE OF SANCTIFICATION

The Christian's response to God's gift of salvation apart from any good works that he has done is a life of good works. Paul's Letter to Titus proclaims that the Christ who redeems us without good works empowers us to respond to that redemption with a life of good works.

Titus 2:11–12 might be rendered, "For the grace of God appeared . . . schooling us, in order that . . . we might live sensibly, righteously, and reverently in this age." The grace of God that appeared with the incarnation and birth of Christ "schools" us; it "educates" us, so that we are able to do what we otherwise could not do: live a righteous life.

---

28. The word "deposit" (παραθήκην) here includes Paul's call to ministry; see 1 Tim 6:20; 2 Tim 1:12, 14; 2:2.

A bit later in the same portion of that letter the apostle adds to our understanding of the entire contribution that the Lord Christ makes to our sanctified living. He writes, "Jesus Christ . . . gave himself for us, in order that he might . . . purify for himself a chosen people, who are zealous for good works" (Titus 2:14). Beyond teaching us how to live, beyond even motivating us to live in a godly way, Christ our savior *enables* us to live in that way. His redemption purifies us, so that we are able to be and to do what we could not be or do without him; we are able to perform good works; in fact, he makes us zealous for good works.

THE CHRISTIAN'S EXISTENCE "IN CHRIST"

See further the entry "In Christ" in the Extended Notes.

A characteristic teaching of the apostle Paul has to do with what it means to be "in Christ." This phrase does not have a merely instrumental meaning, as though the preposition ἐν meant "by" (Eph 2:15);[29] rather, the phrase describes a harmonious relationship with Jesus Christ. God himself creates this relationship (1 Cor 1:30) through baptism (Gal 3:26–27; Rom 6:3, 11) and the gospel (1 Cor 4:15, 17; Eph 1:13; 3:6). This relationship is one of faith directed to Jesus Christ (Gal 3:14, 26; 5:6; Col 2:7). Hence, we are "in Christ" through faith—nevertheless, the expression "in Christ" never designates the object of faith; see further below.

Those who are "in Christ" become partakers of everything that he has accomplished by his redemptive work (1 Cor 1:5, 7; Eph 1:3). Since the relationship of being "in Christ" is one of faith, as one grows stronger in his saving faith, he thereby draws into an even closer relationship with Jesus Christ (Eph 2:21).

The Pastoral Letters mention a number of the blessings that belong to those who are "in Christ." Paul identifies grace (2 Tim 2:1), salvation (2 Tim 2:10), and the love of God (1 Tim 1:14) as gifts received by those who are in Christ. He also mentions the faithfulness of Christ toward those who are in Christ Jesus (1 Tim 1:14).

The way in which the Pastorals associate the phrase "in Christ Jesus" with saving faith helps to demonstrate that the expression ἐν Χριστῷ does not designate the object of faith.[30] When the apostle writes, "The

---

29. Since Christ is the subject of this verse, the phrase ἐν αὐτῷ clearly cannot have an instrumental meaning or be translated "by him" but must have a relational meaning and refer to being in a relationship with our Lord.

30. This is also evident from the apostle's practice of using other means to designate

grace of our Lord was more than abundant with faithfulness and love in Christ Jesus" (1 Tim 1:14), or when he speaks of "sound words which you heard from me in faith and love which are in Christ Jesus" (2 Tim 1:13), it is evident that "in Christ Jesus" is not designating the object of faith; instead, it denotes that relationship with Christ through which we receive his faithfulness, love, and the gift of saving faith.

This points to the correct understanding of two other passages: 1 Tim 3:13 ("Those who served well obtain for themselves a good standing and much courage in faith, which is in Christ Jesus") and 2 Tim 3:15 ("From infancy you have known the holy Scriptures, which are able to make you wise unto salvation through faith, which is in Christ Jesus"). In each case the expression "in Christ" refers to the saving relationship that we have with Christ, a relationship that consists of saving faith that has Christ as its object (on which see "Christ as the Object of Faith" above).

CHRIST AS THE OBJECT OF WORSHIP

In view of what the apostle has to say in these letters about both the person and the work of Jesus Christ, it is not surprising that he should direct prayer and worship to Christ. Near the conclusion of each of his Letters to Timothy he sets forth a doxology to Christ, each concluding with a solemn "amen" (1 Tim 6:16; 2 Tim 4:18).

Along the same lines Paul offers prayer to Christ. In his Second Letter to Timothy he speaks two brief petitions (1:16, 18) to "the Lord," that is, to Jesus Christ, on behalf of Onesiphorus and his household.

PLACING UNDER A SOLEMN OATH

In the Hebrew Scriptures the Lord God had instructed the Israelites that they were to take their oaths by his name (Exod 22:11; Deut 6:13; 10:20). As the apostle professed Jesus to be the "Lord," the one true God revealed in the Old Testament, it is not surprising that when he feels the need to

---

the object of faith (with the genitive [Rom 3:22, 26; Gal 2:16, 20; 3:22; Eph 3:12; Phil 1:27; 3:9; Col 2:12]; with the dative [Rom 10:14 (οὗ = τούτῳ οὐείς); 2 Tim 1:12; Titus 3:8]; with εἰς [Rom 10:14; Gal 2:16; Phil 1:29; Col 2:5]; with ἐπί [Rom 4:5, 24; 9:33; 10:11; 1 Tim 1:16]; with πρός [1 Thess 1:8; Phlm 5]).

give someone a solemn charge, in effect putting that person under oath,[31] he does so before the Lord Jesus Christ.

Paul tells his coworker Timothy, "I adjure you before God and Christ Jesus and the elect angels, that you keep these things without prejudice, doing nothing with partiality" (1 Tim 5:21). The threefold witnesses before whom this charge is given imparts a special gravity to it.

Later in the same letter (6:13) the apostle gives another solemn charge, this time "before God . . . and Christ Jesus." When he here describes Jesus as one "who bore witness to Pontius Pilate about the good confession," he sets before Timothy Christ as both an example that he should follow and as the one who—by his redemptive work to death at the order of the Roman governor—empowers him to do so.

Paul gives a similar charge to Timothy in his Second Letter to him. He enjoins his younger coworker to faithful proclamation of the word "before God and Christ Jesus, who is about to judge the living and the dead, and by his appearing and his kingdom" (2 Tim 4:1).

These charges give an air of special seriousness to the apostle's instructions. They also serve as a testimony to the high regard (equal with God the Father) in which Paul held Jesus.

SUFFERING WITH CHRIST[32]

In his letters Paul does not employ the language of suffering to refer to the redemptive work of Christ.[33] Instead, he uses this vocabulary when speaking of the Christian's life in fellowship with his Lord and savior.

The apostle sometimes speaks of suffering with Christ (Rom 8:17) as the special burden of pastors and others who labor in the word of Christ (2 Tim 2:3). Nevertheless, in agreement with the Lord himself (Matt 16:24–25; Mark 8:34–35; Luke 9:23–24) he makes it plain that suffering for the sake of Christ is the calling of every Christian (2 Tim 3:12).

We must be clear on just what suffering with Christ involves. Not every hardship that befalls a Christian is to be counted as suffering with Christ. Rather, those things that afflict a Christian on account of his/her faith in Christ (2 Tim 2:11), witness to and mission in the word of Christ

---

31. Refer to the textual notes at 1 Tim 5:21; 6:13, and at 2 Tim 4:1.
32. See further "The Afflictions of Christ" in Deterding, *Colossians*, 75–79.
33. By way of contrast, the apostle Peter does do so: 1 Pet 1:11; 2:21, 23; 3:18; 4:1; 5:1.

(2 Tim 2:3; 3:10–11), and godly way of life for Christ (3:12) make up one's life of suffering with Christ.

Paul's words "if we died with him, we will also live with him" (2 Tim 2:11), so reminiscent of his teaching on baptism (Rom 6:3–11; Col 2:11–12), root the believer's life of suffering in his baptism. As one is crucified, buried, and raised from the dead in baptism, he receives the forgiveness and life that Christ acquired by his redemptive work. In that same baptism he is also called on to live out his baptism into Christ by bearing suffering with Christ in this life.[34]

Jesus Christ calls the Christian, especially the Christian pastor, to suffer with him. Nevertheless, he also provides the power to endure the hardships that afflict his people. Christ rescued Paul from all his persecutions (2 Tim 3:10–11), not in the sense that he did not have to experience them, but that he gave him his resurrection power[35] to endure and overcome them. The apostle makes mention of all of this to assure Timothy and "all who desire to live in a godly way in Christ Jesus" that the Lord Jesus will do the same for all his people.

Accordingly, there is this assurance: "If we endure, we will also reign with him" (2 Tim 2:12). With Christ's resurrection power, which we receive in our baptismal incorporation into him, we have the strength to endure suffering with him, until we are raised to reign with him in eternity.

THE NEED FOR FAITHFULNESS TO CHRIST

In these letters the apostle exhorts and encourages his younger coworkers and other pastors to faithful ministry.[36] He also speaks of the need for all Christians to hold intently to their personal faith in Christ, particularly in view of the challenges to faith presented by those sufferings for the sake of Christ that his people bear.

---

34. Note the similar language the apostle uses in Philippians: "To know him and the power of his resurrection and the fellowship of his sufferings, being conformed to his death" (3:10).

35. Note the language of Phil 3. In verse 11 Paul uses the compound verb ἐξανάστασιν to emphasize that there he is speaking of the resurrection of the body *from* the dead. Hence, when in verse 10, in the context of speaking of the fellowship of Christ's sufferings, he refers to the power of Christ's resurrection (the simple form ἀναστάσεως), this designates Christ's resurrection power as that which enables us to endure those things that we must undergo as followers of the crucified and risen one.

36. 1 Tim 1:3–7; 3:6, 9; 4:6–7, 15–16; 5:22; 6:3–5, 11–12, 14, 20–21; 2 Tim 1:13–14; 2:2–3, 14–16, 23–26; 3:5, 14–17; 4:2–5, 15; Titus 1:9, 11, 13; 2:15; 3:8–11.

After alluding to the believers' baptismal death and resurrection with Christ (2 Tim 2:11), Paul continues, "If we endure, we will also reign with him; if we will deny him, he will deny us" (2 Tim 2:12). The apostle does not downplay the harshness of the life of a disciple. Nevertheless, he demonstrates that this is a burden worth bearing (cf. Rom 8:18). Due to the challenges of the Christian faith and life some will fall away; Paul's former coworker Demas was one of them (2 Tim 4:10). Nevertheless, if we remain faithful, we will experience life with the Lord forever.

But the apostle goes beyond telling us of the need for fidelity to Christ. He continues, "If we are faithless, he remains faithful, for he is not able to deny himself" (2 Tim 2:13). The salvation that Christ acquired for us by his death and resurrection is always available to us in his word and sacraments (2 Tim 3:15; Titus 3:4–7). As we hold fast to them, the savior will be holding fast to us.

IN CONCLUSION

The Pastoral Letters set forth a rich portrait of the Lord Jesus Christ. In them Paul presents Jesus as God, savior, and the center of the Scriptures. As such he is the object of the church's proclamation, faith, hope, sanctified service, and worship, and he is proven as one worthy of our absolute faithfulness.

He Saved Us

The Pastoral Letters on the Way of Salvation

The Pastoral Letters are not an evangelism tract. Paul wrote them to give instruction about various matters pertaining to the life of the church and its ministry. Nevertheless, there are portions of these letters that do proclaim the message of salvation.

SALVATION BY GRACE THROUGH FAITH

The central message of the Pauline Letters (and of the entirety of Scripture) is that we are saved by grace through faith in Jesus Christ (Rom 3:19–28; Eph 2:8–9). The Pastorals proclaim that same message. A number of times the apostle speaks of the grace of God by which we are saved.[1] "Mercy" (ἔλεος), "goodness" (χρηστότης), and "love for mankind" (φιλανθρωπία) are synonymous terms that he uses to refer to the saving grace of God.[2] Paul also makes mention of that faith, that act of believing, by which one receives the salvation that God gives by grace.[3]

The salvation that Christ gives has no end; it is eternal life. The Pastoral Letters contain several references to the gift of *eternal* life.[4] That blessed and certain future means that the believer's present existence,

---

1. 1 Tim 1:2, 14; 2 Tim 1:2, 9; 2:1; Titus 2:11; 3:7.
2. Mercy (1 Tim 1:2; 2 Tim 1:2; Titus 3:5), goodness (Titus 3:4), philanthropy (Titus 3:4).
3. 1 Tim 1:4, 5, 16, 19; 3:16; 4:12; 6:10, 12, 21; 2 Tim 1:5; 2:18; 3:10; 4:7; Titus 1:1.
4. 1 Tim 1:16; 6:12; Titus 1:2; 3:7.

however trying it may be, is one of hope. Therefore, these letters also make mention of the hope that is ours because of Christ.[5]

An essential portion of the biblical gospel is that Christ died for all. The Pastorals contain some of the Bible's most explicit statements that God desires the salvation of all people (1 Tim 2:4; Titus 2:11).

THE WORK OF CHRIST

Salvation depends upon the work of Christ; the saving works of Christ are what accomplishes mankind's salvation. The Pastoral Letters often mention the saving works of Jesus Christ.

The incarnation of the Son of God is the necessary prerequisite to his saving work. In these letters Paul speaks of Jesus Christ as both God (1 Tim 1:17; Titus 2:13) and man (1 Tim 2:5).[6] The eternal Christ becoming man is presupposed by several passages in these letters. The apostle writes that Christ "came into the world to save sinners" (1 Tim 1:15) and that he was "manifested in the flesh" (1 Tim 3:16). When in his Letter to Titus he says that "the grace of God appeared, bringing salvation to all people" (2:11) or that "the goodness and love for mankind of God our savior appeared" (3:4), the verb "appeared" presupposes Christ's existence prior to his incarnation; these passages also designate salvation as the purpose for Christ becoming a man.

It was by his death on the cross that Jesus Christ accomplished the salvation of mankind. When Paul writes that our Lord "gave himself" (1 Tim 2:6; Titus 2:14), this refers to his voluntarily giving himself up to death on the cross.

The Pastorals contain the only reference in the New Testament outside of the Gospels and the book of Acts to Pontius Pilate (1 Tim 6:13). What Jesus said—and refrained from saying—to Pilate ultimately led to his death on the cross.[7] This mention of Pilate is another way in which these letters draw our attention to the death of Christ for our salvation.

Christ died for our salvation, but had he remained dead, his death would have been in vain (1 Cor 15:12–20). Hence, it is significant that in the Pastoral Letters the apostle also speaks of that resurrection of which he was an eyewitness (1 Cor 15:8). He calls upon Timothy to remember

---

5. 1 Tim 1:1; 4:10; 5:5; 6:17; Titus 1:2; 2:13; 3:7.
6. See the commentary on these three passages.
7. See the section "Our Lord Jesus Christ" in the commentary on 1 Tim 6:11–16.

Jesus Christ "risen from the dead" (2 Tim 2:8). When in recounting the greatness of the mystery of godliness he identifies Jesus as having been "vindicated in the spirit" (1 Tim 3:16), he speaks of our Lord as having been raised from the dead.[8] In the same passage his words about our Lord as having been "seen by angels" may well refer to the presence of angels at the tomb on the day of Christ's resurrection.[9]

The ascension of Christ also receives attention in the Pastoral Letters. The reference to Jesus being "seen by angels" may refer to the time of his ascension (1 Tim 3:16; see Acts 1:10–11; Eph 1:20–22). Surely that is what is designated by the phrase "taken up in glory" in the same passage.

Paul writes of the work of Jesus Christ when he identifies him as the "one mediator between God and mankind" (1 Tim 2:5). There are two, not mutually exclusive, possibilities as to the apostle's reference here. He might be speaking of our Lord's role of interceding for us before God (Rom 8:34). Another possibility is that he is referring to the sinless Christ being made sin for us, so that we might be righteous before God (2 Cor 5:21). Of course, rather than one or the other, both might be intended here.

The fullness of salvation will be ours when Christ comes again at the last day. In his Second Letter to Timothy Paul makes mention of our Lord's parousia. He speaks of Christ coming as judge (4:1) and references the crown of righteousness that the Lord will give him "on that day" (4:8). When in that latter verse he writes of all those who have loved Christ's "appearing," that too may be speaking of his appearing at the last day.

In the confession-like section of 2 Tim 2:8–13 the apostle makes a pregnant mention of Jesus Christ being "of the offspring of David, according to my gospel" (2:8). From the time of God's covenant with David (2 Sam 7:1–17; 1 Chr 17:1–15) God's people had waited for one from the line of David who would have an eternal rule. The New Testament proclaims that this promise was fulfilled by the person and work of Jesus Christ (Luke 1:31–33). With his reference to Christ being of the offspring of David Paul points to Jesus and his saving work as the fulfillment of God's covenant with David.

---

8. Refer to the commentary on 1 Tim 3:16.
9. See again the commentary on 1 Tim 3:16.

THE PRESENTATION OF SALVATION IN THE PASTORALS

The Scriptures use a rich and varied vocabulary to express and impart the salvation that the crucified and risen Christ acquired for all. The Pastoral Letters themselves exhibit a number of ways of speaking of the salvation that comes from Jesus Christ.

The apostle speaks of himself and his readers as "having been justified through his grace" (Titus 3:7). As the concepts designated by the English words "justification" and "righteousness" are both expressed through the same Greek word group (δικαιόω/δίκαιος/δικαιοσύνη), to be "justified" (δικαιωθέντες, Titus 3:7) will result in receiving the "crown of righteousness" (δικαιοσύνης, 2 Tim 4:8). To be justified is to have the standing before God that is just or "righteous"; it is what is needed to have a right standing before the one who is divine. This standing is ours as a free gift of God's grace for the sake of Christ.[10]

"The wages of sin is death, but the gift of God is eternal life in Christ Jesus our Lord" (Rom 6:23). Thus, it is not surprising that in the Pastoral Letters Paul should speak of the believer's salvation as life,[11] often modifying that term with the adjective "eternal" or pairing it with "incorruption."[12]

The apostle uses other, somewhat related, concepts to describe the believer's eternal salvation. He writes that Christ gave himself to death to "redeem us from all lawlessness" (Titus 2:14). The use of this verb elsewhere in the Greek Scriptures (e.g., Isa 52:3; 1 Pet 1:18) indicates that this verb includes the idea of a payment by which ransom/redemption is accomplished.[13] In a somewhat similar passage Paul states that our Lord "gave himself as a ransom for all" (1 Tim 2:6). The term "ransom" (ἀντίλυτρον) includes the ideas of deliverance and release.[14] The apostle also writes that Christ gave himself to death to "purify for himself a chosen people" (Titus 2:14). The verb "cleanse, purify" (καθαρίσῃ) can refer to physical washing (Matt 23:25–26; Luke 11:39) or to purification from sin (Titus 2:14; Eph 5:26); in that light it may be more than coincidental that shortly thereafter in this letter Paul mentions the "washing of rebirth

---

10. See further the entry "Righteousness/Justification" in the Extended Notes.
11. 1 Tim 1:16; 4:9; 6:12, 19; 2 Tim 1:1, 10; Titus 1:2; 3:7.
12. "Eternal life" (1 Tim 1:16; 6:12; Titus 1:2; 3:7); "incorruption" (2 Tim 1:10).
13. See also *TDNT* 4:350–51.
14. See the entry on "Redeem, Redemption/Ransom" in the Extended Notes.

and of renewal of the Holy Spirit" (baptism) by which God saved us (Titus 3:5). In Titus 2:14 the term embraces both justification (cleansed from sin so as to have eternal salvation) and sanctification (by being purified from sin one is able to lead a godly life "zealous for good works").

"Conscience" (συνείδησις) is a Greek concept. Its sole occurrence in those portions of the Septuagint that are a translation of some portion of the Hebrew Scriptures is at Eccl 10:20, where it renders a Hebrew term (מַדָּע) that is translated differently in all of its other appearances in the canonical Old Testament.[15] Moreover, "conscience" is not found in any of the four Gospels.[16] The term has much in common with both the Old and New Testaments' usage of the term "heart" (Hebrew: לֵב and לֵבָב; Greek: καρδία).[17] Including the Pastorals it occurs nineteen times in the Pauline corpus.[18]

In two different passages Paul describes the unbelieving as having "seared their own conscience" or as having a conscience that has been "defiled" (1 Tim 4:2; Titus 1:15). In contrast, believers have a good or pure conscience.[19] The apostle speaks of this kind of conscience as being equivalent to a pure heart (1 Tim 1:5). Paul often pairs a good conscience with genuine ("unhypocritical") faith; this kind of faith (*fides qua creditur*) results in a good conscience, and in turn the believer holds the teachings of the faith (*fides quae creditur*) with a good conscience.[20]

A good or pure conscience comes from saving faith. Having such a conscience has a wholesome effect on the believer's life and conduct. For example, the apostle speaks of worshiping God "with a pure conscience" (2 Tim 1:3).

At least some Christians are accustomed to speak of salvation from "sin, death, and the devil."[21] The Pastorals also speak of salvation as de-

---

15. The Hebrew term מַדָּע, which in Eccl 10:20 means "mind" or "thoughts," otherwise occurs in 2 Chr 1:10, 11, 12, and Dan 1:4, where it refers to "knowledge." In the LXX συνείδησις is also found at Wis 17:11 and Sir 42:18.

16. It does occur as an addition to the *pericope adulterae* (John 8:9) in a handful of manuscripts.

17. See further the entry "Heart and Conscience" in the Extended Notes.

18. Rom 2:15; 9:1; 13:5; 1 Cor 8:7, 10, 12; 10:25, 27, 28, 29; 2 Cor 1:12; 4:2; 5:11; 1 Tim 1:5, 19; 3:9; 4:2; 2 Tim 1:3; Titus 1:15.

19. 1 Tim 1:5, 19; 3:9; 2 Tim 1:3.

20. 1 Tim 1:5, 19; 3:9.

21. For example, in the Small Catechism Martin Luther says of Jesus Christ that he has "purchased and freed me from all sins, from death, and from the power of the devil" (explanation to the second article of the creed) and says that baptism "brings

liverance from Satan. There are those who have turned away after Satan (1 Tim 5:15), and there is the danger of being in the snare of the devil (1 Tim 3:7).[22] Nevertheless, through God-given, genuine repentance one will "escape from the snare of the devil" (2 Tim 2:26).

There are two other ways in which Paul speaks of salvation with a particular view to its future reality. He notes that "on that day," the day of the final judgment, the righteous judge will give him "the crown of righteousness" (2 Tim 4:8). The term "righteousness" connects this statement with the apostle's teaching on justification (see above), while the word "crown" is royal language. That being the case, this passage looks ahead to another one just a bit later in the same letter, where Paul states that "the Lord will rescue me from every evil work and will save me for his heavenly kingdom" (2 Tim 4:18). Like "crown," "kingdom" is language that easily communicates the idea of highly desirable, extravagant blessings.

THE ROLE OF THE MEANS OF GRACE

Through the work of Christ God has acquired salvation for all. But even beyond providing salvation the Lord also gives that salvation to people individually. The means by which God accomplishes this are also highlighted in the Pastoral Letters.

When the apostle writes of Christ that he was "proclaimed among the nations, believed on in the world" (1 Tim 3:16), the implication—in light of the rest of Paul's letters—is that the proclamation about Christ resulted in people putting their faith for salvation in Christ. Similarly, when Paul states that God "saved us and called us by a holy calling" (2 Tim 1:9), this demonstrates that the act of calling to faith resulted in people receiving salvation. When he adds that for this "I was appointed a proclaimer and apostle and teacher" (2 Tim 1:9), he indicates that this calling takes place through the word.

The saving message that is proclaimed is the message of the Scriptures. In his Second Letter to Timothy Paul unequivocally sets forth the truth that "the holy Scriptures . . . are able to make you wise unto salvation through faith, which is in Christ Jesus" (3:15).

---

about forgiveness of sins, redeems from death and the devil" (answer to the question "What gifts or benefits does baptism grant?"); translations in Kolb and Wengert, *Book of Concord*, 355, 359.

22. The reference to those who desire to be rich falling "into temptation and a snare" (1 Tim 6:9) might well imply that these would fall into the snare *of the devil*.

In these letters the apostle also denotes the place of baptism in God's calling to salvation. He writes that God "saved us ... through the washing of rebirth and of renewal of the Holy Spirit" (Titus 3:5). The baptismal language of 2 Tim 2:11-12, with its verbs compounded with the baptismal preposition σύν (cf. Rom 6:3-11; Col 2:11-12), also point to baptism as a means by which God gives us life and a place in his heavenly kingdom (cf. 2 Tim 4:18).[23]

GOD'S ETERNAL PLAN OF SALVATION

In each of his Letters to Timothy Paul speaks of God's plan of salvation.[24] Similarly he speaks of God promising eternal life (2 Tim 1:1; Titus 1:2); he also notes that God made this plan and promise "before eternal times" (2 Tim 1:9; Titus 1:2).

What was promised in eternity was fulfilled in history. What God promised from eternity he "made known at just the right time by the proclamation of his word" (Titus 1:3). The promise was fulfilled at just the right time;[25] hence, the apostle notes that Christ "gave himself as a ransom for all, as a testimony at the right time" (1 Tim 2:6).

Through the work of Christ God carried out this plan at just the right time. This aids us in our understanding of those passages in these letters when the apostle refers to "the last times" or "the last days" in such a way so as to make it plain that he was speaking of the time in which he was currently living.[26] The days after Christ's resurrection and the day of Pentecost (Acts 2:17) were/are "the last days (times)," for everything necessary for mankind's salvation, in other words, everything that God had planned from eternity for salvation, was completed by the work of Christ (including the sending of the Holy Spirit; John 14:16; 15:26).[27]

All of this helps inform our understanding of Paul's reference to his ministry for the faith of "God's elect ones" (Titus 1:1). That the apostle would refer to God's people with this language in such a brief, almost

---

23. See further Deterding, "Baptism."

24. 1 Tim 1:4: οἰκονομίαν; 2 Tim 1:9: πρόθεσιν.

25. Compare this to what Paul writes in his Letter to the Galatians about God sending his Son "in the fullness of time" (4:4).

26. 1 Tim 4:1 in light of 4:7; 2 Tim 3:1 in light of 3:5.

27. See further the section "The Last Times" in the commentary on 1 Tim 4:1-5 and the section "The Last Days" in the commentary on 2 Tim 3:1-9.

offhanded manner, suggests at least some of the addressees of this letter,[28] at a minimum his fellow servant of the word Titus, would have been familiar with Paul's teaching on the election of grace.

The apostle sets forth the truth regarding God's eternal election of grace in Romans (8:28—9:33) and Ephesians (1:3–14). These would certainly qualify as being among the most significant letters in the Pauline corpus.[29] This would suggest that teaching regarding the believer's eternal election to salvation by God was not some minor, occasional point of Paul's teaching but something he touched on at least on a somewhat regular basis. Hence, he could refer to Christians as "God's elect ones" when writing to a close colleague like Titus, and he would know that his addressee would be familiar with this teaching.

To repeat what was said about this teaching in the commentary on Titus 1:1–4: The biblical teaching of election/predestination must be understood in connection with what the Scriptures have to say about the redemptive work of Jesus Christ.

By his death and resurrection Christ acquired salvation for all (Rom 5:18; 2 Cor 5:14–15). The word of Christ's work dispenses this salvation and creates the faith that receives it (2 Cor 5:18; Rom 10:17). Through faith in Christ, apart from works, one receives God's gift of salvation (Eph 2:8–9). The same faith in Christ that saves without works also moves and empowers the believer to produce good works in his life (Eph 2:10). Through the word that brought one to faith God continues to nourish and so to preserve that faith until the end (Phil 1:6; 4:7), when those who died in the faith will be resurrected and those believers still alive will be glorified (1 Thess 4:16–17; Rom 8:17–18). When all of this is kept in mind, then the individual believer, focusing on the person and work of Jesus Christ, will be able to see that God chose him from eternity for this salvation (Rom 8:29–30).[30]

---

28. The concluding benediction of this letter, "grace be with all of you [plural]" (Titus 3:15), indicates that the apostle intended for it to be read not just by Titus but for a much larger audience.

29. For example, Martin Luther regarded Romans as "the chief part of the New Testament and the purest Gospel" (*Preface to Romans*, para. 1). F. F. Bruce has dubbed Ephesians "the Quintessence of Paulinism" (*Paul*, 424–40).

30. It must be asserted that the Scriptures teach about the eternal election of those saved; it does *not* teach that there was any election by God of anyone for damnation. Note that in Rom 9:22–23 Paul speaks of God in advance (προ-) preparing vessels of mercy for glory (σκεύη ἐλέους ἃ προητοίμασεν εἰς δόξαν); however, when he refers to vessels of wrath, he states that they were prepared for destruction (σκεύη ὀργῆς κατηρτισμένα εἰς ἀπώλειαν); nothing is said about this being done in advance, and

"Our Savior"

All of this brings clarification to the use of the term "savior" in the Pastoral Letters. Should God (the Father) or Jesus Christ be spoken of as our savior?[31] At times in these letters the apostle speaks of "God our savior."[32] In other places he refers to "Christ our savior."[33]

The proximity of these phrases demonstrates that Paul was not simply being casual with his terminology. Instead, his language indicates that both the Father and Christ the Son were involved in our salvation.

God's eternal plan was for our salvation; in that sense the Father is our savior. That plan was carried out in time and history by Jesus Christ; in that sense he is our savior.

In concluding this topic we should take note of one other passage in the Pastorals. In a pericope in which he identifies both God and Jesus Christ as "our savior" (Titus 3:4, 6) the apostle states that God "saved us . . . through the washing of rebirth and of renewal of the Holy Spirit" (3:5). Salvation was the Father's will and plan from eternity. Salvation was the work of the Son of God by his death and resurrection. Salvation becomes one's personal possession through the work of God the Holy Spirit, for example, through baptism. Thus, in the Pastoral Letters Paul proclaims our salvation as the work of God: Father, Son, and Holy Spirit (Amen).

---

it simply states that they were prepared for wrath; God is not identified as the one who prepared them for this. On the scriptural teaching regarding the election of grace see further the Formula of Concord, Article XI (Epitome and Solid Declaration), and Nafzger et al., *Confessing the Gospel*, 1195–261.

31. In the New Testament the vocable "God" (θεός) is almost exclusively reserved for God the Father. The deity of Jesus Christ, the Son of God, is generally indicated by applying to him the Greek term for "Lord" (κύριος), which is the way the Greek Bible (the LXX) renders יהוה, the Old Testament (Hebrew) name of the one true God (BDAG 577 [under II. 2 b, α] and 577–78 [under II. 2 b, γ; ב, א, and ג]). This is also the case in the Pastoral Letters (θεός) for God the Father: 1 Tim 1:1, 2, 4, 11; 2:3, 5 (2x); 3:5; 15 (2x); 4:3, 4, 5, 10; 5:4, 5, 21; 6:1; 2 Tim 1:1, 2, 3, 6, 7, 8; 2:14, 15, 19, 25; 3:4, 16, 17; 4:1; Titus 1:1 (2x), 2, 3, 4, 7, 16; 2:5, 10, 11; 3:4, 8; κύριος for Jesus Christ: 1 Tim 1:2, 12, 14; 6:3, 14; 2 Tim 1:2, 9, 16, 18; 2:7, 19 (2x), 22, 24; 3:11l: 4:8, 14, 17, 18, 22. This is the case, even though the Pastorals contain two passages (1 Tim 1:17; Titus 2:13) which apply the name θεός to Jesus Christ; see the commentary on each of those verses.

32. 1 Tim 1:1; 2:3; Titus 1:3; 2:10; 3:4; 4:10. In 2 Tim 1:9 and Titus 3:5 the apostle states that "God" saved us.

33. 2 Tim 1:10; Titus 1:4; 2:13; 3:6.

In the Last Days

The Eschatology of the Pastoral Letters

Eschatology has to do with more than simply the last chapter in a dogmatics textbook. The Christian's entire life is lived in view of the last things, in view of the way that all things will end. This is because the work of Christ has oriented the believer's entire being toward its blessed outcome.

THE LAST DAYS/TIMES

Paul teaches that God's plan for humanity's salvation was made in eternity (Titus 1:2). That plan was carried out by Jesus Christ, by his death and resurrection (2 Tim 2:8) and by his sending of the Holy Spirit (Titus 3:5) to bring that salvation to individuals through faith. Since everything necessary for the world's salvation—save for Christ's return in glory (at the "right time"; 1 Tim 6:14–15) to take his people to the consummation of that salvation—is already completed, the world has ever since been in "the last days/times" (1 Tim 4:1 in light of 4:7; 2 Tim 3:1 in light of 3:5).[1] The Christian, therefore, already possesses the gift of eternal salvation.

The apostle shows that this becomes our own in baptism (Titus 3:5). In baptism one is crucified, buried, and raised from the dead with Christ (Rom 6:3–11; Col 2:11–12). Having participated with Christ in what he

---

1. See also 1 Cor 10:11 ("These things . . . were written down for our instruction, upon whom the ends of the ages have come"), Acts 2:16–17 ("This was what was spoken through the prophet Joel, 'and it will be in the last days'"), Heb 1:2 ("In these last days he has spoken to us by a Son"), Heb 9:26 ("But now he has been made known one time at the conclusion of the ages for abolishing sin through his sacrifice"), 1 Pet 1:19–20 ("Christ . . . made known at the last of the times"), 1 John 2:18 ("It is the last hour"). See further Deterding, "New Testament View," 385–99.

accomplished for the world's salvation, the Christian is assured of being raised with him for eternity (2 Tim 2:11).[2]

At the time of the writing of the Pastoral Letters there were false teachers who offered a heresy that was perhaps a corrupted version of this teaching. They were "saying that the resurrection has already taken place" (2 Tim 2:18). Evidently, they presented the resurrection as a purely nonmaterial event.[3] Paul's genuine teaching was quite different. Yes, the resurrection of Christ has already taken place as the decisive event in all of history. Nevertheless, the resurrection of his people was to take place in the future. True godliness held its promise "both for the present and for the life to come" (1 Tim 4:8). By putting one's hope in God the believer stores up a good foundation "for the future" (1 Tim 6:19). Virtually the last words from the apostle's pen proclaimed that the Lord "will rescue me from every evil work and will save me for his heavenly kingdom" (2 Tim 4:18; note the future tenses of the verbs). The Pastoral Letters proclaim that Christ achieved our salvation in the past, but he will bring his people to the full realization of that salvation in the future.

A LIFE OF HOPE

To have hope is to have something in the future—something good—for which one can wait expectantly.[4] This content of our hope (*spes quae speratur*) is that on which our act of hoping (*spes qua speratur*) can rest.[5]

---

2. In a similar way, since the Lord's supper is something that Christ will only partake of again when he does so anew in the kingdom of his Father (Matt 26:29; Mark 14:25; Luke 22:18) and is a proclamation of the death of Christ until he comes (1 Cor 11:26), the meal that Christ instituted on the night of his betrayal is, in the words of a hymn, "a foretaste of the feast to come" (LSB 955).

3. See further the section "The Nature of the Heresy" in the Introduction to the Pastoral Letters.

4. The NT word for "hope" is ἐλπίς/ἐλπίζω. In the LXX this word group renders the Hebrew terms קָוָה and יָחַל, meaning "wait" or "await"; this means that the act of hoping involves waiting for God to fulfill his promises. Related to the verb קָוָה is the noun תִּקְוָה, the usual word for "hope" in the Hebrew Scriptures and one which is translated not only by ἐλπίς but also by ὑπομονή ["endurance"]. These various nuances of קָוָה, יָחַל, and תִּקְוָה demonstrate that as the believer waits with hope, he is not just biding time but is waiting with endurance (see Col 1:11); he waits with endurance in anticipation of the consummation of his hope (Rom 8:25; 15:4; 1 Thess 1:3 ["your endurance of hope"]. Note also that in Titus 2:13 Paul describes believers as "awaiting the blessed hope."

5. See further the entry "Hope" in the Extended Notes.

The content of our Christian hope is the eternal life (Titus 1:2; 3:7) that Christ has acquired for us (1 Tim 1:16; 6:12). Thus, Paul can identify Jesus Christ as "our hope" (1 Tim 1:1) and he can speak of a genuine believer as one who has "hoped in God" (1 Tim 5:5).

This, in turn, means that the Christian can face death very differently than can anyone else. The apostle speaks of his impending death as the "time of my departure" (2 Tim 4:6). Death is not the end for the believer; Christ has made it the way of departing this life for "the life to come" (1 Tim 4:8).

THE APPEARING OF JESUS CHRIST

The life to come will be brought to its consummation at the "appearing" (ἐπιφάνεια) of Christ.[6] This noun and its cognate verb can also be used of the appearing of Jesus Christ at his incarnation and birth (2 Tim 1:10; Titus 2:11; 3:4). The close proximity of both uses of this word group (Titus 2:11, 13) points to a truth about our Lord's return. As he came visibly in the fullness of time, so also at his second coming he will come visibly, so that "every eye will see him" (Rev 1:7).

Christ came to fulfill God's plan of salvation in the fullness of time (Gal 4:4). So also, his second appearing will be "at the right time" (1 Tim 6:14–15).

The return of Christ will be both for judgment and salvation. In the Pastorals Paul speaks of the returning Christ as a judge (2 Tim 4:8) and of the judgment that he will carry out on the devil and on the unbelieving.[7] Nevertheless, he also speaks of the salvation that Christ will bestow on his people, as he writes of our "awaiting . . . the glorious appearing of our great God and savior Jesus Christ" (Titus 2:13).

The appearing of Christ will be for salvation for those who have believed the gospel message about him and so have put their faith in him. The apostle indicates this in various ways in these letters: "I was shown mercy for this reason, in order than in me as the foremost Christ Jesus might demonstrate the utmost long-suffering for an example for those about to believe in him for eternal life" (1 Tim 1:16); "godliness has the utmost benefit, having promise . . . for the life to come" (1 Tim 4:8); "lay hold of eternal life, to which you were called, having confessed the good

---

6. 1 Tim 6:14–15; 2 Tim 4:1, 8; Titus 2:13.
7. 1 Tim 3:6; 2 Tim 4:1; see also 1 Tim 5:24; 2 Tim 2:12; 4:14.

confession before many witnesses" (1 Tim 6:12); "command those who are rich in this age ... to put their hope ... in God ... thereby storing up for themselves a good foundation for the future, in order that they might lay hold of what is really life" (1 Tim 6:17–19); "Paul, apostle of Christ Jesus through the will of God in accord with the promise of life which is in Christ Jesus" (2 Tim 1:1); "the promise of life which is in Christ Jesus" (2 Tim 1:10); "for the hope of eternal life, which God, who does not lie, promised before eternal times, and made known at just the right time by the proclamation of his word" (Titus 1:2–3).

Christ will do this on the last day. The Pastorals refer to this, as they speak of Christ's coming on "that day" (2 Tim 1:12, 18; 4:8).

THE NATURE OF THE LIFE TO COME

God's salvation is beyond all that we can comprehend or even imagine (Eph 3:20). That being the case, the Scriptures describe the life to come with a variety of splendid images and concepts. The Pastoral Letters also employ many different ways to describe our salvation.

Perhaps the most noteworthy characteristic of the salvation to come is that it is without end. In these letters Paul regularly uses the adjective "eternal" to describe the life to come.[8]

The prospect of eternal life might not be appealing if that life were beset with all the problems and misery that plague this fallen world. The Scriptures assure us that the life to come is not troubled by any of those. In various ways the Pastoral Letters also describe the splendor of eternal life.

The apostle writes that Christ "brought to light life and incorruption" (2 Tim 1:10). Since the fall the created world has been subject to futility and enslaved to corruption (Rom 8:20–21; Gen 3:16–19), so that Paul speaks of the creation itself agonizingly awaiting the revelation of the glory that the people of God will receive on the last day. Because of this the creation will have freedom from its slavery to corruption (Rom 8:19–22). This is the truth that lies behind the apostle's statement that Christ "brought to light life *and incorruption*" (2 Tim 1:10).

Paul describes the ascension (and ongoing exaltation) of Christ as his being "taken up in glory" (1 Tim 3:16), and he speaks of the eternal glory that belongs to him (1 Tim 1:17).[9] He describes the return of

---

8. 1 Tim 1:16; 6:12; 2 Tim 2:10; Titus 1:2; 3:7.

9. For evidence that 1 Tim 1:17 is referring to Jesus Christ, see the commentary

Christ as his "glorious appearing" (Titus 2:13), and he speaks of believers obtaining salvation "with eternal glory" (2 Tim 2:10). This language indicates that in eternity the life of Christ's people will be one of sharing with him in the glory of his presence.

When the apostle refers to "the gospel of the glory of the blessed God, with which I was entrusted" (1 Tim 1:11), the word "glory" serves as a sort of summary of the message of the gospel. The heart of the message is what Christ has done for our eternal salvation, a salvation that will mean life in his glorious presence. That message of the glory of salvation is one with which Paul was entrusted.[10]

Even for those who live under and who value democratic forms of government the idea of living like royalty has a certain amount of appeal. That would certainly have been no less true of the time during which Paul wrote the Pastoral Letters. Thus, it is not surprising that he uses royal language to describe the believer's salvation. He calls Christ a king (1 Tim 1:17; 6:15), and he speaks of his (heavenly) reign or kingdom (2 Tim 4:1, 18). In view of all of this it is significant that he writes, "If we endure, we will also reign with him [Christ]" (2 Tim 2:12). Our future is a life of glory, for we will share in the glory of Christ. The apostle's declaration, "If we endure, we will also reign with him," is another way of saying this.

LIFE WITH CHRIST

The characteristic Pauline phrase "with Christ" and similar expressions using the Greek word σύν (either as a freestanding preposition or as a prefix to another term) have eschatological significance. Paul roots his declarations about life with Christ in his teaching on baptism. In baptism one dies with, is buried with, and is raised from the dead with Christ (Rom 6:3–11; Col 2:11–12).

This baptismal teaching is the foundation for the apostle's assertion in the creedal/hymnic lines in 2 Tim 2: "If we died with him, we will also live with him; if we endure, we will also reign with him" (11–12). The Christian has already been raised with Christ in baptism. This, therefore,

---

on that verse. Compare the eternal "glory" of this passage with the eternal "honor and might" of 1 Tim 6:16.

10. See further the entry "Glory" in the Extended Notes.

is an assurance of being raised on "that day" (2 Tim 1:12, 18; 4:8) to live with Christ and to reign with him forever.

IN CONCLUSION

The topic of the last things seems to hold perpetual interest for people. While for some this is no more than morbid curiosity, the biblical teachings regarding the end bring great assurance to those who receive them with faith in Christ. The Letters to Timothy and to Titus have a rich and welcome message concerning the last things for all who take the time to read and to study them.

There Is One God

The Pastoral Letters on the Identity of God

Etymologically the word "theology" means "the study of God." In reality, the purview of theological study may include topics (e.g., mankind, ethics) that do not always make explicit mention of the deity. Nevertheless, who God is and what God does/has done/will do is at the heart and center of biblical theology, also of that of the Pastoral Letters.

Paul's statement "there is one God" (1 Tim 2:5) is one to which millions would give assent. However, the apostle is not referring to mere theism. He is writing to fellow Christians,[1] and in doing so he specifies the identity of the one true God.

In the New Testament the vocable "God" (θεός) nearly always refers to God the Father. When the appellation "Lord" (κύριος) is used for Jesus Christ in the Greek New Testament, it has the same significance as it does in the Greek translation of the Hebrew Scriptures; for since the Septuagint renders the Hebrew name of the one true God (יהוה) with κύριος, the identification of Jesus as "Lord" is a way of identifying him with the one true God who revealed himself in the Old Testament.[2]

This practice is also characteristic of the Pastorals. The vocable θεός refers to God the Father;[3] the deity of Jesus Christ is asserted by naming him as *kyrios*.[4]

---

1. Although addressed to individuals, each of these letters concludes with a blessing of grace over many others (1 Tim 6:21; 2 Tim 4:22; Titus 3:15; "you" in each of these occurs in the plural [ὑμῶν]; the Titus passage even says "all of you").

2. BDAG 577 (under II. 2 b, α) and 577–78 (under II. 2 b, γ; ב, א, and ג).

3. 1 Tim 1:1, 2, 4, 11; 2:3, 5 (2x); 3:5, 15 (2x); 4:3, 4, 5, 10; 5:4, 5, 21; 6:1; 2 Tim 1:1, 2, 3, 6, 7, 8; 2:14, 15, 19, 25; 3:4, 16, 17; 4:1; Titus 1:1 (2x), 2, 3, 4, 7, 16; 2:5, 10, 11; 3:4, 8.

4. 1 Tim 1:2, 12, 14; 6:3, 14; 2 Tim 1:2, 9, 16, 18; 2:7, 19 (2x), 22, 24; 3:11; 4:8, 14,

However, the Pastoral Letters do contain two passages that do use the term θεός for Jesus. The most explicit of these occurs in Titus 2:13.[5] There Paul speaks of the appearance of "our great God and savior, Jesus Christ." That this and not "the great God and our savior, Jesus Christ" is the correct translation is demonstrated by the "Granville Sharp Rule," which states that in the New Testament, in the construction article-substantive-*kai*-substantive, when neither substantive is impersonal, plural, nor a proper name, the two substantives are equivalent.[6] The context and content of the phrase also points to this as the proper translation. If, for the sake of argument, we would assume that "the great God" is to be distinguished from "our savior Jesus Christ," it would be impossible to identify an appearance of "the great God" for which believers are waiting other than the parousia of Jesus Christ. Titus 2:13, therefore, stands as one of the New Testament's strongest witnesses to the full deity of "the man Christ Jesus" (1 Tim 2:5).[7]

A comparison of 1 Tim 1:17 ("to the king of the ages; imperishable, unseen, the only God, be honor and glory for ages of ages") with 1 Tim 6:14–16 ("our Lord Jesus Christ . . . who is the blessed and only sovereign, the king of those who are having kingship and lord of those who are having lordship, the only one who has immortality, who dwells in unapproachable light, whom no one among men has seen nor is able to see, to whom be honor and might forever") points to the former passage as another place in which the Scriptures identify Jesus Christ as θεός. As the second passage explicitly refers to Christ, the king to whom belongs eternal honor to whom the apostle refers in the earlier passage, must be Christ Jesus as well. He is the only God, who is imperishable, because risen from the dead he will never die again. He is the only God, who is unseen, because between the time of his ascension (Acts 1:9) and his return in glory

---

17, 18, 22.

5. It is interesting that in this letter Paul never refers to Jesus with the vocable κύριος, not even, as was his custom (Rom 1:7; 1 Cor 1:3; 2 Cor 1:2; Gal 1:3; Eph 1:2; Phil 1:2; 1 Thess 1:1; 2 Thess 1:2; 1 Tim 1:2; 2 Tim 1:2; Phlm 3), in the salutation of the letter. The only other Pauline Letter whose salutation lacks an identification of Jesus Christ as κύριος is Colossians, but that is accounted for by the fact that in this epistle Paul states that in Christ "the whole fullness of deity dwells bodily" (2:9; cf. the similar statement of 1:19).

6. Wallace, *Greek Grammar*, 270–77.

7. On the full deity and humanity of Jesus Christ see further Nafzger et al., *Confessing the Gospel*, 381–418.

(Acts 1:11) he is not seen by us mortals, even though he still dwells bodily (Col 2:9).

Paul sets forth as a basic confession of faith that "there is one God" (1 Tim 2:5), yet these letters are decidedly Trinitarian. A number of places in the Pastoral Letters speak of God (the Father) and Christ together.[8] These "binitarian" statements point to the equality of the Father and the Son, Jesus Christ, as God from all eternity. Particularly relevant here are those passages in which the apostle in effect puts Timothy under oath to follow through on some directive that he is giving him.[9] As oaths are typically taken with the assumption that God is witness to what is pledged, this indicates that Paul regarded Jesus to be nothing less than equal with God the Father.

Moreover, God the Holy Spirit is prominently mentioned in the Pastorals. The apostle refers to what "the Spirit explicitly says" (1 Tim 4:1). He directs Timothy to "guard the good deposit through the Holy Spirit who dwells among us" (2 Tim 1:14). He describes baptism as "a washing of rebirth and of renewal of the Holy Spirit" (Titus 3:5). In light of 2 Pet 1:20–21, Paul's statement that "all Scripture is breathed into by God" (2 Tim 3:16) may be understood as another reference to the Holy Spirit.[10] Along these lines we note that in Titus (3:4–6) the apostle states that God saved us through the washing of the Holy Spirit, whom he poured out through Jesus Christ. All of these passages refer to the Holy Spirit in such a way that the "Spirit" can be understood in no other way than as

---

8. 1 Tim 1:1, 2; 2:5–6; 3:15–16; 5:21; 6:13–14; 2 Tim 1:1, 2, 9; 4:1; Titus 1:1, 4; 2:11–14; 3:4–7.

9. 1 Tim 5:21 ("I adjure you before God and Christ Jesus and the elect angels, that you keep these things without prejudice, doing nothing with partiality"); 6:13–14 ("Before God, who gives life to all things, and Christ Jesus, who bore witness to Pontius Pilate about the good confession, I direct you to keep the commandment spotless and irreproachable until the appearing of our Lord Jesus Christ"); 2 Tim 4:1–2a ("I adjure [you] before God and Christ Jesus, who is about to judge the living and the dead, and by his appearing and his kingdom, preach the word").

10. It is possible that 1 Tim 3:16 and 2 Tim 1:7 might also refer to the Holy Spirit. In the latter passage ("God did not give us a spirit of cowardice but of power and love and prudence") I would argue that the word πνεῦμα is more likely referring to an aptitude that God bestows on us (spirit) rather than to God the Holy Spirit. Of course, since the Holy Spirit bears witness with our spirit (Rom 8:16), this would still be an indirect allusion to God the Holy Spirit. The reference in 1 Timothy ("vindicated in the spirit") seems to be referring to the return of the human spirit to the body of Christ as the cause of his vindicating resurrection (as in Luke 8:55); however, in view of Rom 1:4 πνεῦμα could designate God the Holy Spirit.

being equal in every way with the Father and with his Son, Jesus Christ. Therefore, the Pastoral Letters are most assuredly Trinitarian.

The Trinitarian nature of the Pastorals is seen also in their proclamation of the works of God. In these letters Paul sometimes refers to "God our savior";[11] at other times he speaks of Jesus Christ as our savior.[12] This is a testimony to Christ working out the Father's eternal plan (e.g., 1 Tim 1:4; 2 Tim 1:9) for mankind's salvation.[13] Moreover, the apostle's declaration that "God [the Father] ... saved us ... through a washing of rebirth and of renewal of the Holy Spirit, whom he richly poured out on us through Jesus Christ our savior" (Titus 3:4–6) demonstrates not only the Trinitarian essence of God but also the role that all three persons of the Holy Trinity played in our salvation.

All of this is foundational for understanding Paul's statement "there is one God and one mediator between God and mankind, the man Christ Jesus" (1 Tim 2:5). The one God is Christ (1:17) and the Father (1 Tim 1:2), as well as the Spirit who speaks through the Scripture (1 Tim 4:1). Yet the one mediator between God and man is the one who, still being God, became man to plead for us (Rom 8:34) and to give himself as a ransom for us (1 Tim 2:6; 2 Cor 5:21).[14]

It is at first curious that the Pastoral Letters never use the word "Son" with reference to Jesus Christ as the Son of God. While Paul often uses this language in his letters,[15] it is to be noted that Philippians, 2 Thessalonians, and Philemon also contain no such reference. While this particular terminology is lacking in the Pastorals, they do clearly proclaim the theology inherent in speaking of Christ as the Son of God.

The Pastorals richly proclaim the salvation of God that is in Christ. Therefore, as would be expected, these letters in various ways speak of God and of Christ as the one in whom Christians place their faith and hope.[16] Therefore, to turn away from such faith and hope is to forfeit salvation altogether (1 Tim 5:11).

---

11. 1 Tim 1:1; 2:3; Titus 1:3; 2:10; 3:4; 4:10. In 2 Tim 1:9 and Titus 3:5 the apostle states that "God" saved us.

12. 2 Tim 1:10; Titus 1:4; 2:13; 3:6.

13. See further the essay "He Saved Us: The Pastoral Letters on the Way of Salvation" elsewhere in this commentary.

14. See further the section "The Saving Truth" in the commentary on 1 Tim 2:1–7.

15. Rom 1:3, 4, 9; 5:10; 8:3, 29, 32; 1 Cor 1:9; 15:28; 2 Cor 1:19; Gal 1:16; 2:20; 4:4, 6; Eph 4:13; Col 1:13; 1 Thess 1:10.

16. 1 Tim 1:1, 14; 3:13; 4:10; 5:5; 6:17; 2 Tim 1:13; Titus 1:2; 2:13; 3:7.

God's salvation through the work of Christ has given us hope, the hope of eternal life. Therefore, we wait with hope for the full realization of that salvation at the appearing of Christ.[17] He will come in both judgment and salvation, so we wait for him to appear as both judge and savior.

Worship is to be directed to God alone (Deut 6:13; Matt 4:10). In the Pastoral Letters the apostle offers praise and thanksgiving to God the Father and to Jesus Christ.[18]

In the Pastorals Paul richly presents the work of God as savior. He also makes mention of the Almighty's work of creation (1 Tim 4:4).

Much of the content of the Pastoral Letters has to do with the ministry of the word and of those who carry it out to the church and to the world. As the church is the church of God (1 Tim 3:15), so also the ministry belongs to God.[19] The word and the gospel are the word and the gospel of God,[20] and since God is one who does not lie (Titus 1:2), his word is completely reliable. Since the word and the ministry belong to God, those who proclaim the word are obligated to God. Paul designates this in a number of ways; he refers to himself as a slave of God (2 Tim 2:24; Titus 1:1) and as an apostle of Jesus Christ (1 Tim 1:1; 2:7; 2 Tim 1:1; Titus 1:1). He addresses Timothy as a man of God (2 Tim 3:17); he speaks of his younger coworker as a minister of Christ Jesus (1 Tim 4:6), and he refers to a pastor as a steward of God (Titus 1:7).

Although the thirteen chapters of the Pastoral Letters make up a relatively small percentage of the New Testament, they are rich in their teaching about almighty God. The language of the church's creeds and of systematic theology makes use of much terminology beyond what is found in these letters to proclaim the truth about God as Father, Son, and Holy Spirit. Nevertheless, it can be said that the Letters to Timothy and to Titus richly proclaim the whole counsel of God with respect to the person and work of God Most High.

---

17. 1 Tim 6:14; 2 Tim 4:1, 8; Titus 2:13.

18. 1 Tim 1:17; 4:3–4; 6:16; 2 Tim 1:3; 4:18. See further the essay "Honor and Glory Forever Amen: The Pastoral Letters on Worship" elsewhere in this commentary.

19. 1 Tim 1:1, 11; 2:7; 6:3; 2 Tim 1:1; 2:15; Titus 1:1, 3.

20. 1 Tim 1:11; 4:5; 6:3; 2 Tim 1:10; 2:9, 15; 3:16; Titus 2:5.

Not by Works... Zealous for Good Works

The Pastoral Letters on Justification and Sanctification

Among other things the Pastoral Letters are known for the instruction in godly living that is recorded in them. Some may even think of these letters as overemphasizing instruction for conduct at the expense of proclaiming the saving gospel. In the essay "He Saved Us: The Pastoral Letters on the Way of Salvation" elsewhere in this commentary I have attempted to show that these letters richly and vigorously proclaim the justification of the sinner before God. Nevertheless, it is true that the Pastorals do have much to say regarding Christian ethics.

It is vital to preserve the correct relationship between justification and sanctification, between soteriology and ethics. In this essay I hope to explore in some detail those themes and their relationship to one another. While the main focus of this essay is on the way in which the Pastoral Letters set forth these truths, this piece will also take note of how the New Testament at large deals with these topics.[1]

ATTEMPTS AT SELF-JUSTIFICATION AND SELF-SANCTIFICATION

Although there are exceptions, most people have at least a sense of being separated from what is good; many will associate this with "God." Sensing that they are separated from God—or at least from "good"—many

---

1. On this topic see further Koeberle, *Quest for Holiness*, the English translation of his work *Rechtfertigung und Heiligung* ("Justification and Sanctification").

endeavor to find their way to God/good.[2] For the most part, these efforts fall into one of three categories (or some combination of the three).

Some attempt to conform their will to what is good. This is the approach of moralism.

Others seek to find oneness with God/good/the universe by the actions of their inner being (soul, spirit, etc.). This is the approach of naturalism and mysticism.

Still others endeavor to unite with God/good through their intellect. This may be termed rationalism.

Moralism in its purest form holds to the idea that I can do enough on my own. A less self-confident form of moralism takes the attitude that God will make up the difference if I do the best I can. This attitude may be expressed as, "If I do my part, God will do his part," or "God has done his part; now I need to do my part."[3]

Moralism sees the human will as having at least some capability. Even if my will is not fully sufficient, it is at least capable of doing something "good." The reality, however, is that in the things of God the human will is not merely weak; it is dead (Eph 2:1, 5; Col 2:13).[4] To the extent that the will can do anything, what it does is hostile toward God (Rom 5:10).

Those who pursue God/good in this way end up in one of two predicaments. Some, like Luther, sense that even their best efforts are insufficient.[5] Others, like the rich young man, fall into a smug but erroneous self-righteousness (Mark 10:17–22).

Moralism fails, for the law of God demands perfection. We cannot achieve perfection by what we do.[6]

The attempts at finding God/good through one's "inner being" (soul, spirit, etc.) include naturalism and mysticism. Naturalism focuses on finding God/good in nature. The ancient Canaanite religion of Baal worship (as well as many other ancient and modern forms of paganism) was a form of naturalism.

---

2. Hence, Paul's observation to the men of Athens that "the God who made the cosmos and all things in it" did so in order that every nation of men might "seek God" and perhaps find him (Acts 17:24–27).

3. The former summarizes semi-Pelagianism, the latter synergism.

4. The classic exposition of this truth and its consequences for theology is Luther's *De Servo Arbitrio* (*On the Bondage of the Will*, AE 33).

5. For example, AE 54:94–95, 156–57, 193.

6. Isa 64:6; Matt 5:20–22a, 27–28, 48; 1 Tim 1:9; 2 Tim 1:9; Titus 1:15; 3:5.

God does reveal himself in nature, for it is his creation (Ps 19:1). However, this revelation in nature is inadequate; only the revelation of God by his word is sufficient to overcome our separation from God.[7]

Man is the crown of God's creation, as he was made in the image of God (Gen 1:26–28). However, by his disobedience of God he lost the holiness of the divine image (Gen 5:3) and therefore was driven out from the presence of God and from eternal life (Gen 3:22–24).

Mysticism involves seeking to find God within the self. The Scriptures are filled with warnings against attempts at self-salvation; the Pastorals contain two particularly pointed ones (1 Tim 5:6; 2 Tim 3:2).[8] Paul's repeated warnings against "myths,"[9] which he critiques by labeling them as being "what is falsely named knowledge" (1 Tim 6:20), are also a rejection of any form of self-salvation, including naturalism and mysticism.

Rationalism refers to any attempt to come to God/good by human reason, wisdom, and the like. Human reason is a gift of God the creator and one of the things that distinguishes mankind from the rest of the creation (Dan 4:25, 32, 34, 36).

Human wisdom, however, is incapable of reaching God. In fact, fallen human reason is set in opposition to the truths of God (1 Cor 1:25, 19–21a).

When in the Pastoral Letters the apostle speaks of saving faith as "the knowledge of the truth,"[10] he does so to indicate that faith in Christ and not human reason is the way to God. He speaks of the false teaching troubling the churches as "the corrupt, meaningless talk and the contradictions of what is falsely named knowledge" (1 Tim 6:20), and he warns Timothy to "avoid foolish and uninformed speculations" (2 Tim 2:23; see also 1 Tim 1:4 and 2 Tim 2:16). These observations serve as a rejection of all attempts to come to God/good by our reason.

Moralism, naturalism/mysticism, and rationalism are all insufficient to reach God. No one successfully seeks for God (Rom 3:11). Mankind's efforts at self-justification and self-sanctification mean only that he is without excuse (Rom 1:18–20).

---

7. Ps 19:7, 14; 1 Tim 2:6–7; 3:16; 4:5, 16; 2 Tim 1:10; 3:15; Titus 1:3.

8. 1 Tim 5:6: "One who has lived luxuriously is as good as dead, even while alive"; 2 Tim 3:2: "There will be men who are lovers of self, lovers of money, braggarts, arrogant people, blasphemers, those who are disobedient to parents, ungrateful, unholy."

9. 1 Tim 1:4; 4:7; 2 Tim 4:4; Titus 1:14.

10. 1 Tim 2:4; 2 Tim 2:25; 3:7; Titus 1:1; see also Heb 10:26.

CHRIST'S WORK OF JUSTIFICATION

Mankind's separation from God also meant his inability to do anything that would bridge that separation. Therefore, God came to man in the person of Jesus Christ. The Pastorals contain two of the Bible's most explicit identifications of Christ as God (1 Tim 1:17 and especially Titus 2:13) as well as a number of references to his incarnation.[11] Jesus taught with the authority of God himself (Matt 7:28–29), and his authority was primarily the authority to reconcile God and man through the forgiveness of sins (Mark 2:5–12).

Christ accomplished this through his death on the cross (1 Tim 2:6; Titus 2:14). By giving himself to death on the cross he became our substitute, taking upon himself the sins of all mankind and bearing the punishment these deserved,[12] even the punishment of eternal damnation in hell (Matt 27:46; 2 Thess 1:7–10). Christ's death is often described with the word "blood,"[13] denoting his death as the payment for the forgiveness of sins (Heb 9:22–26).

The resurrection of Jesus Christ from the dead (1 Tim 3:16; 2 Tim 2:8) confirmed that his payment for forgiveness was sufficient (1 Cor 15:17–20). His resurrection is also the cause and source of the resurrection to eternal life of all believers (1 Cor 15:20–23).

The historical death and resurrection of Jesus Christ is the only way to reconciliation with God (John 14:6; 1 Tim 2:5). His one-time death and resurrection is the way of salvation at all times (2 Cor 5:19; 1 Tim 2:6). By his redemptive work Christ objectively acquired salvation for all people (John 3:17; 1 Tim 2:4).

Salvation is described in the Scriptures with a variety of concepts. These include grace,[14] mercy,[15] love (1 Tim 1:14; 2 Tim 1:7, 13), salvation,[16] justification/righteousness,[17] (eternal) life,[18] God's eternal plan that was

---

11. 1 Tim 1:15; 3:16; 6:13–14; 2 Tim 1:10; 2:8; 4:1; Titus 2:11; 3:4.

12. 2 Cor 5:21; 1 Tim 1:15; Titus 2:14; 1 Pet 3:18.

13. Acts 20:28; Rom 3:25; 5:9; Eph 1:7; 2:13; Col 1:20; Heb 9:12, 14; 10:19; 12:24; 13:12; 1 Pet 1:2, 19; 1 John 1:7; Rev 1:5; 5:9; 7:14; 12:11.

14. 1 Tim 1:2, 14; 6:21; 2 Tim 1:2, 9; 2:1; 4:22; Titus 1:4; 2:11; 3:7, 15.

15. 1 Tim 1:2, 13, 16; 2 Tim 1:2, 16, 18; Titus 3:5.

16. 1 Tim 1:15; 2:4 (2:15); 4:16; 2 Tim 1:9; 2:10; 3:15; Titus 2:11; 3:5; also note the references to God and Christ as "savior" (1 Tim 1:1; 2:3; 4:10; 2 Tim 1:10; Titus 1:1, 3; 2:10, 13; 3:4, 6).

17. 1 Tim 1:9; 6:11; 2 Tim 2:22; 3:16; 4:5; Titus 1:8; 2:12; 3:7.

18. 1 Tim 1:16; 4:8; 6:12, 19; 2 Tim 1:1, 10; Titus 1:2; 3:7.

carried out by Christ (2 Tim 1:9–10), Christ being a "mediator between God and mankind" (1 Tim 2:5), "being an heir of eternal life" (Titus 3:7), the fulfillment of God's covenant with David (2 Tim 2:8), redemption/ransom (1 Tim 2:6; Titus 2:14), cleansing/purification (Titus 2:14), having a good or pure conscience,[19] escaping from the snare of the devil (2 Tim 2:26), "the crown of righteousness" (2 Tim 4:8), and rescue from every evil work and being saved for the Lord's heavenly kingdom (2 Tim 4:18).

This universal salvation is offered to all through God's word and sacraments.[20] These not only make available the benefits of his redemptive work but through them God the Holy Spirit actually works that faith in Christ necessary to apprehend these benefits.

The word of God includes both the call to repentance (law)[21] and the gospel that makes one wise unto salvation through faith, which is in Christ Jesus.[22] Thus, the word of God works both repentance (remorse over sin) and saving faith.

Saving faith is more than a knowledge of the facts of Christ's redemptive work; it is also more than an acceptance of the historical truth of the facts of his redemptive work. Saving faith is also and primarily trust in what Christ did for the salvation of all (Rom 4:16–22; 2 Tim 3:15; Titus 1:1, 4).

When a person believes (trusts) in this redemptive work of Christ, his faith is counted to him as righteousness before God (Rom 4:5). Thus, when one believes (trusts) in this redemptive work of Christ, he is personally (subjectively) justified before God (Acts 16:30–31; 1 Tim 4:10). He is saved through faith alone, without the works of the law.[23]

Through the word and sacraments God the Holy Spirit brings an individual to saving faith. Through these same means of grace the Holy Spirit nurtures and preserves saving faith to withstand temptation and to endure unto the end.[24] Hence, the people of God disseminate God's word and sacraments both for their own salvation and for that of others (Matt 28:18–20; Acts 1:8; 2 Tim 4:1–2).

---

19. 1 Tim 1:5, 19; 3:9; 2 Tim 1:3.
20. Acts 2:38; Rom 10:17; 1 Tim 2:7; 3:16; 2 Tim 2:11; Titus 3:5–7; 1 Pet 1:23; 3:21.
21. 1 Tim 1:20; 2 Tim 2:24–26; Titus 1:9, 13; 3:3, 10–11.
22. 1 Tim 2:6–7; 3:16; 4:16; 2 Tim 1:9–11; 3:15; Titus 1:3.
23. Rom 3:28; Eph 2:8–9; 2 Tim 1:9; Titus 3:5.
24. John 20:30–31; 1 Cor 1:4–9; Col 2:8, 11–15; 1 Pet 1:3–5; 2:2–3; 3:21.

Those who persevere in the saving faith unto the end will receive eternal salvation.[25] As Christ was raised from the dead on the third day, never to die again, so at the last day believers will be raised from their graves to life eternal.[26]

All this is entirely the work of God (2 Cor 4:6), as apart from his saving work one is a slave to sin (Titus 3:3). The Scriptures assure us that God planned salvation before the creation of time (Titus 1:2) and, in fact, chose us for this from all eternity (Rom 8:28–30; Eph 1:3–6; 2 Tim 2:10).

Because the believer has the certain prospect of eternal life, his present life is characterized by hope.[27] With the certain hope of eternal life for the sake of Christ, his people have the motivation (and the empowerment) to live the sanctified life (1 Tim 4:10; Titus 2:11–13).

SANCTIFICATION AS THE WORK OF GOD IN THE JUSTIFIED

The term "sanctification" refers to the state of "holiness." The term and its cognates can refer to God's act of dealing with our unholiness by forgiveness (2 Thess 2:13–14); in this use it is a synonym of "justification." More often "sanctification" refers to the holiness of life that is to follow justification (1 Thess 4:3–8). One who is sanctified by God's forgiveness is empowered to live in a sanctified way; therefore, the word group can embrace elements of both meanings.[28]

The Christian life involves knowing what to do that will be pleasing to God, who is holy (John 14:15; 1 Tim 2:3). God reveals this to us through his word, his law. A more important concern has to do with what enables a person to perform works that are holy.

Of ourselves we can do nothing that is holy in terms of either justification or sanctification (John 15:5), for we are spiritually dead (Eph 2:1–2; Heb 9:14; Rev 3:1). God makes us alive through faith in Jesus Christ (Eph 2:4–6, 8); this life-giving faith is created by the word (gospel) of God (Rom 10:17; 2 Tim 3:16–17), through which God the Holy Spirit works (1 Cor 12:3).

---

25. Matt 24:9–13; 1 Tim 1:16; 2 Tim 4:6–8; Rev 2:10.
26. 1 Cor 15:51–53; 1 Thess 4:13–17; 2 Tim 2:11–12a; 4:8, 18.
27. 1 Tim 1:1; 4:10; 5:5; 6:17; Titus 1:2; 2:13; 3:7.
28. 1 Tim 2:15; 4:5; 5:10; 2 Tim 1:9.

This life means eternal life with God in heaven.[29] This life also means the power and ability to do holy works that are pleasing to God (John 15:5; Eph 2:10; 1 Tim 1:12), including the principle virtue of love (1 Tim 1:5).

In baptism we die and are raised with Christ (Rom 6:3-4, 11; Col 2:11-12; 2 Tim 2:11-12a). This means the gift of eternal life in heaven (Rom 6:5; Col 3:1, 4); it also means the power to live a new, holy kind of life (Rom 6:11-12; Col 3:1-3, 5, 12).

The work of justification is entirely God's work, as he makes the dead alive (Eph 2:4-9). We do not cooperate in this being made alive any more than we cooperated in our being born (John 3:3-8). One who has been made alive in this way through the gift of faith thereby becomes one who is actively believing in Jesus Christ (Rom 10:10-11). While our justification is entirely the work of God, in which we do not cooperate, when we have been justified, we do cooperate in the life of sanctification (Rom 8:8-13).

Before faith one is unwilling and unable to do the things that please God (1 Tim 1:13). After coming to faith, one becomes willing and able to do things that are pleasing to God.[30]

In terms of justification God's work for us is already complete (Rom 8:1; Eph 2:8-9). In terms of sanctification this work is never complete in this life (Rom 7:22-25) but is ongoing (Eph 2:10; Col 3:5, 12).

In sanctification we live out what we already are in terms of justification. Therefore, the Scriptures often exhort us to be in our conduct what we already are through faith in Christ (Matt 5:14-16).

In terms of justification, we have already put off the old (sinful) man and put on the new (righteous) man (Col 3:9-10). In terms of sanctification, we are to be continually putting off the old man and putting on the new man (Eph 4:20-24).

Being made alive and empowered to do what is pleasing to God, the Christian lives his entire life in service to and for the glory of God (1 Cor 10:31). The new life of sanctification involves doing those things that are pleasing to God. The law of God as recorded in the Scriptures tells us what those things are that are "good and acceptable to God our savior."[31] This type of life includes specifically religious activity such as

---

29. 1 Tim 1:16; 6:12; 2 Tim 2:10; Titus 1:2; 3:7.
30. Rom 7:22; Titus 1:1; 2:11-14; 3:8.
31. 1 Tim 2:3, 9-10; 5:1-16, 20-24; 6:2-3; 2 Tim 2:21; Titus 3:1, 14.

worship, prayer, and spreading the word of God (1 Tim 2:1–3, 7–10; 2 Tim 1:3). This also means that in terms of those things that God has neither commanded nor forbidden, when the Christian chooses to do any of these (or to refrain from doing them), he does so as a work pleasing to God (Rom 14:5–9; Titus 1:15).

The Scriptures exhort Christians in general and their pastors in particular to hold to the entire truth that is set forth in the Scriptures and to reject all false teachings.[32] Nevertheless, believers are also directed to avoid becoming embroiled in futile disputes over words (2 Tim 2:14, 16; Titus 3:9).

The Christian serves God particularly in his vocation (Luke 3:12–14; Titus 2:1–10). The Christian will hold a number of vocations throughout his earthly life. Among the vocations that Paul mentions in the Pastorals are citizens (1 Tim 2:1–2; Titus 3:1), men (1 Tim 2:8), women (1 Tim 2:9–15), husbands (1 Tim 3:2, 12; Titus 1:6), wives (1 Tim 5:9; Titus 2:4–5), fathers (1 Tim 3:4, 12; Titus 1:6), mothers (1 Tim 2:15; 5:10, 14; 2 Tim 1:5; Titus 2:4), grandparents (2 Tim 1:5), children and grandchildren (1 Tim 5:4), pastors (1 Tim 3:1–7; Titus 1:5–9),[33] "deacons" (1 Tim 3:8–10, 12–13), "deaconesses" (1 Tim 3:11), those enrolled in the order of widows (1 Tim 5:9–16),[34] slaves (1 Tim 6:1–2a; Titus 2:9–10),[35] "those who are rich in this age" (1 Tim 6:17–19), older men (Titus 2:2), older women (Titus 2:3–4), younger women (Titus 2:4–5), and younger men (Titus 2:6–7).

Servants of God's word are to proclaim the word that both empowers godly living and guides the Christian as to the godly works that he is to perform.[36] Servants of God's word, therefore, are to empower and direct sanctified living by both their proclamation and their example.[37]

---

32. 1 Tim 1:3–5; 6:3–4, 20; 2 Tim 3:14–17; 4:1–2; Titus 1:13; 2:15.

33. Throughout the Pastoral Letters are various sections that speak to the pastoral vocation of Timothy, Titus, and/or Paul: 1 Tim 1:3–7, 10, 18; 2:7; 4:6–8, 11–16; 5:1–3; 6:2b, 11–14, 20; 2 Tim 1:8, 11, 13–14; 2:1–3, 14–16, 23–26; 3:5b, 14–17; 4:1–2, 5; Titus 1:3, 11, 13; 2:7–8, 15; 3:1–2, 8–10, 13.

34. See the section "The Office of Widow" in the commentary on 1 Tim 5:3–16.

35. In Eph 6:9 and Col 4:1 the apostle also gives instruction in Christian living for the vocation of masters. See further the entry "Slavery in the New Testament World" in the Extended Notes.

36. 1 Tim 1:3–5; 2 Tim 3:15; Titus 1:1; 2:11, 14.

37. 1 Tim 3:1–13; 4:11; 6:14; Titus 1:5–9.

Grace and Life

SANCTIFICATION AND PRESERVATION IN THE FAITH

Good works are not necessary for salvation, as we are saved by grace through faith in Christ without good works (2 Tim 1:9; Titus 3:5). Nevertheless, good works are a necessary result of that faith which saves without good works, for the faith that saves without good works is never without good works, for the faith that saves without good works always produces good works in the life of the believer.[38] Therefore, someone's lack of good works, his evil works, or his false good works demonstrate that any claim he makes of knowing God is fraudulent (Titus 1:16).

The Christian's life of good works is never perfect in this life, as he is subject to sins of weakness (Rom 7:15–23). However, saving faith is incompatible with deliberate, intentional sins, for these are destructive of saving faith (Heb 10:26–27).

Any sin is a violation of God's law; therefore, any sin makes the sinner worthy of eternal damnation (Jas 2:10; Rom 6:23). Christ came to save sinners (1 Tim 1:15–16); what condemns, therefore, is not the depravity of sin but the absence of repentance over sin and of faith in Christ for forgiveness (Luke 13:1–5).

Good works are a necessary fruit of saving faith. Deliberate, intentional sin is incompatible with genuine faith and brings the loss of salvation (Luke 11:24–26; 12:47–48).

All sin is a violation of God's law; in this regard all sin is equally damning. However, different types of sin have different effects upon the individual and upon others.

Sinful thoughts and desires are every bit as damnable as any other sin against the law of God (Matt 5:21–22, 27–28). These must also be repented of, and forgiveness for them must be found in the crucified and risen Christ.

Sinful words are every bit as damnable as any other sin against the law of God (Matt 5:21–22). In addition, sins of the tongue are harmful not only to the individual but to others as well (Jas 3:6–10). Lies deceive (Prov 26:18–19), and slander harms the reputation of others (Prov 22:1). Thus, sins of speech are sins not only against God but also against others. These must also be repented of, and forgiveness for them must be found in the crucified and risen Christ.

---

38. Gal 2:16; 5:6; 1 Tim 2:10; 5:10, 25; 6:18; Titus 2:7, 14; 3:8, 14.

All sinful deeds are sins against God. Some sins are particularly harmful to one's own self (1 Cor 6:18). Many are also harmful to others: murder, adultery, theft. These must also be repented of, and forgiveness for them must be found in the crucified and risen Christ.

Sinful thoughts and desires are as much a violation of God's law as sinful words and deeds. If left unchecked and unrepented, these may also lead to other sins (2 Sam 11).

The Christian life is never static; one is either growing in faith and in Christian living (Col 1:10; 2 Thess 1:3; 2 Pet 3:18), or he is becoming weaker (Luke 8:13–14). Thus, it is essential to be nurturing one's faith, that he may increase in faith and in the Christian living that follows faith.

In his struggle with sin and the tempter the Christian has no better aid than the word of God (Eph 6:13–17). By the word of God faith (and the holiness of life that follows faith) is nurtured (2 Tim 3:14–17; 1 Pet 2:2–3). To this the Christian adds prayer (Eph 6:18; 1 Tim 2:1–2, 8; 4:5).

SUFFERING AND SANCTIFICATION

Suffering for the sake of Christ is a part of the Christian's new life of sanctification. Jesus himself spoke of the necessity of his followers taking up the cross to follow him.[39] Paul writes of the need to suffer with Christ, that we may be glorified with him (Rom 8:17; 2 Tim 2:12a).

The sufferings of Christ relate to our justification.[40] The sufferings of the Christian have to do not with justification but with sanctification. The sufferings of Christians do not contribute to their justification but are a result of it.

Jesus spoke of taking up the cross; his apostle describes the same reality as suffering with Christ. Bearing the cross and suffering with Christ do not encompass every type of hardship. Some sufferings are the consequence of some specific wrongdoing (Gen 19:15–26; 2 Sam 12:14;

---

39. Matt 10:38; 16:24; Mark 8:34; Luke 9:23; 14:27.

40. It is noteworthy that although in two of his addresses recorded in the book of Acts (17:3; 26:23) Paul speaks of Christ's suffering in connection with his redemptive work, in the apostle's letters he never uses the terminology of suffering with reference to the work of salvation. In his epistles the vocabulary of suffering and affliction always refers to the life of the Christian. Other places in the New Testament that do use the vocabulary of suffering for the redemptive work of Christ are Matt 16:21 (Mark 8:31; Luke 9:22); 17:2 (Mark 9:2); Luke 17:25; 22:15; 24:26, 46; Acts 1:3; 3:18; Heb 2:9–10, 18; 5:8; 13:12; 1 Pet 1:11; 2:21, 23; 3:18; 4:1; 5:1.

2 Tim 4:14). Christians experience other hardships not as a result of any specific sin but because these afflict mankind in general (John 9:3; 2 Tim 4:20). Those sufferings that are a part of the Christian's life of sanctification are those things that he or she endures on account of their Christian faith, life, and/or witness.

In the Pastoral Letters Paul speaks of the sanctified suffering of believers in this way. Sometimes believers suffer for their faith (1 Tim 1:18-19; 2 Tim 1:12). Then again Christ's followers may bear suffering on account of their way of life.[41] Christians also suffer due to their witness to Christ and to his word.[42]

That Christians suffer with Christ as a result of their being justified by Christ is rooted in their baptism. In baptism a Christian is crucified, buried, and raised from the dead with Christ (Rom 6:3-4; Col 2:11-12); the apostle indicates this with verbs compounded with the preposition σύν. As a result of this baptismal incorporation into the redemptive work of Christ, the believer is justified from sin (Rom 6:7). Having been justified with Christ in this way, the baptized is called and empowered to live a new life with (σύν) Christ (Rom 6:4).

This new life of sanctification includes suffering as a result of one's faith, way of life, and/or witness. Our baptismal death with Christ means that we will live with him eternally, and part and parcel of that baptismal death and life is enduring the sufferings that come our way (2 Tim 2:11-12a).

The Christian's suffering with Christ might include such things as imprisonment or martyrdom (2 Tim 2:8-9; 3:11; 4:6). Some followers of Christ may be spared such extreme forms of suffering, but all Christians will experience some type of persecution or harassment.[43]

The life of suffering with Christ is not limited to certain believers. All Christians will bear some form of hardship on account of their faith in Christ, their life for Christ, and/or their witness to Christ (2 Tim 3:12). Nevertheless, it is the special vocation of those who are called to ministry in the word of Christ to bear suffering for his sake.[44]

Our baptismal death and resurrection with Christ calls us to suffer with him, and it also empowers us to endure and to withstand such sufferings (2 Tim 1:7-8). Included in that power is the assurance that our

---

41. 1 Tim 1:18-19; 2 Tim 1:16; 2:3; 3:12.
42. 1 Tim 1:18-19; 2 Tim 1:8, 12, 16; 2:3, 9; 4:5.
43. Gal 6:12; 1 Tim 1:20; 2 Tim 3:12; 4:14.
44. 2 Tim 1:8, 12; 2:3, 9-10; 3:11; 4:5-6.

Lord will preserve us through these until we receive our glorious resurrection with him at the last day (2 Tim 1:12; 2:9; 3:11).[45]

God's people may suffer in the course of their serving others. It is also possible that they may serve others by their suffering. When Paul writes, "I endure all things for the sake of the elect ones, in order that they also may obtain salvation, which is in Christ Jesus with eternal glory" (2 Tim 2:10), he speaks of his service through the word and through suffering. This passage has a meaning similar to that of Col 1:24: "Now I rejoice in my sufferings in your place, and in my flesh I complete the things lacking of the afflictions of Christ on behalf of his body, which is the church." The oneness of believers in the body of Christ means that the sufferings of one Christian may make up for a lack of suffering on the part of fellow believers. See further the section "For the Sake of the Elect Ones" in the commentary on 2 Tim 2:8–13.[46]

THE RELATIONSHIP OF JUSTIFICATION AND SANCTIFICATION

Justification and sanctification must be clearly distinguished in our proclamation and study, lest we confuse the two. If we confuse justification and sanctification, we will have neither justification nor sanctification.

While we distinguish justification and sanctification in our proclamation, these are never separate from one another in the Christian life. True Christianity includes both justification and sanctification. Both are essential for a genuine Christianity.

Justification is the source and cause of sanctification. Without true justification there can be no true sanctification.

Justification that does not produce sanctification is merely masquerading as justification. Sanctification that does not proceed from justification is merely masquerading as sanctification.

---

45. In Phil 3:10–11 Paul speaks of being conformed to Christ's death, knowing the fellowship of his sufferings, and attaining to the resurrection from the dead. The form of the word "resurrection" (ἐξανάστασιν) that the apostle uses in verse 11 emphasizes that he is speaking there of the resurrection *from* the dead. Therefore, when in verse 10 he uses the simple form of the word (ἀναστάσεως) in referring to the power of Christ's resurrection, this indicates that he has reference there to the risen Lord empowering his people to endure and to overcome the sufferings that they experience for being his followers.

46. On the interpretation of Col 1:24 see Deterding, *Colossians*, 75–79.

Without the continual return to justification, sanctification falls into Pharisaism and the wildest exaggeration. When, however, we hold to the condemning word of law and judgment and also to the pardoning word of gospel and forgiveness, sanctification receives its true modesty and its true vitality.

As Luther writes: "God's name is kept holy when the Word of God is taught in its truth and purity, and we, as the children of God, also lead holy lives according to it."[47]

The Epistles often teach this truth by the alternation of indicative and imperative. Indicatives regarding the way of justification (e.g., Rom 1—11) are the basis of the imperatives of sanctification (e.g., Rom 12—16).

Jesus Christ came into the world to bring us salvation and to redeem us to be his own people. Furthermore, he did this to purify us in order that we might renounce ungodliness and be zealous to do good works (Titus 2:11-14).

The word of God gives us life and salvation. The word of God also empowers us to godly living (1 Pet 1:22-25).

Baptism is a death and resurrection with Jesus Christ to bring us the gifts of justification and eternal life (Rom 6:3-4, 7; Col 2:11-12; 2 Tim 2:11-12a). This new life of justification also empowers us for the new life of sanctification (Rom 6:11-12). Hence, the Scriptures often direct us to the meaning of our baptism, that we might thereby be empowered for godly living.

The Lord's Supper gives forgiveness and eternal life (Matt 26:26-29). This forgiving power of the Lord's Supper is, therefore, to be reflected in the lives of the communicants (1 Cor 10:14—11:34).

"You did not choose me, but I chose you and appointed you that you should go and bear fruit and that your fruit should abide" (John 15:16). "Jesus Christ . . . gave himself for us, in order that he might redeem us from all lawlessness and might purify for himself a chosen people, who are zealous for good works" (Titus 2:13-14).

---

47. Small Catechism, Explanation to the First Petition of the Lord's Prayer.

Honor and Glory Forever Amen

The Pastoral Letters on Worship

We might think of the Pastoral Letters as being almost an enchiridion for life in the Christian church. Certainly, one item of interest for Christians would be the church's worship. It is not surprising, then, that the Pastorals touch on a number of facets of Christian worship.

In his First Letter to Timothy (4:4–5) Paul notes that "every creation of God . . . is sanctified by the word of God and prayer." "The word of God and prayer" can be seen as a summary of Christian worship. As believers gather for worship, they read from the word of God and hear it proclaimed to them—also in connection with baptism and the Lord's Supper; they also join together in prayers of requests for themselves and others and acclamations of praise and thanksgiving to God. Thus, the apostle is saying that the church's gathering to worship has as one of its benefits sanctifying believers to live every aspect of their lives in harmony with God and his will.

The most basic statement about worship in the Pastoral Letters is Paul's instruction to Timothy, "Until I come, devote yourself to the public reading [of Scripture], to preaching, to teaching" (1 Tim 4:13).[1] When Paul speaks of reading Scripture and preaching, he is referring to two of the most central elements of the church's public worship. From the Sabbath day worship services conducted in the synagogue the Christian church inherited the practice of reading from the Scriptures and of listening to those who were qualified to do so expound on those Scriptures (Luke 4:16–30; Acts 13:14–41). Therefore, the apostle instructed his younger coworker that he should devote himself particularly to these activities.

---

1. On the translation of this passage see the textual notes on 1 Tim 4:13.

Grace and Life

Paul's mention of these two activities was a synecdoche; by mentioning these two major activities of worship he was including all of the various activities that made up a Christian worship service. In the Pastoral Letters he makes mention of some of the other elements that comprised the church's worship.

Song is a part of worship throughout the Scriptures.[2] In the Pastoral Letters are a number of passages that have the marks of poetry.[3] Perhaps the apostle took these from hymns that were in use in the church of the first century. Equally likely, if not more likely, is the possibility that these are original compositions by Paul, who under divine inspiration (2 Tim 3:16) wrote them in such a way that they could be sung.[4] Either way, the fact that early Christians continued the biblical practice of singing "psalms, hymns, and spiritual songs" (Col 3:16–17; Eph 5:19–20) suggests the possibility that at least some of these verses found their way into the hymnody of the churches served by Timothy and Titus.[5]

When the apostle instructed Timothy to "lay hold of eternal life, to which you were called, having confessed the good confession before many witnesses" (1 Tim 6:12), the "good confession" that Timothy "confessed" refers to his receiving baptism, likely by the hand of Paul himself, as later church history demonstrates that adult baptisms would have included some type of confession of the faith into which the candidates were being

---

2. In addition to the book of Psalms note Exod 15:1; Job 38:4–7; Isa 51:11; Matt 26:30; Luke 1:46–55, 68–79; 2:13–14, 29–32; Eph 5:19–20; Col 3:16–17; Rev 5:9–14. The testimony of the Roman official Pliny the Younger (*Letters* 10.96.7), an unbeliever, that Christians "were in the habit of meeting on a certain fixed day before it was light, when they sang in alternate verses a hymn to Christ, as to a god" also attests to the early Christian practice of singing as a part of their worship.

3. 1 Tim 1:17; 2:5–6; 3:16 (perhaps 6:11–12); 6:15–16; 2 Tim 1:9–10; 2:11–13; Titus 3:4–7. Except for the first of these passages the twenty-seventh edition of the Nestle-Aland edition of *Novum Testamentum Graece* arranges all of them in poetic verse, suggesting that they could have been sung in a manner similar to the way in which biblical psalms were sung.

4. Commenting on a passage in another Pauline Letter and critiquing the notion that it was the apostle's adaptation of an early Christian hymn rather than his own composition, N. T. Wright noted, "Nothing would be more calculated to puzzle a congregation than tampering with a hymn they are in the act of singing" ("Poetry and Theology," 445).

5. In that light it is perhaps significant that of the passages listed in n3 above, only one (2 Tim 2:11–13) is not reflected in the texts of hymns that are included in *Lutheran Service Book*. Language from those passages is attested in thirty different hymn texts from that hymnal (350, 378, 382, 383, 384, 402, 410, 458, 464, 477, 498/499, 526, 556, 559, 565, 566, 571, 588, 594, 599, 661, 664, 689, 714, 745, 802, 822, 847, 905, 922).

baptized.[6] The young man's baptism, therefore, likely took place during a worship service. The apostle also refers to baptism in his Letter to Titus (3:5). Baptism would have been foundational for any Christian as his/her entry into the Christian faith and the fellowship of the Christian church.[7] The circumstances implied by the apostle's reference to Timothy's baptism would indicate that baptism and reflection on the meaning of baptism would have had a place in early Christian worship services.

Timothy's good confession points to the use of some kind of creed as a way of confessing the faith. Later church history demonstrates how early Christian confessions of faith (e.g., "Jesus is Lord") developed into the creeds of Christendom that are still used today.[8] This would indicate that early Christians would have confessed their faith in worship, even if a baptism was not being conducted at that time.

Several passages in the Pastorals have the character of such a creedal confession of faith. In addition to their subject matter, they also lend themselves to being memorized and recited in unison.[9] These include: 1 Tim 1:17 ("To the king of the ages; imperishable, unseen, the only God, be honor and glory for ages of ages. Amen"); 2:5–6 ("For there is one God and one mediator between God and mankind, the man Christ Jesus, who gave himself as a ransom for all, as a testimony at the right time"); 3:16 ("who was manifested in the flesh, vindicated in the spirit, seen by angels, proclaimed among the nations, believed on in the world, taken up in glory"); 6:15–16 ("He who is the blessed and only sovereign, the king of those who are having kingship and lord of those who are having lordship, the only one who has immortality, who dwells in unapproachable light, whom no one among men has seen nor is able to see, to whom be honor and might forever. Amen"); 2 Tim 1:9–10 ("God, who saved us and called us by a holy calling, not according to our works but according to his own plan and grace, which he gave to us in Christ Jesus before eternal times, but now has made known through the manifestation of our savior Christ Jesus, who abolished death and brought to light life and incorruption through the gospel"); 2:11–13 ("For if we died with him, we will also live with him; if we endure, we will also reign with him; if we will deny

---

6. See the section "Timothy's Good Confession" in the commentary on 1 Tim 6:11–16.

7. Note how baptism functions in this way in the episodes of Acts 2:38–41; 8:12–13; 10:44–48; 16:13–16; 18:5–8.

8. On early Christian confessions of faith see Kelly, *Early Christian Creeds*.

9. As noted by Marshall, *Pastoral Epistles*, 56.

him, he will deny us; if we are faithless, he remains faithful, for he is not able to deny himself"); Titus 3:4–7 ("But when the goodness and love for mankind of God our savior appeared, he saved us, not by works in righteousness which we had done, but according to his mercy, through the washing of rebirth and of renewal of the Holy Spirit, whom he poured out on us richly through Jesus Christ our savior, in order that having been justified through his grace, we might become heirs according to the hope of eternal life"). It is possible that one or more of these found their way into early Christian worship services as a confession of faith; certainly, they are reflected to a degree in the earliest confessions of faith known from church history.[10]

We have noted the important place that prayer had in early Christian worship. In 1 Timothy Paul gave instruction for various types of prayer to be offered as a part of public worship, and he marked out the governing authorities as special objects of the church's prayers (2:1–2). In the Pastorals he gave special mention to prayers of thanksgiving (1 Tim 1:12; 4:3–4; 2 Tim 1:3).

Worship is a much broader concept than praise, but praise is certainly an important component of worship. The worship of praise is seen in the Pastoral Letters in three doxologies (1 Tim 1:17; 6:16; 2 Tim 4:18), each of which occur at or near the conclusion of a major portion of the respective letters.

A worship service is a primary way in which Christians offer their worship to almighty God. In his First Letter to Timothy the apostle points out that Christian services of worship (1 Tim 2:8) are to be matched by the believers' worship of service 1 Tim 2:9–10).

Going back at least until the time of Moses and Aaron, biblical worship has involved benediction (Num 6:22–27). Thus, it is no surprise that each of the Pastoral Letters concludes with a benediction (1 Tim 6:21; 2 Tim 4:22; Titus 3:15).

Worship is an important part of the life of the people of God—also in the life to come.[11] That significance of worship is evident also in Paul's Letters to Timothy and to Titus.

---

10. Again see Kelly, *Early Christian Creeds*.
11. See Rev 5:6–14 and also the many other hymns contained in the Apocalypse.

An Excellent Task

The Pastoral Ministry According to the Pastoral Letters

The Pastoral Letters are well known for the list of qualifications for the pastoral office given in 1 Tim 3 and Titus 1. While these requirements are certainly important, these letters have much more than that to say about the office and work of pastors.

We should note at the outset that when Paul instructs Titus that he is to "set right the things that are lacking" by appointing elders (pastors) in every town (1:5), this is an indication that the pastoral office is a necessary part of God's plan for his people. It is the will of God that his people be served spiritually by those who hold the pastoral office. A congregation of God's people needs a pastor, and Christians have the need to receive such ministry from one who holds the pastoral office.

The Pastorals speak to at least five aspects of the ministry of pastors: the qualifications necessary to hold the office, preparation for becoming a pastor, the responsibilities of a pastor, the authority of the pastoral office, and the power with which the pastor carries out his ministry. In this essay we will have a look at each of these; see also the commentary on the various passages that are referred to here.

QUALIFICATIONS

In his First Letter to Timothy Paul warns his younger coworker against hastily laying hands on anyone, that is, against allowing anyone to become a pastor before he is ready (5:22). This presupposes both that a man needs to meet certain qualifications to hold this office, and—by extension—that there will be some way of preparing one to become a pastor.

In 1 Tim 3:1–7 and Titus 1:5–9 the apostle lays out the qualifications for being a pastor. There is considerable overlap between the two lists—sometimes there is even identical vocabulary, so that we can regard the two lists as essentially equivalent. The qualifications they give fall into two broad categories: personal integrity and the aptitude for carrying out the ministry of the word.

The first qualification given in each list, that the overseer/pastor must be "beyond reproach" (ἀνεπίλημπτον, ἀνέγκλητος), serves as a sort of heading and summary of all the remaining attributes. A pastor must be one who leads an exemplary life; the other qualifications given in these lists spell out in detail what constitutes a life "beyond reproach."

Each list indicates that a pastor must be the husband of one wife (1 Tim 3:2; Titus 1:6). We have noted elsewhere that this means the (prospective) pastor must not have ended his marriage and entered into another for reasons other than those deemed acceptable by the Scriptures.[1] Further instruction is given regarding a pastor's oversight of his children (1 Tim 3:4; Titus 1:6). A pastor is to treat those in his care like members of his own family (1 Tim 5:1–2); that being the case, he cannot serve the family of God if his own family life is in disarray due to his negligence or incompetence (1 Tim 3:5).

Other terms common to both lists include "sensible" (σώφρονα), "not a drunkard" (μὴ πάροινον), and "not a bully" (μὴ πλήκτην). Related to this are the requirements that the pastor be "not quarrelsome" (ἄμαχον, 1 Tim 3:3) and "not quick-tempered" (μὴ ὀργίλον, Titus 1:7). These terms, each from a slightly different perspective, describe someone in control of himself both mentally and emotionally (as well as spiritually).

Along the same lines occur other terms with much the same meaning. Paul indicates that a pastor must be "self-controlled" (νηφάλιον, 1 Tim 3:2; ἐγκρατῆ, Titus 1:8), "respectable" (κόσμιον, 1 Tim 3:2), and "a lover of good" (φιλάγαθον, Titus 1:8). These are a part of him having a "good witness from those on the outside" (1 Tim 3:7); such behavior is "necessary" so that even outsiders would have to (however begrudgingly) hold him in respect.

In other instances, the apostle uses different terms in each of the letters to designate similar attributes that are necessary for one who would

---

1. See the textual notes on 1 Tim 3:2; Titus 1:6.

be a pastor. The pastor must be "kind" (ἐπιεικῆ, 1 Tim 3:3), that is, "not arrogant" (μὴ αὐθάδη, Titus 1:7). It is necessary that he be "not quarrelsome" (ἄμαχον, 1 Tim 3:3); in other words, "not quick-tempered" (μὴ ὀργίλον, Titus 1:7). That he is to be "not a lover of wealth" (ἀφιλάργυρον, 1 Tim 3:3) is much the same as his being "not guilty of shameful gain" (μὴ αἰσχροκερδῆ, Titus 1:7).

Near the end of the list in Titus the apostle states that the pastor is to be "righteous" (δίκαιον, 1:8) and "pious" (ὅσιον, 1:8). These are rich terms that comprehensively detail the entirety of the Christian life that emerges from being justified through faith in Christ (see the entries "Righteousness/Justification" and "Gentle, Kind" in the Extended Notes). One who would be a pastor must be one whose faith is active in love and good works (Gal 5:6; Eph 2:8–10).

All of these describe the pastor's personal faith, life, and character. But in addition to all of these, it is equally important that he be "able to teach" (διδακτικόν, 1 Tim 3:2; 2 Tim 2:24), that is, that he "be able both to encourage in the sound teaching and to convince (or reprove) those who speak against it" (Titus 1:9). In order to be able to engage in teaching of this sort, the pastor must adhere to the sound teaching that he has learned (2 Tim 1:13; 3:10–11; Titus 1:9), that is, to the holy Scriptures.[2] For this reason, it is important that he be "not a recent convert" (μὴ νεόφυτον, 1 Tim 3:6); he must have had adequate time to have become sufficiently knowledgeable about the Scriptures.

Related to this is the requirement that the pastor be φιλόξενον (1 Tim 3:2; Titus 1:8, a term often translated "hospitable"). In the commentary on these two passages I have made the case for understanding this in terms of hospitality shown to traveling missionaries in support of their work of spreading the gospel. Therefore, I have translated/paraphrased this word as "a lover of traveling missionaries." In twenty-first-century terms we might think of this as upholding the work of evangelism and missions. The pastor is to champion the spread of the gospel beyond his own immediate concerns.

PREPARATION

One just does not pick up such a task without being prepared for it. The Pastoral Letters presuppose such preparation on the part of Timothy and

---

2. 1 Tim 4:16; 6:3; 2 Tim 2:15; 3:14–15; 4:13.

of others. Timothy has been "instructed [or nourished] in the words of the faith and of the good teaching [or doctrine], after which [he has] followed" (1 Tim 4:6). He is to carry out his ministry according to "those things which [he] heard from [Paul] through many witnesses" (2 Tim 2:2).

In the commentary I have contended that references to "prophecy" made to or about Timothy (1 Tim 1:18; 4:14, which see) refer to his being instructed in the word of God, particularly by the apostle himself. Timothy was taught the Scriptures from childhood by his mother and grandmother (2 Tim 1:4–5; 3:14), but Paul himself was also involved in his instruction in the word (see the commentary on 2 Tim 1:6).[3] Timothy received such instruction; he himself is to instruct others. He is to "entrust those things which [he] heard from [Paul] through many witnesses to faithful men, who will be suited to also teach them to others" (2 Tim 2:2).

Contemporary seminary education has a more formal appearance than that which is presupposed in the Pastoral Letters. Nevertheless, it is cut of the same cloth; it has been structured in order to carry out the sort of preparation for the ministry that lies in the background of the Pastorals.

RESPONSIBILITIES

Throughout these letters Paul instructs Timothy about the responsibilities that he bears. Many of these pertain not just to Timothy himself but to any and all who hold the pastoral office.

A major responsibility that a pastor shoulders is the obligation of fidelity to the word of God. The apostle directs that pastors teach no other doctrine than the truth of what they have been taught.[4] They are to set forth only what is taught in the Scriptures (2 Tim 3:14–17), and they are to teach and preach all that is in the Scriptures (2 Tim 4:1–2, whose commentary see). At certain places within these letters Paul even gives short, creedal-like descriptions of the central message that is to be proclaimed.[5]

And so it is that the major task with which a pastor such as Timothy is to occupy himself is the proclamation of that scriptural word.[6] The

---

3. See the section "Timothy as One in Christ" in the commentary on 2 Tim 2:1–7.
4. 1 Tim 1:3–5; 6:3–4, 20; Titus 1:13; 2:15.
5. 1 Tim 3:16; 2 Tim 1:10–12; 2:8; Titus 2:11–14; 3:4–7.
6. 1 Tim 2:7; 4:6, 11, 13; 5:17; 6:2, 20; 2 Tim 1:11; 2:14–15; 4:1–2; Titus 2:15.

apostle uses a variety of terms for this activity,[7] but all point to the pastor's main task: being a herald of God's word.

The pastor carries out his ministry for the eternal salvation of others (2 Tim 3:15; Titus 2:11). In addition, he proclaims the word to guide and empower believers for a godly life of love and good works (1 Tim 1:3–5; Titus 1:1; 2:14).

That ministry includes rebuking sin (1 Tim 5:19–20; 2 Tim 4:2); in dogmatic terms it includes proclaiming the law as well as the gospel. A pastor rebukes sin in order to bring the sinner to repentance, so that he might be ready for the word of saving truth (2 Tim 2:25).

Related to this is the need to instruct opponents, doing so in the hope that they will come to repentance and saving faith (2 Tim 2:25). Along these same lines a pastor must oppose false teachers, lest these turn others away from the saving faith (2 Tim 4:14–15; Titus 1:11). Thus, the pastor also has a responsibility for church discipline (Titus 3:10–11).

While part of teaching the truth is rebuking error, a pastor must not become distracted by such things from the main focus of his ministry: the message of salvation. As much as possible he must avoid foolish controversies and avoid allowing those in his care to become embroiled in them (2 Tim 2:16, 23; Titus 3:9).

When Paul instructs Timothy to devote himself to "reading" (ἀναγνώσει, 1 Tim 4:13), his reference is to the public reading of Scripture in the church's services of worship (see the commentary on that verse). In the same passage he also directs Timothy to devotion to preaching (παρακλήσει). The apostle also refers to public worship when he calls for prayer for all people, especially the governing authorities (1 Tim 2:1–2; 1 Tim 4:13). These passages make it plain that the church's worship services (of word and sacrament) are to be a main focus and emphasis of a pastor's ministry.

Paul also has some instructions about a pastor's general conduct and demeanor. He tells Timothy to "be sober in all things" (2 Tim 4:5). He exhorts him to be an example to others (1 Tim 4:12; 6:11–14). In his dealings with others he is to show respect for all (1 Tim 5:1–2). The most

---

7. Proclaimer (κῆρυξ), teacher (διδάσκαλος), minister (διάκονος), command (παραγγέλλω), teach (διδάσκω), preaching/proclamation (παράκλησις), teaching (διδασκαλία), preaching (λόγος), proclaim/exhort (παρακαλέω), speak (λαλέω), preach (κήρυξον—2 Tim 4:2), rebuke (ἔλεγξον—2 Tim 4:2), correct (ἐπιτίμησον—2 Tim 4:2), encourage (παρακάλεσον—2 Tim 4:2), convince (ἐλέγχειν—Titus 1:9).

important work, one that brings eternal benefits, is worthy of the most rigorous effort that the laborer can put forth (1 Tim 4:9–10; 2 Tim 2:4–6).

While all believers in him who endured the cross for their salvation are called upon to bear suffering and persecution for the sake of their faith,[8] this is especially true of those who carry out the ministry of the gospel. Therefore, in his final letter, written near the time of his own martyrdom (2 Tim 4:6) and to a fellow proclaimer of the word of Christ, the apostle reminds him repeatedly of his calling to suffer for the sake of Christ.[9]

Paul instructs Timothy to "do the work of an evangelist" (2 Tim 4:5). I propose in the commentary on this verse that a likely understanding of this exhortation is that Timothy is to prepare others for and to supervise them in the task of bringing the gospel to others, especially to those who have not previously received it. If this understanding is correct, it would indicate that a pastor ought to have an interest in the mission of the gospel beyond that of his own local area of responsibility for ministry.

A couple of general, perhaps all-encompassing, exhortations from the apostle to Timothy are to "guard the good deposit" (2 Tim 1:14) and to "fulfill your ministry" (2 Tim 4:5). Men do not promote themselves to the ministry; Christ appoints them to it (1 Tim 2:7; Eph 4:11). The ministry is a sacred deposit entrusted to a man; he is to carry it out in keeping with the standards that the Lord of the church himself, in the holy Scriptures, has given to his church.

AUTHORITY

The Pastoral Epistles also point to the authority of the pastoral office. The office has an authority that exceeds any human authority; a pastor has an authority that comes from God himself.

Paul notes of his own apostolic office that he does not hold it because of anything in himself. Rather, he occupies it by the authority of God (κατ' ἐπιταγὴν θεοῦ, 1 Tim 1:1) and by the will of God (διὰ θελήματος θεοῦ, 2 Tim 1:1).

While the apostolic office was unique to a small number of men in New Testament times,[10] similar things are said that pertain to others who

---

8. 2 Tim 3:12; see also Rom 8:17; Phil 3:10–11; Matt 16:24–28 (Mark 8:35—9:1; Luke 9:23–27).

9. 2 Tim 1:8, 15–18; 2:3, 9–13, 24; 4:5.

10. See the entry "Apostle" in the Extended Notes.

hold the pastoral office. Paul states that Christ appointed him for ministry (θέμενος εἰς διακονίαν, 1 Tim 1:12). Similarly, he states that he was appointed (ἐτέθην) to be a herald and a teacher (1 Tim 2:7; 2 Tim 1:11), and that he was entrusted with the proclamation of God's word according to the authority of God our savior (κηρύγματι, ὃ ἐπιστεύθην ἐγὼ κατ' ἐπιταγὴν τοῦ σωτῆρος ἡμῶν θεοῦ, Titus 1:3). When he refers to Timothy's ministry as that which he received as a "deposit" entrusted to him (παραθήκην, 1 Tim 6:20; 2 Tim 1:14) or as a "gift of God" (χάρισμα τοῦ θεοῦ, 2 Tim 1:6), this indicates that it is God who made his younger colleague a pastor.

It is in view of all of this that the pastor/elder is worthy of "honor" (ἀξιούσθωσαν, 1 Tim 5:17). A pastor is honored as one who has been called to his office by God himself.

POWER

Related to the authority of the pastoral office is its power. Because the pastor ministers by the authority of God and with the word of God, his is a ministry that has power.

Paul writes that Christ himself empowers him for ministry (1 Tim 1:12). His reference to God giving a spirit of power (2 Tim 1:7–8) points to God the Holy Spirit as the one who empowers the church's (and therefore also the pastor's) ministry (2 Tim 1:14).

That power is the power of the holy Scriptures. The inspired Scriptures equip the pastor ("man of God") with all that he needs for carrying out his ministry: "for teaching, for rebuke, for improvement, for instruction in righteousness" (2 Tim 3:16–17).

The heart of the biblical message is the gospel of the crucified and risen Christ (2 Tim 2:8), through which death gives way to life (2 Tim 1:10). That being the case, the gospel is not bound (2 Tim 2:9), so that it will continue to impart the salvation won by Christ. So it is that in the gospel-centered Scriptures the pastor has the only saving power. Moreover, in the gospel-centered Scriptures he also has all the power he needs for his ministry.

FAITHFULNESS, NOT SUCCESS

Throughout these letters the apostle impresses upon his younger coworkers the importance of conducting a ministry that is faithful to Christ and to his word,[11] even if that should result in suffering.[12] He does not impose upon them any requirement that they have apparent success in gaining numbers of followers.

Within these letters are indications of the presence of religious leaders who are acquiring followers by setting forth teachings contrary to the apostolic word.[13] Paul calls on Timothy and Titus to oppose such false teaching with the truth of God's word, even though they may not be outwardly successful and might even experience suffering and persecution for their ministry.[14]

This is true of men of God throughout the Scriptures. The Hebrew prophets were called to be faithful, not necessarily successful. In fact, the three most important prophets were all called to a ministry which, according to human standards, would be a failure.[15] Nevertheless, the books produced by these men whose ministries were "failures" have endured and brought great blessing to all who faithfully use them.

Our Lord himself was not universally accepted. "He came to his own [things that he had established], and his own [people] did not receive him" (John 1:11; see also 5:43; 6:66; Luke 4:28–29). The religious leaders of his own people, who might have most likely been expected to follow him, were instrumental in having him put to death.

The apostle knew from personal experience the truth of all of this. His missionary preaching met with rejection as well as belief.[16] There were those, apparently within at least the outward association of Christianity, who opposed his ministry.[17] That opposition sometimes took the form of active persecution.[18] In spite of this he carried out his ministry in faithfulness to the word of God, and he exhorts his coworkers to do the same.

This is what the Lord expects of all who speak his word. If those who speak his word do so faithfully, they may not have outward success, but their ministry will be blessed by the Lord (cf. 2 Cor 4:8–12).

---

11. 1 Tim 1:14; 4:6–7, 16; 6:3; 2 Tim 1:13–14; 2:2; 3:14–15; 4:2, 5; Titus 1:1–3, 9; 2:1, 7–8, 15.
12. 2 Tim 1:8, 15–18; 2:3, 9–13, 24; 4:5.
13. 2 Tim 2:17–18; 3:6–8, 13; 4:3–4; Titus 1:10.
14. 2 Tim 1:8, 12; 2:3, 9; 3:11–12; 4:5.
15. Isa 6:9–10; Jer 7:27; Ezek 2:3–7; 3:4–11.
16. Acts 13:45–46; 14:4–5; 17:5, 13, 32; 18:6; 28:24.
17. 2 Cor 10:10; 1 Tim 1:19–20; 6:3–5; 2 Tim 1:15; 4:10, 15.
18. Acts 14:19; 16:19–24; 2 Cor 11:23–27; 2 Tim 3:11; 4:6.

THE MAKING OF A THEOLOGIAN

In the preface to the Wittenburg Edition of his German writings Martin Luther spoke of three "rules" that David, in Ps 119, set down for the making of a theologian: *oratio, meditatio, tentatio* ("prayer, meditation [of Scripture], affliction").[19] The Pastoral Letters certainly provide support for that observation of the Reformer.

In these letters Paul speaks of the significance of prayer.[20] The letters also contain references to the apostle's own practice of prayer.[21]

The Pastorals contain one of the Bible's most explicit statements about the nature and power of the holy Scriptures (2 Tim 3:15–16). Paul directs his younger colleague to devote himself to the prophetic and apostolic word of God, and he often speaks of the need to hold to that word and to set it forth in teaching and proclamation.[22]

In these letters the apostle speaks of the reality of suffering and even persecution in the life of the people of God.[23] While this is true of Christians in general, it is especially true of those who labor in the pastoral office,[24] as may be seen from examples recounted in the Pastorals of Paul and Timothy's own sufferings for the sake of the word.[25]

WOMEN AND THE PASTORAL OFFICE[26]

Readers of this commentary are surely aware that not all Christian churches hold to the position set forth here that God intends only men

---

19. See AE 34:283–88. While the term "theologian" is sometimes reserved for those with graduate-level degrees in theology, seminary professors, and the like, it is nevertheless true that every pastor should be a theologian (and, in Luther's words, a "fairly good" one).

20. 1 Tim 2:1–2, 8; 4:5; 5:5; 2 Tim 1:3.

21. 1 Tim 1:12, 17; 2 Tim 1:16, 18; 4:16.

22. 1 Tim 2:7; 3:2; 4:6–7, 13; 5:17; 6:20; 2 Tim 1:13; 2:2, 15; 3:14–17; 4:1–2, 5; Titus 1:9.

23. 2 Tim 2:8, 12; 3:12.

24. Note the observation of Luther (AE 28:219): "Every theologian has been established as a bishop of the church to bear the troubles of everyone in the church. He stands on the battle line. He is the prime target of all attacks, difficulties, anxieties, disturbances of consciences, temptations, and doubts."

25. 2 Tim 1:12, 15; 2:3, 9–10; 3:11; 4:5–6, 10, 14, 16.

26. See also Lockwood, *1 Corinthians*, 503–44; *Women in the Church*, a report of the Commission on Theology and Church Relations of The Lutheran Church—Missouri Synod.

to hold the pastoral office. What follows, therefore, is a brief look at the objections to this position and at answers to those objections.

Some simply reject what the Scriptures have to say on this matter as invalid and/or unauthoritative.[27] A variation of the above is the assertion that certain portions of the New Testament or certain principles set forth in the Scriptures outweigh other sections of the Bible or other standards attested therein.[28] Along these lines is the claim that a passage such as 1 Tim 2:11–15 has to do with a particular situation in that time and place and so is not authoritative for Christ's church of all times and places.[29] A further version of this approach is the claim that in a passage such as 1 Tim 2:11—3:7 Paul is stating a personal opinion that is not authoritative for the church of all ages.[30] Yet another variation of the above is to reject the testimony of the Pastorals as allegedly post-Pauline and therefore late (postapostolic) and hence inferior to other portions of the New Testament.[31]

The Pastoral Epistles set forth the authority of the Scriptures (2 Tim 3:15–17), and various indications in the letters of Paul demonstrate his understanding that what he was writing consisted of more than merely his thoughts and opinions. Instead, what he penned was the word of God that stood alongside the Hebrew Scriptures.[32] Simply to disregard

---

27. For example, Fiorenza, *In Memory of Her*, 260–66, 285–342.

28. This is essentially the argument of Joyce Baldwin in Lees, *Role of Women*, 158–76.

29. This position is taken by Marshall, *Pastoral Epistles*, 437, 441, 455, 521.

30. As noted by Daphne Key in Lees, *Role of Women*, 147. This is essentially the approach taken by Johnson, *Letters*, 203–11.

31. For example, Scroggs, "Paul," 283–303. Similar to this is the claim that 1 Cor 14:34–35 is a later (and hence, inauthentic) interpolation to the letter (Fee, *God's Empowering Presence*, 272–81); in answer to this see Lockwood, *1 Corinthians*, 503–4, 527–34.

32. When he instructs his letters to be "read" (Col 4:16; 1 Thess 5:27), he is directing that these be read in public worship in the same manner as God's people had been reading from the Hebrew Scriptures in their public worship services (Luke 4:16–20; Acts 16:14–15). In the salutations of most of his letters he identifies himself as an apostle (Rom 1:1; 1 Cor 1:1; 2 Cor 1:1; Gal 1:1; Eph 1:1; Col 1:1; 1 Tim 1:1; 2 Tim 1:1; Titus 1:1); "apostle" is a term that denotes that he is speaking as one sent by Christ with the authority of Christ (see the entry "Apostle" in the Extended Notes). He identifies his words in 1 Timothy as what "the Spirit explicitly says" (1 Tim 4:1). When he directs the Thessalonians to hold fast to the things that they were taught "through our letter" (2 Thess 2:15), he demonstrates that his letter to them has all the teaching authority of holy Scripture. He indicates that what he writes to the Corinthians is to be received as a command of the Lord (1 Cor 14:37). He directs the Philippians to do what they "learned and received and heard and saw in" him (Phil 4:9). Thus, when he writes, "I

1 Tim 2:11—3:7 and similar passages of Scripture is to reject the authority of the Scriptures altogether.

Another version of this argument is to try to pit Paul and Jesus against one another. Paul is presented as one who was hostile toward women, while Jesus is depicted as one who was welcoming toward them.

It is to be noted that both Paul and our Lord based their pronouncements regarding women on the biblical doctrine of creation. Both cite favorably the creation of man and woman as the basis of their instruction about the proper roles of each sex.[33] To maintain that Paul had a negative view of women requires ignoring his many cordial relations with them[34] as well as the witness of the Pastoral Letters themselves (1 Tim 5:1–2). Both Jesus and Paul distinguish the roles of men and women from one another. Women served the needs of the Lord and his apostles (Luke 8:1–3), but he chose only men to be among his apostles (Luke 6:12–16). In the Pastorals Paul delineates tasks for women (1 Tim 3:11; 5:9–16), but these were different from those that were to be reserved for men (1 Tim 3:1–7).

Along these lines it is sometimes claimed that the apostle—or even the Bible as a whole—held a hostile, demeaning attitude toward women. As to Paul's actual point of view toward women, attention should be drawn to 1 Tim 5:1–2 ("Do not rebuke an older man, but encourage him as a father, younger men as brothers, older women as mothers, younger women as sisters in all purity"). As to the effect that Christianity, including the teachings of the apostle, had on the treatment of and status of women, one need only look at the standing of women throughout the world. The places where women have the greatest opportunities and freedom are those places where Christianity has had the greatest influence; inferior conditions for women are to be found in those places where the teachings of the Bible have not left their mark on the culture.[35]

Some point to the activity of women in association with the work of Paul.[36] While women were associated with the apostle in his work, they

---

urge" (1 Tim 2:1), "I desire" (1 Tim 2:8), and "I do not permit" (1 Tim 2:12), what he has to say is not simply his opinion but is the directive of the Lord himself.

33. Jesus: Matt 19:4–6; Mark 10:6–9; Paul: 1 Tim 2:13.

34. Priscilla/Prisca (Acts 18:1, 18; Rom 16:3; 1 Cor 16:19; 2 Tim 4:19), Phoebe (Rom 16:1), Mary (Rom 16:6), Tryphaena and Tryphosa (Rom 16:12), Chloe (1 Cor 1:11), Euodia and Syntyche (Phil 4:2–3). Note also 1 Tim 3:11, which I understand to be directed to those who would serve as "deaconesses" in the churches, and 1 Tim 5:9–16, regarding those who would serve the church in the order of widows.

35. See Schmidt, *How Christianity Changed the World*, 97–124.

36. Such as Priscilla/Prisca (Acts 18:2, 18, 26; Rom 16:3; 1 Cor 16:19; 2 Tim 4:19),

were not engaged in the work of the pastoral ministry, which work was clearly reserved for men.

Galatians 3:28 is sometimes cited, particularly by those who deny the Pauline authorship of the Pastorals, as evidence in support of women serving as pastors. However, the subject matter of this passage in Galatians is quite different from that of the Pastorals. In Galatians the apostle is speaking of the equality of men and women in redemption, an equality that the Pastoral Letters affirm (e.g., 1 Tim 5:1–2).[37] All Christians have the same salvation through faith in Christ, but not all Christians are called to serve as pastors. In 1 Timothy and Titus Paul sets forth the creator and redeemer's own standards for those whom he wishes to hold the pastoral office; among these standards is that only men are to serve as pastors.

Some, while acknowledging that 1 Timothy clearly reserves the pastoral office for men, make the claim that this merely reflects the scruples of the time. Women, it is argued, had a diminished place in the culture of the first-century Roman world, which meant that the culture would not have accepted female clergy. It is further argued that since women are not as restricted in our culture, the biblical prohibitions of women pastors do not apply to our place and time.[38]

In actuality, female "clergy" were quite well represented in the first-century Mediterranean world. "Women priests may be found at any time and in any place in the Hellenistic world."[39]

In that light it may be seen that rather than reflecting the culture of the time, the Bible's view of women and the pastoral office is actually countercultural. We must reject the notion that the apostle's statements "apply only to Paul's cultural context, since they are based on principles which are authoritative for all time. They are as binding in the last decades of the twentieth century as they were in the last decades of the first century."[40]

It should also be noted that Christianity's attitude toward women also differs from the negative views of rabbinic Judaism. The attitudes of rabbinic Judaism (attitudes that Paul may well have been taught in his

---

Phoebe (Rom 16:1), Euodia (Phil 4:2), and Syntyche (Phil 4:2).

37. Das, *Galatians*, 383–88; Lockwood, *1 Corinthians*, 535–36.

38. As presented by Joyce Baldwin and I. Howard Marshall in Lees, *Role of Women*; see 162, 165, 179–80, 188, 192–95.

39. Lockwood, *1 Corinthians*, 517.

40. Daphne Key in Lees, *Role of Women*, 148. There is every reason to think that if Ms. Key were writing this today, she would update her remarks to the twenty-first century.

education as a rabbi) are summarized in the prayer a Jewish man was expected to say daily, praising God "who did not make me a gentile . . . a boor . . . a woman."[41]

Thus, the prescriptions of the Pastoral Letters do not reflect the views of either Judaism or of the pagan religious world around them.[42] Instead, through his apostle the Lord of the church communicates his will for his church. In continuity with the exclusively male priesthood of Old Testament Israel and Christ's own selection of twelve men to be his apostles, only men are to be called to the pastoral office.

The Bible's reservation of the pastoral office for men "arises not out of prejudice, but from theological grounds."[43] As set forth both by our Lord (Matt 19:5; Mark 10:6–7) and by his apostle (1 Tim 2:13) the creation of male and female is the basis for this biblical directive. It is the one who made us male or female who desires for his church to receive *pastoral* ministry only from men. As the bride of Christ his church will follow his instruction also in this matter.

---

41. Mishnah, Ber 9.1.

42. In contrast, it can be said that women serving as pastors in the Christian church does reflect the surrounding culture: "The movement to ordain women does not really have its starting point in the Scriptures, but in the sociology and spirit of the modern age (cf. 1 Cor 2:12). It is a novelty, an aberration from the Scriptures and from the universal doctrine and practice of the church for almost two millennia" (Lockwood, *1 Corinthians*, 541).

43. Barrett, *Pastoral Epistles*, 32.

Extended Notes

APOSTLE (ΑΠΟΣΤΟΛΟΣ)

In the salutations of his letters Paul regularly identifies himself as an "apostle"; those letters in which he does not do this[1] are all letters in which he names one or more coworkers who were not apostles as "coauthors" of the letter.[2] Although the word "apostle" can be used in a general sense (as in 1 Thess 2:6–7), it also has a more precise significance. When used in this way (as in the salutation), this term denotes the authority with which Paul is writing. The technical sense of this significant concept is to be understood in light of the Hebrew term *shaliach* (שָׁלִיחַ).[3]

Both ἀπόστολος and *shaliach* are derived from the verb for "send" in their respective languages, yet each has a much fuller meaning than simply "one sent." In Jewish sources a *shaliach* was an authorized representative of the individual or group who sent him, so that the identifying characteristic of a *shaliach* is his *authority*. This can be seen from the rabbinic assertion that "the one sent by a man is as the man himself."

Therefore, one had to subordinate his will completely to that of the sender to be a *shaliach*, as the *shaliach* had the authority of the sender himself in the execution of his commission. The salutations of Paul's letters reflect this. In the greetings of Romans and Titus he also identifies himself as a "slave" of God/Christ Jesus. In five of his letters[4] he specifies that he is an apostle by the "will" of God. In 1 Timothy he indicates

---

1. Namely Philippians, 1 and 2 Thessalonians, and Philemon.
2. The apostle Peter also names himself an apostle in the two letters that bear his name.
3. Refer to *TDNT* 1:414–20 and *DPL* 45–51; the four paragraphs that follow are based largely on these.
4. 1 and 2 Corinthians, Colossians, Ephesians, 2 Timothy.

that he is an apostle by the authority of God and Christ (see the commentary on 1 Tim 1:1), and in the salutation of Galatians he makes an impassioned defense of his claim that he is an apostle "not from men nor through man, but through Jesus Christ and God the Father."

The authority of a *shaliach* can be seen in that engagement and divorce might be executed through a *shaliach*. Among the rabbis Moses, Elijah, Elisha, and Ezekiel were known as the *shaliachim* of God since things normally reserved for God took place through them.

In much the same way those designated as apostles in the New Testament are those to whom Christ has delegated authority; hence "delegate" is perhaps the most nearly equivalent English concept. One who is sent as an authorized delegate has the authority belonging to those who sent him to speak, negotiate, vote, and the like in their stead. Having been commissioned by Christ to preach his word, the apostles had the authority of Christ himself. They had been called by the Lord, and with full submission to his will they were sent with his authority.

The apostles of Jesus Christ were chosen from those who had been eyewitnesses of the resurrected Christ (Acts 1:22; 1 Cor 9:1). The New Testament identifies a limited number of individuals as apostles: the Twelve (Acts 1:21–22); Paul (1 Cor 9:1); James, the brother of the Lord (Gal 1:19; 2:9); and perhaps Barnabas (Acts 14:4, 14).

In his letters Paul bases his apostolic office on his being an eyewitness of the resurrection (1 Cor 9:1) through his calling on the road to Damascus (Gal 1:15–16; cf. 1 Cor 15:7–10). He was called to exercise his apostolate particularly for the benefit of non-Jews (Gal 1:15–16; see also Acts 9:16; 22:21; 26:17, 19, 23); hence, in his Letter to the Romans he identifies himself as the "apostle of the gentiles" (11:13).

The concept of "apostle" contributes to our understanding of the authority of the New Testament documents. Of those New Testament authors whom we can identify, Matthew, John, Paul, James, and Peter were all numbered among the apostles.

Mark was not an apostle, but both church tradition[5] and indications in his Gospel[6] point to him as the "interpreter" of Peter. Therefore, this Gospel can rightly be thought of as the Gospel according to the apostle Peter.

Luke was not an apostle; however, in the preface to his Gospel he indicates that he obtained his information from those who "from the beginning were eyewitnesses and minsters of the word" (1:2), which, in effect, is a definition of an apostle. Therefore, his Gospel can also be rightly considered to be apostolic.

The companion volume to the Gospel according to Luke is the Acts of the *Apostles*. In this second volume Luke accurately recounts the words and deeds of the apostles, who were chosen by Christ to bring his word to the world through the power of the Holy Spirit (Acts 1:2, 5, 8). Luke himself was an eyewitness to some of these.[7]

The Letter of Jude was not written by an apostle, but his identifying himself as "brother of James" (Jude 1) places him in the company of the apostles. Moreover, his exhortation to his readers to remember the words first spoken by the apostles of our Lord Jesus Christ (Jude 17) indicates

---

5. Eusebius, *Ecclesiastical History* 3:39, cites the church father Papias (AD 60–163) as follows: "Mark being the interpreter of Peter whatsoever he recorded he wrote with great accuracy but not however, in the order in which it was spoken or done by our Lord, for he neither heard nor followed our Lord, but as before said, he was in company with Peter, who gave him such instruction as was necessary, but not to give a history of our Lord's discourses: wherefore Mark has not erred in anything, by writing some things as he has recorded them; for he was carefully attentive to one thing, not to pass by anything that he heard, or to state anything falsely in these accounts." These words are often assumed to refer to the composition of the Gospel according to Mark. Similarly, in *Ecclesiastical History* 6:14 Eusebius quotes the church father Clement of Alexandria (AD 150–215) as follows: "When Peter had proclaimed the word publicly at Rome, and declared the gospel under the influence of the Spirit; as there was a great number present, they requested Mark, who had followed him from afar, and remembered well what he had said, to reduce these things to writing, and that after composing the gospel he gave it to those who requested it of him. Which, when Peter understood, he directly neither hindered nor encouraged it."

6. Note these features of Mark's Gospel: (1) passages in Mark in which Peter is mentioned, whereas the parallel passages in Matthew and/or Luke do not mention him (Mark 1:36-38 || Luke 4:42-43; Mark 11:21 || Matt 21:20; Mark 13:3-4 || Matt 24:3 and Luke 21:7; Mark 16:7 || Matt 28:7); (2) Mark 12:42 employs the term κοδράντης for the value of the widow's coins; this is a Roman coin, and only Mark uses this term to explain the value of the widow's two coins; (3) whereas Matthew and Luke regularly employ the Greek term ἑκατόναρχος for a Roman commander of one hundred men, Mark always uses the corresponding Latin term κεντυρίων.

7. Note the "we sections" of the book of Acts (16:10-17; 20:5-15; 21:1-18; 27:1—28:16).

that Jude regarded his letter as accurately conveying apostolic teaching, in contrast to the false teachers against whom this letter is written.

The authorship of the Letter to the Hebrews is unknown, and the author distinguishes himself from those with firsthand contact with our Lord (2:3), which would exclude him from the number of the apostles. However, this same verse indicates that the author of Hebrews understood that the message he proclaimed was confirmed by those with firsthand acquaintance, which would give a mark of apostolicity to what he sets forth in this letter.

Related to this are some of the logia of our Lord spoken to the Twelve in the upper room. On that occasion Jesus told his apostles that he still had many things to say to them, but they were not able to bear them at that time. Nevertheless, he would send them the Holy Spirit. The Spirit would teach them all things, would remind them of what their Lord had said to them, would bear witness to Jesus (so that the apostles themselves would be able to bear witness to their Lord), would lead them into all truth, would bring the word of Christ to them, would speak of things to come, and in all of this would glorify Jesus.[8] At least in part this would refer to the Holy Spirit moving some of those present on that occasion to become authors of various books of the New Testament.

In his letters Paul himself gives evidence that he understood that he had this sort of authority as an apostle of the Lord. In two of his letters (1 Thess 5:17; Col 4:16) he gives instructions to have them "read" to the church; that is, the addresses were to read these in the same way as they were accustomed to read from the Hebrew Scriptures in worship (cf. Luke 4:16-21; Acts 13:14-15). This instruction would indicate that the apostle regarded what he had written as having the same inspiration and authority as the Old Testament Scriptures.[9]

From all of this it is rightly concluded that the apostolic documents that make up the New Testament are authoritative for the church of all times and places. This is also indicated by the designation of the church as being built upon the foundation of the apostles and prophets (Eph 2:20) and by the primacy of place given the apostles among the gifts of God (1 Cor 12:28; Eph 4:11).

All of what is said here about the apostolic authority of the New Testament documents should, of course, be understood alongside the

---

8. John 14:25-26; 15:26-27; 16:7-8, 12-15; 17:20.

9. On the possible identity of the letter "from Laodicea" (Col 4:16), see Deterding, *Colossians*, 192-94.

biblical teaching on the inspiration of the Scriptures. On that topic see the commentary on 2 Tim 3:14–17.

CONSCIENCE

See the entry on "Heart and Conscience."

EPIPHANY, APPEARING (ΕΠΙΦΑΙΝΩ, ΕΠΙΦΑΝΕΙΑ)

Instances of this word family appear ten times in the NT. All but two of these are in the letters of Paul, and of those eight, seven are in the Pastorals.[10] The non-Pauline occurrences refer to the appearance of light (either literally or metaphorically) and need not concern us here.

In nonbiblical Greek the term means "appearing, appearance." "As a t[echnical] t[erm] relating to transcendence it refers to a visible and freq[uently] sudden manifestation of a hidden divinity, either in the form of a personal appearance, or by some deed of power or oracular communication by which its presence is made known."[11] Thus, even prior to the time of the NT the association of the term with deity was firmly established.

The one instance where the LXX uses the term in this sense is at Gen 35:7. There we read that Jacob built an altar at a place that he named Bethel ("house of God"), "for there God appeared [ἐπεφάνη] to him."

Three of the occurrences of this word group in the letters of Paul speak of the incarnation of Jesus Christ (2 Tim 1:10; Titus 2:11; 3:4). The use of this particular term with reference to the coming of Christ into our world presuppose his existence prior to his earthly appearance and serve as ancillary proof of his preexistence and therefore of his deity (see further the commentary on 1 Tim 1:17 and Titus 2:13).

The use of the same word family with reference to Christ's coming at the parousia[12] is significant for several reasons. This serves to indicate that as Jesus lived, died, and rose from the dead in his human body, so he will also return bodily and therefore visibly. This, in turn, demonstrates that he has not abandoned his human body but continues to live bodily

---

10. Luke 1:79; Acts 27:20; 2 Thess 2:8; 1 Tim 6:14; 2 Tim 1:10; 4:1, 8; Titus 2:11, 13; 3:4.

11. BDAG 385; see also *TDNT* 9:7–10.

12. 2 Thess 2:8; 1 Tim 6:14; 2 Tim 4:1, 8; Titus 2:13.

from the time of his earthly ministry until the last day. This also points to the truth that the eternal destiny of humanity involves the resurrection of the body, whether to eternal punishment or to everlasting blessedness.

FAITH, BELIEVE (ΠΙΣΤΙΣ, ΠΙΣΤΕΥΩ)

The noun "faith" (πίστις) and the verb "believe" (πιστεύω) are cognates in Greek. Therefore, many times the noun refers to the act of believing.[13] In dogmatic terminology the act of believing is called *fides qua creditur*.

A related yet distinct meaning to the noun refers to the content of faith as the object of what is believed.[14] In English translation this meaning would often be brought out by the use of the definite article, "*the* faith." In dogmatic terminology the content or object of faith is termed *fides quae creditur*.

Christian faith is never merely the act of believing. Genuine Christian faith always has an object: what God has done in the person and work of Jesus Christ for the world's salvation.[15] Thus, the act of genuine faith/believing (*fides qua creditur*) is always directed to the authentic object of faith (*fides quae creditur*): the person and work of Jesus Christ. This being the case, in some passages the word "faith" has aspects of both meanings.[16]

Genuine faith also shows itself in good works, as articulated in Eph 2:8–10. Therefore, the noun "faith" sometimes also bears the notion of the faithfulness that will be displayed by those with saving faith (1 Tim 2:15; Titus 2:10).

GENTLE (ΠΡΑΰΣ), KIND (ΕΠΙΕΙΚΗΣ)

In the Pastorals the apostle Paul uses the adjective πραΰς, which I have translated as "gentle," and nouns cognate to it (πραϋπαθία, πραΰτης) as well as the adjective ἐπιεικής, which I have rendered "kind," to describe traits that ought to characterize Christians in general and their pastors in

---

13. 1 Tim 1:4, 5, 14, 19 (2x); 4:12; 5:12; 2 Tim 1:5, 13; 2:22; 3:15; Titus 1:1.

14. 1 Tim 1:2; 2:7; 3:9; 4:1, 6; 2 Tim 3:8, 10; Titus 1:4, 13; 2:2.

15. 1 Tim 1:16 ("Christ Jesus might demonstrate the utmost long-suffering for an example for those about to believe in him for eternal life"); 3:16 ("mystery of godliness, who was . . . believed on in the world"); 4:3 ("those who believe and know the truth"); 2 Tim 1:12 ("I know in whom I have believed"); 3:14 ("you continue in the things which you learned and believed"); Titus 3:8 ("those who have believed in God").

16. 1 Tim 3:13; 5:8; 6:10, 11, 12, 21; 2 Tim 2:18; 4:7; Titus 3:15.

particular.[17] As Titus 3:2 and in particular 2 Cor 10:1 demonstrate, the terms are essentially synonymous. In so far as they can be distinguished from one another, ἐπιεικής has to do with not being harsh (1 Cor 4:21; 1 Pet 2:18), while πραΰς refers more to not being arrogant (Matt 21:5).

The King James Version often rendered the πραΰς word group with "meek" and "meekness,"[18] a translation which four centuries later tends to denote weakness. To the contrary, being gentle and kind is not the act of a weak person, as can be seen from its association with both the Lord Jesus Christ and the power of God the Holy Spirit (see below). To be gentle and kind in one's dealings with others requires great strength.

Jesus Christ is the epitome of what it means to be gentle (Matt 11:29; 21:5). The gentle Christ who entered Jerusalem on Palm Sunday shortly thereafter purged the temple of the merchants and rebuked the chief priests and scribes (Matt 21:12–17); this as much as anything indicates that gentleness is not the same as weakness.

But more than the epitome and example of gentleness, Christ is also the one who through the Holy Spirit enables believers to display this virtue. Gentleness is included in the fruit of the Spirit (Gal 5:22–23), and acting with gentleness is part of keeping the unity of the Spirit (Eph 4:2–3). As the Holy Spirit is associated with power and might,[19] this would point to the Spirit being the one who empowers Christians to act gently.

Being gentle and kind has to do with how one deals with others. Treating others with gentleness is the opposite of being harsh with them (1 Cor 4:21; Gal 6:1). To be gentle means that one bears up with the shortcomings (and even the sins) of others (Eph 4:2). This again demonstrates that gentleness is a virtue that requires strength.

All Christians are exhorted to display gentleness in their dealing with others.[20] Nevertheless, it is a virtue that is particularly expected of pastors.[21] A pastor will encounter many situations in which he will be tempted to respond with harshness and/or arrogance. Empowered by the Spirit of Christ, he will be able instead to treat others in a kind and gentle fashion.

---

17. 1 Tim 3:3; 6:11; 2 Tim 2:25; Titus 3:2.

18. Matt 11:29; 21:5; 2 Cor 10:1; Gal 5:23; Eph 4:2; Col 3:12; 1 Tim 6:11; 2 Tim 2:25; Titus 3:2.

19. Isa 11:2; Mic 3:8; Luke 1:17, 35; 4:14; Acts 1:8; 10:38; Rom 15:13, 19; 2 Cor 2:4; Eph 3:6; 1 Thess 1:5.

20. Gal 5:22–23; Eph 4:2; Phil 4;5; Col 3:12; Titus 3:2.

21. 1 Cor 4:21; Gal 6:1; 1 Tim 3:3; 6:11; 2 Tim 2:25.

Grace and Life

GLORY (ΔΟΞΑ)

"The terminology of glory provides a window on virtually the whole of Paul's theology."[22]

As the equivalent of the Hebrew כָּבוֹד (Exod 40:34–35; 1 Kgs 8:11), δόξα is used to describe the being of God himself, especially as this is revealed to mankind (Rom 1:23; 1 Cor 2:8). This being the case, "glory" is a virtual synonym for the image of God (Rom 3:23; 2 Cor 3:18; Phil 3:21).[23]

As a term denoting the being of God, "glory" also serves as an incarnational term: "The Word became flesh.... We beheld his glory, glory as of the only one from the Father" (John 1:14). As an incarnational designation "glory" also serves to describe both Christ's post-resurrection exaltation (1 Tim 3:16) and his second coming (Titus 2:13).

As a term descriptive of eternal life (Rom 8:18; 2 Thess 1:9; 2 Tim 2:10) and the resurrection existence (Phil 3:21) the word "glory" (δόξα) is a highly appropriate term to describe eternal salvation (2 Cor 3:8–11). The resurrection existence, which in this life is hidden under great weakness and dishonor, will be revealed "in glory" (cf. 1 Cor 15:43) at the parousia (Col 3:4). By using a term associated with God's self-revelation for the resurrection life in this last group of passages Paul asserts the same truth as we find in 2 Peter, where it is said that our future salvation involves becoming partakers of the divine nature (1:4).

The association of the word δόξα with the restoration of God's image of righteousness and holiness and with the resurrection life also enriches our appreciation for its use to denote the content of the gospel (2 Cor 4:4; 1 Tim 1:11).

As the Scriptures also employ this term to designate that of which God is worthy for accomplishing humanity's redemption (Eph 1:6, 12, 14), we see that eternity will be characterized by the Lord receiving praise from the redeemed for their salvation.

GODLINESS (ΕΥΣΕΒΕΙΑ, ΘΕΟΣΕΒΕΙΑ)

Other than four occurrences in 2 Peter[24] the term "godliness" in the New Testament is confined entirely to the Pastoral Letters. The word

---

22. DPL 348.
23. On the image of God, see Deterding, *Colossians*, 49–52, 151–53.
24. 1:3, 6, 7; 3:11.

encapsulates the entirety of the Christian faith and as such is virtually a synonym for "Christianity." Since it is such a comprehensive term, in its various uses it has varied shades of meaning.

The all-inclusive nature of this vocable is seen most clearly in 1 Tim 3:16.[25] There Paul writes of the greatness of the "mystery of godliness" and continues with six phrases, each of which refers to some aspect of the saving work of Jesus Christ (see the commentary on that verse). From this it is evident that "godliness" has to do with the right standing before almighty God that is given for the sake of Christ and through faith in him.

Godliness comes to the individual through the word of God. The apostle contrasts the teachings of false teachers with "the sound words of our Lord Jesus Christ and . . . the teaching that is in accord with godliness" (1 Tim 6:3). Only the true word of God brings godliness, for only the true word of God works the faith through which an individual has godliness as his personal possession.

Paul's greeting to Titus (1:1) makes it clear that faith is the way to godliness. There the apostle writes of the "faith . . . that is in accord with godliness." When one has faith in Christ (in that passage also called "knowledge of the truth"), then he has godliness.

But this faith is no mere intellectual assent to some dogmatic propositions. The godliness that is ours through faith in Jesus Christ also shows itself in a life of genuine piety. Paul uses the cognate adverb εὐσεβῶς to describe the kind of life that the Christian will live in response to God's grace in Christ (2 Tim 3:12; Titus 2:12). This can also be seen in his instruction to Christian women (1 Tim 2:10). He indicates that beyond mere outward adornment they are to beautify themselves as is "fitting for women who have professed godliness," namely "through good works." The use of a cognate verb (εὐσεβεῖν) in his instruction about the care of widows by their children (1 Tim 5:4) shows that respect for one's parents is part and parcel of the good work of showing respect for God.

The comprehensive nature of "godliness" is also evident from the apostle's instructions to Timothy about his own personal life of faith (1 Tim 4:7–8). He is to train himself for godliness, since godliness "has the utmost benefit, having promise both for the present and for the life to come." Thus, Paul here names "godliness" as the way to eternal salvation. That is the "great profit" that is to be found in godliness (1 Tim 6:6).

---

25. As noted by Marshall, *Pastoral Epistles*, 523.

Thus, when the apostle instructs Timothy to train himself for godliness (1 Tim 4:7) or to pursue godliness (1 Tim 6:11), he is directing his younger coworker to the word of God (1 Tim 6:3). The word will bring one to and strengthen him in the faith that brings salvation and that will show itself in a life of genuine piety.

Twice in his letters Paul distinguishes genuine godliness from the mere appearance of the same. He warns about the coming of those who have the outward form of godliness without its power (2 Tim 3:5) and about those who think of godliness as a means to profiteering (1 Tim 6:5). Even in these passages we can see that the term "godliness" is a broad term, encompassing the main features of the Christian faith.

GRACE (ΧΑΡΙΣ)

In the New Testament "grace" is largely a Pauline word. Of the 124 occurrences of this term in the NT, eighty-six of them are in the letters of Paul.[26]

The term "grace" emphasizes that salvation is a free gift. By definition a gift is something that is given; it is not earned or paid for by the recipient. That "grace" points to this characteristic of salvation may be seen from those passages in which the word "grace" occurs in conjunction with some Greek term for "gift."[27]

The importance of the concept of grace can be seen in the use of this word in statements that are at the heart and center of the gospel message of salvation. In Romans the apostle writes, "For all have sinned and lack the glory of God, and are justified by his grace as a gift, through the redemption that is in Christ Jesus, whom God put forward as an atoning sacrifice by his blood, to be received by faith" (3:23–25a). In Ephesians are recorded the familiar words, "For by grace you have been saved through faith. And this is not your own doing; it is the gift of God, not a result of works, so that no one may boast" (2:8–9). The apostle uses the word "grace" six times[28] in the significant soteriological exposition of Rom 5.

---

26. See the entry χάρις in any concordance to the Greek New Testament. In addition to this, of the times that the word appears in the book of Acts two of them (20:24, 32) are in places that report the words of Paul.

27. Rom 3:24; 5:15, 17; Eph 2:8; 3:7; 4:7.

28. Rom 5:2, 15 (2x), 17, 20, 21.

Paul uses the word "grace" in the salutations of every one of his letters.[29] Furthermore, he concludes each of his epistles with a blessing of "grace."[30] The fact that the apostle gives grace the first and the last word in each of his letters shows the significance of this concept.

Moreover, these salutations and blessings are more than simply a pious way of saying "hello" and "goodbye." As a word from God through his apostle[31] these greetings and blessings actually impart grace to the readers/hearers. Even as the one true God actually blesses those on whom his name has been placed in the Aaronic benediction (Num 6:27), so God's word of grace through his spokesman actually gives grace to the reader/hearer.

HEART (ΚΑΡΔΙΑ), CONSCIENCE (ΣΥΝΕΙΔΣΙΣ)

In the New Testament the term "heart," καρδία, refers to the entirety of one's true, inner being. This includes the emotional (1 Cor 4:5; Col 4:8), intellectual (Matt 12:34; 24:48), and spiritual (Matt 13:15; 15:8, 18–19; 2 Cor 4:6) elements of human existence. The Hebrew terms לֵב and לֵבָב, regularly translated by καρδία in the Septuagint, have a similar meaning, for these also encompass the emotional (1 Sam 2:1; Isa 65:14), intellectual (Deut 29:4 [MT 3]; 2 Sam 7:3), and spiritual (Deut 29:19 [MT 18]; Job 1:5; Jer 31:33) facets of a person's being.[32] One's καρδία, therefore, refers to the way he really is as opposed to the way he may merely appear to be (1 Sam 16:7; Col 3:22).

Left to himself, one's heart is evil (Matt 12:23). Thus, it is necessary that God himself act (Rom 5:5; 2 Cor 4:6; Eph 1:18), so that one's heart might be enlightened and pure through faith in Christ (1 Tim 1:5).

In ordinary speech we tend to identify conscience as "that little voice from within" that assures us of what is right and bothers us if we have done something wrong. Similarly, in ancient Greek the term referred to

---

29. Rom 1:7; 1 Cor 1:3; 2 Cor 1:2; Gal 1:3; Eph 1:2; Phil 1:2; Col 1:2; 1 Thess 1:1; 2 Thess 1:2; 1 Tim 1:2; 2 Tim 1:2; Titus 1:4; Phlm 3.

30. Rom 16:20; 1 Cor 16:23; 2 Cor 13:14; Gal 6:18; Eph 6:24; Phil 4:23; Col 4:18; 1 Thess 5:28; 2 Thess 3:18; 1 Tim 6:21; 2 Tim 4:22; Titus 3:15; Phlm 25.

31. On the significance of Paul being an apostle see that entry in these Extended Notes.

32. Ladd, *Theology*, 475–76. In all of these verses except Job 1:5 and the first occurrence in Isa 65:14, לֵב or לֵבָב is translated by καρδία. In Job 1:5 לֵבָב is rendered by διάνοια ("mind").

what was within a person that made him or her conscious of an evil act.[33] While that notion is not entirely lacking in the biblical concept of "conscience" (Rom 9:1; 13:5), what the Scriptures mean by that term is much more extensive.

Of itself one's conscience is not an infallible guide. A conscience that is not fully and rightly informed is weak, that is, inadequate (1 Cor 8:7, 10, 12); in fact, it may even be in error (Rom 2:15). Even beyond this Paul speaks of deceivers, liars, and the impure having a "seared" or a "defiled" conscience (1 Tim 4:2; Titus 1:15).

It is necessary that one's conscience be made "good." A good conscience is a result of genuine faith (Titus 1:5, 19). Thus, the apostle can speak of holding faith "with a pure conscience" (Titus 3:9).

When one's conscience has been cleansed of evil and made good in this way, then his conscience can be rightly informed by the word of God. In such circumstances he can live and act with a clear and sincere conscience.[34] One whose conscience has not been rightly informed in this way will fall into error (1 Cor 10:28–29).

Therefore, "conscience" also embraces the use of the mind (2 Cor 4:2; Titus 1:15).[35] A comparison of the biblical use of "conscience" with what the Scriptures have to say about the "heart" will demonstrate that biblically heart and conscience are nearly total synonyms.

HOPE (ΕΛΠΙΣ, ΕΛΠΙΖΩ)

Apart from the faith of the Old and New Testaments "hope" was for the most part absent in the ancient world (Eph 2:12). There were even those who considered it preferable never to have been born.[36] For some the *Pax Romana* under Caesar Augustus led to his birth being hailed as the

---

33. Debelius and Conzelmann, *Pastoral Epistles*, 19; Towner, *Letters*, 117.

34. 1 Cor 10:25, 27; 2 Cor 1:12; 5:11; 2 Tim 1:3. Similarly, Towner (*Letters*, 119) describes a good/clean conscience as "commitment to (belief in, embracing of) the apostolic faith as a basis for godliness in life."

35. BDAG 972–73.

36. Scharlemann, "Apostolic Descant," 11. As proof of the lack of hope in the Mediterranean world of the first century Scharlemann calls attention to an ancient epitaph: "Here I lie, Dionysius of Tarsus, sixty years old, having never married. I wish my father hadn't either." Along these lines he also cites these lines from Sophocles' tragedy *Oedipus Coloneus* (lines 1225–26), spoken by the chorus: "Not to be born at all—that is by far the best fortune; and the second best is as soon as one is born with all speed to return thither whence one has come."

beginning of a new hope.³⁷ However, these hopes quickly faded, as those who succeeded Augustus were unable to prolong those initial expectations.

The ancients' lack of hope had to do with their cyclical view of time. For the most part the Greco-Roman world viewed time as a circle; hence, they could see no goal or meaning to time or history. No less a figure than Aristotle (*Physics* 4:14), for example, stated that "time itself seems to be a sort of circle."³⁸

The faith of the Old and New Testaments, however, was one of hope. Old and New Testament believers viewed history as moving toward a future goal. The people of the Old Testament looked to the future (Jer 29:11; Ps 27:13–14) since the Lord had promised them a coming salvation. Similarly, the authors of the books of the New Testament proclaim that God's activity in the person of Christ has given a goal and meaning to history and time.

Although in the New Testament the word "hope" (ἐλπίς) is occasionally used in the "secular" sense of "wish" (Act 24:26; 1 Cor 16:7), it ordinarily has a rich, theological meaning. The way in which the Septuagint uses the term helps to shape its customary use in the New Testament. The ἐλπίς word group renders terms derived from בָּטַח (the verb meaning "trust" and the noun "security"); this indicates that hope is a trust in the security (certainty) that God will fulfill his promises; hence, the Christian's hope is certain. Similarly, the term is used to translate חָסָה, the verbal form meaning "seek refuge" and the noun form having the meaning "refuge" or "shelter." Since the Christian hope is certain, it brings ultimate safety and security. The ἐλπίς word group also renders קָוָה and יָחַל, meaning "wait" or "await"; this means that the act of hoping involves waiting for God to fulfill his promises. Related to the verb קָוָה is the noun תִּקְוָה, the usual word for "hope" in the Hebrew Scriptures and one which the Septuagint translates not only by ἐλπίς but also by

---

37. Scharlemann, "Apostolic Descant," 11–12. Scharlemann calls attention to the Priene inscription, in which a federation of Greek cities in Asia Minor proposed beginning the year on the birthday of Caesar Augustus as follows: "This day has given the world an entirely new appearance. The world would have gone down to destruction if a new hope had not arisen for all men in him who is born on this day. . . . Now the time is passed when a man regretted having been born."

38. Aristotle, *Physics* 4:14; see Cullmann, *Christ and Time*, 51–52. In much the same way the Stoics taught that the world ran in thousand-year cycles. At the end of each cycle, the world was destroyed by fire, and everything began again (Scharlemann, "Apostolic Descant," 12).

ὑπομονή ("endurance"). These various nuances to קָוָה, יָחַל, and תִּקְוָה demonstrate that as the believer waits with hope, he is not just biding time but is waiting with endurance (see Col 1:11); he waits with endurance in anticipation of the consummation of his hope (Rom 8:25; 15:4; 1 Thess 1:3 ["your endurance of hope"]). Thus, the picture of "hope" that emerges from the Scriptures of both Testaments is that of certain trust in a secure/safe object of trust, so as to produce a waiting with endurance.

What is said in the New Testament about "hope" has much in common with the concept of "faith" (πίστις). The πίστις word group in Greek, like the Hebrew words of the אָמַן family that the Septuagint customarily renders with the πίστις group, refers to the act of placing confident trust in or reliance upon someone or something or to someone or something worthy of such confident dependence (see also the entry on "Faith" in these Extended Notes). Thus, faith and hope may be thought of as two sides of the same coin, for hope is simply faith directed toward the future.

The virtual equivalence of faith and hope may also be seen from 1 Pet 1:21 (where the article τὴν and the personal pronoun ὑμῶν govern πίστιν ["faith"], while ἐλπίδα ["hope"] is in the predicate position; this produces the meaning "your faith is also hope toward God"). This is also demonstrated from 1 Pet 3:5, 15, and Heb 10:23 (where "faith" could be used in place of "hope").

"Faith" (πίστις) may refer either to the subjective act of believing (*fides qua creditur*)[39] or the objective content of faith (*fides quae creditur*),[40] or it may have aspects of both meanings.[41] In the same way "hope" (ἐλπίς) may designate either the subjective act of hoping (*spes qua speratur*)[42] or the objective content or object of hope (*spes quae speratur*),[43] or it may have elements of both meanings.[44] In its objective meaning "hope" is a future worth looking forward to; in its subjective meaning it is the act of looking with assurance toward the future.

---

39. 1 Tim 1:4, 5, 14, 19 (2x); 4:12; 5:12; 2 Tim 1:5, 13; 2:22; 3:15; Titus 1:1.
40. 1 Tim 1:2; 2:7; 3:9; 4:1, 6; 2 Tim 3:8, 10; Titus 1:4, 13; 2:2.
41. 1 Tim 3:13; 5:8; 6:10, 11, 12, 21; 2 Tim 2:18; 4:7; Titus 3:15.
42. 1 Tim 4:10; 5:15.
43. 1 Tim 1:1; Titus 2:13; 3:7.
44. 1 Tim 6:17; Titus 1:2.

EXTENDED NOTES

IN CHRIST (ΕΝ ΧΡΙΣΤΩι)[45]

An important concept in the letters of Paul has to do with what it means to be "in Christ." This may be seen both from the frequency of the use of this prepositional phrase (by one count some 170 times in his thirteen letters) and from its near absence throughout the rest of the New Testament.[46] The apostle uses a variety of designations for Christ in this prepositional phrase[47] without any apparent difference between them; thus, they may all be considered together.

The phrase ἐν Χριστῷ does not have a merely instrumental meaning, as though the preposition ἐν meant "by" (Eph 2:15);[48] rather, the phrase describes a harmonious relationship with Jesus Christ. God himself creates this relationship (1 Cor 1:30) through baptism (Gal 3:26–27; Rom 6:3, 11) and the gospel (1 Cor 4:15, 17; Eph 1:13; 3:6). This relationship is one of faith directed to Jesus Christ (Gal 3:14, 26; 5:6; Col 2:7). Hence, we are "in Christ" through faith (nevertheless, the expression "in Christ" never designates the object of faith[49]).

---

45. An earlier version of this section appeared in Deterding, *Colossians*, 23–25.

46. *DPL* 98.

47. "In Christ": Rom 9:1; 12:5; 16:7, 9, 10; 1 Cor 3:1; 4:10, 15 (2x), 17; 15:18, 22; 2 Cor 1:21; 2:14, 17; 5:17, 19; 12:2, 19; Gal 1:22; 2:4, 17; 3:14, 26; Eph 1:3, 9, 12, 20; 4:32; Phil 2:1; 3:9; Col 1:2, 28; 1 Thess 2:14; 4:16; Phlm 8, 20.
"In the Lord": Rom 14:14; 16:2, 8, 11, 12, 13, 22; 1 Cor 1:31; 4:17; 7:39; 9:1, 2; 11:11; 15:58; 16:19; 2 Cor 10:17; 5:10; Eph 1:15; 2:21; 4:17; 5:8; 6:1, 10, 21; Phil 1:14; 2:19, 24, 29; 3:1; 4:1, 2, 4, 10; Col 3:18; 4:7, 17; 1 Thess 3:8; 4:1; 5:12; 2 Thess 3:4, 12; Phlm 16, 20.
"In Jesus Christ": Rom 3:22; Gal 2:16; 3:22; 1 Thess 1:1, 3; 2 Thess 1:1; 3:12.
"In Christ Jesus": Rom 3:24; 6:11, 23; 8:1, 2, 39; 15:17; 16:3; 1 Cor 1:2, 4, 30; 4:15; 15:31; 16:24; Gal 2:16; 3:14, 26, 28; 5:6; Eph 2:6, 7, 10, 13; 3:6, 11, 21; Phil 1:1, 26; 2:5; 3:3, 14; 4:7, 19, 21; Col 1:4; 1 Thess 2:14; 5:18; 1 Tim 1:14; 3:13; 2 Tim 1:9, 13; 2:1, 10; 3:12, 15; Phlm 23.
Along these lines it is perhaps worth noting that Paul is the only biblical author who refers to Jesus as "Christ Jesus" (in distinction from "Jesus Christ" or simply "Christ"): Rom 1:1; 2:16; 3:24; 6:3, 11, 13; 8:1, 2, 34, 39; 15:5, 16, 17; 16:3; 1 Cor 1:1, 2, 4, 30; 4:15; 15:31; 16:24; 2 Cor 1:1; Gal 2:4, 16 (2x); 3:14, 26, 28; 4:14; 5:6, 24; Eph 1:1 (2x); 2:6, 7, 10, 13, 20; 3:1, 6, 11, 21; Phil 1:1 (2x), 8, 26; 2:5; 3:3, 8, 12, 14; 4:7, 19, 21; Col 1:1, 4; 2:6; 4:12; 1 Thess 2:14; 5:18; 1 Tim 1:1 (2x), 2, 12, 14, 15; 2:5; 3:13; 4:6; 5:21; 6:13; 2 Tim 1:1 (2x), 2, 9, 10, 13; 2:1, 3, 10; 3:12, 15; 4:1; Titus 1:4; Phlm 1, 9, 23. The only "exception" to this is found in Acts 24:24, but since this reports Paul's own testimony, it is not really an exception.

48. Since Christ is the subject of this verse, the phrase ἐν αὐτῷ clearly cannot have an instrumental meaning or be translated "by him" but must have a relational meaning and refer to being in a relationship with our Lord.

49. This may be seen from those passages (1 Tim 1:14; 3:13; 2 Tim 1:13; 3:15) in which Paul modifies the word "faith" with the article plus the expression "in Christ

Those who are "in Christ" become partakers of everything that Christ has accomplished by his redemptive work (1 Cor 1:5, 7; Eph 1:3). Since the relationship of being "in Christ" is one of faith, as one grows stronger in his saving faith, he thereby draws into an even closer relationship with Jesus Christ (Eph 2:21).

All who are "in Christ" are one with Christ and with each other (Rom 12:5; Gal 3:28; Eph 2:15). Thus, phrases such as "in Christ" and "in the Lord" refer not only to the relation of the individual to Christ but also to the believer's relationship to all other believers.

Therefore, when Paul describes some individual or group as being "in Christ,"[50] he is saying more than if he had simply used a word like "Christian" or "believer," for this formulation always denotes the interrelationship of those who are in Christ. Because of the social dimension of this expression the apostle uses it extensively to describe the interaction of the people of God.

One example of this use of the "in Christ" formulations may be found in those passages where Paul employs the expression "in the Lord" to refer to the source of his confidence with regard to certain actions of other believers. He tells the Galatians that he is persuaded "in the Lord" that they will have no other opinion about the matter of justification than the one that he has taught them (Gal 5:10). He writes to the Thessalonians, "We are persuaded in the Lord about you, that you are doing and will do the things that we commanded" (2 Thess 3:4). The apostle's meaning in these passages is that he has based his certainty about his fellow Christians doing the right thing on the fact that he and they have a common relationship to Christ.

In two of his letters Paul instructs his readers to receive "in the Lord" a fellow Christian whom he is sending to them (Rom 16:2; Phil 2:29). The apostle uses the phrase "in the Lord" in these instances to remind his readers of the relationship to Christ that they share with the one who is being sent. They are to receive this person as one who is united with them in Christ.

Jesus," thereby giving the meaning "faith [or 'faithfulness'] which is yours as you are in Christ Jesus." It is also evident from the apostle's practice of using other means to designate the object of faith (with the genitive [Rom 3:22, 26; Gal 2:16, 20; 3:22; Eph 3:12; Phil 1:27; 3:9; Col 2:12]; with the dative [Rom 10:14 (οὗ = τουτῷ οὗ); 2 Tim 1:12; Titus 3:8]; with εἰς [Rom 10:14; Gal 2:16; Phil 1:29; Col 2:5]; with ἐπί [Rom 4:5, 24; 9:33; 10:11; 1 Tim 1:16]; with πρός [1 Thess 1:8; Phlm 5]).

50. Rom 16:3, 7, 8, 9, 10, 11, 12, 13; 1 Cor 7:22; 16:24; 2 Cor 12:2; Eph 1:1; 4:1; 6:21; Phil 1:1, 14; 4:21; Col 1:2; 4:7; Phlm 16, 23.

In his Letter to the Philippians Paul exhorts two women named Euodia and Syntyche to think the same thing "in the Lord" (Phil 4:2). The apostle here appeals to their unity in Christ as a reason why they should resolve their disagreements. Since believers are one in Christ, their life together should be characterized by peace and harmony (cf. Col 3:15; Eph 4:3).

Along these lines two passages from the Letter to the Philippians call for comment. Philippians 1:8, "I long for all of you with the tender mercies of Christ Jesus," is to be interpreted in light of the unity of those who are in Christ. Because in Christ Paul and the Philippian Christians are one new man and the one body of Christ, the apostle identifies the affection that he feels for his readers as the "tender mercies of Christ Jesus." The church is so closely identified with its Lord that the love that one member feels for another is that of Christ himself.[51]

When Paul tells the Philippians, "I rejoiced in the Lord greatly, because now at length you have revived your concern for me" (4:10), the phrase "in the Lord" indicates that this joy has its origin in the relationship to Christ that he shares with the Philippian Christians. The apostle has joy in the Lord because others who are one with him in Christ have shown concern for him.

The unity of the church in Christ is also in view in greetings that are sent "in the Lord" (Rom 16:22; 1 Cor 16:19).[52] This type of salutation expresses the unity in Christ of the one who sends it with those who receive it.[53]

When Paul gave exhortations "in the Lord" to other Christians,[54] he did so cognizant of the fact that his addressees were in Christ, just as he was. Because he and his addressees were one in Christ, the apostle's admonitions "in the Lord" carry a brotherly connotation. In these passages Paul appeals to his readers as his equals in the sight of God.[55]

Because the church is united in Christ Jesus, it gives glory to God the Father with one voice. This is the implication of the apostle's statement

---

51. Fee, *Philippians*, 94–95; Bruce, *Philippians*, 35.

52. In Phil 4:21 ἐν Χριστῷ Ἰησοῦ probably goes with "every saint" rather than "greet"; Bruce, *Philippians*, 157.

53. Bouttier, *En Christ*, 93.

54. Eph 4:17; 1 Thess 4:1; 2 Thess 3:12.

55. Morris, *Epistles to the Thessalonians*, 256; Bouttier, *En Christ*, 91, 93.

recorded in Eph 3:21: "To him be glory in the church and in Christ Jesus unto all generations forever and ever."[56]

When the mission of the church is described as being "in Christ," this denotes that Christ himself works through the proclamation of judgment and salvation (2 Cor 2:15–17). Because of their relationship to Christ those who are in him will live a life of good works (Eph 2:10); hence, Paul can speak of the ethical behavior of believers as their conduct "in Christ" or "in the Lord" (Col 3:18, 20).

On account of this mission and lifestyle "in Christ" all who are "in Christ" will suffer (2 Cor 13:3–4; 2 Tim 3:12), for they are living out their baptismal incorporation into the death (Rom 6:3–4, 11) of him who suffered death for their salvation. Nevertheless, since those "in Christ" have also been incorporated by way of their baptism into his resurrection (Col 2:11–13), they receive the power of the resurrection to endure these sufferings (2 Cor 1:5–7; 13:4; Phil 3:10–11),[57] and they will be raised at the parousia (1 Thess 4:16; 1 Cor 15:22).

This favored phrase of Paul's is interrelated with some of his other customary expressions. When one is baptized "into Christ" (εἰς Χριστόν), he finds himself to be "in Christ"[58] and to have participated in some event "with Christ" (σὺν Χριστῷ).[59] The equivalence of the expressions "in Christ" and "with Christ" may also be seen in the apostle's use of ἐν- forms together with σύν- forms when he speaks of our relationship to Christ.[60] The interrelation and equivalence of these phrases (ἐν Χριστῷ, εἰς Χριστόν, σὺν Χριστῷ) demonstrate that they represent three different ways that Paul uses to describe the single reality of salvation and all of the blessings that salvation involves.

---

56. Abbott, *Ephesians and Colossians*, 103–4.

57. Note that in Phil 3:10–11 the apostle uses two slightly different forms of the Greek term for "resurrection." In verse 11 he uses the compound noun ἐξανάστασιν to emphasize that he is speaking of the resurrection *from* the dead at the eschaton. That being the case, he uses the simple form ἀναστάσεως in verse 10, for there he is referring to the *power* of Christ's resurrection that enables the believer to endure "the fellowship of his sufferings."

58. Compare Gal 3:27 and Rom 6:3 with Gal 3:26 and Rom 6:11.

59. Compare Rom 6:3 with the σύν- forms in verses 4, 5, 6, and 8.

60. 2 Cor 13:4; Col 2:11–13; Eph 2:5–7, 22; 3:6; Rom 6:4–8, 11.

EXTENDED NOTES

KNOW, KNOWLEDGE (ΟΙΔΑ, ΓΙΝΩΣΚΩ, ΓΝΩΣΙΣ, ΕΠΙΓΝΩΣΙΣ)

In Greek usage the γνῶσις word group designates "intelligent comprehension of an object or matter."[61] Another word group for "knowing," οἶδα, is used without any significant difference in meaning from the γνῶσις word group.[62]

The New Testament use of "knowledge" is more heavily influenced by the use of the Hebrew word יָדַע in the Old Testament Scriptures than by classical Greek usage. In the Old Testament Bible "to know" someone or something implies having a relationship; hence, Adam "knew" his wife, and she conceived and gave birth (Gen 4:1). Of the two Greek terms for "knowledge" that occur in the NT, only γινώσκω is used of sexual intimacy (Matt 1:25). Thus, even though γινώσκω and οἶδα are used essentially synonymously, the former seems to carry more of the connotations of the Hebrew יָדַע.

In the Pastoral Letters Paul uses both of these Greek words to speak about "knowing." For the most part he seems to use the different word families to refer to different types of "knowledge."

In the Pastorals the apostle sometimes speaks of "knowing" in the ordinary, "secular" sense of the function of the human mind.[63] In most of these instances the word Paul uses for "knowing" is from the root οἶδα.[64]

The OT background seems to inform the apostle's use of οἶδα in 1 Tim 3:5. When Paul writes of the necessity for a pastor to "know" how to keep his own household in order, the verb "know" implies more than mere intellectual information. The term here refers rather to an aptitude for ordering one's family in a godly way.

The most significant use of this concept in the Pastoral Letters is as a synonym of saving faith. Several times the apostle speaks of faith as the "knowledge of the truth."[65] The only one of these instances in which Paul uses a form of οἶδα rather than of γνῶσις is 2 Tim 1:12. However, there he

61. *TDNT* 1:689.

62. *TDNT* 5:116.

63. 1 Tim 1:8; 3:15; 2 Tim 1:18; 2:23; 3:14; Titus 3:11.

64. The one exception is 2 Tim 1:18; in this passage Paul refers to what Timothy knows about the service of a fellow Christian. As Christians have a unity through their common faith in Christ, this would perhaps account for the apostle using a term (γινώσκεις) that more fully carries the connotation of a relationship and not mere intellectual knowledge.

65. 1 Tim 2:4; 4:3; 2 Tim 1:12; 2:25; 3:7; Titus 1:1.

writes, "I know him in whom I have believed [πεπίστευκα]." As the word "believed" itself denotes the relationship of faith, that word provides the sense of relationship beyond mere intellectual knowledge.

The relational connotation of "knowledge" is also seen in 2 Tim 2:19, where the apostle writes that "the Lord knows those who are his." God not only knows that they are his; he has also put them in a saving relationship with him.

A special use of this concept in the Pastorals is with reference to the heresy troubling the churches. Paul writes against that which is "falsely called knowledge" (γνῶσις, 1 Tim 6:20), and he speaks of those who claim to know (from οἶδα) God but who deny him by their evil deeds (Titus 1:16). This points to a feature of the false teaching that was disturbing the churches served by Timothy and Titus. The heretics claimed a special "knowledge" that others did not have. In these verses the apostle asserts that the false teachers' claims of "knowledge" are false. Therefore, the teaching of these heretics does not save but leaves them under the wrath of God. See further "The Nature of the Heresy" in the Introduction to the Pastoral Letters.

LOVE (ΑΓΑΠΗ, ΦΙΛΙΑ)

In the Pastorals Paul uses forms of the word ἀγάπη as well as those of the word group φιλία. He does so to refer to both God's love and human love.[66] His use of the term φιλία often occurs in compound words.

By definition your enemy is one who is hostile toward you. God loved us while we were his enemies (Rom 5:8, 10). In this we see the undeserved nature of God's love toward us.

It was because of God's love for humanity (φιλανθρωπία) that he saved us (Titus 3:4). The love of God was shown to us "in Christ Jesus" (1 Tim 1:14; 2 Tim 1:13). To be in that saving relationship with Christ that the apostle describes with the phrase "in Christ [Jesus]" is to have saving faith in Christ.[67] Through faith in Christ we have his love, and such faith empowers us to show love to others.

---

66. The distinction between these two word groups is not hard and fast. In addition to the "indiscriminate" way the apostle uses the two terms in the Pastorals, note that in the Johannine phrase "the disciple whom Jesus loved," while the verb ἠγάπα is used four times (13:23; 19:26; 21:7, 20), ἐφίλει is used once (20:2).

67. See Deterding, *Colossians*, 23; on Paul's use of the phrase "in Christ" and equivalents, see the entry "In Christ" in these Extended Notes

God's love for us moves us to love him in return. The Johannine sentiment "we love, because he first loved us" (1 John 4:19) captures the Pauline view as well. In the Pastorals Paul speaks of believers in Christ as those who have loved his appearing (2 Tim 4:8).

The virtue of love has its origin in biblical faith. This may be seen in the fact that prior to the first Christian century there is no certain reference in nonbiblical Greek literature to love as a moral quality.[68] Thus, viewing love as a virtue is essentially a uniquely Christian contribution to culture.

The use of the English word "love" may tend to suggest that love is a more intense form of liking. The meaning of ἀγάπη and φιλία in the NT is rather different. Love as a feeling depends upon some lovable trait in the object of love, and it will ebb and flow as the "lovableness" of the object of that love is greater or lesser. Love, both as an expression of God's attitude toward mankind and as a virtue of the Christian life, is not a feeling. Instead, ἀγάπη/φιλία designates an act of the will.

Like most of the virtues of the Christian life, love cannot be practiced in isolation. Instead, to exercise the virtue of love one must show it to others.

The Christian virtue of love as a product and reflection of the love of God for us is an act of the will. As God loved us, unconditionally, while we were his enemies, so our love for others will be unconditional. Because love as a virtue of the Christian life is not a feeling but an act of the will, believers can be *commanded* to love (Rom 13:8, 10; Gal 5:14).

Hence, love is to be characteristic of the Christian life.[69] Christians are specifically directed to love for others (Titus 2:4; 3:15).

As love is the chief virtue of the Christian life (1 Cor 13:13; Col 3:14), so misplaced love is a vice to be avoided. The Pastorals contain several warnings about the dangers of misdirected love.[70]

Christian pastors are to be an example for others of such love (1 Tim 4:12). In fact, Paul offers himself up to Timothy as an example of love for him to imitate (2 Tim 3:10).

---

68. *TDNT* 1:37; Quinn, *Titus*, 132; Spicq, *Notes de Lexicographie*, 26.
69. 1 Tim 6:11; 2 Tim 1:7; 2:22; Titus 2:2.
70. 1 Tim 3:3; 6:10; 2 Tim 3:2, 4; 4:10.

GRACE AND LIFE

MERCY (ΕΛΕΟΣ)

The Greek word ἔλεος referred to pity or kindness shown to another (e.g., Rom 12:8). However, the Septuagint, by customarily using this term to render the Hebrew word חֶסֶד,[71] gave a whole new level of meaning to the New Testament use of ἔλεος.

In the Hebrew Scriptures חֶסֶד expressed both the undeserved character of Yahweh's favorable attitude as well as its enduring character (e.g., Exod 34:6–7); hence, it has been translated into English by the phrase "steadfast love." Therefore, in the Greek New Testament ἔλεος denotes that God's favor is both undeserved and everlasting.

This character of ἔλεος can be seen from its use in the Pastorals. Salvation is due to the ἔλεος of God, not because of our works (Titus 3:5). Paul presents himself as the prime example of this; although he was a blasphemer and a persecutor of Christ, indeed, the foremost of sinners, he was shown mercy (1 Tim 1:13–16). God's ἔλεος reaches its apex at the day of resurrection, as may be seen from 2 Tim 1:16, 18.

"Mercy" is grouped together with "grace" in the salutations of both of the apostle's Letters to Timothy (1 Tim 1:2; 2 Tim 1:2). This serves to demonstrate that ἔλεος, like χάρις, is a comprehensive term for all that God has done, does, and will do (in Christ) for the salvation of mankind. See further the entry "Grace" in these Extended Notes.

MYSTERY (ΜΥΣΤΗΡΙΟΝ)[72]

"Mystery" (μυστήριον) is a significant kerygmatic term and one used far more often by Paul than any other New Testament author. By definition a mystery is something hidden; it may be made known through revelation (ἀποκάλυψις).

The apostle uses μυστήριον with reference to God's plan of salvation.[73] This plan is a mystery, because although present during Old Testament times, it was hidden in shadows and types (Col 2:17). Conversely, the mystery has been revealed or made known (ἐφανερώθη) in the New Testament era (the "now" of Col 1:26).[74] The plan itself predates the

---

71. Hatch and Redpath, *A Concordance to the Septuagint*, 451–52.
72. An earlier version of this section appeared in Deterding, *Colossians*, 73–75.
73. Rom 11:25; 1 Cor 2:7; Eph 1:9; 1 Tim 3:9.
74. See also Rom 16:25–26; 1 Cor 2:7; Eph 1:9; 3:3–6, 9.

Old Testament period, for its origin is in eternity (Col 1:26 ["ages" and "generations"]; see also Rom 16:25-26; 1 Cor 2:7; Eph 3:9).

Christ himself is the μυστήριον (Col 1:27;[75] 2:2), so that his coming is the revelation of this mystery. The phrase "hope of glory" in Col 1:27 designates our Lord as the source of the future glory of eternal salvation; as such, he reveals the mystery of God's plan (see also 1 Tim 3:16; cf. 2 Cor 3:13-16). Christ is the hope of glory in that from him we will receive glory, that is, the fullness of eternal life in the resurrection of the body; it is to all of this that our hope is directed. This revelation of Christ as savior also for the gentiles (see also Rom 16:26; Eph 3:6) marks another characteristic of the New Testament era; much of the narrative of Jesus' ministry and of the history of the earliest church was bound up with making known that Christ had come for all and not only for the chosen people of Old Testament times.

In the Septuagint μυστήριον is significant as the translation of רָז ("mystery"), which occurs only in the Aramaic portions of Daniel and, in fact, apart from 4:9 [4:6 MT], is confined entirely to chapter 2. There (18-19, 27-30, 47) the mystery is not simply anything hidden but has to do with the coming of Christ's kingdom (the rock of verses 44 and 45).

This mystery is revealed by the Holy Spirit (Eph 3:5) through both the written word (Rom 16:26) and the oral proclamation of the word.[76] For this reason Paul refers to proclaimers of the gospel as stewards of the mysteries (1 Cor 4:1), for, as he says, the μυστήριον is given them to proclaim (Eph 3:3-4, 6, 8-9; Col 1:28). The μυστήριον is proclaimed to all (Rom 16:26; Eph 3:8-9; 1 Tim 3:16); in fact, its scope involves all of creation (Eph 3:10).

The revelation of the mystery via the word means that the mystery is "Christ in you," or perhaps "Christ *among* you" (Col 1:27), for this mystery is revealed through Christ's making himself known to the community gathered about his word and sacraments. Through these the

---

75. In this passage the relative clause "which/who is Christ in/among you" stands in apposition to μυστηρίου. The textual witnesses are divided between the neuter ὅ, agreeing in gender with μυστήριον, to which it stands in apposition, and the masculine ὅς, which would agree in gender not with the grammatical antecedent, μυστήριον, but with the understood one, "Christ." While scribes might be inclined to correct what they felt to be a grammatical slip [changing an original ὅς to ὅ], it is equally possible for them to have accommodated the gender of the relative to correspond to the person referred to. The external evidence seems to give slight preference to the neuter. The decision in this matter of textual criticism does not, of course, change the overall meaning of the passage.

76. Note that "the mystery" in Col 1:26 is in apposition to "the word of God" in 1:25; see also Col 4:3; Rom 16:25; 1 Cor 2:7; 4:1; Eph 3:3, 6, 8-9; 6:19.

mystery is revealed and hence made known to faith. The nature of this mystery as the *hope* of glory is revealed also through the sacraments, for in baptism one is already raised from the dead with Christ (Rom 6:3–11; Col 2:12) and in the Lord's Supper one receives a foretaste of the banquet of eternity (Matt 26:29; Mark 14:25).

The mystery is known through faith (Rom 16:26; 1 Tim 3:9, 16). Among all nations it is those who have saving faith who know the riches of the glory of this mystery, for it was God's desire (Col 1:27), that is, his eternal plan of salvation (οἰκονομία), that this be experienced through saving faith (Col 1:25; Eph 3:2, 9; refer also to 1 Tim 1:4).

This Pauline usage of μυστήριον is in harmony with the one use of the concept by our Lord, namely, in connection with his commencing to teach in parables. In explaining to his disciples the reason for his parables, Jesus indicated that while his parables would hide the kingdom from those rejecting it, they would further reveal it to the believing, to those to whom the μυστήριον of the kingdom had been given. Mark's Gospel (4:11) uses the singular at this point, denoting that the mystery is Christ himself. Both Matthew (13:11) and Luke (8:10) employ the plural, indicating that our Lord reveals the mystery through his works and teachings.

The apostle's use of μυστήριον is also similar to that in Rev 10:7. There the mystery is something fully known at the end, even as it is now proclaimed by God to (and hence also through) prophets (stewards of the mysteries) for faith (theirs and their hearers').

The Dead Sea Scrolls use the concept of mystery in a similar manner with reference to their community. In the scrolls we find the assertion that God, who alone can reveal them (1QS 11:18–20), made known to the Teacher of Righteousness all the mysteries (the Hebrew term is identical to that used in Dan 2 and 4) of his servants the prophets (1QpHab 7:4–5). Therefore, in the thanksgiving hymns God is praised for having given knowledge of his wonderful mysteries to the hymnist (1QH 2:13; 4:27–28), who may again be the Teacher of Righteous or a representative member of the Qumran community, to which the Teacher has imparted this knowledge.

Both the Dead Sea community and the church of which Paul was a minister viewed itself as the community in which the promises were fulfilled and the mystery was revealed. But whereas the Qumran community viewed this as being accomplished through the teaching of ideas, the apostle understood it as having taken place because of Christ's work of reconciliation.

EXTENDED NOTES

PARAKLESIS (ΠΑΡΑΚΛΗΣΙΣ, ΠΑΡΑΚΑΛΕΩ)

The Greek noun παράκλησις and its cognate verb παρακαλέω have such a broad range of meanings that no single English translation can capture them all. "Encourage," "comfort," and "exhort" are some of the more common renderings. Only context will determine what would be the most suitable translation for any given use of these words.

Occasionally this word group is used of the comfort (soothing) that persons give to one another.[77] However, more often it has a more profound meaning.

Perhaps the most basic meaning to this word family is seen from its synonymous use with terms that denote the proclamation of the word of God. In the letters of Paul it is grouped with "prophecy," "teaching," and "preach/proclaim."[78] The παράκλησις of the Scriptures gives hope (Rom 15:4); similarly, by the word about the resurrection of believers at the last day Christians are able to comfort/encourage one another (1 Thess 4:18).

The word is a word of "comfort," as it brings the blessings of salvation. For example, the apostle calls on the Christians at Corinth "to forgive and to comfort" (χαρίσασθαι καὶ παρακαλέσαι) the sinner in their midst who has been brought to repentance (2 Cor 2:7). While "comfort" would certainly include kind and soothing treatment of the individual, the real "comfort" comes from the word of forgiveness.

In this light it is not surprising that the term can be used of formal preaching. Paul's synagogue sermon recorded in Acts 13 (16–41) is given in response to the invitation to him to speak, if he has any word of παράκλησις for the people assembled there (Acts 13:15). The author of Hebrews describes his entire composition as a "word of exhortation/encouragement" (παρακλήσεως, 13:22). Thus, "preaching" (in worship) seems to be called for as the meaning of the noun in 1 Tim 4:13.

This is significant in light of two other connotations of the word group. Comfort/encouragement is sometimes designated to be the work of God himself.[79] Since God works through his word, it would be expected that the proclamation of his word would be a means by which he would provide such comfort/encouragement. The message that provides such divine encouragement is the message of eternal

---

77. 2 Cor 7:4, 13; 1 Thess 3:7; Phlm 7.
78. Rom 12:7–8; 1 Cor 14:3, 31; 1 Tim 6:2b; 2 Tim 4:2; Titus 1:9.
79. Rom 15:5; 2 Cor 1:3–4; 2 Cor 7:6–7; Phil 2:1.

salvation (2 Thess 2:16–17). This word provides "comfort" by creating and strengthening saving faith.[80]

Related to this is the use of the cognate noun παράκλητος ("Paraclete") with reference to Jesus as our "advocate" before God (1 John 2:1) and to the Holy Spirit as another "advocate" whom Christ would send to his followers.[81] These passages designate each of these as one who speaks for the benefit of others. As both Christ (2 Cor 4:5–6) and the Holy Spirit (2 Tim 3:16) work through the word, encouragement through the word would indicate that encouragement through speaking the word involves the power of Christ and of the Holy Spirit through that word.

The word of exhortation/comfort/encouragement is more than mere words. This may be seen from those passages that speak of the comfort of the "heart,"[82] "heart" referring to one's true inner being (see the entry "Heart and Conscience" elsewhere in these Extended Notes). That being the case, in many instances the rendering "comfort," although it is commonly used for this word group, may not be the best translation, as the English word may tend to connote attempts to soothe feelings apart from any objective reality that would actually provide genuine relief.

This gives insight to Paul's statement to Titus that he should "exhort and convince of these things *with all authority*" (Titus 2:15). As God himself works through the exhortation of his word, that word could be proclaimed with all the authority of God himself.

This helps to explain those passages where the apostle speaks of "encouraging" others to an action rather than commanding them to do it.[83] The "encouragement" of God's word has authority, the authority of God the Holy Spirit himself. Beyond any human power of persuasion or compulsion the Holy Spirit has the power to create in the hearers the willingness to do those things that he would have them do.

The divine power of this word of encouragement is demonstrated in any and every circumstance. Paul speaks of the giving and receiving of encouragement/comfort even in the face of suffering and affliction.[84]

The power of encouragement in the word of God is seen in other effects that it produces in the lives of those to whom it comes. The apostle

---

80. 2 Cor 5:20; 6:1; 1 Thess 3:2; 5:11.
81. John 14:16; 15:26; 16:7.
82. Eph 6:22; Col 2:2; 4:8; 2 Thess 2:17.
83. 1 Thess 2:3; 1 Tim 5:1; Phlm 9–10.
84. 1 Cor 4:13; 2 Cor 1:4, 5, 6, 7.

often speaks of exhorting others to action,[85] in particular to godly living.[86] The authority associated with this term means that these exhortations are not mere suggestions but directives that are to be followed (as well as being directives that actually empower the hearer to do what is directed). Corresponding to this are those passages where the noun should be translated with something like "strong appeal," "urgent request," or "earnestness."[87] In fact, Paul even uses the verb with reference to his earnestly beseeching the Lord to remove from him his "thorn in the flesh" (2 Cor 12:8).

The divine power inherent in this term also means that those exhorted to godly living are not left to their own wherewithal to follow these exhortations. Rather, the power of the Holy Spirit is available to empower their following what has been directed.

This word group is multifaceted in its meaning. The student of the Scriptures should be aware that there is often more involved in any given use of these terms than what any particular English translation might convey.

PEACE (EIPHNH)

The NT concept of peace is greatly influenced by the Hebrew term שָׁלוֹם, a word which can have the meaning "whole, unbroken" (1 Kgs 6:7; 8:61). The state of שָׁלוֹם is the status of having a relationship with God in which everything is as it should be; it is whole and unbroken.

Such peace is a fruit of having been justified before God through faith in Jesus Christ (Rom 5:1). The justifying and reconciling work of Christ brings peace with God, and this peace with almighty God means peace also with all those who are at peace with the Lord (Eph 2:14–18). That peace is then reflected in the life of the justified, as they strive to live at peace with all (Rom 12:18).

As with "grace" (see the entry by that name elsewhere in these Extended Notes) Paul's greeting of "peace" in the salutations of his letters is more than a polite greeting or a pious wish. The power of the word of God is such that it actually bestows on the hearer/reader the peace of which it speaks.

85. 1 Cor 16:12; 2 Cor 6:8; 8:6; 9:5; 10:1; 12:18 1 Tim 1:3.
86. Rom 12:1; 15:30; 16:17; 1 Cor 1:10; 4:16; 16:15–16; Eph 4:1; Phil 4:2; 1 Thess 2:12; 4:1, 10–11; 5:14; 2 Thess 3:12; 1 Tim 2:1; Titus 2:6.
87. 2 Cor 8:4, 17; BDAG 766.

REDEEM, REDEMPTION/RANSOM
(ΛΥΤΡΟΩ, ΑΝΤΙΛΥΤΡΟΝ)

The range of meaning of the word group that includes ἀντίλυτρον and λυτρόω includes the ideas of deliverance and release. This can be seen from its use in Heb 11:35, which refers to heroes of faith from the past who refused to accept deliverance (ἀπολύτρωσιν) from death in order that they might obtain a better resurrection.

This word group is used in the Septuagint with various shades of meaning. Through Moses Yahweh foretells that he will redeem Israel from its bondage in Egypt (Exod 6:6). Later Moses tells the Israelites that because of God's love and his oath to their ancestors the Lord redeemed them from their slavery (Deut 7:8).

The word can also be used in a broader sense. David asserts that Yahweh redeemed his life from every affliction (2 Sam [LXX 2 Kingdoms] 4:9).

In secular Greek the word group is used of the release of someone from slavery. Specific mention might be made of an amount of money that was the price of the slave's manumission.[88]

In the New Testament era Jesus himself first applies the concept of redemption to his work. Two of the evangelists record his statement that he came not to be served but to serve and to give his life as a ransom for many (Matt 28:20; Mark 10:45).

Pauline passages that employ the concept of redemption often make explicit mention of the price paid by which the redemption was accomplished. When the apostle writes to the Romans concerning the "redemption that is in Christ Jesus" (3:24), he adds that Christ himself was put forward by God (the Father) as the redemption price (3:25).[89] Similarly, in Ephesians (1:7) Paul asserts that in Christ we have redemption "through his blood," that is, through his sacrificial death on the cross.

In the Pastoral Letters the apostle uses this concept twice, each time with a similar meaning. In 1 Timothy Paul notes that Christ gave himself as a ransom (ἀντίλυτρον) for all, pointing to the truth that Christ's redemptive work was sufficient for all (2:6). In writing to Titus, the apostle

---

88. Spicq, *Theological Lexicon*, 2:426–27.

89. This is the case regardless of how the translator renders the term ἱλαστήριον into English ("propitiation" [ESV], "expiation" [RSV], "atoning sacrifice" [CSB], "mercy seat" [NET]).

notes that Jesus Christ gave himself (to death) for us in order that he might redeem us from sin and purify us to be zealous of good works (2:14).

This concept contributes richly to our understanding of both justification and sanctification. Christ has redeemed us, so that we may receive eternal life. He has also redeemed us, so that belonging to him we will live in keeping with his will and to his glory.

RIGHTEOUSNESS/JUSTIFICATION (ΔΙΚΑΙΟΣΥΝΗ)

The Greek word group δικαιόω/δίκαιος/δικαιοσύνη can be translated into English with two different word groups: "justify/just/justification" (from Latin) and "declare righteous/righteous/righteousness" (by way of Old English). The translator will decide which rendering to use based on which reads better in a given passage. When students of the Bible are studying the Scriptures in English, they would do well to keep this in mind in order to pick up on connections between words in a given passage that will be apparent in Greek but not in English.[90]

The Greek word group describes things as they ought to be.[91] Even in secular Greek the word connotes what man owes to the divine.[92]

Jesus speaks of a penitent sinner being justified (Luke 18:14), and there are a few references to justification by faith in the Letter to the Hebrews[93] and in the Letter of James.[94] Otherwise righteousness/justification in the New Testament is a distinctively Pauline concept. The significance of this concept for the apostle is seen in the more than sixty uses of the δικαιόω/δίκαιος/δικαιοσύνη word group in his letters.

Despite what Paul had once believed as a Pharisee (Phil 3:6), righteousness before God is not a human achievement. Instead, this is entirely the work of God.[95]

---

90. A good example of this would be Rom 3:20–30.
91. Spicq, *Theological Lexicon*, 1:320.
92. Spicq, *Theological Lexicon*, 1:321.
93. 10:38; 11:4, 7; 12:23.
94. On the proper interpretation of Jas 2:21, 24, 25, see Giese, *James*, 236–81.
95. Rom 3:26; 3:30; 8:30, 33.

We are justified by the grace of God;[96] justification is not by works or by the law.[97] It is not by works; rather, it is received through faith in Jesus Christ.[98]

Faith in Christ justifies, because justification is the work of Christ;[99] for example, when one is put to death and raised from the dead with Christ in baptism, he is justified from sin (Rom 6:7). Jesus Christ was "put to death for our trespasses and raised for our justification" (Rom 4:25). When one has righteousness before God through faith in Christ, then he has the gift of eternal life (1 Tim 4:8).

The righteousness that is received by grace through faith shows itself in the life of the believer. One who is righteous through faith in Christ will be able to produce righteous deeds in his life.[100]

SAVE, SAVIOR, SALVATION (ΣΩιΖΩ, ΣΩΤΗΡ, ΣΩΤΗΡΙΑ)

On its most basic level the verb σῴζω means to "rescue" or to "deliver." Thus, when the disciples are in danger at sea, they implore Jesus to "save" them (Matt 8:25; 14:30). Similarly, while he is being crucified, both passersby and the members of the Sanhedrin taunt Jesus by challenging him to "save" himself by coming down from the cross (Matt 27:40–42). When Jesus delivers individuals from infirmities such as hemorrhage (Mark 5:34), blindness (Mark 10:52), and "leprosy"[101] (Luke 17:19), he tells these recipients of his power, "Your faith has saved you."

Episodes in the ministry of our Lord such as these are to be understood in light of the use of "save" to refer to eternal salvation. These acts of deliverance from the consequences of mankind's fall into sin

---

96. Rom 3:24; 5:16, 21; Titus 3:7.

97. Rom 3:20, 21; 4:6, 13; 2 Cor 3:9; Gal 2:16 (3x), 21; 3:11; 5:4. On the proper interpretation of Jas 2:21, 24, 25, see Giese, *James*, 236–81.

98. Rom 1:17; 3:22, 26, 28, 30; 4:3, 5 (2x), 9, 11, 13, 22; 5:1, 9, 18; 9:30; 10:4, 6, 10; Gal 2:16 (3x); 3:6, 8, 11, 24; 5:5; Phil 3:9.

99. Rom 4:25; 5:17, 19, 21; 6:7; 8:10; 10:4; 1 Cor 1:30; 6:11; 2 Cor 5:21; Gal 2:21; Phil 3:9.

100. Rom 6:13, 16, 19; 2 Cor 6:14; 9:10; Eph 4:24; 1 Thess 2:10.

101. The terms customarily translated "leper" and "leprosy" refer to a wide variety of ailments and not only to the neurological disorder that is more properly termed "Hanson's disease."

demonstrate that Christ had come not simply to deal with these consequences of the fall but to deal with the root cause itself: sin.

The vocable "save" is used more than one hundred times in the New Testament[102] (including twenty-nine times in the thirteen letters of Paul),[103] the majority of which refer to the work of Jesus Christ in delivering from sin and eternal damnation. Familiar Pauline passages such as 1 Cor 1:21 and Eph 2:8 are examples of this meaning of "save."

Related to this is the use of the term "savior" (σωτήρ) with reference to God (the Father) and/or Jesus Christ.[104] "The activity implicit in [this] title permeates the whole of Paul's soteriology."[105] This can be seen from the relative frequency with which the apostle uses this title; the twelve places in the letters of Paul where this title is used[106] far outnumber those passages that employ other related titles, such as "redeemer" (1), "justifier" (1), "advocate" (0), or even "the Christ/Messiah" (3).[107]

This preference for "savior" over other terms that the apostle might have used indicates that for Paul the vocable "savior" had become a general, all-embracing term for the work of Christ. Thus, "save" and "savior" cover the entire panorama of designations for the redemptive work of Christ.

SLAVERY IN THE NEW TESTAMENT WORLD[108]

Biblical passages such as 1 Cor 7:20–22, 1 Pet 2:18–25, Eph 6:5–8, Col 3:22–25, 1 Tim 6:1–2, Titus 2:9–10, and the Letter to Philemon raise

---

102. BDAG 982–83.

103. Rom 5:9, 10; 8:24; 9:27; 10:9, 13; 11:14, 26; 1 Cor 1:18, 21; 3:15; 5:5; 7:16 (2x); 9:22; 10:33; 15:2; 2 Cor 2:15; Eph 2:5, 8; 1 Thess 2:16; 2 Thess 2:10; 1 Tim 1:15; 2:4, 15; 2 Tim 1:9; 4:16, 18; Titus 3:5.

104. God (the Father): 1 Tim 1:1; 2:3; Titus 1:3; 2:10; 3:4 (In 2 Tim 1:9 and Titus 3:5 the apostle states that "God" saved us); Jesus Christ: 2 Tim 1:10; Titus 1:4; 2:13; 3:6.

105. *DPL* 359.

106. Eph 5:23; Phil 3:20; 1 Tim 1:1; 2:3; 2 Tim 1:10; Titus 1:4; 2:13; 3:6; Titus 1:3; 2:10; 3:4. In addition the synagogue homily of Paul recorded in Acts 13:23 also identifies Jesus as "savior."

107. The term ὁ Χριστός, "the Christ," was originally the Greek equivalent of הַמָּשִׁיחַ, "the Messiah" (John 1:41), "the Anointed One," that is, the promised one (from David's line) for whose coming religious Jews were waiting (Luke 20:41; 22:67). Over time the Greek term (ὁ) Χριστός morphed into a name: "Jesus Christ," "Christ Jesus," or simply "Christ"; this is most often the meaning that the vocable has in the letters of Paul. However, there are three Pauline passages (Rom 9:3, 5; 1 Cor 10:4) in which the term seems to preserve its original sense of "the Messiah."

108. An earlier version of this section appeared in Deterding, *Colossians*, 171–76.

the issue of Christianity's view toward the institution of slavery. To understand the biblical position, we must also be familiar with slavery as practiced in the Roman Empire in New Testament times,[109] realizing that "slavery must have meant something quite different in antiquity from what it means to many people today."[110]

In the ancient world a slave was not a person but a piece of property: Aristotle called a slave "a living tool"[111] and mere property,[112] and under Roman law a slave was a thing rather than a legal person. Nevertheless, the picture that the word "slavery" may conjure up in our minds of a cruel taskmaster cracking a whip over the bare backs of men laboring knee-deep in muck fails to consider many of the factors that made up the complex phenomenon of slavery in the Roman world.

Slaves in the Roman Empire worked under a wide variety of conditions and circumstances.[113] Owners had the legal power of life and death over their slaves, but they exercised the same power over their sons. Thus, as little as one can imagine this right regularly leading to cruel and inhuman treatment of an owner's sons, so little should we assume that an owner's rights over his slaves automatically led to cruelty and mistreatment of them.[114] Furthermore, under Roman law slaves possessed (at least theoretically) the right to protest to the authorities when their masters treated them cruelly, even though practical access to such legal protection varied from place to place.[115] While at times Roman slaves were dealt with very cruelly,[116] it was clearly in the interests of the slave owners to treat their slaves decently and fairly; such treatment would help to diminish the threat of hostility from one's slaves and would help to promote cooperation from them.[117]

---

109. The following two paragraphs summarize the extensive research and primary source references found in Bartchy, *MALLON XRESAI*. See especially 38–40, 63–75, and 82–87.

110. Nordling, *Philemon*, 46.

111. Aristotle, *Nicomachean Ethics* 8.11.

112. Aristotle, *Politics* 1.2, 4–5.

113. Bradley, *Slaves and Masters*, 15.

114. Nordling, *Philemon*, 52.

115. Bradley, *Slaves and Masters*, 123–26.

116. Hopkins, *Conquerors and Slaves*, 1:118; note the observation (and criticism) of Seneca in Quinn, *Titus*, 146.

117. Quinn, *Titus*, 146–47. S. Scott Bartchy ["Slavery (Greco-Roman)," in *ABD* 6:66] notes that while in much of Roman law slaves were regarded as things (*instrumentum vocale*—a "speaking tool"), they nevertheless "were regularly treated as

Another factor to consider is that slaves in the Roman world did not perform only menial, physical labor. Slaves might also serve in "white-collar" professions such as artisans, administrators, tutors, doctors, writers, and scholars; for example, the three "slaves" (δοῦλοι) of the parable of Matt 25:14–30 are entrusted respectively with five talents, two talents, and one talent; clearly they hold positions of significant responsibility.[118]

It should also be noted that many slaves lived with the prospect of eventual manumission. While this matter was complex and differed from place to place, it did make the life of a slave more hopeful than that word might suggest to us of the twenty-first century.[119]

Moreover, since the entire economic order of the empire depended on slave labor, to a great extent a condition of "mutual interdependence" existed in the Roman world between masters and slaves.[120] In that light, it was in the interest of the masters to keep their slaves willing to work well by providing them with both fair treatment and the prospect of eventual freedom.[121]

Additionally, we note that race played little if *any* role in the institution of Roman slavery. Indeed, "Latins, Greeks, dark-skinned Syrians, black Ethiopians, and blond, blue-eyed Germans could be slaves together under one owner."[122]

Thus, slavery was taken for granted in the Roman Empire during New Testament times. Slaves would be a part of even a comparatively modest household,[123] with perhaps 85 to 90 percent of the population of Rome consisting of people who were slaves or of slave origin.[124] The literature of the time indicates that there was no great need felt, even by

---

well as free human beings and were normally granted Roman citizenship when set free, as happened regularly." Even Hopkins (*Conquerors and Slaves*, 132), who emphasizes the cruel realities of Roman slavery, begrudgingly admits that "the human factors" of the generosity and kindness of masters and the corresponding gratitude of slaves who had been freed "have often been exaggerated, but [these factors] should not be ignored."

118. Nordling, "Christ Leavens Culture," 47. See also the many examples cited in Nordling, *Philemon*, 76–86.

119. Bradley, *Slaves and Masters*, 87–89, 95–122; Nordling, *Philemon*, 50–52.

120. Nordling, *Philemon*, 58–59.

121. Nordling, *Philemon*, 99–102, 108.

122. Osiek, "Slavery," 151. See also Nordling, *Philemon*, 69–76, 89–91; Nordling, "Christ Leavens Culture," 46–47; Sherwin-White, *Racial Prejudice*; Snowden Jr., *Before Color Prejudice*, 46–47, 89–90.

123. Dunn, *Colossians and Philemon*, 252n26.

124. *DPL* 881.

slaves, for abolishing the institution; for many, even some former slaves, spiritual and metaphorical freedoms were considered as valuable and desirable (perhaps even more so) than manumission from slavery.[125] Furthermore, we should note that when a slave in the Roman world was freed, he had to assume responsibility for feeding, clothing, and housing himself, obligations that heretofore the master had assumed. Thus, a slave who had been reasonably well treated might have preferred the security afforded by his master to the life of a freedman.[126] There were even instances of free individuals submitting to being sold into slavery with a view to having a better life in the household of a well-off master than they would have had on their own.[127]

All of this gives us a more nuanced view of slavery in the New Testament world than what we might assume. The master/slave relationship encountered by Paul was, in some significant ways, closer to our modern employer/employee relationship than to the institution of slavery, with all its abuses, practiced in the United States prior to the Civil War.[128]

Of special interest to the situation of the Letter to Philemon is that of fugitive slaves. These were subject to seizure and punishment,[129] although there was legal recognition of a slave finding refuge at certain sacred sites for the purpose of having his grievances heard.[130]

Neither Paul nor any other New Testament author sought to abolish the institution of slavery or otherwise to overthrow the social order by violence; this, in fact, would have been contrary to the apostle's teachings on retribution and social order.[131] Instead, he and other New Testament authors instructed Christians to live and to serve in their station(s) in life, even if that was as a slave. In fact, Christian slaves were to carry out their service in a more godly manner than they would have done apart from being believers in Christ (Col 3:22–23); this was to be especially true if their masters were fellow Christians, for now they would be serving not

---

125. Nordling, *Philemon*, 52–53, 56–57.

126. Nordling, *Philemon*, 52–53, 56–57, 108. It is also worth noting that in another time and setting the Hebrew scriptures made provision for the circumstance when a slave, even though he had the right to obtain his freedom, chose to remain permanently with the master whom he loved (Exod 21:2–6; Deut 15:12–17).

127. Nordling, *Philemon*, 94–98.

128. Bartchy, "Slavery (Greco-Roman)," in *ABD* 6:66; Nordling, *Philemon*, 69, 138; Quinn, *Titus*, 146–47.

129. Bartchy, *MALLON XRESAI*, 44; Moule, *Colossians*, 34–37.

130. Bartchy, *MALLON XRESAI*, 105.

131. Martin, *Colossians and Philemon*, 121.

only a master but also a brother in Christ (1 Tim 6:1–2). Moreover, even if set free, Christian slaves were to continue, now as freedmen, to live according to God's call (1 Cor 7:20–24[132]).

In both Ephesians (6:9) and Colossians (4:1) the apostle lays obligations on masters as well as on their slaves. He instructs masters to treat their slaves justly and equitably. As both a check on their actions and a motivation for doing as they are directed, Paul reminds them that they themselves have a master—in heaven.

Christian freedom is a freedom from sin, death, and the law won by Christ (Gal 4:21—5:1); this freedom both transcends earthly freedom or bondage and transforms the obligations of one's earthly status into a service of God and for one's fellowman.[133] This freedom, therefore, does not mean that all human servitude must be abolished (contrary to, for example, the claims of liberation theology).

These attitudes are reflected in the Letter to Philemon. In it the apostle "is not really dealing with the question of slavery as such or the resolution of a particular instance of slavery."[134] He does not ignore the legal claims of Philemon over Onesimus. Even in his delicate request that Philemon do "more than what I ask" (21), he does not call for the emancipation of Onesimus (Philemon could have kept Onesimus as a slave and then assigned him to work for Paul).

All of that being said, the way in which Paul and the other biblical writers deal with the question of slavery did serve to transform the way in which it was viewed. As a result, as Western society as a whole became influenced by Christian thought and values, the very institution of slavery itself, because it was intrinsically liable to grave abuses, came to be viewed as unacceptable.[135] In broad terms we may note five things that Christian teaching and practice did to bring about the abolition of slavery in much of the modern world:

1. Christianity treated slaves as equals in the church (Gal 3:28; 1 Cor 7:20–24). In Rom 16:21–23 the names Tertius and Quartus

---

132. On the interpretation of this passage see Bartchy, *MALLON XRESAI*, 155–59.

133. On this subject see Luther's masterful treatise *The Freedom of a Christian* (AE 31:333–77), in particular the following two sentences (344): "A Christian is a perfectly free lord of all, subject to none. A Christian is a perfectly dutiful servant of all, subject to all."

134. O'Brien, *Colossians, Philemon*, 298.

135. For a survey of the role of Christianity in the abolition of slavery see Schmidt, *How Christianity Changed the World*, 272–91.

seem to be those of slaves; these are listed on the same level as Erastus, the city's director of public works, and Timothy, Paul's fellow worker.[136] From later church history we learn that the Christian church opened church offices to slaves:[137] Onesimus, bishop of Ephesus about AD 100, may have been the Onesimus of Colossians and Philemon;[138] Calixtus, an ex-slave, was sixth bishop of Rome [AD 217–22];[139] possibly Pius, bishop of Rome, was a slave or at least the brother of a slave.[140] Furthermore, there are accounts of slave girls and their mistresses sharing martyrdom for the Christian faith.[141]

2. Paul reminded the masters that they too had a master, in heaven (Col 4:1; Eph 6:9). This set the slaves on an equal spiritual footing with their masters.

3. The New Testament addressed slaves and treated them as persons with both rights and responsibilities (Col 3:22–25; 1 Pet 2:18), which was a significant step beyond the circumstances of the day (contrast the views of Aristotle cited above). The duty codes of both Judaism and Stoicism, which in many respects parallel such passages as Col 3:22—4:1, Eph 6:5–9, and 1 Pet 2:18–25, impose no moral demands on slaves, only masters.[142]

4. Christianity asserted the dignity of manual labor (Eph 4:28). Although work in a trade was advocated by others in the first-century Roman world, for the most part people looked upon having to engage in manual labor as humiliating and most certainly as unbecoming anyone of privilege.[143]

5. The New Testament pointed to the example of Christ as one who suffered unjustly (1 Pet 2:21). This is particularly pertinent in view of the fact that crucifixion was known as the "slaves' punishment"

---

136. Pokorný, *Colossians*, 178–79.
137. Bruce, *Galatians*, 189.
138. Ignatius, *Ephesians* 1:3.
139. Hippolytus, *Refutation of All Heresies* 9:11–12.
140. Compare Muratorian Canon 73–77 with Shepherd of Hermes, *Visions* 1:1.
141. Eusebius, *Ecclesiastical History* 5:1:17–19, 37–42. See also Bruce, *Colossians*, 151, and Perpetua, *Passion of S. Perpetua*, 90–95.
142. Davids, *First Peter*, 105; Dunn, *Colossians and Philemon*, 252.
143. Hock, *Social Context*; see especially 36, 40, 44–45, 64, and the primary source material in the notes.

(even though not everyone in the Roman world who died by crucifixion was a slave).[144] In doing so Christianity gave a new dignity to those who were slaves, particularly when they bore unwarranted mistreatment.

What is the message of these portions of the Scriptures to Christians living in a culture that has significant differences from that of the New Testament world, particularly in that the formal institution of slavery has been abolished? To determine this, we must here distinguish what is constant from what is contingent.

The structure of social orders (government, family, economic systems) may change from age to age: monarchies, oligarchies, parliamentary systems, and representative democracies are rather different from one another; the large, extended families of earlier times have dissimilarities from the so-called nuclear family; a free market economy with employers and employees has important differences from the slavery-based economy of the Roman Empire. Nevertheless, the orders themselves, as creations of God (1 Pet 2:13), are changeless until the new creation of the resurrection.

The New Testament paraenesis regarding the relationships between slaves and masters is applicable to modern relationships between employees and employers or other superiors in the workplace.[145] The Christian employee is to serve his employer and supervisor in the same manner as the first-century Christian slave was instructed by Paul to act toward his master. The Christian employer or supervisor is to show the same consideration toward his employees or subordinates as the apostle directed the masters among the readers of Colossians and Ephesians to display toward their slaves.

These passages of God's word provide guiding principles for our relationships within the various orders of society rather than giving us detailed rules, which would have quickly become time-bound and hence irrelevant. Thus, these constant principles are applicable to a variety of changing and contingent situations within culture and within one's own personal experience.

---

144. Nordling, *Philemon*, 111–12.
145. Nordling, *Philemon*, 59.

TEACHING/DOCTRINE (ΔΙΔΑΣΚΑΛΙΑ, ΔΙΔΑΣΚΩ, ΔΙΔΑΧΗ)

The English words "teaching" and "doctrine" are alternate ways of rendering a term that carries a great deal of meaning in the Scriptures. The translation "doctrine" accents the content of the teaching. The rendering "teaching" includes that emphasis but also includes the notion of the act of teaching.

There are times when the New Testament employs this word in such a way that the reference is primarily to the teaching of salvation in Jesus Christ (1 Tim 1:3; 2 Pet 2:1). Nevertheless, the use of this term throughout the New Testament indicates that most often it refers to the whole of Christian doctrine.

The entire Sermon on the Mount (Matt 5:1—7:29) is identified as "teaching" (5:2; 7:28, 29). Included in this teaching are a number of guidelines for sanctified, Christian living. This use of the concept of teaching is also found in several places in the Pauline correspondence.[146] According to Matt 5:19 one might teach contrary to some such ethical prescription and still remain within the pale of the Christian faith.

The concept of "teaching" is also applied to matters of the Christian faith other than the rudimentary essentials necessary for salvation. The teaching of Jesus in the Sermon on the Mount dealt with prayer (Matt 6:5–15), fasting (Matt 6:16–18), and being reconciled to a brother (Matt 5:23–26). Jesus taught his disciples to pray (Luke 11:1). One finds a similar use of the idea of "teaching" in Paul. In 1 Corinthians the apostle refers to what nature teaches about proper attire of men and women in Christian worship (11:14–15). He also uses the concept of "teaching" with reference to instruction concerning marriage and foods (1 Tim 4:1, 6, 11) and on the relationship between Christian slaves and their masters (1 Tim 6:2–3).

Furthermore, the idea of "teaching" is sometimes used in connection with the entire biblical revelation. In the book of Acts Paul is described as teaching the word of the Lord (15:35) or again the word of God (18:11). In the apostle's instruction to Timothy to "preach the word, be ready at opportune times and at inopportune times, rebuke, correct, encourage with all long-suffering and teaching" (2 Tim 4:2) the word "teaching" must be understood in an inclusive sense, referring to all articles of the Christian faith. This can be seen in the connections between

---

146. Eph 4:21; Col 2:7; 1 Tim 1:10; Titus 2:1.

this passage and the Pauline description of those things for which the Scriptures are profitable (2 Tim 3:16–17, where the terms διδασκαλίαν and ἐλεγμόν are recalled in 4:2 by the cognates ἔλεγξον and διδαχῇ). In Matt 28:20 the risen Lord instructs his disciples to teach the nations to observe *all* things that he has commanded. In 2 Tim 3:16 Paul indicates that *all* Scripture is profitable for teaching.

The apostle's statement in 2 Thess 2:15, "Hold to the traditions which you were taught, either by [spoken] word or by our letter," contributes much towards understanding the concept of "teaching." The object of teaching is identified as "traditions," the plural form suggesting that Paul has a number of doctrines in mind. Moreover, the Greek term for "traditions" (παραδόσεις) is a cognate of the verb "delivered" (παραδίδωμι), one of the two Greek equivalents of the rabbinic technical terms (the other is παραλαμβάνω, "received") which the apostle uses in 1 Cor 11:23 (cf. the use in 15:3) to refer to the Lord's Supper as part of the apostolic tradition (the ultimate origin of which was Christ himself) that he handed on to his readers.[147] This demonstrates that the Lord's Supper was among the "traditions" to which Paul's readers were to adhere. In 2 Thess 2:15 the apostle indicates that the teaching of this apostolic tradition is done not only orally but also by way of his letter, a portion of the Scriptures.[148] This suggests that the whole of the apostolic Scriptures form the content of biblical "teaching."

The way in which the idea of "teaching" is used throughout the Scriptures illumines the meaning of Rom 16:17: "I appeal to you, brothers, to watch out for those who cause divisions and create obstacles contrary to the doctrine [or "teaching"] that you have been taught; avoid them." From this it is evident that this passage cannot refer only to non-Christians who dissent from the essentials of the Christian faith necessary for salvation. Instead, the word "doctrine/teaching" in this passage must refer to Christian doctrine in all its articles. This means that in this passage Paul directs his readers to avoid religious fellowship with those who create divisions

---

147. Barrett, *First Corinthians*, 264–66.

148. On the relationship of the apostles as authoritative teachers in Christ's church and the Scriptures, see the entry "Apostle" in these Extended Notes. That Paul understood his letters as being on a level with the Hebrew Scriptures that were read in worship (as in Luke 4:16–19 and Acts 13:15) is seen in his instruction to have his letters read (in worship) by his addressees (Col 4:16; 1 Thess 5:27).

and offenses within the Christian community by departing from any of the teaching contained in the biblical revelation.[149]

Thus, when we encounter the term "teaching/doctrine," we ought not immediately limit the meaning of the word to certain teachings of the faith. Instead, in the absence of other factors, we should think of the entirety of Christian doctrine.

TRUTH (ΑΛΗΘΕΙΑ)

"What is truth?" With those words (John 18:38) Pontius Pilate dismissed our Lord's claims about the truth, but this is a question that might legitimately be asked. What is "truth," and what does it mean that something/someone is "true?" Biblically there are at least three distinct but related denotations to the concept of "truth."[150] While one or another of these might be the main emphasis in a given passage, none of them would be entirely lacking.

That someone or something is "true" might mean that he/it is real and not imaginary. Such a meaning predominates in passages where Paul contrasts the "truth" with "myths" or "falsehood" (Eph 4:25; 2 Tim 4:4; Titus 1:14).

To be "true" could denote what is accurate and factual in distinction from what is erroneous or false. This would be what is indicated in passages where the apostle uses "truth" to emphasize the factual nature of what he is saying (Rom 9:1; 2 Cor 12:6). He sets forth the truth, for he is an apostle and "slave" of him "who does not lie" (Titus 1:1–2).

For someone or something to be "true" might involve the person or thing being trustworthy. In passages where Paul talks about "the knowledge of the truth" as the way to salvation[151] the word "truth" would have this as its primary meaning; hence, one can put his/her trust for eternal salvation in it.

Moreover, the vocable "truth" must be understood in light of the content (and context) of what is being referenced by the term. It is not enough simply to use the word "truth"; it must be made clear just what is being characterized by that term.

---

149. On the interpretation of Rom 16:17 see Franzmann, "Exegesis on Romans 16:17ff," 13–20.

150. BDAG 42–43.

151. 1 Tim 2:4; 2 Tim 2:25; 3:7; Titus 1:1.

For Paul "the truth" has to do with the truth from and about God (Rom 1:25; 3:7). This truth is known through the word of God (2 Tim 2:15, 18). While the heart of that truth is the gospel of salvation (Eph 1:13; Col 1:5–6), the truth also includes the law of God that rebukes sin (Gal 4:16) and his law that directs the believer to godly living (Eph 4:21).

Truth is the object of saving faith (2 Thess 2:13); through this faith one grasps the truth. In the Pastoral Letters[152] the apostle often refers to this faith as "the knowledge of the truth."

The era in which we have been living for the past half century or so is often described as the postmodern era. A characteristic of postmodernism is a denial of the truth. It is thought that each person has his or her own truth; it may even be claimed that there is no such thing as "the truth."

An analysis of postmodernism is far beyond the scope of the present work.[153] However, what the authors of the Scriptures, especially Paul, have to say about "the truth" will equip the student of their writings to meet the challenges that the postmodern mindset poses. The testimony of the Scriptures will benefit the reader for this life and especially for the life to come.

---

152. 1 Tim 2:4; 2 Tim 2:25; 3:7; Titus 1:1.
153. For a survey and critique of the postmodern era, consult Veith, *Postmodernism*.

Bibliography

Abbott, T. K. *The Epistles to the Ephesians and to the Colossians*. The International Critical Commentary. Edinburgh: T. & T. Clark, 1897.

Achtemeier, Paul J., et al. *Introducing the New Testament: Its Literature and Theology*. Grand Rapids: Eerdmans, 2001.

Althaus, Paul. *The Ethics of Martin Luther*. Translated by Robert C. Schultz. Philadelphia: Fortress, 1972.

Arndt, William F. "*Egno*, 2 Tim. 2:19." *Concordia Theological Monthly* 21 (1950) 299–302.

Arnold, Clinton. *The Colossian Syncretism: The Interface Between Christianity and Folk Belief at Colossae*. Grand Rapids: Baker, 1996.

Barrett, C. K. *The First Epistle to the Corinthians*. New York: Harper & Row, 1968.

———. *The Pastoral Epistles in the New English Bible*. Oxford: Clarendon, 1963.

———. *The Second Epistle to the Corinthians*. London: A. & C. Black, 1973.

Bartchy, S. Scott. *MALLON XRHSAI: First-Century Slavery and the Interpretation of 1 Corinthians 7:21*. Society of Biblical Literature Dissertation Series 11. Missoula: University of Montana, 1973.

Bartelt, Andrew H. "Dialectical Negation: An Exegetical Both/And." In *"Hear the Word of Yahweh": Essays on Scripture and Archaeology in Honor of Horace D. Hummel*, edited by Dean O. Wenthe et al., 57–66. St. Louis: Concordia, 2002.

Bauer, Walter, et al. *Greek-English Lexicon of the New Testament and Other Early Christian Literature*. 3rd ed. Chicago: University of Chicago Press, 2000.

Blass, Friedrich, and Albert Debrunner. *A Greek Grammar of the New Testament and Other Early Christian Literature*. Translated and revised by Robert W. Funk. Chicago: University of Chicago Press, 1961.

Bouttier, Michel. *En Christ*. Etudes d'Histoire et de Philosophie Religieuses 54. Edited by R. Mehl. Paris: Presees Universitaires de France, 1962.

Bradley, K. R. *Slaves and Masters in the Roman Empire: A Study in Social Control*. Oxford: Oxford University Press, 1987.

Brown, Shelby. "The Getty Villa Guide to the Ancient Olympics." Getty, August 13, 2016. https://www.getty.edu/news/the-getty-villa-guide-to-the-ancient-olympics/.

Bruce, F. F. *1 & 2 Thessalonians*. Waco: Word, 1982.

———. *The Book of the Acts*. Grand Rapids: Eerdmans, 1954.

———. *The Epistles to the Colossians, to Philemon, and to the Ephesians*. New International Commentary on the New Testament. Grand Rapids: Eerdmans, 1984.

———. *Galatians*. New International Greek Testament Commentary. Grand Rapids: Eerdmans, 1982.

———. *New Testament History*. Garden City, NY: Doubleday, 1969.

BIBLIOGRAPHY

———. *Paul: Apostle of the Heart Set Free*. Grand Rapids: Eerdmans, 1977.
———. *Philippians*. Peabody, MA: Hendrickson, 1989.
Commission on Theology and Church Relations of The Lutheran Church—Missouri Synod. *Theses on Justification*. May 1983.
———. *Women in the Church: Scriptural Principles and Ecclesial Practice*. September 1985.
Concordia Seminary, St. Louis. "Master of Arts (M.A.) with Deaconess Certification." https://www.csl.edu/academics/programs/master-arts-m-deaconess-certification/.
Cranfield, C. E. B. *The Epistle to the Romans*. 2 vols. The International Critical Commentary. Edinburgh: T. & T. Clark, 1975, 1979.
Cullmann, Oscar. *Christ and Time: The Primitive Christian Conception of Time and History*. Translated by Floyd V. Filson. Rev. ed. Philadelphia: Westminster, 1964.
Das, A. Andrew. *Galatians*. Concordia Commentary. St. Louis: Concordia, 2014.
Davids, Peter H. *The First Epistle of Peter*. New International Greek Testament Commentary. Grand Rapids: Eerdmans, 1990.
Debelius, Martin, and Hans Conzelmann. *The Pastoral Epistles*. Translated by Philip Buttolph and Adela Yarbro. Hermeneia. Philadelphia: Fortress, 1972.
Deferrari, R. J., ed. *Fathers of the Church: A New Translation*. Washington, DC: Catholic University of American Press, 1947.
Deissmann, Adolf. *Light from the Ancient East*. Grand Rapids: Baker, 1978.
Deterding, Paul E. "Baptism According to the Apostle Paul." *Concordia Journal*, 6.3 (May 1980) 93–100.
———. *Colossians*. Concordia Commentary. St. Louis: Concordia, 2003.
———. "The New Testament View of Time and History." *Concordia Journal* 21.4 (October 1995) 385–99.
Dowley, Tim, ed. *Eerdman's Handbook to the History of Christianity*. Grand Rapids: Eerdmans, 1977.
Dunn, James D. G. *The Epistles to the Colossians and to Philemon: A Commentary on the Greek Text*. New International Greek Testament Commentary. Grand Rapids: Eerdmans, 1996.
Easton, Burton Scott. *The Pastoral Epistles*. New York: Charles Scribner's Sons, 1947.
Eisenstein, Ron. "MLK: 'Street Sweeper' Portion of 'What Is Your Life's Blueprint?' Speech." YouTube. January 17, 2022. Video, 00:00–00:40. https://www.youtube.com/watch?v=QMrCAQcAFeo.
Evans, Craig A., and Stanley E. Portner. *Dictionary of New Testament Background*. Downers Grove, IL: InterVarsity, 2000.
Fee, Gordon D. *God's Empowering Presence: The Holy Spirit in the Letters of Paul*. Grand Rapids: Baker Academic, 2009.
———. *Paul's Letter to the Philippians*. Grand Rapids: Eerdmans, 1995.
Fiorenza, Elizabeth Schussler. *In Memory of Her: A Feminist Theological Reconstruction of Christian Origins*. New York: Crossroad, 1983.
Forde, Gerhard. *On Being a Theologian of the Cross: Reflections on Luther's Heidelberg Disputation, 1518*. Grand Rapids: Eerdmans, 1997.
Franzmann, Martin H. "Exegesis on Romans 16:17ff." *Concordia Journal* 7.1 (January 1981) 13–20.
———. *The Word of the Lord Grows*. St. Louis: Concordia, 1961.
Gibbs, Jeffrey A. "'Following' Matthew 18: Interpreting Matthew 18:15–20 in Its Context." *Concordia Journal* 29.1 (January 2003) 6–25.

BIBLIOGRAPHY

———. *Matthew 1:1—11:1*. Concordia Commentary. St. Louis: Concordia, 2006.
———. *Matthew 21:1—28:20*. Concordia Commentary. St. Louis: Concordia, 2018.
Giertz, Bo. *The Hammer of God*. Translated by Clifford Ansgar Nelson and Hans Andrae. Rev. ed. Minneapolis: Augsburg, 2005.
Giese, Curtis P. *James*. Concordia Commentary. St. Louis: Concordia, 2021.
Goodreads. "Martin Luther King Jr. > Quotes > Quotable Quote." https://www.goodreads.com/quotes/21045-if-a-man-is-called-to-be-a-street-sweeper.
Gorday, Peter, ed. *Colossians, 1–2 Thessalonians, 1–2 Timothy, Titus, Philemon*. Ancient Christian Commentary on Scripture, New Testament 9. Downers Grove, IL: InterVarsity, 2000.
Grant, Robert M. *Gnosticism: A Source Book of Heretical Writings From the Early Christian Period*. New York: Harper, 1961.
Guthrie, Donald. *New Testament Introduction*. Downers Grove, IL: InterVarsity, 1970.
———. *The Pastoral Epistles*. 2nd ed. Grand Rapids: Eerdmans, 1991.
———. *The Pastoral Epistles and the Mind of Paul*. London: Tyndale, 1956.
Harris, Murray J. "Titus 2:13 and the Deity of Christ." In *Pauline Studies: Essays Presented to Professor F. F. Bruce on His 70th Birthday*, edited by Donald A. Hagner and Murray J. Harris, 262–77. Grand Rapids: Eerdmans, 1980.
Harrison, P. N. *The Problem of the Pastoral Epistles*. London: Oxford University Press, 1921.
Harstad, Adolf. *Deuteronomy*. Concordia Commentary. St. Louis: Concordia, 2022.
Hatch, Edwin, and Henry A. Redpath. *A Concordance to the Septuagint*. 3 vols. Grand Rapids: Baker, 1983.
Hawthorne, Gerald F., et al eds. *Dictionary of Paul and His Letters*. Downers Grove, IL: InterVarsity, 1993.
Hennecke, Edgar, et al., eds. *New Testament Apocrypha*. 2 vols. Philadelphia: Westminster, 1963–64.
Hock, R. F. *The Social Context of Paul's Ministry: Tentmaking and Apostleship*. Philadelphia: Fortress, 1980.
Hoerber, Robert G. "Galatians 2:1–10 and the Acts of the Apostles." *Concordia Theological Monthly* 31.8 (August 1960) 482–91.
Hopkins, Keith. *Conquerors and Slaves*. Sociological Studies in Roman History 1. Cambridge: Cambridge University Press, 1978.
Huegli, Albert G., ed. *Church and State Under God*. St. Louis: Concordia, 1964.
Hughes, Philip E. *The Second Epistle to the Corinthians*. Grand Rapids: Eerdmans, 1962.
Johnson, Luke Timothy. *The First and Second Letters to Timothy*. The Anchor Yale Bible Commentaries. New York: Doubleday, 2001.
Just, Arthur A. *Luke 1:1—9:50*. Concordia Commentary. St. Louis: Concordia, 1996.
Kaveny, M. Cathlene. "The Order of Widows: What the Early Church Can Teach Us About Older Women and Health Care." *Christian Bioethics* 11 (2005) 11–34.
Kelly, J. N. D. *Early Christian Creeds*. New York: D. McKay Co., 1972.
———. *The Pastoral Epistles*. London: A. & C. Black, 1963.
King, Martin Luther Jr. "What Is Your Life's Blueprint." https://www.goodreads.com/quotes/21045-if-a-man-is-called-to-be-a-street-sweeper.
Kleinig, John. "Scripture and the Exclusion of Women from the Pastorate." *Lutheran Theological Journal* 29/2–3 (1995) 74–81, 123–29. https://www.angelfire.com/ny4/djw/KleinigExclusionOfWomen.pdf.

BIBLIOGRAPHY

Knight, George W. *The Pastoral Epistles*. New International Greek Testament Commentary. Grand Rapids: Eerdmans, 1992.

Koeberle, Adolf. *The Quest for Holiness*. Translated by John C. Mattes. Minneapolis: Augsburg, 1936.

Kolb, Robert, and Timothy J. Wengert, eds. *The Book of Concord: The Confessions of the Evangelical Lutheran Church*. Minneapolis: Fortress, 2000.

Kummel, Werner Georg. *Introduction to the New Testament*. Translated by Howard Clark Kee. Rev. ed. Nashville: Abingdon, 1975.

Kuriakose, Manish, and Elizabeth Shaji. "Parental Influence in the Formation and Sustenance of Spiritual Attitude in Christian Adolescents." *The International Journal of Indian Psychology* 7.4 (October–December 2019) 327–35. https://ijip.in/wp-content/uploads/2020/03/18.01.036.20190704.pdf.

Ladd, George Eldon. *A Theology of the New Testament*. Grand Rapids: Eerdmans, 1974.

Lees, Shirley, ed. *The Role of Women: When Christians Disagree*. Downers Grove, IL: InterVarsity, 1984.

Lewis, C. S. *The Lion, the Witch, and the Wardrobe*. New York: Scholastic, 1995.

———. "Modern Theology and Biblical Criticism." In *Christian Reflections*, edited by Walter Hooper, 152–66. Reprint. Grand Rapids: Eerdmans, 1997.

Lockwood, Gregory J. *1 Corinthians*. Concordia Commentary. St. Louis: Concordia, 2000.

Lumen. "Influences on Moral Development." https://courses.lumenlearning.com/adolescent/chapter/influences-on-moral-development/#:~:text=In%20the%20formation%20of%20children's,the%20values%20of%20their%20culture.

Marshall, I. Howard. *The Pastoral Epistles*. The International Critical Commentary. Edinburgh: T. & T. Clark, 1999.

Martin, Ralph. P. *Colossians and Philemon*. New Century Bible. Grand Rapids: Eerdmans, 1973.

Meeks, Wayne A. *The First Urban Christians*. New Haven, CT: Yale University Press, 1983.

Metzger, Bruce M. *The Text of the New Testament: Its Transmission, Corruption, and Restoration*. New York: Oxford University Press, 1968.

Middendorf, Michael P. *Romans 1—8*. Concordia Commentary. St. Louis: Concordia, 2013.

———. *Romans 9—16*. Concordia Commentary. St. Louis: Concordia, 2016.

Morris, Leon. *The First and Second Epistles to the Thessalonians*. Grand Rapids: Eerdmans, 1959.

Moule, C. F. D. *The Epistles of Paul the Apostle to the Colossians and to Philemon: An Introduction and Commentary*. Cambridge Greek Testament Commentary. Cambridge: Cambridge University Press, 1957.

Mounce, William D. *Pastoral Epistles*. Nashville: Thomas Nelson, 2000.

Murphy-O'Connor, Jerome. *St. Paul's Corinth: Text and Archaeology*. Good News Studies 6. Collegeville, MN: Liturgical, 2002.

Nafzger, Samuel H., et al., eds. *Confessing the Gospel: A Lutheran Approach to Systematic Theology*. St. Louis: Concordia, 2017.

The Nag Hammadi Library in English. Translated by members of the Coptic Gnostic Library Project of the Institute for Antiquity and Christianity, Claremont, California. 3rd ed. San Francisco: Harper, 1988.

BIBLIOGRAPHY

Neuhaus, Richard John. "The Ambiguities of 'Christian American.'" *Concordia Journal* 17.3 (July 1991) 285–95.

Nordling, John G. "Christ Leavens Culture: St. Paul on Slavery." *Concordia Journal* 24 (January 1998) 43–52.

———. *Philemon*. Concordia Commentary. St. Louis: Concordia, 2004.

O'Brien, Peter T. *Colossians, Philemon*. Word Biblical Commentary. Waco, TX: Word, 1982.

Orthodox Wiki. "Serapion of Antioch." October 9, 2017. Orthodoxwiki.org/Serapion_of_Antioch.

Osiek, C. "Slavery in the New Testament World." *Bible Today* 22 (May 1984) 151–57.

Penner, Glenn M. *In the Shadow of the Cross: A Biblical Theology of Persecution and Discipleship*. Bartlesville, OK: Voice of the Martyrs, 2021.

Perpetua. *The Passion of S. Perpetua*. Edited by J. Armitage Robinson. Cambridge: Cambridge University Press, 1891.

Pieper, Francis. *Christian Dogmatics*. 4 vols. St. Louis: Concordia, 1950–53.

Plummer, A. *The Second Epistle of Paul the Apostle to the Corinthians*. Cambridge: Cambridge University Press, 1903.

Pokorný, Petr. *Colossians: A Commentary*. Translated by Siegfried S. Schatzmann. Peabody, MA: Hendrickson, 1991.

Quinn, Jerome D. *The Letter to Titus*. The Anchor Yale Bible Commentaries. New York: Doubleday, 1990.

Ramsey, William M. *Historical Commentary on the Pastoral Epistles*. Edited by Mark Wilson. Grand Rapids: Kregel, 1996.

———. *Pauline and Other Studies in Early Christian History*. 2nd ed. Grand Rapids: Hodder and Stoughton, 1906.

Reicke, Bo. *The New Testament Era*. Translated by David Green. Philadelphia: Fortress, 1968.

———. *Re-Examining Paul's Letters: The History of the Pauline Correspondence*. Edited by David P. Moessner and Ingalisa Reicke. New York: Trinity, 2001.

Richardson, Cyril C., trans. and ed. *Early Christian Fathers*. Library of Christian Classics 1. Philadelphia: Westminster, 1953.

Rudolph, Kurt. *Gnosis: The Nature and History of Gnosticism*. Translated by P. W. Coxon et al. San Francisco: Harper, 1987.

Scharlemann, Martin H. "An Apostolic Descant." *Concordia Journal* 2.1 (January 1976) 9–17.

———. "The Secret of God's Plan: Studies in Ephesians." *Concordia Theological Monthly* 40.8 (September 1969) 532–44.

———. "A Theology of Freedom." *Concordia Journal* 7.3 (May 1981) 103–8.

Scheidel, Walter. "Population and Demography." *Princeton/Stanford Working Papers in Classics* (April 2006) 209–26.

Schmidt, Alvin. *How Christianity Changed the World*. Grand Rapids: Zondervan, 2004.

Schneider, Johannes. *Die Passionsmystik des Paulus*. Untersuchungen zum Neuen Testament. Leipzig: J. C. Hinrichs, 1929.

Schuchard, Bruce G. *1–3 John*. Concordia Commentary. St. Louis: Concordia, 2012.

Scroggs, Robin. "Paul and the Eschatological Woman." *Journal of the American Academy of Religion*. 40.3 (September 1972) 283–303.

Sherwin-White, A. N. *Racial Prejudice in Imperial Rome*. London: Cambridge University Press, 1967.

Snow, Kyle. "Learning Begins at Birth." The Children's Reading Foundation. https://www.readingfoundation.org/learning-begins-at-birth#:~:text=From%20the%20time%20a%20child,of%20his%20or%20her%20life!.

Snowden, F. A. Jr. *Before Color Prejudice*. Cambridge: Harvard University Press, 1983.

Spicq, Ceslas. *Notes de Lexicographie Neo-Testamentaire*. Vol 1. Goettingen: Vandenhoeck & Ruprecht, 1978.

———. *Theological Lexicon of the New Testament*. Translated and edited by James D. Ernest. Peabody, MA: Hendrickson, 1991.

Staab, K., ed. *Pauluskommentare aus der griechischen Kirche: Aus Katenenhandsschriften gesammelt und herausgegeben*. NT Abhandlungen 15. Muenster: Aschendorff, 1933.

Steinmann, Andrew E. *Proverbs*. Concordia Commentary. St. Louis: Concordia, 2009.

Towner, Phillip H. *The Letters to Timothy and Titus*. New International Commentary on the New Testament. Grand Rapids: Eerdmans, 2006.

Veith, Gene Edward Jr. *God at Work*. Wheaton, IL: Crossway, 2002.

———. *Postmodern Times*. Wheaton, IL: Crossway, 1994.

———. *Reading Between the Lines*. Wheaton, IL: Crossway, 1990.

———. *The Spirituality of the Cross*. Rev. ed. St. Louis: Concordia, 2010.

Wallace, Daniel B. *Greek Grammar: Beyond the Basics*. Grand Rapids: Zondervan, 1996.

Walther, C. F. W. *The Proper Distinction Between Law and Gospel*. Translated by W. H. T. Dau. St. Louis: Concordia, 1928.

Wegener, G. S. *6000 Years of the Bible*. Translated by Margaret Shenfield. New York: Harper & Row, 1963.

Winger, Thomas M. *Ephesians*. Concordia Commentary. St. Louis: Concordia, 2015.

Wright, N. T. "Poetry and Theology in Colossians 1.15–20." *New Testament Studies* 36.3 (July 1990) 444–68.

Subject Index

Aaronic benediction, 456, 481
Adam, 92, 98, 221, 489
Age, ages, 63, 267–70, 429n
    Past, 63, 116, 412
    Present, 63, 88, 116, 122, 186, 202, 262, 264, 385, 414
    To come, 63, 264, 275
Alexander, 10n, 70, 71, 72, 384, 387, 388, 390, 391
Alienation from God, 64, 77
Amanuensis, 206, 288, 398n
Angels, 17, 111, 112, 116, 163, 226, 407, 422, 455
    Fallen, 96, 112
Anger, 87, 89, 231
Antioch of Pisidia, 132
Antioch of Syria, 13, 209, 210, 356
Apollos, 288, 396
Apostasy, 352, 374
Apostle, 22–25, 84, 86, 91, 92, 97–98, 110, 114, 120–21, 130, 179–80, 218, 225, 276, 295, 322, 363, 413, 471–75
Aristotle, 483, 502, 506
Artemas, 285, 288
Asceticism, 19
Attire, 86, 508
Augustine, 81n
Authority,
    Of government, 76, 81, 173
    Of God/Christ, 48, 50, 55, 120, 162, 216–17, 276, 295, 443, 496–97
    Of Paul, the apostle, 22–25, 74, 84, 86, 91–92, 97–98, 110, 114, 120–21, 130, 179–80, 218, 225, 276, 322, 363, 413, 471–75
    Of Paul's letters, 50, 121, 179–80, 363, 466
    Of the pastoral office, 91, 92, 162, 229, 237, 266, 270, 462–63

Baptism,
    Christian, 54, 120, 142, 196, 275, 281, 282, 304, 308, 319, 321, 327–31, 334, 415, 418, 424, 426, 428, 429, 433, 446, 450, 452, 455, 485, 488, 494, 500
    Of Timothy, 40, 196, 200, 321, 454–55
Baptismal confession, 40, 195–96, 197, 200, 328, 454
Barnabas, 13, 79, 134, 138, 209, 225, 303, 391, 472
Beloved, 172, 285, 295, 301, 386
Benediction, 390, 414, 427n, 456, 481
Blasphemy, 61, 62, 65, 74, 178, 181, 226, 348, 492
Blood of Christ, 443, 480, 498
Bodily training/athletics, 128, 129, 138, 190, 228, 256, 320, 322, 380, 382
Body of Christ,
    Church as, 332, 333, 399, 451, 487
    Physical, 19, 63, 115, 199, 264, 331, 406, 421, 475
Body, human, 17, 111, 170, 332, 338, 343, 389, 476, 493
Brother, brothers, 127, 146, 287, 398, 399
Buried with Christ in baptism, 418, 429, 433, 450

SUBJECT INDEX

Busybodies, 91, 108, 128, 147, 151, 155, 162, 186

Canonization of scripture, xi, 4, 11n, 24, 50, 121, 179–80, 363, 400, 466
Call,
    To faith, 61, 142, 305, 310, 320, 322, 425, 426, 444, 455
    To the pastoral office, 73, 100, 137, 138, 146, 195, 296, 308, 414n
Carpus, 10n, 11
Child, children,
    Literal, 95, 101, 148, 162, 231, 235, 255, 338n, 364, 447, 458, 479
    Metaphorical, 49, 70, 73, 217, 296
Chosen, 65, 244, 265, 407, 413, 423, 452, 472, 473, 493
Christ, Christology, 403–19
    Death, 122, 193, 221, 268, 275, 282, 310, 352
    Deity, 19, 49, 63, 66, 192, 199, 217, 269, 403–6, 435–39
    Eschatological return, 116, 123, 164, 198, 269, 370, 378, 382, 387, 408, 431–32
    Example for Christians, 93, 95, 257, 417
    Faith in, 23, 57, 65, 71, 123, 141, 184, 189, 193, 221, 360, 411
    Faithfulness of, 64, 68, 414
    Humanity, 77, 82, 405–6
    Incarnation, 19, 77, 82, 87, 115, 219, 262, 268, 274, 280, 403–5
    Incorporation into, 9, 321, 331, 366, 372, 415–16, 485–88
    Preexistence of, 66n, 405, 406
    Resurrection, 79, 91, 112, 116, 122, 192, 193, 221, 275, 282, 310, 325, 328, 352
    Saving work of, 19, 64, 76, 81, 83, 129, 142, 189, 193, 221, 268, 280, 406–9, 420–28, 443–45
Chrysostom, 72
Church,
    Local, 39
    Universal, 3, 25, 43, 44, 50, 56, 73, 80–82, 86, 97–100, 113–16, 137–41, 153–57, 166–71, 229–33, 313, 321–23, 391–92, 409–10, 453–56
Circumcision,
    Hebrew/Jewish, 15, 20, 39, 196n, 209, 235, 241
    Into Christ, 196n
Citizenship, 80–81, 174, 282–83, 456, 461
Commands,
    Divine, 22, 54, 55, 58, 98, 121, 146, 348
    Human, 15, 223, 238, 239, 241
Conscience, 15, 57, 73, 104–5, 123, 235, 244, 413, 424, 481–82
Controversies, 14, 15, 223, 277, 283, 461
Conversion of Paul, 12, 13, 60, 61, 62, 65, 78, 84, 130, 209, 331, 472
Corinth, 12, 23, 40, 41, 42, 72, 113, 210, 211, 286, 395, 396, 397, 495
Covenant
    New, 77
    Old, 84
    With David, 326, 328, 329, 422, 444
Covetousness, 55, 58
Creation, 119, 125, 232, 349, 442, 453,
    Christ as agent of, 197, 439
    Christ as goal of, 413, 493
    Christ's sovereignty over, 116, 199
    Fallen, liberation of, 113, 432
    New, 89, 244, 332, 432, 442, 507
    Of humanity, 92, 98, 113, 124, 257, 360, 442, 467, 469
    Orders of, 80, 124, 173, 257, 467, 507
Creator, 54, 64, 98, 102, 124, 138, 190
Creed, 68, 108, 115–16, 196, 309, 328, 407, 433, 454–56, 460
Crescens, 10n, 385
Crete, 13, 19, 22, 43, 51, 53, 210–12, 224–25, 229–30, 236–37, 243, 246, 283, 288, 291–92
Cross,
    Of Christ, 19, 20, 77, 115, 150, 265, 268, 280, 310, 406, 408, 421, 443, 462, 498
    Of Christians, 312, 329, 449
Crucifixion, 198, 506, 507

SUBJECT INDEX

Dalmatia, 211, 291, 384
David, 8, 326, 328, 329, 382, 403, 405, 422, 444, 465, 498
Day and night, 301n
Dead Sea Scrolls, 494
Death
  Eternal, 57, 199, 299, 306, 310, 407, 408, 409, 423, 424, 455, 463, 505
  Spiritual, 148, 149, 441, 445, 446
  Temporal, 63, 101, 111, 115, 141, 300, 307, 316, 358, 373, 375, 379, 381, 382, 389, 391, 392, 394, 397, 405, 421, 431, 463, 498
  With Christ, 327, 329, 331, 366, 372, 418, 419, 450, 452, 488, 500
Demas, 211, 385, 386, 390, 419
Demiurge, 17
Demon(s), devil, 14, 71, 90, 94, 96, 99, 113, 118, 123, 142, 152, 183, 227, 245, 248, 249, 303, 335, 343, 349, 365–67, 424–25, 431, 444
Dietary prohibitions, 15, 19, 119, 123–24, 244
Discipline, 74, 162, 164, 167n, 170, 263, 461
Disputes, 14, 15, 89, 181, 223, 272, 277, 283, 335, 341, 345, 346, 447
Divorce, 94, 106, 149, 226, 231, 472
Doctrine, 23, 55–56, 91, 127, 136, 177, 190, 208, 228, 232, 251, 253, 258, 307, 365, 370, 371, 374, 460, 508–10
Doxologies, 65–67, 192, 199, 270, 390, 394, 398, 416, 456
Drink, Drunkenness, 94, 95, 104, 106, 165, 226, 248, 249, 330, 372, 458

Economic order, 256, 503, 507
Election of grace, 221, 221n, 345n, 427, 427n, 428n
Emanations, Gnostic teaching of, 17, 18
Employer/employee relationship, 259, 504, 507
Encouragement, 41, 95, 99, 145, 146, 150, 167, 198, 211, 228, 232, 237, 246, 317, 355, 370–77, 381, 393, 459, 467, 495–97, 508

Endurance, 189, 194, 254, 334, 382, 430n, 484
Ephesus, 19, 41, 43, 51, 53, 55–56, 84, 113, 114, 169, 210, 211, 224–25, 229–30, 285–86, 292, 301, 316, 349, 386, 396, 506
Erastus, 397, 506
Eschatology, 117–25, 184, 305n, 307, 327, 347–55, 367, 373–74, 380, 381, 406, 408, 412, 422, 426, 429–34, 445, 451, 476, 495
Ethics, 19, 56, 92, 344, 440–52
Eunice and Lois, 39, 195, 308, 364
Eve, 92, 98, 100, 101, 221
Example, model, 64–65, 85, 93, 95, 100, 131–32, 140–41, 157, 228, 242, 254, 257–58, 288, 289, 365, 366, 417, 431, 447, 461, 477, 491, 506
Eyewitnesses of resurrection, 112, 421, 472, 473

Faith, 420–21, 424–25, 476
  And baptism, 196, 197, 364, 415, 426
  Fall from, 15, 72, 73, 95, 96, 117, 151, 194, 314, 338, 419
  Firmness of, 57, 73, 136, 141, 193, 243, 254, 301, 367, 382, 427, 445, 448–49
  Reception/transmission of, 23, 40, 65, 84, 120, 124, 142, 220, 313, 362, 425, 427, 444
Faithfulness, 100, 141, 151, 193, 195, 329–30, 344, 416, 418–19, 463–64
Fall into sin, 82, 98, 101, 124, 331, 432, 500, 501
Family, 95, 152, 153, 154, 159, 173, 231, 242, 255, 288, 300, 322, 364n, 458, 489, 507
Father, God the, 48, 50, 63, 66, 76, 77, 91, 98, 119, 129, 142, 163, 190, 192, 197, 199, 217, 222, 250, 253, 255, 269, 274–76, 280, 281, 310, 369, 404, 409, 417, 428, 435–39, 472, 478, 487, 498, 501
Fathers, 54, 58, 148, 259, 348

521

SUBJECT INDEX

Fides qua creditur, 49, 52, 53, 71, 132, 149, 184, 189, 190, 205, 215, 237, 249, 301, 338, 357, 380, 424, 476, 484

Fides quae creditur, 49, 52, 71, 79, 104, 117, 127, 149, 184, 190, 205, 215, 237, 249, 288, 351, 357, 380, 424, 476, 484

Flesh, 17, 18, 19, 72, 112, 115, 124, 170, 264, 330, 332, 338, 389, 406, 421, 451, 455, 478, 497

Foods, 15, 19, 119, 120, 123–25, 183, 184, 244, 508

Forgiveness,
    From God, 64, 119, 122, 133, 146, 315, 328, 331, 334, 418, 443, 445, 448, 449, 452
    To others, 495

Fornication, 51, 146

Foreshadows/ types of Christ, 353n, 412, 492

Freedom,
    As a synonym of salvation, 274, 432, 505
    Christian freedom where scripture has not spoken, 157, 165
    Political, 467, 503

Galatia, 385
Gallio, 12, 13n
Gamaliel, 12, 12n
Gaul, 385
Genealogies, 14, 17, 52, 56, 223, 238, 272, 277, 283
Gentiles, 5, 9, 39, 79, 113, 209, 210n, 238, 393–94, 410, 413, 469, 493
Gentleness, 194, 245, 283, 344, 345, 477
Glory, 55, 56, 79, 98, 112, 113, 116, 122, 191, 259, 260, 270, 307, 333, 346, 382, 405, 407, 411, 412, 422, 429, 432, 433, 436, 446, 451, 456, 453–56, 478, 487, 493, 494
Gnosticism, 14–21, 53, 56, 83, 115, 124, 207, 238, 240, 241, 277, 326, 343
God, 435–39

Goodness, 173, 222, 273, 274, 280, 281, 406, 412, 420, 421, 456
Gospel, 12, 23, 53, 55, 56, 65, 95, 110, 136, 145, 184, 193, 212, 217, 231, 286, 304n, 310–13, 328–29, 332, 346, 376–77, 393–94, 410, 439, 462–63, 485
Gossip, 108, 128, 140, 147, 151, 155, 156, 162, 252, 254, 258
Government, 76, 80–81, 155, 174, 507
Grace, 480–81
Graciousness, 140

Heart, 193, 226, 235, 244, 424, 481–82
Hellenists, 210n
Heresy, 14–21, 83, 124, 206–7, 244, 343
Hermogenes, 10n
Holiness, 93, 100, 228, 333, 442, 445, 449
Holy Spirit, see Spirit, Holy
Hope, 482–84
Hospitality, 94–95, 149–50, 277, 459
Humility, 146, 150, 189, 194, 202, 257
Husbands, 94, 105, 231, 250, 255, 256, 257, 259, 447, 458
Hymenaeus, 10n, 71, 72, 337, 343
Hymns in the Pastorals, 89, 112, 115n, 328n, 411, 413, 454, 454n, 456n
    Authorship, 328, 454

Iconium, 40, 356
Idolatry, 226
Image of God,
    Christ as, 333, 478n
    Lost in fall, 123, 442
    Restored in Christ, 333, 478
Immorality, 226
In Christ relationship, 485–88
Incarnation, 19, 21, 62, 66, 77, 82, 111, 219, 262, 264, 268, 274, 281, 305, 333, 405, 406, 414, 421, 431, 443, 475, 478
Inheritance, 160, 167, 226, 276, 411
Inscription, Gallio, 12, 12n
Inspiration of scripture, 71, 121, 177, 360, 362–63, 377, 400, 409, 454, 463, 474–75
Irenaeus, 16, 17n

SUBJECT INDEX

Jannes and Jambres, 351, 352
Jerome, 156n, 389n
Jewish Christians, 79, 301, 395, 396
Jews, 5, 12, 39, 79, 113, 190, 198, 388, 393–96, 410
John of Damascus, 56n
Josephus, 197, 389n
Joy, 301, 393, 400, 487
Judaism, 12, 53, 110, 130, 134, 135, 309, 468, 469, 506
Judge, Christ as, 22, 122, 198, 373, 380, 387, 408, 412, 417, 422, 424, 431, 439
Judgment, final, 90, 96, 99, 123, 164, 165, 178, 186, 191, 242, 316, 352, 380, 381, 408, 425, 431, 439
Justification, 9, 122, 129, 189, 193, 227, 263, 277, 282, 284, 328, 363, 407, 423–25, 440–52, 499–500

Kerygma, 115, 212, 279, 284, 389, 393–94, 410, 412, 413, 492
Kindness, 250, 283, 459, 476–77
King, Martin Luther, 259n
Kingdom of God, 138, 243, 329, 370, 373, 378, 384, 393, 406, 408, 411, 417, 425, 426, 430, 433, 444, 493, 494
Kingdoms, two, 82, 82n, 174
Knowledge,
 Of the truth, 52, 64, 83, 84, 96, 123, 124, 215, 220, 221, 245, 335, 342, 343, 351, 367, 442, 479, 489–90, 510, 511
 Role of in Gnosticism, 14, 17, 18, 19, 56, 83, 115, 177, 178, 180, 205, 207, 239, 240, 343, 352, 354, 360

Labor, 129, 323, 503, 506
Last Day, 184, 307, 327, 352, 367, 380, 381, 382, 406, 408, 412, 422, 432, 445, 451, 476, 495
Last days/times, 121–23, 348, 350, 352, 373–74, 426, 429–34
Law of God, 53, 57–58, 77, 93, 110, 145, 146, 168, 254, 265, 273, 279, 370, 441, 444, 445, 446, 448, 449, 452, 461, 505, 511
Laying on of hands, 134–38, 164, 169, 195, 302–3, 311, 457
Letters,
 Copies, 391–92
 Style in NT world, 21, 50
Lewis, C. S., 141n, 156n,
Light, 19, 192, 199, 306, 310, 406–9, 432, 436, 455
"Lord," Jesus as, 66, 269–70, 280, 315, 404, 428n, 435, 455
Lord's Prayer, 183, 389, 452n
Lord's Supper, 23, 120, 142, 430n, 452, 453, 494, 509
Love shown by Christians, 19, 41, 57, 87, 92, 100, 107, 114, 132, 141, 193, 228, 232, 249, 253, 254, 257, 287, 303–4, 308, 312, 344, 349, 353, 399, 446, 459, 487, 490–91
Love shown by God/Christ, 65, 68, 155, 274, 280, 308, 406, 414, 415, 420, 443, 490–91
Luke, 5, 132, 161, 197, 229, 385–86, 390, 393, 398, 399, 473
Luther, Martin, 56n, 57n, 65n, 81n, 82n, 87n, 88n, 97n, 102n, 131n, 140n, 152n, 163n, 164n, 174n, 194n, 206n, 212n, 217n, 222n, 233n, 243n, 259n, 375n, 424n, 427n, 441, 452, 465
Lying, 58, 84, 85, 220, 243, 448
Lystra, 39, 40, 49, 195, 196, 217, 296, 309, 357, 358

Macedonia, 41, 42, 43, 51, 210, 211, 292, 397
Man/men,
 Males, 54, 86, 98, 251, 257, 319, 348, 351, 469
 Older, 131, 144, 145, 248, 253–54, 447
 Younger, 145, 251, 257–58
Marcion, 4, 17
Mark, 256n, 386, 391, 392, 473, 473n

SUBJECT INDEX

Marriage, 15, 58, 94, 119, 123, 124, 125, 151, 152, 156, 226, 132, 244, 256, 458, 508
Master(s), 172–75, 447n, 501–7
Mediator, 77, 82, 83, 407, 408, 422, 438, 444, 455
Mercy, 49, 64, 65, 280, 282, 296, 297, 316, 397, 408, 420, 431, 443, 492
Messiah, Jesus as, 8, 60, 101, 102, 115, 161, 309, 315, 326, 329, 334, 395, 403, 405, 501
Miletus, 292, 395
Mind, 93, 179, 180, 239, 244, 353, 354, 424n, 481n, 482, 489
Ministry,
    Of Paul, 61, 65, 79, 84–85, 169n, 302–3, 311, 393
    Of Timothy, 41, 73, 322–23
    Of Titus, 210, 224, 229
    Of others, 224–34, 386
    Of the Word, 99–100, 126–43, 224–34, 335–46, 457–69
    Of Word and Sacrament,
Missions, 100, 150, 153, 155, 157, 203, 227, 233, 259, 377, 409–10, 417, 459, 462, 488
Moses, 77, 134, 345, 351, 352, 354, 355, 456, 472, 498
Music of Worship, 89, 453–56
Mystery, 115–16, 412–13, 492–94
Mystery religions, 106, 110

Name of God, 49, 61, 173, 280, 315, 404
    See also Yahweh
Natures in Christ, two, 115, 191n, 333, 405, 478
Nero, 389n
New creation, 124, 507
New man, 446, 487
Nicopolis, 286, 292
Night and day, 301
Nympha, 152

Oath, 163, 190, 320, 336, 369, 370, 374, 378, 416–47, 437, 498
Old man, 446
Old Testament, 17, 21, 24, 39, 49, 61, 66, 110, 115, 121, 122, 130, 132, 161, 162, 167, 195, 217, 241, 243, 295, 300, 301, 309, 359, 363, 391, 412, 413, 416, 424, 435, 469, 474, 483, 489, 492, 493
Onesimus, 186, 505, 506
Onesiphoros, 292, 315, 316, 396, 416
Orderliness, 91, 95, 98, 258
Origen, 10n, 112n
Outside the church, 90, 96, 100, 125, 140, 152, 181, 205, 257, 260, 287, 354, 376, 458
Overture, 44, 46, 70, 212, 222, 293, 298

Paganism, 81, 238, 257, 441, 469
Paraenesis, Christocentricity of, 414–15, 477
Parents, 148, 149, 239, 364, 479
Parousia, 24, 64, 122, 123, 157, 191n, 198, 264, 269, 270, 352, 355, 371, 381, 382, 387, 400, 408, 410, 412, 422, 429, 431, 432, 436, 475, 478, 488, 429–34,
Passion of Christ, 197, 198, 352
Pastoral concern of Paul, 169n, 170, 210, 343
Pastors
    Discipline, 74, 164, 461
    Preparation, 137, 138, 164, 169–71, 311, 321–23, 457, 459–60
    Qualifications, 64, 94, 99–100, 105, 162, 164, 227, 229, 230–33, 311, 341, 457–59
    Supervision, 168–71, 210
Patience, 189
Paul,
    As apostle, see Apostle
    As example, 63, 64–65, 366, 381, 383, 431, 492
    As persecutor of Christians, 64
    As Pharisee, 12, 499
    Authority of, see Authority of Paul, the apostle,
    Call of, 9, 13, 60–63, 78, 84, 130, 209, 414n, 472
    Chronology of, 12–13
    Conversion of, 12, 13, 6062, 65, 78, 130, 209, 331

Life of, 11–13
Mission work of, 5, 12, 13, 39–42, 130, 135, 138, 169n, 196, 210, 225, 233, 303, 357, 391, 395, 397, 399, 464
Suffering of, 312–13, 326–27, 330, 332–33, 379–83, 390
Pauline authorship of Pastorals, 4–11, 386
Pauline letters, authority of, xi, 4, 11n, 22–25, 50, 121, 74, 84, 86, 91–92, 97–98, 110, 114, 120–21, 130, 179–80, 218, 225, 276, 322, 363, 400, 413, 466, 471–75
Pax Romana, 482
Peace, spiritual, 21, 48, 87, 218, 296, 303, 340, 487, 497
Peace, worldly, 80, 81
Persecution,
    By Paul, 64
    Of believers, 150, 293, 322, 331, 345, 362–67, 373, 383, 393, 450, 462, 464, 465
    Of Paul, 304, 330, 331
Philemon, the man, 186, 292, 505
Philetus, 10n, 337, 343
Philo, 140n, 274
Philosophy, 18, 19, 20, 106, 179, 207, 211, 229, 236, 241, 304n, 336
Phygelus, 10n, 314
Plan of God, 48, 52, 78, 83, 115, 122, 198, 219, 280, 305, 310, 313, 357, 373, 405, 408, 412, 413, 426–28, 429, 431, 438, 443–44, 455, 457, 492–94
Plato, 20, 241
Plutarch, 140n, 165n
Pontius Pilate, 22, 190, 197–98, 200, 408, 417, 421
Prayer, 75–76, 80–81, 87, 89, 107, 120, 148, 154, 316, 390, 416, 447, 449, 453, 456, 461, 465, 508
Preaching, 99, 132–33, 139, 166–67, 218, 226, 370–71, 374–75, 453, 460, 461, 464, 472, 495
Predestination, see Election of grace
Pride, 150, 202
Priene Inscription, 483n

Prisca/Priscilla and Aquila, 152, 250, 315, 395, 396, 467n
Prison/prisoners, 5, 150, 291, 304, 387, 389, 391
Proclamation, 5, 55, 78–79, 84–85, 99, 107, 116, 131, 134, 139–40, 144, 219, 220, 284, 306–7, 311, 332, 370, 374–75, 393, 394, 410, 413, 417, 425–26, 432, 447, 451, 463, 465, 488, 493, 495
Promise, fulfillment, 5, 122, 219, 296, 309, 328–29, 393, 394, 405, 412, 422, 426, 430, 432, 479, 483
Prophecy, 70, 71, 133–35, 137, 164, 169, 302–3, 377, 460, 464,
Psalms, 89, 454
Putting off/ putting on, 466

Quartus, 505
Qumran, 351n, 494

Rabbinic exegesis, 472, 509
Raised with Christ, 327, 331, 419, 430, 433, 446, 450–51, 452
Ransom, 81, 83, 94, 265, 406, 408, 423–24, 426, 438, 444, 455, 498–99
Reconciler, Christ as, 443, 494
Recreation, 170
Redeemer,
    Christ as, 57, 88, 122, 142, 190, 265, 267, 268, 333, 373, 406, 407, 414, 415, 423, 444, 452, 478, 480, 498–99, 501
    Role of in Gnosticism, 16–19
Religion, manmade, 53, 106, 110, 179, 181, 236, 336, 355, 441
Repentance, 59, 64, 74, 96, 162, 168, 245, 278, 335, 341, 342, 367, 425, 444, 448, 449, 461, 495
Rescue, 141, 358, 366, 367, 389, 392, 418, 430, 444, 500
Resurrection
    Of believers, 15, 19, 66, 71, 122, 191, 275, 327, 329, 331, 333, 334, 338, 343, 355, 382, 405, 411, 419, 430, 443, 450, 451, 452, 476, 478, 488, 492, 493, 495, 498, 507

SUBJECT INDEX

Of Christ, 19, 23, 63, 79, 111, 112, 115, 116, 122, 193, 199, 221, 275, 280, 281, 282, 305n, 306, 310, 325, 326, 328, 330, 334, 343, 352, 367, 373, 380, 407, 418, 419, 421–22, 426–28, 429–30, 443, 472, 478

Revelation, 57, 65, 115, 116, 134, 193, 219, 220, 301, 311, 333, 374, 404, 412–13, 416, 432, 435, 442, 445, 478, 492–94, 508, 510

Rich, riches, 88, 184, 186–87, 201–3, 432, 441, 447

Righteousness, see Justification

Rome, 5, 42–43, 211, 386, 387, 389, 393, 395–96, 410, 503

Rule of God/Christ/the Messiah, 122, 326, 329, 405, 422

Sabbath, 58, 453

Sacraments, 80, 85, 120, 173, 196n, 222, 409, 419, 444, 461, 493, 494

Salutations, 22, 42, 50, 142, 179, 212–14, 218, 220, 222, 295, 296, 299, 328, 436n, 471, 481, 497

Salvation,
 Eternal, 219, 222, 264, 270, 276, 333, 393, 411, 420–28, 500–501
 God's plan of, 48, 52, 78, 83, 115, 122, 198, 219, 280, 305, 310, 313, 357, 373, 405, 408, 412, 413, 426–28, 429, 431, 438, 443–44, 455, 457, 492–94
 Universal, 81–82, 83, 129, 140, 142, 221, 263, 279, 444

Sanctification,
 Basis of, 120, 414–15, 424, 440–52
 Growth in, 446, 448–49
 Relationship to justification, 451–52

Satan, 72, 73, 112, 123, 147, 152, 186, 205, 321, 342, 358, 366, 372, 376, 382, 389, 390, 425

Scripture,
 Inspiration of, 121, 177, 360, 362363, 400, 409, 454, 463, 474–75

 Public reading of, 22, 121, 132, 139, 363, 453, 461, 474

Servant/slave of Christ, 215, 218, 231, 274, 285, 341, 344, 439, 471, 510

Sex/sexuality, 19, 54, 58, 226, 228, 344, 489

Sexes, roles of, 92, 98, 102, 110, 249, 467

Shaliach, 471–72

Shame, 252, 260, 304n, 307, 336

Silas/Silvanus, 40, 41, 42, 186, 296n

Sin, 23, 24, 54, 57–59, 62, 64, 82, 83, 92, 94, 101, 110, 145, 146, 151, 163, 165, 167–68, 170, 180, 183, 192, 227, 244, 248, 249, 265, 268, 278, 279, 284, 327, 330, 336, 340, 344, 348, 349, 350, 351, 357, 407, 408, 422, 423, 424, 444, 445, 448, 449, 450, 461, 499, 500, 501, 505, 511

Slander, 178, 181, 226, 249, 252, 254, 258, 273, 283, 349, 448

Slavery, 501–7

Social order, 80, 88, 110, 173, 256, 504, 507

Soteriology, xii, 420–28
 See also Salvation,

Soul, 106, 441

Speech,
 Of Christians, 132, 140, 252, 258
 Persuasive, 14, 133, 336, 496
 Sinful, 140, 252, 448

Spes qua speratur, 264, 430, 484

Spes quae speratur, 264, 276, 430, 484

Spirit, Holy, 8, 22, 24, 25, 40, 50, 57, 79, 114, 120–21, 133–35, 176, 179, 180, 217, 230, 232, 275, 281, 301–8, 302n, 312, 313, 344, 351, 354, 362, 363, 409, 413, 424, 426, 428, 429, 437, 438, 439, 444, 445, 456, 463, 473, 474, 477, 493, 496, 497

Spirit, human, 18, 111, 115, 124, 180, 211, 303, 312, 351, 407, 414, 422, 455

Steward(s), pastors as, 232, 413, 439, 493, 494

Stoicism, 506

526

SUBJECT INDEX

Strength, 141, 193, 194, 197, 198, 228, 305, 319, 321, 334, 357, 383, 410, 418, 477, 480
Struggle, 129, 140, 382, 449
Subjection, 91, 98, 250, 255–57, 258, 282
Suffering with Christ, 304, 305, 313, 322, 326, 327, 329–32, 366, 417–18, 449–50
Sufficiency of Christ, 19, 116, 265, 305, 332, 443, 498
Synagogue, 110, 132, 139, 453, 495

Teacher of righteousness, 494
Teachers,
    False, 14–16, 20, 52–53, 56, 58, 72, 73–74, 82, 84, 115, 118, 123–24, 165, 177–81, 184, 195, 205, 207, 236, 238–42, 244, 245, 277, 287, 336–39, 342–43, 350–55, 358, 360, 365–66, 371–72, 374, 430, 461, 464, 474, 479, 490
    True, 67, 70, 79, 84, 91, 133, 139n, 195–99, 217, 249, 302, 307, 311, 323, 359n, 376, 377, 425, 461n, 463, 509n
Teaching,
    False, 14–16, 20, 43, 52–56, 71–74, 115, 118, 123, 125, 142, 144, 163, 178, 180–81, 195, 202, 205–7, 233, 238–42, 244–45, 277, 283–84, 287, 314, 336–39, 341, 343–45, 351–55, 374, 376, 391, 430, 442, 490
    True, 8, 19, 23, 24, 55, 56, 58, 65, 68, 77, 82–84, 91, 94, 95, 98, 99, 103, 104, 107, 115, 117, 118, 122, 127–28, 130, 133, 135–39, 149, 166–67, 177–80, 208, 228, 232–33, 243, 248, 254, 258, 287, 302, 311–12, 323, 355–56, 365, 370–72, 374–75, 380, 409, 424, 427, 453, 459–61, 463–65, 467, 479, 494, 508–10
Ten Commandments, 58
Tertius, 505
Tetragrammaton, see Yahweh

Thanksgiving, 42, 67, 76, 120, 125, 244, 259, 300, 300n, 309, 313, 364, 439, 453, 456
Theodoret of Cyr, 105n, 115n, 256n, 314–15, 332, 385
Theology of cross, 20
Thessalonica, 23, 40, 41, 113, 341, 385
Time, view of, 121–23, 123n, 267–70, 373–74, 429–34, 482–84
Timothy, 39–42
Titus, 209–11
Torah, 23, 50n, 362, 363
Tradition(s),
    Biblical, 23, 509
    Church, 85
    Human, 23
    Jewish, 351
    Of elders, 309
Trinity, 82, 284, 438
Troas, 11, 42, 210, 387, 391
Trophimus, 397
Truth, 510–11
Tychicus, 285, 288, 292, 386
Typology, 219, 353n, 412, 492

Understanding, 149, 179, 180, 257, 321, 360, 413
Unity of church, 287, 289, 399, 477, 487, 489n

Vocation, 102, 152, 152n, 180, 202, 212, 247–61, 289, 447

Wages, 160–61
Wickedness, 243, 274, 279, 353
Will of God, 25, 48, 85, 174, 254, 267, 295, 296, 342, 393, 432, 457, 462, 471
Wisdom,
    And creation, 232
    From God/Christ/the Holy Spirit, 79, 220n, 307, 360
    Mere human wisdom, 106, 352, 360, 442
    Synonym of saving faith, 64, 273, 277

SUBJECT INDEX

Witness, Christian, 5, 78, 257, 304, 307, 313, 322, 330, 334, 366, 383, 417, 450

Woman/Women,
  Older, 128, 146, 248–49, 254–57, 264, 447, 467
  Younger, 94, 146, 151–52, 156, 226, 248–50, 254–57, 260, 264, 447, 467

Word,
  And Sacrament, 85, 120, 173, 196, 222, 409, 419, 444, 461, 493–94
  Christ as chief content of, 110, 114, 139, 192, 334, 409, 413, 419

Workers, fellow, 49, 170, 171, 180, 207, 210, 220, 233, 240, 245, 270, 285, 289, 296, 385, 394, 400, 427, 462, 506

Works,
  Evil works expose false faith, 14, 240, 244, 260, 273, 353, 448
  Faith saves without works, 57, 183, 193, 221, 274, 280, 282–83, 414, 427, 440–50, 455–56, 480, 492, 500
  Fruit of saving faith, 88, 89, 114, 148, 149, 150, 157, 165, 168, 189, 193, 203, 221, 224, 249, 253, 258, 259, 260, 267, 268, 274, 276, 277, 282–83, 287, 289, 305, 353, 365, 414–15, 424, 427, 440–52, 459, 461, 476, 479, 488, 499

Worship, xii, 22, 54, 58, 80–82, 85, 87, 89, 99, 107, 114, 120, 121, 124, 132, 133, 139, 148, 153, 207, 242, 249, 259, 281, 289, 309, 363, 374, 379, 382, 383, 398, 400, 416, 419, 439, 447, 453–56, 461, 474, 495, 508

Wrath, 141, 221n, 357, 372, 490

Yahweh, 66, 81, 280, 315, 404, 428n, 435, 498

Zenas, 288

Scripture Index

Genesis

Ch 1	124, 227
1:26–28	442
1:26–27	251
1:31	349
Ch 2	124
2:7	24, 92, 360
2:18–24	251
2:24	54
Ch 3	98, 101
3:13	92
3:16–19	432
3:16	101
3:22–24	442
4:1	83, 221, 489
5:3	442
14:14	186
18:1–8	149, 227
19:15–26	449
24:53	88n
35:7	475
35:16–20	101

Exodus

3:8	358
6:6	498
7:11–12	351, 355
7:22	351, 355
8:7	351, 355
8:18–19	351, 352, 355
9:11	351, 352, 355
19:5	265
20:1–17	348
22:11	416
33:20	192
34:6–7	492
40:34–35	333, 478

Leviticus

22:17–25	191

Numbers

6:22–27	456
6:27	481
16:5	338, 345
16:26	339, 346
23:19	215

Deuteronomy

5:1–21	348
6:4	77
6:13	416, 439
7:6	265
7:8	498
10:20	416
14:2	265
19:15	162
21:17	160
25:4	37, 161, 166n
29:4	481
29:19	481
31:10–13	132

SCRIPTURE INDEX

1 Samuel

2:1	481
4:19–22	101
16:7	481

2 Samuel

4:9	498
7:3	481
7:1–17	8, 326, 328, 403, 405, 422
7:12	329
7:14	329
7:16	329
Ch 11	449
12:14	449

1 Kings

6:7	497
8:11	333, 478
8:61	497
19:10	355
19:14	355
19:15–18	355

1 Chronicles

17:1–15	8, 326, 328, 403, 405, 422

Nehemiah

8:1–8	132

Job

1:5	481
1:21	183
28:28	64
33:4	24

Psalms

19:1	442
27:13–14	483
62:12	387
104:14–15	95, 104, 226
104:24	232
Psalm 119	465

Proverbs

3:6	336
3:19–20	232
10:14	349
11:5	336
13:3	349
22:1	448
22:6	364
26:18–19	448
30:7–9	187

Ecclesiastes

5:11–15	183
10:20	424

Isaiah

3:16–26	87
40:6–8	355
52:3	265, 423
65:14	481

Jeremiah

29:7	81
29:11	483
31:33	481
Ch 50	81
Ch 51	81

Daniel

Ch 2	494
2:18–19	493
2:27–30	493
2:44	493
2:45	493
2:47	493
Ch 4	494
4:9	493
4:25	442
4:32	442
4:34	442
4:36	442

Matthew

1:25	489

3:15	88	13:46	87
4:10	439	14:30	141, 500
4:11	111	15:8	481
5:1—7:29	508	15:18–19	481
5:2	508	16:21	134, 160n
5:14–16	446	16:24–25	329, 417
5:16	88, 141	16:24	313
5:19	508	18:15–17	278
5:21–48	344	18:16	162
5:21–24	54, 58	18:17	163
5:21–22	448	19:1–12	94, 226
5:22	140	19:5	54, 319, 348, 351, 469
5:23–26	508	19:21	356
5:27–28	448	19:28	275
5:42	238	20:28	265, 498
5:48	265	21:5	477
6:5–15	508	21:12–17	477
6:10	389	21:37	117
6:13	183	22:15	118
6:16–18	508	22:18	118
6:25–34	129	23:13	240
6:33	101, 138	23:25–26	265, 423
7:17–19	353	23:34	340
7:28–29	443	24:9–13	352, 374
7:28	508	24:14	393, 410
7:29	162, 508	24:15	239
8:4	78	24:23–26	374
8:19	356	24:48	481
8:25	500	25:21	168
8:28	348	25:23	168
9:2	70, 217	25:14–30	252, 503
9:9	356	25:31–46	94, 150n
9:22	141	25:31–32	352
10:10	161	25:39–40	150
10:19–20	375	25:41	96
10:33	327	26:26–29	452
11:8	54	26:29	494
11:20	96	26:60	117
11:22	96	27:9	148, 160n
11:23	96	27:11	190
11:24	96	27:29	380
11:29	477	27:39–44	115
12:5	205	27:39	61
12:23	481	27:40–42	500
12:28	122	27:46	443
12:34	481	28:2–7	111
13:11	494	28:15	130
13:15	481	28:18–20	444

Matthew (continued)

28:18	360
28:19	275, 281
28:20	91, 130, 509

Mark

1:13	111
1:15	219
2:5–12	443
2:5	70, 217
4:11	494
5:15	94, 227, 248
5:34	500
6:5	134, 302
6:11	78
8:34–35	329, 417
10:1–12	94, 226
10:6–7	469
10:7	54
10:17–22	441
10:45	265, 498
10:52	500
12:13	118
12:15	118
13:10	393, 410
13:11–12	375
13:11–13	352, 374
13:21–23	352, 374
13:14	239
14:3	87
14:5	87
14:25	494
14:68	263n, 327n
14:70	263n, 327n
15:2	190
15:17	380
15:29	61
16:5–7	111

Luke

1:2	473
1:3	356
1:17	239
1:31–33	405, 422
1:51	348
1:70	63
2:8–14	111
2:22–40	308
2:51	91, 250, 255
2:52	136
3:12–14	447
3:18	133
4:16–30	453
4:16–20	121, 466n
4:16–21	22, 474
4:16	132
4:28–29	464
4:32	162
5:5	129
5:7	184
5:10	342
5:17	53
5:21	61
6:12–16	467
6:15	266
6:16	349
6:35	349
7:25	54
7:36	149, 227
7:44–46	149, 227
8:1–3	250, 467
8:2–3	186, 256n
8:2	105
8:10	494
8:13–14	449
8:35	94, 227, 248
8:55	111, 437n
9:23–24	329, 417
10:7	161
10:33	96
10:34	96
11:1	508
11:4	183
11:20	122
11:24–26	448
11:39	265, 423
12:3	216
12:9	327
12:16–21	148
12:27	129
12:33	178
12:47–48	448
13:1–5	448
15:13	226

SCRIPTURE INDEX

16:1–9	252	10:36	119
16:2–4	52	11:42	277
16:13	131n, 228	11:51	236
17:19	500	12:3	87
18:14	499	12:23	219
18:22	224	13:1	219
19:11–27	252	13:10	340
19:17	168	14:6	176, 443
20:20	118	14:15	445
20:26	118	14:16	133, 232, 426
20:32	117	14:19	66
21:12–19	352, 374	14:26	176, 232, 336
21:13–15	375	14:27	303
21:24	350	15:2	287
21:35	183	15:4–5	289
22:57	263n, 327n	15:4	287
22:61	336	15:5	287, 445, 446
22:65	61	15:8	287
23:3	190, 198n	15:13–15	22
23:43	111	15:16	287, 306n, 452
23:46	111	15:20	344
24:4–7	111, 407n	15:26	133, 176, 232, 426
24:25	183, 273	16:7	133, 176, 232
24:39	111, 405	17:1	219
		17:17	243
		17:19	119
John		18:36–37	190, 198n
Entire Gospel	15n	18:36	129, 189, 380
1:11	464	18:38	510
1:14	111, 269n, 333, 478	19:2	380
1:18	63, 66	19:5	380
2:1–11	95, 104	19:11	190, 198n
2:5	103, 127	19:30	111
2:6	215	20:12–13	111
2:9	127	20:22	24
2:15	236, 242, 338	21:1	111
		21:14	111
3:3–8	446		
3:17	101, 443	**Acts**	
5:25	122	1:1—6:7	5
5:39–40	360	1:2	113, 473
5:43	464	1:5	473
6:66	464	1:8	134n, 444, 473
9:3	450	1:9	436
10:33	61	1:10–11	407, 422
10:34–36	362	1:10	111
10:34–35	243	1:11	113, 437
10:35	24		

533

Acts (continued)

1:21–22	112, 472
1:22	113, 472
2:1–4	135n
2:3	302
2:17–18	134
2:17	122, 135n, 352, 373, 426
2:27	228
2:36	360
2:40	132
3:21	315
5:2–3	252
5:12	134, 302
5:29	273, 283
5:32	273
5:34	53
6:1–7	103, 154
6:4	107
6:5	376
6:6	135, 303
6:8—9:31	5
7:22	263
7:26	273
7:27	71
7:39	71
7:52	349
7:58—8:3	13
7:58	39, 130
8:1	357
8:3	61
8:4–13	376
8:14–17	135n
8:17	134, 135n, 302
8:26–40	376
9:1–31	13, 311
9:1–20	60
9:1	61
9:4–5	331
9:4	64
9:11	12
9:15	65
9:16	472
9:26–30	13
9:32—28:31	5
9:36	89
10:42	370
10:44–48	135n
11:20	210
11:25–26	13, 209
11:27–30	13, 209n
12:8	386
12:25	135n, 209n
Ch 13	138
13:1—14:28	13, 39, 357
13:1	209
13:2–3	135, 303
13:9	11, 12n
13:13–14:23	357
13:14–41	453
13:14–15	22, 12, 474
13:15	132, 495
13:16–41	495
13:25	178
13:35	228
13:46	71
Ch 14	229
14:3	302
14:4	472
14:14	472
14:5–20	309
14:5–19	196
14:6–23	39, 49, 217, 296
14:19	258
14:23	137n
15:1–35	13
15:23	21
15:35	508
15:36—18:22	13, 39
15:36–41	386
15:36	39
15:39	391
16:1–5	309
16:1–3	39, 49, 196, 217, 296
16:1	29, 130, 196, 301, 357
16:2	40
16:3	130
16:8–12	387
16:8	387
16:11	387
16:14–15	152, 186
16:14	250
16:30–31	444
16:37–38	11
16:40	152

17:1–3	309	22:3	12, 263
17:13–15	40, 41	22:6	387
17:23	148	22:7–8	331
17:28	12, 236	22:21	472
18:2–3	250	22:25–28	11
18:2	395	23:6	12
18:3	396	23:26	21
18:5	40	23:33—26:32	13
18:11	40, 508	24:2	149
18:18–21	396	24:5	277
18:18	395	24:6	205
18:23—21:16	210	24:14	277
18:23—21:17	13	24:26	483
18:24–28	396	25:7	277
18:26	395	25:18	178
19:1–10	210	26:4	130
19:1–6	135n	26:5	12, 277, 309
19:1	225	26:14–15	331
19:6	134, 135n, 302	26:14	11
19:8–9	53	26:17	472
19:8–10	41, 169n, 225	26:19	472
19:12	303	26:23	472
19:22	397	27:1—28:31	13
19:24	285	27:1—28:16	161n, 385
19:27–28	285	Ch 27	71
19:32	110	27:9–44	397
19:33–34	388	27:12	286
19:34–35	285	27:27	178
19:36	349	Ch 28	388
19:40	110	28:11	286
20:1–6	113, 397	28:16–31	316
20:3–6	42	28:20	315
20:4	285	28:22	277
20:17–35	230	28:30–31	13, 42, 51, 381
20:17	6, 154, 160, 225	28:31	41
20:27	374		
20:28	6, 93, 160, 225	**Romans**	
20:29–30	123	Chs 1–11	452
20:31	169n	1:1–7	222
20:32	119	1:1	137, 215
20:33	179, 236	1:2–4	326
21:8	376	1:2	359
21:27—28:31	42	1:3–4	328
21:29	397	1:3	35, 36, 326
21:33	315	1:4	35, 111, 329
21:39	12	1:10–13	399
21:40	76	1:14	183, 273
22:2	76, 91		

SCRIPTURE INDEX

Romans (continued)

1:16–17	306
1:16	311, 312
1:17	382
1:18–20	442
1:23	333, 478, 511
1:25	110, 192
1:28–32	353
1:28	180
1:29	151
1:30	61, 239
2:6–11	370
2:6	387
2:14–15	149
2:15	257, 482
2:18–20	57
2:21	216, 370
3:3	327
3:4	111, 215
3:7	110, 511
3:8	146
3:11	442
3:19–28	420
3:19	57
3:20	57
3:21	57
3:23–25	480
3:23	333, 478
3:24–25	57
3:24	111, 498
3:25	498
3:28	57, 111
4:2	111
4:5	444
4:7–8	264
4:8	388
4:16–22	444
4:25	122, 328, 500
Ch 5	480
5:1	111, 497
5:4	194
5:5	304, 481
5:8	490
5:9–10	29
5:9	100, 111, 142
5:10	100, 441, 490
5:12–21	92
5:14	92
5:17–21	194
5:18	221, 427
6:1–2	146
6:3–11	275, 329, 418, 426, 429, 433, 494
6:3–4	304, 319, 366, 446, 450, 452, 488
6:3	327, 415, 485
6:4	450
6:5	446
6:7	450, 452, 500
6:11–12	446, 452
6:11	415, 446, 485, 488
6:14	57
6:17	24
6:18	274
6:20—7:6	57
6:22	274
6:23	423, 448
Ch 7	93
7:6	57
7:7–8	58
7:7	57
7:8	57
7:12	57
7:15–25	231
7:15–23	448
7:22–25	446
7:23	180, 351
7:25	180, 351
8:1	446
8:2	57, 58
8:3–4	57
8:8–13	446
8:9	178
8:11	111
8:15–17	351
8:16	180, 303
8:17–18	221, 367, 427
8:17	322, 326, 327, 329, 331, 417, 478
8:18	333, 357, 383, 419, 478
8:19–22	432
8:20–21	432
8:25	484
8:28—9:33	427

8:28–30	445	14:21	165
8:28	305	14:23	92
8:29–30	221, 427	15:3	96
8:31–32	129	15:4	194, 484, 495
8:33	326	15:8	276
8:34	75, 407, 422, 438	15:14—16:27	399
8:37	305	15:16	119
9:1	482, 510	15:18–19	393
9:3–5	300	15:18–20	308
9:4–5	309	15:22	399
9:5	63, 66, 192, 390	15:24	5, 13, 292, 385
9:11	252, 305	15:28	5, 13, 51, 292, 385
9:20–21	92	15:30	304
9:31–32	57	16:1–3	6n, 152
10:3	62	16:2	486
10:4	57	16:3–5	396
10:10–11	446	16:3	395
10:14–15	370	16:13	326
10:17	116, 120, 136, 142, 221, 427, 445	16:17	91, 192, 228, 278, 509
		16:21–23	505
11:9	183	16:21	42
11:13	113	16:22	206, 288, 487
11:14	136	16:23	397
11:22	237	16:25–26	412, 493
11:26	360	16:25	216, 305
11:36	63, 66, 192	16:26	134, 359, 413, 493, 494
Chs 12–16	452		
Ch 12	133	16:27	63, 66, 192, 390
12:2	180, 275, 351		
12:3	304	**1 Corinthians**	
12:5	486		
12:6–7	133	1:1	137
12:6	302	1:2	119
12:8	95, 344, 492	1:5	415, 486
12:18	340, 497	1:6	276
12:19	387	1:7	415, 486
12:20	350, 372	1:9	305
13:1–7	174, 273, 282	1:10–13	87
13:5	482	1:11	152
13:8	491	1:16	316, 397
13:8–10	57, 254	19–21	442
13:13	266	1:21	64, 501
13:14	149	1:23	370
Ch 14	238	1:25	442
14:3	124	1:30	415, 485
14:5–9	447	2:4–5	308
14:6	124	2:4	79, 307
14:15	165	2:7	412, 493

1 Corinthians (continued)

Reference	Pages
2:8	333, 478
4:1	166, 226, 413, 493
4:2	266
4:5	481
4:15	415, 485
4:17	41, 113, 415, 485
4:19	113
4:21	477
5:1	149
5:5	72
5:9–10	391
5:9–11	178, 284
6:9	54
6:11	119, 120
6:18	449
7:1–16	226
7:1	124, 319, 348, 351
7:6–9	124
7:6–8	94
7:7	225
7:9	228
7:12–16	94
7:14	119
7:20–24	505
7:20–22	501
7:22	174
7:25	61
7:29	122
7:32–40	94
8:7	482
8:13	165
9:1–7	100
9:1	112, 472
9:3–14	166
9:3–12	160
9:5	94, 226
9:7	319
9:12–14	100
9:15	109
9:17	52
9:22	136
9:24–27	128, 380
9:25	63, 66, 129, 189, 228, 380
9:27	129
10:1–13	309
10:11	122
10:14—11:34	452
10:28–29	482
10:31	446
10:33	136
11:3	98
11:14–15	508
11:17–22	87
11:19	277
11:23–26	23
11:23–25	177
11:23	509
Ch 12	133
12:1–11	304
12:3	116, 142, 362, 445
12:4	302
12:9	302, 397
12:12–27	332
12:28	133, 302, 397, 474
12:30	302, 397
12:31	133, 302
Ch 13	93, 312
13:5	257
13:13	132, 193, 344, 353, 491
14:20–33	6
14:31	91
14:33	255
14:37	22, 121
15:1–11	112
15:1–4	23
15:3	509
15:7–10	472
15:8	421
15:9–10	64
15:10	62
15:12–20	421
15:17–20	443
15:19–21	199
15:20–23	443
15:21–22	92
15:22	488
15:24–28	255
15:28	91, 250, 255, 257
15:32–33	338
15:33	12, 236
15:39	111
15:43	478

15:44–46	111	7:13	211
15:45–49	92	8:16–17	211
15:52	63, 66	8:16	210
15:53	191	8:23	210
15:54–57	306	9:2	266
16:7	483	9:8	182
16:10–11	41, 113, 131	10:1	95, 273, 477
16:16	161	11:3	92
16:17	316, 397	11:4	52
16:19	152, 395, 487	11:5	72
16:20	287	11:23–27	4
		11:25	71
		12:1–10	72

2 Corinthians

		12:6	510
1:1	41	12:8	497
1:5–7	488	12:10	184, 185
1:6–7	330	12:11	72
1:19	40	12:18	211
2:7	495	12:20	151
2:12	387	13:3–4	331, 488
2:13	210	13:4	331, 488
2:15–17	488	13:12	287
3:8–11	333, 478		
3:13–16	493		

Galatians

3:14	132		
3:18	333, 478	1:1	84
4:2	482	1:1–5	222
4:3–6	79, 307, 312	1:3–4	385
4:4	333, 478	1:5	63, 66, 192, 390
4:5–6	496	1:6–9	52
4:6	445, 481	1:10–17	311
4:8–12	464	1:11–12	65
4:10–11	331	1:13–17	60
Ch 5	74	1:13–16	64
5:8	389	1:13–14	309
5:10	252, 370	1:13	340
5:14–15	221, 427	1:14	136
5:17	124	1:15–16	84, 472
5:18	221, 427	1:18–24	13
5:19	388, 443	1:19	472
5:21	83, 382, 408, 422, 438	1:23	340
6:6	304	2:1–10	13
6:9	148	2:1–3	217
6:14	192	2:1	209
7:4	106	2:3	209
7:5	273	2:6–10	113
7:6	211	2:7–9	79
7:8	391	2:9	394, 410, 472

Galatians (continued)

2:11–14	163, 278
2:16	57
3:1	183
3:3	183
3:10–13	57
3:13	57
3:14	415, 485
3:19–20	77
3:26–27	415, 485
3:26	448n
3:28	110, 486, 505, 467
4:4	57, 78, 83, 219, 431
4:16	110, 511
4:21—5:1	505
5:6	57, 107, 108, 120, 141, 148, 189, 193, 232, 249, 254, 308, 353, 459
5:10	486
5:11	216
5:14	491
5:18–23	259
5:20	277
5:22–23	289, 344, 477
5:22	304, 344
6:1	477
6:6	160
6:7	366
6:10	174, 277, 287, 154
6:11	109
6:17	331
6:18	398

Ephesians

1:3–14	46n, 427
1:3–6	445
1:3	415, 486
1:6	333, 478
1:7	498
1:10	52, 83, 219
1:11	305
1:12	333, 478
1:13	110, 415, 485, 511
1:14	333
1:18	481
1:20–23	113, 116, 199
1:20–22	422
2:1–2	445
2:1	441
2:4–9	446
2:4–6	445
2:5	29
2:8	100, 101, 445, 501
2:8–10	120, 189, 353, 459, 476
2:8–9	142, 221, 420, 427, 446, 480
2:10	88, 89, 148, 221, 339, 361, 427, 446, 488
2:12	482
2:14–18	497
2:15	415, 485, 486
2:20	474
2:21	415, 486
3:1	304
3:2	52, 412, 494
3:3–4	413, 493
3:5	413, 493
3:6	413, 415, 485, 493
3:8–10	219
3:8–9	413, 493
3:9	52, 412, 412, 493, 494
3:10	413, 493
3:11	305
3:12	106
3:13	332
3:20	432
3:21	63, 66, 192, 488
Ch 4	376
4:1	304, 305
4:2–3	477
4:2	477
4:3	487
4:11	154, 462, 474
4:17–18	351
4:17	180
4:20–24	446
4:21	110, 511
4:23	180, 351
4:25	510
4:28	506
4:30	93
5:18	165, 226
5:19–20	454

5:22–25	105	4:8	120
5:24	252, 256	4:9	121
5:25	257	4:10–13	184
5:26	265, 275, 423	4:10	487
5:31	319, 348, 351	4:11	182, 184, 185
6:4	364	4:13	388
6:5–9	506	4:20	63, 66, 192
6:5–8	501	4:22	287
6:9	88, 505, 506	4:23	398
6:10–17	71, 73, 99, 320		
6:13–17	449	**Colossians**	
6:18	449	1:5–6	110, 511
6:20	315	1:6	393
6:21	285, 386	1:8	304
		1:10	449
Philippians		1:11	484
1:1	6, 93, 215	1:20	332
1:6	221, 427	1:22	332
1:7	276	1:23	393
1:8	487	1:24	330, 331, 332, 451
1:19–26	381	1:25–27	219
1:20	106	1:25	52, 494
1:21–26	291	1:26	393, 412, 492, 493
1:22–23	389	1:27	413, 493, 494
1:23	340, 371	1:28	413, 493
2:1–11	150	2:1	399
2:3–4	257	2:2	413
2:5–11	257	2:7	415, 485
2:14	87	2:9	63, 437
2:17	379	2:11–13	488
2:19	114	2:11–12	304, 319, 329, 418, 426, 429, 433, 446, 450, 452
2:22	40		
2:24	114		
2:29	486	2:12	275, 327, 331, 494
3:4–7	309	2:13	441
3:5	11, 12	2:17	412, 492
3:6	499	2:18	180, 351
3:9	275	3:1–3	446
3:10–11	327, 330n, 367, 488	3:1	327, 446
3:10	313, 327, 329, 331, 344, 366	3:4	116, 327, 333, 446, 478
3:11	330n	3:5	340, 446
3:21	333, 478	3:8–9	140
4:1	128, 487	3:9–10	446
4:2	487	3:12	326, 446
4:5	122	3:14	132, 193, 344, 353, 491
4:7	221		

Colossians (continued)

3:15	487
3:16–17	454
3:16	89
3:17	120
3:18	256, 488
3:20	488
3:21	364
3:22–25	501, 506
3:22–23	504
3:22	252, 481
4:1	88, 505, 506
4:7–18	399
4:7–8	6n
4:7	285, 386
4:8	481
4:14	315, 385, 386
4:15	152
4:16	22, 121, 363, 398, 474

1 Thessalonians

	42
1:1	41
1:3	484
1:5–6	308
1:5	303, 307, 312
2:2	106
2:5	179, 236
2:6–7	471
2:7	341
3:1–3	41
3:2	41, 113
3:6	41, 113
4:3–8	445
4:11	155
4:16–17	221, 427
4:16	488
4:18	495
5:1–2	191
5:3	184
5:6–8	372
5:10	389
5:12–13	161
5:12	95, 159
5:27	22, 121, 363, 398, 474

2 Thessalonians

	11, 42
1:1	41
1:3	448
1:5–10	387
1:6–10	370
1:7–10	443
1:9	184, 333, 478
2:1–12	123
2:8	191
2:13–14	84n, 445
2:13	120, 511
2:14	120
2:15	23, 91, 121, 127, 139, 391, 509
2:16–17	496
3:4	486
3:6–12	186
3:6	278
3:8–9	160
3:11–12	108, 156
3:11	128, 151
3:12	76, 91
3:14–15	284
3:15	278

1 Timothy

1:1	431, 439, 462, 472
1:2	217, 309, 404, 438, 492
1:3–11	300
1:3–5	461
1:3	13, 22, 224, 291, 292, 316, 508
1:4	14, 438, 442, 494
1:5	104, 105, 123, 238, 340, 424, 446, 481
1:6–7	14
1:6	14, 205, 235
1:7	14, 264
1:8	265
1:9	128, 205, 235, 349
1:11	333, 433, 478
1:12–17	129, 276, 279, 327
1:12	68, 308, 388, 410, 446, 456, 463
1:13–16	492

SCRIPTURE INDEX

1:13	348, 446	3:2	22, 105, 167, 225, 227, 248, 264, 287, 319, 341, 344, 447, 458, 459
1:14	68, 308, 414, 415, 416, 443, 490		
1:15–16	448		
1:15	67, 68, 142, 198, 281, 406, 481	3:3	458, 459
		3:4–5	106, 226
1:16	329, 411, 431	3:4	76, 251, 447, 458
1:17	192, 270, 274, 404, 405, 421, 432, 433, 436, 443, 455, 456, 475	3:5	458, 489
		3:6	459
		3:7	183, 425, 458
		3:8–13	6
1:18–19	450	3:8–10	447
1:18	73, 309, 460	3:8	76, 165, 248, 249, 254
1:19–20	15	3:9	238, 413, 494
1:19	104, 105, 123	3:10	225
1:20	337, 387, 388	3:11	68, 76, 248, 349, 447, 467
2:1–3	447		
2:1–2	447, 449, 461	3:12–13	447
2:2	76, 274	3:12	447
2:3–4	142	3:13	416
2:3	283, 445	3:14–16	219
2:4	123, 310, 351, 421, 443	3:15	22, 439
		3:16	55, 177, 185, 405, 406, 407, 411, 413, 421, 422, 425, 432, 443, 477, 479, 493, 494
2:5–6	455		
2:5	405, 407, 421, 422, 435, 436, 437, 438, 443, 444		
2:6	265, 310, 405, 406, 409, 421, 423, 726, 438, 443, 444	4:1–5	127, 320, 350, 352, 371
		4:1–3	15
2:7–10	447	4:1	14, 22, 24, 113, 308, 348, 363, 429, 437, 438, 508
2:7	9, 439, 462, 463		
2:8	22, 228, 447, 456		
2:9–15	447	4:2	424, 482
2:9–10	456	4:3–4	456
2:9	264	4:3	123
2:10	193, 479	4:4–5	453
2:11—3:7	319, 466, 467	4:4	439
2:11–15	97, 466	4:5	383
2:12	22, 249	4:6	107, 410, 439, 460
2:13	469	4:6–16	73, 311
2:15	87, 447, 476	4:7–8	187, 479
3:1–7	97, 137, 292, 311, 321, 341, 447, 458, 467	4:7	128, 278, 337, 429, 480
		4:8–10	97
3:1–2	6	4:8	430, 431, 500
3:1	67, 68, 133	4:9–10	68, 462
		4:9	67

1 Timothy (continued)

4:10	142, 444, 445
4:11	22
4:12	41, 266, 340, 461, 491
4:13	107, 228, 453, 461, 495
4:14	302, 303, 311, 377
4:16	43, 142, 410, 460
5:1–2	131, 134, 350, 458, 461, 467, 468
5:2	128
5:4	447, 479
5:5	431
5:6	441
5:7	22
5:9–16	157, 447, 467
5:9	447
5:10	89, 447
5:11–14	94
5:11	438
5:12	194
5:13–14	254
5:13	250
5:14	226, 447
5:15	205, 425
5:17	133, 166, 225, 463
5:18	197
5:19–20	461
5:20	178
5:21	22, 112, 204, 417
5:22	135, 250, 303
5:23	95, 104, 226, 249
5:25	168
6:1–2	447, 501, 505
6:2–3	508
6:2	22, 88, 127
6:2b–5	228
6:3	187, 409, 479, 480
6:4	14, 277, 336, 349
6:5	236, 242, 480
6:6	179, 479
6:7	113
6:9–10	96
6:9	371
6:10	93, 95, 185, 348
6:11–16	301
6:11–14	461
6:11	340, 361, 480
6:12	40, 305, 309, 310, 380, 431, 432, 454
6:13–14	22
6:13	80, 421
6:14–16	270, 436
6:14–15	429, 431
6:14	406, 408
6:15–16	390n, 454n, 455
6:15	63, 78, 404, 405, 406, 408, 433
6:16	405, 406, 416, 456
6:17–19	432, 447
6:17	186
6:18	89
6:19	430
6:20	14, 128, 239, 319, 337, 342, 343, 360, 441, 463, 490
6:21	15, 84, 88, 266, 398, 456

2 Timothy

1:1	426, 432, 439, 462
1:2	309, 404, 492
1:3	67, 104, 424, 447, 456
1:4–5	460
1:5	39, 49, 130, 195, 217, 250, 295, 350, 447
1:6	71, 133, 135, 460, 463
1:7–8	450, 463
1:7	308, 443
1:8	409
1:9–10	198, 411, 444, 455
1:9	142, 216, 339, 408, 425, 438, 448
1:10	406, 407, 408, 409, 426, 431, 432, 463, 475
1:11	463
1:12	411, 414, 432, 434, 450, 451, 489
1:13	22, 121, 137, 167, 416, 443, 459, 490
1:14	204, 437, 462, 463
1:15	238
1:16	492

SCRIPTURE INDEX

1:18	397, 405, 406, 408, 434, 492	3:7–8	298
2:1	309, 415	3:7	14, 52, 91, 178, 239, 342, 343, 360
2:2	67, 68, 121, 134, 137, 460	3:9	358, 366
2:3	417, 718	3:10–15	273
2:4–6	462	3:10–11	167, 418, 459
2:4	76	3:10	491
2:7	413	3:11	450, 451
2:8–13	313, 422, 451	3:12	80, 141, 313, 322, 330, 331, 344, 377, 382, 383, 417, 450, 479, 488
2:8–9	450		
2:8	382, 405, 422, 429, 443, 444, 463	3:13	365
2:9	451, 463	3:14–17	56, 218, 232, 449, 460
2:10	55, 333, 406, 411, 415, 433, 445, 451, 478	3:14	121, 134, 460
		3:15–17	466
		3:15–16	409, 465
2:11–13	455	3:15	24, 142, 273, 277, 308, 362, 416, 419, 444, 461
2:11–12	9, 426, 433, 446, 450, 452		
2:11	67, 68, 417, 418, 419, 430	3:16–17	24, 400, 445, 463, 509
		3:16	24, 114, 177, 243, 437, 453, 496, 509
2:12	382, 418, 419, 433, 449		
2:13	65, 68, 414, 419	3:17	339, 345, 439
2:14	447	4:1–2	444, 460
2:15	110, 114, 351, 511	4:1	22, 191, 387, 406, 408, 417, 433
2:16	128, 205, 277, 442, 447, 461	4:2	132, 139, 461, 508
2:17–18	15, 19, 71, 194	4:3–4	15
2:18	74, 110, 236, 430, 511	4:4	128, 205, 314, 510
2:19	490	4:5	461, 462
2:21	119	4:6	80, 431, 450, 462
2:22	238, 411	4:7–8	128
2:23	14, 15, 128, 273, 277, 278, 442, 461	4:7	129, 189, 249
		4:8	191, 316, 367, 387, 397, 408, 411, 412, 423, 425, 431, 434, 444, 491
2:24–26	367		
2:24	167, 319, 344, 439, 459		
		4:9–15	211
2:25–26	74, 96, 245, 278	4:9–11	392
2:25	245, 351, 461	4:9	292, 386
2:26	183, 425, 444	4:10–11	399
3:1	121, 122, 429	4:10	113, 211, 291, 315, 419
3:2–7	15		
3:2	239, 442	4:11	340
3:4	96	4:12–13	315
3:5	122, 193, 278, 429, 480	4:12	285, 292
		4:13	11

2 Timothy (continued)

4:14–15	461
4:14	71, 408, 450
4:15	204
4:16	387, 398
4:17	9, 410
4:18	63, 66, 192, 270, 329, 408, 416, 425, 426, 430, 433, 444, 456
4:19	292, 315
4:20	292, 450
4:21	292, 386
4:22	340, 414, 456

Titus

1:1–4	271
1:1–2	510
1:1	185, 274, 326, 351, 426, 439, 444, 461, 479
1:2–3	432
1:2	24, 305, 362, 426, 429, 431, 439, 445
1:3–4	142
1:3	78, 426, 463
1:4	406, 444
1:5–9	99, 137, 222, 271, 292, 300, 311, 321, 341, 376, 447, 458
1:5–7	154, 160
1:5	6, 13, 22, 25, 51, 144, 154, 160, 212, 291, 292, 482
1:6–7	105
1:6	162, 447, 458
1:7	6, 93, 154, 160, 439, 458, 459
1:8	94, 248, 264, 287, 458, 459
1:9	68, 167, 195, 206, 246, 319, 341, 344, 459, 482
1:10–16	271
1:10	15, 20, 53, 336
1:11–15	11
1:11	461
1:12	12
1:13–16	253
1:14	15, 128, 314, 510
1:15–16	214
1:15	424, 447, 482
1:16	14, 15, 342, 343, 360, 448, 490
2:1–10	270, 271, 447
2:1	222
2:2	76, 94, 104, 264, 447
2:3–8	11
2:3–4	447
2:3	106, 349
2:4–5	447
2:4	264, 447, 491
2:5	94, 260, 264
2:6–8	266
2:6–7	447
2:6	264
2:7	76, 89
2:8	260
2:9–10	447, 501
2:9	256
2:10	260, 476
2:11–15	220
2:11–14	268, 270, 452
2:11–13	445
2:11–12	414
2:11	142, 406, 421, 431, 461, 475
2:12–13	266
2:12	371, 479
2:13–14	142, 452
2:13	55, 63, 66, 76, 111, 142, 191, 274, 404, 406, 408, 412, 421, 431, 433, 436, 443, 444, 475, 478
2:14	88, 405, 407, 415, 421, 423, 424, 443, 461, 499
2:15	48, 216, 222, 270, 271, 496
3:1–3	271, 276
3:1–2	174
3:1	447
3:2	95, 477
3:3	183, 371, 445

3:4–7	271, 276, 280, 419, 456	6:16	276
3:4–6	437, 438	6:18	215
3:4	406, 428, 431, 475, 490	7:25	75
		7:26	228
3:5–7	53	9:14	445
3:5–6	409	9:15	77
3:5	40, 142, 222, 308, 424, 426, 429, 437, 448, 455, 492	9:22–26	443
		9:26	122
		10:23	484
3:6	428	10:26–27	448
3:7	407, 411, 423, 431, 444	10:33	96
		11:1	266
3:8	67, 68, 88, 95, 159	11:3	63
3:9–11	214	11:16	93
3:9	14, 15, 336, 461, 482	11:35	498
3:10–11	14, 271, 461	12:1	189
3:10	128	12:2	131
3:12–13	222	12:16	128
3:12	13, 291, 292	12:24	77
3:13	95, 224, 227	12:25	238
3:14	88, 95, 159	12:28	87
3:15	242n, 266, 398, 456, 491	13:4	54
		13:22	133, 495

James

1:12	380
2:10	273, 448
2:17	149
2:26	149
3:2–12	140
3:6–10	448
4:1	273
4:6	348
5:5	148
5:8–9	122

Philemon

	11, 42, 130, 156, 291, 385, 398, 438, 501, 504, 505, 506
1	186, 304
2	11, 319
9	130, 156, 186, 288, 301
16	186
21	505
22	5, 192, 292
24	315, 385
25	398

1 Peter

1:2	49, 217, 296
1:13	372
1:18	265, 423
1:19	191
1:20	111, 122
1:21	484
1:22–25	355, 452
1:23	360
2:2–3	449

Hebrews

1:2	122
2:3	276, 474
2:10	88
2:14	306
4:12	360
5:4	84, 137

1 Peter (continued)

2:7	148
2:13–17	173, 174
2:13	76, 173n, 507
2:18–25	173, 501, 506
2:18	256, 477, 506
2:21	506
2:25	93
3:1–7	173
3:5	484
3:7	250
3:13	266
3:15	375, 484
3:16	152
3:18–22	112
3:19	216
3:21	142
4:4	226
4:6	216
4:7	372
4:9	87
4:10	226
5:2	154
5:4	380
5:5	348
5:8	372, 389
5:12	133

2 Peter

1:2	49, 217, 296
1:4	333, 478
1:16	128
1:20–21	114, 121, 134, 362, 437
1:21	24
Ch 2	478
2:1	277, 508
2:4	163
2:10	226
2:16	266
3:3	122
3:18	449

1 John

2:1	133, 232, 496
2:18	122
3:3	132, 145
4:19	491

2 John

3	49, 217, 296

3 John

5–8	94
10	150n, 151, 227n

Jude

1–4	245, 341
1	472
2	49, 217, 296
3	73, 195
6	163
17	472
18	122

Revelation

1:7	66, 352, 431
2:10	380
2:20	238
3:1	445
3:11	380
5:12–13	199
7:2	338
8:12	144
11:18	178
12:9	366
15:1	95, 227
15:4	228
15:6	95, 227, 340
15:8	95, 227
16:9	95, 227
17:14	191
19:16	191
20:3	366
20:8	366
20:10	366
21:18	340

www.ingramcontent.com/pod-product-compliance
Lightning Source LLC
Chambersburg PA
CBHW052110010526
44111CB00036B/1605